D0753153

Temperament
A Psychological Perspective

PERSPECTIVES ON INDIVIDUAL DIFFERENCES

CECIL R. REYNOLDS, *Texas A&M University, College Station*
ROBERT T. BROWN, *University of North Carolina, Wilmington*

Current Volumes in This Series

ASSESSMENT OF INTELLECTUAL FUNCTIONING, Second Edition
Lewis R. Aiken

BEHAVIOR GENETIC APPROACHES IN BEHAVIORAL MEDICINE
Edited by J. Rick Turner, Lon R. Cardon, and John K. Hewitt

COGNITIVE ASSESSMENT
A Multidisciplinary Perspective
Edited by Cecil R. Reynolds

DEAFNESS, DEPRIVATION, AND IQ
Jeffery P. Braden

DEMENTIA
Allen Jack Edwards

EXPLORATIONS IN TEMPERAMENT
Edited by Jan Strelau and Alois Angleitner

FIFTY YEARS OF PERSONALITY PSYCHOLOGY
Edited by Kenneth H. Craik, Robert Hogan, and Raymond N. Wolfe

INDIVIDUAL DIFFERENCES IN CARDIOVASCULAR RESPONSE TO STRESS
Edited by J. Rick Turner, Andrew Sherwood, and Kathleen C. Light

INTERNATIONAL HANDBOOK OF PERSONALITY AND INTELLIGENCE
Edited by Donald H. Saklofske and Moshe Zeidner

PERSONALITY, SOCIAL SKILLS, AND PSYCHOPATHOLOGY
An Individual Differences Approach
Edited by David G. Gilbert and James J. Connolly

SCHIZOPHRENIC DISORDERS
Sense and Nonsense in Conceptualization, Assessment, and Treatment
Leighton C. Whitaker

TEMPERAMENT
A Psychological Perspective
Jan Strelau

TEST ANXIETY
The State of the Art
Moshe Zeidner

A Continuation Order Plan is available for this series. A continuation order will bring delivery of each new volume immediately upon publication. Volumes are billed only upon actual shipment. For further information please contact the publisher.

Temperament
A Psychological Perspective

Jan Strelau

University of Warsaw
Warsaw, Poland, and
Silesian University
Katowice, Poland

Plenum Press • New York and London

Library of Congress Cataloging-in-Publication Data

Strelau, Jan.
    Temperament : a psychological perspective / Jan Strelau.
      p. cm. -- (Perspectives on individual differences)
    Includes bibliographical references and index.
    ISBN 0-306-45945-0
    1. Temperament. I. Title. II. Title: Temperament, a psychological
perspective III. Series.
    BF798 .S66 1998
    155.2'6--ddc21
                                                        98-41542
                                                            CIP

ISBN 0-306-45945-0

© 1998 Plenum Press, New York
A Division of Plenum Publishing Corporation
233 Spring Street, New York, N.Y. 10013

http://www.plenum.com

10 9 8 7 6 5 4 3 2 1

All rights reserved

No part of this book may be reproduced, stored in a retrieval system, or transmitted in any form or
by any means, electronic, mechanical, photocopying, microfilming, recording, or otherwise,
without written permission from the Publisher

Printed in the United States of America

To the memory of Boris M. Teplov and Hans J. Eysenck
and to Alexander Thomas and Stella Chess
all pioneers of contemporary temperament research

Preface

More than 40 years have elapsed since I was a psychology student at the University of Warsaw and wrote a seminar paper on temperament, specifically, on Teplov's contribution to this field. My first published paper, which appeared in 1958, was devoted to Pavlov's typology of higher nervous activity, and to assessing temperament in children. These four decades of my academic career can be summarized in two statements: (1) My professional activity has always been rooted at the University of Warsaw as its center; and (2) from its inception, my research has concentrated on temperament. These statements require some elaboration.

Although I was in my 40th year before the Polish authorities of the period granted me permission, for the first time, to travel outside the socialistic sphere, I was nonetheless fortunate in having had numerous opportunities during the previous two decades to visit academic centers and establish direct contact with experts in temperament research from around the world.

In 1966, before the gates to the West were opened to me, I spent 6 months in Teplov's Laboratory of Differential Psychophysiology in Moscow. This visit was very fruitful. I was able to realize my own research projects which concentrated on EEG and photochemical correlates of the Pavlovian temperament constructs, and became acquainted with the whole range of methods and theoretical issues related to CNS properties as developed by Boris Teplov, Vladimir Nebylitsyn, and their coworkers. During my stay in Moscow, the Eighteenth International Congress of Psychology took place. There would be no reason to mention this if this event had not accorded me the opportunity to meet and talk with, among others, Hans Eysenck and Jeffrey Gray, whom I knew only from the literature. Under the influence of their theories, I extended my temperament interests beyond the Pavlovian typology. This meeting resulted in close research contacts with both of them, which have lasted until the present day.

My first visit to the West was in 1971 when I was awarded a scholarship by the U.S. IREX Foundation which afforded me a one-year stay in the United States. While doing research on *Drosophila melanogaster* in the laboratory of Professor Jerry Hirsch at the University of Illinois (Urbana-Champaign), I obtained my initial education in behavior genetics, for which there was no opportunity in Polish universities at that time. The stay in America was nevertheless a crucial step in my research activities, mainly because of the numerous contacts I was able to establish with American scientists engaged in research on temperament and related areas. Of special significance to me were personal contacts with Alexander Thomas and Stella Chess, the founders of contemporary temperament research in the United States. They in turn provided contacts with most of their followers and colleagues, including Robert Plomin, Mary Rothbart, Hill Goldsmith, Bill Carey, Adam Matheny, Roy Martin, Ted Wachs, and many others, with whom I have had continuous research relationships through correspondence and more or less regular meetings.

The fact that my research interests have concentrated for such a long time on temperament might imply a rather narrow orientation in my scientific activity. This is true only in the sense that temperament constitutes a very small part of psychological phenomena. At the same time, to speak of a narrow orientation is inappropriate since my studies on temperament are based on a very broad perspective. As expressed in many of my publications, my interests embrace all kinds of issues and problems related to temperament in humans (both children and adults) and animals. Further, development of my own conceptualizations into the "regulative theory of temperament" has led to my interest in determining how my theory relates to the contributions of others in this field of study. This is most clearly addressed in my book *Temperament—Personality—Activity*, published by Academic Press in 1983.

As a result of my study of the literature on temperament, as well as my participation in numerous international meetings dedicated to this field, I have become increasingly convinced that many temperament researchers are not likely to extend their scientific efforts beyond the narrow topic or issue on which they are focused. This is most evidenced by the fact that child-oriented temperament scientists are frequently unfamiliar with studies and concepts of adult-oriented researchers, and vice versa. In many publications on temperament within a given theoretical approach, minimal attention is given to links with other conceptualizations in this domain. Geographical isolation among temperament scientists is more the rule than the exception. I could quote hundreds of papers in which references are limited to authors of one nation, even though much research has been conducted in the same temperament domain in other countries. Furthermore, for political reasons, an impassable geographical barrier affecting scientists from the former socialist countries existed for many years. This barrier no longer exists, but researchers from these countries still experience intellectual deprivation that is characterized mainly by lack of professional books and journals, and this is true for temperament researchers, including myself. However, during the past decade there has been noticeable progress in mutual contact.

Efficient research activity under such conditions of intellectual deprivation requires compensatory mechanisms which I have been able to develop with some success. With access to *Current Contents,* I have systematically collected reprints from my domain of research which most authors mailed to me at my request. Also, since my first visit to the United States a quarter century ago, I have used every opportunity while abroad to make copies of papers and chapters of interest to me. Many researchers working in the domain of temperament and other personality areas have donated copies of their books as gifts. The monograph of Boris Teplov mailed to me in 1961 with a personal dedication opened this collection, which today covers the most representative books on temperament. As a result of the generous support of friends and colleagues around the world, as well as my own efforts, I have been able to collect almost 5,000 reprints, most of which are on temperament and related areas.

The factors that stimulated me to work on a book that brings together knowledge on temperament in children and adults, that goes beyond geographical isolation, and that reports research based on different paradigms and conceptualizations include the conviction that knowledge on temperament is still not sufficiently integrated, the belief that my over 40 years of research in this domain has led to development of a broad view on a variety of issues related to temperament, and, finally, access to an almost complete temperament literature.

The idea of writing a monograph of this kind had already taken shape in my mind in the mid 1980s. It was Robert Brown, coeditor of the Plenum Press Series *Perspectives on Individual Differences* who, while working in 1990 on Strelau and Angleitner's *Explorations in Temperament: International Perspectives on Theory and Measurement,* encouraged me to write an integrated volume on temperament.

Authors know that writing a book requires particular tolerance for delay in getting positive reinforcement, with the risk that it may not happen at all. I have managed to overcome this hurdle and to pass the critical point of reaching this tolerance level, even though it took me a full six years to prepare this text. The preliminary synopsis of the book and the first chapter were written in 1991–1992 during my second one-year stay at the University of Bielefeld. The Max Planck Award given to me and Alois Angleitner by the German Max Planck Society and the Alexander von Humboldt Foundation provided conditions for efficient concentration on this task. I was fortunate to be able to continue work on the book in almost ideal circumstances at the Netherlands Institute for Advanced Study in the Humanities and Social Sciences (NIAS) in Wassenaar, where in 1992–1993 I was a fellow-in-residence. Almost exclusive concentration on completing this book resulted in preparing Chapters 2, 3, 4, and 5 at NIAS. During the next two years, I prepared Chapters 6 and 7. During the last year, I also updated the chapters written in the initial stage. The preparation of Chapter 7 ("Functional Significance of Temperament"), the content of which precisely reflects my recent research activity, was financially supported by a grant from the Polish Research Foundation (KBN 1HO1F 06609).

My original plan was to cover as many topics related to temperament as possible. However, in order not to extend the volume size, selectivity was necessary and such decisions are always influenced by a person's own views and experiences. I have tried to present in the chapters the most important issues in the temperament domain, but I can appreciate that some readers may have a somewhat different view of what is most significant regarding our knowledge of the subject.

An essential question concerns the readership of this book. The most obvious audience is, of course, students of psychology. In writing this book, however, I had a broader audience in mind. Experts in given fields of temperament research, whether psychologists, physicians, or educational scientists, may profit from this monograph as a source for a variety of temperament topics. The ample list of references provides a good starting point for extended studies. Specialists in biological aspects of temperament and behavior genetics need not read the introductory parts of Chapter 4 ("Physiological and Biochemical Correlates of Temperament") and Chapter 5 ("Behavior-Genetic Research on Temperament"), which I consider useful for readers with minimal biological orientation. In the applied domains, there are many areas of professional enterprise, such as education, health, and organization or management, where temperament is a subject of interest. Not infrequently, attempts are made to assess this aspect of personality and to make given predictions regarding an individual's future functioning. Chapters on temperament theories (2 and 3), diagnostic matters related to temperament (6), as well as the discussion on the functional significance of temperamental traits (Chapter 7), provide bases for extending the theoretical background of applied issues.

It rarely happens that authors publish books that are entirely new with respect to content. The material needed for writing a book grows to a certain extent as a result of partial presentation in the form of papers and chapters written on different occasions, and this is the case with *Temperament: A Psychological Perspective.* Several ideas and phrases presented may be found in some of my previous publications. Nevertheless, even when published elsewhere, they have been included in this volume in a new context in order to contribute to a more synthetic, integrative picture on temperament.

The list of persons to whom I owe so much in preparing the final version of the manuscript is very long, and incomplete, hence I beg those colleagues who were helpful in some way, and are not mentioned here, to forgive me.

Chapter 1 ("The History and Understanding of the Concept of Temperament"), was read by Alois Angleitner, Marvin Zuckerman, and Rebecca Geiger. Their critical remarks led to essential changes. I mailed Chapter 2 ("The Initiators of Contemporary Research on Temperament") and Chapter 3 ("Current Theories of Temperament") to all authors whose temperament theories are presented therein (excluding the late Teplov), asking for critical remarks and comments. All ten authors responded to my request, and from nine of them I received constructive remarks, comments, and friendly support. Chapter 4 ("Physiological and Biochemical Correlates of Temperament") was reviewed by Jan Matysiak and Petra Netter. The detailed corrections and supplements by Professor Netter were extremely helpful. My coworker, Włodek Oniszczenko, made useful comments on Chapter 5 ("Behavior-Genetic Research on Temperament") and Chapter 6 ("Assessment of Temperament: Diagnosis and Methodological Issues"). The latter was also constructively reviewed by Alois Angleitner, Jerzy Brzeziński, and Bogdan Zawadzki, the last mentioned a coworker of mine. In addition, Bogdan Zawadzki kindly prepared the statistics of our questionnaire data presented in Chapters 1 and 6. Very helpful were the comments of Stevan Hobfoll on a large part of Chapter 7 ("The Functional Significance of Temperament"). I would like to express my cordial thanks to all my friends, colleagues, and coworkers just mentioned for their important aid and valuable contributions to the final version of my book.

Although my English is far from adequate, I wrote the book in this language. Frankly, it was not easy, if even possible, to express some subtle ideas which I could have formulated in Polish. Professor Grace W. Shugar, a distinguished scientist in child psycholinguistics, was generous in working on my text as English-language editor. Her very detailed corrections and remarks improved the manuscript considerably. I wish to express my most cordial thanks for Dr. Shugar's assistance. Chapter 1 was corrected for English language errors by Helena Grzegołowska-Klarkowska to whom I also owe much for the work she has done.

All drawings in the book which are not photoprinted, and there are more than 40 of them, were prepared by Dr. Wojtek Pisula, a colleague from my department. I am not sure that he was aware how much work was entailed when he willingly agreed to provide the figures for this book. I am exceedingly grateful to him and appreciate his altruistic attitude.

I am deeply indebted to each of my twelve coworkers at the Department of Individual Differences. Whenever the need arose, they were always helpful and very cooperative. Their constructive criticism during our scientific meetings helped to clarify several problems confronting me in writing the book. I thank my efficient secretary, Grażyna Młodawska, whose essential contribution involved preparing the final drafts for the publisher.

My greatest debt is to my wife, Krystyna, who was able to create an atmosphere and conditions which were very conducive to my work. Without her tolerance and the support I received continuously from her while writing this book, completion of such a long-lasting task would have been impossible.

I am very grateful to the Senior Editor, Eliot Werner, for his personal involvement in the publication of *Temperament: A Psychological Perspective.*

JAN STRELAU

Contents

1

The History and Understanding of the Concept of Temperament

For several decades there has been a tendency in psychology to ignore or at least to underestimate the contribution of the previous generations in a given field of study. Many concepts, even theories, are presented in such a way as to give the reader the impression that they are new discoveries or original contributions, whereas in fact similar ideas or thoughts have been formulated decades and sometimes hundreds of years ago. This state of affairs is definitely true for research on temperament. The historical perspective allows a better understanding of the recent conceptualizations on temperament; it helps in making the distinction between the concepts of temperament and personality that are recently quite often used interchangeably. This perspective also shows that our knowledge of temperament developed step by step, rather than by sudden discoveries as is often the case in natural or exact sciences.

Temperament from a Historical Perspective

To give a comprehensive historical review of conceptualizations of temperament that go back to antiquity several hundred pages should be written. In order to characterize thinking on temperament to be found only in the German 15th-century literature Schönfeld (1962) published a book of about 200 pages. Historical reviews regarding temperament may be found in somewhat older publications (Diamond, 1957; Ewald, 1924; Roback, 1931; W. Stern, 1921; see also H. J. Eysenck & Eysenck, 1985; Kagan, 1989b, 1994; Kohnstamm, 1989a; Strelau, 1969).

I limit my review to selected concepts and to only a few empirical studies on temperament which seem to be of special importance for a better understanding of current research in this area.

The Speculative Approach to Temperament

The beginning of research on temperament consisted mainly of speculations regarding the nature of this phenomenon. Many philosophers and physicians may be mentioned here as having some influence on further development in this field of study. For example, Kagan (1989b, 1994), who centers his research on the emotional components of temperament, acknowledged the contributions of Alexander Bain, Franz Gall, Joseph Spurzheim, and Sigmund Freud, among others.

In making a selection of views and speculations that are presented in this chapter I concentrated on these researchers and thinkers who contributed in a way that essentially influenced further development of temperament research.

The Ancient Greek Typology of Temperament

The concept of temperament has its roots in the thought of ancient Greek philosophers and physicians. The father of medicine, Hippocrates (4th century B.C.) developed a theory of humors to explain the states of health and illness and his follower, Galen (2nd century A.D.), also a Greek physician, supplemented this theory with a psychological interpretation.

The Four Humors Distinguished by Hippocrates as the Basis for Individual Differences. The starting point for Hippocrates' theory presented in the dissertation *On the Nature of Man* was the concept of primary elements of the universe introduced by Empedocles (5th century B.C.). From these four elements—earth, air, fire, and water—Hippocrates educed four qualities: warmth, cold, moisture, and dryness, as well as four fluids (humors) of the organism. The humors were regarded as a manifestation of the four qualities. "The human body consists of blood, phlegm and two kinds of bile (chole)—white and black. These fluids determine the nature of his body and due to them man is healthy or ill. He is most healthy when the mixture of these fluids, their activity and amount are in a proper relationship" (Hippocrates, 1895, p. 195). An optimal relationship between these fluids is a source of health whereas an imbalance between them causes illness. Recovery consists mainly in the restoration of a proper balance among these four fluids. Several factors influence illness: among other things, nutrition and seasons of the year. For example, during winter the phlegm, the coldest of the fluids, plays the dominant role. In winter phlegm is the greatest secretion of human body. During this season most common illnesses are related to the secretion of phlegm. Blood dominates during spring; during summer, white bile (chole), and in winter, black bile. According to Hippocrates the fluids derive from the following organs of the body: blood from the heart, phlegm from the head, white bile from the liver, and black bile from the spleen. In Hippocrates' theory one finds no references to temperament, nor did he describe relationships between the proportion of humors and behavioral characteristics.

Galen's Four Temperaments. Taking advantage of Hippocrates' theory of the four humors Galen developed the first typology of temperament, described in his monograph *De Temperamentis* (L. *temperare*—to mix, to combine in a proper proportion). He distinguished and described nine temperaments. The four that depend directly on the dominance of one of the qualities—warmth, cold, moisture, and dryness—he considered to be the primary (ordinary) temperaments. The four temperaments that are the result of pairs of these qualities (warmth–dryness, warmth–moisture, cold–dryness, cold–moisture) were considered secondary (derivative). The ninth temperament, which is a result of a steady mixture of the four qualities, was regarded as the ideal (optimal) temperament.

Galen's four primary temperament types, also well known among laymen, were named according to the humors that predominated in the body. These are the four types: sanguine (L. *sanguis*—blood), choleric (Gr. *cole*—bile), melancholic (Gr. *melas*—black, *cole*—bile) and phlegmatic (Gr. *phlegma*—phlegm, mucus). Galen gave a psychological (behavioral), although unsystematic and incomplete, description of these temperaments. A detailed description of Galen's theory with reference to its roots and also its relationship to extraversion and neuroticism has been given by Stelmack and Stalikas (1991; see also Howarth, 1988; Lester, 1990; Merenda, 1987; Ruch, 1992) and the theory recently has been viewed from a broader perspective by Kagan (1994).

The Merit of the Hippocrates–Galen Typology. A major contribution of the ancient Greeks to the knowledge of temperament is that they postulated individual differences in behavior that can be explained by physiological mechanisms. The variety of behaviors in which individuals differ can be reduced to a small number of basic (primary) temperament categories. Galen's typology must be regarded as a prototype of a causal, explanatory theory of temperament.

This fantastic conceptualization, in which the categories of temperament were linked to the excess or dominance of given humors in the organism, has found some support in recent studies regarding the biological bases of temperament. Namely, it has been shown that some temperament characteristics, especially those referring to emotions, are related to the activity of the endocrine system (see, e.g., Kagan, 1994; Netter, 1991; Zuckerman, 1991c).

The ancient typology of temperament gained remarkable popularity among philosophers, physicians, and psychologists especially in the 19th and the begin-

ning of the 20th centuries. Most of the contributions to the development or modification of Galen's temperament typology stem from Germany, from such authors
as Ach (1910), Hellwig (1872, 1888), Hirt (1905), and Rumelin (1890). Also in
other countries, many papers were published on the issues of temperament by taking the Hippocrates–Galen typology as a starting point, for example, in the United
States (e.g., Ashmun, 1908; H. Davis, 1898), in France (e.g., Fouillee, 1895; Ribot,
1887; see also Balleyguier, 1989), in Italy (De Giovanni, 1891; Viola, 1906; see
also Attili, 1989), and in Poland (Falkiewicz, 1874).

Two German scholars, Immanuel Kant and Wilhelm Wundt, were the most
influential researchers and theorists on temperament of the two centuries preceding modern times. Their typologies of temperament were based on the formal
characteristics of behavior.

Immanuel Kant: Temperament Expressed in Actions and Emotions

Kant (1912) presented a theory of temperament in his *Anthropology* published in 1798. According to him the biology of temperament consists of the bod-
ily constitution and the humors as proposed by Galen. Kant believed that
temperament as a psychological phenomenon consists of psychic traits determined
by the composition of blood. Thus, like Aristotle (4th century B.C.), he mentioned
blood as the component underlying temperament.

Kant's Typology. Two properties of blood determine to which category of temperament an individual belongs: the ease or difficulty of blood coagulation and the
temperature of the blood (cold versus warm). Taking advantage of the labels introduced by Galen, Kant distinguished four temperament types. He used two criteria for
separating them. The first was life energy (*Lebenskraft*) which oscillates from excitability to drowsiness: "Each temperament may be characterized by means of life
energy (*intensio*) or by release (*remissio*)" (Kant, 1912, p. 228). The second criterion
was the individual's dominant behavior characteristics (emotions versus actions).

In two of the temperaments, the sanguine and the melancholic, emotions
dominate. The sanguine temperament is characterized by strong, quick but super-
ficial emotions, whereas for the melancholic slow, long-lasting and deep emotional reactions are typical. The two remaining temperaments were separated with
respect to the characteristics of actions. The choleric acts rapidly and impetuously
whereas the phlegmatic acts slowly and inertly with a simultaneous lack of emotional reactions. Kant emphasized that there are only four simple temperaments
analogous to the four syllogistic figures. This means, among other things, that
there are no combined (e.g., sanguine–choleric) temperaments.

The Biotonus as a Concept Based on Kant's Theory. Kant's considerations on
temperament no doubt influenced further thinking about this phenomenon. Two of

his statements seem to be of special importance. First, temperament refers to the energetic characteristics of behavior. The energetic characteristics belong to the formal traits which play a crucial role in many temperament theories. Kant's description of temperament by means of energetic characteristics of behavior was elaborated more than a hundred years later by G. Ewald (1924), a German psychiatrist who introduced the concept of the *biotonus*. There are stable individual differences in the biotonus that are determined by the quality and speed of metabolism. Individuals with high biotonus are resistant to strong stimuli and fatigue and their typical vital energy recovers after a short period of relaxation. The opposite occurs in individuals with low biotonus. They are prone to fatigue, not resistant to strong stimuli, and need much time to recover (achieve good balance). Also, temperament expresses itself in human actions, and not only in emotions as some theories suggest.

Wilhelm Wundt: Temperament Limited to Formal Characteristics of Emotions

Wundt, when studying emotions and reaction time in his laboratory, with the aim of establishing general laws of psychic characteristics, was confronted with individual differences in the reactions under study. This led him to the conclusion that individuals differ in temperament. According to him temperament is a disposition that applies to drives and emotions. "Temperament is in relation to drive and emotion as excitability is in relation to sensory sensitivity" (Wundt, 1887, p. 422). Taking as a point of departure two features of emotional reactions—strength and speed of change—Wundt distinguished, as Galen did, four temperament types (see Figure 1.1). Cholerics and melancholics are characterized by strong emotions, sanguines and phlegmatics by weak emotions. Rapid emotional changes are typical for sanguines and cholerics and slow emotional changes for melancholics and phlegmatics.

According to Wundt each temperament has its advantages and disadvantages and the art of life consists in making use of each of the four temperaments depending on the specific situation with which the individual is confronted. This means that individuals can be characterized by more than one temperament.

Wundt's rather marginal considerations of temperament had, nevertheless, significant influence on the further development of temperament theories. This is probably due to the distinguished position he gained in psychology. Some issues raised by Wundt are worth mentioning here. Temperament refers to the domain of emotions (and drives) only. Exclusively formal features of emotions constitute the basis for characterizing temperament. In addition to the energetic aspect of reactions (strength of emotions) Wundt also considered the temporal characteristic (speed of changes). In contrast to Kant, who regarded temperament types as strictly separate categories, Wundt introduced the concept of a two-dimensional system for distinguishing temperament types.

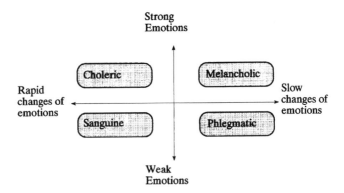

Strong
Emotions

Choleric | Melancholic

Rapid
changes of
emotions

Slow
changes of
emotions

Sanguine | Phlegmatic

Weak
Emotions

FIGURE 1.1. The two-dimensional typology of temperament as proposed by Wundt.

Whatever the specificity of theoretical considerations regarding temperament in the pre-empirical state of studies in this area, most of the authors were strongly fixed on the number of four types of temperament as well as on the labels proposed by Galen. To exemplify this statement, W. Stern (1921) described 16 typologies of temperament, developed mainly at the turn of the 19th and 20th centuries; 11 are based on the classification of four types with labels the same as those proposed by the ancient Greeks.

At the beginning of the 20th century psychiatrists became very active in developing ideas that were important for further developments in research on temperament. Whereas some of them conducted empirical studies based mainly on a constitutional approach, others, mostly psychoanalysts, developed more or less speculative theories. A distinguished representative of the latter theorists was C. G. Jung.

The Extravert and Introvert: Two Psychological Types Distinguished by Carl Gustav Jung

On the basis of psychiatric practice and under the influence of long-lasting collaboration with Sigmund Freud, Jung (1923), a Swiss psychoanalyst, developed his own theory of personality which had a great influence on studies in the field of temperament. His theory, described in 17 volumes and known as "analytical psychology" is a very complex one that tries to explain the interplay of the conscious and unconscious elements of personality by referring to different constructs. Among them were such concepts as libido, understood as a general psychological energy not limited to the sexual drive (as had been proposed by Freud), psychic functions, attitudes, ego, persona, and personal and collective unconsciousness with the symbolic part represented in the concept of archetypes. These constructs were used to explain in a very speculative way the structure and dynamics of the individual's psychological entirety (*psychische Totalitaet*).

For researchers on temperament Jung's (1923) view according to which people have two sorts of attitudes—extraverted and introverted—played the most crucial role. Jung understood extraversion and introversion as two types of general attitudes anchored in the biological endowment and reflecting the direction in which the general psychic energy, libido, expresses itself.

The two attitudes reveal themselves in four basic psychic functions: sensation, thinking, feeling, and intuition (regarded as psychic activity that takes place independently of the content of activity). In normally developing persons one of the four functions plays a dominant role. Thus, taking into account that four types of psychic functioning may be distinguished and all of them may be expressed in an extraverted or introverted attitude, the final classification consists of eight types.

The description of the extravert and introvert given by Jung is very rich. In general, the extravert is oriented in ways of adaptation and reactions to the outside, is ruled by the expectancies and needs of the social milieu, shows outward physical activity. The introvert's libido realizes itself by means of inner subjective states and psychic processes. The introvert is inclined to disregard objects, and withdrawal is the first reaction to the unknown physical and social milieu.

Taking as a point of departure the idea of interplay between the consciousness and unconsciousness Jung (1923) postulated that extraversion and introversion are to some extent complementary. An extraverted attitude in the conscious part of personality goes together with a compensatory introverted attitude in the unconscious domain and vice versa. The unconscious of the introvert is extraverted. In some individuals the unconscious attitude becomes visible in the conscious domain of personality; this results mostly in behavior disorders. Extraverts in case of neurotic breakdown tend toward hysteria, introverts to psychasthenia.

The two attitude types, extraversion and introversion, became the most popular personality or temperament dimensions ever known. They have been incorporated in personality theories of many researchers, among whom Cattell (1965), Guilford (1959), and H. J. Eysenck (1970) are the best known. As is shown in the next chapter, Eysenck developed a causal theory of extraversion–introversion taking Jung's contribution, among others, as a starting point. Jung's ideas were also very influential in the development of other lines of temperament research, for example, the conceptualization of the inhibited and uninhibited temperament (Kagan, 1994). Jung's theory, combined with clinical experience, resulted in the construction of the Myers–Briggs Type Indicator (MBTI) which allows the measurement of extraversion and introversion in combination with the four basic functions distinguished by Jung (I. B. Myers & McCaulley, 1985). This inventory gained a visible popularity in the last decade (see McCaulley, 1990; McCrae & Costa, 1989; Tzeng, Ware, & Bharadwaj, 1991).

The First Empirical Studies on Temperament

At the beginning of the 20th century there was a growing tendency in psychology to move from purely theoretical and philosophical considerations to empirical studies. This is also true for temperament. In the first quarter of the century empirical research on temperament gained popularity mainly in Europe. It is impossible to mention all of the studies conducted during this period. However, the most influential contributions to further studies on temperament came from three researchers, from three different countries: Gerard Heymans from the Netherlands, Ivan P. Pavlov from Russia, and about two decades later Ernst Kretschmer, a psychiatrist from Germany.

Gerard Heymans's Psychometric and Genetic Approach to Temperament

Gerard Heymans was one of the typical 19th-century scholars with broad interests in philosophy and psychology. His contribution to our knowledge of temperament consists mainly in undertaking a huge study with the aim of describing the basic dimensions of the structure of temperament and determining to what degree heredity and environment contribute to the development of temperamental traits.

Empirical Study Undertaken by Heymans and Wiersma. In 1905 Heymans and his coworker, Enno D. Wiersma, distributed a 90-item questionnaire to more than 3,000 physicians requesting them to assess the behavior and psychic characteristics of families they knew well; these families were to be composed of father, mother, and at least one child. The questionnaire consisted of six categories of items expected to cover all domains of human psychic and behavioral characteristics.

More than 400 physicians returned completed inventories and this yielded data from 437 families including father, mother, and 1 to 12 children. Altogether the research project comprised 2,415 subjects. After preliminary selection, data from 400 families were analyzed. The study was described in detail in nine consecutive papers, all of them published under the same title: *Contributions to Special Psychology Based on a Large-Scale Research* (Heymans & Wiersma, 1906a, 1906b, 1906c, 1907, 1908a, 1908b, 1909, 1912, 1918). Without going into details I describe the main findings of this research.

The Three Basic Temperament Dimensions. Three basic temperament dimensions were distinguished: activity, emotionality and primary–secondary function (to some extent a synonym of perseveration). The concept of primary–secondary function, probably not well known to the reader, was taken from Otto Gross (1902). This Austrian physician, referring to primary and secondary functions of the nerve cells in the cortex, had introduced a distinction between primary effects of the contents of consciousness and secondary effects. Secondary effects occur as long-lasting states when the original content leaves the center of consciousness. Under the influence of Gross's ideas Heymans (1899–1909) and Wiersma (1906–1907) conducted a series of experiments aimed at studying the aftereffect phenomenon in sensory sensations.

These experiments, as well as Gross's theoretical considerations, led Heymans to introduce the concept of *primary–secondary function* to studies on individual differences. *Primary function* is typical for individuals in whom the actual content of consciousness determines behavior and psychic processes. For individuals in whom the former experiences and states of consciousness influence behavior and reactions, the *secondary function* is typical. These characteristics suggest that the primary–secondary function is the temporal aspect of behavior and psychic processes, that is, the duration of these processes and behaviors or the speed with which they switch from one state to another.

According to Heymans and Wiersma, the term *emotionality* refers mainly to the formal characteristics—sensitivity or excitability—of emotions, both negative and positive. *Activity* refers mainly to goal-directed, operant behavior, and is characterized by the amount of time a person spends performing given kinds of action.

The Typology of Temperaments (Characters). Taking into account the possible compositions of these three temperament dimensions—emotionality, activity and primary–secondary function—each trait represented by two opposite poles, the authors developed a typology of temperaments, most often referred to as types of character. As a result eight temperament types emerged, known as the "Heymans cube" (Van der Werff, 1985). Table 1.1. gives an overview of the types distinguished by the authors.

TABLE 1.1 The Typology of Temperaments Introduced by Heymans and Wiersma

Emotionality	Activity	Dominance of P or S	Type of temperament
–	–	P	Amorphous
–	–	S	Apathetic
+	–	P	Nervous
+	–	S	Sentimental
–	+	P	Sanguine
–	+	S	Phlegmatic
+	+	P	Choleric
+	+	S	Passionate

Note. P = primary function, S = secondary function, "+" = high level of the given trait, "–" = low level of the given trait. From "Beiträge zur speziellen Psychologie auf einer Massenuntersuchung [Contribution to Special Psychology Based on Large-Scale Investigation]," by G. Heymans and E. Wiersma, 1909, *Zeitschrift für Psychologie, 51,* p. 6.

On the basis of data collected during the study, the authors give detailed characteristics of the three temperament dimensions as well as of each of the eight types. Heymans and Wiersma concluded that the temperament dimensions are not orthogonal. For example, primary functions correlate positively with emotionality and negatively with activity. They also stated that the temperament dimensions are gender-specific.

A biographical study conducted by Heymans (1908) on 110 eminent or popular persons from the period between the 15th and 19th centuries yielded similar results regarding the characteristics of the separate temperament traits as well as their relationships and configurations resulting in types.

Factors Determining Individual Differences in Temperament. Since their large-scale study was aimed at assessing temperament characteristics in parents (mother and father) and children, Heymans and Wiersma were able to analyze the data from the genetic point of view. At that time behavior genetics was not yet developed; thus the outlook on heredity was influenced by Mendelian genetics.

Using the terms *heredity-coefficient* (*Erblichkeitskoeffizient*) and *gender-coefficient* (*Geschlechtskoeffizient*)[1] the authors were able to state that temperament characteristics are to a high degree inherited and that, in most of the cases, same-sex inheritance is dominant. But Heymans and Wiersma were cautious enough to state that their empirical evidence allowed them to conclude only that there is an interrelated influence of both factors—heredity and education—in determining temperament traits (Heymans & Wiersma, 1907, p. 3).

The data collected by these authors also permitted the conclusion that intellectual traits and preferences (also measured by means of their inventory) differ from temperament traits. Whereas the former, due to assimilation and choice, are similar among married couples (assortative mating), traits belonging to the temperament domain undergo only negligible changes during human life and they are distributed differently among spouses (Heymans & Wiersma, 1907, p. 2).

Heymans as the Pioneer of Empirical Studies on Temperament. To summarize, Heymans's contribution to research on temperament or, more generally, personality is of special importance. This has been especially stressed by H. J. Eysenck (1981), who stated that Heymans's achievements "entitle him to be called the father of experimental personality research" (p. 9). The Dutch scholar's research is so important for temperament for the reasons mentioned here.

Heymans undertook the first systematic empirical research on temperament by using the experimental, psychometric, and biographical approach. The Hey-

---

[1] These coefficients are based on descriptive statistics. The gender coefficient expresses the hypothetical frequency with which a trait would occur in individuals of a given sex if factors other than gender were absent. The heredity coefficient expresses the strengthening or weakening of a disposition (tendency) caused by the presence or absence of a given trait in father or mother.

mans–Wiersma project was the first psychometric approach to temperament or personality. Heymans and Wiersma's method of quantitative analysis of these data suggests that the authors were "in essence anticipating factor analysis" (H. J. Eysenck, 1981, p. 8).

As mentioned by H. J. Eysenck (1981), Heymans introduced the hypothetical-deductive method to studies on temperament (personality). The concept of three temperament dimensions is not a result of empirical studies only. Heymans, on the basis of Kant's, Gross's, and Wundt's theoretical considerations as well as his own empirical studies in the domain of sensory aftereffects, hypothesized the existence of the three temperament dimensions. The dimensions distinguished by Heymans, especially activity and emotionality, gained high popularity among temperament researchers. In most of the contemporary theories both dimensions are included in the structure of temperament, although their meaning differs.

The temperament study, in which data from parents and their children were analyzed from the point of view of genetic contribution to individual differences in temperamental traits, was the forerunner of behavior genetic studies on temperament and personality. The temperament study conducted by Heymans and Wiersma and their contribution to our knowledge on temperament recently has been described by H. J. Eysenck (1992c) and Strelau (1994b).

Studies Referring to Heymans's Research on Temperament. Heymans's conceptualizations on temperament as well as the many data collected by him and stored in the archives of the University of Groningen, where Heymans was a professor for almost forty years (1890–1928), almost unknown in the United States, attracted considerable interest among many psychologists in Europe. Thus, for example, the French psychologist Le Senne (1945) used Heymans's typology of characters and treated these characters as the constitutional components of personality. His extension and modification of the Dutch typology gained great popularity among French researchers, especially in the 1950s and 1960s.

Making the assumption that the three dimensions of temperament—emotionality, activity, and primary–secondary function—are constitutionally determined, Le Gall (1950) hypothesized that each of these three dimensions has its specific physiological mechanism. Emotionality was assumed to be determined by the balance of the autonomic nervous system, activity by the subcortex, and primary–secondary function, by the speed of recovery in the nerve tissues, as hypothesized previously by Gross (1902).

Several authors have undertaken the effort to compare Heymans and Wiersma's temperament dimensions with contemporary concepts in this area. Thus, for example, Feij (1984, after Van der Werff, 1985) hypothesized that Heymans's primary–secondary function dimension is related to impulsivity and to sensation seeking. Feij and Orlebeke (1974), taking into account experimental studies on the spiral aftereffect and impulsivity as measured by questionnaire concluded that there is a parallel between impulsivity and Heymans's secondary function.

H. J. Eysenck (1970), when analyzing the data collected by the two Dutch temperament researchers from the perspective of his own temperament or personality theory concluded that Heymans and Wiersma's emotionality corresponds with neuroticism, and primary and secondary function with extraversion and introversion respectively. According to him, activity correlated with both extraversion and neuroticism is not an independent dimension (H. J. Eysenck & Eysenck, 1985, pp. 54–55; see also H. J. Eysenck, 1992c).

Recently the original data collected by Heymans and Wiersma have been reanalyzed by means of factor analysis. In two studies conducted by Van der Werff (1985) and Van der Werff and Verster (1987) two of Heymans's temperament dimensions—emotionality and activity—were replicated. The primary–secondary function did not emerge as an independent factor. Items representing this temperament dimension, along with items representing activity (the impulsive component of this trait) and emotionality (the violent component) made up a separate factor. On the basis of these data Van der Werff and Verster (1987) suggested that the primary–secondary function dimension resembles the impulsivity–reflection dimension.

Pavlov's Typology Based on Properties of the Central Nervous System

It was at the end of the first decade of this century that the Nobel Prize winner, Ivan P. Pavlov, giving a lecture at a meeting of the Association of Russian Physicians in St. Petersburg, introduced the concept of the type of nervous system (TNS). The first experimental study on types of nervous system (NS) was conducted, however, not by Pavlov but by one of his students—Nikiforovsky. In his doctoral dissertation defended in 1910 (Nikiforovsky, 1952) and devoted to the pharmacology of conditioned reflexes, he gave a behavioral description of three types of dogs distinguished on the basis of conditioned reflex (CR) characteristics. From that time on the concept of TNS and a detailed description of the central nervous system (CNS) properties were presented in several of Pavlov's publications. Pavlov, under the influence of experimental studies conducted on dogs, often changed his views on these types and properties. Experts in this field of study generally agree that the most up-to-date and representative theory of types of nervous system and CNS properties was presented by Pavlov (1951–1952) in his 1935 paper *General Types of Higher Nervous Activity in Animals and Man.* I use this paper as the main frame of reference for presenting Pavlov's typology in this chapter.

The assumption that any behavior is governed and regulated by the CNS ("nervism") was for Pavlov the starting point for studying conditioned reflexes in dogs. Observations during the many experiments on dogs conducted in his laboratory showed that individual differences in conditioning exist. These differences are expressed in such characteristics as speed, efficiency, and accuracy of conditioning and intensity, durability, and changeability of CR. Pavlov hypothesized that certain properties of the NS are responsible for individual differences in these characteristics. He distinguished the following four fundamental properties of the CNS: strength of excitation, strength of inhibition, balance (equilibrium), and mobility of nervous processes (NP; excitation and inhibition). The combination of these properties constitutes the types of the nervous system regarded as the physiological equivalent of temperaments.

Strength of Excitation. Strength of excitation (SE) was regarded by Pavlov as the most important property of the CNS because individuals are often confronted with extraordinary events of high stimulative value. Strength of excitation means the working capacity of cortical cells. There is little information in Pavlov's publications concerning the essence of strength of excitation. He limited himself to the statement that the fundamental ability to work is borne by a hypothetical "excitable substance" underlying the ability of the nerve cells to work. Working capacity or endurance is manifest in the withstanding of either prolonged or short-lived, but exceedingly strong, excitation without slipping into protective (transmarginal) inhibition. On the behavioral (or physiological) level the individual's functional endurance is expressed in responses to strong prolonged or recurrent stimulation.

The terms *strength of excitation* and *strength of the nervous system* were used by Pavlov interchangeably and he treated them as a property (not a state) of the CNS. As may be assumed, a reverse relation occurs between the strength of the nervous system understood as a property and the intensity of the excitatory process as a state. The stronger the nervous system, that is, the more resilient it is to strong or long-lasting stimuli, the smaller the excitatory process, understood as an evoked state.

Physiological methods for diagnosing the SE in dogs were elaborated by Pavlov, all of them referring to different aspects of conditioning. These methods were aimed at (a) determining the intensity of stimuli to which the individual is able to react adequately, (b) increasing the excitability of the nerve cells by means of food deprivation or caffeine, (c) using prolonged stimulation. Their common function was to assess the level of stimulus intensity at which protective inhibition occurs.

Protective Inhibition. Protective or transmarginal inhibition, regarded by Pavlov as unconditioned inhibition, protects the central nervous system against overloading. Pavlov (1951–1952) regarded the intensity and efficiency of conditioned reflexes as a function of the intensity of stimuli ("law of strength"). When the intensity of stimuli surpasses the capacity (endurance) of the CNS the law of strength no longer works because of the onset of protective inhibition. As illus-

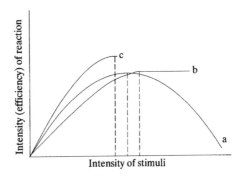

FIGURE 1.2. Protective inhibition: Different manifestations and individual differences.

trated in Figure 1.2, this inhibition may be manifest in several ways: (a) decrease of intensity (amplitude) of reaction, (b) lack of changes in the intensity of reaction or (c) disappearance of reaction in spite of increasing intensity of stimuli. In individuals with a weak nervous system, protective inhibition occurs at lower stimulus intensities as compared with individuals with a strong nervous system.

Strength of Inhibition. This feature of the nervous system plays a secondary role in Pavlov's typology. In his publications information as to the meaning of strength of inhibition (SI) is scarce. All we find are statements indicating that inhibition is related to the process of assimilation or that excitation and inhibition are inseparable. Conditioned inhibition comprises all kinds of acquired (learned) inhibitions, that is, extinction, delay, differentiation, and conditioned inhibition in its narrow sense as used by Pavlov.

The ease of evoking inhibitory CRs and their stability are, according to Pavlov, indicators of conditioned inhibition, especially its strength. Pavlov assumed SI to be a trait, as was SE. He described several methods used at his laboratory for assessing SI. Most of them were aimed at elaborating different kinds of inhibitory CRs (see Strelau, 1983). As a rule, SI was diagnosed only when the equilibrium of nervous processes—excitation and inhibition—needed to be estimated.

In general, Pavlov's views on SI were unclear and confused (see, e.g., Strelau, 1969; Teplov, 1964). Thus there was reluctance among Pavlov's students and followers to refer to this trait.

Balance (Equilibrium) of Nervous Processes. Balance or equilibrium of the nervous processes (BA) was the first NS property distinguished by Pavlov. When analyzing the essence of BA Pavlov regarded this feature from the functional point of view, as was the case with other properties of the NS. During the life of humans and animals it is often necessary to inhibit certain excitations in order to evoke other reactions, which are adequate and appropriate for new stimuli in the environment (Pavlov, 1952, p. 540).

When writing about BA Pavlov was referring to the equilibrium between SE and SI. This position remained unchanged from the 1920s up to the last period of his life, when he wrote that the equilibrium of nervous processes should be regarded as the ratio of the strength of excitatory process to the strength of inhibition (Pawłow, 1952, pp. 543, 602). Pavlov did not refer to the assessment of BAP. Probably he diagnosed the equilibrium of NP by comparing the ratio of strength of excitation to strength of inhibition.

Mobility of the Nervous Processes. According to Pavlov (1952), the essence of mobility is "the ability to give way—according to external conditions—to give priority to one impulse before the other, excitation before inhibition and conversely" (p. 540). In other words, mobility of nervous processes (MO) manifests itself in the speed with which a reaction to a given stimulus, when required, is inhibited in order to yield to another reaction evoked by other stimuli. In Pavlov's publications there is no information about the hypothetical neurophysiological mechanism of MO.

The methods used to diagnose MO are all based on the idea that this feature refers to the speed of alteration of excitation into inhibition and vice versa that takes place during different kinds of conditioning.

The Status of CNS Properties. The terms used by Pavlov, such as strength of excitation, mobility of nervous processes, and so on suggest that Pavlov was exploring the nature of these features by studying neurophysiological mechanisms underlying individual differences in the formal characteristics (e.g., speed, intensity) of conditioning. In fact, Pavlov, when defining the basic CNS properties did not refer to physiological mechanisms. He characterized them from the functional point of view, stressing the role they play in the process of the individual's adaptation to the environment. One may say that Pavlov took the behaviorist position in defining and studying CNS properties (Strelau, 1983; Windholz, 1987). He used the terms for CNS properties as explanatory concepts (Strelau, 1969), based on a nervous system theory.

Types of the Nervous System. Different configurations of the properties of the CNS just described constitute the types of nervous system also referred to by Pavlov as types of higher nervous activity. He did not construct his typology in a logical manner by simply combining the basic properties of the CNS; this would have resulted in distinguishing dozens of types. Because he was under the influence of the Hippocrates–Galen typology, Pavlov argued consistently that, taking into account the adaptive functions of individuals, four TNS should be distinguished. They correspond to the ancient Greek types of temperaments.

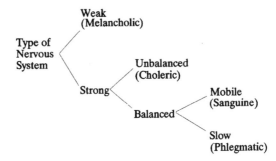

FIGURE 1.3. Pavlov's nervous system typology and its relation to the Hippocrates–Galen typology of temperaments.

Referring to the SE, Pavlov distinguished the strong and the weak TNS. The equilibrium between the SE and SI allowed him to make the next distinction (though within the strong type only), that of the balanced and unbalanced types. The unbalanced type occurs in the form of predominance of excitation over inhibition. Finally, taking mobility as the next criterion, strong, balanced individuals may be divided into the mobile and the slow types. The four types as distinguished by Pavlov, with the four temperaments to which they correspond, are presented in Figure 1.3.

Pavlov conceptualized the TNS as innate and, hence, relatively immune to environmental influences, including rearing. He referred to it as the genotype, in contradiction to the traditional meaning of the term, thus giving rise to various misinterpretations of his position.[2] The terms TNS and temperament have sometimes been used by Pavlov interchangeably. According to Pavlov, the types of nervous system established in animals justifiably could be extended to humans. "The mentioned types [the TNS] are what we call temperament in man. The temperament constitutes the most general characteristic of every man, the most general and most essential characteristic of his nervous system" (Pawłow, 1952, p. 389). The details regarding the behavioral characteristics of the four TNS may be found in several of Pavlov's publications. They are also described in the literature (see Gray, 1964a; Mangan, 1982; Nebylitsyn, 1972a; Strelau, 1983; Teplov, 1964). Pavlov strongly related the TNS to the individual's ability to adapt to the environment: the two strong, well-balanced types are best able to adapt and the weak TNS is less able.

The Importance of Pavlov's Typology for Temperament Research. Pavlov's theory of TNS gained high popularity, mainly in his country but also abroad. He un-

---

[2]*Genotype* refers to the genetic program inherited by a given individual, whereas innate traits are the result of the interaction between genotype and the prenatal environment. The term *phenotype* was used by Pavlov to characterize the ongoing nervous activity that is the outcome of the TNS properties (genotype) and the whole system of temporal connections formed during the individual's life. The phenotype has been identified with what psychologists call "character" (Pavlov, 1952, p. 594).

derlined, as no one had before, the functional significance of temperament, the role of CNS properties in the individual's adaptation to the environment. Conducting studies in laboratory settings he was able to show the links between temperament characteristics and the conceptual nervous system, that is, the hypothesized CNS properties. By making use of the CR paradigm, Pavlov introduced objective and psychophysiological measures to experimental studies on temperament.

The concept of strength of excitation, which refers in fact to individual differences in the chronic level of excitation, should be considered a forerunner of the concepts of arousal and arousability. By using bromine and caffeine in order to experimentally decrease or increase the actual level of excitation when diagnosing strength of the NS, Pavlov introduced the model for manipulating the level of arousal by means of pharmacological substances. This procedure is often used in studies on temperament dimensions related to the level of arousal (e.g., extraversion). The concept of protective inhibition used by Pavlov as an indicator of the endurance (capacity) of the CNS has been applied in several temperament-personality theories as a hypothetical construct to explain the decrease in reactions or level of performance under highly stimulating conditions.

The First Attempts to Transfer Pavlov's CNS Typology to Humans: Studies on Children

At the end of the first quarter of the 20th century two of Pavlov's students and coworkers—A. G. Ivanov-Smolensky and N. I. Krasnogorsky—made an attempt to adapt Pavlov's theory on TNS to children. As already mentioned, Pavlov's research on TNS was based on the CR paradigm. This approach has also been consistently used by his students.

Ivanov-Smolensky's Typology. Taking into account two CNS properties, mobility and equilibrium of NP, Ivanov-Smolensky (1935, 1953) distinguished four types of higher nervous activity in children. The criteria for separating them were the ease and speed with which CRs are elaborated; therefore he called them types of reflex-forming activity. These are the following: the mobile type (positive and inhibitory reflexes are formed easily and quickly), the slow type (both kinds of reflexes are formed slowly, with difficulty), the excitable type (positive reflexes are formed easily and quickly, and inhibitory reflexes slowly and with difficulty), and the inhibited type (positive reflexes are formed slowly, inhibitory reflexes easily and quickly).

In his studies, conducted mainly on children of kindergarden age, Ivanov-Smolensky used a kind of reaction time (RT) procedure consisting in pressing a rubber bulb in response to conditioned stimuli (CS)—auditory and visual. Verbal commands such as "press," "eh," "well," "bad" were used as "unconditioned stimuli" (UCS). This verbal conditioning procedure, also known as the Ivanov-

Smolensky method, has been strongly criticized. The main criticism was that the kind of verbal instructions Ivanov-Smolensky used in his experiments had little in common with UCS as used in the CR procedure (Strelau, 1969).

Krasnogorsky's Typology. The first attempts by Krasnogorsky to study the TNS in children go back to 1917 (Krasnogorsky, 1939). Investigating the inhibitory reaction in children he distinguished two types of nervous system: the normal and the inert (slow) type of higher nervous activity (HNA). In the 1930s his conception of the TNS was further elaborated by referring mainly to three basic Pavlovian properties of the CNS—the strength, balance, and mobility of NP (Krasnogorsky, 1939, 1953). Krasnogorsky's preferred procedure for the assessment of the NS properties in children was the salivary conditioned reflex.

Using unconditioned and conditioned reactions (UCR, CR) and taking into account verbal and global behavior of the children, Krasnogorsky identified four TNS and linked them, as had Pavlov, to the ancient typology of temperament. There was an essential difference, however, between him and Pavlov concerning the criteria for distinguishing TNS. Krasnogorsky did not assign balance of the NS to the relation between the strength of excitation and inhibition, as Pavlov did, but referred instead to the relationship between the strength of excitation in the cortex and strength of excitation in the subcortex. Hence the equilibrium of excitation between the cortex and subcortex areas became the major criterion of his typology. The introduction of this criterion changed to some extent the characteristics of the four types as distinguished by Krasnogorsky. The four types are (1) the sanguine—the strong type with optimal excitation, balanced and quick, with harmonious cooperation of all segments of the brain; (2) the phlegmatic—a strong type, with optimal excitation, balanced in the activity between cortex and subcortex, and slow; (3) the choleric—a strong type, excitable, immoderate, unbalanced, with dominance of excitation in the subcortical centers; and (4) the melancholic—characterized as the weak type, with low excitation of both cortical and subcortical centers.

A detailed description of the four types distinguished by Krasnogorsky has been presented by Strelau (1983). It is noteworthy that, according to Krasnogorsky, the types of HNA are not immutable as Pavlov assumed. They may be subject to changes due to learning, nutrition, social events, education, and various diseases (Krasnogorsky, 1939, 1953).

When estimating the contribution of Krasnogorsky to the knowledge of temperament it must be stressed that he was probably the first who paid attention to the cortex–subcortex ratio in explaining individual differences in temperament characteristics. He was also one of the very few Pavlovian typologists to recognize the possibility of temperament changes due to environmental factors, including education. Krasnogorsky and Ivanov-Smolensky were the first who applied Pavlov's typology of the CNS to humans.

The Constitutional Typologies of Temperament

At the beginning of the 20th century a view was spread according to which there is a relationship between the makeup of the body and the traits of the temperament. This view was developed under the influence of anthropologists and psychiatrists. The former paid attention to the diversity in the constitution of the human body whereas the latter concentrated on the convergences between the makeup of the body and individual differences in predispositions to psychiatric diseases. The constitutional approach[3] was popular mainly among Italian, German, and French researchers and found a representative expression in the constitutional theory developed in the second decade of the 20th century by a French pathologist, Claude Sigaud (1914).

Sigaud's constitutional typology was based on an assumption that the varieties of human body and its pathology are determined by both inherited dispositions and the environment. Each system in the organism corresponds to an aspect of the environment which in turn affects the given system. Air is the source of respiratory reactions, food delivered to the alimentary system lies at the root of digestive reactions, motor reactions are caused by the physical environment, and the social environment is responsible for cerebral reactions. Depending on which of the four systems in the organism is dominant, Sigaud distinguished the following four body types: the respiratory, the digestive, the muscular, and the cerebral. These body types had been distinguished almost a century earlier by L. Rostan (1824), to whom Sigaud refers. The differences in the physical makeup are especially expressed in the anatomy of the face, as can be seen in Figure 1.4. The dominance of one of the four systems causes individuals to react in a specific way to changes in the environment, this resulting in different temperament characteristics ascribed to the four body types.

Kretschmer's Constitutional Typology of Temperament

A German psychiatrist, Ernst Kretschmer, developed the most systematic constitutional theory of temperament, published in 1921 in his *Körperbau und Charakter.* In 1944 this monograph, to which I mainly refer in presenting Kretschmer's views, was already running its 18th edition, which speaks for the popularity of this theory in the first half of the 20th century. The title of the monograph suggests that Kretschmer concentrated in his research on the relationship

---

[3]The term *constitutional* is used in this section as well as in further considerations in a narrow meaning. In a more general sense constitution comprises all inherited and inborn anatomical, physiological, and psychic properties of the individual. In this book the notion *constitutional typology* or *constitutional approach* has been reserved for these conceptualizations according to which temperamental traits, or more broadly, personality characteristics, are linked (directly or indirectly) to the morphology (anatomy) of the body, to the structural (static) aspects of the physical makeup.

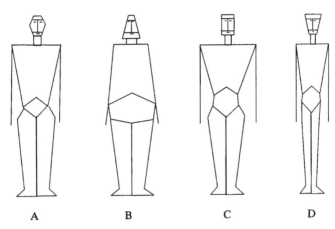

FIGURE 1.4. Body types according to Sigaud: A—respiratory, B—digistive, C—muscular, and D—cerebral.

between the makeup of the body and character. However, the subtitle of this monograph, *Research Concerning Problems of Constitution and Knowledge on Temperaments,* indicates Kretschmer's tendency to use the concept of temperament defined rather consistently as follows:

> The temperaments. They are, as we empirically know for sure, blood-chemical, humoral co-determined. Their bodily representative is the brain–gland system. The temperaments are the part of the psyche which, through the mediation of the humoral system, correlates with the physical make-up. (p. 298)

Body Types and Psychiatric Disorders. Kretschmer was under the influence of the early constitutional typologies, especially Hippocrates' distinction between the two body types, *habitus apoplecticus* and *habitus phthisicus.* On the basis of clinical observations Kretschmer arrived at the conclusion that there is a contingency between patients' physical makeup and their psychiatric disorders. Manic-depressive patients are mostly pyknics (short-thick physique, typical for the *habitus apoplecticus* type), schizophrenics are dominantly leptosomatics or asthenics (long-thin physique, characteristic of the *habitus phthisicus* type) and epileptics come mainly from the athletic types. The description of physical makeup was based on a detailed anthropological examination as well as on a photographic technique, later further developed by Sheldon. For example, Kretschmer (1944, pp. 2–3) distinguished in his "Constitutional Schema" 17 parts of the face and skull which were described by 86 different items. The body types are schematically illustrated in Figure 1.5.

Kretschmer's statement regarding the relationship between body types and psychiatric disorders was supported by empirical data. On the basis of 8,099 indi-

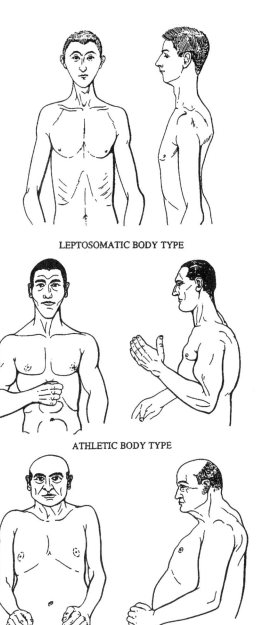

LEPTOSOMATIC BODY TYPE

ATHLETIC BODY TYPE

PYKNIC BODY TYPE

FIGURE 1.5. The physical makeup types distinguished by Kretschmer. *Note.* From *Körperbau und Charakter: Untersuchungen zum Konstitutionsproblem und zur Lehre von den Temperamenten* [Physique and Character: Research concerning Problems of Constitution and Knowledge on Temperaments] (17th–18th ed., pp. 18, 23, 27), by E. Kretschmer, 1944, Berlin, Germany: Springer. Copyright 1944 by Springer Verlag. Reprinted with permission.

vidual cases the following findings emerged: among schizophrenics 50.3% are leptosomatics, 64% of manic-depressive individuals are pyknics, and epileptics are mostly found among athletics (28.9%) and dysplastics (29.5%), as presented in Figure 1.6. The dysplastic type comprises all kinds of departures from the normal physique (Kretschmer, 1944).

Body Types and Temperaments. Taking these findings as a point of departure, Kretschmer put forward a hypothesis stating that in healthy, normal people there is also a relationship between the physical makeup and temperaments, including the inclination to psychiatric disorders. Normal people with a given type of physique have temperaments that are somewhat like the psychiatric disorders typical for their physical makeup. Kretschmer distinguished the following three types of temperament: schizothymic, cyclothymic, and ixothymic.

The *schizothymic* temperament has a leptosomatic (asthenic) body type. In case of illness individuals representing this type are prone to schizophrenia, are autistic (withdrawn), their emotions oscillate between irritability and coldness,

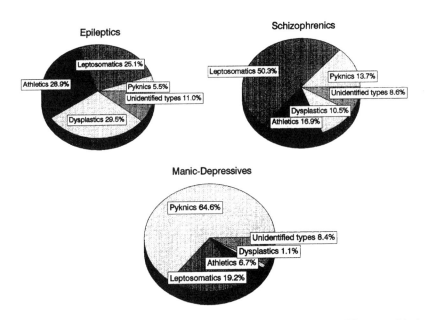

FIGURE 1.6. The distribution of physical makeup types among individuals with different psychiatric disorders. *Note.* From *Körperbau und Charakter: Untersuchungen zum Konstitutionsproblem und zur Lehre von den Temperamenten* [Physique and Character: Research concerning Problems of Constitution and Knowledge on Temperaments] (17th–18th ed., p. 35), by E. Kretschmer, 1944, Berlin, Germany: Springer. Copyright 1944 by Springer Verlag. Adapted with permission.

they are rigid in habits and attitudes, they withdraw from reality, and they have difficulty adapting.

The *cyclothymic* temperament, named from the cyclical psychosis known as manic-depression, is mostly found among pyknics. Pyknics are prone to manic-depressive psychosis; their emotions vary from joy to sadness. They have easy contact with their environment and are realistic in their views.

The *ixothymic* (Gr. *ixos*—sticky) temperament has an athletic body type. When psychiatric disorders occur, individuals with this temperament have a tendency toward epilepsy, are quiet, have low sensitivity, are modest in gestures and mimicry, have low plasticity, and have difficulty adapting to their environment.

On the basis of his research and experiences Kretschmer described the characteristic qualities of temperament. The temperaments are present in the following four psychological domains: (1) psychasthesia (*Psychaestesie*) expressed in over- or undersensitivity to psychic stimuli, (2) mood, which may vary from pleasure (joy) to unpleasantness (sadness), (3) psychic tempo expressed in the acceleration or inhibition of psychic processes in general as well as in their specific rhythmicity, and (4) psychomotility (*Psychomotolitaet*), the general tempo of motions as well as specific modes of locomotion (Kretschmer, 1944, p. 298). It is clear that these temperament characteristics spotlight the formal aspect of human behavior.

In Europe Kretschmer's constitutional typology gained exceptional popularity, especially in the 1930s. Many psychologists and clinicians were under the influence of Kretschmer. During World War II a German psychiatrist, K. Conrad (1941), referring to Kretschmer's theory, published a constitutional typology based on a genetic approach. His view, according to which temperament characteristics as well as more complex psychic phenomena (e.g., attitudes, beliefs) are, like the physical makeup, genetically determined has been rejected by most psychologists. Such views were conducive to the development of racist attitudes.

To treat the physical makeup as an indicator of human psyche, or at least temperament, was an attractive and easy route to psychological and psychiatric diagnostics. After World War II Kretschmer's typology lost its popularity. In recent decades few papers referring to his theory have been published.

The Constitutional Theory of Temperament Developed by Sheldon

The popularity that Kretschmer gained in Europe did not spread to American psychologists and physicians. Twenty years after Kretschmer's famous monograph W. H. Sheldon and coworkers (Sheldon & Stevens, 1942; Sheldon, Stevens, & Tucker, 1940) published a constitutional theory of temperament that earned popularity in the United States. Sheldon's theory of temperament has been described in almost all U.S. handbooks of personality; thus I limit the presentation of his concept to the most important issues.

Sheldon's constitutional theory, which developed under the influence of Kretschmer and to test his theory, was based on the assumption that body and temperament constitute two integral aspects of the same object: the human being. The body, viewed structurally, determines temperament which in turn is a function of the body. The interdependence of structure and function is masked by the complexity of the organism and the psyche. In order to grasp the relationship between the physical and psychological characteristics, the basic variables (physical and psychological) must be separated.

The Morphological Taxonomy. The starting point of Sheldon's theory was the description of basic morphological components by means of a standardized photographic technique and anthropometric studies (Sheldon *et al.,* 1940). He distinguished 17 different measures (parameters expressed as ratios to stature) based on a 7-point rating scale. This procedure led him to the distinction of three primary components (dimensions) of the physical makeup. Using embryological terminology, he called the morphological components endomorphy, mesomorphy, and ectomorphy, referring to the three tissue layers.

The composition of the three components results in the *somatotype* which provides the basis for a morphological taxonomy. The strength of these components is expressed by means of a 7-point scale. Thus the *endomorphic* type, in which the digestive viscera are massive and highly developed, is symbolized by the numbers 7-1-1. The *mesomorphic* type, with strongly developed bones, muscles, and connective tissue has the numbers 1-7-1. The numeral configuration 1-1-7 represents the *ectomorphic* type, in whom the nervous system, sensory tissue, and skin are dominant. The configuration 4-4-4 is typical for an average (mixed) somatotype.

In contrast to Kretschmer, Sheldon and his coworkers conducted studies on normal subjects. Most of his more than 4,000 subjects were males, normally nourished and in a broad age range (Sheldon *et al.,* 1940).

The Temperament Components. Whereas the morphological components represent the static aspect of constitutional psychology, temperament refers to the dynamic aspect. By temperament Sheldon and Stevens (1942) meant "the level of personality just above physiological function and below acquired attitudes and beliefs" (p. 4). The starting point for the study of temperament, which lasted over 5 years, was a list of 650 alleged temperament trait terms. No information was given about the sources from which they were derived apart from indicating that most of them refer to extraversion or introversion. On the basis of prolonged observations and dozens of interviews conducted with each subject the authors distinguished 60 trait terms which represent three clusters, also called components or factors.

Borrowing the suffix *-tonia* from Eppinger and Hess (1910), who conducted studies on vagotonia, the authors labeled the three primary temperament components viscerotonia, somatotonia, and cerebrotonia. The names illustrate the functional dominance of given organs of the body. As with the morphological measures, the temperament components, as well as the separate traits constituting the components, were estimated by means of a 7-point scale. *Viscerotonia* comprises temperamental traits closely related to the functional predominance of the digestive viscera (endomorphic physique). *Somatotonia* is characterized by traits associated with the functional predominance of the somatic structures (mesomorphic physique) and *cerebrotonia* refers to the functional prepotency of the higher centers of the NS, especially to attentional consciousness (ectomorphic physique). Thus the numeral configuration 7-1-1 represents the viscerotonic temperament, the configuration 1-7-1, the somatotonic temperament, and the numbers 1-1-7 illustrate the cerebrotonic temperament. In Table 1.2 each of the three primary temperament components has been described by means of 10 traits which constitute

TABLE 1.2. The Short Form of the Temperament Scale Developed by Sheldon and Stevens

Viscerotonia	Somatotonia	Cerebrotonia
Relaxation in posture and movement	Assertiveness of posture and movement	Restraint in posture and movement, tightness
Love of physical comfort	Love of physical adventure	Overly fast reactions
Slow Reaction	The energetic characteristic	Love of privacy
Love of polite ceremony	Need and enjoyment of exercise	Mental overintensity, hyperattentionality, apprehensiveness
Sociophilia	Love of risk and chance	Secretiveness of feeling, emotional restraint
Evenness of emotional flow	Bold directness of manner	Self-conscious motility of the eyes and face
Tolerance	Physical courage for combat	Sociophobia
Complacency	Competitive aggressiveness	Inhibited social address
The untempered characteristic	The unrestrained voice	Vocal restraint, and general restraint of noise
Smooth, easy communication of feeling, extraversion of viscerotonia	Overmaturity of appearance	Youthful intentness of manner and appearance

Note. From *The Varieties of Temperament: A Psychology of Constitutional Differences* (p. 26), by W. H. Sheldon and S. S. Stevens, 1942, New York: Harper & Brothers. Copyright 1942 by Harper & Brothers. Adapted with permission.

the short form of the Temperament Scale developed by Sheldon and Stevens (1942, p. 26).

Studies conducted by Sheldon and Stevens (1942) on a sample of 200 men aged from 17 to 31 showed that there is a highly significant and strong correlation between the physical makeup and temperament characteristics: for viscerotonia and endomorphy, .79; for somatotonia and mesomorphy, .82; and for cerebrotonia and ectomorphy, .83.

Sheldon and his coworkers also conducted studies in which the somatotypes and temperament components were related to psychiatric disorders. Wittman, Sheldon, and Katz (1948) showed that, in general, somatotypes, as well as temperament components, correlate with psychiatric disorders in the hypothesized direction.

Critical Remarks Regarding the Constitutional Approach

There is at least one common denominator for all constitutional approaches, explicitly present in both Kretschmer's and Sheldon's typologies. This is the assumption that human physique, being inherited, does not change during ontogenesis. The dualistic doctrine, typical for the constitutional approach, postulates that temperament (personality) is a parallel of the physical makeup, which means that temperament also does not change during ontogenesis. Ignorance of the environment (physical and social) as a factor codetermining temperament or personality has consequently led to the rejection of the constitutional typologies. This rejection was particularly expressed in the United States but was also present in Europe. Psychologists, physicians, and educators became more interested in changes occurring in human behavior; they concentrated on factors other than inheritance contributing to the development of human psyche. The static, purely descriptive approach and a fatalistic view of human temperament and personality as proposed by constitutional typologies were probably the main reasons for the loss of interest in the theories of Kretschmer and Sheldon, the most prominent investigators in this field of study.

There is also a more detailed critique regarding the constitutional theories, specifically referring to the concepts of Kretschmer and Sheldon. Most of the critical remarks, some of which are mentioned in the following sections, were made several decades ago.

Kretschmer's Typology. The typology of Kretschmer was developed with pathology as the starting point. It was based on the assumption, not commonly accepted, that psychiatric disorders differ from normal mental states quantitatively rather then qualitatively. Kretschmer's methods of data collection and the findings of him and his coworkers have been subject to criticism from several angles. For example, it has been shown that college students essentially differing in body types (pyknics versus leptosomes) do not differ in a series of psychological tests, including temperament characteristics (Klineberg, Asch, & Block, 1934) which speaks against the temperamental specificity of the body types under study.

Brengelmann (1952), in a study conducted on 100 normal subjects showed that the tests used by Kretschmer (1944) and his students (Enke, 1930) as experimental markers for the schizothymic and cyclothymic temperament did not allow for differentiation of individuals according to the cyclothymia–schyzothymia hypothesis as proposed by Kretschmer. The tendency to mental diseases, as well as to given body types, is to some extent age specific—a finding not taken into account by Kretschmer. In general, schizophrenics and leptosomes are about 10 years younger than manic-depressive individuals and pyknics (e.g., Burchard, 1936). Kretschmer ignored the essential changes in the physical makeup that occur during and after puberty (Homburger, 1926).

The empirical data presented by Kretschmer, limited to descriptive statistics, are handicapped by lack of statistical sophistication (H. J. Eysenck, 1970) as well as by ignorance of other methodological requirements, especially the matching of samples for age and socioeconomic status (SES).

Sheldon's Typology. The fact that Sheldon distinguished three morphological components, the combination of which resulted in somatotypes, differentiates his typology from Kretschmer's, which is based on traditional typological thinking, where categorization referring to extreme characteristics leads to the distinction of separate types. Sheldon's typology refers to dimensions and different combinations of dimensions, thus allowing for quantitative gradations among types. His constitutional theory has been criticized for several reasons, some of which are given in the following discussion.

Factor analytic studies have shown that the three-dimensional system as proposed by Sheldon in the morphological and temperament domains can easily be reduced to two dimensions. Extreme ectomorphy may be regarded as the absence of either the endomorphic or the mesomorphic component (G. Ekman, 1951); ectomorphy and endomorphy are opposite manifestations of one factor (Howells, 1952). Humphreys (1957), criticizing the statistical and empirical bases of Sheldon's theory, pointed out that when proper statistics were used to analyze his data, measures of any two of the dimensions enabled the prediction of a third dimension.

The correlations between somatotypes and objective tests used as measures of the three temperament components are much lower than postulated by Sheldon, often not significant at all (Janoff, Beck, & Child, 1950; H. C. Smith, 1949). The estimations of the somatotypes and temperament components were often conducted by the same person, thus leading to a strong halo effect which in turn biased the objective relationship between the physique and temperament (Adcock, 1948; Tyler, 1965).

Definite opinions and stereotypes exist regarding the relationship between the physical makeup and behavioral characteristics. They are mainly based on folk wisdom and in line with Sheldon's findings. These kinds of stereotypes regarding the physique–temperament relationship influenced the collection of data (Gacsaly & Borges, 1979; Wells & Siegel, 1961). The fact that somatotypes correspond with temperament components does not necessary mean that the latter are determined by the body type. The stereotypes and opinions regarding the physique–temperament relationship may influence the educational treatment of a child in such a way as to favor the kind of activity that corresponds with the individual's physical makeup. Also, changes in morphology may occur due to special child-rearing events (Lindzey, 1967).

Sheldon, presenting the idea of interdependence of the structure (body) and the function (temperament), did not make use of the embryological hypothesis (H. J. Eysenck, 1970) that was his starting point for the three morphological dimensions. He limited his theory to a purely descriptive level.

There are hundreds of publications, starting from antiquity, in which authors have tried to define temperament. A few years ago a roundtable discussion by child-oriented temperament researchers aimed at answering the question "What Is Temperament?" was published in the journal *Child Development*. In four presentations four different views regarding the definition of temperament were delineated (Goldsmith *et al.*, 1987). As demonstrated in the following sections, in spite of many differences in the understanding of this phenomenon, there are several characteristics on which most temperament scholars agree.

The Concept of Temperament

One of the main aspects on which temperament scholars differ is the domain of behavior characteristics and psychic functioning to which the concept temperament refers. To consider the extremes, according to some researchers temperament characteristics should be limited to emotions only, whereas to others behavioral expressions of temperament are present in all kinds of human functioning.

The Emotion-Oriented Understanding of Temperament

It is difficult, if not impossible, to determine the extent to which the contributions of former researchers have influenced our own ideas and inquiries. From my own reading on temperament over my 40 years of studies in this area, it is apparent that the conceptualization of temperament presented in the 1920s and 1930s by Gordon Allport is one of the most influential contributions in the attempt to determine the meaning of the concept of temperament, at least in Western countries. His definition of temperament constitutes the basis for all or almost all emotion-oriented temperament researchers.

Gordon Allport's Definition of Temperament

G. W. Allport (1897–1967) is regarded as the founder of trait-oriented personality psychology. This statement is not neutral for our considerations on temperament, since with but a few exceptions temperament is viewed as a structure consisting of traits.

Allport's starting point in his task of describing temperament was a deep penetration of the temperament literature, including the contributions of German and French researchers, and his creative understanding of personality. I contend that G. W. Allport (1937) regarded temperament as one of the components of personality. According to him:

> Temperament refers to the characteristic phenomena of an individual's emotional nature, including his susceptibility to emotional stimulation, his customary strength and speed of response, the quality of his prevailing mood, and all peculiarities of fluctuation and intensity in mood; these phenomena being regarded as dependent upon constitutional make-up, and therefore largely hereditary in origin. (p. 54)

In an article written by G. W. Allport and Vernon (1930) we find a very similar definition of temperament, quoted, however, after Floyd H. Allport (1924), the brother of Gordon Allport.

G. W. Allport's understanding of temperament as referring to individual differences in emotions, especially in the formal characteristics of these phenomena, has its historical forerunners. As shown previously, Wundt, as well as many other authors, limited temperament to emotional characteristics. The ancient Greek typologists also considered individual differences in emotions as the core of temperament when they claimed that "humors" were the physiological basis of temperament.

Further statements from Allport's classic monograph *Personality: A Psychological Interpretation* add to our knowledge of his understanding of temperament. For example, for Allport temperament, like intelligence and physique belongs to the class of raw material from which personality is fashioned. Temperament being dependent on the biochemical constitution should be regarded as psychobiological.

Temperament belongs to the category of dispositions that are almost unchanged from infancy throughout life. "The more anchored a disposition is in native constitutional soil the more likely it is to be spoken of as temperament" (G. W. Allport, 1937, p. 53). The behavioral expressions of temperament are present since early infancy.

According to Allport (1937) two aspects of temperament may be characterized by means of quantitative continua (dimensions): broad emotions–narrow emotions, which refers to the range of objects and situations to which an individual reacts emotionally, and strong emotions–weak emotions. The latter dimension, which pertains to the intensity of feeling evoked by objects and situations can be measured objectively by means of blood pressure, pulse rate, and psychogalvanic skin response (pp. 407–408).

Allport's writings were of utmost importance in further considerations and studies regarding temperament. As seen in the next sections of this chapter, many of Allport's ideas still hold today and modifications made by others usually go in the direction of less radical ascertainments and expanding the domain of temperament.

Emotion-Centered Definitions of Temperament in Contemporary Research

The emotion-oriented definitions of temperament, of which Allport's is regarded as the classic one, have also gained popularity in contemporary psychology. In his earlier publications H. J. Eysenck (1970), referring Allport, among others, defined temperament as a "more or less stable enduring system of affective behaviour ('emotion')" (p. 2). However, Eysenck, whose temperament theory is described in Chapter 2, has seldom used the term "temperament."

The most popular emotion-oriented definitions of temperament may be found in Mehrabian's and Goldsmith and Campos's conceptualizations regarding this phenomenon. Since about the mid-1970s Albert Mehrabian (1978b, 1991; Mehrabian & Falender, 1978; Mehrabian & O'Reilly, 1980) has presented an emotion-based theory of temperament (see Chapter 3) which refers to the following understanding of this concept: "Temperament is viewed as a characteristic emotional state" (Mehrabian & Falender, 1978, p. 1120). Probably to avoid misunderstanding in defining temperament in terms of states, Mehrabian (1991) supplemented this definition by stating that "'Temperament' is defined here as a 'characteristic emotion state' or as an 'emotion trait'" (p. 77).

By using the term *state* the author wanted to underscore that temperamental characteristics are present only in states. The rather confusing term *characteristic* has been used by Mehrabian to stress that only those emotional states that are typical and unique for the given individual, that is, the emotional states in which individuals usually differ, are the subject of study in temperament research. The definition of temperament as presented by Mehrabian and his coworkers is rarely cited by other researchers, even when these others are centered on emotions as the core concept of temperament.

Whereas Mehrabian's concept of temperament was developed by studying adults, Goldsmith and Campos (1982, 1986, 1990; see Chapter 3) were centered on infants. The analysis of infant behavior led them to the conclusion that the motoric, facial, and vocal behavior of infants all are expressions of the affective systems (Goldsmith & Campos, 1982); temperament in infants is expressed mainly in emotional behavior. As the authors write:

> We conceive of *temperament* as individual differences in emotionality. . . . This includes individual differences in the primary emotions—fear, anger, sadness,

pleasure, interest, and so forth—and more generalized arousal, as expressed in the temporal and intensive parameters of behavioral response. We delineate temperament from individual differences in cognition, perception, and emotional states (as opposed to traits). (Goldsmith & Campos, 1986, p. 231)

Taking a more general view Goldsmith and Campos (1990) proposed to define infant temperament "as individual differences in tendencies to express the primary emotions" (p. 1945). Temperament dimensions form the emotional substrate of some later personality characteristics (Goldsmith et al., 1987). The authors make clear that in the understanding of temperament they follow a tradition dating to Hippocrates and Galen and resurrected by Allport.

Conclusion

To close the presentation of the emotion-centered conceptualizations of temperament one may conclude that the most conspicuous common denominator of the definitions of temperament as proposed by Allport, Eysenck (in his earlier writings), Mehrabian, and Goldsmith and Campos is the statement that temperament should be regarded as a construct referring exclusively to emotional behavior. Explicitly or implicitly these definitions say that more or less stable individual differences in emotions are the subject of temperament research. For these authors temperament is a synonym of the expression, "individual differences in emotional behavior."

Temperament Understood as a Style of Behavior

One of the most popular definitions of temperament was formulated in the 1960s by Alexander Thomas and Stella Chess (1977; A. Thomas, Chess, & Birch, 1968), the founders of contemporary temperament research in children. Considering temperament as a behavioral style the authors described temperament thus:

Temperament may best be viewed as a general term referring to the *how* of behavior. It differs from ability, which is concerned with the *what* and *how well* of behaving, and from motivation, which accounts for *why* a person does what he is doing. Temperament, by contrast, concerns the *way* in which an individual behaves. (A. Thomas & Chess, 1977, p. 9)

Thomas and Chess considered temperament as a phenomenological term, with no implications as to etiology and immutability. Temperament is defined on a purely descriptive level without any inference to the determinants of individual differences in temperament. However, on different occasions the authors assumed that temperament has a genetic background (Chess & Thomas, 1989; A. Thomas &

Chess, 1977). There is a high consistency in the authors' understanding of temperament which is defined in recent publications of the two eminent temperament scholars as it was 25 years ago (Chess & Thomas, 1986, 1989, 1991).

Giving some more detailed explanation to their definition of temperament Thomas and Chess (Goldsmith *et al.,* 1987, pp. 508–509) emphasized that temperament is an independent psychological attribute; must at all times be differentiated from motivations, abilities, and personality; is always expressed as a response to an external stimulus, opportunity, expectation, or demand; and is an attribute of the child that modifies the influence of the environment.

Every behavior, irrespective of its content, may be characterized by means of the stylistic component; it might be concluded that temperament understood as a behavior style reveals itself in all kinds of behavior and it refers rather to the formal characteristics and not to the content of behavior. J. V. Lerner and Lerner (1983) paid attention to the fact that it is difficult to define the concept of style. Bates (1987) argued that the concept of style does not apply to all temperament dimensions, even those distinguished by Thomas and Chess (see Chapter 2).

Many temperament researchers, especially in the United States, take the stylistic definition of temperament as formulated by Thomas and Chess as a starting point for their studies, centered mostly on infants and older children (see, e.g., W. B. Carey, 1983; P. S. Klein, 1984; Maziade, 1988; McDevitt & Carey, 1978; Persson-Blennow, McNeil, & Blennow, 1988; Rutter, 1982; Sameroff, Seifer, & Elias, 1982; Windle, Iwawaki, & Lerner, 1988).

Biology-Oriented Definitions of Temperament

Most researchers in the area of temperament take the fact that individual differences in temperament are determined or codetermined by some biological mechanisms as the basic or one of the basic criteria for defining temperament. This is not to say that the biology-oriented understandings of temperament compose a class of concordant or convergent definitions. They differ mostly in the number of criteria to be represented in the definition, such as heritability, stability, population, and age to which temperament refers. As illustrated in Chapters 2 and 3, they also differ in the understanding of biological mechanisms underlying temperament. Because most of the definitions refer to more than one criterion in defining temperament, it is not easy to present a clear-cut distinction between them. Even some of the definitions of temperament presented until now, especially the one by Allport, emphasize the importance of the constitutional factor as one of the criteria to be applied in order to distinguish temperament from other phenomena. Several groups of definitions representing the biological approach to temperament are given in the following sections.

Temperament as an Expression of the Type of Nervous System

Since Pavlov there has existed in the former Soviet Union, especially in Russia, a tradition according to which temperament is regarded as the psychological expression of the type of higher nervous activity (e.g., Golubeva & Rozhdestvenskaya, 1976; Leites, 1956, 1972) or as the dynamic characteristics of behavior as expressed in individual differences in speed and intensity of reaction (behavior) and determined by the type of nervous system (Ilin, 1978; Merlin, 1973; Rusalov, 1979; Teplov, 1985).

The fact that temperament is determined by the type of nervous system regarded as a given composition of the basic properties of the central nervous system was commonly accepted among Russian psychologists at least until the 1980s. Also established was the view that temperament refers to formal traits, such as the energetic and temporal characteristics of behavior.

The understanding of temperament as presented by Russian psychologists in the period from the 1950s to the 1980s influenced research on temperament in Eastern Europe to some extent (see, e.g., Halmiova & Sebova, 1986; Strelau, 1969; Zapan, 1974). However, such a comprehension of temperament did not gain much popularity in Western countries (see Mangan, 1982; Strelau, 1983).

Temperament as an Inherited Component of Personality

The inheritance of temperament traits had already been pointed out by G. W. Allport (1937). One of the most influential theoreticians on temperament in the 1950s, Solomon Diamond (1957), considered temperament as the inherited (though influenced by environment) component of personality. He pointed to the similarities between temperament characteristics in humans and other mammals, as well as to the evolutionarily determined adaptive function of temperament. When referring to the understanding of temperament by Allport, Diamond (1957) preferred to define temperament "in terms of the ease of arousal of *unlearned* [emphasis added] patterns of adaptive behavior, and to define its dimensions in terms of whole classes of adaptive response, rather than in terms of emotional expression" (p. 95). Both Allport and Diamond, as well as Thomas and Chess, influenced to some extent the theory of temperament as developed by Buss and Plomin (1975, 1984). According to their theory (see Chapter 3) temperament must be defined by taking into account two basic criteria that distinguish this phenomenon from other personality traits: inheritance and presence in early childhood. Thus the authors define "temperaments as *inherited personality traits present in early childhood*" (1984, p. 84).

This definition of temperament emphasizes most consistently the fact that temperament is inherited. It also excludes from the domain of temperament all personality traits that originate solely in environmental events. The definition does not specify, however, the domain of behavior in which temperament is expressed, thus giving way to the search for temperament characteristics among a broad range of behaviors, assuming they fulfil the definitional criteria—inheritance and presence since early infancy. In most definitions of temperament the exposition of inheritance is absent, even when referring to biological bases of temperament.

A contemporary Russian psychologist, V. M. Rusalov (1985, 1989c), also makes inheritance one of his basic criteria when defining temperament. According to him, the basis of temperament consists in the general constitution of the human organism which should be considered a composite of physical and physiological properties of the individual. These composites are rooted in the inherited apparatus (Rusalov, 1985, p. 25).

In studies conducted during the past two decades the inheritance criterion has lost its strength. It has been shown in several studies that the heritability index does not differentiate between the traditionally recognized temperament traits and other personality characteristics (Holden, 1987; Loehlin & Nichols, 1976).

Temperament as Referring to the Formal Characteristics of Behavior

The fact that temperament refers not to the content of behavior but to formal characteristics of human functioning has been emphasized by many authors. When temperament is limited to emotional behavior, such formal characteristics as intensity, duration, speed, fluctuation of emotions, and so on are the basic criteria for describing individual differences in temperament. The conceptualizations of temperament offered by Wundt, Allport, Goldsmith, and Campos may serve as examples here. The stylistic definition of temperament as presented by Thomas and Chess also refers mainly to the formal characteristics of behavior. The speed and intensity of behavior have been used as definitional criteria of temperament by Russian investigators as well.

In some biologically oriented definitions of temperament the formal characteristics of behavior are particularly exposed. To some extent the statement that temperament refers to formal features of behavior implies the biological roots of temperament, the fact that temperament refers not only to emotions but to all kinds of behavior, its specificity as compared with other personality traits. In definitions given by Strelau (1983, 1989b), Eliasz (1990), Rusalov (1985, 1989c), and partly also by Rothbart (1989b; Rothbart & Derryberry, 1981), the formal characteristics of behavior serve as a definitional criterion of temperament.

As mentioned previously, in most definitions of temperament more than one criterion is used for specifying the nature of temperament. For some authors the relative stability of temperamental traits has been regarded as an essential feature. The requirement of stability is explicitly exposed in definitions of temperament given by Kagan (1982a, 1989b), Hagekull (1989), Eliasz (1990), and Rusalov (1985). As Kagan (1982) wrote:

If there is a correlated cluster of qualities that seems intuitively to belong together (for whatever reason), and the composite of the cluster is *stable* [emphasis added], that cluster is a reasonable candidate for temperamental status. (p. 24)

Concluding Remarks Regarding the Understanding of Temperament

In spite of the differences in defining temperament, there seems to be some agreement regarding the definitional criteria by means of which this phenomenon is characterized. At least there is more consistency in the understanding of this concept as compared with such notions as "personality" (see, e.g., Hall & Lindzey, 1978; Pervin, 1990, 1996; Wiggins, Renner, Clore, & Rose, 1971) or "intelligence" (e.g., Sternberg, 1982; Vernon, 1979).

The Most Common Features Determining the Understanding of Temperament

Most temperament researchers, whether emotion-oriented or expanding this phenomenon to other kinds of behavior as well, agree, explicitly or implicitly, with the view that temperament is a phenomenon that may be characterized by the following features:

(a) Temperament refers to behavior characteristics in which individuals differ. These differences are described by such concepts as *disposition* (e.g., Betz & Thomas, 1979; Diamond, 1957), *trait* (e.g., Allport, 1937; Buss & Plomin, 1984; Strelau, 1983), *quality* (e.g., Kagan & Reznick, 1986; Roback, 1931), *attribute* (e.g., Stevenson & Graham, 1982; Windle, 1989b), *factor* (e.g., Cattell, 1934–1935; J. P. Guilford, 1975), *dimension* (e.g., H. J. Eysenck, 1990b, 1991a; J. P. Guilford & Zimmerman, 1950), *type* (e.g., Kagan, 1989b; Zapan, 1974), and *category* (e.g., Chess & Thomas, 1989; Kagan, 1989b); these concepts are used interchangeably by many researchers.

(b) Temperament is relatively stable as compared with other phenomena and is also characterized by considerable cross-situational consistency. The terms "stability" and "consistency," however, should not be understood literally. In the context of temperament research they underline only that temperament, as compared with other behavior characteristics, belongs among the most stable and cross-situationally consistent phenomena.

(c) Temperament has a biological basis; however, as shown in Chapters 2 and 3, a variety of views regarding the kind and quantity of anatomic structures and physiological mechanisms underlying temperament can be found.

(d) Temperament refers mainly to formal characteristics of behavior or reactions, such as intensity, energy, strength, speed, tempo, fluctuation, and mobility. In some conceptualizations regarding the nature of temperament these characteristics are limited to emotions only (e.g., G. W. Allport, Goldsmith, Campos); in others they spread to all kinds of behavior (e.g., Rothbart, Strelau).

The Status of Temperamental Traits as Exemplified by a Methaphor

For a better understanding of the nature of temperament I refer to an analogy with the characteristics of the automobile which I have applied in my lectures on temperament since the end of the 1960s. In order to explain the nature of temperament some authors have used the functioning of a steam engine or a car as a metaphor of temperament features in man (e.g., Buss & Plomin, 1975; Eliasz, 1990; Ewald, 1924).

Acceleration of the car seems to illustrate the concept of temperament better than any other feature. As we know, each type of car has given acceleration characteristics, which are expressed in time units (seconds), that is, the time needed to move the car from standstill for a given distance under optimal and fully controlled conditions. The acceleration characteristic is one of the most important features of the car and may be found in every car catalog. No statistics are needed to state that there are differences in acceleration between cars.

By using the term "acceleratability," treated here as an analogy to temperament traits, I underscore the fact that cars differ from each other in acceleration and that these differences, being relatively stable, have the status of a feature resembling traits or dimensions in psychology. Acceleratability can be measured in time units, suggesting that we are dealing with a property that objectively exists. However, it does not have the ontological status of a feature as does the color or shape of a car. The latter are permanently observable features of the car, whether the car is moving, has stopped, is operating, or is damaged. In contrast, acceleratability reveals itself under specific conditions and can be measured only when the car moves (behaves), similar to temperament traits which are expressed exclusively in behavior and reactions. Thus acceleratability, like temperament traits, has the status of a *latent* property, which is activated and expressed under specific conditions, such as movement (car), or behavior and reactions (man and animals). Acceleratability, like temperament traits, should be understood as the *tendency* of a car to move (behave) with a given speed.

The mechanisms determining acceleratability of a car throw some light on our understanding of the determinants of temperamental traits. They also exemplify how to understand cross-situational stability and temporal consistency of temperament traits. Acceleratability of the car depends on many of its aggregates and elements, the most important of which seem to be the following: type of engine, capacity of cylinders, ignition, carburetor, shape, size, and weight of the body, and type of wheels. Other conditions being equal, the interaction of these aggregates and the "makeup" elements of the car determine its acceleratability. One may also say that these composite features of the car ensure stability and cross-situational consistency of the acceleratability characteristics, as the biochemical and physiological mechanisms underlying temperament do.

Drivers know, however, that such factors as a dirty spark plug, disordered ignition, choked carburetor, leaky cylinder, and so on, directly influence the acceleratability of a car by lowering its capacity. Even one element in the system of aggregates determining acceleratability, for example, leaky cylinders, may essentially decrease this feature. This gives the erroneous impression that acceleratability is determined by the one factor only. Such a state of affairs is often found in temperament research. A disorder or change in a given physiological mechanism, causing changes in temperament characteristics, was used by some researchers (e.g., Kretschmer, 1944) as an argument proving that a given temperament trait is predominantly or only determined by this mechanism. The number of aggregates and elements of the car the interaction of which determines such a simple trait as acceleratability suggests that the biochemical and physiological bases of any temperament trait in man and animals must be much more complex and cannot be reduced to single biological mechanisms.

When assessing acceleratability of the same car but under different conditions we easily observe differences in scores expressing this "trait." We then find that acceleratability also depends on such factors as air pressure of the wheels, quality of gasoline, temperature of the engine, kind and quality of the road (highway), weather (e.g., rain, wind, snow). Only when these environmental conditions are comparable for the two cars may we expect similar scores on the acceleratability dimension. Under constant conditions the scores expressing this feature are stable, that is, they are predictable.

The fact that the actually measured acceleration depends not only on the anatomy and functional capacity of the aggregates (the interaction of which determines acceleratability) but also on other (environmental) conditions shows distinctly that the expression of this trait is a result of interaction between the composite mechanisms of the car and a variety of environmental conditions. This is all the more true when referring to temperament characteristics. The more constant the environmental variables, the stronger their influence on the stability of a given characteristic. A car that always runs on a dust track will always show lower acceleration characteristics as compared with the same car tested on free highways. This is also the case with temperament characteristics that may be expressed differently depending on the particular environment.

Some external conditions, especially permanent ones, may cause changes in the elements and aggregates of the car that in turn lead to changes in its acceleratability. For example, the way the new car has been run in, the mode of exploitation, the quality of gasoline usually applied, and so on, are factors that codetermine the acceleratability of the car. Again, the analogy with temperament is obvious. Educational treatment, especially in the first period of life (the analogy to the running in of a new car), and permanently acting environment (social and physical) cause changes in the biological bases of temperament and therefore also lead to changes in temperament characteristics.

Acceleratability has the status of a formal trait, as most temperament characteristics do. Each car may be characterized by means of this property, measured in time units (in analogy to tempo, duration, or mobility in temperament).

Finally, acceleratability understood as the car's property is not the speed with which the car passes a given distance from starting point, yet it expresses itself in speed units. Neither can acceleratability be reduced to the mechanisms and factors underlying this property. Acceleratability is the latent property of the car which results from the interaction among the different aggregates and elements. In my understanding temperament traits have a similar status.

Temperament traits are expressed in behavior characteristics but cannot be reduced to these characteristics. They are determined by internal (inborn and acquired) mechanisms but, again, cannot be reduced to these mechanisms. Temperament traits are the result of a given interaction among a variety of internal mechanisms; they have a specific status expressed in the tendency to behave (react) in a given way. This tendency, because it is more or less consistent and stable, may be modified by external conditions. As shown in Chapter 4 and 5 the biological bases determining temperament traits are far from familiar and identified, thus *temperament traits have the status of hypothetical constructs* as some authors have mentioned (e.g., Bornstein, Gaughran, & Homel, 1986; Kagan & Reznick, 1986; Eliasz, 1990). Several years ago I emphasized that temperament "does not exist as such; it is a type of a theoretical construct, referring to existing phenomena, just like the theoretical construct of intelligence" (Strelau, 1986, p. 62).

Temperament and Personality

Much less agreement occurs, however, regarding the relationship between temperament and personality. This is mainly due to the ambiguity of the concept of "personality" itself, already shown most explicitly by G. W. Allport (1937) who distinguished 50 definitions of this concept (see Fig 1.7).

The tendency to distinguish between temperament and personality has a long-standing tradition. Whereas Galen used the term *temperament* to describe behavior characteristics that have their roots in the individual's organism (endogenous factors), others have tried to explain human behavior characteristics by means of external conditions. The monograph *Characters* by Theophrastus (4th–3rd century B.C.), who explained individual differences in character[4] mainly in terms of environmental settings (exogenous factors) exemplifies this view.

---

[4]In more contemporary writings the term *character* has been substituted by the term *personality* or temperament and character have been treated as two separate components of personality (see G. W. Allport, 1937; Roback, 1931).

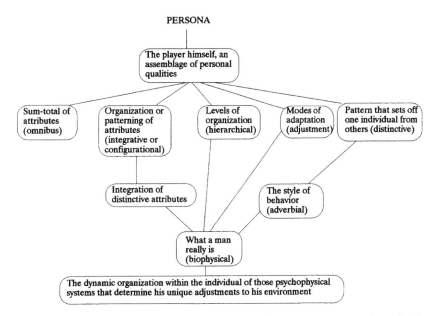

FIGURE 1.7. Psychological meaning of the notion "personality." *Note.* From *Personality: A Psychological Interpretation* (p. 46), by G. W. Allport, 1937, New York: Holt.

Temperament as a Component of Personality or as a Concept Synonymous with Personality

As already mentioned, research on temperament has its roots in the individual-differences approach (see, e.g., W. Stern, 1921). This is also one of the most popular and classic perspectives from which contemporary personality has been viewed (see, e.g., Amelang & Bartussek, 1990; Royce & Powell, 1983). G. W. Allport (1937), one of the founders of the individual-differences approach to personality, treated the concept of personality as a very general one, comprising such phenomena as habits, specific and general attitudes, sentiments and dispositions; the last are described in terms of traits which also include temperamental characteristics. For Allport, individual differences constituted a definitional component of personality. According to him (G.W. Allport, 1937), "Personality is the dynamic organization within the individual of those psychophysical systems that determine his *unique* [emphasis added] adjustments to his environment" (p. 48). In very recent conceptualizations of personality this concept has also been defined by personological or trait-oriented psychologists in terms of individual differences (see, e.g., H. J. Eysenck & Eysenck 1985; Royce & Powell, 1983). For example, Hofstee (1991) proposes "to define psychology of personality as the study of traits" and argues that "the specific assignment of personality psychology is to explain behavior in terms of individual differences" (p. 177).

If we take the individual-differences approach according to which differences among people are described by means of traits or similar concepts, such as factors and dimensions, the place of temperament in the domain of personality is quite legitimate. As proposed by many authors (G. W. Allport, 1937; Buss & Finn, 1987; Diamond, 1957; Endler, 1989; J. P. Guilford, 1975; Roback, 1931; Strelau, 1987a), temperament, as illustrated by Figure 1.8, should be regarded as one of the constituents of personality.

Taking the trait approach to personality as a starting point we may say that (a) temperament refers to the raw material out of which personality is fashioned (G. W. Allport, 1937; Endler, 1989), thus it constitutes the primary (elementary and fundamental) personality traits; (b) these personality traits belong to the domain of temperament that has been present since early childhood (Buss & Plomin, 1984); and (c) temperament comprises those personality traits which have a biological background (Buss & Plomin, 1984; Rothbart, 1989a; Strelau, 1983, 1994a).

The literature on trait-oriented personality and temperament describes two other tendencies. First, the concepts of personality and temperament are regarded as synonyms; second, the term *temperament* is not used at all, even when studying personality traits which have traditionally been regarded as belonging to the domain of temperament.

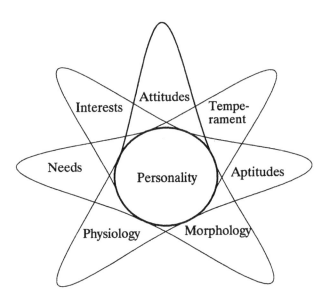

FIGURE 1.8. Modalities of traits representing different aspects of personality. *Note.* From *Personality* (p. 7), by J. P. Guilford, 1959, New York: McGraw-Hill. Copyright 1959 by McGraw-Hill. Adapted with permission.

G. W. Allport (1937, p. 53) noted that it is apparently a British tradition to equate temperament with personality. This statement is exemplified in the conceptualizations of H. J. Eysenck and J. A. Gray, two prominent researchers in the domain of individual differences. According to Eysenck (H. J. Eysenck & Eysenck, 1985) "personality, as we look at it, has two major aspects: temperament and intelligence. Most textbooks of personality deal with temperament only" (p. vii). Concepts such as values, interests, and attitudes although related to personality do not usually form part of its central core (H. J. Eysenck, 1991a). According to Eysenck the personality structure consists of three basic dimensions—extraversion, neuroticism, and psychoticism—which, depending on the context, are labeled personality or temperament dimensions (factors). Gray has a similar view. When discussing the main issues of anxiety, impulsivity, extraversion, and neuroticism he used the terms *personality* and *temperament* as synonyms (e.g., Gray, 1973). As Gray wrote: "I use the terms 'temperament' and 'personality' interchangeably; I take them both to mean what remains of individual differences once general intelligence and such special cognitive characteristics as visuo-spatial or verbal ability have been removed" (Gray, 1991, p. 122). Also in North American literature such a view on the relationship between temperament and personality has gained some popularity (see, e.g., Stelmack, 1990; Zuckerman, 1985, 1991c).

It must be added that researchers who treat the terms temperament and personality as synonyms represent, as a rule, a biological approach to personality, and the dimensions that they describe have the status of source traits (H. J. Eysenck & Eysenck, 1985), major dimensions (H. J. Eysenck, 1991a), or basic dimensions (Zuckerman, 1991a) of personality.

The view according to which the concepts of temperament and personality are used as synonyms (assuming that intelligence and abilities are excluded from the personality domain) implies that all personality traits may be characterized by features typical for temperament, such as presence since early childhood and strong biological determination. This, however, is not true.

The most prominent representatives of trait-personality have emphasized that temperament traits constitute only part of the personality structure. For example Allport's scheme of fundamental traits of personality used at the Harvard Psychological Laboratory comprised intelligence, temperament, self-expression traits, and the sociality domain (F. H. Allport & Allport, 1921/1922). According to Diamond (1957), the concept of personality encompasses temperament traits (typical for men and animals) and traits that develop only in human beings. The specifically human personality traits refer to the self-concept, to interests and motivation, and to characteristics that develop under the influence of culture. In the 1950s C. J. Adcock (1957), in his paper *The Differentiation of Temperament from Personality,* strongly advocated for the distinction between the terms *temperament* and *personality.* According to him, temperament refers to innate differences that underlie personality. Temperament characteristics change due to influences that produce physiological effects, such as nutrition, chemical agents, and temperature. Adcock contrasted differences in temperament "with personality differences which are the product of learning in any form" (p. 103).

J. P. Guilford (1975) distinguished 58 personality factors, among which 18 refer to temperament and 35 to the motivational area (interests and needs); 5 are attitude dimensions. His view on personality as a structure composed of several modalities, including temperament, is illustrated on Figure 1.8. Also Cattell (1934/1935, 1965) distinguished within the personality structure traits that belong to temperament and ones that refer to the dynamics of behavior (character, will-factor). Royce and Powell (1983), to whom Eysenck (e.g., H. J. Eysenck & Eysenck., 1985) often referred as the authors who confirmed his concept of the three major dimensions of personality (read also "temperament") are far from reducing personality to these dimensions. Taking the individual-differences approach as their starting point, Royce and Powell distinguished the following six systems, assumed to be components of personality: value, style, affective, motor, cognitive, and sensory systems. Although they do not use the term *temperament,* one may assume that the affective system that comprises the three Eysenckian dimensions belongs to the temperament domain.

The richness of personality traits, which goes far beyond temperament characteristics, has been shown by Buss and Finn (1987) in an attempt to present a conceptual classification of personality traits as schematized in Table 1.3. The following three criteria constituted the basis for this taxonomy: (a) the traditional division into instrumental, affective, and cognitive aspects of behavior, (b) the dichotomy of social versus nonsocial traits, and (c) the distinction between traits related to self and nonself. The authors present a list of 32 personality traits of which only about one third belong to the temperament domain. Table 1.3 also illustrates the developmental differentiation of personality traits. At the age of 18 months individuals are characterized almost exclusively by temperament traits. With age the number of personality traits increases, especially in the cognitive domain. By the age of ten years all traits typical for adult personality are present. Whether one agrees or disagrees with the taxonomy of personality traits presented by Buss and Finn (1987), it cannot be denied that it reveals a richness of personality structure that goes far beyond temperament.

The use of the terms *personality* and *temperament* interchangeably should be regarded as useless reductionism and has several disadvantages for both temperament and personality scholars. Let me turn to some of them.

Ever since the ancient Hippocrates–Galen typology the concept of temperament has had a strong biological connotation. Thus the interchangeable use of the concepts of temperament and personality suggests that personality is mainly biologically determined. In fact this statement is in accordance with H. J. Eysenck's (1986) position when he wrote:

> Genetic factors are very much involved in the causation of individual differences
> and personality, and constitute the strongest single element. When it is realized

TABLE 1.3. Classification of Personality Traits for 18-Month-Old Children (I), 5-Year-Olds (C), and Adults (A)

Instrumental traits		Affective traits		Cognitive traits	
Power	Prosocial	Self	Non-self	Self	Non-self
Social traits					
Aggressiveness (I, C, A)	Sociability (I, C, A)	Shyness (C, A)	Resentment (C, A)	Public self-consciousness (C, A)	Interpersonal trust (C, A)
Rebelliousness (I, C, A)	Succorance (I, C, A)	Shame (A)	Empathy (A)	Locus of control (A)	Perspective of others (A)
Dominance (C, A)	Nurturance (C, A)			Morality (A)	Sensitivity to expressive behavior in others (A)
Machiavellianism (A)	Altruism (A)				
Impression managememt (A)					
Non-social traits					
Impulsivity (I, C, A)		Guilt (A)	Fear (I, C, A)	Private self-consciousness (C, A)	Absorbtion (A)
Activity (I, C, A)		Well-being (A)	Anger (I, C, A)	Self-esteem (C, A)	Blunter-monitor (A)
Excitement seeking (I, C, A)				Gender identity (C, A)	
Achievement (C, A)					

Note. From "Classification of Personality Traits," by A. H. Buss and S. E. Finn, 1987, *Journal of Personality and Social Psychology, 52,* pp. 435, 438–439. Copyright 1987 by American Psychological Association. Adapted with permission.

that the measuring instruments are usually much less reliable than those used in intelligence testing, it will become clear that *personality is determined almost as much by genetic factors as is intelligence.* [p. 217; emphasis added]

No doubt, many personality psychologists disagree with this statement as I do.

When we consider temperament to be equivalent to personality we are unable to grasp the specificity of temperament mechanisms or traits as compared with other personality characteristics, namely those for which the variance is primarily determined by social factors. Of course, the same argument is valid if one takes the point of view of a socially oriented personality researcher.

The interchangeable use of the concepts of temperament and personality, or the packing of all behavioral characteristics typical of broadly understood personality into the temperament concept (as was the case in constitutional psychology) not only should be regarded as a kind of reductionism but it also may lead to socially harmful consequences. We know from experience that constitutional typologies have been utilized as theoretical arguments justifying racist attitudes as exemplified by the Nazis' ideology concerning the concept of *Übermensch* (see Kagan, 1994).

Treating the concepts of temperament and personality as synonyms also leads to misunderstandings. To give one example among the many cases in the literature, Prior, Crook, Stripp, Power, and Joseph (1986) in an attempt to study the relationship between temperament and personality empirically, used the Dimensions of Temperament Survey (DOTS) as a measure of temperament traits and the Eysenck Personality Questionnaire (EPQ) as a measure of personality traits. On the basis of the results obtained in this study the authors drew groundless conclusions regarding the relationship between temperament and personality. In fact, the EPQ is a measure of personality understood, according to Eysenck, as a synonym of temperament. Thus, what Prior and colleagues really did was to compare one set of temperament traits (as measured by the EPQ) with another set of temperament traits (as measured by the DOTS).

As already mentioned, often even biologically oriented personality psychologists (see, e.g., Barratt & Patton, 1983; Haier, Sokolski, Katz, & Buchsbaum, 1987; Petrie, 1967) avoid using the concept of temperament, probably due to the socially negative connotation of this term derived from constitutional psychology. The authors representing this position speak about biologically based personality dimensions (considered synonymous with temperament) rather than temperament.

The fact that this group of researchers tends to avoid using the concept of temperament, yet regards personality research as the study of biologically based individual differences, does not solve the problem since the disadvantages already mentioned remain.

Aspects in Which Temperament and Non-Trait-Oriented Personality Concepts Differ

As is well known, the concept of personality developed in a variety of directions, demonstrating that researchers of different theoretical and methodological backgrounds perceive the essence of human nature in different ways, the Skinnerian model of man as a rat being one of the extremes and Kelly's model of man as a scientist representing the other pole (see, e.g., Caprara & Van Heck, 1992; Hall & Lindzey, 1978; Pervin, 1990; Wiggins *et al.,* 1971). The perspective from which most non-trait psychologists represent the different theories of human personality is usually devoid of temperament. Whatever the specific concepts of personality, a full understanding of the nature of human beings requires, among other things, the study of those behavior characteristics that are present from early childhood and that have a strong biological foundation.

The following theories of personality, in which there is no place at all or only marginal attention paid to the concept of temperament, may be mentioned as examples: psychoanalytic and neopsychoanalytic theories, learning theories of personality, especially the socially oriented ones, phenomenological self-concepts of personality, and cognitive theories, whether based on the concept of personal constructs as developed by Kelly (1955) or on regulatory mechanisms, cognitive in nature, as presented by East European psychologists (see, e.g., Leontev, 1978; Lukaszewski, 1974; Reykowski, 1979).

The question arises as to why researchers representing the different theoretical orientations do not pay attention to the kind of behavior embraced by the notion of temperament or why they treat temperament as a phenomenon not belonging to the domain of personality. Several reasons are mentioned here. Common to all personality theories that fail to notice temperament is the fact that the paradigms on which they are based do not refer to the type of thinking representative of the individual-differences approach with which trait-oriented personality theories, as well as temperament concepts, are bound. We also discern some other essential differences between theories of personality and temperament that call for a broader discussion. In fact these differences explain the failure of temperament scholars and non-trait-oriented personality investigators to find a common language.

In a paper published several years ago (Strelau, 1987a) I expressed some ideas regarding the concept of temperament in personality research. Among other things I referred to aspects in which temperament and personality differ, assuming that personality is considered a non-trait phenomenon, that is, a construct not used in the individual-differences approach. Some authors have misunderstood my ideas (see, e.g., Hofstee, 1991), thus I would like to make it clear that the temperament–personality relationship discussed in this section refers to personality understood as a construct that is not composed of traits.

It is not my purpose to exhaust the list of features in which the non-trait construct of personality and temperament differ. Therefore, this presentation is limited to such aspects as determinants of development, the developmental stage in which temperament and personality are thought to be shaped, the population to which they refer, the degree to which they are saturated with behavior contents, and the role both personality and temperament play in integrating behavior. It should be added that, to some extent, the differences between temperament and personality discussed in the following sections also refer to the concept of personality viewed from the individual-differences perpective, assuming that temperament is compared with non-temperament traits of personality.

TABLE 1.4. Differences between Temperament and Non-Trait-Oriented Personality Concepts (and Non-Temperamental Traits of Personality)

Temperament	Discriminatory features	Personality
Biological factor	Determinants of development	Social factor
Infants	Developmental stages in which the phenomenon occurs	Older children and adults
Animals and man	Populations to which the phenomenon refers	Man
Absent	Content-saturated behavior	Present
Moderation	Regulatory functions	Integration

Note. From "The Concept of Temperament in Personality Research," by J. Strelau, 1987), *European Journal of Personality, 1,* p. 112. Copyright 1987 by John Wiley & Sons, Ltd. Adapted with permission.

Since temperament and personality seldom manifest extreme values of the discriminatory features mentioned previously it is convenient to regard them as dimensions on which temperament and personality characteristics occupy different places as shown in Table 1.4. The greater the distance between the positions held by personality and temperament characteristics on a given dimension, the higher the probability that we are dealing with different phenomena. A central position on these dimensions suggests that it is difficult to decide whether the subject under study belongs to the category of temperament or personality; taking the individual-differences approach, to temperament or non-temperament traits of personality.

Biological versus Social Factors

It has already be mentioned that biological factors play a crucial role in determining temperament. In Chapters 4 and 5 the biological backgrounds of temperament traits are discussed in detail.

Personality theories, especially those based on social learning (e.g., Bandura & Walters, 1963; Dollard & Miller, 1950; Rotter, 1972) and on the cognitive approach (e.g., Cantor & Zirkel, 1990; Epstein, 1990; Kelly, 1955; Leontev, 1978; G. A. Miller, Galanter, & Pribram, 1960; Reykowski, 1975) regard the social environment as the only or the most important factor in the development of personality.

I do not intend to say that the social factor does not influence the molding of temperament traits. Research conducted on temperament in children (see, e.g., Stevenson-Hinde & Hinde, 1986; Super & Harkness, 1986; A. Thomas & Chess, 1977) has shown that the social environment, especially parental treatment and family interactions, essentially influences the expression of temperament characteristics. However, there is no temperament theory known to me that claims that the social environment plays the most crucial role in the development of temperament traits. Some years ago I (Strelau, 1983) argued that the social environment, to the extent to which it influences the molding of temperament traits, acts not so much by means of its content (specificity), but through certain formal attributes of the social environment, such as excessive tension, threat, aggressive behavior, or other situations and reactions evoking permanent over- or understimulation.

Summing up, one can say that whereas temperament is mainly a result of biological evolution, personality is a product of the social environment; however, this product emerged on the basis of the biological endowment regarded as a component of personality.

Childhood versus Later Developmental Stages

In many studies, especially those conducted by A. Thomas and Chess (1977) and by their students and followers, much evidence shows that temperament features may be identified from early childhood (see Kohnstamm, Bates, & Rothbart, 1989; Rothbart, 1989c).

Since personality as understood by non-trait psychologists is mainly a product of learning and socialization it is clear that a newborn child does not yet have a personality. The structures and mechanisms of personality develop in ontogenesis and the stage at which one may say that personality, however differently qualified, has formed, falls at some later period of development. Even if we take a trait approach to personality it can be demonstrated that nontemperament traits composing the structure of personality occur in later developmental stages. As already mentioned, Buss and Finn (1987) have shown that it is at the age of approximately 10 years that the whole repertoire of personality traits may be observed, whereas temperament traits are already present in infancy (see Table 1.3).

Man and Animals versus Humans Only

The personality concept itself suggests that it refers to humans only (L. *persona*—actor's face, mask, character, person). It comprises psychological phenomena that are molded by the human-specific environment. Thus it would be rather strange to speak about personality in animals. When we apply the notion of personality to characterize animal behavior we tend to use it parenthetically.

This is not so with temperament, a concept applied to characterize both human and animal populations. The first experimental studies on temperament in animals were conducted by Pavlov and his students. All the research on dogs, rats, mice, and other animal species and aimed at studying individual differences in anxiety and emotionality (P. L. Broadhurst, 1975; Gray, 1982a), extraversion–introversion (Garau & Garcia-Sevilla, 1985; Simonov, 1987), stimulation seeking (Matysiak, 1985, 1993), and so on should be classified as belonging to the sphere of temperament. As Diamond (1957) stated, it is of great advantage "to be able to study the temperament foundations of personality as they appear in the culture-free behavior of animals" (p. 4). Buss and Plomin (1984) argued that since the early-developing temperament traits have an evolutionary heritage it is obvious that temperament traits, which play an adaptive role, are present in animals as well.

Formal Characteristics of Behavior versus Content of Behavior

A whole section in this chapter was intended to show that temperament traits refer mostly, though not exclusively, to formal characteristics of behavior. Such expressions as style, intensity, energetic characteristics, or temporal components of behavior illustrate this view.

On the other hand, personality, irrespective of the specific theory to which it refers, embraces the contents of behavior; these reflect the specificity of reactions, the relation of humans to themselves, to each other, and toward the world, their motivations, desires, and other psychological phenomena (Pervin, 1996). The content of behavior is a product of human activity under the impact of the specific human environment.

It is highly probable that there are still some characteristics of behavior that have elementary contents still belonging to the sphere of temperament because of their biological determination. Individual differences in primary emotions, for example, anxiety or aggression, may be mentioned here. There is evidence to show that, for example, anxiety, which reflects a given relation of an individual (man and animal) toward the external world, is determined, at least primarily, by biological factors. Gray's (1982a) studies on the behavioral inhibition system (BIS) provide an example. One may predict that in the case of temperament traits, which have a special adaptive meaning, physiological mechanisms, determining to some extent the substantial component of behavior expressed mainly in emotional traits, have developed.

Moderation of Behavior versus Integration of Behavior

The fifth discriminatory feature that distinguishes temperament from the construct of non-trait personality refers to the fact that temperament and personality play different roles in human behavior. Personality psychologists, in spite of their differences regarding the development, structure, and mechanisms of personality, generally agree with the assumption that the concept under discussion refers to integrative functions of human behavior, to mechanisms that ensure the consistency of goal-directed activity or which act as a central regulatory system, or some combination of these aspects. Such concepts as ego, self, superego, cognitive maps operations systems, value systems, and program-oriented schemata, used in different schools and theories, reflect this point of view. Trait-oriented personality psychologists too are far from reducing the essence of personality to the composition of given traits. G. W. Allport (1937) emphasized in his definition of personality that it refers to the *dynamic organization* of the psychophysical systems. Diamond (1957), who considered temperament as a composition of traits common to man and animals, believed the specificity of personality lay in the formation of the self-concept which is essential for the integration of human behavior.

> *The human capacity to observe oneself and to judge oneself* gives rise to a variety of complex phenomena, which are perhaps more distinctively human than any other aspect of our behavior. For more than one psychologist, these phenomena have seemed to constitute the core of human personality. (p. 230)

More recently one of the temperament researchers on children, Rutter (1987), who also considered personality a phenomenon that cannot be reduced to a composition of traits, emphasized that personality refers to the coherence of human functioning that assures the conceptual whole.

The fact that temperament refers mainly to emotions or (and) formal characteristics of behavior implies that its integrative functions are not so significant as those of other personality characteristics. As opposed to personality, temperament refers mainly to traits or mechanisms that play a role in modifying behavior or in the way behavior expresses itself. The modification of behavior consists, for example, in regulating the stimulative value of the surroundings or the individual's own activity (see Eliasz, 1985; Rothbart, 1989b; Strelau, 1983). In turn, the way behavior is expressed may be exemplified by emotional reactions or stylistic characteristics to which temperament refers (see, e.g., A. Thomas & Chess, 1977).

Final Remarks

As mentioned before, temperament and personality characteristics very rarely occupy an extreme position on one of the five discriminatory dimensions. It can be concluded, therefore, that the closer we are to one of the poles the higher the probability that we know whether we are dealing with temperament or non-trait-oriented personality. Viewing the relationship between temperament and personality from an individual-differences perspective we may say that the more extreme the characteristics on the separate dimensions, the stronger the arguments for distinguishing personality traits that belong to the domain of temperament from those personality characteristics that are not temperament-related.

Temperament and the Big Five Factors of Personality

One of the issues that has gained considerable attention in the past decade is the discussion regarding the relationship between the "Big Five" personality factors, considered to be a comprehensive taxonomy of personality characteristics, and temperament. Assuming that the relationship between the Big Five and temperament will be one of the most thoroughly explored domains in the individual-differences approach for the next few years I devote a separate section to this issue. The volume edited by Halverson, Kohnstamm, and Martin (1994) in which several chapters are devoted to the relationship between temperament and personality considered within the big five approach and drawn from a developmental perspective should be considered one of the first steps in approaching this topic.

After the publication of Norman (1963), who showed that when analyzing different personality scales, and especially the personality factors as distinguished by Cattell, one can classify personality characteristics into five factors, interest in taxonomies of personality increased. Lexical studies on terms (mainly adjectives) describing personality characteristics conducted mainly in the past decade (see Angleitner, Ostendorf, & John, 1990; Digman & Takemoto-Chock, 1981; L. R. Goldberg, 1990; John, 1990; John, Angleitner, & Ostendorf, 1988; Wiggins & Pincus, 1992) have, in general, given support to Norman's idea that personality may be described by means of the "Big Five" factors. They have been labeled by Norman (1963, p. 577) as follows: Extroversion or Surgency (Factor I), Agreeableness (Factor II), Conscientiousness (Factor III), Emotional Stability (Factor IV), and Culture (Factor V). Different names have been used for describing the Big Five. A perspicuous list of these labels, in accordance with the numbering proposed by Norman, has been presented by Digman (1990). To avoid misunderstandings in labeling the Big Five I will usually refer to their numerical symbols as presented in Table 1.5.

The lexical approach to the taxonomy of personality traits has been followed by psychometric studies, many of which have given support to the Big Five (see Costa & McCrae, 1988; John, 1990; McCrae, 1989; McCrae & Costa, 1987; Ostendorf & Angleitner, 1992; Zuckerman, Kuhlman, Thornquist, & Kiers, 1991).

Speculations on the Relationship between the Big Five and Temperament

For several years now the question of the relationship between the Big Five personality factors and temperament has been pursued. There are several reasons for asking this question. At least two of the Big Five factors (I and IV) have already been identified by Eysenck—Extraversion and Neuroticism. As mentioned before, these factors, labeled differently by different authors (see Wiggins, 1968) are classified by Eysenck as well as by others as personality or temperament factors interchangeably.

The first stage of searching for relationships between the Big Five and temperament traits consists mainly in making speculations and hypotheses. According to Angleitner (1991), one may treat "the first four factors of the Big Five as primarily temperamental dimensions" (p. 190), assuming that temperament is understood as defined by Strelau (1987a). Hofstee (1991), who considers temperament the core of personality, hypothesized that Introversion (Factor I) and Emotional Stability (Factor IV) have the strongest temperament connotation. This assumption

TABLE 1.5. The Five Robust Dimensions of Personality from Fiske to Present

Author	I	II	III	IV	V
Fiske (1949)	social adaptability	conformity	will to achieve	emotional control	inquiring intellect
H. J. Eysenck (1970)	extraversion	psychoticism		neuroticism	
Tupes & Christal (1961)	surgency	agreeableness	dependability	emotionality	culture
Norman (1963)	surgency	agreeableness	conscientiousness	emotional stability	culture
Borgatta (1964)	assertiveness	likeability	task interest	emotionality	intelligence
Cattell (1957)	exvia	cortertia	superego strength	anxiety	intelligence
Guilford (1975)	social activity	paranoid disposition	thinking introversion	emotional stability	
Digman (1988)	extraversion	friendly compliance	will to achieve	neuroticism	intellect
Hogan (1986)	sociability & ambition	likeability	prudence	adjustment	intellectance
Costa & McCrae (1985)	extraversion	agreeableness	conscientiousness	neuroticism	openness
Peabody & Goldberg (1989)	power	love	work	affect	intellect
Buss & Plomin (1984)	activity	sociability	impulsivity	emotionality	
Tellegen (1988)	positive emotionality		constraint	negative emotionality	
Lorr (1986)	interpersonal involvement	level of socialization	self-control	emotional stability	independent

Note. From "Personality Structure: Emergence of the Five-Factor Model" by J. M. Digman, 1990, *Annual Review of Psychology, 41*, p. 423. Copyright 1990 by Annual Review of Psychology. Reprinted with permission.

is based on the fact that both factors have the highest fundamentality ratings and "the more temperamental a trait is, the more fundamental it is judged to be with respect to the concept of personality" (p. 184). The so-called Nature criterion ("He or she is [adjective] by nature") was regarded as an indicator of fundamentality. John (1990), when analyzing the relationship between Buss and Plomin's four temperaments—Emotionality, Activity, Sociability, and Impulsivity—and the Big Five, speculated that "Activity and Emotionality can easily be matched to Factors I and IV of the Big Five" (p. 85).

The search for the Big Five factors of personality can also be observed among child-oriented temperament researchers. For example, Prior (1992) has hypothesized that an analogy exists between the approach–withdrawal tendencies of the child and Extraversion. Agreeableness may be compared with the temperament factor known as cooperation/manageability/positive mood, and Conscientiousness with Rothbart's temperament concept of "self regulation." Hagekull (1994) hypothesized that Factors III and IV (Conscientiousness and Emotionality) may have some roots in the infant's temperament persistency and mood. Intensity of the child's activity is considered by Hagekull as constituting the roots for factors I and II (Extraversion and Agreeableness). Eaton (1994) suggested that developmentally specific molded activity becomes in adulthood a component of Extraversion and Conscientiousness.

Developmentally oriented researchers interested in the relationship between temperament and the Big Five personality factors mostly consider infant's temperament characteristics to be precursors of these Big Five that are met in adolescents and adults (Ahadi & Rothbart, 1994; Graziano, 1994; R. P. Martin, Wisenbaker, & Huttunen, 1994). Assuming that temperament characteristics may be understood as early-appearing personality traits (Buss & Plomin, 1984; Hagekull, 1994) it seems reasonable to speculate and to study the relationship between temperament and the Big Five starting from early infancy.

Preliminary Empirical Studies regarding the Relationship between the Big Five and Temperamental Traits

There is also preliminary empirical evidence throwing some light on the relationship between temperament and the Big Five. McCrae and Costa (1985b) have shown that the Activity and Sociability scales from Buss and Plomin's EASI-TS have the highest loadings on Factor I and Emotionality on Factor IV. The authors (McCrae & Costa, 1985a) have also shown that there are some relationships between the Big Five factors and the temperament dimensions as measured by the Guilford–Zimmerman Temperament Survey (GZTS); however, only data for three factors (I, IV and V) from the Big Five are presented in this study. The GZTS extraversion scales (General Activity, Ascendance, Sociability) were found to correlate with Extraversion (Factor I) as measured by Costa and McCrae's (1989) NEO Personality Inventory (NEO PI), and the emotional health scales of the GZTS (Emotional Stability, Objectivity, Friendliness, Thoughtfulness) with the NEO PI Neuroticism scale (Factor IV).

A study conducted by McCrae (1987) justified the conclusion that sensation seeking, a temperamental trait separated by Zuckerman (1979), correlates with Factor V (Openness). In a study aimed at measuring the validity of the Strelau Temperament Inventory–Revised, Ruch, Angleitner, and Strelau (1991) showed that the Strength of Excitation and Mobility scales have high loadings on Factor I and Factor IV (with a minus sign). In a factor analysis study Zuckerman and colleagues (1991) were able to show that 46 scales derived from many inventories, including such temperament scales as the EASI, Eysenck Personality Questionnaire, and the

Sensation Seeking Scale (Form V) have resulted in extracting three as well as five factors. However, in this study criterion markers for the Big Five were not used.

The largest empirical studies on the relationship between the Big Five and temperament traits have been conducted by Angleitner and Ostendorf (1994) and by Strelau and Zawadzki (1996). In both studies apart from measures of the Big Five temperament inventories have been used. In the Angleitner and Ostendorf study the Strelau Temperament Inventory–Revised (STI-R; now known as the Pavlovian Temperament Survey, PTS), Zuckerman's SSS, Buss and Plomin's EASI-III, and Windle and Lerner's DOTS-R have been administered whereas in the Strelau and Zawadzki study instead of the SSS the newly developed Formal Characteristics of Behavior–Temperament Inventory (FCB-TI; Strelau & Za-wadzki, 1993) was used. In addition, the EPQ-R inventory was applied.

To go into some details of these findings I present selected data obtained in our study (Strelau & Zawadzki, 1996) conducted on 527 subjects (259 males and 268 females) ages from 20 to 77 years. In this study the Big Five were measured by means of the NEO-FFI (Costa & McCrae, 1989).

Table 1.6 gives some information about the relationships between the Big Five and the temperament traits under study. The upper part of the table presents the result of a forced 5-factor solution (the scree test suggested a 6-factor model) obtained by means of the principal component analysis with Varimax rotation in which all scales administered in this study were included. The bottom part of Table 1.6 presents coefficients of correlation between five factors obtained from an analysis in which only scores from temperament inventories were included (FCB-TI, PTS, EAS-TS, and DOTS-R) and the five NEO-FFI scales.

If we consider the results of factor analysis comprising all scales included in this study the first factor can be identified as Emotionality or Neuroticism. It has the highest loadings on the following scales: Emotional Reactivity, Neuroticism (EPQ-R and NEO-FFI), Emotionality and Perseveration. A clear Extraversion is represented by the second factor, which has the highest loadings on both Extra-version scales, and on the Activity, Sociability, Approach–Withdrawal and Mood Quality scales.

The third factor resulted as a combination of energeticness (Briskness, Activity, Activity-general), attentional focus or task orientation (Distractibility and Persis-tence), and Conscientiousness. Since the number of traits referring to energeticness and attentional characteristics is dominant, there are stronger arguments to identify this factor as Energeticness/Attentional Focus than to label it as Conscientiousness.

The fourth factor is a clearly expressed Rhythmicity (with negative signs on all three scales), accompanied by moderate positive loadings on the Openness and Flexibility–Rigidity scales. There are no sufficient reasons to identify this factor as Openness.

The last factor has the strongest loadings on Agreeableness and low level of Psychoticism. Since there is a negative correlation between Agreeableness and

TABLE 1.6. The Big Five and Temperament Traits

Inventory	Scale	I	II	III	IV	V	H2
				Factors			
A. Factors with NEO-FFI and EPQ-R scales included							
FCB-TI	BR	−.36		.60			.58
	PE	.74					.61
	SS					.39	.28
	ER	.82					.76
	EN	−.59		.38	.35		.64
	AC		.75				.64
PTS	SE	−.60	.34	.35			.72
	SI	−.50				.45	.54
	MO	−.44	.54				.63
EAS-TS	EMO	.79					.71
	ACT		.48	.55			.58
	SOC		.65				.49
DOTS-R	A-G		.47	.49			.50
	A-S	.30					.15
	A-W		.65				.56
	F-R	−.50	.32		.40		.53
	MQ		.64				.52
	R-S				−.68		.49
	R-E				−.69		.52
	R-H				−.74		.57
	DIS			.60			.44
	PER			.65			.51
EPQ-R	EXT		.81				.71
	NEU	.81					.73
	PSY					−.74	.59
NEO-FFI	E		.84				.74
	N	.72					.63
	O				.43		.28
	A					.71	.52
	C			.66		.38	.64
B. Factors with EPQ-R and NEO-FFI scales excluded							
FCB-TI	BR	.48			.52		.58
	PE	−.76					.67
	SS					.79	.64
	ER	−.84					.75
	EN	.72					.66
	AC		.71				.59
PTS	SE	.69			.31		.68
	SI	.52				.42	.47
	MO	.51	.56				.67

TABLE 1.6. The Big Five and Temperament Traits (*Continued*)

Inventory	Scale	Factors					
		I	II	III	IV	V	H2
EAS-TS	EMO	−.71					.61
	ACT		.33		.71		.64
	SOC		.68				.48
DOTS-R	A-G		.33		.69		.63
	A-S	−.32					.18
	A-W	.30	.67				.62
	F-R	.54	.42				.59
	MQ		.71				.58
	R-S			.73			.54
	R-E			.78			.62
	R-H			.79			.65
	DIS				.56		.50
	PER			.36	.51	.40	.57

C. Correlations of temperament factors (four inventories) with the Big Five

		I	II	III	IV	V	
NEO-FFI	E		.70*		.31*		
	N	−.59*	−.26*	−.14*			
	O		.23*	−.20*		.29*	
	A		.14*			.20*	
	C	.12*		.27*	.43*	.22*	

Note. The abbrevations of scales are as follows: Formal Characteristics of Behavior—Temperament Inventory (FCB-TI): Briskness (BR), Perseverative (PE), Sensory Sensitivity (SS), Emotional Reactivity (ER), Endurance (EN), Activity (AC); Pavlovian Temperament Survey (PTS): Strength of Excitation (SE), Strength of Inhibition (SI), Mobility of Nervous Processes (MO); EAS Temperament Survey (EAS-TS): Activity (ACT), Sociability (SOC), Emotionality (EMO—combined score of Distress, Fear and Anger); Revised Dimensions of Temperament Survey (DOTS-R): Activity-General (A-G), Activity-Sleep (A-S), Approach-Withdrawal (A-W), Flexibility-Rigidity (F-R), Mood Quality (MQ), Rhythmicity-Sleep (R-S), Rhythmicity-Eating (R-E), Rhythmicity-Daily Habits (R-H), Distractibility (DIS), Persistence (PER); Eysenck Personality Questionnaire–Revised (EPQ-R): Extraversion (EXT), Neuroticism (NEU), Psychoticism (PSY); NEO Five Factor Inventory (NE-FFI): Extraversion (E), Neuroticism (N), Openness (O), Agreeableness (A), Conscienscicousness (C).
*$p. < .01$

Psychoticism (L. R. Goldberg & Rosolack, 1994; John, 1990) this factor may be identified as Agreeableness, with only moderate, but reasonable, loadings on two temperamental scales: Sensory Sensitivity and Strength of Inhibition.

When only temperamental scales were taken into account the five factors separated at the following points: Factor I, Emotional Stability; Factor II, Extraversion; Factor III, Rhythmicity; Factor IV, Energeticness/Attentional Focus; and Factor V, Sensory Sensitivity. Taking into account the coefficients of correlation between the NEO-FFI scales and these five temperament factors we see that the Neuroticism and Extraversion scales show correlations with the first two temperament factors as predicted. The relationships between the three remaining NEO scales and the temperament factors III, IV, and V are much less clear.

Final Remarks

The issue of whether the Big Five should be regarded as temperament or as personality factors will remain unresolved until sufficient empirical findings are collected and as long as the domains of temperament and personality are imprecisely delineated. We may say that those of the Big Five which have a biological background, which are present since early childhood, and may be found both in man and animals, fulfill the criteria of temperament. There is ample evidence showing that if factors I and IV (Extraversion and Neuroticism) are understood as they have been conceptualized by H. J. Eysenck (1967, 1970, H. J. Eysenck & Eysenck, 1985), they should be regarded as dimensions belonging to the domain of temperament. At the same time it seems reasonable to assume that the three remaining factors—Agreeableness, Conscientiousness, and Intellect or Openness—refer rather to the phenomenon known in psychology as character (Strelau & Zawadzki, 1996). This view seems to be reasonable if we take into account the level of facets that represent Agreeableness and Conscientiousness as described by the NEO Personality Inventory–Revised (Costa & McCrae, 1992b). Such facets as trust, straightforwardness, altruism, compliance, modesty, tender-mindedness (Agreeableness), competence, order, dutifulness, achievement striving, self-discipline and deliberation (Conscientiousness) do not reflect the nature of temperament and they may be identified as typical character traits that develop, however, in individuals with a given temperament endowment.

Costa and McCrae (1992a) have proposed four criteria for basic dimensions of personality. In the authors' opinion the Big Five fulfill these criteria. These are as follows: (1) the reality of the factors, expressed in stability, cross-observer validity, and practical utility of the factors; (2) the pervasiveness of the factors, that is, their presence in innumerable forms throughout all personality concepts; (3) the universality of the factors, by which is meant that they are present in both sexes, in various age groups, in all races, and in different cultures; and (4) the biological bases of the factors mainly reduced to heritability scores. Some of these criteria, for example, criteria (1), (3), and (4) seem to be similar to the ones discussed in the context of temperament. Also Zuckerman (1992) has proposed four criteria for a basic trait of personality. They differ to some extent from Costa and McCrae's and are closer to the criteria used for temperament traits. One of the four criteria refers to the identification of similar kinds of behavior traits in nonhuman species. This is a requirement not fulfilled by such factors from the Big Five as II (Agreeableness), III (Consciensciousness), and V (Culture).

The similarities and differences between temperament traits and the concept of the Big Five would be clearer if we had evidence throwing more light on the issue of the extent to which the Big Five are present from early infancy and whether they can also be found in animals—two crucial criteria by which temperament traits are distinguished from other personality characteristics.

One has to be very careful, however, in formulating statements that say that temperament traits may be reduced to the Big Five or that the Big Five factors describe the whole of personality, including temperament. One may also inquire about the explanatory power or predictive value of a procedure that leads to classifying a given set of temperament traits within the five factor *taxonomy* of personality. We know from biology (e.g., biological species), chemistry (chemical elements), and many other sciences, that taxonomies are very useful tools in explaining and predicting given phenomena (see, e.g., Meehl, 1992). The theoretical backgrounds of the Big Five taxonomy are trivial, if they exist at all. The most thorough and detailed critique of the big-five approach conducted by Block (1995) led him to the conclusion that "The Big Five factors, as they have evolved and become differently understood which remaining similarly labelled by different Big Fivers, represent striking instances of the jingle fallacy" (p. 209). The five-factor model of personality is a purely empirical outcome, and recent findings force us to reflect on the relationship between some of the Big Five factors and temperament traits.

To exemplify this need for reflection it must be stated that Factor V, known under the labels Openness (to Experience), Intelligence, Intellect, or Culture (see Digman, 1990), has little in common with temperament characteristics, although this factor in Angleitner and Ostendorf's (1994) study correlated positively with strength of excitation and mobility. Costa and McCrae (1992a, p. 654) included the following facets in the Openness scale of the NEO PI: fantasy, aesthetics, feelings, actions, ideas, and values. One may assume, as Angleitner and Ostendorf did, that the only domain that refers to temperament is the preference for experience, expressed in actions. But a conclusion based on a correlation between openness and strength of excitation that this Pavlovian NS property is related to aesthetics, ideas, and values of which openness is composed leads to nonsense. The impression that Factor V, when its content characteristics are taken into account, is far removed from temperament traits, is expressed even more clearly when the Factor V content characteristics are described by means of adjectives. Ostendorf and Angleitner (1992) have shown that Factor V (Culture, Intellect, Openness) had the highest loadings on the following adjectives: artistically sensitive–artistically insensitive, intellectual–unreflective (narrow), creative–uncreative, broad interests–narrow interests, intelligent–unintelligent, imaginative–unimaginative. It is obvious that all these adjective descriptions are far removed from the temperament area. Thus the inclusion of several temperament traits in Factor V of the Big Five reduces the specificity of temperament characteristics, that is, ascribes them a meaning that they do not have, and may lead to many misunderstandings.

Why then, in spite of the spectacular differences between the content characteristics of several factors of the Big Five (V, II and III) and temperament, do some temperament scales have loadings on those factors? A satisfactory explanation can be given only when more empirical evidence is collected. Some speculations on this matter may be offered: (a) Temperament traits are present from the very onset of the human life and therefore they contribute to the development of all other personality characteristics; (b) all Big Five factors have several elements that may be more or less directly attributed to temperament (e.g., preference for variety in Factor V, good-natured–irritable in Factor II, or hardworking–lazy in Factor III); (c) questionnaires aimed at measuring the Big Five include items formulated in the same way or very similarly to those present in temperament questionnaires; (d) when we factor analyze the many scales of inventories, which differ in their contents, the common denominator to which they refer when reduced to a small number of factors (e.g., the Big Five) consists mainly of certain formal characteristics of behavior rather than of the specific content by means of which the separate scales are described. The closer we are to grasping the formal characteristics common to the separate scales, the closer we come to the temperament domain.

We are still far from a satisfactory answer to the question regarding the relationship between temperament and personality, including the big-five approach. More empirical research is needed that goes beyond the psychometric and lexical approach (see Kagan, 1994) and that takes into account the developmental specificity (Kohnstamm *et al.,* 1989), the cardinal influence of the environment (Wachs, 1992, 1994), and genetic contribution (Goldsmith, Losoya, Bradshaw, & Campos, 1994) in grasping the relationship between temperament and personality and in the process of molding the structure of personality based on temperament endowment.

2

The Initiators of Contemporary Research on Temperament

In describing the theories of temperament I limit the presentation to contemporary conceptualizations. A historical background which helps in explaining the development of recent tendencies in temperament research has been provided in Chapter 1. If we take Popper's (1959) or Kuhn's (1970) criteria for defining what a theory is, the conceptualizations presented in this chapter hardly fulfill these criteria. Many of the assumptions and theoretical proposals discussed here cannot be subject to the criterion of falsification as proposed by Popper, and most temperament theories do not fully correspond with the Kuhnian paradigm of so-called normal science, which refers to conceptual, theoretical, instrumental, and methodological requirements.

The label *theory* is used in this chapter as well as in Chapter 3 in a more tolerant way. The conceptualizations presented here implement at least the three following criteria: (1) They offer new views and/or solutions in the domain of temperament, (2) they present conceptual problems that are susceptible to verification, and (3) they are based on empirical evidence. The conceptualizations regarding temperament differ in the range of problems they embrace, from very broad perspectives (e.g., Eysenck's PEN theory) to rather narrow ones (e.g., Petrie's augmenting/reducing dimension which is an extention of Eysenck's theory of extraversion). In spite of these differences all of them have the status of a microtheory (see Pervin, 1990), for they touch on only a small fragment of psychological phenomena. They are limited to issues of temperament regarded by most authors as a component of personality. Even Eysenck's attempt to include in his theory all major problems of personality (H. J. Eysenck, 1970; H. J. Eysenck & Eysenck, 1985) is far from reality; many central themes of personality psychology, for example, motivation and the self (see Caprara & Van Heck, 1992; Pervin, 1990), although studied in H. J. Eysenck's (1965) laboratory are not covered by his theory.

The review of temperament theories is divided into two main parts. The first, presented in this chapter, deals with theories that have been developed in the 1950s by researchers who should be considered initiators of the contemporary study of temperament. In the next chapter the conceptualizations delineated are those that developed during the past two decades and which, together with theories described in this chapter, reflect the current state of research on temperament.

Introduction

When we attempt to tap the beginnings of the new interests in temperament, accompanied by the original approaches, our attention concentrates particularly on the following scholars active in three different research centers: Alexander Thomas and Stella Chess, psychiatrists from the New York University Medical Center; Borys M. Teplov at the Institute of Psychology, Academy of Pedagogical Sciences in Moscow; and Hans J. Eysenck at the Maudsley Hospital, University of London.

In 1956 Thomas and Chess launched a longitudinal study on temperament known in the literature as the New York Longitudinal Study which is still in progress. Their primary objective was to show that behavior disorders in infants and preschool children are the outcome of interaction between environment (mainly child-rearing variables) and temperament. The significance of Thomas and Chess's work in promoting modern research on temperament has been widely recognized. Characterizing contemporary research on temperament Plomin (Plomin & Dunn, 1986) stated: "The modern history of temperament research began in the late fifties with the New York Longitudinal Study conducted by Alexander Thomas, Stella Chess, and their colleagues" (p. ix). This statement is, however, only partly true since it is limited to the United States.

Somewhat earlier, at the midpoint of the 20th century, Teplov and his collaborators, of whom the leading role was played by Vladimir D. Nebylitsyn, undertook to adapt Pavlov's typology of the central nervous system to the human adult population. The principal activity of these researchers focused on studying the nature of basic nervous system properties and on developing laboratory methods for the assessment of these properties. The research of Teplov and his collaborators was a cornerstone in the development of several approaches to temperament, especially those stressing the physiological mechanisms determining temperament traits.

An adequate sketch of the beginnings of contemporary research on temperament cannot omit the contribution of Eysenck. This English scholar, of German origin, was the first to attempt to explain individual differences in temperament traits in terms of physiological constructs by undertaking a broad range of empirical studies. The three superfactors he distinguished, namely, psychoticism, extraversion, and neuroticism (PEN) are considered to comprise one of the most popular taxonomies of personality (temperament). Eysenck, who considered personality and temperament synonyms, used mainly the term *personality* in referring to his PEN dimensions (for details see Chapter 1). This fact in itself explains why Eysenck's contribution was for so long unknown to many temperament researchers. The work of Eysenck, which started as early as the 1940s, had a crucial influence on the development of those theories of temperament that incorporated the construct of arousal.

In my attempts to show the links and the integrative aspects between the different approaches to temperament (Strelau, 1991b; see also Strelau & Angleitner, 1991; Strelau & Plomin, 1992) I noticed that for a period of about three decades these three important research centers were almost completely isolated from each other. To my knowledge, Thomas and Chess never referred to studies conducted by Teplov or Nebylitsyn and hardly ever to the British scholar. Eysenck devoted some attention to the Pavlovian approach, but, with one or two exceptions, never referred to the contribution of Thomas and Chess. Teplov, probably mainly for political reasons, had no idea about the extensive research conducted by Thomas and Chess, and only marginally mentioned Eysenck's contribution when commenting on A. Anastasi's 1958 monograph *Differential Psychology.*

Among the initiators of contemporary research on temperament such influential scholars as Cattell and Guilford will be passed over here. The reason for doing so is the following: Cattell's (1950, 1957) theory touches on temperament issues only to the extent to which temperament constitutes a part of personality; his theoretical approach goes far beyond the problems at the core of this book. The same argument holds for J. P. Guilford's (1959) theory of personality. However, Guilford's temperament inventory—The Guilford–Zimmerman Temperament Survey (GZTS, J. P. Guilford & Zimmerman, 1950; J. S. Guilford, Zimmerman, & Guilford, 1976), has gained considerable popularity since the 1950s. But neither Cattell nor Guilford developed a temperament theory as such.

Diamond (1957) was also one of the initiators who had a significant influence on thinking about temperament, especially among some American researchers. In his extensive monograph covering the domain of temperament and personality, he took an evolutionary approach which led him to distinguish four basic dimensions of temperament: impulsivity, affiliativeness, aggressivity, and fearfulness. According to Diamond, these traits are shared by man and other mammals. As mentioned in Chapter 1, Diamond too made a clear-cut distinction between the terms temperament and personality, the latter comprising such psychological phenomena as the self, interests, and cognitive characteristics. Diamond's original and stimulating considerations on temperament have, however, the status of speculations, and do not fulfill the criteria of a theory as dealt with in this chapter.

Eysenck's Biological Theory of PEN

The theory of temperament as developed by Eysenck over almost 50 years of study has been described in several hundred publications, starting from the 1940s (H. J. Eysenck, 1944) and still in progress (H. J. Eysenck, 1993, 1994a). Among the many publications there are some that give a complex picture representing different stages of his theory (H. J. Eysenck, 1947, 1957, 1967, 1970; H. J. Eysenck & Eysenck, 1985). From a temporal perspective several modifications of his theory may be noted, but the core ideas are to be found at all stages of theory development, namely, that temperament has a biological background, temperamental traits are universal, and the structure of temperament may be described by a few independent superfactors—extraversion and neuroticism, to which psychoticism was added later. Eysenck's PEN theory, firmly based on the sources of individual differences in temperament, belongs to those theories that fulfill most of the criteria of a paradigm as postulated by Kuhn. In presenting his theory I refer to the following issues: roots of the PEN theory, postulated dimensions and structure of temperament, biological background of PEN, assessment procedures, temperament in relation to performance and social behavior, and critical remarks. This scheme is applied in this chapter, whenever possible, in presenting all conceptualizations and theories of temperament.

Roots of the PEN Theory

Unlike many other researchers on temperament, Eysenck in describing his theory of temperament refers to numerous historical sources where some of the ideas present in his theory are to be found. Without pretending to cite all the historical sources (see H. J. Eysenck, 1970; H. J. Eysenck & Eysenck, 1985) those that Eysenck considers of special importance are mentioned here. Going back to ancient times, he emphasized that the dimensions of extraversion and neuroticism were anticipated by Hippocrates and Galen, and in most of his publications he noted the similarity between these two basic temperament dimensions and the Hippocrates–Galen typology as illustrated on Figure 2.1. The dimensional concept of temperament that allowed Eysenck to search for continuity between normal characteristics and pathology already had been developed by Wundt (1887). Eysenck took the term extraversion–introversion from Jung (1923) but gave it a different meaning. Also the idea that extraversion and neuroticism are two independent dimensions may be found, according to Eysenck, in Jung's writings. Jung regarded neurosis as independent of extraversion–introversion, and suggested that in the case of neurotic breakdown extraverts are predisposed to hysteria and introverts to psychasthenia. The causal approach to temperament present in Eysenck's theory was ascribed to Gross (1902) who gave a neurophysiological interpretation

FIGURE 2.1. Relation between the four ancient temperaments and the neuroticism-extraversion dimensional system. *Note.* From *Personality and Individual Differences: A Natural Science Approach* (p. 5), by H. J. Eysenck and M. W. Eysenck, 1985, New York: Plenum Press. Copyright 1985 by Plenum Press. Reprinted with permission.

of the primary–secondary function (see Chapter 1) that became one of the three temperament dimensions in the Heymans–Wiersma typology. The research conducted by Heymans and Wiersma (1906–1918) was regarded by Eysenck as the first model in which the psychometric approach was combined with laboratory tests and empirical data were statistically analyzed under the guidance of a general theory. In a contemporary and even more complex fashion, this model has been superseded by Eysenck. The historical perspective present in most of H. J. Eysenck's (1947, 1967, 1970; H. J. Eysenck & Eysenck, 1985) writings allowed him to construct a theory of temperament that shows how earlier findings and ideas can contribute to new developments in personality psychology.

The Dimensions and Structure of Temperament

Eysenck's first attempts to develop a temperament theory consisted in a description of the main dimensions of the structure of personality or temperament (here used as synonyms). It should be emphasized once again that, according to Eysenck, "temperament, that is the noncognitive aspects of personality" (H. J. Eysenck & Eysenck, 1985, p. 353) is regarded as the phenomenon that comprises the dimensions discussed here.

As early as 1944, Eysenck, under the influence of Jung's ideas and Mac-Kinnon's (1944) confusing considerations regarding the place of extraversion and neuroticism in the structure of personality, conducted a psychometric study on 700 neurotic soldiers. The data from this study led him to separate two independent factors: neuroticism, and hysteria versus dysthymia, where hysteria was typical for the breakdown of extraverts and dysthymia for the breakdown of introverts.

Viewed chronologically, the main temperament dimensions distinguished by H. J. Eysenck (1947, 1952, 1970) were extraversion and neuroticism. Early in the 1950s H. J. Eysenck (1952) suggested that psychoticism might be regarded as a third dimension of temperament, but this idea was fully elaborated only in the 1970s (H. J. Eysenck & Eysenck, 1976; see also H. J. Eysenck, 1992a), especially after an inventory was constructed which permitted measurement of this trait (H. J. Eysenck & Eysenck, 1975).

Exhaustive factor analytic studies conducted by Eysenck over several decades on a variety of populations as well as findings of psychometric techniques (self-ratings and other-ratings) and laboratory experimentation led him to conclude that the structure of temperament consists of three basic factors: psychoticism (P), extraversion (E), and neuroticism (N), often identified as superfactors (H. J. Eysenck, 1978, H. J. Eysenck & Eysenck, 1985), biological dimensions (H. J. Eysenck, 1990b), major dimensions (H. J. Eysenck, 1990a), or types (H. J. Eysenck & Eysenck, 1985) of personality. The three superfactors are orthogonal to each other. They have a hierarchical structure and are composed of first-order factors (primary traits) which, in turn, result from a group of correlated behavioral acts or action tendencies. The hierarchical structure of the PEN superfactors is illustrated on Figure 2.2.

Curiously enough, it is difficult, if not possible, to find in Eysenck's publications a typical definition of these factors. The three superfactors "are defined in terms of observed intercorrelations between traits" (H. J. Eysenck, 1990b, p. 244). Thus extraversion, as opposed to introversion, is composed of such traits as sociability, liveliness, activity, assertiveness, and sensation seeking. Neuroticism, for which emotionality is used as the synonym, has the following components: anxiety, depression, guilt feelings, low self-esteem, and tension. The opposite pole of neuroticism is emotional stability. Psychoticism, the opposite of which is impulse control, consists of such primary traits as aggression, coldness, egocentrism, impersonality, and impulsiveness.

The psychoticism dimension differs basically from E and N in that it is directly related to pathology. According to Eysenck psychoticism represents a dimensional continuity which at one pole may be described by such characteristics as altruism, empathy, and socialization and at the opposite pole by such psychotic syndromes as criminality, psychopathy, and schizophrenia (H. J. Eysenck, 1992a) as shown on Figure 2.3.

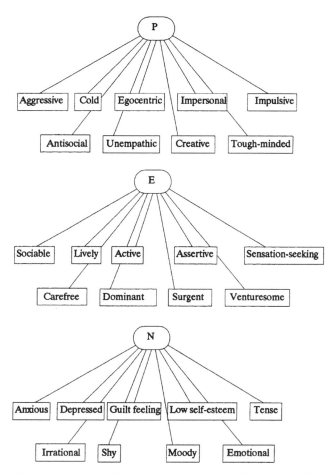

FIGURE 2.2. Hierarchical structure of Eysenck's three superfactors: Psychoticism (P), Extraversion (E), and Neuroticism (N). *Note.* From *Personality and Individual Differences: A Natural Science Approach* (p. 14–15), by H. J. Eysenck and M. W. Eysenck, 1985, New York: Plenum Press. Copyright 1985 by Plenum Press. Reprinted with permission.

Although it is not unlikely that other superfactors will be discovered in the future, H. J. Eysenck (1990b; H. J. Eysenck & Eysenck, 1985) claimed that for the current state of personality research the PEN superfactors comprise the whole personality (excluding intelligence), and they have been identified in scores of culturally diverse countries (see, e.g., Barrett & Eysenck, 1984). Thus, the three superfactors may be used as the most universal taxonomy by which personality can be described.

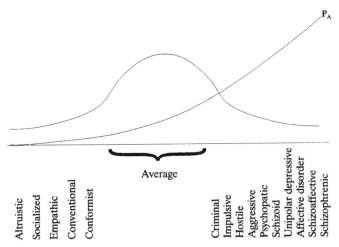

FIGURE 2.3. Diagrammatic representation of the continuity theory of "psychoticism." *Note.* From "The Definition and Measurement of Psychoticism," by H. J. Eysenck, 1992, *Personality and Individual Differences, 13,* p. 758. Copyright 1992 by Elsevier Science Ltd. Reprinted with permission.

The Biological Background of PEN

It was in the early 1950s that Eysenck started to concentrate on the question: "What are the causes of individual differences in extraversion and neuroticism?" The study conducted by H. J. Eysenck and Prell (1951) on the inheritance of neuroticism is regarded as the first behavior-genetic research in the personality domain. Since then, a series of behavior-genetic studies were conducted by Eysenck and his associates (see Chapter 5) which led Eysenck to the following conclusion: "Broadly speaking, twin studies suggest a narrow heritability of temperamental traits of around 50%, which, when corrected for attenuation, suggests heritabilities between 60% and 70%" (H. J. Eysenck & Eysenck, 1985, p. 96). The conviction, which accompanied Eysenck from almost the initiation of his studies in the domain of extraversion and neuroticism, that individual differences in temperament traits have a strong genetic determination, led him to search for the biological bases of these dimensions. This inquiry was grounded on the following assumption: "Genetic factors cannot directly influence behavior or cognitions, of course, and the intervening variables must inevitably be physiological, neurological, biochemical, or hormonal in nature" (H. J. Eysenck, 1990b, p. 247). Conceptualizations and empirical studies regarding the biological bases of temperament traits concentrated mainly on extraversion, less on neuroticism, and almost not at all on psychoticism.

The Physiological Basis of Extraversion

Two stages in Eysenck's theorizing about the physiological mechanisms me-diating individual differences in extraversion need to be distinguished: the "inhi-bition theory" and the "arousal theory" (H. J. Eysenck & Eysenck, 1985). In his monograph *Dynamics of Anxiety and Hysteria,* H. J. Eysenck (1957), referring to Hull's (1943) concept of reactive inhibition and to Pavlov's (1951–1952) typolog-ical theory of excitation and inhibition, presented two postulates that guided the physiological and behavioral study of extraversion for at least the next ten years. Briefly, these postulates state: (1) Individuals differ with respect to the speed and strength of produced excitation and inhibition, and to the speed at which inhibition disappears; (2) individuals in whom excitatory potential is generated slowly and weakly, and in whom reactive inhibition is generated rapidly and strongly and is dissipated slowly are predisposed to develop extraverted patterns of behavior; the opposite characteristic is typical for introverts.

On the dimension of cortical excitation–inhibition balance, introverts occupy the excitation pole and extraverts are located at the inhibition pole. By means of drugs the position of individuals on the dimension of excitation–inhibition balance can be changed, and this led H. J. Eysenck (1957) to develop a third, so-called drug postulate. This postulate says that depressant drugs increase inhibition and de-crease excitation, thus producing extraverted patterns of behavior. In turn, stimu-lant drugs decrease inhibition and increase excitation, thereby producing introverted patterns of behavior.

Under the influence of Moruzzi and Magoun's (1949) discovery that the brain stem reticular formation produces unspecific activation which is expressed in spontaneous EEG activity, and known as cortical arousal (see Chapter 5), Eysenck broadened his view on the physiological mechanism underlying extraversion. The causal chain has been taken a bit further back by considering excitation as a prod-uct of cortical arousal. In his 1967 book *The Biological Basis of Personality* he postulated that individual differences in the activity of the corticoreticular loop are responsible for the individual's position on the extraversion–introversion dimen-sion. "Introverts are characterized by higher levels of activity than extraverts and so are chronically more cortically aroused than extraverts" (H. J. Eysenck & Eysenck, 1985, p. 197).

Since cortical arousal is mainly reflected in EEG activity, indices of this ac-tivity, such as alpha rhythm (frequency, amplitude, total energy, alpha index) and different characteristics of evoked potentials, have been studied in relation to ex-traversion (for details see Chapter 4). The results, together with studies in the do-main of electrodermal activity (EDA) and some other indices of physiological arousal, have yielded partial support for Eysenck's hypothesis that extraverts are chronically less aroused than introverts.

The Physiological Basis of Neuroticism

Research aimed at investigating the physiological basis of neuroticism developed in parallel with that of extraversion. Studies that have shown that emotions are mainly mediated by the activity of the autonomic nervous system (ANS), and especially Wenger's concept of autonomic imbalance (see Chapter 4), which says that the predominance of the sympathetic branch is responsible for such emotional states as emotional excitability, anxiety, emotional tension, and so on led H. J. Eysenck (1957) to the hypothesis that differential responsivity of the sympathetic nervous system must be regarded as the physiological basis mediating differences in neuroticism. In neurotic individuals responsivity of the sympathetic nervous system is higher than in emotionally stable individuals.

In 1967 Eysenck modified his physiological interpretation in respect to both extraversion and neuroticism. He located the physiological center of neuroticism in the visceral brain (see Figure 2.4 later in this chapter); more precisely, differences in responsivity of such centers of the CNS as the hippocampus, amygdala, cingulum, septum, and the hypothalamus are responsible for individual differences in neuroticism (H. J. Eysenck, 1967; H. J. Eysenck & Eysenck, 1985). When speaking about activity of the visceral brain Eysenck referred to the term *activation,* whereas for cortical activity he used the term *arousal.* The many studies conducted on the physiological markers of neuroticism (some of which are presented in Chapter 4) brought H. J. Eysenck (1990b) to the conclusion that "studies within the normal population have not been successful in giving strong support to the theory linking N with psychophysiological measures of activation" (p. 266).

Biological Correlates of Psychoticism

Eysenck did not develop a physiological theory of psychoticism. There is evidence that psychoticism has heritability scores comparable to those found in the domain of extraversion and neuroticism (Eaves & Eysenck, 1977; H. J. Eysenck, 1990a, 1992a; H. J. Eysenck & Eysenck, 1985). Some biological markers of psychoticism have been found as, for example, low MAO activity in individuals characterized by psychotic behaviors (Schalling, Edman, & Asberg, 1983; Zuckerman, 1991c). Although some biological correlates of psychoticism have been recorded (H. J. Eysenck, 1992a), the biological basis of this trait is unclear. According to Claridge (1985), one of the leading researchers in this temperament domain, psychoticism is associated with a kind of dissociation of CNS activity, especially when related to performance indices. Eysenck sympathizes with the view that

> [t]he crucial psychophysiological quality of psychoticism is *not* hyperresponsiveness (or hyporesponsiveness) *per se.* It lies rather in an increased tendency to-

ward dissociation of the autonomic, motor, and cortical components of arousal, possibly due to a characteristic, weakened form of excitatory and inhibitory regulation in the nervous system (Claridge, 1987, p.145).

Assessment Procedures Used for Diagnosing PEN

Although a special chapter is devoted to presenting the main issues concerning assessment of temperament traits, a complex view of Eysenck's PEN theory requires specific information regarding basic assessment techniques as developed by Eysenck and his associates (for a review, see Amelang & Bartussek, 1990; Morris, 1979).

Eysenck's psychometric study on the main temperament dimension was initiated by developing the Maudsley Medical Questionnaire (MMQ) aimed at diagnosing neuroticism (H. J. Eysenck, 1947). The MMQ was composed of items which referred mainly, as the title of this inventory suggests, to medical symptoms of neuroticism.

The need to assess the two main temperament dimensions postulated by Eysenck in the 1950s led to the development of the Maudsley Personality Inventory (MPI; H. J. Eysenck 1956, 1959), composed of two scales: Extraversion and Neuroticism. The MPI items referred to psychological and behavioral characteristics typical of normal individuals. A large number of MPI items were taken from Guilford's temperament scales. The Extraversion scale consisted partly of items from Guilford's Rhathymia and Social Introversion scales, and for the Neuroticism scale several items were taken from the Depression and Nervousness scales (J. P. Guilford, 1975). Some items from the MMQ were included as well. Whereas in samples representing normal subjects the E and N scales were more or less orthogonal to each other, in neurotic patients they correlated negatively to an extent that motivated Eysenck to develop a new version of his inventory.

In 1964 Eysenck and his wife, Sybil B. G. Eysenck, constructed the Eysenck Personality Inventory (EPI) which became one of the most popular measures of extraversion and neuroticism. This inventory, which had two parallel forms (A and B), consisted of three scales: Extraversion, Neuroticism, and a Lie scale. The third scale, aimed at measuring dissimulation, is considered a control scale. The Extraversion scale had two basic components, sociability and impulsivity, which could be measured separately. For more than a decade the EPI was the main instrument in Eysenck's laboratory for assessing extraversion and neuroticism. Considerable data which relates EPI extraversion to behavior and performance as well as to physiological correlates refer to extraversion as composed of impulsivity and sociability (H. J. Eysenck & Eysenck, 1964). The Eysenck Personality Inventory has also been constructed for children and adolescents (S. B. G. Eysenck, 1965).

Eysenck's idea, which dates from the early 1950s, that psychoticism can be distinguished as a separate dimension as well as the fact that some aspects of impulsivity, such as nonplanning, are typical for behaviors comprising this dimension, resulted in the development of a new inventory known as the Eysenck Personality Questionnaire (EPQ, H. J. Eysenck & Eysenck, 1975, 1976). The EPQ consists of four scales: Extraversion, Neuroticism, Psychoticism, and a Lie scale. The Extraversion scale differs from the EPI-E scale in that many of the impulsivity items have been replaced by the Psychoticism scale. The latter was constructed in such a way as to measure psychoticism in normal, nonpsychotic groups. A thorough critique of the Psychoticism scale was undertaken (see D. V. M. Bishop, 1977; Block, 1977); this critique showed that the mean scores of the P scale are too low, the standard deviations as compared to the mean scores too high, and the distribution of scores grossly skewed. This critique forced Eysenck (S. B. G. Eysenck, Eysenck, & Barrett, 1985) to modify the Psychoticism scale, and this modification resulted in the development of the Eysenck Personality Questionnaire–Revised (EPQ-R). On the P scale of the EPQ-R some new items were added and others removed with the result that the shape of the P score distribution was improved, the mean was increased, and standard deviations lower than the mean scores were obtained. The EPQ-R, now adapted like the EPI in many countries and languages, is at the present time the most popular questionnaire in use for measuring the PEN superfactors.

Recently H. J. Eysenck, Wilson, and Jackson (1996) published the *Eysenck Personality Profiler* (EPP), a package that consists of 22 inventories aimed for measuring separately 22 traits of which the PEN factors are composed. The evidence is not yet sufficient to allow an estimation of the usefulness of this instrument.

The ambiguous status of impulsivity expressed in the fact that this trait shows high scores on all three superfactors (PEN) motivated the Eysencks (S. B. G. Eysenck & Eysenck, 1978, 1980; S. B. G. Eysenck, Pearson, Easting, & Allsopp, 1985) to develop impulsivity scales that would allow for the measurement of separate components of impulsivity in its broad sense, such as narrow impulsiveness, venturesomeness, and empathy. These inventories, known as the I.V.E. Scale (S. B. G. Eysenck & Eysenck, 1978), the I_7 Impulsiveness Questionnaire (S. B. G. Eysenck, Pearson, *et al.,* 1985), and a version for children and adolescents, the Junior I.V.E. Scale (S. B. G. Eysenck & Eysenck, 1980), are recommended by Eysenck for a proper location of the impulsivity components in the three-dimensional space of the PEN superfactors.

The Eysenckian Superfactors in Relation to Performance and Social Behavior

The inhibition theory, as well as the arousal theory, which should be considered an extension of the inhibition theory (H. J. Eysenck & Eysenck, 1985), allowed for several predictions regarding different kinds of social behavior and performance under a variety of conditions depending on the individuals' position on the extraversion–introversion dimension.

Theoretical Bases for Relating the PEN to Behavior

From the postulates derived from the inhibition theory, it follows that excitatory processes are chronically higher in introverts as compared with extraverts and, similarly, the arousal theory says that introverts are chronically more highly aroused than extraverts. If so, both theories predict that stimuli of the same intensity or situations of a given stimulative value will produce different effects in extraverts and introverts. This has been shown to be the case in different domains.

As we know from the two Yerkes and Dodson (1908) laws, there is an inverted-U relationship between the level of arousal (motivation, emotional tension) and efficiency of performance, and this relationship is mediated by task difficulty. For difficult tasks (more generally, for high stimulation) the optimal level of arousal is lower as compared with easy tasks (low stimulation). If so, for extraverts, who have a chronically low level of arousal, stronger stimulation is needed to generate the optimal level of arousal as compared to introverts. The decrease in performance under high stimulation has been interpreted by H. J. Eysenck (1981, 1990b; H. J. Eysenck & Eysenck 1985), by means of transmarginal inhibition, a theoretical construct introduced by Pavlov (see Chapter 1). In introverts, who have a chronically higher level of arousal, transmarginal inhibition (i.e., decrease in reactions or performance) occurs for stimuli of lower intensity than is the case with extraverts.

Looking at the relationship between arousal level and extraversion–introversion from another (motivational) perspective, Eysenck hypothesized that stimuli of the same intensity evoke in extraverts and introverts different emotional states due to their differences in chronic arousal level. "Just as there is an optimal level of arousal for *performance,* so there is an optimal level of arousal for subjective feelings of contentment, happiness or generally preferred *hedonic tone*" (H. J. Eysenck, 1981, p. 18). Referring to Wundt's (1887) idea that stimuli of low intensity generate positive emotions whereas stimuli of high intensity produce negative emotions, Eysenck hypothesized that the relationship between level of sensory input and experienced hedonic tone depends on the individual's position on the extraversion–introversion dimension. This is illustrated in Figure 2.4, originally constructed by H. J. Eysenck (1963) at the time when the inhibition theory was still in force. As can be seen, extraverts and introverts experience an optimal level of hedonic tone (O.L.) at different intensities of stimuli: introverts at a lower stimulation level than extraverts. Weak stimuli (A) will be positively hedonic for introverts and negatively hedonic for extraverts, whereas the opposite is the case under strong stimulation (B). In consequence, in order to experience a positive hedonic tone extraverts seek strong stimulation whereas introverts seek low stimulation. Extraverts are charac-

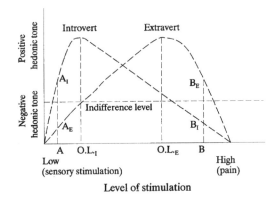

FIGURE 2.4. Relation between level of sensory input and hedonic tone as a function of personality. *Note.* From "General Features of the Model," by H. J. Eysenck. In H. J. Eysenck (Ed.), *A Model for Personality* (1981, p. 18), Berlin, Germany: Springer Verlag. Copyright 1981 by Springer Verlag. Adapted with permission.

terized by *stimulus hunger* (sensation seeking, arousal seeking) and introverts, who favor activities of a relatively unstimulating nature, by *stimulus aversion* (H. J. Eysenck, 1967, p. 111; H. J. Eysenck & Eysenck, 1985, p. 249).

Of great importance for studying the relationship between individual differences in extraversion, and the degree of socialization as well as susceptibility to various psychiatric disorders, was H. J. Eysenck's (1957) conditionability postulate. This postulate has its roots in Pavlov's (1951–1952) finding that conditioning is more efficient in dogs with strong types of CNS than in the weak type. The conditionability postulate, consequent to H. J. Eysenck's (1957) two basic postulates, says that because of higher excitatory and lower inhibitory potential in introverts, as compared with extraverts, introverts elaborate conditioned reflexes more easily and more rapidly than is the case with extraverts. According to the arousal theory, a reverse relationship can occur when conditioning is based on high intensive stimuli, owing to transmarginal inhibition present in introverts exposed to strong stimuli (H. J. Eysenck & Eysenck, 1985).

Three major statements follow from these situations: (a) The relationship between performance level and stimulus intensity is mediated by extraversion, (b) extraverts seek stimulation whereas introverts avoid stimulation, and (c) introverts condition, in general, more easily than extraverts. These statements guided Eysenck's studies on the relationship between extraversion and different kinds of performance and behaviors in laboratory settings, field studies, and observations in real-life situations.

As for neuroticism, Eysenck's predictions on the relation of this temperament trait to performance and to social behavior have not been elaborated to such an extent as in the case of extraversion. Regarding neuroticism as a tendency to express negative emotional states, such as anxiety and emotional tension, Eysenck hypothesized that this temperament trait would mediate performance and behavior in situations that increase activity of the visceral brain (under high activation). Any adequate test of the hypothesis that high and low neurotics differ as to level of autonomic activation requires "the use of relatively stressful conditions in which differences in responsivity of the sympathetic nervous system as a function of neuroticism would have a reasonable chance of manifesting themselves" (H. J. Eysenck & Eysenck, 1985. p. 206).

As concerns psychoticism, which in Eysenck's theory has not such a clear causal status as compared with extraversion and neuroticism, predictions relate only to psychosis and antisocial behaviors treated as expressions of a high position on this temperament dimension. No hypotheses or data have been reported by Eysenck which allow for any conclusion regarding the relationship between psychoticism and performance.

Empirical Evidence Supporting the Functional Significance of PEN

Over four decades of studies allowed Eysenck and his coworkers to collect enormous amounts of data in different fields of human activity showing that the three superfactors play a significant role in codetermining a variety of behaviors in different situations. Some findings are reported here.

PEN and Performance. It is impossible here to mention the scores of experiments and studies conducted by Eysenck and his associates in which performance has been related to extraversion, so only some general findings are mentioned. Experimental studies of different kinds of performance, such as classical and operant conditioning, vigilance, verbal learning and memory, the reminiscence phenomenon as revealed in psychomotor tasks, as well as psychophysical studies on sensory thresholds, aftereffects, and critical flicker fusion, reported in many publications (H. J. Eysenck, 1957, 1967, 1970; H. J. Eysenck & Eysenck, 1985) have often, but not always, given support for Eysenck's hypotheses. In general, the findings show that under experimental conditions characterized by stimuli or situations of high stimulative value efficiency of performance was higher in extraverts than in introverts. And conversely, when stimuli of low intensity were used, performance of introverts was more efficient than that of extraverts. The evidence on the relationship between neuroticism and performance is scanty and inconsistent, and mainly relates to anxiety which, according to Eysenck, is but one of the components of neuroticism (see Figure 2.2).

PEN and Social Behavior. As regards different aspects of social behavior some data show that extraverts prefer social interaction of high stimulative value whereas introverts show a tendency for reducing social contacts (e.g., Furnham, 1981; G. D. Wilson, 1981). Studies have also shown that extraverts prefer professional activity and university courses that allow for active social contacts whereas introverts seek activities that are more theoretically oriented (see H. J. Eysenck & Eysenck, 1985).

PEN and Sexual Behavior. One of the domains in which all three superfactors have been related to social activity is sexual behavior which can be characterized by strong emotional states, high physiological arousal, and strong rewards and punishments (H. J. Eysenck & Eysenck, 1985). If such is the case, this explains the importance of relating PEN to this behavior. It has been demonstrated that in general extraverts are sexually more active than introverts, neurotics seek more substitute sexual outlets (pornography, masturbation), and psychotics like oral sex (H. J. Eysenck, 1976; Giese & Schmidt, 1968). From a study in which 14 sexual attitudes were related to all three superfactors Eysenck distinguished two broader factors: libido and satisfaction. It turned out that the libido factor, which reflects a general sex drive (active sexuality and permissiveness) was most strongly associated with psychoticism, while the satisfaction factor, which is the opposite of sexual difficulty and deprivation, was most typical for emotionally stable individuals (H. J. Eysenck, 1976).

PEN and Education. Several studies related extraversion and neuroticism to educational achievement. Summarizing the data, which include cross-cultural studies, H. J. Eysenck and Eysenck (1985) concluded that "it is generally true at all ages from about 13 or 14 upwards that introverts show superior academic attainment to extraverts" (p. 321). In respect to neuroticism the relation to educational achievement is more equivocal, which suggests that this temperament dimension may influence learning efficiency depending on the teaching strategy used. Neurotics prefer supportive teaching strategies, and emotionally stable individuals exploratory strategies (H. J. Eysenck & Eysenck, 1985).

PEN and Antisocial Behavior. Eysenck and others have conducted a number of studies in which antisocial behavior, primarily crime, was related to the superfactors, especially to extraversion and neuroticism. H. J. Eysenck's (1964, 1977) theory of crime at its earlier stage predicted that individuals characterized by higher conditionability, that is, introverts, are less prone to commit crime than extraverts, due to the fact that conditioned fear, which prevents antisocial behavior, develops more easily in introverts. Furthermore, the lower conditionability of extraverts does not allow them to acquire social rules as effectively as do introverts. The theory also predicted that criminals are more neurotic than normal individuals. "Their anxiety acts as a drive that multiplies with habit" (H. J. Eysenck & Eysenck, 1985, p. 330). After developing the concept of psychoticism H. J.

Eysenck (1977) added psychoticism to his criminality theory as a dimension that contributes to criminal behavior. Thus, according to Eysenck, criminals are considered to occupy high positions on all three dimensions: extraversion, neuroticism, and psychoticism. H. J. Eysenck and Gudjonsson (1990) showed that extraversion is more powerful in children, neuroticism in adults. This is explained by the theory that conscience becomes conditioned in childhood, hence extraversion is important; in adults neuroticism, as a drive variable in the sense of Hull becomes more important because conscience is already formed. The empirical data are not very consistent as regards the contribution of extraversion and neuroticism, but support almost without exception the hypothesis that criminals occupy a high position on the psychoticism dimension (H. J. Eysenck & Gudjonsson, 1990; see also Hare, 1982; Putnins, 1982).

PEN and Psychiatric Disorders. H. J. Eysenck's (1970) assumption that there is a continuity between normal and pathological behavior and that neurotics as well as psychotics differ from normals only quantitatively (occupy different positions on the same dimensions) motivated him to search for relationships between the superfactors, as measured by inventories, and different psychiatric disorders. The search for links across temperament characteristics in normals, and pathological expressions of these traits, was present in H. J. Eysenck's (1944, 1947) research from the very beginning of his work. The data Eysenck collected by means of the EPQ support his statement that psychotic patients, as compared with normals, score significantly higher on the psychoticism dimension, while neurotic patients differ essentially from normals with respect to the place they occupy on the neuroticism dimension (H. J. Eysenck & Eysenck, 1976).

In summarizing the data reflecting the relationship between the PEN factors and social behavior H. J. Eysenck and Eysenck (1985) arrived at the following conclusions:

> The personality dimensions of extraversion, neuroticism, and psychoticism all have predictive and explanatory power across a heterogeneous collection of real-life situations. . . . We are now in a position to claim categorically that social phenomena such as criminality and mental illness depend in part on genetically determined individual differences in personality. (p. 342)

Critical Remarks

Eysenck's theoretical and empirical work on the major dimensions of temperament began almost half a century ago. It is natural that the wealth of ideas and enormous amount of data he and his coworkers produced have given many opportunities for critical comment and analysis. Some of them that seem to be of special importance from the temperament perspective are presented in this section.

One of the cardinal criticisms of Eysenck's extraversion and neuroticism dimensions treated as two basic, orthogonally related factors, came from his most eminent student, Gray (1981). Gray's temperament theory is presented in the next chapter in detail, thus only those points that refer to Eysenck's theory will be raised here. According to Gray (1981, 1987), extraversion and neuroticism are secondary consequences of the interaction between anxiety and impulsivity which Gray regarded as the two basic temperament dimensions. Extraverts are characterized by high impulsivity (+I) and low anxiety (–A), introverts by –I and +A, the emotionally stable by –I and –A, and neurotics by +I and +A.

Gray (1981) noted that Eysenck's conditionability postulate, that introverts condition more readily and rapidly than extraverts, does not explain a variety of phenomena, including social behavior. For Gray, individual differences in conditionability relate differently to the two poles of the E dimension. Whereas introverts condition with greater speed and ease than extraverts to punishment (aversive UCS), extraverts are superior to introverts in conditioning to rewards (appetitive UCS).

Increasing amounts of data (see H. J. Eysenck & Eysenck, 1985; Revelle, Humphreys, Simon, & Gilliland, 1980; Revelle, Anderson, & Humphreys, 1987) have shown that there are diurnal changes in arousal level along the extraversion dimension. Whereas introverts are more highly aroused in the morning, extraverts increase their level of arousal in the evening. This lack of stability in arousal level seriously undermines Eysenck's postulate regarding the chronic level of arousal typical of extraverts and introverts (Gray, 1981). A study conducted by G. D. Wilson (1990), reported in detail in Chapter 4, did not confirm the diurnal changes in arousal as related to extraversion.

The important modification in the structure of extraversion which consisted in the removal from this dimension of an essential part of the impulsivity component (H. J. Eysenck & Eysenck, 1976; S. B. G. Eysenck, Pearson, *et al.,* 1985) to which the construct of arousal mainly refers (Revelle *et al.,* 1987; Rocklin & Revelle, 1981; Zuckerman, 1991c) should have led to a modification of Eysenck's theory on the physiological basis of extraversion, but this did not take place.

A serious criticism is addressed to Eysenck's psychoticism dimension on several grounds. First, the construction of the Psychoticism scale is unsatisfactory. Although Eysenck corrected the P scale under the criticism of Block (1977) and D. V. M. Bishop (1977), the distribution of P scores is still essentially skewed to the right (H. J. Eysenck, 1992a) and therefore not normal. The Gaussian curve is typical for biologically rooted phenomena to which psychoticism, according to Eysenck, refers. Second, the findings regarding the genetic determination of individual differences in psychoticism are contradictory. Eaves, Eysenck, and Martin (1989) report data that are supportive for Eysenck's view regarding the heritability of P in some studies but no confirmation was obtained. A thorough behavior-genetic study, conducted on almost 3,000 adult subjects by Heath and Martin (1990), has not supported Eysenck's assumption that individual differences in psychoticism, as measured by EPQ items, have a strong genetic determination. Third, studies conducted within the framework of the Big Five approach suggest that psychoticism should not be considered as an independent factor but rather a combination of low agreeableness and low conscientiousness (L. R. Goldberg & Rosolack, 1994; John, 1990; McCrae & Costa, 1985a). Very recently the strong but also the weak parts of Eysenck's theory have been broadly discussed by his students and proponents (Nyborg, 1997).

In many of his publications H. J. Eysenck (1970, 1990b, 1992a, 1992b; H. J. Eysenck & Eysenck, 1985) responded to the criticisms of the PEN theory. The discussion between Eysenck and his opponents shows that other views on the nature of temperament are possible.

The Neo-Pavlovian Typology: Teplov and His School

Teplov belongs to the group of eminent Russian psychologists who influenced the mode of thought and conduct of research over the first three decades of postwar psychology in the former Soviet Union. His scientific activity was very broad and strongly oriented to experimental approaches (Teplov, 1985). Working as a military psychologist from the 1920s he conducted a series of experiments on the psychological aspects of camouflage. Until the 1940s visual sensitivity and perception were his main scientific interests. He pioneered in Russian psychology in such domains as mental and musical abilities. He was also the founder of differential psychophysiology.

Teplov's interests in Pavlov's typology dates from the early 1950s. In 1951 he set up the Laboratory of Psychophysiology of Individual Differences at the Institute of Psychology in Moscow, and the first results of Teplov's research on nervous system properties were published in 1954. From the beginning Teplov attracted a group of psychologists who worked collectively until his death (1965) and continued to develop his ideas over at least the next two decades. Among Teplov's most eminent coworkers and students were Golubeva, Gurevich, Leites, Nebylitsyn, Ravich-Shcherbo and Rozhdestvenskaya. From the collective work of this group of researchers it is not always possible to identify the contribution of Teplov. Nevertheless, most of the original ideas stem from Teplov, Nebylitsyn, or both. Nebylitsyn was not only Teplov's most creative student but also his successor as head of the laboratory. It is therefore reasonable to speak of the Teplov-Nebylitsyn School (see Strelau, 1983).

The published contribution of Teplov and his coworkers is contained in 10 volumes, 5 of which (1 to 5) were edited by Teplov (1956, 1959, 1963a, 1965, 1967) under the title: *Typological Features of Higher Nervous Activity in Man.* The consecutive 5 volumes (6 to 10), entitled *Problems of Differential Psychophysiol-*

ogy were edited by Nebylitsyn (1969, 1972b, 1974), Borisova and colleagues (1977), and Golubeva and Ravich-Shcherbo (1981). For the English reader the books edited by Gray (1964a), Nebylitsyn and Gray (1972), and the monographs written by Nebylitsyn (1972a), Mangan (1982), and Strelau (1983), give the most comprehensive information on the contribution of the Moscow School to the physiological and behavioral components of temperament.

Roots of Teplov's Approach to Studies on Nervous System Properties in Man

The list of precursors who motivated and oriented Teplov's research in the domain of nervous system properties is not as lengthy as in the case of Eysenck. Three sources are mentioned here: Pavlov's typology, the critique of Pavlov's successors in studying types of nervous system, and Teplov's long experience in psychophysics.

Teplov was fascinated by Pavlov's (1951–1952) contribution to the understanding of individual differences in behavior. Certain features of Pavlov's approach to the study of types of nervous system in dogs strongly influenced Teplov's theory and methodology in the study of central nervous system (CNS) properties. These features were concentration on CNS properties for an interpretation of individual differences in behavior, objective methods for the study of CNS properties, and the functional significance ascribed by Pavlov to these properties.

The state of research on types of nervous system by Pavlov's students and followers was extensively criticized by Teplov in his most comprehensive paper (Teplov, 1956; in English 1964). Teplov was critical of the attempts to assess nervous system types in man by means of anamnesis and observations in clinical settings (e.g., Birman, 1951; Lang-Belonogova & Kok, 1952). In his view these studies lacked objectivity and did not allow a grasp of the nature of CNS properties. His critique was addressed mainly to two of Pavlov's students, Krasnogorsky and Ivanov-Smolensky. They had undertaken, independently of each other, to adapt the Pavlovian typology to children (for details see Chapter 1; also Nebylitsyn, 1972a; Strelau, 1983; Teplov, 1964). Krasnogorsky (1939, 1953) applied the conditioned reflex (CR) method, especially the salivary CR, for diagnosing nervous system types in children. Using criteria that took into account the balance between excitatory and inhibitory processes in the cortex and subcortex Krasnogorsky distinguished, like Pavlov, four types of CNS, but different ones from Pavlov's. Teplov criticized Krasnogorsky's approach mainly as a simplified application to man of Pavlov's ideas and methods used in studies of CNS types on dogs.

Ivanov-Smolensky (1935, 1953), also fixed on the CR method as the main way to assess types of nervous system in children, using verbal reinforcement as a substitute for unconditioned stimuli (UCSs). Taking account of facility and speed in the elaboration of motor CRs Ivanov-Smolensky, too, distinguished four types which he called "types of CR activity." Teplov's criticism of this approach was mainly an attack on the verbal reinforcement procedure. Verbal reinforcement does not allow for examination of the nature of CNS processes. Furthermore, irregular reinforcement, of which the Ivanov-Smolensky method consisted, was given without any instruction as to what the subject was to do when verbal reinforcement (e.g., the command: "press the bulb") was absent. This kind of unstructured experimental setting was, as noted by Teplov, confusing for the subject.

Almost all the studies by Pavlov's students and followers, regardless of the criteria and methods used in assessing CNS types in man and animals, focused on the magic number of four types as proposed by Pavlov. This was true for all approaches previously discussed. Teplov was very critical of this kind of typological thinking which to his mind failed to capture the nature of CNS properties.

Not without influence on Teplov's neo-Pavlovian approach to the study of CNS properties was his former experience, especially his more than 15 years of research in the domain of sensory sensitivity. While studying visual sensitivity he discovered that the absolute visual threshold changes in the presence of an additional stimulus in the field of vision (Teplov, 1936). He interpreted this phenomenon by means of irradiation and concentration of excitatory and inhibitory processes. His studies on visual sensitivity had a direct influence on the development of the "induction method" aimed at assessing CNS strength (for description of this method see Gray, 1964a; Mangan, 1982; Nebylitsyn, 1972a; Strelau, 1983). Teplov's experience in laboratory studies on sensory sensitivity influenced his preference for physiological and psychophysical methods in studying CNS properties.

The Concept of Temperament and Its Postulated Structure

Under the influence of Pavlov, Teplov and his coworkers considered temperament the behavioral and psychological expression of CNS properties. Temperament was regarded as the dynamic characteristic of behavior expressed in individual differences in speed and intensity of reactions (Golubeva & Rozhdestvenskaya, 1978; Leites, 1956; Teplov, 1964). Temperament reveals itself mainly in the way an activity is performed and not so much in the result of the performance (Teplov, 1964). In general, it is to be noted that Teplov's and his students' conceptualizations regarding temperament understood as a behavioral concept are very theoretical and scanty.

The most elaborated view on the understanding of temperament and its postulated structure was presented by Nebylitsyn (1976) in his 1961 paper published in the *Pedagogical Encyclopaedia*. For him temperament is an individual characteristic expressed in such aspects of behavior as tempo, speed, and rhythm, and consists of three major components: activity, movement, and emotionality (Nebyl-itsyn, 1976, pp. 178–185). Activity, which reveals itself in all kinds of behavior, may vary in intensity characteristics from passive at one pole to energetic at the other. The motoric component, strongly related to activity, is expressed in such aspects of movement as speed, strength, impetuousness, rhythm, and amplitude. Nebylitsyn regarded emotionality as a complex trait expressed in the emergence, course, and termination of different kinds of emotions and moods, and composed of impulsivity and emotional lability.

According to Teplov (1964, 1972) and Nebylitsyn (1976), temperament traits are not susceptible to change. The fact that temperament is considered innate, but not necessarily inherited, was used by Teplov and his associates as the main argument in favor of temperament stability. However, in Teplov's laboratory data collected by Leites (1956, 1972) showed developmental changes in CNS properties, such as developmental shift from weakness to strength and from lack of balance (with predominance of excitation) to a balanced type of nervous system. Leites assessed these CNS properties in preschool and elementary school children not by physiological methods but mainly on behavioral indices and motor performance in laboratory settings. This suggests that the developmental changes recorded by Leites refer not so much to CNS properties but to temperament characteristics.

It is important to note that in Teplov's laboratory temperament as a psychological construct was rarely, if ever, a subject of study.[1] All conceptualizations regarding the structure of temperament, its dimensions, and its stability were purely speculative.

Studies on Properties of the Central Nervous System

The physiological bases of temperament were not apprehended by Teplov and his coworkers in the Pavlovian type of CNS, as most former Soviet psychologists had done, but in the separate CNS properties (Nebylitsyn, 1972a; Teplov, 1964). These became in Teplov's laboratory the focus of research guided by several pos-

---

[1] Intensive studies on temperament as measured mainly by means of behavior characteristics were conducted during the 1950s to 1970s by Merlin and his students. A detailed description of these studies published in many Russian-language books and papers (e.g., Merlin, 1955, 1970, 1973) has been provided by Strelau (1983). The very fact that these researchers published their studies almost exclusively in local journals or in local publishing houses has meant that their research did not greatly influence studies conducted in other centers of the former Soviet Union. Merlin's research was almost unknown internationally. His popularity among Warsaw temperament researchers was an exception (see Strelau, 1983, 1985). As a point of interest, Merlin and his associates worked in a Siberian town, Perm, saturated with military industry. Foreigners were not allowed to visit it and inhabitants were greatly restricted in traveling outside their area. To make a meeting with me possible, Professor Merlin had to go to Moscow. Political factors were strong reasons for Merlin's isolation from other temperament research centers.

tulates formulated by Teplov (1954, 1955, 1964) and Nebylitsyn (1972a; Teplov & Nebylitsyn, 1963a, 1963b) of which the most important were the following:

(1) For a proper understanding of the physiological bases of temperament it is necessary to study the nature of the separate CNS properties. Configurations of these properties, which result in nervous system types, should be studied only after the CNS properties are identified and their substance understood.

(2) The CNS properties are clearly manifested only in involuntary movements, undisguised by the individual's experience. The way to study them is to concentrate on physiological phenomena which are not influenced by verbal behavior or by other voluntary acts. Therefore mainly psychophysiological, eventually psychophysical, methods should be used for assessing the CNS properties.

(3) Each property of the CNS is associated with a specific form of adjustment by the organism to the environment. CNS properties are therefore neither good nor bad, and their behavioral significance depends on the specific situation in which the individual acts.

Following these postulates, which became a kind of methodological "credo," Teplov and his associates were able to identify or specify several CNS properties. Research in the domain of such physiological phenomena as photochemical and pupillary reflexes, vascular, muscular, electrodermal, and electroencephalographic activity resulted in modifying some of Pavlov's original constructs of CNS properties as well as in distinguishing new properties of the CNS which are described in the following sections.

Strength of Excitation as a Dimension Characterized by Endurance and Sensitivity

On the basis of data collected over many years Teplov and Nebylitsyn (1963a) concluded that there is a direct relationship between Pavlov's understanding of strength of excitation regarded as the capacity to work (endurance), and the CNS's response threshold, that is, its sensitivity (reactivity). The endurance of nerve cells and their sensitivity can be viewed as two facets of strength of excitation. The authors postulated an opposite relationship between endurance and sensitivity of the CNS: the higher the endurance the lower the sensitivity, and vice versa. Nebylitsyn (1972a) interpreted individual differences in strength of excitation by means of the ionic theory which refers to the mechanism of the sodium-potassium pump (see Hodgkin, 1951). In short, during physiological rest the nerve cell is in a state of ionic asymmetry (ionic gradient) characterized by equilibrium between the potassium ions inside and outside the cell. Stimulation of the nerve cell initiates a process of excitation which results in lowering the ionic asymmetry. Decrease in asymmetry (increase in ionic symmetry) produces a reduced level of functioning in the nerve cell resembling the state of transmarginal inhibition. There are "individual differences in speed at which the critical level of ionic asymmetry is reached. On this assumption, this critical level defines strength of the excitatory process" (Nebylitsyn, 1972a, p. 137). Strong cells are able to efficiently reestablish the ionic gradient (ionic asymmetry) during interstimulus intervals, whereas in weak nerve cells a progressively slower and weaker recovery occurs.

Lability of the CNS

Ravich-Shcherbo (1956) using the procedure of photochemical conditioning applied different indices of broad-sense mobility in reference to all temporal characteristics of CNS functioning (Teplov, 1964). The results of this study, replicated in further experiments using factor analysis (Borisova *et al.,* 1963; Nebylitsyn, 1972a), showed that broad-sense mobility must be split into two independent properties: mobility in the narrow sense and lability. Mobility (narrow) as expressed in ease of switch from excitation to inhibition and vice versa, is identified with Pavlov's understanding of this CNS property. In turn, lability is manifested in the speed with which nervous processes are initiated and terminated (Teplov, 1963b).

Dynamism of Nervous Processes

Nebylitsyn's (1963) detailed review of the literature concerning the relationship between speed and efficiency of conditioning and strength of the nervous system, including his own studies, led him to conclude that the speed at which positive and negative CRs are elaborated does not correlate with the strength of nervous processes, as postulated by Pavlov. According to Nebylitsyn (1963, 1972a), the dynamism of nervous processes is manifested in the formation of temporal connections in the brain. This property, which is independent of the others, was understood by Nebylitsyn as well as by Teplov (1972) as the facility and speed with which the processes of excitation (dynamism of excitation) and inhibition (dynamism of inhibition) are generated during the formation of CRs. "The balance of both nervous processes as regards dynamism, their equilibrium, should be considered as the equilibrium of the reticular formation system and the cortex" (Nebylitsyn, 1963, p. 18). This hypothesis enhanced the use of EEG activity as an indicator of dynamism.

Balance of CNS Processes as a Secondary Property

Pavlov (1951–1952), who considered the ratio between strength of excitation and strength of inhibition as the measure of balance (equilibrium) of CNS processes, had already given this property secondary status. Nebylitsyn (1963, 1972a) extended the meaning of balance by attributing to it the role of a general organizing principle of NS properties. In his view, balance of CNS processes comprises strength, mobility, lability, and dynamism, and is expressed as a ratio between excitation and inhibition in reference to each of these four properties separately. Nebylitsyn also proposed a global estimation of balance expressed in one score arrived at from the ratio between the sums of the indices of excitation and inhibition for the four CNS properties (strength, mobility, lability, and dynamism). This global index of balance between excitation and inhibition, reminiscent of Eysenck's concept of excitation–inhibition balance, was, however, never applied in Teplov's laboratory.

Other CNS properties also have been distinguished in Teplov's laboratory, such as concentratability (Borisova, 1959, 1972) understood as the tendency of nervous processes to concentrate, and activatability. The latter, which closely resembles Gray's (1964c) concept of arousability, refers to stable and inborn individual differences in activation (arousal) as expressed in "EEG balance" (Golubeva, 1975, 1980). Only marginal attention was paid in Teplov's laboratory to these two individual characteristics of CNS activity.

Genetic Studies on CNS Properties

Teplov's (1964) assumption that CNS properties are inborn was interpreted in such a way that at least part of the variance of these properties was to be attributed to the genes. A series of studies was conducted by Ravich-Shcherbo (1977; Ravich-Shcherbo, Shlakhta, & Shibarovskaya, 1969) for the purpose of verifying this assumption. The studies conducted in Teplov's laboratory from the end of the 1960s to the end of the 1970s have been summarized by Strelau (1983). Because of the small number of subjects, limitation to one twin design only (MZ and DZ twins reared together), and lack of adequate statistical procedures, no reasonable conclusion could be drawn. In general, the results were inconsistent, but they did not contradict the assumption that individual differences in CNS properties are to some extent genetically determined (Strelau, 1983). Studies regarding heritability of CNS properties are still in progress (e.g., Ravich-Shcherbo, 1988).

General and Partial CNS Properties

According to Teplov (1964), one of the main tasks in studying the CNS properties was to distinguish between general and partial properties. General properties characterize the work of the brain hemispheres as a whole, and they constitute the physiological bases of temperament. Partial CNS properties, considered by Teplov as the physiological bases of special abilities, characterize the activity of separate parts of the cortex. Empirical support for the distinction between general and partial CNS properties was provided mainly by Nebylitsyn (1957) but also by others (see Strelau, 1983). Summarizing the data collected in Teplov's laboratory Nebylitsyn (1972c) arrived at the conclusion that the partiality phenomenon refers to about 15%–20% of subjects. It consists of differences in assessment of the separate CNS properties depending on the kind of (a) analyzer (e.g., visual versus auditory modality), (b) effector from which recordings are taken, and (c) rein-forcement applied in the experimental design. In other words, it has been found that in about 20% of subjects assessments of CNS properties are lacking cross-sit-uational consistency. The problem of general and partial CNS properties has been studied in detail by Strelau (1958, 1965, 1972b) and in the domain of EEG activ-ity by Rusalov (1977). In a series of laboratory experiments using different kinds of CS and UCS stimuli, and taking records from different kinds of effectors, Stre-lau demonstrated that the results are lacking in generalizability, which makes for difficulties in identifying the general properties of CNS.

Methods Used for Assessing the CNS Properties

As already mentioned, Teplov and his associates were interested mainly in studying the physiological bases of temperament. This explains why they neither constructed nor applied methods for the diagnosis of temperament traits. However, they contributed substantially to the development of many experimental tech-niques addressed to the assessment of CNS properties. It is impossible to present the score of methods developed by Teplov (1964, 1972), Nebylitsyn (1972a), and other members of the Moscow group. These methods have been described in de-tail by Gray (1964c), Mangan (1982), and Strelau (1983).

Several assumptions underlay the development of methods to assess CNS properties. First, as already mentioned in the methodological credo, to avoid the masking effect of environmental influences involuntary reactions have to be in-vestigated. Second, the elaboration of conditioned reflexes enables the study of in-voluntary reactions unaffected by the individual's experience. Third, the best way to study the general properties of the CNS, as distinct from the partial ones, is to record the brain's bioelectrical activity. Fourth, coming closer to human behavior, simple voluntary reactions, as measured in classical RT experiments, can also be taken as expressions of CNS properties. In addition, in the domain of strength of excitation, assuming the bipolarity of this CNS property Teplov and his associates developed methods to measure the sensitivity pole of the strength dimension. Prior to Teplov, assessment of this CNS property was based exclusively on measuring the individual's capacity (endurance) under strong or lengthy stimulation. Most of the methods applied in Teplov's laboratory refer to three domains: conditioning, sensory sensitivity, and bioelectrical activity of the brain. Some of these methods are briefly presented in the following sections.

Assessments of CNS Properties Based on the CR Paradigm

The conditioned reflex (CR) phenomenon which served in Teplov's labora-tory for measuring strength of excitation, mobility, and dynamism of CNS processes was studied by recording such events as the photochemical reflex, EEG alpha-blocking, EDA and electromyography (EMG). The most popular method in the domain of strength of excitation was "extinction with reinforcement." Essentially this method consists in comparing the magnitude of CR before and after intense stimulation, as schematically presented in Figure 2.5. After the CR to a given stimulus is consolidated its amplitude is measured. Next, a series of CS–UCS pairings are presented and, again, CR amplitude is measured after the final pairing has been presented. The two amplitudes (before and after the series of CS–UCS expositions) are then compared. A decrease of CR amplitude after stimulation was taken to indicate a weak nervous system, and no change or amplitude increase indicated a strong nervous system. The greater the number of CS–UCS applied, the shorter the interstimulus interval, and the higher the intensity of stimuli used, the more easily the threshold of transmarginal inhibition (as expressed in the decrease of CR amplitude) is reached.

Mobility of the CNS processes was measured in Teplov's laboratory mainly by means of the classical CR method developed by Pavlov (see Chapter 1). As underlined by Teplov (1963b), "mobility is that property of the nervous system which is characterized by alteration of stimulus signs" (p. 37). Essentially, this technique consists of elaborating a positive CR to one stimulus and a negative CR (inhibitory response) to another. The two stimuli are presented alternately. After the positive and negative CRs are consolidated the signal values of the stimuli are switched. The positive stimulus, no longer reinforced, becomes negative, and the negative stimulus, now reinforced, changes to positive. The speed with which the subject is able to react adequately to the reversed presentations is the most popular index of CNS mobility. Mobility is higher when fewer stimuli are needed to adequately react to the changed value of the stimuli.

Dynamism also was measured by use of the CR paradigm. Dynamism of the excitatory and inhibitory processes were measured separately according to the number of trials required to develop positive (dynamism of excitation) or negative (dynamism of inhibition) conditioned reflexes (Nebylitsyn, 1972a; Strelau, 1983).

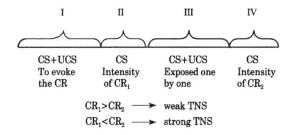

FIGURE 2.5. Extinction with reinforcement.

Sensory Sensitivity Phenomena as the Basis for Diagnosis of CNS Properties

As mentioned earlier, Teplov's experience in psychophysics, and his assumption regarding the reverse relationship between sensitivity and endurance, contributed to the development of a series of diagnostic methods based on sensory phenomena, especially in respect to visual sensitivity. At the beginning of research on CNS properties a procedure known as the Induction Method was elaborated by Rozhdestvenskaya (1955). Teplov's (1936) earlier finding that a point of light in peripheral vision changes the sensitivity threshold to the target stimulus was the starting point for developing this method. The rather complicated procedure (for detailed description see Gray, 1964a; Strelau, 1983), used mainly in the 1950s in Teplov's laboratory, was based on an assumption that changes in visual sensitivity under additional stimuli depend on the shifts from irradiation to concentration and from concentration to irradiation (the "law of induction" established by Pavlov). These shifts were supposed to be different depending on the strength of the CNS.

Several studies were conducted in which sensory thresholds (visual, auditory) were used as indices of strength of excitation. It was assumed that the higher the sensitivity (the lower the sensory threshold) the weaker the nervous system. This method was recommended by Teplov (1972) and Nebylitsyn (1972a) as a referent indicator of NS strength.

One of the most popular methods used in Teplov's laboratory for assessing strength of excitation was the "slope of RT curve" which also refers to the phenomenon of sensory sensitivity. As we know, the law of strength predicts that simple reaction time (RT) decreases with increasing intensity to stimuli. Nebylitsyn (1960, 1972a) predicted that in individuals with low sensory thresholds a stimulus of low intensity evokes higher excitation, thus also shorter RT, than in individuals with a high sensory threshold. This means that RT to stimuli of low intensity will be shorter in weak CNS individuals (who have low sensory thresholds) as compared with individuals with strong CNS. This assumption has been verified in several experiments which have shown that individuals with a weak nervous system display shorter RTs as compared with strong individuals. The differences between weak and strong individuals disappeared when strong stimuli were exposed (see Figure 2.6).

Phenomena of sensory sensitivity were also broadly used for assessing CNS lability, as, for example, adequate optical chronaxie, critical frequency of flicker-fusion, or speed of visual sensitivity restoration. In all these methods speed of initiation and/or termination of visual phenomena served as the main index of lability. According to Teplov and his associates, the higher the speed of initiation and the shorter the termination time of visual phenomena evoked by stimuli of different intensity, the more labile the CNS processes (Nebylitsyn, 1972a; Shvarts, 1965).

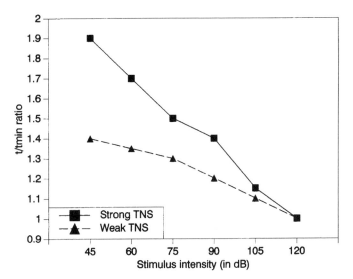

FIGURE 2.6. Reaction time (as measured by t/t_{min}) as a function of intensity of auditory stimuli for individuals with strong and weak NS.

EEG Activity and the Diagnosis of CNS Properties

Since the mid-1960s EEG methods have gained maximal popularity in diagnosing strength, lability, and dynamism of CNS processes. As already mentioned, in EEG activity the general properties of the CNS were supposed to be most evident. Additional arguments in favor of these methods were the substantial individual differences in EEG activity and the highly stable EEG records.

The photic driving reaction (PDR) was the most popular method for assessing CNS strength based on EEG activity (Klyagin, 1974). It is known that the expression of the PDR grows, to some degree, with the increasing intensity of rhythmic exposure to light stimuli. In the diagnosis of strength this method was used on the assumption that, in individuals with a weak nervous system, because of their high sensitivity, the PDR would be more strongly expressed than in strong CNS individuals (Nebylitsyn, 1964). This method was used for diagnosing strength with stimuli frequencies referring mainly to theta band (see Strelau, 1983). Attempts have also been undertaken to apply the amplitude of evoked potentials (EP) as a measure of strength of excitation. Bazylevich (1974), taking into account that strong stimulation, due to transmarginal inhibition, may result in a decrease of reaction intensity, applied somatosensory evoked potentials (SEP) to measure this CNS property. This property "is directly reflected in the SEP understood as a function of the intensity of proprioceptive stimulation" (p. 91). A decrease in the amplitude of EP to strong stimuli was regarded as an indicator of a weak type of CNS (see also Bazylevich, 1983).

The photic driving reaction was also used for diagnosing lability of the CNS, although in the high frequency band. According to Golubeva (1972a), who most frequently applied the PDR for diagnosing lability, "labile subjects are persons in whom excitation arises faster, but their restorative processes also operate fast after the action of stimuli" (p. 23). This explains why high efficiency of PDR to stimuli of high frequency has been regarded as an indicator of lability.

Nebylitsyn (1965, 1972a) found that speed of conditioning to positive and negative stimuli correlated with indices of alpha activity, especially with the alpha index. "Alpha index similarly reflects both dynamism of inhibition and dynamism of excitation" (Nebylitsyn, 1972a, p. 92). From the mid-1960s the alpha index and the total energy of the alpha rhythm became the principal measures of balance in dynamism of CNS processes. According to Nebylitsyn and other associates of Teplov, a high alpha index and a high score of total energy of alpha rhythm reflect the predominance of inhibition over excitation, whereas low scores on both measures indicate the domination of excitation over inhibition.

Properties of CNS in Relation to Behavior

According to Nebylitsyn (1972a), the role of temperament in human behavior is particularly pronounced when the balance between organism and environment is disturbed, which occurs in stressful situations. Gurevich (1970; Gurevich & Matveyev, 1966) conducted a field study that exemplifies this line of thinking. The authors demonstrated an interrelation between CNS strength as measured by laboratory methods and performance efficacy of operators during a breakdown in a power plant. Under these conditions, which may be characterized as extreme stress, the behavior of operators representing a weak type of CNS was disorganized, especially as regards perception, memory, and thinking. On the other hand, subjects with a strong CNS displayed considerable endurance in the face of stress.

Most of the studies in which performance efficiency was related to CNS properties have been conducted in laboratory settings. For example, Rozhdestvenskaya (1980; Rozhdestvenskaya, Golubeva, & Yermolayeva-Tomina, 1969) in a series of experiments was able to demonstrate that, when subjects perform tasks consisting of memorizing verbal material under high tension and high motivation, performance efficiency is higher in strong than in weak CNS individuals. In experiments characterized by monotonous situations a reverse relationship holds between performance efficiency and CNS strength: efficiency was higher in individuals with a weak CNS.

Teplov (1964) hypothesized that inertia of the nervous system, as opposed to mobility, seems to be one of the most important physiological mechanisms underlying memory. This hypothesis gave impetus to a series of studies by Golubeva (1972b, 1980). Studying the efficiency of voluntary and involuntary memorizing in relation to NS properties, Golubeva found that lability correlates positively with efficiency of involuntary memorizing, whereas in voluntary memorizing individuals with a low level of lability are more efficient. Golubeva (1972b) also found that individuals with a strong CNS reveal higher efficiency in memory tasks involving large quantities of material and a low degree of comprehension. In Teplov's laboratory many studies have been conducted with respect to different functions of memory under a variety of conditions, always related to CNS properties (Golubeva, 1980). The results of these studies are rather equivocal (Strelau, 1983) and do not allow for general conclusions regarding the relationship between CNS properties and efficiency of memorizing.

Critical Remarks

Research conducted by Teplov and his associates represents a typical bottom-up approach, with large amounts of data at the bottom and almost no empirical evidence regarding the top. From this point of view one can agree with Powell's (1979) statement that "Russian work as propounded by Pavlov, Teplov and Nebylitsyn begins with properties and types of nervous activity—and stops there" (p. 25). My own research covering more than a decade in the domain of CNS properties (Strelau, 1958, 1965, 1969), and a review of almost all of the studies conducted by the Teplov school, have led me to formulate several critical comments (for details see Strelau, 1983), some of which are mentioned in the following paragraphs.

In using the concept "property" of the CNS Teplov and his coworkers assumed that this concept has the status of a trait, with relatively high stability and satisfactory cross-situational consistency. Stability of CNS properties remained only an assumption in Teplov's laboratory, since no empirical studies were conducted on this issue. As regards cross-situational consistency of the CNS properties, the data collected in Teplov's laboratory (for a review, see Strelau (1969, 1983), and Strelau's (1965, 1969) own experiments, have shown beyond any doubt that CNS properties lack generalizability. Assessments of CNS properties are highly influenced by the specificity of laboratory conditions under which they are studied.

The postulated orthogonality of the CNS properties, as distinguished by Teplov and Nebylitsyn, has not been confirmed. As shown by Strelau (1983), there is also much inconsistency in the interrelations of the separate CNS properties. Sometimes the same experimental procedures were applied for measuring different CNS properties, as, for example, photic driving reaction in the same frequency band as a measure of strength and lability, or speed of conditioning as a measure of dynamism but also of lability. Also, the same CNS property was assessed by means of different indicators which did not correlate with each other. For example, dynamism, measured by speed of elaborating positive and negative conditioned reflexes, did not correlate with EEG alpha activity, also regarded as an indicator of dynamism (Nebylitsyn, 1972a). Indeed, speed of conditioning was used as an index for all the CNS properties (see Mangan, 1982; Strelau, 1983), which testifies against its being an appropriate measure for this purpose. It also contradicts the idea that the separate NS properties are orthogonal.

The Interactional Theory of Temperament Developed by Thomas and Chess

Factors such as the strong criticism of the constitutional approach to temperament, the deep belief that environment is the only determinant of the development of human personality, and fascination for the psychoanalytic approach as developed by Freud and his followers created the atmosphere in which Thomas and Chess, two American psychiatrists, launched their studies on temperament. Contrary to popular views, these scientists underlined the importance of individual differences in human behavior as well as the role of interaction between individual characteristics and the social environment in human development from early childhood onward. The interactions between the factors—temperament as well as other individual characteristics, and environment (especially social demands and expectations) were considered by Thomas and Chess to be the main causes of normal development as well as of many behavior disorders. The interactional approach with its strong emphasis on developmentally specific phenomena is the most typical feature of their temperament theory.

In 1956 the two psychiatrists undertook a longitudinal study of temperament, known as the New York Longitudinal Study (NYLS), still continuing today. The results of this study, which has lasted more than 30 years, a duration unique in the temperament domain, have been published in many books (Chess & Thomas, 1984; A. Thomas & Chess, 1977; A. Thomas, Chess, Birch, Hertzig, & Korn, 1963; A. Thomas, Chess, & Birch, 1968). This research, as well as Thomas and Chess's theoretical considerations, were, and still are, very influential in the development of several contemporary conceptualizations on temperament, to mention only the theories of Buss and Plomin (1975, 1984), Goldsmith and Campos (1982), or Rothbart and Derryberry (1981).

Roots of the Interactional Theory of Temperament

Thomas and Chess, who combined their research interests with clinical practice, were struck by the obvious individual differences in children's behavior from the first weeks of life. Their attempts to explain these differences, as well as behavior disorders,by reference to parental attitudes and rearing practices failed. Observations conducted by the two clinicians showed that the same parental attitudes and practices resulted in different courses of development and behavior disturbances depending on the child's individual characteristics. Thomas and Chess's thinking in terms of individual differences in behavior characteristics which emerged from their own experience was influenced by the research conducted in the period between 1930 and 1950. A number of studies looking for the causes of development in children underlined the existence and importance of individual differences in human behavior. For example, individual patterns in behavior in early infancy were demonstrated by Escalona (1968) and by Gesell and Ames (1937). Individuality in physiological and biochemical responses already present in neonates was also demonstrated (Richmond & Lustman, 1955; Williams, 1956).

In studying the interaction between temperament characteristics and environment the authors referred to the evolutionary concept of "goodness of fit" as introduced by Henderson (1913) and Dubos (1965). Goodness and poorness of fit became a crucial construct in their interactional theory of temperament. Further, the idea formulated in the 1950s by some researchers that human development is the outcome of reciprocal relations between the organism and the environment in which the organism plays an active role (Schneirla, 1957) influenced Thomas and Chess's approach to studies on temperament.

The NYLS as Source and Evidence for the Interactional Theory of Temperament

The temperament theory developed by Thomas and Chess, their measurement techniques for assessing temperament and environment variables, as well as their conclusions and interpretations regarding the relationship between temperament and behavior, and behavior disorders, all have their roots in the longitudinal study initiated by the two psychiatrists in 1956. This study was guided by two cardinal assumptions: (1) children show individual differences in temperament and (2) temperament plays an important role in normal and deviant development.

The NYLS Project

Eighty-five families representing the middle and upper-middle class of New York's population agreed to take part in this study, which comprised altogether 138 children. Most of the families had one or two children, and the age of the children when the initial interview with their parents was scheduled was between 2 and 3 months. From this sample 133 subjects were followed from early infancy until the 1980s. Depending on the subjects' age the manner of data collection differed; the number and kind of measured variables also varied. At all stages of development, temperamental traits, parental attitudes and practices were assessed, and clinical evaluation, when necessary, was conducted. The investigation included also observations and interviews collected in nursery school, kindergarten, elementary school, and at home; self-report data, and ratings by parents and teachers were also used. The consecutive stages of the longitudinal temperament study have been reported for infancy and early childhood (A. Thomas *et al.,* 1963), for childhood (A. Thomas *et al.,* 1968), for adolescence (A. Thomas & Chess, 1977), and for adulthood (Chess & Thomas, 1984).

At the beginning of the NYLS research, A. Thomas and Chess (1957, p. 351), in referring to individual differences in behavior characteristics, applied the term *individual reaction patterns.* These patterns depend on the character of the responses to external and internal stimuli. A case study of seven individuals from the NYLS resulted in classifying the reaction patterns into five categories. These included intensity of reaction and positive versus negative responses, which became the starting point for the temperament categories distinguished by the researchers. After realizing that individual characteristics not only refer to reactive behavior but also interact actively with the environment, the authors introduced the term *temperament.* Temperament refers to the *how* of behavior and, thus, may be equated to the term *behavioral style.* The authors emphasized that "temperament is a phenomenologic term and has no implication as to etiology or immutability" (A. Thomas & Chess, 1977, p. 9).

The Categories of Temperament and Their Constellations

At the beginning of their study Thomas and Chess distinguished nine temperament categories. This distinction was made on the basis of an inductive content analysis of parents' reports about their children's behavior in the infancy period. Twenty-two interview protocols were analyzed, and on the basis of item scoring, each category was assessed on a 3-point rating scale (A. Thomas *et al.,* 1963). The nine temperament categories proposed by Thomas and Chess more than 30 years ago have remained unchanged in their most recent publications (Chess & Thomas, 1989, 1991; A. Thomas & Chess, 1985). The essential description of these categories follows:

- *Activity level:* the motor component in a child's behavior and the diurnal proportion of active to inactive periods.
- *Rhythmicity (regularity):* the regularity or irregularity of biological functions (e.g., sleep-wake cycle).
- *Approach or withdrawal:* the nature of the initial response to a new stimulus (e.g., food, toy, person). Approach is regarded as a positive response, withdrawal as a negative one, both expressed in emotions and/or motor activity.
- *Adaptability:* ease with which behavior can be changed in a desired direction expressed in reactions to new stimuli.
- *Threshold of responsiveness:* the intensity of stimulation required to evoke a discernible response.

- *Intensity of reaction:* the energy level of response, irrespective of its quality or direction.
- *Quality of mood:* the extent of positive emotions (mood) as contrasted with negative ones.
- *Distractibility:* the effectiveness of extraneous stimuli in drawing attention away from the ongoing behavior.
- *Attention span and persistence:* the uninterrupted length of time a particular activity can be pursued (attention span), and ability to continue activity in the face of distractors (persistence); the categories are related to each other.

Qualitative examination of the functional significance of temperament, supported by factor analysis, led the authors to distinguish the three following temperamental constellations: difficult child, easy child, and slow-to-warm-up child (A. Thomas *et al.,* 1963; A. Thomas & Chess, 1977); the term "child" was later replaced by the term "temperament" (Chess & Thomas, 1984; A. Thomas & Chess, 1986; A. Thomas, Chess, & Korn, 1982). The "easy temperament" (about 40% of the NYLS sample) has been characterized by high scores in the following categories: regularity, approach and adaptability, mild or moderately intense reactions, and predominance of positive mood. For the "difficult temperament" (about 10% of the sample) an opposite temperamental constellation is typical: irregularity, withdrawal, nonadaptability, intense reactions, and negative mood. The constellation of the "slow-to-warm-up temperament" (about 15% of subjects) comprises negative reactions to new stimuli with slow adaptability, predominance of negative mood but with mild intensity of reactions, and a moderate position on the regularity dimension.

The terms "easy" and "difficult" have their justification in the reports of parents who considered children with one of the temperament constellations as easy to bring up and a joy to their parents, whereas children with the opposite constellation were regarded as troublemakers (A. Thomas *et al.,* 1963).

According to the authors the constellation of the difficult temperament "clearly placed a child at greater risk for behavior disorder development than did any other set of temperamental characteristics" (Chess & Thomas, 1984, p. 186). However, the authors limited this statement to families as represented by the NYLS population. In other cultures, with different demands and expectations, the difficult temperament may not have the same high-risk potential for the development of behavior disorders.

The Concept of Goodness of Fit

The lack of a direct relationship between the temperament constellations (easy versus difficult) and behavior disorders led Thomas and Chess to introduce the concept of *goodness of fit* (A. Thomas *et al.,* 1968; Chess & Thomas, 1989,

1991), which fully corresponds with their interactional approach to temperament. Goodness of fit occurs when the individual's capacities, temperament, and other individual characteristics are in accord with the opportunities, demands, and expectations of the environment (especially parents, teachers, and peers). Such a consonance between organism and environment assures optimal development. When a significant and long-lasting dissonance between the individual's characteristics and the environmental conditions occurs, "there is poorness of fit, which leads to maladaptive functioning and distorted development" (Chess & Thomas, 1984, p. 21). A minor dissonance resulting in conflict and stress experienced by new demands and expectations is basically positive for developmental processes, but excessive stress resulting from poorness of fit leads to behavior problems. In most of their publications Thomas and Chess have emphasized that temperament categories and their constellations are not by themselves causes of behavior disorders. Temperament categories of themselves are neither good nor bad, and they have to be always considered in relationship to, or in interaction with, other individual characteristics and environmental factors.

Temporal Consistency of Temperament Characteristics

The longitudinal study has yielded some evidence regarding the continuity of temperament. The longer the NYLS subjects were under investigation the less categorical the conclusions of Thomas and Chess regarding the continuity of the separate temperament categories. Whereas the expressions of temperament change over time, which is due to developmental changes in range and quality of behaviors, "what remains consistent over time is the *definitional identity* of the characteristic" (A. Thomas & Chess, 1977, p. 159). The scores for the nine temperament categories taken for ages from 1 to 5 years and correlated with temperament measures for adults are rather pessimistic when considered as indicators of continuity. No one coefficient reached the value of .30 and most of the correlations were statistically insignificant (A. Thomas & Chess, 1986). However, a comparison of temperament characteristics across ages (from early childhood to adulthood), in which the constellation of difficult temperament was taken into account, has given a more optimistic picture. It turned out that negative temperament attributes at the age of 3 years were significantly related to the difficult temperament in adulthood. This relationship was mediated by such variables as maternal attitude in childhood and adjustment in adulthood (Chess & Thomas, 1984).

In line with their descriptive theory of temperament, without any attempt to answer the question of the etiology of temperamental categories, Thomas and Chess did not hypothesize about the biological background of the phenomena under study. However, they assumed that temperament has its roots in physiological mechanisms, and that individual differences in these behavioral characteristics have some genetic determination (see Torgersen's study reported in Chapter 5).

Temperament Measures Applied by Thomas and Chess

When Thomas and Chess started their studies on temperament, their subjects, who are now adults, were several-weeks-old infants. This fact in itself determined to a high degree the kind of methods used for assessing temperament. In early childhood parents were the main source of information regarding children's temperament. On the basis of structured interview protocols taken from parents, the nine categories of temperament were assessed by using a 3-point rating scale. The interviews focused on factual descriptions of behavior, such as questions relating to feeding, elimination, sleep–waking cycle, and so on. At school age classroom observations lasting 1–2 hours and teacher interviews were added as sources of temperament assessment.

For the ages between 3 and 7 years a 72-item questionnaire was constructed for parents and a 64-item questionnaire for teachers. Both questionnaires had a 7-point rating scale (from "hardly ever" to "almost always") for judging the frequency of given behaviors (A. Thomas & Chess, 1977). For adult subjects, a self-report measure was constructed. A. Thomas, Mittelman, Chess, Korn and Cohen (1982) developed a 140-item temperament questionnaire for early adult life. Like the two former psychometric measures, this inventory had a 7-point rating scale on which frequency of given behaviors was assessed. In contrast to the other assessment techniques developed by Thomas and Chess, the inventory for early adulthood has more complete psychometric characteristics, including reliability and validity scores.

In general, it is clear that the diagnostic procedures developed by Thomas and Chess for assessing temperament are rather simplistic, with little psychometric background. Some of their students and associates have developed questionnaires which are widely used in assessing the nine NYLS temperament categories for early infancy (W. B. Carey & McDevitt, 1978), for 1–3-year-old children (Fullard, McDevitt, & Carey, 1984), for 3–7-year-old children (McDevitt & Carey, 1978), and for 8–11-year-old children (Hegvik, McDevitt, & Carey, 1982).

Temperament and Behavior Disorders

More than three decades of NYLS research on temperament, together with studies conducted on other samples, such as mildly retarded children, children prenatally infected with the rubella virus, prematurely born infants, and children from working-class families, allowed the authors to study in detail the relationship between temperament characteristics, especially the three temperament constellations mentioned earlier, and different kinds of behavior disorders. Behavior disorders were defined by the authors (Chess & Thomas, 1984, 1986; A. Thomas & Chess, 1977) according to the *Diagnostic and Statistical Manual of Mental Dis-*

orders in terms of adjustment disorder, conduct disorder, and anxiety disorder. As summarized by the authors:

> These are the disorders in which a significant degree of disturbance in behavioral function has resulted from a poorness of fit between the child's temperament and/or other characteristics and the demands and expectations of the environment. . . . In most cases it is a poorness of fit with the child's temperament which is a major or even decisive factor in the unfavorable course of psychologic development. (Chess & Thomas, 1986, p. 159)

This conclusion is based on a variety of quantitative and qualitative data reported by the two psychiatrists in most of their books and papers.

The Pattern of Difficult Temperament and Behavior Disorders

A quantitative analysis of 108 NYLS children at ages 3, 4, and 5 years, among whom 42 were assessed as having behavior disorders, showed that before and after the development of behavior disorders the clinical sample differed essentially in temperament characteristics from the nonclinical group. Within the clinical sample two subgroups were distinguished, with active and passive symptoms of behavior disorders. Children with passive symptoms, characterized as nonparticipators, differed at the age of 5 years from the nonclinical group in such temperament characteristics as mood, activity, approach/withdrawal, and persistency. Children with active symptoms, who were in the majority of the clinical sample, were characterized by various expressions of anxiety, such as tantrums, stuttering, and sleep problems. As compared with the nonclinical group, these children were characterized at all three ages (3, 4 and 5 years) by such temperament categories as high activity, irregularity, low threshold, nonadaptability, intensity, persistence, and distractibility, and these differences were statistically significant (A. Thomas & Chess, 1977).

In a sample of 52 mildly retarded children, ages 5 to 11 years, assessed for temperament scores, those identified as having behavior disorders had a pattern of difficult temperament significantly more often than was the case for mildly retarded children without behavior disorders (A. Thomas & Chess, 1977). A 6-year clinical follow-up of 44 children from this mentally retarded sample showed that the constellation of a difficult temperament has a predictive value for behavior disorders present 6 years after temperament assessment.

A study conducted by Chess, Korn, and Fernandez (1971) on 243 2½- to 4-year-old children with congenital rubella has shown that, in children with a constellation of difficult temperament, behavior disorders occurred significantly more often than in children without difficult temperament. The relationship "difficult temperament–behavior disorder" was especially evident in rubella children suffering from deafness, which may be explained by the difficulties these children have in communication with the social environment. A 4-year follow-up of the rubella sample showed that occurrence of four to five categories comprising the difficult temperament constellation diagnosed at the beginning of this study predicted behavior disorders 4 years later (A. Thomas & Chess, 1977).

Considering the three samples just mentioned—NYLS, mentally retarded, and rubella children—it is noteworthy that there was no difference among them regarding the frequency with which the constellation "difficult temperament" occurred. However, in both clinical samples, the relationship between difficult temperament and behavior disorders seemed to be more strongly expressed than in the normal (NYLS) sample. As A. Thomas and Chess (1977) stressed, "the Difficult Child is more vulnerable to behavior disorder development even without intellectual or physical handicap, as seen in the NYLS findings, but the presence of handicap increases this vulnerability" (p. 62). In order to obtain goodness of fit between the constellation of difficult temperament and a cognitive or physical handicap, much more effort from the social environment (parents and teachers) is required than for normal children with difficult temperament. This explains to some extent why a difficult temperament in handicapped children leads more often to behavior disorders then in normal cases.

Environment as a Factor Mediating the Relationship between Difficult Temperament and Behavior Disorders

In order to show whether the categories of temperament and temperament constellations identified in the NYLS sample can be replicated in populations from different socioeconomic backgrounds a longitudinal study was also conducted by A. Thomas and Chess (1977) on 95 children of Puerto Rican working-class parents. These children were followed from early infancy to the age of 6 years. In general, the Puerto Rican children did not differ temperamentally from the NYLS sample. However, the most striking result was that the two samples differed in symptoms of behavior disorders, which result was due to differences in social demands and expectancies typical for the contrasted social classes. When dissonance occurred in the interactional process between temperament and environment, symptoms of behavior disorders occurred in the NYLS sample mainly in sleep, discipline, mood disturbance, speech, peer relationship, and learning. In the Puerto Rican sample, these symptoms referred to physical activity, feeding, and elimination. A comparison of the two studies led to the conclusion that environmental factors, such as high need for achievement and well-organized time schedules in NYLS families and crowded housing and many offspring in the Puerto Rican families, played an essential role in determining the areas in which symptoms of behavior disorder developed.

It has been demonstrated by A. Thomas and Chess (1977; A. Thomas et al., 1968), mainly by qualitative analyses based on case studies, that behavior disorders also occurred, although more rarely, in children with a constellation of easy temperament. In these children poorness of fit, regarded as the main determinant of behavior disorders, resulted from the fact that during the rearing process there was a chronic discrepancy between the social demands and expectancies and the children's temperament characteristics.

Critical Remarks

Thomas and Chess exemplify investigators who were able to combine in their research on temperament two different attitudes, that of the scientist and that of the clinician. The composite of the two attitudes influenced the direction and manner of their work. A great deal of attention was paid to the subjects themselves and to procedures such as prevention, treatment, and parental guidance (Chess & Thomas, 1986) which contribute to a proper development of the children under study. Such an attitude (what is best for the subjects) did not make for optimal control of the variables under study. As already mentioned, the longitudinal study was the main source of data regarding temperament and its relation to behavior. One of the features of such studies is that conceptualizations and methods of investigation introduced at the beginning of research must be continued throughout, even if the original choice was not optimal. Only such a procedure can ensure comparability of data across different developmental stages. This background explains some of the weaknesses of the temperament studies conducted by the two psychiatrists.

Thomas and Chess's intuitive distinction of nine temperamental categories from their analysis of 22 parental protocols on infant behavior remained unaltered. Empirical data collected over 30 years did not influence the authors' view regarding the number of temperamental categories nor their understanding of their developmental specificity. This has been criticized by many authors who have demonstrated that the number of temperamental traits in children can be reduced (Buss & Plomin, 1984; Gibbs, Reeves, & Cunningham, 1987; Hagekull, 1989; R. P. Martin, 1988b; Martin, Wisenbaker, & Huttunen, 1994; Prior, Sanson, & Oberklaid, 1989) and that there are developmental changes in the structure of temperament traits not taken into account by Thomas and Chess (Prior *et al.,* 1989; Rothbart, 1989c).

The concept "difficult child" and its synonym "difficult temperament" does not correspond with Thomas and Chess's interactional theory of temperament. The label "difficult child" underscores the significance of the temperament categories (the personological context) in determining difficulties (in behavior, education, etc.). Temperament traits have different meanings and values, depending on the external (environmental) and internal components with which they interact, as shown by the very authors of the "difficult child" concept. As Rothbart states: "What is seen as difficult in one situation may not be difficult in another" (Goldsmith *et al.,*

1987, p. 521). The evaluation of temperament by use of such adjectives as "easy" or "difficult" is misleading and, as studies on intelligence tells us, labels such as "difficult child" or "difficult temperament" can be socially harmful. The concept of "difficult child" has been criticized by several authors (Bates, 1980, 1986; Buss & Plomin, 1984; Rothbart, 1982; Strelau, 1991b) from different perspectives (for details see Chapter 7).

Assessment methods applied in the Thomas and Chess studies rarely go beyond interviews, observations, and ratings. The psychometric tools developed for diagnosing temperament in 3- to 7-year-old children by parents and teachers (A. Thomas & Chess, 1977) are lacking in the basic psychometric characteristics. Data that refer to the only psychometrically elaborated inventory aimed at diagnosing temperament in adults (A. Thomas, Mittelman, et al., 1982) argue for a reduction of the number of traits from nine to three (second-order factors). They also speak for a rather low validity of this psychometric measure. Coefficients of correlation between interviewer's ratings and scales were for seven temperament categories between .32 and .47.

Many conclusions drawn by the authors on the basis of longitudinal studies conducted on samples representing different populations refer to the relationship between temperament characteristics and behavior disorders. I was unable to find in Thomas and Chess's publications information regarding a sufficient operationalization of the concept "behavior disorder." In spite of thorough medical (psychiatric) examinations conducted in semi-standardized situations the authors did not go beyond statements that behavior disorders include adjustment disorders, conduct disorders, and so on as defined in DSM-III, classified into mild, moderate, and severe (Chess & Thomas, 1984). Furthermore, there is no information regarding the indices and measurement procedures of the categories of adjustment and conduct disorders separated by the authors. The lack of operationalization meant that Thomas and Chess studied behavior disorders taking into account a poorly qualitative approach. There was no quantitative specification regarding classes or kinds of disorders that might be different for specific categories of temperament and for specific developmental stages from infancy to adulthood.

A thorough critique of Thomas and Chess's research on temperament has been carried out by Buss and Plomin (1984), who characterized the NYLS project as a pediatric approach, and by Goldsmith and Campos (1982), for whom the theory of the two American psychiatrists represent a stylistic approach. In spite of the critical remarks, of which only a few are mentioned here, I fully agree with Buss and Plomin (1984), who summarized their critical review of Thomas and Chess's contribution to research on temperament by concluding that "none of this critique, however, can detract from their pioneering efforts, which have spawned a generation of resrach on temperament" (p. 31).

3

Current Theories of Temperament

As already mentioned, Eysenck, as well as Thomas and Chess, are still very active in generating ideas and conducting studies on temperament. Their theories and research, together with the contribution of the late Russian psychologists Teplov and Nebylitsyn, have stimulated many researchers to develop new conceptualizations or theories of temperament or to modify the existing ones. It is impossible to mention the whole variety of proposals to be met in the literature. Several attempts have been made to bring some order into this diversity. For example, Meyer (1988), in grouping contemporary concepts of temperament, mentioned such approaches to temperament as descriptive (Thomas and Chess), behavior-genetic (Buss and Plomin), psychophysiological (Strelau, Rothbart and Derriberry, Goldsmith and Campos) and developmental. The last mentioned approach has been presented in modifications such as stylistic (Thomas and Chess), behavior-genetic (Buss and Plomin), constitutional (Rothbart and Derryberry) and emotional (Goldsmith and Campos). Goldsmith and Campos (1982), in classifying theories of temperament with developmental orientation, distinguished the following four approaches: stylistic (Thomas and Chess), criterial (Buss and Plomin), psychobiological (Rothbart), and neonatal (Brazelton). To this classification Endler (1989) added the emotional approach (Goldsmith and Campos). Strelau and Plomin (1992) distinguished three approaches to temperament: clinical (e.g., Thomas and Chess), infancy (e.g., Goldsmith and Campos), and personality-oriented (e.g., Buss and Plomin). Recently Strelau (1991b) adopted three criteria for classifying contemporary conceptualizations of temperament: (1) focus on children (e.g., Rothbart) versus adults (e.g.,Eysenck), (2) explanatory (e.g., Zuckerman) versus descriptive (e.g., Thomas and Chess) theories, and (3) applicational (clinical or educational) versus theoretical approaches as represented, respectively, by Thomas and Chess, and Eysenck.

TABLE 3.1. Classifications of Temperament Theories

Criterion	Author
(1) *Child vs. Adult*	
(a) Child	Buss & Plomin, Goldsmith & Campos, Kagan, Rothbart & Derryberry, Thomas & Chess
(b) Adult	Eysenck, Gray, Mehrabian, Rusalov, Strelau, Teplov & Nebylitsyn, Zuckerman
(2) *Descriptive vs. Causal*	
(a) Descriptive	Goldsmith & Campos, Mehrabian, Thomas & Chess
(c) Causal	Buss & Plomin, Eysenck, Gray, Kagan, Rothbart & Derryberry, Rusalov, Strelau, Teplov & Nebylitsyn, Zuckerman
(3) *Mono- vs. Multi-dimensional*	
(a) Mono-dimensional	Kagan, Zuckerman
(b) Multi-dimensional	Buss & Plomin, Eysenck, Goldsmith & Campos, Gray, Mehrabian, Rothbart & Derryberry, Rusalov, Strelau, Teplov & Nebylitsyn, Thomas & Chess
(4) *Emotion vs. Whole Behavior*	
(a) Emotion	Goldsmith & Campos, Gray, Mehrabian, Kagan
(b) Whole behavior	Buss & Plomin, Eysenck, Rothbart & Derryberry, Rusalov, Strelau, Teplov & Nebylitsyn, Thomas & Chess, Zuckerman

As can be seen from the classifications presented, a clear-cut taxonomy of currently developed conceptualizations of temperament is hardly possible; the solution depends largely on the perspective from which the theories are viewed. Most of the conceptualizations and theories of temperament combine different approaches and are more or less eclectic. To show the diversity in temperament theories I have taken into account four criteria by which they may be classified, as follows: (1) child (developmental)- versus adult (nondevelopmental)-oriented, (2) descriptive versus causal (biological: behavior-genetic- or arousal-oriented), (3) monodimensional versus multidimensional, and (4) emotion versus whole-behavior–oriented. As can be seen from Table 3.1. the same theory (or author) can be classified in different groups, depending on which criterion is used. For example, the Thomas–Chess interactional theory of temperament can be characterized as child-oriented, multidimensional, descriptive, and centered not only on emotions but on entire behavior.

The review of temperament theories presented in this chapter cannot be done by using all of the criteria just mentioned. Table 3.1, which may be helpful in searching for links between the theories of temperament, shows that most theories can be classified under each of the criteria. The decision as to which of them is applicable for presenting the theories is arbitrary. Taking into account the tradition in temperament research I decided to use the first criterion, "child versus adult" for presenting the theories.

Child-Oriented Theories of Temperament

Categorization makes it possible to bring some order among the various temperament theories, but it also has some disadvantages in that it makes sharp distinctions between the classes of theories; frequently this does not correspond with reality. For example, Thomas and Chess's theory of temperament was concentrated on infancy, whereas now the subjects followed for more than 30 years are adults. Buss and Plomin's theory of temperament originated in studies on children, but has been expanded to adults. Some authors (e.g., Windle, 1991, 1992) concentrate mainly on adolescents, thus their conceptualizations of temperament have to be located somewhere on the borderline of child- and adult-oriented theories.

The criterion adopted for assigning a conceptualization to child-oriented theories of temperament was its starting point, or the way it originated. The number of researchers concentrating on studying children's temperament has grown enormously over the past two decades. Many of them have presented original ideas on specific issues, such as measurement of child temperament (e.g., Bates, 1986; Goldsmith & Rothbart, 1991; N. C. Hubert, Wachs, Peters-Martin, & Gandour, 1982; R. P. Martin & Halverson, 1991; Rothbart & Goldsmith, 1985), continuity and stability of child temperament (Asendorf & Van Aken, 1991; Hagekull, 1989; Matheny, Wilson, & Nuss, 1984; Rothbart, 1989c), the contextual approach to temperament (J. V. Lerner, 1984; J. V. Lerner, Nitz, Talwar, & Lerner, 1989; Talwar, Nitz, Lerner, & Lerner, 1991), and temperament as related to clinical and educational issues (W. B. Carey & McDevitt, 1989; Keogh, 1986; R. P. Martin, 1988a; Maziade, 1988). The most comprehensive review of ideas and findings in the domain of child temperament has been presented by Kohnstamm, Bates, and Rothbart (1989) and in a very condensed form by Bates (1987) and Prior (1992). The selection of theories to be presented here was arbitrary, as was the classification criterion. The conceptualizations that fulfill more or less the criteria of a microtheory (see Chapter 2) are the following: the behavior-genetic theory of Buss and Plomin, the developmental model of temperament by Rothbart and Derryberry, the emotion-oriented theory of Goldsmith and Campos, and Kagan's psychobiological theory of temperament.

I decided to exclude in the following presentation Hinde's (1989; Hinde & Stevenson-Hinde, 1987) biosocial theory of temperament as well as Brazelton's (1973; Brazelton, Nugent, & Lester, 1987) neonatal approach to this domain of personality, although their research has been important for the development of conceptualizations on children's temperament. The reasons were that Hinde's conceptualization of temperament lacks operationalization and measurement proposals; in Brazelton's studies measurements, which go far beyond the temperament domain, are not founded on a specific neonatal theory of temperament.

Buss and Plomin's Behavior-Genetic Theory of Temperament

The most systematic and methodologically grounded approach to studies on temperament in children has been followed during the past two decades by Buss and Plomin. Among child-oriented conceptualizations on temperament their theory is the closest to fulfilling the requirements of a theory as postulated by Popper and Kuhn (see Chapter 2). Referring to the criteria depicted in Table 3.1, the child-oriented theory of temperament developed by Buss and Plomin may be characterized as a causal (behavior-genetic), multidimensional, and whole-behavior–oriented conceptualization. This theory, although centered from its very beginning on children, is one of the few that offers a broad developmental perspective, including conceptualizations and studies on adult temperament.

Theoretical Background

Reviewing Buss and Plomin's publications in the domain of temperament, it is not easy to gain a full picture of the origins of their temperament theory. Influential for their view on temperament was undoubtedly the comparative approach to temperament as represented by Diamond (1957), whom Buss and Plomin (1975) regarded as the initiator of modern temperament research. Diamond's idea that four basic temperaments—fearfulness, aggressiveness, affiliativeness, and impulsiveness—are shared by man and our mammalian predecessors was important for developing their conception of the nature of temperament. Also, G. W. Allport's (1937) popular definition of temperament, in which not only the emotional nature but also the constitutional component of temperament was underlined, played an important role in Buss and Plomin's theorizing about temperament.

At the time that Buss and Plomin started their studies on temperament, Eysenck's theory of extraversion and introversion and his pioneering behavior-genetic studies in this domain were already known to personality psychologists. Thomas and Chess's studies on children's temperament also created a favorable context for Buss and Plomin's research on the temperament domain of personality.

The authors' own experience also influenced the construction of the behavior-genetic–oriented theory of children's temperament. Arnold H. Buss (1961), from the University of Texas, conducted one of the most systematic studies on human aggression. This involved him in studying a personality/temperament dimension present in both humans and animals. His empirical investigations led him to elaborate a broad evolutionary and developmental perspective on personality research (Buss, 1988, 1989a; Buss & Finn, 1987). Robert Plomin was a student of Buss. His 1974 doctoral dissertation (cited in Buss & Plomin, 1975) was aimed at studying parent–child interaction, with temperament the main variable under study. From the very start of his academic career Plomin became involved in intensive behavior-genetic studies (DeFries & Plomin, 1978; Plomin, 1976; Plomin,

DeFries, & Loehlin, 1977) at the University of Colorado, one of the leading centers in this domain of research. The combination of Buss's interests in aggression and Plomin's concentration on behavior genetics led these investigators to begin thinking about those aspects of personality that might be most heritable, fundamental, and present in early developmental stages.

The EAS Temperaments

Buss and Plomin's theory of temperament has been described in detail in two monographs (Buss & Plomin, 1975, 1984) and in several papers (see Buss, 1989b, 1991; Buss & Plomin, 1986; Strelau & Plomin, 1992). The authors defined "temperaments as *inherited personality traits present in early childhood*" (Buss & Plomin, 1984). This short definition comprises the core elements of their theory.

According to Buss and Plomin (1984), two definitional and inseparable criteria must be fulfilled to classify behavior characteristics as belonging to temperament. They have to be present from early childhood (during the first 2 years of life), and there must be an essential contribution of the genetic factor to individual differences in these behavior characteristics. Thus, a trait that shows essential heritability but is not present in early childhood as, for example, conscientiousness, cannot be considered temperament. The same refers to a behavior characteristic present in early infancy, the variance of which is not genetically determined, for example, smiling or laughter.

In the first version of their temperament theory, Buss & Plomin (1975) considered inheritance as the crucial criterion for deciding which trait should be referred to as temperament. Such criteria as stability over childhood, retention into maturity, adaptive value, and presence in primates and other mammals were considered secondary to inheritance. These criteria have not been treated recently as imperative, although they remain important in Buss and Plomin's theory. Thus, the authors assume that temperaments are characterized by some continuity that assures that "such early traits [temperaments] are likely to be the foundation on which later personality traits are built" (Buss & Plomin, 1984, p. 84). Temperament traits have an essential impact on personality development. Temperament, according to the authors, is a crucial part of human personality. In early childhood, characterized by lack of internal cognitive structures and limited experience, the child's temperament constitutes his or her whole personality, assuming that cognitive functioning (intelligence) is not included in the construct "personality" (Buss & Plomin, 1984; Buss & Finn, 1987). Buss and Plomin also postulated that temperament traits must be broad, referring to a wide class of behaviors and situations. Temperaments must show functional significance documented by the role they play in different kinds of human adjustment (Buss & Plomin, 1975).

Taking these criteria and considerations into account, as well as the data from many studies, Buss and Plomin (1984, 1986; Buss, 1991) distinguished three basic temperaments: emotionality, activity, and sociability—EAS, an acronym by which their temperament theory has often been labeled. The notion "temperament" has been used by Buss and Plomin in two different meanings. First, according to the definition just given, it refers to all three traits of which the structure of temperament is composed. Second, temperament is used as synonymous with temperamental trait; thus, according to the authors' view, there are three temperaments.

Emotionality. The authors defined emotionality as the tendency to be aroused easily and intensely; this tendency is expressed in a primordial emotion identified as distress. "Emotionality equals distress, the tendency to become upset easily and intensely" (Buss & Plomin, 1984, p. 54). Distress, which can be observed from the first day of life (the presence of crying), differentiates during infancy into fear (at the age of 2–3 months) and anger, the latter developing at the age of about 6 months. Fear is expressed in an attempt to escape (flight) from threatening (aversive) stimuli, whereas anger reveals itself in attacking and complaining as a response to annoying or frustrating stimuli.

Taking into account three components of emotions—expression, feeling, and arousal—the authors (Buss & Plomin, 1975, 1984) argued that the only component that makes it possible to measure genetically determined individual differences in intensity and temporal characteristics of emotions is arousal. The only emotions characterized by level of arousal exceeding the level of nonemotional states (e.g., orienting reaction) are distress, fear, and anger. Although a fourth emotion—sexual arousal—is high, it is not present in early childhood and, according to the authors, there is no evidence for genetic determination of individual differences in respect to sexual emotion. As can be seen, the authors did not include positive emotions in their emotionality temperament. The reason is simple. The level of arousal typical for positive emotions is below that of negative emotions and, moreover, they do not fulfill the definitional criteria of temperament. There are gender-specific characteristics of emotionality, boys scoring higher on the anger component of emotionality and girls scoring higher on the fear component. The authors hypothesized that these differences are determined by inherited gender differences as well as by gender role socialization.

Activity. According to Buss and Plomin (1975) the "level of *activity* refers to total energy output. . . . Activity is equivalent to movement" (pp. 31–32). Since movement refers to all behavior, it also means that activity may be expressed in any kind of behavior. The activity temperament in reference to individual differences in activity consists of two components: vigor and tempo, mostly positively correlated with each other. A very active person is strongly motivated to be energetic; that is, she or he expends energy in vigorous activity performed with rapid tempo. "The twin aspects of activity—vigor and tempo—are best seen in *how* a response is delivered (style)" (p. 33). In some individuals, or for some kinds of activity, the components of activity may not be correlated with each other.

Activity occupies a special place among the three temperaments. Every response is accompanied by expended energy, and thus varies in vigor (intensity) and tempo. This means that activity has a more diffused character as compared with the two other temperaments and so may be considered a stylistic trait. The authors' view on activity did not change in their revised theory of temperament (Buss & Plomin, 1984).

Sociability. In contrast to the other temperaments sociability has a directional component: seeking other persons. "Sociability is the tendency to prefer the presence of others to being alone" (Buss & Plomin, 1984, p. 63). This tendency has its roots in intrinsic rewards which result from social interaction with other persons. Buss and Plomin (1984) postulated that there are five social rewards underlying sociability: (1) presence of others, (2) sharing an activity, (3) receiving attention from others, (4) mutual responsivity expressed in such responses as agreement, disagreement, surprise, and interest, and (5) initiation of social interaction. These social rewards can be characterized by their extremes—absence and excess of reward. Absence of reward is seen as lack of social stimulation and, thus, as a source of low level of arousal, whereas excess of reward may be regarded as highly intensive social stimulation (resulting in a high level of arousal). Individuals high on sociability are more reinforced by social rewards and more upset by their deprivation.

The authors emphasize that any social interaction can be rewarding, and it is not the content of social rewards, such as sympathy, respect, or praise that is linked to sociability. Sociability as expressed in social interaction is developmentally specific. In infancy it plays a role in mother–infant interactions; it affects the type of attachment. Once mobile, infants and older children enlarge the range of social interactions significantly, especially in behavior with peers. Buss and Plomin (1975, 1984) suggested that the sociability temperament may be considered one of the two crucial components of extraversion, as postulated by H. J. Eysenck (1970), when extraversion was measured by means of the EPI.

In the 1975 version of their temperament theory, Buss and Plomin (1975) postulated that there are four temperaments, with impulsivity added to the three presented earlier. Thus, the theory in its first version was labeled by the acronym EASI. The main reason impulsivity has been removed from the list of traits composing the structure of temperament was lack of sufficient evidence regarding the heritability of this trait. Furthermore, impulsivity came out as a complex trait composed of inhibitory control, decision time, persistence in ongoing tasks and sensation seeking. Some of these components—sensation seeking and inhibitory control—are not present in early childhood (Buss & Plomin, 1984).

The Biology of EAS Temperaments

Since inheritance became the most crucial criterion for treating a trait as a part of temperament, Buss and Plomin devoted some effort to examining the genetic contribution to trait variance. Five studies in which the three temperaments were measured in MZ and DZ children (average age 43 months to 7;6 years) provided unequivocal evidence for the contribution of the genetic factor to individual differences in all three temperaments (Buss & Plomin, 1984). Table 3.2, which contains the average twin correlations across the five studies in which inventories constructed by the authors were applied, summarizes these data. The authors explained the (too) low intracorrelations for DZ twins by referring to contrast effects. A contrast effect, strongly present in fraternal twins, is the tendency to be perceived and treated by others as different. More recent data which correspond with the findings presented in Table 3.2 are discussed in Chapter 5.

After distinguishing three levels of arousal—behavioral, autonomic, and brain arousal, Buss and Plomin (1984) referred to them in the context of the three temperaments. As regards behavioral arousal that may vary from deep sleep to high excitement, its most obvious aspect is activity. Individual differences in autonomic arousal refer mainly to emotional behavior. The authors hypothesized that the sympathetic dominance of the autonomic nervous system (ANS) is linked to emotionality. The two components of emotionality, fear and anger, are probably indistinguishable on the basis of autonomic arousal indices. "What is inherited in emotionality is the tendency to become physiologically aroused (sympathetic reactivity) regardless of whether the particular emotion is distress, fear, or anger" (Buss & Plomin, 1984, p. 54). In the authors' publications there is no direct statement regarding the postulated biological correlates of sociability. The authors' remarks that Eysenck's extraversion has its physiological background in the physiology of brain structures, and that sociability has a part in regulating the level of arousal (Buss & Plomin, 1975), leads to the assumption that brain arousal is a physiological correlate of sociability. To conclude the discussion of the biological bases of temperament, it is noted that, while there is plenty of evidence regarding the genetic contribution of individual differences in EAS temperaments, Buss and

TABLE 3.2. Twin Correlations for EAS Questionnaires

			Twin correlations for EAS Scales					
	No. of Twins		Emotionality		Activity		Sociability	
Sample	MZ	DZ	MZ	DZ	MZ	DZ	MZ	DZ
1	81	57	.64	.03	.62	.09	.62	.13
2	60	51	.58	.12	.49	−.27	.47	−.12
3	36	31	.70	.06	.65	−.38	.48	−.16
4	51	33	.60	.27	.73	.05	.56	.05
Total	228	172	.63	.12	.62	−.13	.53	−.03

Note. The table is based on data taken from Buss and Plomin (1984, pp. 20–22). Sample 1—Buss and Plomin (1975), sample 2—Plomin (1974), sample 3— Plomin and Rowe (1978), sample 4—Plomin (unpublished doctoral dissertation). The mean age of the total number of subjects (samples 1–4): 61 months.

Plomin did not conduct studies that examined the physiological correlates of these temperaments.

Measurement of EAS

Buss and Plomin, in discussing the temperaments, presented a series of methods for the assessment of the traits under discussion. For example, for measuring activity, such methods as mechanical measures (actometer, fidgetometer, experimental indices), locomotion in open field, observational ratings, and self-report questionnaires have been presented (Buss & Plomin, 1975). However, the original contribution of Buss and Plomin to the assessment of temperament consists in developing inventories that made it possible to measure the EAS or EASI traits in children and adults, according to their theory.

Without going into detail regarding the historical background of the versions of the EASI scales (see Buss & Plomin, 1975), two inventories (in self-report and parent-rating versions) are in use to study temperaments according to Buss and Plomin's theory: the EASI-III Temperament Survey (EASI-III-TS, described in detail in Buss & Plomin, 1975) and the EAS–Temperament Survey (EAS-TS; Buss & Plomin, 1984). Several versions of the EASI-TS have been recently used by several authors (e.g., Neale & Stevenson, 1989; Ruch, Angleitner, & Strelau, 1991; Windle, 1989b), although Buss and Plomin, as a consequence of their modified temperament theory, recommend the application of the EAS-TS.

The EAS-TS, which is a modification of the EASI-III-TS, is composed of 20 items, and contains five scales, each with four items (scored on a 5-point rating scale). Three scales refer to the emotionality temperament: Distress (E-d), Fear (E-f) and Anger (E-a); the two other scales—Activity (Act) and Sociability (Soc) represent the two remaining temperaments. Reliability of the EAS-TS, in spite of the very short scales, is satisfactory (ranging from .75 to .85). As regards intercorrelations between the scales, the emotionality scales correlate positively with each other (from .28 to .63). Also the Act scale correlates positively with the Soc scale (.31 for male and .21 for female) but only for males (.26) with the E-a scale.

In parallel with the EAS-TS, for the study of temperament in adolescents and adults, the authors also developed a parental rating version of the EAS-TS under the label EAS Temperament Survey for Children (EAS-TSC). The EAS-TSC is a modification of two former parental rating scales, the EASI-II-TS (Buss & Plomin, 1975) and the Colorado Childhood Temperament Inventory (CCTI; Plomin & Rowe, 1977; Rowe & Plomin, 1977) for the assessment of 1- to 6-year-old children's temperament. The EAS-TSC also contains 20 items (with a parental 5-point rating scale), but with scales different from the EAS-TS. EAS-TSC contains the following four scales: Emotionality (distress only), Activity, Shyness, and Sociability. The Sociability scale is regarded by the authors as an experimental scale for which no standarization data are as yet available. Detailed information is lacking regarding the age of children to which the EAS-TSC refers, but from the description given by the authors (Buss & Plomin, 1984) one may assume that this parent-report inventory is designed for children from 1 to 9 years.

As a general remark in reference to both inventories (EAS-TS and EAS-TSC), the assessment methods developed by Buss and Plomin are attractive because of the small number of items, clear and short formulation of the items, satisfactory orthogonality of the scales, and, in the case of EAS-TS, acceptable reliability scores.

Final Remarks

Buss and Plomin (1975, 1984) postulated that temperament plays an important role in human adaptation; however, insufficient empirical evidence has been provided by the authors to confirm this hypothesis. Several interesting suppositions, speculations based on their theory, can be found in their writings. For example, Buss and Plomin (1984) hypothesized that individual differences in elation and depression may result from a combination of the activity and sociability temperaments. Hyperactivity in children may be affected by the combination of an extreme position on the activity dimension with accompanying lack of control, that is, high impulsivity. In turn, individual differences in aggressive behavior may result from a combination of two temperaments: activity and the anger component of emotionality (Buss, 1991; Buss & Plomin, 1975).

Buss and Plomin's (1975, 1984) theory makes some predictions regarding matches and mismatches between the child and the social environment, especially his or her parents. For example, if mother and child are characterized by high emotionality, the emotional mother by her emotional reactions intensifies the child's fear, which may result in neurotic behavior. Matches between parents and children seem to be best for activity and for sociability (Buss, 1981; Buss & Plomin, 1984). Several predictions have also been made regarding interaction between the individual's temperament and the environment. First, one may assume that only extreme temperaments (e.g., high versus low activity) influence the environment, whereas the opposite influence (environment on temperament) occurs mainly when temperament is in the middle range. Second, the influence of temperament on environment may consist in selecting environments, affecting social environments, and modifying the environmental impact (Buss & Plomin, 1984). The person–environment interactions specific for the three temperaments have been presented in more detail by Buss (1991).

Critical remarks regarding Buss and Plomin's theory of temperament deal mainly with the speculative character of that part of the EAS theory in which the functional significance of temperament is discussed (Goldsmith & Campos, 1982). The authors' suppositions regarding the temperament–environment interaction and the role temperaments play in human adaptation may, however, serve as a good starting point for further investigations in areas that are still lacking.

The concept of emotionality presented in the EAS theory has some weak points. The authors' hypothesis that fear, anger, and sexual behavior are the only emotions beyond the level of baseline arousal does not rest on empirical evidence. We know from everyday observation that specific human emotions, for example, hate or shame, usually have a strong arousal component that often goes beyond that typical for anger (for more detailed remarks see Strelau, 1987b).

Goldsmith and Campos (1982), in criticizing Buss and Plomin's theory of temperament, drew attention to the fact that the evidence for heritability of the EAS temperaments is not very convincing. This conclusion is based mainly on the lack of similarity between fraternal twins in respect to activity and sociability. To be honest, the evidence for the heritability of the EAS traits is certainly better than for many other temperament dimensions.

A criticism to be found in several publications says that the genetic contribution to the variance of temperamental traits, as defined by Buss and Plomin, is not higher than that met in other genetically determined personality traits. However, this statement refers to all temperament constructs assumed to have an inherited background. In answer to this criticism it should be pointed out that the authors of the EAS temperaments regard as temperament traits only those that fulfill simultaneously two inseparable criteria: heredity and presence in early childhood.

Taking a historical perspective regarding the precursors of the EAS temperaments, one easily finds several elements in common with the Heymans–Wiersma typology of temperaments, not mentioned by Buss and Plomin. These authors also included activity and emotionality among their three temperaments. Much attention in Heymans's research was given to the genetic component of these traits; temperament traits were analyzed in combination with each other and almost always within a broader concept of personality. Although the EAS conceptualization and the Dutch temperament theory came from different perspectives it is noteworthy that they converged on similar traits.

The Developmental Model of Temperament: Rothbart and Derryberry

The theory of temperament proposed in the beginning of 1980s by Rothbart and Derryberry (1981; Derryberry & Rothbart, 1984, 1988) can be described as a developmental (child-oriented), constitutional-psychobiological (causal), and multidimensional approach, with concentration on children's whole behavior. This theory, further developed by Rothbart and her associates (Rothbart, 1989a, 1989b, 1989c, 1991; Rothbart & Mauro, 1990; Rothbart & Posner, 1985), gained great popularity among child-oriented temperament researchers. The attractive aspect of this theory was chiefly in showing the developmental changes in temperament by reference to the interactional dynamics of behavioral and biological phenomena.

Theoretical Background

In describing their developmental model of temperament Mary Rothbart and Douglas Derryberry took advantage of many findings, concepts, and theories of temperament reported in the literature. The NYLS study, although critically viewed by the authors (Rothbart, 1989c; Rothbart & Derryberry, 1981), was profitable for their temperament research in that it has shown the richness of possible temperament categories present in infants. Diamond's (1957) understanding of temperament as a phenomenon present in man and animals, with individual characteristics rooted in physiological structures, was influential for Rothbart and Derryberry's constitutional approach to temperament.

In the authors' considerations about temperament one easily notes the influence of temperament theories in which such physiological constructs as excitation–inhibition, arousal, optimal level of arousal, and arousability, were applied to interpret the biological background of temperament (H. J. Eysenck, 1967; Gray, 1972; Nebylitsyn, 1972a; Pavlov, 1951–1952; Strelau, 1974; Zuckerman, 1979).

As the label suggests, the developmental model of temperament is firmly based on theories and findings taken from developmental psychology. Of special importance in the construction of Rothbart and Derryberry's theory were those conceptualizations and findings that showed the significance of individual differences in neonates and infants as well as reports on early evidence of infants' individuality (Brazelton, 1973; Escalona, 1968; Gesell & Ames, 1937).

The developmental model offers a highly original theory of temperament. At the same time, it is supplemented with information that makes it possible to search for links between Rothbart and Derryberry's theory and other conceptualizations of temperament, including studies on adults.

Temperament as Constitutionally Based Individual Differences in Reactivity and Self-Regulation

Rothbart and Derryberry (1981, p. 37; Derryberry & Rothbart, 1984, p. 132), defined temperament as constitutional differences in reactivity and self-regulation. *Constitutional* refers to the individual's relatively enduring biological makeup influenced over time by heredity, maturation, and experience. *Reactivity* refers to arousability of the physiological and behavioral systems, which include somatic, autonomic, neuroendocrine, and cognitive reactivity (Rothbart, 1989b, 1991). It is reflected in the response parameters of threshold, latency, intensity, rise, and recovery time. By *self-regulation* Rothbart and Derryberry meant processes that modulate (facilitate or inhibit) reactivity. These processes include attention, approach, withdrawal, attack, behavioral inhibition, and self-soothing). Although developed independently, the "constructs of reactivity and self-regulation are very similar to Strelau's" (Rothbart, 1989a, p. 59).

There is a continuous interaction between reactivity and self-regulation, with a developmentally determined increase in the influence of self-regulation on the modulation of reactivity (Rothbart & Ahadi, 1994). With growth, self-regulation becomes more and more under conscious (effortful) control. Effort, identified with the concept of will, is regarded by Rothbart (Rothbart & Posner, 1985) as "the ability to inhibit responses to stimuli in the immediate environment while pursuing a cognitively represented goal" (Rothbart, 1989c, p. 208). The framework of the developmental model of temperament is depicted in Figure 3.1.

As can be seen from this model, reactivity is considered not only as a tendency to react in terms of intensity and speed (arousability), but also as a process or state determined by such factors as stimulus intensity, its meaning (signal qualities), internal state, and novelty. Under low or moderate stimulation individuals experience positive reactions (feelings of pleasure), described in Figure 3.1 as positive reactivity. Under strong stimulation negative reactions, experienced as feelings of distress (in Figure 3.1, negative reactivity), are dominant. Depending on

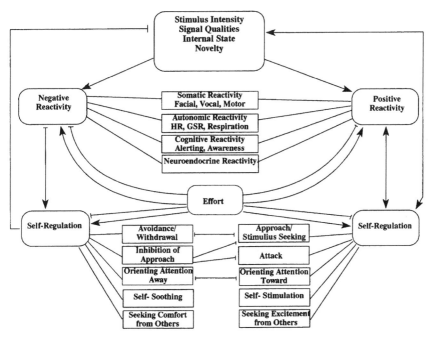

FIGURE 3.1. A framework for temperament. *Note.* From "Temperament: A Development Framework," by M. K. Rothbart. In J. Strelau and A. Angleitner (Eds.), *Explorations in Temperament: International Perspectives on Theory and Measurement* (1991, p. 7), New York: Plenum Press. Copyright 1991 by Plenum Press. Reprinted with permission.

their level of temperament reactivity, individuals differ in experiencing negative or positive reactivity to stimuli of the same intensity.

> Individuals are then posited to differ in their thresholds for and intensity of posi-
> tive and negative reactions, and the rise and recovery time of these reactions, so
> that the effect of a stimulus will be stronger for some [high-reactive] individuals
> than for others [low-reactive individuals]. (Rothbart, 1989b, p. 64)

Temperamental differences refer also to the ease with which self-regulatory processes (reactions) are initiated. By means of self-regulatory processes, the list of which is shown in Figure 3.1, the individual is able to modulate reactivity (e.g., negative reactivity may be reduced by lowering the stimulative value of the situation), approach or avoid stimuli, orient attention toward or away from given situations or activities, and so on. With age, self-regulatory processes become more and more cognitive and conscious.

Temperamental traits are expressed in such behaviors as attentional, emotional, and motor activity; however, these behaviors have a developmentally specific organization (Rothbart & Ahadi, 1994). For example, if we take into account emotional activity, in the neonatal period only negative emotionality (susceptibility to distress) occurs. In early infancy, positive emotionality, expressed in smiling and vocalization, can be observed as well. Rothbart and Derryberry (1981; Derryberry & Rothbart, 1984, 1989c; Rothbart & Posner, 1985; Rothbart, Derryberry, & Posner, 1994) have described in more detail than anyone else the developmentally specific structure of temperament starting from their temperament framework. Table 3.3 gives a general view of the ontogenetic changes in temperament from the neonatal period until the school years.

The continuing development of effortful control indicated in Table 3.3 consists of qualitative differences in the mechanisms involved in the control of the individual's behavior. Whereas in infants the effortful control consists mainly in orienting attention toward or away from objects or persons (Rothbart, Posner, & Rosicky,

TABLE 3.3. Temperament in Development During Early Childhood

Developmental period	Temperament components
Newborn	Distress and soothability, activity, orienting and alertness (attention), approach–withdrawal
Early infancy	All of the above and smiling and laughter, vocalization, stimulus seeking and avoidance, frustration
Late infancy	All of the above and inhibition of approach, effortful control, fear
Preschool years and beyond	All of the above with continuing development of effortful control

Note. From "Temperament and Development," by M. K. Rothbart. In G. A. Kohnstamm, J. E. Bates, and M. K. Rothbart (Eds.), *Temperament in Childhood* (1989, p. 196), Chichester, England: Wiley. Copyright 1989 by John Wiley & Sons, Ltd. Reprinted with permission.

1994), at an older age verbal control becomes dominant. By means of verbal self-regulative acts (instructions and self-instructions), the individual may behave in ways that are not neccessarily expressions of her or his temperament characteristics.

Biological Processes in Temperament

Rothbart and Derryberry's (1981; Derryberry & Rothbart, 1984) view on the biological bases of temperament has been consistently subordinated to the developmental model of temperament. Developmental changes in temperament characteristics go along with the maturation of the nervous system. In early infancy, lower-level excitatory influences arising from brain stem projections are relevant to temperament. The authors, referring to findings reported in the literature, hypothesized that three such projections—norepinephrine, dompamine and serotonin—are of particular importance. Inhibitory control, which increases with the infant's development, is accompanied by maturation of the limbic and cortical areas of the CNS. The self-regulatory processes observed in the infant's developing temperament are facilitated through the maturation of the forebrain. Taking fear as an example of a temperamental characteristic, Rothbart and Posner (1985) have shown how developmental changes in this trait are accompanied by neurophysiological and neurochemical changes across age, starting from the neonatal period up to the age of 4 years, at which time verbal self-regulation already plays an important role.

As described in detail by Rothbart (1989a; Rothbart & Posner, 1985; Rothbart, Derryberry, & Posner, 1994), the biological bases of temperament traits are considered to be complex. This means that arousability of the ANS and CNS, hemispheric laterality, activity of the neurotransmitters and endocrine processes all play important roles in determining individual differences in temperament characteristics. Hitherto no studies have come to light that permit any conclusion regarding the biological specificity of the temperament characteristics as distinguished by Rothbart and Derryberry. Taking the developmental perspective as a point of departure some suggestions based on literature review have been proposed by Rothbart, Derryberry, and Posner (1994). Figure 3.2 gives a summary of these considerations.

Behavior genetic studies on infant twins in which Rothbart's Infant Behavior Questioniare was used have shown that, for such temperament traits as activity, fear, and distress to limitations, identical co-twin similarity is greater than fraternal co-twin similarity. This speaks for a significant contribution of the genetic factor to individual differences in these traits (Goldsmith, 1996).

Measurement of Temperament in Infancy

Rothbart (1981) developed a caretaker-report instrument aimed at assessing temperament in 3- to 12-month-old children. This psychometric measure, known as

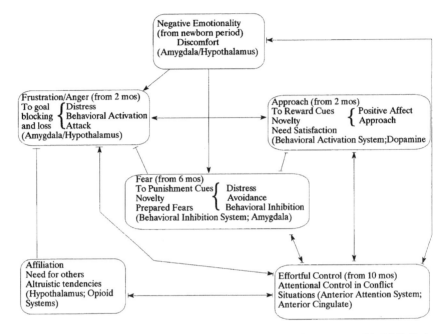

FIGURE 3.2. "A Psychobiological Approach to the Development of Temperament," by M. K. Roth-bart, D. Derryberry, and M. I. Posner. In J. E. Bates and T. D. Wachs (Eds.), *Temperament: Individual Differences at the Interface of Biology and Behavior* (1994, p. 107), Washington, DC: American Psychological Association. Copyright 1994 by the American Psychological Association. Reprinted with permissions.

the Infant Behavior Questionnare (IBQ), is composed of 87 items and consists of the following six scales: Activity Level, Smiling and Laughter, Fear, Distress to Limitations, Soothability, and Duration of Orienting. Reliability of these scales as measured by comparing mother's scores with those for father or babysitter, was not very high (varying from .45 to .69) but was consistent with data reported by others.

In a study (Rothbart, 1986) in which IBQ scores were compared with observations in the home, the coefficients of correlation varied between .30 and .90. Alpha estimates scored at 3-month intervals (from 3 to 13 months) were satisfactory for all six scales, varying from .67 (duration of orienting at 6 months) to .85 (smiling and laughter at 3 months), with the majority of scores not lower than .75 (Goldsmith & Rothbart, 1991). Stability as measured in a longitudinal study at 3-month intervals between the ages of 3 and 12 months varied in Rothbart's 1981 study from .06 (fear, 3–12 months) to .80 (smiling and laughter, 9–12 months) and in her 1986 study from .16 (distress, 3–9 months) to .63 (activity level, 6–9 months). In general, stability scores were rather high when temperament characteristics were compared between the ages of 9 and 12 months (Rothbart, 1981). As can be easily noted, the IBQ does not include all characteristics as proposed by the temperament framework. A currently developed inventory, known as the Children's Behavior Questionnaire (CPB; Ahadi, Rothbart, & Ye, 1993; Rothbart, Ahadi, Hershey, & Fisher, 1995) is much more differentiated.

The CBQ, which is a caregiver report measure aimed for assessing children ages from 3 to 8 years, is composed of 15 scales and contains 195 items with a 7-point answer format. The scales are as follows: Approach, High Intensity Pleasure, Smiling, Activity, Impulsivity, Shyness, Discomfort, Fear, Anger, Sadness, Soothability, Inhibitory Control, Attention, Low Intensity Pleasure, and Perceptual Sensitivity. Internal consistency of these scales varies from the .60s (Perceptual Sensitivity, Attention, LoPleasure, Soothability and Discomfort) to the .90s (Shyness). Parental agreement on the CBQ scales varies from <.20 to >.70, and when aggregated accross samples and averaged for all scales, reaches the score over .40 (Rothbart *et al.,* 1995). The CPQ scales when factor analyzed resulted in a three-factor solution—Surgency, Negative Affectivity, and Effortful Control. Cross-cultural studies conducted on American, Chinese, and Japanese samples have shown that these factors are stable across cultures (Ahadi *et al.,* 1993; Rothbart *et al.,* 1995).

Recently laboratory assessment batteries were constructed by Goldsmith and Rothbart for diagnosing temperament in infants. They assess the following temperament traits: fear, anger, joy/pleasure, interest/persistence, and activity in 6-month-old infants (prelocomotor version; Goldsmith & Rothbart, 1992b) and in 12- to 18-month-old infants (locomotor version; Goldsmith & Rothbart, 1992a). These batteries describe in detail the standardized episodes presumed to evoke behaviors typical of the temperamental traits under study and the procedures of temperament assessment. Studies which make possible an estimation of reliability and validity of these original and promising temperament measures have so far not been published.

Final Remarks

The developmental model of temperament was published by Rothbart and Derryberry less than two decades ago, hence it would be unrealistic to expect much empirical evidence for or against this theory. One of the central issues to which the Rothbart–Derryberry's child-centered theory of temperament refers is the development of inhibitory mechanisms underlying the control of behavior still absent in early infancy. A study conducted by Rothbart (1988) on 6.5- to 13.5-month-old infants has shown that, although at the age of 6.5 months individual differences in approach tendencies are clearly present and relatively stable across age, inhibition of approach, measured by means of latency to approach and grasp high-novelty/intensity toys was present only in older infants. Individual differences in hesitation, accompanied by feelings of fear and regarded as the behavioral expression of inhibition of approach, are present not earlier than 1 year of age. Hesitation was more strongly expressed in boys than in girls.

A more advanced behavioral control is guided by inhibitory self-control which develops from toddlerhood through kindergarten age and beyond. This control mechanism is essentially more voluntary, involves attentional mechanisms (Rothbart, Posner, & Rosicky, 1994), and is not necessarily accompanied by negative emotions. A study by Reed, Pien, and Rothbart (1984) on older children (40 to 49 months), in which inhibitory self-control was measured during different games performed in laboratory settings, supported the existence of individual differences in levels of inhibitory self-control. As Reed and colleagues (1984) suggest, the concept of individual differences in self-control has much in common with the Pavlovian concept of internal (conditioned) inhibition.

Though Rothbart and Derryberry's developmental model of temperament is among the most interesting temperament theories, the theory has its weak points, and several issues can be raised which await solution in further studies. Some of them are mentioned here.

Not all temperamental characteristics included in the framework for temperament (see Figure 3.1) have been sufficiently operationalized and investigated. One may expect that assessment techniques will be constructed that permit the measurement of all the temperament characteristics postulated by the theoretical model. The construction of CPQ suggests that the authors are close to the goal at a behavioral level.

The concept of reactivity, as presented in the developmental model, has different meanings which the authors do not clearly distinguish. Reactivity is considered a tendency to react in a given way (arousability), and this meaning permits reactivity to be treated as a temperament characteristic. But it also is a process (state) determined by several factors as shown in Figure 3.1. In fact, among the determinants of state reactivity temperament reactivity is lacking. Finally, reactivity is reaction. For example, Rothbart (1989b) in referring to negative and positive reactivity wrote: "Both positive and negative reactions are expressed via *somatic, autonomic, cognitive, and neuroendocrine reactions*" (p. 65).

The constructs "reactivity" and "self-regulation" have in Rothbart and Derryberry's theory two essentially different uses. In one context, when the authors are attempting to measure these phenomena, they are descriptive terms. In another context they are used as explanatory constructs, by means of which the authors try to interpret behavior as measured by their temperament inventories.

Although original, the concept of effort seems to be outside the temperament domain. Effort, treated as synonymous with "will," should be regarded as belonging to the domain of character, a personality structure that develops after infancy (as suggested by Rothbart in respect to effort). Studies relating effort characteristics to those of temperament can be expected to throw some light on the developmentally determined integration of temperament within the structure of personality.

Buss and Plomin (1984) drew attention to the fact that Rothbart and Derryberry's theory, in which reactivity and self-regulation refer to behavioral and neural processes that are typical for all kinds of behavior, does not allow for a distinction between temperament traits and other behaviors. A similar criticism was raised by Goldsmith and Campos (1982) who noted that the explication of Rothbart and Derryberry's theory is so wide-ranging that it is difficult to decide what individual differences in infant behavior are not temperament related. The criticism that emphasizes that reactivity and self-regulation extends to all kinds of behavior seems to be too overwhelming if we consider that such behaviors as cognition, attribution, learning, and many other aspect of human functioning are not temperament related (Rothbart, personal communication, June 1995).

The Emotion-Centered Theory of Temperament Developed by Goldsmith and Campos

Goldsmith and Campos's conceptualizations on infant temperament are descriptive, multidimensional and emotion-oriented. This theory, also developed from the early 1980s has much in common with Rothbart and Derryberry's view on temperament, but with two main differences. First, Goldsmith and Campos, while not ignoring the biological aspects of temperament do not consider them as a definitional component of this construct. Second, they limit temperament to emotions whereas Rothbart and Derryberry extended temperament characteristics over all behavior. For several years Goldsmith and Rothbart, working at the same department of psychology at the University of Oregon, have closely collaborated in the domain of temperament, and have produced several joint publications, particularly on temperament assessment (Goldsmith & Rothbart, 1991, 1992a, 1992b; Rothbart & Goldsmith, 1985).

Theoretical Background

The roots of Goldsmith and Campos's view on infant temperament are similar to those already mentioned in the presentation of Rothbart and Derryberry's developmental model. As stressed by the authors of the emotion-centered theory, the Hippocrates–Galen view on temperament, and especially G. W. Allport's (1937) understanding of temperament as a phenomenon which refers to individual differences in the emotional domain of human functioning, were of particular significance in the development of their own theorizing about temperament (Goldsmith & Campos, 1990).

In the development of the emotion-centered theory of child temperament an esential role was played by the different research experiences contributed by the authors to their joint work on temperament. At the beginning of his scientific career Hill Goldsmith was involved in searching for the genetic determination of individual differences in personality traits (G. Carey, Goldsmith, Tellegen, &

Gottesman, 1978). This study, using the California Personality Inventory, showed that the temperamental factor extraversion–introversion was the most heritable trait among those measured. A longitudinal study conducted by Goldsmith and Gottesman (1981) on twins at the ages of 8 months, 4 years, and 7 years showed that the genetic contribution to the temperament traits is developmentally specific and that, among the nineteen temperament characteristics measured, strong genetic evidence was found for only activity and persistence.

Joseph Campos, whose research took an experimental approach to emotions, was interested in studying the normative patterns of emotional development in early life (Campos & Stenberg, 1981; Campos, Barrett, Lamb, Goldsmith, & Stenberg, 1983). These studies led him to penetrate deeply into the nature of emotions in children.

The normative studies on affect expression by Izard (1977), on methods for measuring nonverbal behavior (Scherer & Ekman, (1982), on negative and positive affect by Tomkins (1982), and the evolutionary approach to research on emotions as represented by Plutchik (1980), were also important factors for the development of the emotion-centered theory of temperament.

Temperament as Individual Differences in Emotionality

Individual differences in the primary emotions, such as disgust, distress, fear, anger, sadness, pleasure, joy, surprise, and interest, are considered by Goldsmith and Campos (1982, 1986; Goldsmith, 1993) to be temperament. The primary emotions are regarded as content dimensions of temperament. Apart from the specificity of the separate primary emotions, these dimensions can be expressed behaviorally in different modalities which comprise facial, vocal, postural, gestural, and motoric expressive systems. The expressive systems can be measured using relatively stable temporal and intensive parameters that refer to the construct of general arousal. The structure of temperament as postulated by Goldsmith & Campos (1986) consists of the dimensions of emotion, their expressions, and the parameters of behavioral responses.

As distinct from other temperament theories, emotionality according to Goldsmith and Campos is not a single dimension but refers to individual differences in respect to all primary emotions, including both positive and negative. The authors emphasize the fact that their definition of temperament is a behavior-based one, without reference to the biological basis of temperament, whether genetic or neurophysiological. Two main arguments speak in favor of the behavioral approach to temperament. First, behavioral expressions from earliest infancy serve an essentially social communicative function. Second, individual differences in behavioral expressions of emotions can be easily detected and measured (Goldsmith & Campos, 1982).

As suggested by Goldsmith and Campos, their theory of temperament, especially the temperament structure, should be limited to infants. Emotions are in infants the dominant reactions by which they regulate their relationship with the external world. In view of developmental change one assumes that the structure of adolescent and adult temperament may differ. Individual differences in emotionality refer also to behaviors that cannot be identified as emotions; emotions can be expressed in different kinds of activity.

Goldsmith (1993) postulates the application of a systems theory to emotion-centered studies of temperament.

> A property of some systems is sensitivity to initial conditions, and temperament is a prime candidate for an initial condition. . . . Emotional regulatory processes can be considered either as internal (or specific) to emotional systems or as other external (or more general) systems that interact with emotion developmentally. . . . Individuals show wide variability in outcome of these regulatory processes. At least early in development, such differences are often considered as temperamental. (p. 360)

The systems approach to temperament in Goldsmith and Campos's theory is futuristic thinking without postulating how this idea could be satisfactorily operationalized.

The Measurement of Infant Temperament

In Goldsmith and Campos's theory of temperament assessment procedures play an essential role. The authors (Goldsmith & Campos, 1986, pp. 258–259) formulated several principles of temperament measurement among which the most important state that (a) the method of temperament measurement should be theory-based, (b) a single behavioral act or inventory item cannot be used as a measure of temperament, (c) the situational context used to assess temperament must be considered, (d) in developmental studies temperament should be assessed only within narrow age brackets, and (e) parental perception of infant temperament may be biased by several factors, thus temperament measurement should not be equated with parental rating or interview.

Like Rothbart, Goldsmith strongly advocated a multimethod assessment of infant temperament, which includes inventories, laboratory methods, and caretaker interviews (Goldsmith & Rieser-Danner, 1990; Goldsmith & Rothbart, 1991, 1992a, 1992b; Rothbart & Goldsmith, 1985).

Goldsmith (1996; Goldsmith & Rieser-Danner, 1990; Goldsmith & Rothbart, 1991) developed a questionnaire for assessing infant temperament in the age range of 16–36 months. This inventory, known as the Toddler Behavior Assessment Questionnaire (TBAQ) was thought to be a parallel to Rothbart's IBQ for infants at a younger age (3–12 months). The TBAQ, guided by the Goldsmith–Campos emotion-oriented theory of temperament, is a 108-item inventory composed of the following five scales: Activity Level, Pleasure, Social Fearfulness, Anger Proneness, and Interest/Persistence. Reliability of the five scales as measured by Alpha scores is satisfactory (from .78 to .83; for 18-month-old toddlers from .86 to .89) and intercorrelations between the scales do not extend beyond the value of .37 (Pleasure versus Interest/Persistence). For 18-month-old children the highest correlation was between the Activity and Anger Proneness scales—.48 (Goldsmith, 1996). Correlations with other measures of temperament, such as the Toddler Temperament Scale developed by Fullard, McDevitt, and Carey (1984) and the EASI (Buss & Plomin, 1975) are in most of the comparisons in the predicted direction. Studies in which measures from the Laboratory Temperament Assessment Battery (LAB-TAB) were compared with the TPAQ scores promise convergent validation for both methods (Goldsmith & Rothbart, 1991).

As already mentioned in the foregoing sections, Goldsmith and Rothbart (1992a, 1992b) developed two parallel LAB-TAB measures for assessing temperament in 6-month-old infants and in toddlers. The authors regarded the LAB-TAB as a behaviorally based, theoretically grounded, and objective laboratory procedure which in a videotape-equipped laboratory allows recording of children's behavior in a variety of standardized episodes. Following the methodological principles just mentioned, Goldsmith and Rothbart recommended the use of the LAB-TAB procedure along with psychometric measures of temperament by means of IBQ or TBAQ.

Final Remarks

As already mentioned, Goldsmith and Campos did not postulate any specific biological basis for the temperament dimensions which they distinguished, although in recent studies physiological correlates, including EEG, peripheral psychophysiological measures, and cortisol assessment have been included (Goldsmith, personal communication, January 1995). As regards heritability of temperamental traits, their view was rather pessimistic. Referring to Loehlin and Nichols's (1976) data, as well as to their own reviews (Goldmith, 1983, 1989), the authors share a rather common view that the heritability criterion does not differentiate temperament from other components of personality (Goldsmith & Campos, 1986). They also raised the question, still unanswered, how heritable a dimension of personality must be to qualify as a temperament trait.

In spite of his attitude to the genetic determination of temperament, Goldsmith, probably influenced by his early research experiences, conducted some behavior-genetic studies aimed at examining the genetic contribution to infant temperament. The results of these studies (see Goldsmith, 1983) showed that, among the temperament dimensions as measured in infants by means of Rothbart's IBQ, distress to limitations has the highest heritability score (.77). Individual differences in activity level are moderately determined by the genetic factor (.36). For such traits as smiling and laughter, and soothability, heritability was close to zero (.08 and .04 respectively). A behavior-genetic study conducted recently by Goldsmith, Losoya, Bradshaw, and Campos (1994) on parents and children aged from

8.5 months to 8 years showed that there is some resemblance in parents and their offsprings' temperament characteristics. Positive emotionality in parents (measured by means of the Multidimensional Personality Questionnaire, MPQ) was associated with IBQ-pleasure scores in infants, and MPQ-contraint with TBAQ-fearfulness in toddlers. Goldsmith (1994) collected some data which show that in respect to the TBAQ scales applied to toddlers fraternal twin correlations tend to be at least one-half the value of the identical twin correlations.

The emotion-centered theory of infant temperament was introduced only a decade ago, hence little evidence has come to light on the many issues postulated by the authors, especially in the domain of communicative and broadly viewed social behavior. Since temperament refers to emotional behavior, a close relationship between temperament characteristics and attachment has been postulated by Goldsmith and Campos (1982; Goldsmith, Bradshaw, & Rieser-Danner, 1986).

> Affect is closely linked to social interaction, and the quality of mother–infant social interaction is thought to influence greatly the attachment process. This nexus of relationhips suggests the plausiblity of functional relationships between temperament and attachment, which might take several forms. (Goldsmith & Campos, 1982, p. 185)

The empirical evidence supporting the temperament–attachment relationship is rather scanty. A meta-analysis of data in which infant temperament was related to attachment allows us to conclude that negative emotionality predicts distress when the infant is separated from the mother in a strange situation (Goldsmith & Harman, 1994).

As I review the Goldsmith–Campos theory of temperament, I have some critical remarks. First, the assessment techniques developed by Goldsmith and Campos are far from embracing all components of the infant's temperament structure as postulated by the emotion-centered theory. Among the primary emotions listed by the authors, certain ones such as disgust, distress, sadness, joy, and surprise are not included in the TBAQ, the most representative measure of temperament dimensions distinguished by Goldsmith and Campos.

Second, in their use of the IBQ and TBAQ inventories intended to measure the temperament dimensions of the Goldsmith–Campos theory, the authors are not consistent in their distinction between content dimensions of temperament and expression of temperament. All the IBQ and TBAQ scales, with one exception, refer to the emotional dimensions of temperament. In this context the Activity scale, present in both inventories, should be regarded as irrelevant. According to Goldsmith and Campos's view, activity is not a dimension of emotion but an expressional component of emotions. Goldsmith's (1996) main argument for including the Activity scale in the TBAQ refers to the assumption that activity is related to a general level of emotional arousal (Goldsmith & Campos, 1982). Also, Buss and Plomin (1984) argued that activity cannot be considered emotional in nature, and therefore does not belong on the list of temperament traits as defined by Gold-smith and Campos.

Third, Buss and Plomin questioned the affiliation of interest/persistence with the emotionality domain. Interest/persistence, which involves curiosity and attention, refers to the cognitive aspect of behavior. "If interest/persistence and activity are examples of affect, it is hard to see which behaviors would not also be examples of affect" (Buss & Plomin, 1984, p. 4). To be fair, it should be noted that many emotion researchers view interest as a central dimension of affect (e.g., P. Ekman, 1992; Izard, 1993).

Fourth, by using the construct "arousal" as one of the core concepts in their theory, the authors entered, in spite of their declaration regarding a purely behavioral approach, the biological domain. For emotion investigators, whether normative or differential oriented, arousal constitutes the physiological component of emotions (see Buss & Plomin, 1975; Strelau, 1987b). The emotion-centered theory makes no suggestions as to how the concept of arousal should be operationalized for studies on infant temperament.

Kagan's Inhibited and Uninhibited Temperaments

In referring to the classifications of temperament conceptualizations presented in Table 3.1, Kagan's theory can be described as a causal, monodimensional (typological) one tending to an emotion orientation, strongly concentrated on infancy and early childhood. In spite of Kagan's long career in developmental psychology, his interest in temperament, stimulated by his own experience as well as by ideas and findings in the literature, began less than two decades ago.

Theoretical Background

As delineated by Jerome Kagan (1989b, 1994; Ellis & Robbins, 1990), two events developed his interest in temperament research. First, Kagan and Moss (1962) conducted an *ex post* analysis of data from the Fels Longitudinal Study which comprised about 100 normal subjects followed from early childhood to adulthood. One of the conclusions from this analysis was that the only individual characteristic to remain stable across the developmental period under study was shy, timid behavior as opposed to outgoing, sociable behavior. Influenced by the environmentalistic *Zeitgeist* Kagan and Moss interpreted these stable individual differences in terms of environmental factors. Second, a study conducted about 15 years later by Kagan, Kearsley, and Zelazo (1978) on 3- to 29-month-old children showed that Chinese children differ essentially from Caucasian children in some behavior characteristics that could not be explained in terms of rearing practices. Chinese children were quieter and more fearful than Caucasian children. This fact alone bolstered Kagan's belief that it was the biological factor that contributed to the behavioral differences between the two samples under study.

Before his involvement in studies on temperament, Kagan (1974) had already put forward a temperament hypothesis for the interpretation of changes in infants' behavior following presentations of discrepant objects. He suggested that temperament dispositions, probably genetically determined, contribute to whether a child confronted with unexpected events tends to react with smiling or crying.

At least three different lines of research influenced Kagan's interests in temperament: Jung's (1923) theory of biologically determined extraversion–introversion, Thomas and Chess's studies on temperament which had shown the uniqueness of behavioral style from early infancy, and animal research. Animal research had given evidence that the tendency to approach or to avoid novelty is biologically determined (Royce, 1955; Schneirla, 1965; Scott & Fuller, 1965).

The Two Basic Temperament Categories

According to Kagan (1989a, p. 668; Kagan, Snidman, Julia-Sellers, & Johnson, 1991, p. 332), the concept *temperament* refers to inherited profiles (categories, qualities, types) of behavior and biology which are present in the infant and which mediate different phenotypic displays depending on childhood experiences. Kagan (1989a, 1994), who does not deny the existence of many temperament categories or traits, developed his theory and research around one dimension, the extremes of which result in two qualitatively different categories—the *inhibited* and *uninhibited* temperament. These two categories refer to the child's initial reaction to unfamilar events (people, objects, situations). The encounter with unfamiliar events develops a state of uncertainty, which may be compared to a state of stress (Kagan, 1983), to which children react in different ways.

A child who is consistently shy, quiet, cautious, emotionally reserved, and timid, when confronted with unfamiliar events, is characterized as having an inhibited temperament. A child who under the same conditions is consistently sociable, talkative, affectively spontaneous, and minimally fearful, has an uninhibited temperament (Kagan, 1989a, 1989b, 1994; Kagan & Snidman, 1991; Kagan, Reznick, & Snidman, 1988). In an unselected Caucasian population there are about 10% inhibited children and 25% uninhibited children. The two categories are considered by Kagan and his collaborators not as a dimension but as the extremes of a continuum, with qualitatively different temperament characteristics.

> The constructs inhibited and uninhibited to the unfamiliar refer to children who fall at the extremes of a phenotypic continuum from shyness and restraint to sociability and affective spontaneity. (Kagan, Reznick, & Gibbons, 1989, p. 838)

These constructs have behavioral, genetic and physiological patterns specific for the inhibited and uninhibited temperaments.

The two temperaments are relatively stable. Longitudinal studies conducted for several purposes in different cohorts of children aged from 2 months (Kagan & Snidman, 1991) to over 7 years (e.g., Kagan *et al.,* 1988; Reznick *et al.,* 1986) showed that the majority of inhibited and uninhibited infants selected from Caucasian samples did not change their temperament characteristics even in late childhood. The categories of inhibited and uninhibited temperament typical of children are somewhat analogous to the approach–withdrawal individual characteristics encountered in animals, especially in monkeys (e.g., Stevenson-Hinde, Stillwell-Barnes, & Zunz, 1980; Suomi, 1987), as well as to the extraversion–introversion dimension studied in adults (Kagan, 1989b; Kagan & Reznick, 1986).

Biological Bases of Inhibited and Uninhibited Temperament

Kagan (1982b, 1989a, 1989b, 1994) and his coworkers (Kagan, Reznick, & Snidman, 1987; Kagan *et al.,* 1988) developed a theory of the biological bases of inhibition–uninhibition which had an essential influence on the majority of studies conducted in Kagan's laboratory.

Individual differences in the threshold of reactivity in the limbic system, especially the amygdala and hypothalamus, and the systems connected with the latter (pituitary–adrenal axis, reticular activating system, and sympathetic chain of the ANS) are regarded as the physiological bases of the two temperament categories. Inhibited children are characterized by lower reactivity thresholds in these systems.

> The physiological signs that are characteristic of inhibited children could be due to tonically lower thresholds of reactivity in these brain structures. As a result, the inhibited children show increases in muscle tension, a rise and stabilization of heart rate, pupillary dilation, or increased cortisol to minimally unfamiliar or challenging events, whereas most children would not show these physiological reactions to the same relatively innocuous experiences. (Kagan *et al.,* 1987, p. 1469)

In Kagan's (1994; Kagan *et al.,* 1988) laboratory a whole set of physiological and biochemical markers of behavioral inhibition has been used. Heart rate, heart rate variability, heart rate acceleration, pupillary dilation, and urinary norepinephrine level reaction to psychological stress have served as indices of sympathetic reactivity. For measuring the activity of the hypothalamic–pituitary–adrenal axis cortisol levels from samples of saliva were taken. Skeletal muscle tension of the larynx and vocal cords measured by such indices as vocal perturbation and variability in the fundamental frequency of verbal utterances were used as measures of activity of the limbic system. Since the correlations between the physiological measures were rather low, varying between –.20 and +.30 (with the exception of heart rate and heart rate variability), an aggregate index of physiological activity was often used as the physiological marker of inhibited temperament. "There was a substantial positive relation between this composite physiological index and the index of inhibition at every age ($r = 0.70$ with the index at 21 months, and $r = 0.64$ with the index at 7.5 years of age)" (Kagan *et al.,* 1988, p. 170).

Behavioral inhibition as measured by Matheny (1989) in a longitudinal study of MZ and DZ twins aged from 12 to 30 months reared together showed that MZ twins as compared with DZ twins have significantly higher intrapair correlations. This speaks for the importance of the genetic factor in determining individual differences with respect to this temperament category. A study conducted by Emde and colleagues (1992) in which several temperament characteristics were measured in 200 pairs of 14-month-old twins has given support for this statement. Data from this study show that inhibited temperament as measured by means of behavioral observations had a heritability score of .62, one of the highest scores among the temperament characteristics under study.

Assessment Procedures Used in Kagan's Laboratory

In contrast to most researchers on temperament in children, Kagan and his coworkers did not use psychometric procedures for diagnosing the inhibited versus uninhibited temperament. When assessing children's temperament, according to Kagan (1994; Ellis & Robbins, 1990), one cannot rely on the reports of parents or teachers; therefore, in Kagan's laboratory observation of children's behavior under standardized conditions was the main method for studying temperament (see Garcia-Coll, Kagan, & Reznick, 1984; Kagan, 1989b; Kagan & Snidman, 1991; Kagan *et al.,* 1989; Reznick *et al.,* 1986).

The behavioral sessions during which temperament characteristics were assessed consisted of different episodes, depending on the child's age and the specific aim of the study. Separation from the mother, reactions to unfamiliar objects, such as unusual toys, robots, and sounds, and to an unknown person or group of persons (children, adults) were considered the most critical situations provoking behavior typical for the inhibited and uninhibited temperament. Observations and judgments of temperament characteristics were conducted by more than one examiner. The intercoder reliability measured for the behavioral indices of inhibited–uninhibited temperament, for example, latency to play, latency to first approach, and time proximal to mother, was mostly very satisfactory, reaching the value of .80 to .90. The behavioral study was almost always accompanied by psychophysiological recordings taken after or during the behavioral sessions. For school-age children classroom behavior recorded during different experimental settings was also taken as a temperament measure.

Since different situations provide a different set of incentives for the manifestation of inhibited–uninhibited behavior, an aggregate index of inhibition was often used by Kagan and his coworkers. For example, in a study conducted by Reznick and colleagues (1986) on 5.5-year-old children, average standard scores of the following five indices were used for calculating an aggregate index of inhibition: peer play inhibition, laboratory inhibition, school inhibition, risk avoidance in laboratory settings, and number of times the child looked at the examiner). The correlations among these indexes are given in Table 3.4.

In general, assessment of inhibited or uninhibited temperament was based on a complex of behavioral and physiological indices. Standardized batteries consisting of age-specific laboratory situations were often supplemented by parental reports and maternal interviews.

Final Remarks

Only a few studies have been conducted by Kagan and his associates in which the inhibited–uninhibited temperaments were related to behaviors that were not considered to be expressions of the two temperament types. In a recent study, Kagan and colleagues (1991) demonstrated a relationship between children's inhibited temperament and allergic symptoms in first- and second-degree relatives. Relatives of inhibited children reported more often, as compared with those of uninhibited children, the occurrence of such allergic symptoms as hayfever and eczema. This finding suggests a genetic background that relates shy and timid behavior in children to factors influencing immunological vulnerability to selected allergies.

Kagan and his coworkers considered cognitive functioning in unfamiliar experimental settings (objects and persons) as well as physiological patterns recorded during these states in terms of stressor and stress (Kagan, 1983; Reznick *et al.,* 1986). Findings suggest that inhibited children, being shy and restrained, experience higher stress than uninhibited children under unknown and unfamiliar situations. According to Kagan the difference between inhibited and uninhibited children bears some resemblance to Pavlov's distinction between weak and strong types of nervous system. Inhibited children have a weak nervous system and uninhibited children a strong nervous system (Reznick *et al.,* 1986, p. 677). It may be expected that studies relating Kagan's temperamental categories to behavior under

TABLE 3.4. Correlations among the Major Behavioral Indexes of Inhibition at 5.5 Years of Age

Variable	1	2	3	4	5	6
1. Peer play inhibition		.21	.04	.26	.30*	.63***
2. Laboratory inhibition			.45**	.41**	-.09	.64***
3. School inhibition				.22	-.31	.37**
4. Risk avoidance					.21	.73***
5. Look examiner						.51***
6. Aggregate inhibition						

Note. $^* = p < .05$, $^{**} = p < .01$, $^{***} = p < .001$. From "Inhibited and Uninhibited Children: A Follow-up Study," by J. S. Reznick, J. Kagan, N. Snidman, M. Gersten, K. Baak, and A. Rosenberg, 1986, *Child Development, 57,* p. 666. Copyright 1986 by the Society for Research in Child Development. Reprinted with permission.

different kinds of stress will throw some light on the functional significance of the inhibited and uninhibited temperament types.

Kagan's postulate which says that inhibited and uninhibited children represent two qualitatively different temperaments has no empirical support. Studies conducted in his laboratory did not lead to the distinction of two qualitatively different physiological mechanisms underlying these two temperament categories. Further, by using an aggregate index combining qualitatively different physiological indices in one quantitative measure of inhibited–uninhibited temperaments, Kagan contradicts his own view regarding the qualitative difference between the two temperaments (Strelau, 1995d).

According to Buss and Plomin (1984), Kagan's term *inhibited temperament* may be misleading because the infants thus labeled do not inhibit behavior in the usual sense of this notion. This temperament does not refer to inhibited behavior in terms of delaying response or resisting temptation. What is essential is fear or distress in a novel situation, so Kagan and his colleagues are in fact dealing with a temperament dimension known as emotionality. Buss and Plomin (1984) drew a conclusion which in my opinion is inadequate, that the conceptualization developed by Kagan, however promising, cannot be classified as a specific theory of temperament.

Adult-Oriented Theories of Temperament

From a geographical vantage point, contemporary research on child temperament initiated by New Yorkers Thomas and Chess has been located in the United States. All theories discussed in the first part of this chapter have been developed in this country. Adult temperament research initiated in the second half of the century was launched mainly in Europe (Eysenck and Teplov). Contemporary theories in this domain,however, have been developed in both hemispheres.

At first glance, the list of candidates for presentation in this chapter as authors of temperament theories is rather lengthy. It is not easy to make a compilation, since frequently researchers in the domain of adult temperament, to mention only Zuckerman and Gray, prefer to use the concept *personality* rather than *temperament* (for a detailed discussion, see Chapter 1). Taking into account the criteria adopted at the beginning of Chapter 2, I decided on introducing the following five conceptualizations: Gray's neuropsychological theory of temperament, Zuckerman's sensation seeking theory, Mehrabian's emotion-centered theory of temperament, Rusalov's functional-systems theory of temperament, and Strelau's regulative theory of temperament.

Taking into account other criteria than those applied here would have admitted numerous other researchers. For an adequate grasp of the variety of investigations going on in the domain of temperament some examples will suffice. Claridge (1985, 1987) developed a theory of psychoticism which might be regarded as a dimension of temperament. His conceptualization, although original, especially as regards his view on the physiological basis of psychoticism, is close to that of Eysenck. Claridge, like his mentor, considered psychoticism one of the three superfactors—PEN.

The temperament construct of reducing–augmenting was elaborated by Petrie (1967) and later modified by Buchsbaum (1978; Buchsbaum & Silverman, 1968). Petrie's theory has its roots in her clinical observations in which she found individual differences in the extent that patients suffer pain. The reason the reducing–augmenting construct has not been included in the list of temperament theories is the following. This conceptualization, most systematically presented in Petrie's (1967) monograph, has not been further developed, except for some attempts to elaborate psychometric measures of this dimension (e.g., Barnes, 1985). In turn, Buchsbaum's neurophysiological modification of Petrie's dimension, which consisted mainly in applying evoked potential (amplitude) measures of the augmenting–reducing phenomenon, should be considered more in terms of neurophysiological correlates of temperament (see Zuckerman, 1991c) than as a temperament dimension per se.

An interesting general theory of heritable personality traits, which according to the understanding of temperament accepted in this book may be regarded as temperament traits, recently has been developed by Cloninger (1986; Cloninger, Svrakic, & Przybeck, 1993). The author distinguished three independent dimensions: novelty seeking, harm avoidance, and reward dependence which have much in common with Gray's conceptualizations. Cloninger's theory which concentrates on links between temperament and different aspects of pathology (Joyce, Mulder, & Cloninger, 1994; Svrakic, Whitehead, Przybeck, & Cloninger, 1993), deserves in the near future a detailed presentation.

Tellegen, whose main research activity was focused on examining the genetic contribution to individual differences in personality, distinguished three second-order personality dimensions: positive emotionality, negative emotionality, and constraint (Tellegen, 1985; Watson & Tellegen, 1985). Two of these dimensions, which resulted from factor analysis of data from different measures of mood states and mood traits, are comparable to Eysenck's extraversion (positive emotionality) and neuroticism (negative emotionality). The author of this emotion-oriented view on personality did not develop a specific theory of the proposed temperament structure.

Recently a construct of affect intensity has been introduced by Larsen and Diener (1985, 1987; Larsen & Ketelaar, 1991). Affect intensity, defined in terms of the typical strength of an individual's response to stimuli that generate positive and negative affect, has its roots in Allport's understanding of temperament, and has some elements in common with the dimension of emotionality as introduced by Goldsmith and Campos. Larsen and Diener (1987) also developed an inventory, the Affect Intensity Measure (AIM), that enables the assessment of individual differences in emotion intensity. Their conceptualizations on affect intensity, accompanied by assessment proposals, have been broadly developed (see, e.g., Emmons, Diener, & Larsen, 1986; Larsen & Ketelaar, 1991; Larsen & Zarate, 1991). The only reason for my decision to exclude this conceptualization from my review is that the affect intensity dimension is a very narrow concept, referring to only one, albeit important, aspect of emotional behavior.

Finally, a student and former coworker of mine, Andrzej Eliasz, developed a transactional model of temperament. This theory, presented in several publications (Eliasz, 1981, 1985, 1990), underlines the role of the social environment and its reciprocal relationships with temperament in determining the individual's behavior. The individual's temperament is considered an important variable in a more general system of regulation of stimulation. The transactional model of temperament is a modification of Strelau's regulative theory of temperament. Further, the model does not postulate any specific operationalization procedures by means of which the theory could be tested for validity.

As can be seen from this brief overview, the variety of conceptualizations in the domain of adult temperament is much broader than is presented in the five theories mentioned. Still, it is my belief that the theories described in the following sections embody the mainstream of research on adult temperament.

Mehrabian's PAD (Pleasure–Arousability–Dominance) Temperament Model

At the beginning of the 1980s, when Goldsmith and Campos introduced their emotion-centered theory of infant temperament, there already existed in the United States a broadly elaborated emotion-based theory of adult temperament developed in the 1970s by Mehrabian. It is strange that Mehrabian's contribution to studies on temperament was not cited by Goldsmith and Campos. Furthermore, temperament researchers, including those who deal with adults, have very rarely referred to Mehrabian's work. No review of temperament theories in which Mehrabian's important contribution to the understanding of human temperament is not taken into account can be considered adequate.

Mehrabian's theory of adult temperament is a descriptive, multidimensional and emotion-centered conceptualization (see Table 3.1). A broadly summarized review of his theorizing and findings in the domain of temperament has been published in an extensive monograph (Mehrabian, 1980) mainly comprised of his papers and those of his coworkers written in the 1970s.

Theoretical Background

For a proper understanding of Albert Mehrabian's contribution to temperament note should be taken of the fact that his first period of psychological research was apparently far from temperament issues. During the first decade of his academic career he was mainly interested in problems of communication, especially nonverbal (e.g., Mehrabian, 1965, 1972), attitudes, achievement, affiliation, and other social-behavior characteristics (e.g., Mehrabian, 1968, 1969; Mehrabian & Ksionzky, 1974). Those studies directed his attention to the importance of situations and environment in human behavior (e.g., Mehrabian, 1976b; Mehrabian & Ksionzky, 1972). In his studies on human–environment interaction he arrived at the conclusion that emotions, understood as states, play an important role in this interaction. They are also the phenomena by means of which the individual categorizes environments (Mehrabian & Russell, 1974a, 1974b).

A search for the roots of Mehrabian's theory of temperament reaching beyond his own experience shows that the contribution of a number of scholars was of particular importance for his research. His temperament theory takes off from studies based on the concept of semantic differential as developed by Osgood (Snider & Osgood, 1969). The three dimensions (evaluation, activity, and potency) by means of which Osgood described human responses to social and physical situations were viewed in Mehrabian's theory from an emotional perspective.

As we see in the next section, influential in the development of Mehrabian's emotion-based theory of temperament were studies that demonstrated the existence of individual differences in the intensity and duration of orienting reflexes (see Maltzman & Raskin, 1965). Also of importance was the neo-Pavlovian approach to investigating the CNS properties, especially strength of excitation (see Nebylitsyn, 1972a), and its interpretation by Gray (1964c) in terms of arousability. The construct of arousal, which plays an important role in Mehrabian's theory, was taken from Berlyne (1960), to underline the behavioral components of arousal.

Emotions as the Basis for Three Temperament Dimensions

Mehrabian's (1972) extensive studies on nonverbal communication led him to the conclusion that the diversity of motoric expressions and movements by means of which the individual interacts with others can be described in terms of communicative meanings, at the core of which are emotions. Emotions constitute the primary referents of nonverbal and implicit verbal messages. They "serve as mediating variables between situational and personality variables on the one hand and specific behavioral variables (e.g., actions, verbalizations) on the other" (Mehrabian, 1991, p. 75). Extensive studies, based mainly on the semantic differential type of measure, enabled Mehrabian and Russell (1974a, 1974b) to identify three independent and basic bipolar dimensions of emotion states: pleasure–displeasure, arousal–nonarousal and dominance–submissiveness (PAD Emotion Model). Russell and Mehrabian (1977) demonstrated that all kinds of emotion states may be described in terms of these three dimensions. Different configurations of the three basis emotion states play an important role in human adaptation and they are important concepts for understanding the phenomena of anxiety and depression (Mehrabian, 1995–1996).

There are individual differences in habitual emotional reactions to a variety of stimuli, and a comprehensive evaluation of averages of emotional states leads directly to the description of temperament.

> "Temperament" is defined here as "characteristic emotion state" or as "emotion trait." In accordance with standard usage, "state" refers to a transitory condition of the organism, whereas "trait" refers to a stable, habitual, or characteristic condition of the organism. (Mehrabian, 1991, p. 77)

According to the three emotion factors, three basic bipolar temperament variables were distinguished: trait pleasure–displeasure, trait stimulus screening–arousability, and trait dominance–submissiveness.

Pleasure–Displeasure. The temperament dimension of pleasure–displeasure has been defined as a characteristic (typical for an individual) feeling state with such behavioral indicators as smiles and laughter, or, more generally, in terms of positive versus negative facial expressions especially during social interaction (Mehrabian, 1980). One pole of this dimension is characterized by pain and unhappiness, and the opposite pole by ecstasy and happiness (Mehrabian, 1978b).

Dominance–Submissiveness. Dominance is a characteristic feeling state behaviorally expressed in postural relaxation. This feeling is a function of the extent to which an individual feels unrestricted or free to act in a variety of ways (Mehrabian, 1980). At one extreme this dimension refers to feelings of lack of control or influence on the surroundings, and at the other, to feelings of being influential, powerful, and in control over the situation (Mehrabian, 1978b).

Stimulus Screening–Arousability. Of the three dimensions of temperament the most attention was paid to the trait stimulus screening–arousability. Several findings contributed to the identification of this temperament dimension. Studies have shown that there are individual differences in the amplitude of the orienting reflex to strong and novel stimuli, in habituation to this reflex, and in the degree to which individuals are behaviorally aroused by the acting stimuli. Pavlovian typologists have argued that individual differences in these characteristics are mediated by "strength–weakness" of the nervous system. Mehrabian and Russell (1974a) used an information theory approach to develop a hypothesis according to which aspects of stimulation such as variety, complexity, and novelty comprise an "information rate" which determines the level of arousal. The more complex, variegated, and novel the acting stimuli, the higher the information rate. The level of information rate may be regulated by means of screening considered as an information-processing state. There are individual differences in screening of irrelevant stimuli and rapidity of habituation to distracting and irrelevant cues. Stimulus screening is an automatic, not intentional, information-processing state and individuals differ in the degree to which they habitually process information (Mehrabian, 1991). These speculations and observations led Mehrabian (1977b) to the following definition of arousability.

> "Arousability," then, may be defined as an individual difference dimension that subsumes the following intercorrelated qualities: the initial amplitude of the orienting reflex; number of trials for GSR habituation; various indexes of arousal response to increases in information rate of stimulation; and "weakness" of the nervous system. (p. 91)

Arousability is inversely related to stimulus screening. Arousable individuals (nonscreeners) screen less of the irrelevant stimuli and, as a consequence, experience a higher information rate of acting situations, which leads to higher arousal levels and slower declines in arousal as compared with screeners (unarousable individuals). In turn, screeners are able to screen irrelevant stimuli and thus reduce their random character, leading to a lower level of arousal and a more rapid decrease of arousal in comparison with nonscreeners. Mehrabian (1977b, p. 92) emphasized that it is the temporary spikes in arousal rather than the chronic level of arousal over time and across situations that is most relevant to the differences in behavioral arousal between screeners and nonscreeners.

According to Mehrabian (1978b, 1991), temperament traits are among the most stable behavior characteristics. They are related to behaviors expressed in a wide range of situations, thus satisfying the criterion of generality. Temperament refers to genetic predispositions rather than to learned patterns of behavior; at least 50% of temperament traits are determined by genetic factors. Since temperament traits are classed among the most general and stable individual characteristics, modification of behavior can be achieved mainly through changes in the environment (Mehrabian, 1991).

Mehrabian viewed his temperament dimensions as fundamental for personality description. In a study in which the three temperament dimensions: pleasure (+P)–displeasure (–P), arousability (+A)–stimulus screening (–A), and dominance (+D)–submissiveness (–D), were dichotomized, Mehrabian and O'Reilly (1980) described, by means of regression analysis, the following eight personality types: exuberant (+P+A+D) versus bored (–P–A–D), relaxed (+P–A+D) versus anxious (–P+A–D), hostile (–P+A+D) versus docile (+P–A–D), and disdainful (–P–A+D) versus dependent (+P+A–D).

Measures of Temperament

At the beginning of the emotion-centered studies on temperament, Mehrabian and Russell (1974a) constructed semantic differential scales under the lengthy heading "Semantic Differential Measures of Emotional State or Characteristic (Trait) Emotions" (SDMESCTE). Depending on the instruction given to subjects, this technique allowed the assessment of any of the three basic emotion states or traits: pleasure, dominance, and arousal. Each of the three scales was composed of 6 pairs of antonymic adjectives (e.g., happy–unhappy in the Pleasure scale). Used as a temperament measure, these adjectives were rated in terms of *general* feelings on a 9-point rating scale. It turned out, however, that these three scales, when used as measures of traits, were not sufficiently reliable.

Taking the SDMESCTE as a starting point, Mehrabian (1978b) developed, in four consecutive studies conducted on undergraduate students, a new semantic differential format for assessing the three temperamental traits. This method is currently known as the Pleasure–Arousal–Dominance scales (PAD; Mehrabian, 1995a). The PAD scales developed in 1978, which I labeled the Mehrabian Temperament Scale (MTS: Strelau, 1991b). are composed of 47 pairs of adjectives, 24 for the Trait-Pleasure scale, 8 for the Trait-Arousal scale, and 15 for the Trait-Dominance scale. Like the former semantic differential format, adjective pairs were rated on a 9-point scale with emotionally reversed adjectives at the two poles [e.g., tired (1) versus inspired (9)]. The MTS has appropriate Trait-Pleasure and Trait-Dominance scales with reliability coefficients .91 and .84 respectively. The reliability of the Trait-Arousal scale, the construction of which afforded the greatest difficulty, was still not satisfactory (.60). This led Mehrabian to conclude that trait-arousal is a difficult concept to measure because of the unreliability of subjects' reports. The revised 1995 version of PAD is composed of 34 items. The scales are orthogonal to each other and they contain 16 Pleasure items, 9 Arousal items and 9 Dominance items, with reliability coefficients of .97 (P), .89 (A) and .80 (D).

Since in the 1970s the semantic differential approach did not make it possible to develop a satisfactory Trait-Arousal scale, Mehrabian (1976a, 1977a, 1977b) constructed an inventory aimed at measuring the temperament dimension of stimulus screening–arousability and known as the Trait Arousability Scale (TAS; also labeled the Stimulus Screening Scale, SSS). TAS is a measure of an emotional predisposition to be aroused. This inventory consists of 40 items balanced for direction of wording and scored on a 9-point rating scale. The construct of stimulus screening is represented in the TAS by the nine following intercorrelated factors: low general arousability, rapid habituation, low arousability to sudden changes and events, thermal screening, low arousability in novel or changeable settings, auditory screening, tactual and kinesthetic screening, olfactory screening and low arousability in multicomponent or complex settings. A high score on the TAS is indicative for screeners (unarousable individuals) whereas a low score indicates non-screeners (high arousability).

The TAS yields high reliability scores (.92) and adequate convergent as well as discriminant validity characteristics. Curiously, the Stimulus Screening Questionnaire did not correlate with scales that also refer to the concept of arousal and arousability, such as Extraversion and Arousal Seeking Tendency (Mehrabian, 1976a, 1977a). In a recent review of studies in which TAS was applied Mehrabian

(1995b) presented data that support high reliability and validity (construct, convergent, and divergent) of this inventory.

Mehrabian and Falender (1978) also developed a psychometric measure of stimulus screening–arousability in children as a questionnaire based on maternal report. The Child Stimulus Screening Scale (CSSS; so labeled by Strelau) is a 46-item inventory with a 9-point rating scale (from very strong agreement to very strong disagreement). The Kuder–Richardson formula 20 reliability coefficient, used by Mehrabian in all his psychometric studies as a measure of reliability, was very high for the CSSS (.92).

Mehrabian and Hines (1978) also developed a questionnaire aimed at measuring the third temperament dimension: dominance–submissiveness. This questionnaire, also composed of 40 well-balanced items and with very satisfactory reliability (.95) was considered a more effective measure of dominance than the SDMESCTE–Trait Dominance Scale (Mehrabian, 1978b).

In sum, it may be noted that the only assessment technique that succeeds in measuring all three emotion-centered temperament dimensions involves the PAD scales. However, for a reliable measure of stimulus screening–arousability, which is the most interesting of Mehrabian's temperament dimensions, the TAS is recommended.

Temperament as Related to Behavior and Environment

The emotion-centered theory of temperament is based on assumptions that allow a search for a variety of links between temperament and other behaviors and behavior disorders in a diversity of situations and environments. A series of studies has been conducted by Mehrabian (1980) and his associates to illustrate the links between temperament and such phenomena as eating characteristics and disorders (Mehrabian, 1987; Mehrabian & Riccioni, 1986; Mehrabian, Nahum, & Duke, 1985–1986), chronic stimulant use (Mehrabian, 1986; 1995b), sexual desire and dysfunction (Mehrabian & Stanton-Mohr, 1985), illness (Mehrabian, 1995b; Mehrabian & Bernath, 1991; Mehrabian & Ross, 1977), emotional empathy (Mehrabian, Young, & Sato, 1988), and environmental preferences (Hines & Mehrabian, 1979; Mehrabian, 1978a). It is impossible to refer to all these studies; however, two lines of research mentioned in the following paragraphs illustrate Mehrabian's approach to the study of temperament characteristics as related to behavior and environment.

Mehrabian and his associates gave much attention to the search for links between eating-related characteristics, including such disorders as obesity and anorexia, and temperament. There was no specific and theoretically grounded rationale behind these studies except for the fact that up till then most research in this domain had been conducted using a clinical approach and/or referred to inadequate personality traits assumed to mediate eating characteristics. In Mehrabian and his coworkers' studies (Mehrabian, 1987; Mehrabian & Riccioni, 1986; Mehrabian *et al.*, 1985–1986) eating-related characteristics were measured in normal populations (always undergraduate students) by means of specially constructed questionnaires, and related to the three basic temperament factors. In general, the findings suggested several conclusions, which include the following. Three factors of eating-related characteristics—predisposition to obesity, uncontrollable urges to eat, and predisposition to anorexia, were significantly correlated with trait arousability. Most striking, predisposition to obesity was associated with arousability and submissiveness. Persons engaged more in joyless eating tended to have more unpleasant temperaments, and so on. In general, the association between eating-related characteristics and emotions was stronger when the latter were measured not as traits (temperament) but as states.

Mehrabian's studies on the relationship between temperament and environment were theoretically grounded. Referring to the Yerkes–Dodson law, Mehrabian (1977a) developed a pleasure-arousal hypothesis directly related to the screener–nonscreener temperament dimension. According to this hypothesis, "a high rate of information in a setting maximizes approach versus avoidance as a function of the pleasure versus displeasure elicited" (Mehrabian, 1977a, p. 247). This hypothesis is based on an assumption that in pleasant situations approach behavior is a direct correlate of arousal, whereas in unpleasant situations it is avoidance behavior that directly correlates with arousal. Mehrabian's theory postulates that screeners are less arousable in situations of high information rate than nonscreeners. If this is the case, one may assume that nonscreeners, more than screeners, will approach a pleasant environment and avoidance of an unpleasant environment will also be more strongly expressed in nonscreeners than in screeners (see Figure 3.3); both tendencies should be most strongly expressed under a high information rate of stimulation.

In several studies where approach was operationalized in terms of situation preferences, desire to work or socialize, and avoidance was scored by measuring physical avoidance of the surroundings, avoidance of work and social interaction, the pleasure-arousal hypothesis as applied to screeners and nonscreeners was partially confirmed (Hines & Mehrabian, 1979; Mehrabian, 1978a, 1980, 1995b).

Final Remarks

In spite of Mehrabian's assumption that individual differences in temperament are essentially determined by the genetic factor, to the extent of my knowledge, none of the studies conducted by him or his coworkers can be treated as evidence for his claim. Mehrabian's conceptualizations although pertaining to such biologically rooted concepts as arousal and arousability, did not refer to any specific biological mechanisms or correlates of the three emotion-based temperament dimensions.

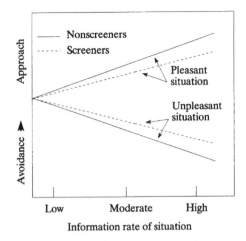

FIGURE 3.3. The pleasure-arousal hypothesis for screeners and nonscreeners. *Note.* From "A Questionnaire Measure of Individual Differences in Stimulus Screening and Associated Differences in Arousability," by A. Mehrabian, 1977, *Environmental Psychology and Nonverbal Behavior, 1,* p. 248. Copyright 1977 by Duke University Press. Reprinted with permission.

In using the construct of arousability in his writings, Mehrabian made mention of Gray (1964c) who introduced this concept, but ascribed to it a different meaning. For Gray, arousability was considered to be a chronic (more or less stable) level of arousal on which individuals differ, while for Mehrabian (1977a) this term referred to the temporary states (spikes) of arousal. The application of the construct "arousability" to refer to phasic arousal is unusual in personality or temperament research (see Chapter 5).

Most interesting, however, is the fact that Mehrabian differs from all other scholars in his view regarding the basis of individual differences in arousal. Other authors, in interpreting the sources of individual differences in arousal or in using the concept of arousability, refer to different anatomic structures of the nervous system, to physiological or biochemical mechanisms or both (for a detailed discussion see Chapter 5). In contrast, Mehrabian (1995b) discerns the causes of individual differences in behavioral arousal as automatic information-processing phenomena, which he identifies as habitual screening of irrelevant stimuli. Mehrabian did not develop any hypothesis which allows for assumptions as to the kinds of biological determinants expected to mediate these automatic and habitual information-processing states.

In analyzing the construct of dominance–submissiveness, "one has the feeling" that this temperament dimension, as defined by Mehrabian, does not correspond with the understanding of the term "feeling" as applied by most researchers of emotions. In defining dominance Mehrabian uses the term "feeling" as I have used it in the preceding sentence. Dominance is characterized as "Feelings of being influential and powerful" (Mehrabian, 1978b, p. 1107). In this context, feeling is rather a synonym of consciousness, for example, in the context "feeling safety." This has not much in common with feelings as the content component of basic emotions.

However interesting Mehrabian's theory of temperament is, one has to bear in mind that all of his findings as well as the data collected during the two decades are based exclusively, or more cautiously, almost exclusively, on undergraduate student samples. From this point of view, Mehrabian's theory is a biased one, since in fact it is a theory of university students' temperament. Only recently studies have been extended to other populations (Mehrabian, 1995a, 1995b) as well as to other personality traits throwing some light on the relationship between Mehrabian's PAD constructs and other conceptualizations regarding adult temperament.

The Neuropsychological Model of Temperament Developed by Gray

In the 1970s Eysenck's most prominent student, Gray, undertook a thorough critique of his master's theory of extraversion and neuroticism, which led to the development of Gray's own neuropsychological theory of temperament or personality (Gray used the terms interchangeably; Gray, 1991). This theory differs from all other temperament conceptualizations in that it is the most physiologically oriented one, supported by rich neurophysiological, pharmacological, and biochemical evidence, collected, however, mainly in studies on rats.

Applying the four criteria by which temperament theories have been classified (see Table 3.1), Gray's neuropsychological model of temperament is seen as oriented to adults, and a causal, multidimensional, and emotion-centered theory. His temperament model has developed over the past two decades and has been described in many papers and books. To write about the biological basis of personality or temperament without reference to Gray's contribution reflects ignorance.

Theoretical Background

From the beginning of his research career Jeffrey Gray was involved in studying arousal as related to temperament. In his Ph.D. thesis, written in 1968 under the supervision of Peter Broadhurst (in Eysenck's laboratory), he studied the relationship between level of arousal and behavioral indices of extraversion (cited in H. J. Eysenck & Eysenck, 1985). Eysenck's initial interpretation of extraversion in terms of Pavlov's concepts of excitation and inhibition motivated Gray (1964b) to undertake a thorough examination of the Pavlovian and neo-Pavlovian typology, with special reference to the construct of strength of excitation. In order to bring the concept of strength of excitation to the attention of biologically oriented personality researchers, Gray (1964c) undertook a reinterpretation of strength of excitation in terms of arousal and arousability; the latter construct was introduced by him (for details see Chapter 5). His theoretical considerations regarding arousal were based on a profound knowledge of research in this domain, with special reference to the contributions of Duffy, Malmo, Hebb, Berlyne, and Lindsley (for references see Chapter 5). Gray was also deeply involved in studying classical and operant conditioning, particularly as related to behavior and behavior disorders. His own research on rats (Gray, 1967; Gray & Smith, 1969) showed the role of reward and punishment in animal learning and made him aware of the importance of individual sensitivity to the effects of reward and punishment in classical and operant conditioning (Gray, 1975). Gray's studies on animal learning were deeply rooted in the learning theories of Pavlov (1951–1952), Hull (1952), Mowrer (1960), Amsel (1962), and Spence's (Spence & Spence, 1966) learning theory of anxiety, as well as on empirical evidence regarding the role of brain structures as rewarding or punishing loci (McCleary, 1966; Olds & Olds, 1965).

   Although he concentrated on experimental research concerning the physiological and biochemical mechanisms and neural structures underlying anxiety in rats, Gray used animal data to develop a neuropsychological theory of human temperament. His studies on temperament were also strongly influenced by Eysenck and the Russian neo-Pavlovian typologists Teplov and Nebylitsyn.

Anxiety and Impulsivity: The Two Basic Temperament Dimensions

   Gray (1970, 1981) undertook a major revision of Eysenck's theory of temperament, mainly by questioning the conditionability paradigm and the physiological mechanisms mediating extraversion and neuroticism (see Chapter 2). Analysis of data collected in the domain of eyeblink conditioning in man as related to extraversion and neuroticism, and studies on rats which showed that barbiturate drugs and alcohol, similarly to lesions of the frontal cortex, tend to lead to extraverted behavior, led Gray to the following conclusions: (a) Introverts are more susceptible to punishment and nonrewards than are extraverts, whereas extraverts are more sensitive to rewards and nonpunishment; and (b) neuroticism is a dimension which may be characterized in terms of general sensitivity to reinforcing events, both rewards and punishments; neurotics, in comparison with emotionally stable individuals, are characterized by increased sensitivity to rewards and punishments.

   The critical approach to extraversion and neuroticism, and studies on the biological mechanisms of anxiety in rats, including his own findings, allowed Gray to conclude that extraversion and neuroticism are secondary traits emerging from a combination (interaction) of two basic temperament traits—anxiety and impulsivity—as illustrated in Figure 3.4. These two traits, orthogonally related, are a result of a 45° rotation of Eysenck's neuroticism and extraversion.

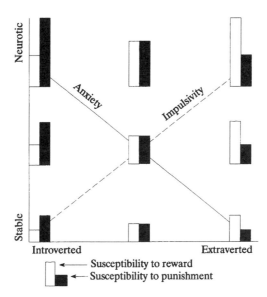

FIGURE 3.4. Relation between sensitivity to stimuli associated with reward (impulsivity) and with punishment (anxiety), neuroticism and introversion–extraversion. *Note.* From "The Neuropsychology of Temperament," by J. A. Gray. In J. Strelau and A. Angleitner (Eds.), *Explorations in Temperament: International Perspectives on Theory and Measurement* (1991, p. 124). Copyright 1991 by Plenum Press. Reprinted with permission.

Influenced by N. E. Miller's (1951), Amsel's (1962), and Mowrer's (1960) animal learning theories which postulate that emotions consist of states elicited by stimuli having the capacity to act as reinforcers for instrumental behavior, Gray developed two assumptions which guided his studies on temperament, and postulated

> (1) that temperament reflects individual differences in predispositions towards particular kinds of emotions and (2) that emotions are states of the CNS elicited by reinforcing events. . . . Reinforcer is any stimulus (or more complex event) which, if made contingent upon a response, alters the future probability of emission of that response. (Gray, 1991, pp. 106–107)

Anxiety as a trait is mediated by sensitivity to signals of punishment, nonreward, and novelty. High sensitivity determines a high level of anxiety (see Figure 3.4). Individual differences in impulsivity depend on sensitivity to signals of reward and nonpunishment. The higher the sensitivity to these signals, the higher the impulsivity (Gray, 1981).

Taking this model as a point of departure, extraversion may be characterized as being composed of low anxiety and high impulsivity, whereas neuroticism is a combination of high anxiety and high impulsivity (see Figure 3.4). In other words, extraverts are characterized by high sensitivity to signals of rewards and low sensitivity to signals of punishment, whereas introverts are more sensitive to punishment than to reward. As regards neurotics, effects of all reinforcing stimuli (punishment and reward) are amplified. Figure 3.4 illustrates also that neurotics differ from emotionally stable individuals in that they are more susceptible to both kinds of conditioned stimuli (punishment and reward) than are emotionally stable individuals.

In his recent publications, Gray (1991) postulated further the existence of a third basic temperament trait which may be called defensiveness. This trait is expressed in defensive aggression or escape bahavior. As opposed to anxiety and impulsivity, which are mediated by sensitivity to conditioned reinforcers, defensiveness is determined by susceptibility to unconditioned aversive stimuli.

Susceptibility of the BIS, BAS, and F/FLS as Biological Bases of Temperament Traits

Gray's most significant contribution to research on temperament consists in his development of empirically grounded hypotheses regarding the biological mechanisms mediating temperament characteristics. As mentioned in the preceding citation, emotions, to which temperament refers, are states of the CNS. By the abbreviation CNS Gray (1987, 1991) intended to underline that in his physiological studies on temperament he is referring to the "central nervous system" as well as to the "conceptual nervous system," for both of which this abbreviation holds.

Gray hypothesized that in the brain there are three distinguishable systems for the control of emotional behavior, composed of specific structures and functions that constitute the neurological basis for the three temperament dimensions, each of these dimensions "corresponding to individual differences in the sensitivity or reactivity of one emotion system" (Gray, 1987, p. 494). I limit the present account to more general issues concerning the physiological mechanisms underlying the three basic emotions and the corresponding emotion-traits. The details which refer to neurophysiological, biochemical, and pharmacological data may be found in Gray's (1982a, 1982b, 1991; Gray, Owen, Davis, & Tsaltas, 1983; Gray, Feldon, Rawlins, Hemsley, & Smith, 1991) publications.

The Behavioral Inhibition System. Sensitivity to signals of punishment, nonreward, and novel stimuli, as well as reactions to these stimuli (behavioral inhibition, increment in arousal, and increased attention) regarded as expressions of anxiety, are mediated by the Behavioral Inhibition System (BIS). The core structure for BIS is the septohippocampal system which comprises the following three basic neural structures: the hippocampal formation, the septal area, and the Papez circuit.[1] BIS activity is accompanied by a subjective state identified as anxiety.

---

[1]Some details regarding the anatomy, physiology, and biochemistry of the central nervous system are presented in Chapter 4.

This is "a state in which one responds to threat (stimuli associated with punishment or nonreward) or uncertainty (novelty) with the reaction, 'stop, look, and listen, and get ready for action'" (Gray, 1991, p. 110). Reactivity (susceptibility) of the operating parameters of BIS (e.g., thresholds, ease of excitation, speed of operation) determines individual differences in anxiety as a trait (Gray, 1983).

BIS should be regarded as a unified system that may be identified by means of pharmacological treatment. The administration of drugs, such as alcohol, barbiturates, and benzodiazepines, on the one hand, causes a decrease in the susceptibility of the BIS and, on the other, reduces anxiety (Gray, 1982a, 1982b). In turn, ascending monoaminergic pathways (both noradrenergic and serotonergic) originating in the brain stem have a boosting effect on the activity of the septohippocampal system. These pathways are activated in stress-inducing situations, especially those which are of biological significance (Gray, 1983).

The Behavioral Approach (Activation) System. Much less elaborated are the physiological and neuroanatomical bases for impulsivity which Gray identified with reactivity of the Behavioral Approach System (BAS), often termed also the Behavioral Activation System (Fowles, 1980). Recently Gray (1991), in discussing the temperament dimension corresponding to BAS, hypothesized that high sensitivity (reactivity) of BAS may be associated with behavior motivated by positive reinforcement, thus related to positive emotionality which comprises such emotions as hope, happiness, and elation.

The neurological structure of BAS consists of the following hypothesized key components: basal ganglia, dopaminergic fibers ascending from the mesencephalon, thalamic nuclei, and neocortical areas (motor, sensorimotor, and prefrontal cortex), all of them interacting with each other. They constitute two motor systems: the caudate motor system and the accumbens motor system. The function of the caudate motor system is to encode the relationships between input (signals of reward and nonpunishment) and output (responses) in a goal-directed motor program. The accumbens motor system is responsible for switching between the consecutive steps in the motor program (Gray, 1991; Gray *et al.,* 1991). The motor program is guided by the projection to nucleus accumbens from the amygdala. The BAS closely interacts with the BIS in that the septohippocampal system controls the matches between the actual outcome and expected outcome of a particular motor step.

Release of dopamine from the terminals of neurons whose cell bodies are in the ventral tegmental area, and especially in the nucleus accumbens, activates the BAS. As a consequence, dopamine release elicits approach behavior similar to that which occurs as a response to positive reinforcers such as food, a sexually receptive partner, and chemically diverse drugs such as amphetamines, nicotine, alcohol, heroin, and cocaine (Gray, 1991; Gray *et al.,* 1991).

The Fight/Flight System. As already mentioned, Gray (1987, 1991) in his recent publications distinguished a third system for the control of emotional behavior: the Fight/Flight System (F/FLS). Reactivity of F/FLS determines individual differences in defensiveness, a basic temperament trait that may be identified in human beings as anger.

F/FLS responds to unconditioned aversive stimuli with unconditioned defensive aggression or escape behavior. There are three major neural structures of which F/FLS is composed: amygdala, medial hypothalamus, and central gray. The septohippocampal system, through its connections with the medial hypothalamus, influences the functioning of F/FLS. The medial hypothalamus inhibits the final output pathway in the central gray; the amygdala inhibits the medial hypothalamus (Gray, 1991). Some authors (e.g. Adams, 1979; Panksepp, 1982) made detailed analyses of the anatomy involved in the F/FLS.

As can be seen from this short presentation of the neuropsychological basis of temperament dimensions, "much of the above analysis is inevitably speculative" (Gray, 1991, p. 113). The hypothetical constructs of BIS, BAS, and F/FLS, although referring to structures and functions of the central nervous system, are themselves conceptual nervous system concepts.

Psychometric Attempts to Measure Temperament Traits Elicited on the Basis of BIS, BAS, and F/FLS Constructs

Starting from the assumption that the three neuropsychological systems responsible for the control of emotional behavior make it possible to predict the structure of temperament, G. D. Wilson, Barrett, and Gray (1989) constructed an inventory directly related to the inputs and outputs of BIS, BAS and F/FLS. This inventory, known as the Gray–Wilson Personality Questionnaire (GWPQ), consists of the following six scales: (1) Approach and (2) Active Avoidance which are deduced from the BAS construct, (3) Passive Avoidance and (4) Extinction which are supposed to refer to BIS, (5) Flight and (6) Fight which are related to F/FLS. The GWPQ is composed of 120 well-balanced items, 20 for each scale. A study conducted on 243 adult men and women has given reliability scores varying from .35 (Active Avoidance in women) to .71 (Approach in men, and Fight and Flight in women), which should be considered unsatisfactory. Most important, however, is the fact that the intercorrelations of the six scales did not correspond with the predictions of Gray's theory. For example, approach and active avoidance should correlate positively, but the results were just the opposite. Also, Fight and Flight, having the same neurological basis, were expected to correlate positively but the results obtained in this study did not confirm this assumption. From their data the authors concluded that "these results present a difficulty for Gray's theory of personality as applied to human subjects" (Wilson *et al.,* 1989, p. 513). Sosnowski and Bialski (1992) also failed in a questionnaire investigation of Gray's three-dimensional theory. A correlational and factor analysis of items from the six scales of which their inventory was constructed supported the existence of two orthogonal factors, similar to impulsivity and anxiety. S. A. Ball and Zuckerman (1990) were more successful in developing a two-factor scale based on Gray's theory. Their Generalized Reward and Punishment Expectancy scales (GRAPES) showed reasonable convergent validity when related to the SSS and EPQ-R scales.

Final Remarks

Except for the unsatisfactory GWPQ there is no reasonable diagnostic measure that enables an assessment to be made of the temperament traits that directly correspond with the three physiological systems controlling emotional behavior, as postulated by Gray. Among the most popular diagnostic instruments aimed at measuring the BIS and BAS constructs are EPQ-R, the State-Trait Anxiety Inventory (STAI; Spielberger, Gorsuch, & Lushen, 1970) and Cloninger's Tridimentional Personality Questionnaire (TPQ; Cloninger, Svrakic, & Przybeck, 1991). This has been demonstrated in several publications (see, e.g. Boddy, Carver, & Rowley, 1986; Derryberry, 1987; Gray *et al.*, 1991; MacAndrew & Steele, 1991).

Pickering (1997) reviewed his own studies in which the aforementioned inventories as well as some other psychometric instruments suggesting associations with BIS and BAS were applied. He arrived at a conclusion that the findings regarding links between BIS and BAS and other temperament dimensions which are supposed to be related to these constructs are contradictory.

Comparing Gray's theory with his own, Eysenck concluded that, in fact, they are very similar. One of the main differences lies in their different predictions. Whereas Eysenck's theory predicts superior conditioning in introverts when appetitive (rewarding) unconditioned stimuli are used, Gray expects extraverts to be more susceptible to rewards, thus more efficient in conditioning (H. J. Eysenck & Eysenck, 1985). These differences derive from different physiological interpretations postulated by the two authors. A vigorous critique of Gray's theory from an Eysenckian point of view was made by Robinson (1986) who came to the extreme conclusion that "Gray's theory is really not much more than a theory of anxiety. So much so that it can barely claim to be a theory of personality at all; let alone one that might replace the Eysenckian paradigm" (p. 467).

If we look at Gray's neuropsychological model of temperament from the standpoint of human temperament, we need to bear in mind that this model was developed on the basis of animal studies, centered mainly on the physiological bases of rat anxiety (Gray, 1978, 1982a, 1982b). The failure to develop a psychometric measure of human temperamental traits based on Gray's animal learning paradigms exemplifies the difficulties and problems in making human–animal analogies or comparisons in this domain of study (see Gray, 1973; Robinson, 1986). This does not deny the fact that Gray's extensive studies on the biological basis of temperament in animals are of great importance for an understanding of the neurophysiological backgrounds of human temperament (see, e.g., Cloninger, 1986; H. J. Eysenck & Eysenck, 1985; Rothbart, 1989a; Zuckerman, 1991c).

Zuckerman (1991c), in his biological interpretation of a variety of biologically based personality dimensions, has most convincingly shown how useful Gray's neuropsychological model of temperament is for bringing us closer to an understanding of the nature of temperament. Zuckerman's main criticism of Gray's theory was also directed toward the rat bias in his approach to temperament, in which behavior was limited mainly to habituation, conditioning, and reinforced instrumental learning. The spectrum of the human personality expressed in social behavior is different from animal behavior in its variety and content. To take physiological mechanisms as a starting point in studying temperament dimensions leads to a "bottom-up" approach. This approach, which Gray represents, is based on the assumption that temperament dimensions and specific neurological and neurotransmitter systems are isomorphic (Zuckerman, 1991c, 1992). There is, however, no empirical evidence for temperament–biology isomorphism.

Several authors aim their criticism at the biological model underlying temperament traits. A detailed critique of this model was presented in an Open Peer Commentary to Gray's 1982b paper. This critique shows that experts who study the anatomical, physiological, and biochemical basis of anxiety, although recognizing Gray's major contribution to this field of study, are far from agreement (expressed even in contradictory statements) regarding the answer to the question: "What are the neuropsychological bases of anxiety?"

Gray's neuropsychological approach to temperament, which to my knowledge is the approach most deeply rooted in experimental data and in the neurological sciences and biochemistry, exemplifies, better than any other temperament theory, how far we still are from answering the question posed in the preceding paragraph.

The Biological Theory of Sensation Seeking Developed by Zuckerman

Marvin Zuckerman is one of the very few differential psychologists who have been able to develop a theory of a temperament dimension, one which skillfully combines the correlational with the experimental approach, studies on humans with research on animals, and behavior characteristics with biochemical and psychophysiological measures. This multidirectional approach made it possible for the author to develop a causal theory of individual differences in sensation seeking. In terms of the criteria presented in Table 3.1, the sensation seeking theory represents a monodimensional approach that developed in studies conducted on adults (and on animals). This theory has been presented by Zuckerman in scores of publications, some of which contain a general and comprehensive review (Zuckerman, 1979, 1984c, 1994). Recently Zuckerman's research interests have been concentrated on the Big Five issue. Taking part in the discussion regarding the number and nature of basic personality factors Zuckerman (1992; Zuckerman, Kuhlman, Joireman, Teta, & Kraft, 1993) arrived at a solution that proposed the following five factors: impulsive sensation seeking, neuroticism-anxiety, aggression-hostility, activity, and sociability. Together with coworkers (Zuckerman, Kuhlman, Teta, Joireman, & Carroccia, 1992) he developed an inventory aimed at measuring these constructions. For reasons given in chapters 1 and 2 I am not presenting Zuckeramn's contribution to the Big Five issue.

Theoretical Background

Zuckerman, working in the 1950s as a clinical psychologist, became sensitive to individual differences in human behavior. His clinical experience led him to construct an adjective checklist for measuring state and trait anxiety (Zuckerman, 1960).

In the initial stage of his research career Zuckerman (1969) was involved in studies on sensory deprivation. He paid attention to the fact that individuals behave differently under such circumstances. Some are resistant to sensory deprivation, while others react in a way that suggests that perceptual isolation is for them a stress situation (Zuckerman, 1964). To grasp the individual differences in the need for stimulation, Zuckerman, Kolin, Price, and Zoob (1964) developed a sensation seeking scale, the first of consecutive versions of this inventory constructed by Zuckerman.

The concept of optimal level of arousal, developed by Hebb (1955) from studies on sensory deprivation, became one of the crucial constructs that Zuckerman incorporated into his theory of sensation seeking. Of special importance for the application of the concept of arousal to the study of individual differences, and for a biological interpretation of the sensation-seeking trait, was Zuckerman's close contact with Eysenck and Gray. Eysenck's personality (temperament) theory, especially the biological basis of extraversion, as well as Gray's neuropsychological model of reward and punishment systems underlying individual differences in anxiety and impulsivity, were influential in molding Zuckerman's theory of sensation seeking.

The contemporary tendency to concentrate on neurotransmitters in the explanation of excitatory and inhibitory functions of brain activity present in Gray's theory, but also strongly advocated by others, especially in studies on reward pathways by Stein (1974, 1983), together with Zuckerman's educational background in biochemistry, contributed to the extension of the biological interpretation of the sensation seeking trait. Zuckerman devoted much attention to the biochemical correlates, especially to the brain monoamine systems, in determining individual differences in sensation seeking (Zuckerman, 1987a, 1994).

The Concept and Structure of Sensation Seeking

Zuckerman's research on sensation seeking from the beginning of the 1960s has undergone several changes. Zuckerman's interest in the sensation seeking phenomenon stems from studies on sensory deprivation conducted by the McGill School in the 1950–1960s (Hebb, 1955; Zubek, 1969) and by Zuckerman (1969) himself. Records taken during deprivation have shown that individuals behave, and react physiologically, in different ways to prolonged sensory deprivation. Taking into account this observation and the classic conceptualizations on motivation, such as instincts, drives, and needs (Hull, 1952; McDougall, 1923; G. Murphy, 1947), as well as a variety of arousal theories (e.g., Berlyne, 1960; Hebb, 1955; Fiske & Maddi, 1961; Leuba, 1955), Zuckerman introduced in the early 1960s the concept of sensation seeking understood as a "simple sensory need based on the optimal level of stimulation" (1979, pp. 98). Individual differences in the need for external stimulation permit predictions of stress reaction to sensory deprivation. Sensation seeking was considered by Zuckerman as a general factor, and the Sensation Seeking Scale–Form I was used for measuring this trait (Zuckerman *et al.,* 1964).

An essential step in the construction of the sensation seeking theory consisted in formulating ten postulates (Zuckerman, 1969); the most important of these refers to individual differences. It states that, for such behaviors as cognitive and motor activity as well as for experiencing a positive emotional state there are individual specific optimal levels of stimulation and arousal. The optimal level of stimulation varies depending on such factors as age, learning experience, recent levels of stimulation, task demands, diurnal cycle, and, most important, the individual's constitutional characteristics. These characteristics, responsible for more or less stable individual differences in sensation seeking, comprise such components as reactivity of the CNS and ANS to specific classes of stimulation and strength of excitatory and inhibitory centers in the CNS.

Extensive psychometric studies conducted by Zuckerman in the 1970s led to the development of inventories for the assessment of the sensation seeking trait. But their main contribution was to the development of the sensation seeking construct. According to Zuckerman (1979): "Sensation seeking is a trait defined by the need for varied, novel, and complex sensations and experiences and the willingness to take physical and social risks for the sake of such experience" (p. 10). This definition, only slightly modified in recent publications (Zuckerman, 1994), emphasizes that it is not the physical value of stimuli that is the source of stimulation but their meaning, which varies depending on individual-specific experience.

It has also been shown that sensation seeking is not an undifferentiated, general factor, but has a structure composed of the following four subfactors: thrill and adventure seeking, experience seeking, disinhibition, and boredom susceptibility (see Zuckerman, 1979, 1984c, 1994).

Thrill and Adventure Seeking (TAS) is a trait that refers to the interest or desire to engage in outdoor, physical risk-taking activities and exciting sports, such as skiing, parachuting, and fast driving.

Experience Seeking (ES) is characterized by "seeking of arousal through the mind and senses through a nonconforming life-style" (Zuckerman, 1979, p. 102), such as unplanned traveling, associating with unusual types of persons, and an inclination to drug-taking.

Disinhibition (Dis), which has the strongest biological background, is a trait expressed in the tendency toward seeking release and social disinhibition through drinking, sex, gambling, partying, and so forth. It applies to activities performed in the hedonistic pursuit of pleasure.

Boredom Susceptibility (BS) reflects aversion for repetitive experience, routine work, and boring people, and is expressed in restlessness in an invariable environment.

Zuckerman's view on the nature and structure of the sensation seeking construct has remained constant. What has changed over his many years of study is the biological interpretation of the sensation seeking trait.

The Biology of Sensation Seeking

Under the influence of Eysenck's biological interpretation of extraversion, Zuckerman (1974; Zuckerman, Murtaugh, & Siegel, 1974) formulated a hypothesis according to which the cortico-reticular feedback arousal system is responsible for individual differences in sensation seeking. Individuals differ in the need for optimal stimulation. Sensation seekers need high stimulation for maintaining the optimal level of arousal whereas sensation avoiders need low stimulation for maintaining the same level of arousal.

Standard measures accepted as indices of arousal, such as amplitude (intensity) characteristics and orienting reflexes (ORs) expressed in electrodermal and cardiovascular activity as well as the augmenting–reducing phenomenon in the domain of evoked potentials (EPs)[2] were used by Zuckerman (1979, 1983a, 1984b, 1984c, 1990; Zuckerman, Buchsbaum, & Murphy, 1980) as basic markers of the sensation seeking trait.

According to Zuckerman, data seem to support the hypothesis that high sensation seekers characterized by a need for novel sensations have a stronger OR as compared with low sensation seekers. Experiments in which EP amplitudes were used as physiological correlates of sensation seeking refer to the relationship between the level of cortical arousal and the intensity of stimulation. These studies

---

[2]Studies on electrodermal and cardiovascular activity and EP measures related to temperament, including the sensation seeking dimension, are presented in detail in Chapter 4.

have mostly shown that, in high sensation seekers, increases in intensity of stimuli go together with increases of EP amplitude (augmenting phenomenon). In low sensation seekers the opposite phenomenon occurs: increases in stimulus intensity, particularly at high intensities, cause a decrease in EP amplitudes, a reducing phenomenon explained by the Pavlovian construct of protective inhibition (see Chapter 1).

Under the influence of his own findings as well as of those reported in the literature regarding the biochemical correlates of sensation seeking behavior in man and animals, Zuckerman (1991a, 1991c) modified his view on the biological bases of the sensation seeking trait. An experiment conducted by Carrol, Zuckerman, and Vogel (1982) showed that high and low sensation seekers did not report different feelings and did not show differences in behavioral efficiency in performance tests under depressant (diazepam) and stimulant (D-amphetamine) drugs, as predicted by the optimal level of arousal theory. Both high and low sensation seekers reported positive feelings and functioned best after administration of amphetamine, that is, with a higher level of arousal.

Many studies, mainly on animals, have shown the importance of the limbic system and the monoamine neurotransmitters[3] which mediate the reward mechanism underlying the approach behaviors that can be identified as sensation seeking (Gray, 1973; Olds & Olds, 1965; Schneirla, 1965; Stein, 1974, 1983). Influenced by these studies, Zuckerman (1979) put forward the following hypothesis:

> Sensation-seeking trait is in some part a function of the levels of the catecholamines norepinephrine and dopamine in the reward areas of the limbic system, as well as the neuroregulators that control their availability at the synapses within these neural systems. (p. 372)

Studies by Zuckerman and others (see Chapter 4) in which platelet MAO activity was related to sensation seeking have shown that, in general, sensation seeking is negatively correlated with platelet MAO activity. The relationship between MAO activity and sensation seeking is explained by the fact that limbic DA sensitizes exploratory tendencies and behavioral activity. High levels of MAO activity serve the function of degrading dopamine, thus decreasing the sensation seeking tendency (Zuckerman, 1983a, 1983b, 1984c, 1994).

Psychometric studies on sensation seeking have shown that this temperament trait is higher in males than in females, and decreases with age. This suggested that sensation seeking is related to gonadal hormones. Studies by Daitzman and Zuckerman (1980, see also Zuckerman, 1984c, 1991c) pointed out that individuals who score high on the Disinhibition scale (high disinhibitors) are higher than low disinhibitors on testosterone, estrone and estriadol. Thus, besides physiological and

---

[3]The biochemical correlates of temperament, especially the monoaminergic neurotransmitters, serotonine, norepinephrine (NE), and dopamine (DA) and the enzyme that inactivates these neurotransmitters—monoamine oxidase (MAO)—are discussed in detail in Chapter 4.

neurochemical correlates, hormonal markers of the sensation seeking traits were also found by Zuckerman and his coworkers.

Since sensation seeking has an evident biological basis, it is logical to expect that the biological endowment has a genetic origin. If so, heredity plays an important role in determining individual differences in sensation seeking. Only a few behavior-genetic studies have been hitherto conducted. Some of them have shown that heritability of the sensation seeking trait is about $h^2 = .60$ (H. J. Eysenck, 1983a; Fulker, Eysenck, & Zuckerman, 1980; Koopmans, Boomsma, Heath, & van Dornen, 1995) which is one of the highest scores among temperament dimensions. As reported by Zuckerman (personal communication, June 1994) an unpublished study by Lykken and coworkers shows the same results for twins separated during their formative years and raised in different families.

To summarize, the range of physiological and biochemical correlates of sensation seeking is very broad. If we add the studies regarding heritability of this temperament trait, it follows that the biological model for sensation seeking, merely outlined here, is a highly complex one, as illustrated in Figure 3.5.

The Psychometric Measures of Sensation Seeking

As already mentioned, the first attempt to measure individual differences in the sensation-seeking tendency was made by Zuckerman in studies on deprivation,

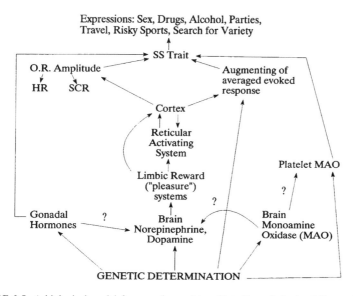

FIGURE 3.5. A biological model for sensation seeking. *Note.* From *Behavioral Expressions and Biosocial Bases of Sensation Seeking* (p. 24), by M. Zuckerman, 1994, New York: Cambridge University Press. Copyright 1994 by Cambridge University Press. Reprinted with permission.

which resulted in the development of the first form of the Sensation Seeking Scale (SSS–Form I; Zuckerman *et al.*, 1964). This 50-item scale was expected to measure sensation seeking as a general factor, understood as a simple sensory need based on the optimal level of stimulation (Zuckerman, 1979, p. 98). Since then, the Sensation Seeking Scale has undergone several changes and, altogether, six forms have been developed by Zuckerman.

Form II of the Sensation Seeking Scale consisted of a reduced number of items (34), of which 22 composed the General sensation seeking scale and 12 referred to gender-specific behavior characteristics.

Taking as a starting point 50 items from the SSS–Form I and 63 new items, Zuckerman (1971) constructed the SSS–Form III, which made it possible to grasp the specific components of the sensation seeking trait. Factor analysis of the items resulted in the construction of scales which remained in the two consecutive forms of the SSSs—Thrill and Adventure Seeking, Experience Seeking, Disinhibition, and Boredom Susceptibility, the last scale more typical for men than for women. The factor structure which consists of the four sensation seeking traits has been replicated in many countries (Zuckerman, 1994).

Forms IV and V of the SSS gained their greatest popularity among sensation seeking researchers. SSS–Form IV consists of 72 items. It includes the General scale from Form II and four factor scales which developed from work with the SSS–Form III. On the basis of an extensive investigation conducted on American and English male and female samples, the number of items for each of the four scales—TAS, ES, Dis, and BS, was reduced to 10, resulting in a 40-item questionnaire known as the SSS–Form V (Zuckerman, Eysenck, & Eysenck, 1978). As distinct from SSS–Form IV, Form V does not have a separate sensation seeking general scale. Sensation seeking as a general factor (tendency) may be measured by taking into account the total score from the four subscale scores (from all 40 items).

For all five forms of the SSS, forced-choice items were constructed so that one item represents one pole of the sensation seeking tendency and the other the opposite pole, as for example:

A: I have tried marijuana or would like to (+ES).
B: I would never smoke marijuana (–ES).

Zuckerman (1979) presents the details regarding the psychometric characteristics of the Sensation Seeking Scales Forms IV and V. Alpha Cronbach correlations for the TAS scale vary between .77 and .88 and for ES and Dis between .61 and .85. Unsatisfactory reliability scores, ranging from .38 to .66, were obtained for the Boredom Susceptibility scale.

In the 1980s, Zuckerman (1984a) developed the SSS Form VI, but it did not gain much popularity. This scale is constructed around the distinction between sensation seeking items which refer, on the one hand, to past experiences of the reporting person, and, on the other, to desired or intended future experiences. Since the TAS scale and the Dis scale are more orthogonal to each other than the remaining scales, the SSS–Form VI refers only to these two subtraits. In consequence, Zuckerman developed the following four scales: Experience-TAS, Intention-TAS, Experience-Dis, and Intention-Dis. The SSS-VI comprises 128 items with three response options for each item.

The Behavioral Correlates of the Sensation Seeking Trait

Several studies have been carried out in which sensation seeking, as measured by means of the SSSs (Forms IV and V), was related to different risk-taking activities and to behavior in situations differing in stimulative value. Further, the relationship between sensation seeking and different kinds of behavior disorders (e.g., drug use, delinquency, criminal behavior, pathology) was frequently investigated. The results reported by Zuckerman and his coworkers, as well as by researchers from other laboratories, have been summarized by Zuckerman in several monographs (1979, 1984c, 1994).

As suggested by the definition of sensation seeking, the majority of findings support the assumption that sensation seekers prefer activities and situations that are novel, rich in stimulation, or both, which require risky behavior or which satisfy hedonistic needs, regardless of whether these activities are socially accepted or whether they represent normal or abnormal behavior, including pathology. For example, there is evidence that among sensation seekers there are significantly more alcoholics, drug abusers, criminals, psychopaths, and delinquents than among sensation avoiders (Zuckerman, 1979, 1984c, 1987b, 1994). After two decades of research on the nature of sensation seeking Zuckerman (1994) concluded that

> [t]he only thing constant in the life of high sensation seekers is change. They change activities, sexual and marital partners, and drugs, just as they switch from one channel to another if compelled to watch television for any length of time. (p. 374)

The need for change seems to be the most typical behavior characteristic for a sensation seeker.

To explain the relationship between the sensation seeking trait and behavioral expressions of sensation seeking, Zuckerman refers to the concept of optimal level of arousal. In contrast to his former view adapted from H. J. Eysenck (1967) according to which the cortico-reticular loop was responsible for regulating the level of arousal, Zuckerman developed a biochemical theory of arousal. This theory is based on the concept of optimal level of the catecholamine systems activity (Zuckerman, 1984c, 1987a, 1994). The catecholamines, dopamine and norepinephrine, are regarded as activating systems (see Chapter 4).

> The general term *catecholamine systems activity* (CSA) is used to summarize the net effect of production, rate of release, metabolism, disposal, and receipt sensitivity on the general level of activity in these systems. . . . Adaptability in general

is postulated to be a function of CSA activity, neuroregulators such as MAO, and neurotransmitters such as serotonin and endorphins that generally seem to regulate actions of the catecholamines. There is a tonic level of CSA . . . that is *adaptively optimal* [emphasis added] for mood (positive hedonic tone), general activity, and social interaction. (Zuckerman, 1984c, p. 431)

As illustrated in Figure 3.6, there is an inverted U relationship between adaptability and the activity of the catecholamine system. From the point of view of adaptation, expressed by mood, activity, social interaction, and clinical condition, an average level of CSA (point C in Fig. 3.6) is optimal. At both extremes of CSA levels (points A and E, F) a low level of adaptability occurs, which is expressed by behavior disorders and negative mood, such as anxiety or panic.

The sensation seeking tendency, expressed in the need for intense and novel stimuli, in engagement in risky and fear-provoking activities, and in inclination to drugs, may be explained by the chronically low level of CSA typical for high sensation seekers who tend to search for stimuli and to perform activities that increase the tonic level of CSA. The opposite tendency occurs in sensation avoiders who, because of their chronically high level of CSA, tend to behave in a way that leads to a decrease of the tonic level of CSA.

Final Remarks

Among contemporary temperament theories the sensation seeking conceptualization belongs to those with well-established traditions. The intensive and extensive studies of Zuckerman and his coworkers over two decades have yielded a large amount of evidence in favor of his ideas and hypotheses. His theory, which exemplifies a complex and interdisciplinary approach to the sensation seeking ten-

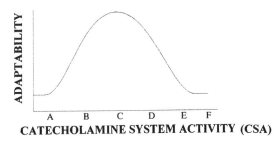

CATECHOLAMINE SYSTEM ACTIVITY (CSA)

MOOD	1. Depression 2. Anxiety	Boredom, Apathy	Positive Feelings	Euphoria	1. Anxiety 2. Depression	Panic
ACTIVITY	Minimal	Limited	Active	Hyperactive	Aimless Limited	Stereotyped
SOCIAL INTERACTION	Withdrawn or Hostile	Introverted (state)	Sociable	Hypersociable	Unsociable	Agressive-Hostile, Interactive
CLINICAL CONDITIONS	Major Depression	Normal	Normal	Cyclothymic, Hypomanic	Anxiety Disorder	Paranoid Disorder

FIGURE 3.6. A model for the relationships of mood, activity, social interaction, and clinical conditions to catecholamine system activity (CSA). *Note.* From "Sensation Seeking: A Comparative Approach to a Human Trait," by M. Zuckerman, 1984, *Behavioral and Brain Sciences, 7,* p. 431. Copyright 1984 by Cambridge University Press. Reprinted with permission.

dency, has gained considerable popularity among differential psychologists. The data collected by Zuckerman and others, however, include some results that are not compatible with the expectations postulated by the theory. Furthermore, the theory is ambitious and has some shortcomings. The most extensive critique of Zuckerman's sensation seeking approach was presented in his target article: "Sensation Seeking: A Comparative Approach to a Human Trait" (Zuckerman, 1984c). I refer first to those comments on which some reviewers agree.

Zuckerman's sensation seeking model does not offer a specific sensation seeking profile of physiological and biochemical markers. These biological correlates may also be found for such traits as extraversion or impulsivity (Barratt; Neufeld; Panksepp, & Siviy; Stelmack—in Zuckerman, 1984c).

The global treatment of catecholamines, as expressed in the CSA concept, does not have empirical support. Data regarding the relationship catecholamines–sensation seeking are contradictory. Further, neurotransmitters, depending on their location and concentration, and on the interaction with other neurotransmitters and hormones, have a variety of different functions unaccounted for by Zuckerman's CSA construct (Von Knorring; Mason; Redmond—in Zuckerman, 1984c).

The sensation seeking model underestimates the role of environment, especially the social context, in determining the specific aspects of sensation seeking as expressed in the four sensation seeking traits—TAS, ES, Dis, and BS. For these components of sensation seeking as well, no specific physiological or biochemical markers have been postulated by Zuckerman (Baldwin; Strelau—in Zuckerman, 1984c).

Questions passed over by the reviewers of the target article refer to the sensation seeking scales and to the population on which these scales have been used. A careful reader of Zuckerman's publications will easily conclude that most of his work has been conducted on students. His findings have therefore a kind of academic bias, and may not apply to populations that extend beyond the university sphere. It must be added, however, that data collected by others on nonstudent populations are consistent with Zuckerman's (1994) findings.

Among the many personality and temperament questionnaires known to me, the sensation seeking scales are the most culturally biased. Many items refer to behaviors (e.g., I have tried marijuana), situations (e.g., "wild" uninhibited parties), attitudes (e.g., I dislike "swingers"), and activities (e.g., parachute jumping) unknown or rarely met in other cultures, and, even when known, hardly ever experienced by the subjects under study. These features of the SS scales render it difficult to adapt the SS inventories to other countries or languages (see Andresen, 1986; Oleszkiewicz, 1982).

Over the past few years much of Zuckerman's research has been devoted to the structure of so-called basic personality dimensions (see Chapter 1). Among these, a particular kind of sensation seeking—Impulsive Unsocialized Sensation Seeking (P-ImpUSS)—constitutes one of the five postulated factors (Zuckerman, 1993; Zuckerman, Kuhlman, Thornquist, & Kiers, 1991). Logically and linguistically the phrase "impulsive unsocialized sensation seeking" suggests that this general factor covers only a part of the sensation seeking trait, and thus should be regarded as an additional component of TAS, ES, Dis, and BS. This, however, is contrary to Zuckerman's view according to which the abbreviation P-ImpUSS means a factor composed of impulsivity, socialization, and sensation seeking with "psychopathy" as the extreme, clinical, manifestation.

Rusalov's Theory of Temperament Based on a Functional Systems Approach

In the 1960s Rusalov, originally an anthropologist, joined the Teplov–Nebylitsyn group which consisted of about a dozen researchers, among them Borisova, Golubeva, Gurevich, Leites, Ravich-Shcherbo, and Rozhdestvenskaya (for detail, see Strelau, 1983). All of them were involved in studying different aspects of CNS properties, thus contributing basically to the development of Teplov and Nebylitsyn's neo-Pavlovian theory. In the 1980s Rusalov introduced some new ideas to the neo-Pavlovian approach, resulting in the development of an original, albeit speculative, theory of temperament. In terms of the criteria depicted in Table 3.1, Rusalov's theory may be regarded as centered on adults, causal, multidimensional, and oriented to whole human behavior.

Theoretical Background

Vladimir M. Rusalov's first studies in the domain of CNS properties, as understood by Teplov and Nebylitsyn (see Chapter 2), attempted to measure the lower threshold (the sensitivity pole) of strength of the nervous system as postulated by Nebylitsyn (1972a). His anthropological training influenced these studies in that he tried to relate sensory sensitivity to two body types ("fatty" and "osteomuscular"), but without much success (Rusalov, 1972). Furthermore, his attempts to measure visual, auditory, and cutaneous sensitivity showed that correlations between the separate sensory thresholds, even when statisically significant, were low or wholly lacking (Rusalov, 1967, 1972). These findings supported the conclusion that CNS properties, when measured by peripheral indices, are modality specific (the so-called partiality phenomenon).

In order to "grasp" CNS properties not influenced by peripheral phenomena, Rusalov (1974, 1979), guided by Nebylitsyn's ideas, undertook to measure the EEG components of CNS properties. These studies led him to conclude that the polarity–amplitude asymmetry of evoked potentials reflects a general brain factor which might be identified as a general CNS property.

In view of the shortage of appropriate electrophysiological equipment, and his increasing interest in the psychological aspects of human individuality, Rusalov's attention turned to theoretical issues of individual differences; this change in direction was significant for the development of his theory of temperament. Especially significant for his theory were Teplov's (1964) considerations on CNS properties and Nebylitsyn's (1976) view of the structure of temperament as composed of activity and emotionality. Also influential were Rubinstein's (1946) and Leontev's (1978) theories of activity, which regarded activity as the source of human development, as well as Merlin's (1986) theoretical considerations on individuality, in the molding of which activity plays a crucial role. These were significant landmarks for Rusalov's theory, but most important was Anokhin's (1978) physiological theory of functional systems.

Temperament as a Substructure of Human Individuality Composed of Object-Related and Social-Related Traits

According to Rusalov (1989c), temperament is one of the most important substructures of human individuality. Individuality is understood as the most general psychological concept, one that comprises individual-specific innate prerequisites, temperament, and such personality traits as abilities (intellect) and character (Rusalov, 1985, 1986). Rusalov defined temperament "as a totality of formal characteristics of behavior as distinguished from the totality of content properties constituting personality features" (Rusalov, 1989c, p. 817). Temperament is a psychobiological category, whereas personality is a sociopsychological category. A trait that fulfills the following seven criteria can be considered as belonging to the domain of temperament: (a) refers not to the content but to formal characteristics, (b) reflects the dynamic aspect of behavior, (c) is expressed in all kinds of behavior, (d) is present since childhood, (e) is stable across a long period of life, (f) has close relationship with biological systems, and (g) is inherited (Rusalov, 1985, 1986, 1989a).

In his first writings on temperament Rusalov (1982, 1985, 1986) distinguished, following Nebylitsyn (1976), two basic temperamental traits: activity and emotionality. General activity is expressed in the extent of the dynamic-energetic tension in the individual's interaction with the physical and social environment. The basic indicators of activity are tempo, rhythm, speed, intensity, plasticity, and endurance.[4] Emotionality refers to formal-dynamic characteristics which comprise sensitivity, impulsivity, and prevailing mood in terms of positive versus negative emotions (Rusalov, 1985, 1986).

Rusalov's (1979) and his coworkers' (Bodunov, 1986) studies on EEG correlates of CNS properties and their relationship to some aspects of activity, such as

---

[4]The term *indicator* used by Rusalov means in this context rather "aspect" or "component" of activity. In his criticism of Strelau for considering temporal characteristics as independent temperamental traits (which Rusalov himself also postulates in his recent theory) Rusalov (1986) regarded these characteristics as composing the syndrome of activity.

tempo, speed, and endurance, led to the conclusion that the CNS properties, as well as temperamental characteristics related to these properties, have a hierarchical structure and are a result of interacting physiological systems. The theory of functional systems as developed by Anokhin (1978) was adopted by Rusalov (1989a, 1989c) as the most adequate for interpreting the origins and nature of temperament as well as for composing the structure of temperament. Since this theory is unknown to most temperament psychologists, some basic information is needed for a better understanding of Rusalov's conceptualization. The essence of Anokhin's theory of functional systems, from the behavioral point of view, can be briefly presented in the following three postulates:

(1) Each behavior is a result of functional systems which consist of dynamic structures comprising the whole organism. By means of modification and change, these structures interact in such a way as to assure the attainment of given adaptive behavior (a useful result).

(2) The systems are hierarchically organized, which means that the results of lower-level subsystems contribute to the results of higher-level systems (from the biochemical to the behavioral level); all systems, independent of their level of organization, have the same functional architecture.

(3) The architecture of functional systems underlying behavioral acts consists of the following mutually interacting components: (a) afferent synthesis which serves to establish the result (goal) of behavior to be achieved; this is a process in which the dominant motivation and its physiological correlate (excitatory processes) plays a basic role; (b) decision making during which, from a variety of possible behavioral options, a selection is made of those enabling the result to be obtained; (c) execution of behavioral acts; and (d) acceptor of behavioral results which, on one hand, serves for programming behavior, and, on the other, evaluates behavior; evaluation consists of comparing the obtained result with the planned one by means of feedback afferentation.

Referring to Anokhin's theory, Rusalov regarded temperament as a result of "systems generalization" composed of components involved in the functional systems of behavior. An initial, genetically determined, set of systems of individual-specific biological properties, engaged in various kinds of activity, results from successive restructuralization and reorganization in the formation of a generalized system of individual behavior (temperament) of invariant properties. The nature of these qualitatively new properties is not just biological, but psychobiological. They are regarded as formal properties independent of behavioral content (Rusalov, 1989a, 1989c).

> If we accept that the formal properties of individual behavior are formed as a result of "systems generalization" of individual biological properties serving the functional state of human behavior, then, in the context of the internal four-state structure of the functional system, we can derive four fundamental parameters of formal organization of human behavior. (Rusalov, 1989c, p. 818)

The components of the architecture of functional systems, as delineated by Anokhin, led Rusalov (1989c) to distinguish the following four temperamental traits: ergonicity (endurance), plasticity, tempo (speed), and emotionality. The first three were treated as components of the most general temperamental trait: activity.

Ergonicity is derived from the width–narrowness characteristic of afferent synthesis, which applies to the excitatory processes of the CNS. Plasticity refers to Anokhin's decision-making component, in that it characterizes the ease or difficulty in switching from one decision (behavioral program) to another. Tempo as a temperament trait is associated by Rusalov with the degree of speed in realization of behavioral programs. Emotionality refers to the evaluatory aspect of the acceptor of behavioral results. It reflects the sensitivity to discrepancy between planned and realized behavior, or between input information and expectancy. As is known, this discrepancy is a source of emotional tension (Festinger, 1957; Simonov, 1984).

According to the Russian tradition in psychology, activity, understood as goal-directed behavior, is the most crucial concept in psychology. By means of activity human beings regulate their relationship with the external world—objects and persons (Rubinstein, 1946; Leontev, 1978). Guided by the idea that man's activity may be directed toward objects (things) or toward people (social world), Rusalov (1989b, 1989c) extended the structure of temperament by separating two facets of each of the four temperament traits. Thus, depending on whether a given temperament characteristic is expressed in behavior directed toward objects (things) or toward people (social interaction), Rusalov developed the following eight-dimensional structure of human temperament: object-related ergonicity (Er), social (communicative) ergonicity (SEr), object-related plasticity (P), social plasticity (SP), object-related tempo (T), social tempo (ST), object-related emotionality (Em), and social emotionality (SEm).

The Measure of Object-Related and Social Temperament Traits

In line with his theoretically postulated structure of temperament, Rusalov (1989b, 1989c) developed a questionnaire known as the Structure of Temperament Questionnaire (STQ) aimed at measuring the eight temperamental traits just mentioned. Three consecutive studies designed for constructing the STQ were conducted on student samples numbering 118 to 190 subjects of both sexes. These studies resulted in a selection of 96 items (12 for each scale) from 160 formulated at the beginning of this project. The STQ has a Yes–No format and includes as well a Lie scale adapted from the Eysenck Personality Inventory.

In constructing the STQ, Rusalov (1989b, 1989c) applied the latent-structure analysis technique which enabled him to relate the empirical data to the theoretically postulated items and scales. Those items that showed highest loadings on the so-called theoretical scale Rusalov considered as reflecting the "essence" of the scale. For a better understanding of the separate traits and scales distinguished by Rusalov the most "basic" (reference) item for each of the eight scales is given below.

- *Er*—Are you so energetic that you need the challenge of a difficult job?
- *SEr*—Are you the life of the party?
- *P*—Do you switch easily from one task to another?
- *SP*—Do you often express your first impressions without thinking them through?
- *T*—Do you prefer to work slowly?
- *ST*—Is it difficult for you to talk very quickly?
- *Em*—Do you often get excited about errors committed at work?
- *SEm*—Are you sometimes inclined to overemphasize a negative attitude that familiar persons have about you?

Reliability scores of the STQ scales obtained by Rusalov (1989b, 1989c) vary from .71 (SEm scale) to .84 (Em scale). Intercorrelations between scales have shown that object-related scales (as well as scales referring to the social domain) correlate with each other more highly than do object-related and social scales referring to the same temperament trait. A four-factor solution, preferred by Rusalov (1989c), has shown that Factor I comprises scales that refer to object-oriented activity (Er, P, T), Factor II unites the equivalent social scales of the activity components (SEr, SP, ST), Factor III consists of emotionality scales (Em, SEm), and Factor IV refers to the Lie scale. This factor solution explained 72 percent of the total phenotypic variance.

The STQ, originally constructed in the Russian language (Rusalov, 1989b), has been published in an English translation by Rusalov (1989c), and also used in English-speaking countries (D. Bishop, Jacks, & Tandy, 1993; Brebner & Stough, 1993; Stough, Brebner, & Cooper, 1991), as well as in Germany (e.g., Ruch, Angleitner, & Strelau, 1991) and Poland (Zawadzki & Strelau, in press).

Final Remarks

Only a few years have elapsed since Rusalov published his conceptualization of temperament with reference to Anokhin's theory, and the STQ has not yet been used in many studies. Accordingly, there are almost no data relating the eight temperamental traits postulated by Rusalov to behavior and performance in laboratory or field investigations. In a study conducted on 56 adults Rusalov and Parilis (1991) showed that a cognitive style characterized in terms of simplicity–complexity correlates with several STQ scales (Plasticity, Social Plasticity, and Social Emotionality). The authors interpreted these relationships as showing that temperament, a more primitive construct, constitutes the basis for the development of more complex cognitive structures of personality.

In view of the recency of Rusalov's theory, there has not been time for other authors to make critical appraisals of this conceptualization. Some comments which seem to me most important are given here.

If we consider the original Pavlovian typology, as well as Teplov's view on the CNS properties, to be rather static, it seems reasonable that Rusalov adopted Anokhin's theory regarding the dynamic interaction between the hierarchically organized functional systems as a kind of heuristic basis for his own conceptualization. However, the derivation of the four temperamental characteristics from Anokhin's theory of functional systems is not obvious. First, there is no logical reason why, for example, plasticity should be limited to the decision-making component, or tempo to the realization of behavioral programs, as postulated by Rusalov. In fact, each of the temporal sequences of a behavioral act, as proposed by Anokhin, may be characterized in terms of tempo and plasticity. Second, three among the four basic temperament dimensions—ergonicity, plasticity, and tempo—had been distinguished by Rusalov (1985) and Bodunov (1986) before Rusalov made use of Anokhin's idea regarding the components of behavioral acts.

In using the English version of the STQ we must take into account the fact that the English translation of the STQ (Rusalov, 1989c) is not the best. Several items in the English version differ from the original items of the Russian STQ. To give one example, item 67, regarded as the best reference for the Social Ergonicity scale reads in English: "Are you the life of the party?" while its Russian (original) version is as follows: "Are you relaxed in a large company?" (Russ. "Derzhites' li svobodno v bolshoi kompanii?"). No studies have been undertaken regarding the specificity of the populations and languages to which the Russian STQ is to be adapted to permit such changes. In short, the English STQ, as published by Rusalov (1989c), is not equivalent to its original Russian version (this was also the case with the STI; Strelau, 1972a).

The object-related items of the STQ refer mainly to work (see Brebner & Stough, 1993), thus limiting the area of object-related traits to very specific activity. This may be exemplified by the reference items (see the preceding discussion) of the four object-related scales. Other studies conducted using the STQ (Bodunov, 1993; Ruch et al., 1991) do not confirm Rusalov's postulate that object- and social-related temperament traits are orthogonal to each other.

Exploratory as well as confirmatory factor analyses conducted on the Polish STQ version by Zawadzki and Strelau (in press) suggest that whereas ergonicity, plasticity, and tempo can be separated as object- and social-related traits, and emotionality occurs as a common, indivisible trait. Thus Rusalov's dichotomy—toward objects and toward people—seems to be limited only to those traits which refer to the broad, Russian, construct of activity (ergonicity, plasticity, and tempo).

Rusalov's theory of temperament needs stronger empirical support in order to demonstrate its advantages over other conceptualizations on temperament. Data showing the functional significance of the object- and social-related temperament traits would be the best argument in favor of Rusalov's conceptualization. Whatever the further development of his theory, Rusalov has clearly contributed essentially to the neo-Pavlovian approach to temperament by offering a new perspective.

Strelau's Regulative Theory of Temperament

One of the few centers where research on temperament has developed under the strong influence of Pavlov's typology is the University of Warsaw. Benefiting from the Russian ideas on temperament, Strelau and his coworkers also focused almost from the start on the research and theories of temperament developing in the 1950s and 1960s in both western Europe and the United States. Due to these influences the regulative theory of temperament (RTT) is rooted in many concepts and findings. My own research of nearly 40 years which aimed at the study of different aspects of temperament had its measure of influence upon the current state of the RTT. In terms of the criteria depicted in Table 3.1, the RTT may be characterized as concentrated on adults, presenting a causal theory that postulates a multidimensional structure of temperament and is based on the assumption that temperament refers to all kinds of human behavior.

Theoretical Background

As a student I conducted a study to assess the Pavlovian properties of the nervous system by means of the CR paradigm applied to electrodermal activity (Strelau, 1960). Following further psychophysiological and psychophysical studies in the domain of EDA, EEG, and RT experimentation, I arrived at the conclusion that the Pavlovian CNS properties, as assessed by these methods, lack generality. Their assessment depends on the kind of stimuli (CS and UCS, sensory modality) and on the kind of reaction (effector) applied (Strelau, 1965, 1972b). This partiality phenomenon stimulated me to elaborate a psychological interpretation of the Pavlovian typology (Strelau, 1969, 1974). As a by-product of my failure to find general CNS properties, I developed a temperament questionnaire aimed at assessing the behavioral expressions of the Pavlovian CNS properties (Strelau, 1972b).

In 1966 I had the opportunity to work for 6 months with Vladimir Nebylitsyn and his coworkers. This experience and closer studies of Teplov's contribution to temperament broadened my view on the nature of the CNS properties. During my stay in Moscow I had several meetings with Volf Merlin, whose research on the relationship between CNS properties and style of action (Merlin, 1973) motivated me to incorporate the concept *style of action,* but with a different meaning, into the RTT.

In the same year I first met Eysenck and Gray at the International Congress of Psychology in Moscow. From that time on I developed closer contacts with both of these scholars, which significantly extended my perspectives on temperament. Under their influence I came to know the whole range of arousal theories as well as the temperament conceptualizations based on these theories, for example, Marvin Zuckerman's sensation seeking concept.

In 1971, during my first visit to the West, I had my first "lessons" in behavior genetics from the eminent behavior geneticist, Jerry Hirsch, at the University of Illinois. For a period of 8 months I studied the genetic determination of individual differences in locomotor activity in *Drosophila melanogaster*. For 3 months I attended a seminar chaired by Richard Lazarus at the University of California at Berkeley. These meetings made me aware of the important role temperament plays in functioning under stress. My 1-year stay in the United States resulted also in personal contacts with Alexander Thomas and Stella Chess. Their view on temperament, their longitudinal study, especially in respect to behavior disorders in children, and the concept of "difficult temperament" were very important for my own thinking on the functional significance of temperament. They also enabled me to participate in the Occasional Temperament Conferences. This opportunity led to a close acquaintance not only with the ideas but also with the persons in the leading group of American temperament researchers, such as Robert Plomin, Mary Rothbart, Hill Goldsmith, Jack Bates, and Ted Wachs. Their original contributions to temperament had an impact on the development of my own ideas.

From the very beginning of my research on temperament I was under the strong influence of the theory of action developed by my mentor, Tadeusz Tomaszewski (1963, 1978). His concept of activity, basically modified as compared with the theories of the Russian psychologists Rubinstein and Leontev, facilitated investigation of temperament features from the point of view of the reciprocal relations between the individual and his or her environment, where human activity plays the most important role in regulating these relations. My students and their work, especially the creative ideas and detailed studies of Andrzej Eliasz, Tatiana Klonowicz, and Jan Matysiak, also contributed to the development of the regulative theory of temperament.

As is illustrated, the RTT has many roots, sometimes even difficult to locate in a given theory or conceptualization or ascribed to a specific person.

Temperament as a Phenomenon That Refers to Formal Characteristics of Behavior

The regulative theory of temperament as formulated at the different stages of its development has been presented in several monographs and papers (see Strelau, 1983, 1985, 1989b, 1993, 1995a, 1996a; Strelau & Plomin, 1992). The history of the research and the considerations that led to the construction of RTT aside, the main idea is that temperament refers to the formal characteristics of behavior. This point was strongly expressed in a paper published by Strelau in 1974 under the title

"Temperament as an Expression of Energy Level and Temporal Features of Behavior." This assertion remains one of the basic assumptions of the RTT. On the energy level I distinguished reactivity and activity as the two basic temperament traits. Reactivity, which has its roots in the concept of strength of excitation (see Nebylitsyn, 1972a; Pavlov, 1951–1952; Teplov, 1964), is understood as a dimension revealed in sensitivity (sensory and emotional) at one pole, and efficiency (resistance to intensive stimulation) at the other. High-reactive individuals (the equivalent of the Pavlovian weak CNS type) may be characterized in terms of high sensitivity and low endurance, whereas low-reactive individuals (Pavlovian strong types) have a low level of sensitivity and a high level of endurance (see Figure 3.7). It was assumed, after Teplov and Nebylitsyn, that there is a more or less stable relationship between the sensitivity and endurance thresholds (Strelau, 1974, 1983).

Activity was defined as a temperament trait that refers to the frequency and intensity of actions individuals engage in. By means of activity the individual regulates the stimulative value of behavior, situations, or both in such a way as to satisfy his or her need for stimulation (Eliasz, 1981; Matysiak, 1985; Strelau, 1983). Activity "is one of the sources and regulators of arousal level. Owing to the inflow of appropriate stimuli it renders possible the maintenance of this excitation at an optimum level" (Strelau, 1974, p. 124).

The RTT has developed to a certain extent asymmetrically in respect to both aspects of the formal characteristics of behavior. Less attention has been paid to the temporal features. Of the several traits referring to this domain of temperament (speed, tempo, persistence, recurrence, regularity, and mobility) studies were con-

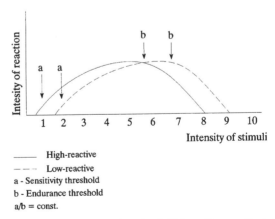

FIGURE 3.7. Model of intensity (magnitude) of reaction in high- and low-reactive individuals. *Note.* From *Temperament, Personality, Activity* (p. 178), by J. Strelau, 1983, London: Academic Press. Copyright 1983 by Academic Press. Reprinted with permission.

ducted on mobility understood as the ability to react quickly and adequately in response to environmental changes (Strelau, 1983, 1989b). The mobility of the CNS, as understood by Pavlov (1951–1952) and Teplov (1964), served as an explanatory concept for individual differences in behavioral mobility.

Under the influence of several arguments presented elsewhere (Strelau, 1993; 1995a; Strelau & Zawadzki, 1993, 1995) I revised the RTT, which is now based on several postulates leading to the following definition of temperament:

> *Temperament refers to basic, relatively stable, personality traits expressed mainly in the formal (energetic and temporal) characteristics of reactions and behavior. These traits are present from early childhood and they have their counterpart in animals. Primarily determined by inborn biological mechanisms, temperament is subject to changes caused by maturation and individual-specific genotype–environment interplay.*

After a detailed theoretical analysis of the status of temperament traits proposed by the 1983 RTT, and a thorough psychometric study conducted on more than 2,000 subjects (aged 15 to 80 years) representing both genders, Strelau and Zawadzki (1993, p. 327) described the structure of temperament by the following six traits.

1. *Briskness* (BR): tendency to react quickly, to keep a high tempo in performing activities, and to shift easily in response to changes in the surroundings from one behavior (reaction) to another.
2. *Perseveration* (PE): tendency to continue and to repeat behavior after cessation of stimuli (situations) evoking this behavior.
3. *Sensory sensitivity* (SS): ability to react to sensory stimuli of low stimulative value.
4. *Emotional reactivity* (ER): tendency to react intensively to emotion-generating stimuli, expressed in high emotional sensitivity and in low emotional endurance.
5. *Endurance* (EN): ability to react adequately in situations demanding long-lasting or high stimulative activity and under intense external stimulation.
6. *Activity* (AC): tendency to undertake behaviors of high stimulative value or to supply by means of behavior strong stimulation from the surroundings.

These traits are first-order factors and are not necessarily orthogonal to each other. It is assumed that temperament traits, as postulated by the RTT, take part in the regulation of the relationship "man–environment." The essence of regulation consists in moderating all those behaviors and situations in which the energetic aspect (e.g., intensity of stimulation, behavior under stressors, risk-taking activity) and/or the temporal component (e.g., speed of changes in the environment, tempo of consecutive reactions), play an important adaptive role (Strelau, 1996a).

The Biological Bases of the RTT Traits

As the definition of RTT says, temperamental traits are assumed to have a biological background. A study by Strelau, Oniszczenko, Zawadzki, Bodunov, and Angleitner (1995) on a Polish sample of 463 pairs of twins (250 MZ and 213 DZ pairs) aged from 16 to 63 years, in which model-fitting analyses were applied, showed that broad-sense heritability varies for the six traits as follows: briskness (.50), perseverance (.43), sensory sensitivity (.42), emotional reactivity (.34), endurance (.46), and activity (.54) (see also Strelau, 1995a). Angleitner and colleagues (1995) in a parallel study conducted on a German sample of 860 twin pairs (698 MZ and 162 DZ pairs) aged from 14 to 80 years obtained similar results.

In contrast to some arousal-oriented temperament theories, such as Eysenck's, Gray's, or Zuckerman's, the RTT does not postulate trait-specific neurophysiological or biochemical mechanisms. It is assumed that behavior, in which the energetic and temporal characteristics of temperament are expressed, is an outcome of the interaction of all the physiological and biochemical mechanisms that take part in the regulation of speed components and level of arousal. As shown in chapters 4 and 5, specific physiological and biochemical mechanisms regulate different kinds of arousal. This explains why different measures show a diversity of arousal levels. However, in real behavior, in which the motor, cognitive, and emotional components are inseparably interacting with each other, the behavioral arousal results from interaction of the specific arousal components. The same behavioral arousal may be determined by different specific physiological and biochemical kinds of arousal, and the reverse (Mason, 1984; Netter, 1991). As L. von Knorring (1984) indicated, there are at least 34 neurotransmitter systems in the CNS, and our knowledge of the complicated interactions among these systems is very meager. Thus, ascribing to the different temperament traits a biology-specific mechanism that mediates individual differences in these traits is no more than wishful thinking, although useful for generating hypotheses.

From the postulate that temperament refers to formal characteristics of behavior, one can speculate that such features as sensitivity of neuron postsynaptic receptors or their sensitivity in synaptic transmission, amount of neurotransmitters released, and reactivity of neural structures (from receptor to neocortex) to different kinds of stimuli take part in mediating individual differences in arousal-oriented temperament traits. The action-oriented traits (sensory sensitivity, endurance, activity) probably refer mainly to the physiology and biochemistry of cortico-reticular structures. In turn, emotional reactivity is to be related to susceptibility characteristics of the limbic system and the autonomic nervous system (Strelau & Zawadzki, 1993). The temporal traits can probably be explained by neurophysiological and biochemical mechanisms responsible for the speed of elicitation, termination, and course of nervous processes, as well as the interaction between them (1993).

Generally speaking, in the RTT the biological basis of temperament is regarded as a *neuroendocrine individuality* (Strelau, 1983; Strelau & Plomin, 1992) which means that temperament is determined by an individual-specific configuration of neurological (physiology and biochemistry of CNS and ANS) and endocrine systems regulating the energetic and temporal components of behavior. There are intra- and interindividual differences in the functioning of these mechanisms.

The Psychometric Measures of RTT Traits

For about two decades the Strelau Temperament Inventory (STI, Strelau, 1972a, 1983; Strelau, Angleitner, & Ruch, 1990) was the main instrument for measuring two of the RTT traits: reactivity and mobility. The Strength of Excitation (SE) scale was used as a measure of reactivity (the endurance pole), with high scores indicating low reactivity level. The Mobility of Nervous Processes (MO) scale served as an indicator of behavioral mobility. Activity was mainly assessed on the basis of the so-called *style of action,* estimated by means of observation. An adjunctive style of action (predominance of auxiliary activity over basic activity) was considered to indicate a low level of activity, whereas a straightforward style of action (balance between auxiliary and basic actions or a predominance of the latter) was used as a measure of high level of activity (see Strelau, 1983, 1988). For measuring the temporal characteristics of behavior—speed, tempo, persistence, recurrence, regularity, and mobility—the Temporal Traits Inventory (TTI, Goryńska & Strelau, 1979; Strelau, 1983) was used, though rarely.

Because of unsatisfactory psychometric characteristics (see Strelau, Angleitner, & Ruch, 1990), the STI has been thoroughly revised and published under the title of Strelau Temperament Inventory–Revised (STI-R; Strelau, Angleitner, Bantelmann, & Ruch, 1990; Ruch *et al.,* 1991). Like the STI, it contains three scales: Strength of Excitation, Strength of Inhibition, and Mobility of Nervous Processes. The STI and STI-R inventories gained international popularity (for a review see Strelau, Angleitner, & Ruch, 1990). They were often considered to be measures referring directly to the RTT, which was against Strelau's intention. In fact, the STI-R is aimed at assessing the three classic Pavlovian temperament properties; therefore, Strelau and Angleitner (1994) decided to rename this inventory the Pavlovian Temperament Survey (PTS).

For measuring the six temperament traits as postulated by the recent version of the RTT, Strelau and Zawadzki (1993) constructed a new inventory—the Formal Characteristics of Behavior–Temperament Inventory (FCB-TI). The reliability scores, as measured by Cronbach's alpha, obtained from five independent studies (Strelau & Zawadzki, 1993) which comprised altogether more than 3,500 subjects (aged from 15 to 80 years) vary for the six scales as follows: Briskness (.77–.79), Perseveration (.79–.81), Sensory Sensitivity (.72–.78), Emotional Reactivity (.82–.87), Endurance (.85–.88), and Activity (.82–.84). Long-term stability as measured by a 6-month interval varies for the six scales from .69 to .90 (but .55 for sensory sensitivity in the student sample). The FCB-TI scales also show satisfactory validity measures by means of convergent and divergent validity criteria (Strelau & Zawadzki, 1995).

Temperament and Behavior

A belief that has guided me from the very beginning of my research on temperament is that temperament characteristics are of special importance when an individual is confronted with stressors or performs highly demanding activity. This belief has support in Wright and Mischel's (1987) competency-demand hypothesis, which says that "psychologically demanding situations constitute one category of conditions in which individual differences in certain domains (e.g., aggressiveness, withdrawal) may be observed with particular clarity" (p. 1163). The temperament domain on which the Warsaw group focused their studies was reactivity as measured by means of the STI-SE scale. The reasoning underlying these studies was as follows.

High-reactive individuals, in whom physiological and biochemical mechanisms augment stimulation, need only low levels of stimulation to attain an optimal level of arousal, regarded here as a standard of stimulation intensity regulation (Eliasz, 1981, 1985; Strelau, 1983). Such individuals therefore avoid stimulation and activities that involve strong stimulation. Low-reactive individuals, in whom arousal mechanisms tend to suppress stimulation, have a high need for stimulation in order to maintain an optimal level of activation. Thus they undertake activities and seek out situations that possess high stimulation values. A lack of correspondence between the stimulative value of activity or situations in which activity is performed, and the individual's level of reactivity, leads to several consequences (Strelau, 1983, 1985, 1988).

(1) When subjects are able to regulate the stimulation value of their activity or situation by developing a style of action that corresponds with their level of reactivity, level of performance and psychophysiological costs usually do not distinguish low-reactive individuals from high-reactives. The difference between them consists, however, in the fact that they use different styles of action in order to cope with the stimulation value of the situation. In high-reactive individuals an adjunctive style of action, aimed at decreasing the stimulation value of activity or of the situation in which activity is performed, is dominant. For low-reactives the straightforward style of action is typical; this style is aimed at supplying stimulation (Friedensberg, 1985; Klonowicz, 1986; Strelau, 1983, 1985).

(2) When the possibility of using the preferred style of action is blocked, or for some reason a style of action has not developed, stimulation of extreme values (very high or very low) produces in individuals differing in reactivity different lev-

els of performance. In high-reactive individuals a decrease of performance occurs, whereas the level of performance in low reactives does not change or even increases. This finding has been recorded in field studies as well as under laboratory conditions for a variety of activities and situations (Eliasz, 1981; Klonowicz, 1986; 1987b; Strelau, 1983, 1988, 1989a).

(3) If, for some reason (e.g., motivation, social pressure, or other controlled and uncontrolled variables), a situation of high stimulation value does not lead to differences in the level of performance between high- and low-reactive individuals, one may expect that differences in psychophysiological or psychological costs will occur. Several of our studies showed that the costs of performance under high stimulation are high in high-reactives compared with low-reactives, and the reverse. Under stimulation of very low intensity the costs of performance may be higher in low-reactive individuals (Klonowicz, 1974, 1987b, 1992; Strelau, 1983, 1988).

(4) Long-lasting discrepancy between level of reactivity and the stimulative value of behavior and/or situations under which individuals develop or act, causes a high level of reactivity to become a temperament risk factor (TRF) leading to different kinds of disturbances or anomalies in behavior. Findings in respect to hyperactive children (Strelau, 1989c), patients suffering from ulcer disease (Strelau, 1983), and especially studies on Type A behavior pattern (Eliasz & Wrześniewski, 1986; Strelau & Eliasz, 1994) support this view.

Final Remarks

It is much easier to criticize someone else's views or findings than one's own. Weaknesses of a theory or shortcomings in methodology to which the author is blind, others see immediately. Nevertheless, I attempt a critical review of some aspects of the RTT.

As readily noted, the starting point of my research was the Pavlovian typology on which I concentrated for many years. After developing the regulative theory of temperament, the main instrument for measuring reactivity and mobility was the STI (in the case of activity, observation methods were applied). But as the scales of the STI indicate, this inventory is aimed at measuring the behavioral expressions of strength of excitation, strength of inhibition, and mobility of nervous processes. This fact meant that the RTT was often identified as a Pavlovian approach to temperament. The RTT could not have been developed if not for the contributions of the arousal-centered theories, the theory of action, and my own long experience. Nevertheless, the lack of an adequate instrument for measuring the RTT constructs was one of the weakest points of the theory. This weakness recently has been overcome in the development of the FCB-TI.

One of the main RTT postulates states that temperament has a biological background. The biological determination is also used as a definitional criterion for the construct "temperament." The facts that support the biological background of the RTT traits are, however, scanty. The only data that refer directly to the RTT traits stem from our behavior-genetic research (see Chapter 5). No studies addressed to a search for neurophysiological or biochemical correlates have been reported yet from our laboratory. There are several reasons for this shortcoming, the main one being the lack of appropriate equipment. There are, however, some studies in which the STI dimensions have been related to biological markers (see, e.g., Danilova, 1986; De Pascalis, 1993; Kohn, Cowles, & Lafreniere, 1987), but, as already mentioned, STI does not refer directly to traits postulated by the RTT.

Only recently de Pascalis, Strelau, and Zawadzki (in press) conducted a study in which event-related potentials and heart rate measures during cognitive task performance were related to the six traits postulated by the RTT. The results are promising in showing that endurance, sensory sensitivity, perseveration, and emotional reactivity play a specific role in moderating physiological changes during task performance.

With a few exceptions (e.g., Friedensberg, 1985), the RTT developed on the basis of studies conducted on adults and adolescents. For a better understanding of the mechanisms underlying temperament characteristics and of the contribution of temperament to the maturing of other personality structures, developmental studies are needed; the lack of a developmental approach is a shortcoming of the RTT.

Apart from the neo-Pavlovian approach to temperament which developed in Russia mainly in the 1950 to 1960s, the RTT was for about 20 years the only original approach to temperament to be found in the former socialist countries. Only recently Rusalov (see this chapter) developed a theory distinct from the conceptualizations of Teplov and Nebylitsyn (see Chapter 2). Up to the present the RTT is in eastern and central Europe the only theory of temperament that has incorporated more or less effectively certain ideas not only from Pavlov and other Russian researchers but also from the findings and theories developed in western Europe and in North America.

4

Physiological and Biochemical Correlates of Temperament

Introduction

Most definitions of temperament, apart from their specificity, emphasize the fact that temperament has some biological background, which may be expressed in different ways. Some authors refer rather generally to the constitutional makeup (e.g., G. W. Allport, 1937), or to the fact that temperament is inherited (e.g., Buss & Plomin, 1984). Others (e.g., H. J. Eysenck, 1970; Gray, 1982a, 1982b; Kagan, 1994; Zuckerman, 1979) specify the anatomo-physiological mechanisms and/or the biochemical factors underlying temperament characteristics. Very often researchers on temperament, when discussing the biology of this phenomenon, refer to all possible levels constituting the biological foundation of temperament (e.g., H. J. Eysenck, 1990b; Rothbart, 1989a; Strelau, 1983; Zuckerman, 1991c).

When posing questions about the biological bases of temperament, regardless of what might be included in the term "biology," we are confronted with at least two basic difficulties. First, what do we understand by temperament? Many discussions have arisen around this question (see Chapter 1), showing that, depending on the theory that researchers have followed, the population studied (children, adults, animals), or methods used, the definition of temperament differs. Thus the question arises: What is the phenomenon we are seeking a biological basis for? Since the probability is almost nil that there is a consistent biological basis for temperament in general, whatever the definition of this concept may be, the answer to this question may not be so important for studies on the biology of temperament. Much more important is the kind of traits (dimensions) we include in the structure of temperament.

In studying the biology of temperamental traits we face a key problem so far unsolved and from this emerges the second question: What temperamental traits are to be studied, and how many of them? Recently Strelau (1991b) has identified 81 traits within the domain of temperament, and Table 6.4 in Chapter 6 presents a list of 71 traits measured by means of temperament inventories. Independent of differences in quality, these traits also have a different degree of generality. Some are very specific traits (e.g., motor impulsiveness), most of them are first-order factors (e.g., impulsivity), and some are second-order factors (e.g., extraversion).

According to Zuckerman (1992), narrower traits are probably closer to biological levels than broader ones, which might be taken as a recommendation to focus biological studies on the very specific traits and first-order factors. On the other hand, the most cogent evidence on the biology of temperament traits has been acumulated with reference to second-order factors, for example, extraversion and neuroticism. As a matter of fact, many researchers departing from different definitions of temperament agree that extraversion is an important temperament trait, but this does not mean that authors agree on what extraversion is (e.g., Cattell, 1965; H. J. Eysenck, 1970; Gray, 1991; Kagan, Reznick, & Snidman, 1988). Such a state of affairs has far-reaching consequences for conclusions regarding the biology of the trait under study.

The present state of affairs regarding the understanding of temperament, the quality and number of dimensions comprised by this term (see Strelau, 1991b), and the diversity of meanings referring to the same temperament label, does not permit unequivocal conclusions regarding the biological bases of temperament.

The definitional postulate that temperament has biological backgrounds is based on several assumptions or findings, some of which are not necessarily specific for this domain of research. Seven are presented in the following paragraphs.

(1) As argued by Gray, any psychological function depends on the activities of the brain. Therefore, if there is a psychology of temperament (as well as of any other psychological function or trait) then there is *ipso facto* a neuropsychology of temperament (Gray, 1991, p. 105). This assumption, however, cannot be used as an argument for the study of the biology of temperament.

(2) Behavior-genetic studies on temperament have shown the importance of the genetic factor in determining individual differences in temperament traits (e.g., H. J. Eysenck, 1990b; Loehlin,1986; Matheny & Brown-Dolan, 1980; Pedersen, Plomin, McClearn, & Frisberg, 1988; Plomin & Rowe, 1977; Segal, 1990; Torgersen, 1985; R. S. Wilson & Matheny, 1986). It should be noted, however, that personality traits not belonging to the domain of temperament, for example, traditionalism (Bouchard, Lykken, McGue, Segal, & Tellegen, 1990) or conservatism (N. G. Martin & Jardine, 1986), have heritability scores that do not differ essentially from those ascribed to temperament characteristics.

(3) If genetic factors play an essential role in determining individual differences in temperament, there must be intervening variables of a biological nature,

such as physiological, neurological, biochemical, and hormonal, that are transferred genetically through generations (H. J. Eysenck, 1990b). One must agree with Zuckerman's (1992) claim that

> [w]e do not inherit [temperament] traits directly, but we do inherit variations in structure and biochemistry of the nervous system and it is these that dispose us to certain types of behavioral, affective, or even cognitive reactions to the environment. (p. 676)

Temperament researchers make the assumption that the physiological and biochemical mechanisms (at least markers) of temperament traits are rather specific to them, as compared with other phenomena.

(4) The universality of temperament traits across cultures implies that there must be species-specific carriers of these traits which have a biological (genetic) background. This assumption has been used by H. J. Eysenck (1982; 1990b) as one of the strongest arguments in favor of the biological origin of the PEN dimensions. The weakness of this assumption consists in the fact that universality of psychic or behavioral phenomena can also be explained by environmental factors. As suggested by Costa and McCrae (1992a), who claim that the Big Five factors are universal, the basic features of human nature may result from the fact that the human social environment has some elements in common across cultures such as abstract thinking, use of language, and so on. We also know from the cross-cultural literature that psychological phenomena that are universal across cultures can be explained by environmental commonality (see, e.g., Tooby & Cosmides, 1990; Triandis, 1978; Triandis et al., 1980–1981).

(5) One of the strongest assumptions in favor of biological bases of temperament traits says that the presence of temperament traits and clear-cut individual differences in this domain from early childhood cannot be explained by environmental factors (see, e.g., Buss & Plomin, 1984). Ample evidence has been gathered over the past two decades that shows that temperament traits are among the first more or less stable behavior characteristics present from birth (see, e.g., Kohnstamm, Bates, & Rothbart, 1989); some authors even argue for their presence in prenatal life (e.g., Eaton & Saudino, 1992). The evidence that temperament traits exist in neonatal human infants is a strong argument in favor of the importance of biological factors in determining individual differences in temperament.

(6) The presence of temperament traits not only in human beings but also in other mammalian species serves as the basis for two important assumptions: (a) In the process of biological evolution temperament traits must have played an important adaptive function, as emphasized already in the 1950s by Diamond, (1957; see also Buss & Plomin, 1984; Strelau, 1987a; Zuckerman, 1991c); (b) there must be some biological mechanisms in common for both humans and other mammalians mediating temperament traits (H. J. Eysenck, 1967, 1990b; Pavlov, 1951–1952; Strelau, 1983; Zuckerman, 1991c). The biological mechanisms underlying tem-

perament traits across mammalian species refer to hormones, to the autonomic nervous system, and to lower-level structures of the central nervous system.

(7) The stability of temperament traits has also been used as a basis for the assumption that temperament traits have a biological background. This assumption was strongly advocated by Teplov (1964). Recently this view has been presented by H. J. Eysenck (1990b), who argues that temporal consistency of the three major temperament dimensions (PEN) "in the face of changing environments points strongly to a biological basis for individual differences" (p. 247). Existing evidence shows, however, that temporal consistency (stability) has not been found unequivocally in temperament studies, especially among children (Plomin & Dunn, 1986), and that stability or change in temperament characteristics is a weak argument for or against the importance of the genetic factor (Plomin & Nesselroade, 1990). In the face of these data the assumption regarding the biological background of temperament based on the stability phenomenon has only weak empirical support.

Summarizing, I underline that the strongest support for the importance of the biological bases in determining individual differences in temperament stems from (a) behavior-genetic studies, (b) studies on neonatal infants, and (c) research aimed at identifying the physiological and biochemical variables presumed to mediate temperament characteristics (in man and other mammalian species). Whereas the first two approaches, (a) and (b) allow only for general statements (yes or no) regarding the biological bases of temperament, the third one, (c) aims to provide more specific information concerning the kind of biological mechanisms underlying temperament or, at least, the categories of biological markers to which given temperament characteristics refer. In this chapter I will concentrate on the third approach by trying to show some general findings and statements rather than going into specific details which are available elsewhere (see Gale & Eysenck, 1992; Gray, 1982b; Janke, 1983; Rothbart, 1989a; Strelau & Eysenck, 1987; Zuckerman, 1983a, 1991c).

It is not easy to find a common term for the biological approaches aimed at identifying specific structures and functions of the organism underlying temperament characteristics. For studies aimed at identifying physiological mechanisms or correlates of given behaviors or traits, without inquiring into the structures underlying them, we use the term psychophysiology, as proposed by J. A. Stern (1964). In this case, most often though not always, the independent variable is a given behavior or trait under study, and the physiological changes such as electrodermal activity, heart rate, or amplitude of evoked potentials are treated as dependent variables. The relationship between the two variables (physiology and behavior) is more like correlation than causation, hence we usually use such terms as physiological "correlates" or "markers" instead of mechanisms. We may say that the psychophysiology of temperament consists of identifying the physiological markers or correlates typical for the temperament traits under study.

Research aimed at examining the anatomical structures hypothesized to underlie the physiological and biochemical bases of temperament belongs to the domain of *physiological psychology* (see Schwartz, 1978). The goal of this discipline, based on animal studies, is to establish causal relationships between given anatomical structures and behaviors by means of electrical stimulation, lesions, low temperature, and so on. Changes in anatomical structures are considered independent variables and changes in behavior (or traits) are dependent variables. When brain structures in man are studied in relation to mental processes or behavior, often the term *neuropsychology* is used. This discipline, popularized in studies on temperament by Gray (1982a), has in this context a specific meaning. He uses the term *neuropsychology* "to mean the study, quite generally, of the role played by the brain in behavioral and psychological function, whether in human or animal subjects, and whether there is structural damage to the brain or not" (Gray, 1991, p. 105). According to this understanding, which has gained popularity in the domain under discussion, neuropsychology of temperament comprises studies on the structures, physiology, and biochemistry of the brain in relation to temperament traits.

In the past two decades study on biochemical components of behavior has become very popular and this is also true in the domain of temperament, especially in relation to such traits as anxiety (e.g., Gray, 1982a, 1982b; Janke & Netter, 1986) and sensation seeking (Zuckerman, 1991c). Since neurotransmitters of the brain, to which most biochemical studies on temperament refer, are structure-specific, this kind of research can hardly be conducted without referring to the anatomy of the brain. Studies on the biology of temperament comprise many more approaches than mentioned here, for example, the relationhip between temperament and the hormonal system, body build, blood groups, and responsivity to drugs (see Janke, 1983; Janke & Kallus, 1995).

The Structure, Physiology, and Biochemistry of the Nervous System as Related to Temperament Characteristics

From a review of the literature on biological mechanisms or correlates related to temperament, at least three lines of research, in the main interconnected, can be distinguished. Some authors center on the specific brain structures related to temperament characteristics, as, for example, Gray (1982a) in research on anxiety. Others concentrate on the physiological correlates (markers) of temperament traits; studies by H. J. Eysenck (1967, 1970) and his followers on the biological bases of extraversion and neuroticism may be mentioned here. In the past decade a strong tendency to search for biochemical markers of temperament traits, especially neurotransmitters, has been observed, as, for example, in studies on sensation seeking (Zuckerman, 1984c). There are also attempts to search for links and to integrate the different levels of biological mechanisms and correlates underlying temperament characteristics (e.g., Zuckerman, 1991c).

A proper understanding of the biology of temperament requires basic knowledge about the anatomy, physiology, and biochemistry of the nervous system, which may be found in relevant textbooks. To find a common language with the reader and to avoid misunderstandings in this and the remaining chapters, the most essential information is given with account taken of the specificity of biological mechanisms as related to temperament. Attention is paid mainly to the mechanisms responsible for regulating (1) the energetic (intensity) aspect of stimulation and excitation, (2) the inhibitory processes participating in the individual's activity, and (3) the emotional characteristics of behavior. Detailed information regarding the mechanisms under discussion is to be found in monographs edited by Gale and Edwards (1983a) and by Wittrock (1980), and in Zuckerman's (1991c) *Psychobiology of Personality,* the three references on which the following presentation is largely based.

The Neuron

The basic functional unit of the nervous system is the neuron. The neuron receives information from receptors and other neurons, and transmits information to other neurons, muscles, internal organs, or all of these. Bioelectrical and biochemical processes going on in the neuron also participate in regulating the energetic relationship between input and output of transmitted information. The human nervous system contains enormous numbers of neurons differing in function and structure and comprising different neural systems. It is estimated that the brain alone consists of about 10^{12} neurons.

The Anatomy

Each neuron, irrespective of the variety in anatomical structure, consists of four major components: the cell body (soma), the dendrites, the axon, and the axon terminal, each of which has a widely differentiated structure not discussed here. At the center of the soma, which is the central feature of the neuron, is the cell nucleus. The nucleus contains the genetic material (deoxyribonucleic acid, DNA; ribonucleic acid, RNA) that controls the production of proteins and enzymes. The dendrites, which branch extensively like the crown of a tree, constitute the receptive surface of the neuron. The information from other neurons is transmitted to the cell body by means of dendrites. In turn, the information from the cell body is transferred to other neurons by the axon which in humans may vary in length from less than 1 millimeter up to 3 meters. When the axon reaches another neuron or muscle, it branches into a terminal ending known as the synaptic knob.

Neurons are separated from each other, thus the axon terminal does not directly contact the membrane of the adjacent nerve cells. The output information of the nerve cell is transmitted across the synapse, known also as the synaptic cleft (see Figure 4.1). The synapse consists of the presynaptic axon terminal (from which the information is transmitted) and the postsynaptic receptor area (to which the information is transmitted). In the presynaptic axon terminal, sacs called synaptic vesicles are located; these contain transmitters (neurotransmitters) the release of which allows the transmission of information from the presynaptic terminal to the postsynaptic receptors.

The Physiology

Leaving aside the details regarding the processes of potassium, sodium, and chlorine ions, as well as of the various organic anions (protein molecules) on the inside and outside of the cell membrane, let us say that the essence of neuronal activity consists of two basic processes: synaptic transmission and action potential. These are the two basic modes of coding processes by means of which external events are transformed into brain activity. When the neuron is not transmitting information (is at rest), it is characterized by a potential difference between the inside and outside of the cell membrane of about -70 millivolts, the *resting potential*. Information received by a neuron results in two events: (1) a decrease in the membrane potential (depolarization), known as the *excitatory postsynaptic potential* (EPSP), and/or (2) an increase in the membrane potential (hyperpolarization), termed an *inhibitory postsynaptic potential* (IPSP).

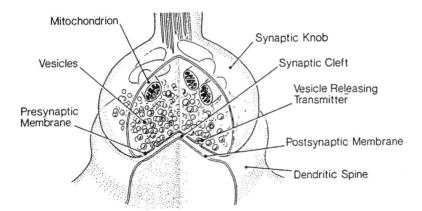

FIGURE 4.1. A single synapse. *Note.* From "The Nervous System: Structure and Fundamental Processes," by J. Boddy. In A. Gale and J. A. Edwards (Eds.), *Physiological Correlates of Human Behaviour: Basic Issues* (1983, Vol. 1, p. 26), London: Academic Press. Copyright 1983 by Academic Press. Reprinted with permission.

Postsynaptic transmission (EPSP and IPSP), which occurs only in the dendritic regions and in the cell body, is a graded (continuous) one. This means that the amplitude of EPSP and IPSP is proportional (to a given point) to the strength of the incoming stimulus. An increasing intensity of stimuli (expressed in spatial and temporal summation of EPSPs) results in reaching a threshold at which the EPSP converts into an action potential, the latter being a qualitatively different kind of neuronal transmission. Whereas the EPSP, by increasing the depolarization of the cell membrane, drives the latter closer to the threshold point, IPSP acts in the opposite way. By causing greater hyperpolarization it leads the cell membrane further from the threshold. It is always the summation of postsynaptic potentials (PSPs; EPSPs and IPSPs) that decides whether an action potential will be generated. Assuming that individual differences are universal, one may hypothesize that individuals differ in the intensity of stimuli needed to reach the postsynaptic threshold or (and) they differ in the magnitude of the threshold needed to convert PSPs into action potential.

The amplitude of the action potential is an all-or-none phenomenon. This means that its amplitude is constant and not proportional to the intensity of input. By means of action potentials neuronal information is transmitted from the cell body to the axon and axon terminals. The two modes of neuronal information processing are schematically presented in Figure 4.2. Since an action potential is a bi-

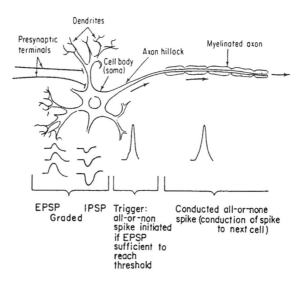

FIGURE 4.2. Neuronal transmission of information. *Note.* From "Introduction to the Anatomy, Physiology and Chemistry of the Brain," by R. F. Thompson, T. W. Berger, and S. D. Berry. In M. C. Wittrock (Ed.), *The Brain and Psychology* (1980, p. 13), New York: Academic Press. Copyright 1980 by Academic Press. Reprinted with permission.

nary event (all-or-none), like a digital computer, the varieties of external and internal events are represented in the neurons by a series of action potentials which differ on such parameters as duration, temporal pattern, or frequency. The summed electrical change in the many thousands of neurons acting in concert, produced by all PSPs and action potentials in given brain areas, may be recorded by means of the electroencephalogram (EEG).

The Biochemistry

Because neurons are anatomically separated from each other, the ionic currents which occur during postsynaptic potentials (EPSP and IPSP) and action potentials cannot cross over the synaptic gap. It is the transformation of an electrical event into a chemical one that makes the transmission of informations across neurons possible. As already mentioned, this process occurs due to neurotransmitters located in the presynaptic vesicles (see Figure 4.1). When the action potential reaches the axon terminal, the vesicles release their neurotransmitter contents into the synaptic cleft which enables contact to be made with the postsynaptic membrane. This membrane is provided with special receptors (protein molecules) which, being activated by transmitters, retransform the chemical events into ionic ones. After release from presynaptic terminals, neurotransmitters are partly deactivated by degradative enzymes present in the extracellular space. The enzymes catabolize neurotransmitters into their metabolites, most of which are nonactive. Another form of clearing neurotransmitters is reuptake into the cell body where they are metabolized by enzymes located in the mitochondria.

The process of synaptic transmission is common for all kinds of brain synapses; however, different neurons contain different neurotransmitters. In recent studies on the biological bases of temperament, attention has been paid to the biochemical components of the neuron. Apart from the specific functions mediated by synaptic transmission, one may also consider the synaptic processes as mediating the energetic (intensity) component of transmitted information, which brings us close to the way of thinking typical in temperament studies. It is known from studies in biological psychiatry that there is large within- and between-subject variation in receptor number and sensitivity. Thus it might be conjectured that receptor sensitivity in the postsynaptic membrane differs across individuals, who may also differ in the quantity of secreted neurotransmitters, this being dependent on individual differences in the size of synaptic terminals and/or in the number of presynaptic vesicles releasing neurotransmitters.

There are several groups of neurotransmitters; only those to which temperament researchers refer are presented here.

Acetylcholine (ACh). ACh is a neurotransmitter which was identified almost a century ago in studies on the ANS, and is known to function at the neuromuscular junctions, in the cholinergic pathways of the brain, and in the preganglionic part of both sympathetic and parasympathetic neurons in the peripheric nervous system. ACh is synthesized from acetylcoenzyme A and choline. The enzyme acetylcholinesterase inactivates ACh after release.

Catecholamines. Catecholamines include three important neurotransmitters: epinephrine (E), norepinephrine (NE), also termed noradrenaline, and dopamine (DA). DA is also a precursor of NE; E is derived from NE, but covers only about 5% of brain neurotransmitters and plays a minor biological role in the brain. The synthesis of catecholamines involves a complex chain of metabolic processes which is illustrated in Figure 4.3. Norepinephrine is synthesized from the amino acid tyrosine, which is converted to dihydroxyphenylalanine (DOPA), and then enzymatically to dopamine. Dopamine is converted to norepinephrine by an enzyme called dopamine beta-hydroxylase (DBH). Dopamine catabolism leads to homovanillic acid (HVA), a final breakdown product of dopamine. NE is inactivated by two enzymes, by catechol-O-methyltransferase (COMT) in the synaptic cleft and by monoamine oxidase (MAO) type A in the cell body, and converted to 3-methoxy-4-hydroxyphenylglycol (MHPG). The biosynthesis and degradation of dopamine is similar to that of NE except that its metabolism to HVA is mediated by MAO type B. Norepinephrine, concentrated mainly in the locus coeruleus from which a major bundle of noradrenergic neurons originate, also occurs in neurones of the brainstem, in the limbic system, and the ANS. Dopamine is concentrated mainly in the basal ganglia and in the nucleus accumbens of the limibic system connected by dopaminergic pathways (from the brain stem up to the cerebral cortex). Catecholamines, as well as acetylcholine, play a role in mediating the level of excitation in the nervous system.

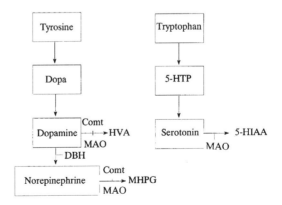

FIGURE 4.3. Biosynthesis and breakdown of the monoamines dopamine, norepinephrine, and serotonin. *Note.* From *Psychobiology of Personality* (p. 177), by M. Zuckerman, 1991, New York: Cambridge University Press. Copyright 1991 by Cambridge University Press. Adapted with permission.

Serotonin. Serotonin or 5-hydroxytryptamine (5-HT), is synthesized from the amino acid tryptophane. Fibers of this neurotransmitter system originate in the raphe nuclei and are distributed in areas roughly paralleling those of NE and DA. Serotonin is also degraded by MAO-A and converted to 5-hydroxyindoleacetic acid (5-HIAA). 5-HT mediates a great variety of functions such as the sleep–waking cycle, feeding, temperature regulation, pain threshold. It may be regarded as mainly responsible for inhibitory processes.

Because of similarities in molecular structures, the catecholamines (NE and DA) and serotonin are considered monoamine systems. It is important to note that MAO, the most widely used biochemical marker in temperament studies, is an enzyme that degrades all three monoamine neurotransmitters, NE, DA, and 5-HT, although by different MAO isoenzymes. MAO is present in all neural tissues with its highest concentration in the hypothalamus.

Amino acids. These include several neurotransmitters such as glutamic acid, acting as a stimulator of neurones in the spinal cord. Around glutamic acid and its metabolites a complex of neurotransmitters is formed. Among them gamma-aminobutyric acid (GABA) is the most relevant for research in temperament because of its role in inhibiting emotional arousal. GABA, which produces IPSPs, is known as one of the clearly identified inhibitory neurotransmitters.

Neuropeptides. Besides neurotransmitters there is an ever increasing number of neuropeptides which are partly released as "cotransmitters" from the same neurons as monoamines and have a modulating effect on neurotransmission but also act partly as neurotransmitters on their own. One of the most prominent groups are the endorphins (a term constructed from *endo*genous mor*phine*). They are opiate-like (morphinelike) peptides that act as neurotransmitters. One of them, beta-endorphin, has been most widely investigated. It is produced in a variety of brain areas including the pituitary. High concentrations are found particularly in the limbic system, mainly in the amygdala. It exerts its functions on opioid receptors and is believed to influence pain thresholds by inhibitory functions.

The Autonomic Nervous System

The autonomic nervous system (ANS), together with the somatic nervous system, are the two subdivisions of the peripheral nervous system. For temperament research the ANS is of special interest. Many physiological reactions that are regulated by means of the ANS are considered physiological correlates of several temperament characteristics. A few examples of such phenomena are electrodermal activity (EDA), cardiovascular changes (e.g., heart rate, blood pressure), respiratory movements, and salivation may be mentioned.

The autonomic nervous system, which controls many vegetative and involuntary body functions, has two major divisions differently organized, namely, the sympathetic and the parasympathetic branches. Most organs innervated by the ANS are under the control of both branches, but in opposite relationships. In general, the parasympathetic NS is concerned with the storage and preservation of energy in the body; it tends to reduce the level of functioning. The sympathetic NS, on the other hand, is active during energy release, especially in situations demanding high concentration of energy mobilization, when the individual acts under stressful situations. The sympathetic NS, also responsible for the manifestation of emotions, tends to increase the level of the organism's functioning.

The neurotransmitter involved in the activity of the parasympathetic NS is acetylcholine, produced in the cholinergic terminals. The terminals of the sympathetic NS are noradrenergic, that is, they release noradrenaline. The sympathetic NS innervates not only the viscera and blood vessels but also the adrenal gland. Thus adrenaline and to some extent also noradrenaline are secreted from the adrenal gland when activated by the sympathetic NS which, however, in this section is mediated by acetylcholine. Table 4.1 provides summarized information about the functional differences between the sympathetic and parasympathetic branches of the ANS.

Despite the old belief that the ANS acts independently of the CNS, it has now become clear that the brain regulates the functions of the ANS. According to the hierarchical organization of the brain, lower nervous structures are under the control of higher nervous centers.

TABLE 4.1. The Functional Differences between the Sympathetic and Parasympathetic Branches of the ANS

Autonomous Nervous System	
Sympathetic	Parasympathetic
Catabolism	Anabolism
Activity of noradrenaline	Activity of acetylcholine
Diffuse, long lasting activity	Discrete, short-lasting activity
Dilates pupil of eye	Constricts pupil of eye
Scanty secretion of salivary glands	Profuse secretion of salivary glands
Increase of HR	Decrease of HR
Constricts blood vessels	Slight effect on blood vessels
Dilates bronchial tubes of lungs	Constricts bronchial tubes of lungs
Regulates ejaculation	Regulates erection
Stimulates sweat glands	Stimulates lacrimal gland
Contracts sphincters	Relaxes sphincters

Note. From *Psychobiology of Personality* (p. 257), by M. Zuckerman, 1991, New York: Cambridge University Press. Copyright 1991 by Cambridge University Press. Adapted with permission.

The Central Nervous System

Among the structures of the CNS, the brainstem, the hypothalamus, the limbic system, the thalamus with basal ganglia, and the cerebral cortex deserve special attention in studies on the biological bases of temperament. Most of the structures of interest to us may be seen on the sagittal section of the brain as depicted in Figure 4.4.

The Brainstem

On its dorsal part the spinal cord extends to a neural structure known as the brainstem, considered as the evolutionary oldest and lowest part of the brain. The brainstem consists of three basic neural structures: medulla oblongata (medulla), pons, and the midbrain (see Figure 4.4). From the central core of the midbrain there ascends a network of neurons which has extended connections with a variety of cerebral structures, including the cortex. This diffuse multisynaptic ascending network is known as the brainstem reticular formation (BSRF) and receives nonspecific excitatory input from virtually every system of the body. Among the many basic functions of the organism under control of the brainstem (e.g., respiration), the BSRF participates in the regulation of the sleep–waking states. It also transmits arousal signals to the cortex and other cerebral structures, thus modulating the ex-

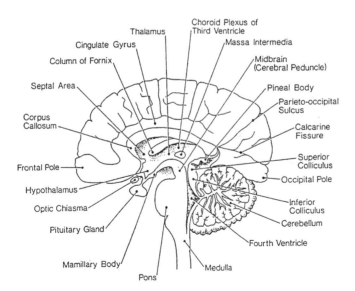

FIGURE 4.4. The principal structure of the brain as seen from a sagittal plane. *Note.* From "The Nervous System: Structure and Fundamental Processes," by J. Boddy. In A. Gale and J. A. Edwards (Eds.), *Physiological Correlates of Human Behaviour: Basic Issues* (1983, Vol. 1, p. 38), London: Academic Press. Copyright 1983 by Academic Press. Reprinted with permission.

citatory states of these nervous centers. Taking into account its basic functions the BSRF is often termed the reticular activating system (RAS, see Figure 4.5). The BSRF also plays a role in mediating the orienting reflex and attention processes.

The basic neurotransmitters located in the BSRF are acetylcholine, noradrenaline, dopamine, and serotonin. Originating in the brainstem, they ascend to widespread diencephalic and neocortical centers. The BSRF acetylcholine mediates the processes of arousal and attention, noradrenaline mediates the reinforcing (activating and inhibiting) effects of behavior, dopamine mediates motor activity, and serotonin participates in the production of sleep.

The Hypothalamus and Its Control over the Endocrine System

Anterior to the brainstem is the hypothalamus (see Figure 4.4). This rather small neural structure, composed of many nuclei and pathways, plays an important role in regulating metabolic, hormonal, sexual, and emotional behavior, especially emotional arousal. The hypothalamus has extensive afferent and efferent connections to lower and higher brain structures. Of great importance is its efferent connection with the pituitary gland (see Figure 4.4) by means of which the hypothalamus controls the endocrine system.

The pituitary gland (or hypophysis) consists of two major lobes connected by an intermediate lobe: the posterior lobe, which has a direct neuronal connection

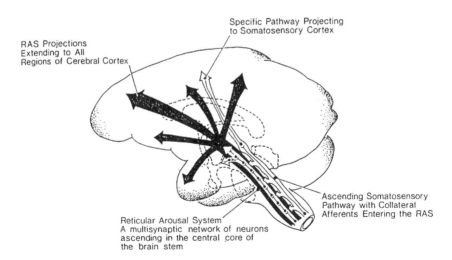

FIGURE 4.5. Schematic diagram of the reticular activating system. *Note.* From "Information Processing and Functional Systems in the Brain," by J. Boddy. In A. Gale and J. A. Edwards (Eds.), *Physiological Correlates of Human Behaviour: Basic Issues* (1983, Vol. 1, p. 67), London: Academic Press. Copyright 1983 by Academic Press. Reprinted with permission.

with the hypothalamus, and the anterior lobe. The anterior lobe secretes many glandotropic hormones, for example, the adrenocorticotropic hormone (ACTH), the thyrotropic hormone (TSH), or gonadotropic hormones (GTH), which influence the activity of the peripheral glands—thyroid, adrenals, and gonads. Acting as a relay station between the CNS and the endocrine system the pituitary is considered the pivotal endocrine gland.

The hypothalamic–pituitary–hormone system is illustrated in Figure 4.6. This system, however, is not complete. As already mentioned, by means of the adrenal gland (the inner segment termed adrenal medulla), the hormonal system is directly connected with the ANS. During emotional arousal and energy mobilization, especially in states of stress, the ANS activates the adrenal gland, which secretes adrenaline, and to a given extent also the neurotransmitter noradrenaline, remaining in reciprocal interaction with the ANS. In turn, the adrenal cortex, when activated by ACTH, produces glucocorticosteroid hormones, of which cortisol is the best known; these are secreted under states similar to those producing adrenaline and noradrenaline.

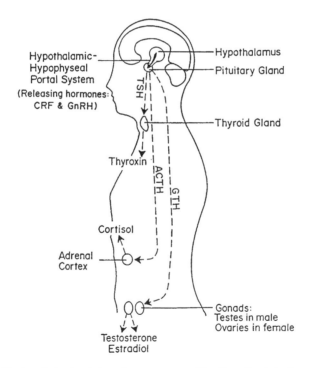

FIGURE 4.6. The hypothalamic–pituitary–hormone system. *Note.* From *Psychobiology of Personality* (p. 182), by M. Zuckerman, 1991, New York: Cambridge University Press. Copyright 1991 by Cambridge University Press. Adapted with permission.

The pituitary–adrenocortical mechanism was regarded by Selye (1956) as an important mediator during the alarm, resistance, and exhaustion stages of his general "adaptation syndrome." The two gonadal hormones—androgens produced in the testes in males, and estrogens produced in the ovaries in females—which also play a role in stress responses (Janke & Kallus, 1995), are of crucial significance in the development of primary and secondary sexual characteristics (Nyborg, 1994), including behavior traits.

The bloodstream transports hormones to the target organs. As hypothesized by Leshner (1978), hormones should not be considered to be causes of behavior but they are essential factors regulating the intensity of behavior characteristics. This conclusion is of special interest in the context of temperament studies related to the endocrine system. The hormones not only have reciprocal links with the hypothalamus and the ANS, but are also under the control of the limbic system.

The Limbic System

The limbic system (L. *limbus*—border, rim), also known as the visceral brain, is located between the brainstem and the cerebral cortex, and its structures consti-

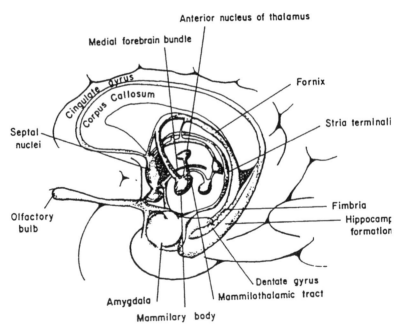

FIGURE 4.7. The limbic system. *Note.* From "Introduction to the Anatomy, Physiology and Chemistry of the Brain," by R. F. Thompson, T. W. Berger, and S. D. Berry. In M. C. Wittrock (Ed.), *The Brain and Psychology* (1980, p. 25), New York: Academic Press. Copyright 1980 by Academic Press. Reprinted with permission.

tute a shape like a rim. The amygdala, septum, hippocampus, cingulate gyrus, and the limbic areas of the frontal cortex are considered to be the major parts of the limbic system (see Figure 4.7). The hippocampus, which is the largest structure of the limbic system, constitutes a band of fibers called fornix. These fibers descend to the hypothalamus. Because of this connection, which assures control over the endocrine system, the hypothalamus is sometimes considered to be a part of the limbic structure. The limbic system is connected through collaterals with the BSRF. Thus emotional arousal generated in the visceral brain stimulates the cortex via BSRF. All neurotransmitters of the brain are found in the limbic system: beta-endorphin, noradrenaline, serotonin, and dopamine.

The limbic system is regarded as the center of emotional reactivity, and is involved in motivational and learning processes. It constitutes the anatomical basis for the Behavioral Inhibition System and the Fight/Flight System as postulated by Gray (1982a, 1982b; for details, see Chapter 3). The amygdala is considered a sensory gateway to the emotions (Aggleton & Mishkin, 1986), especially in reference to rage, anxiety, and fear. The hippocampus is thought to mediate memory processes.

Thalamus and Basal Ganglia

The thalamus, which is the largest diencephalic structure, is located dorsally from the hypothalamus (see Figure 4.4). It is composed of three types of nuclei: reticular, intrinsic, and relay. The reticular nuclei, which receive input from the BSRF, project nonspecific arousal diffusely into the cortex. Because of this function, these structures are often termed the diffuse thalamic projection system (DTPS). It is conjectured that DTPS mediates processes of selective attention and awareness investigated mainly by use of measures of evoked potentials (EPs). Intrinsic nuclei are responsible for communication within the thalamic structures. The relay nuclei assure transsynaptic transmission; they transfer information from all sensory receptors to the cerebral cortex.

The thalamus, which has extensive cortical and subcortical connections, is surrounded by basal ganglia. The functions of this complex pattern of structures are as yet unclear, but basal ganglia appear to mediate motor activity. Lack of adequate levels of dopamine in the dopaminergic neurons of the basal ganglia leads to Parkinsonism. According to Gray (1982a, 1982b) the thalamus and basal ganglia, together with motor and sensorimotor areas of the neocortex, constitute the neurological basis for the Behavioral Approach System (for a detailed description, see Chapter 3).

The Cerebral Cortex

The concentration of cell bodies on the surface of the cerebral hemispheres comprises the gray matter, approximately 2 mm thick, known as the cerebral cortex. The cortex consists of six layers which differ according to the size and shape of the nerve cells. The human cortical surface is a complex of deep sulci and convolutions (gyri); therefore, the cortical surface of the brain can contain a great number of neurons. The cerebral cortex is, phylogenetically and ontogenetically, the youngest neural structure.

The two cerebral hemispheres of the brain are joined by the corpus callosum (see Figure 4.4) which plays the role of a relay station transferring information between the two hemispheres. Like most brain structures, the cerebral hemispheres are in the sagittal plane parallel to each other. The cortical surface consists of the following four lobes: frontal, parietal, temporal, and occipital (see Figure 4.8). Motor functions are localized in the frontal lobe and somatosensory functions in the parietal. The two lobes are separated from each other by the central sulcus. The occipital lobe comprises the visual area and the temporal lobe the auditory area, as illustrated in Figure 4.8. The central fissure (known as the fissura Rolandi) divides the cortex functionally into the motor and sensory areas, the former being located in front of the central fissure and the latter behind it. The cortex also includes areas that are not clearly sensory or motor (the "association" cortex), which play an important role in the higher cognitive functions, such as memory and thinking.

The 19th century discoveries by Broca and Wernicke, that the sensory and motor speech areas are located in only one of the hemispheres (the left hemisphere for right-handed persons), provided the first evidence that there is a hemispheric

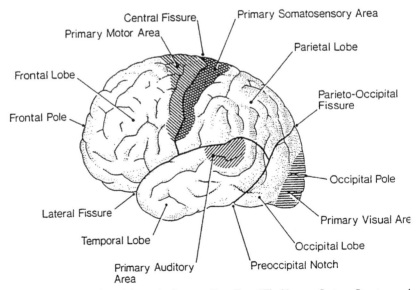

FIGURE 4.8. A lateral view of the cerebral cortex. *Note.* From "The Nervous System: Structure and Fundamental Processes," by J. Boddy. In A. Gale and J. A. Edwards (Eds.), *Physiological Correlates of Human Behaviour: Basic Issues* (1983, Vol. 1, p. 44), London: Academic Press. Copyright 1983 by Academic Press. Reprinted with permission.

asymmetry concerning the functional significance of the cortex. Language functions are mainly associated with the left hemisphere, and spatial abilities and some perceptual functions with the right. The left hemisphere seems to be dominant in processes involved in analytic approaches, while the right hemisphere dominates in the more global and emotion-oriented activity. In general, however, the evidence regarding cerebral lateralization, mainly based on clinical findings, is equivocal and insufficiently documented. This holds true as well for studies in which hemispheric asymmetry has been related to temperament characteristics.

Final Remarks

The foregoing selective review of the structure, physiology, and biochemistry of the nervous system leads to the conclusion that there are no functional systems of the brain that can be directly related to temperament characteristics. It has been shown that there are many different structures and chemical components that serve similar (e.g., excitatory or inhibitory) functions, as well as the reverse. The same neural structure, because of its many links with other structures, may serve different functions, and the same holds true for the biochemical components. The same neurotransmitter fulfills various roles in different structures. The nervous system (ANS and CNS) should be considered a complex integrated unit. To conclude, I share the view vividly expressed by Boddy (1983a) in the following way:

> The brain does not consist of a series of separate boxes which are switched "on" or "off" in specific situations (e.g. hunger) and perform their functions in isolation. The brain must be viewed as a dynamic organization of interacting subsystems. Barry Commoner's (1972) first law of ecology that "everything is connected to everything else" is entirely applicable to the brain. (p. 73)

Psychophysiological Correlates of Temperament

In the prescientific period of psychology, the biology of temperament consisted mainly in speculations about relationships between temperament traits and given biological functions, or in relating more or less apparent characteristics, such as physical makeup (see Chapter 1), with temperament. Empirical studies searching for the biological backgrounds of temperament became possible only with the development of psychophysiology, psychological physiology, neuropsychology, and biochemistry. The majority of these studies, published in hundreds of papers, have been conducted during the last decades of this century.

Chapters 2 and 3, in which temperament theories were presented, provided information about the biological background of the traits under discussion. In this chapter, the presentation takes another perspective, starting from the physiological and biochemical correlates of temperament characteristics. The sections in this chapter presenting the structure, physiology, and biochemistry of the nervous system clearly showed that the complex connections between the separate structures and functions makes it difficult, if not impossible, to decide which specific structure and function of the NS is related to given temperament characteristics. For example, electrodermal activity (EDA), in temperament research one of the most popular physiological correlates, has a multifold determination. EDA is mediated by the autonomic nervous system, but at the same time is codetermined by the activity of higher nervous centers such as the hypothalamus, the limbic system, and the BSRF. Because of its multiple determination, electrodermal activity, depending on the context and the theory within which this measure is used, is considered an indicator of the activity of the autonomic nervous system, of the visceral brain, or even of cortical arousal. The same refers to other physiological correlates. Such a state of affairs leads to much confusion and misunderstanding.

To avoid judgments regarding the neural structures underlying the specific physiological correlates, a broad distinction has been made in this section between correlates that refer to autonomic arousal (including the ANS and visceral brain), to cortical arousal as expressed by spontaneous and reactive EEG activity, and to biochemical components (including neurotransmitters and hormones).

Arousal, whether related to BSRF and cortical structures, to the visceral brain, or to the ANS, can be described in terms of tonic and phasic arousal. By *tonic* arousal is meant the basal activity of given neural structures when no stimuli are present or the level of arousal that occurs prior to stimulation. When recordings are taken during a state of rest (when no stimuli are exposed), it is assumed that physiological measures under this state reflect tonic arousal. The term *chronic arousal* also refers to the tonic level of arousal, with the additional assumption that the tonic level of arousal is more or less stable, as already noted by Wenger (1941). *Phasic* arousal occurs as a result of any kind of stimulation (external or internal), and might be considered to be a change from the tonic level. Usually, after cessation of stimuli, phasic arousal decreases until the level of tonic arousal has been reached. In a temporal perspective one may say that phasic arousal, as a response to stimuli, is a short-lived phenomenon, whereas tonic arousal is a durable one. Some authors also distinguish *spontaneous* arousal, reflecting changes in arousal that are not under the control of the experimenter (mostly internal stimulation). A state of spontaneous arousal is particularly evident in the preliminary step of experimentation, when the experimental situation is unfamiliar to the subject.

The distinction between tonic and phasic levels of arousal is of great importance in temperament research. Depending on the theory on which temperament traits are based, different predictions have been made regarding the relationship between the traits under discussion and the physiological markers referring to phasic and tonic levels of arousal. In temperament studies, where physiological phenomena are measured during different kinds of performances, different situations (e.g., stress versus relaxation) and expositions of stimuli (e.g., novel, un-expected, simple versus complex), the physiological markers refer mostly to phasic arousal.

Depending on the specific relationship between a given temperamental trait and the variables being manipulated (performance, situation, stimuli), the physiological markers (different measures of arousal) may vary for the same temperamental trait and across traits or may be the same for different traits. The links between EDA and extraversion may serve as an example of the variety of relationships. A high level of electrodermal response may be a physiological marker of extraversion when strong stimuli are applied to individuals differing on this temperament dimension. This is in accordance with H. J. Eysenck's (1970, 1990b) theory of extraversion, which predicts that in extraverts the intensity of arousal increases as a function of intensity of stimuli, whereas in introverts stimuli of high intensity evoke protective inhibition, that is, a decrease in EDA. But high levels of electrodermal activity may also be a marker of introversion when reactions to new stimuli are recorded for individuals differing with respect to the extraversion–introversion dimension. Again, the theory predicts that in introverts, because of their higher reactivity, the orienting reflex to new stimuli should be stronger as compared with that in extraverts (Eysenck, 1970, 1990b).

Physiological Correlates of Temperament Referring to Autonomic Arousal

In the first stage of psychophysiology much attention was devoted to the activity of the autonomic nervous system, and this line of research has also been developed in temperament studies. Since the ANS controls many vegetative and involuntary body functions, from the very beginning these studies were aimed at searching for links between given temperament characteristics and a whole pattern of physiological phenomena regarded as expressions of the ANS activity.

A Multivariate Approach

Studies considered to be among the first attempts to relate a wide range of physiological correlates to temperament were conducted by M. A. Wenger in the first half of this century. Wenger's study on the physiological basis of temperament served as a kind of model for a multivariate approach in this field of research, hence they deserve a more detailed description.

Wenger—The Pioneer of a Multivariate Approach. Three assumptions may be considered as the starting point of Wenger's study. (1) Individual differences, based on everyday observations, are often expressed by means of such descriptive terms as: "bundle of nerves," "restless," "nervous," "tense," "jittery," "energetic," and so on. Thus there must be a close relationship between temperament and muscular processes. (2) Pavlov invoked inhibitory processes to explain why some dogs under experimental conditions fall into drowsiness and others are excited, but this is not a satisfactory explanation. These differences may be explained instead by an increase or reduction in muscular tension. (3) The autonomic nervous system plays an important role in mediating the organism's level of activation, as has already been postulated by Eppinger and Hess (1910) who developed the concepts of vagotonia (parasympatheticotonia) and sympatheticotonia.[1]

On these assumptions Wenger (1938, 1941, 1943, 1947, 1966) conducted a series of studies on school children. The variables used in these studies comprised temperament characteristics [mainly measured by Downey's (1923) Will-Temperament Test], observational data, including measures of overt muscular activity (collected by parents, teachers, and experimenter), and more than a dozen physiological measures. Multiple regression, and factor analysis were applied to integrate the numerous data. It is impossible to report the detailed results obtained by Wenger. However, the main conclusions from his studies, because of their importance for understanding the biological bases of temperament, are outlined in the following paragraphs.

(1) Factor analysis of the physiological data showed that an autonomic factor, identified as the Nu factor, which represents the functioning of the ANS may be separated. Nu has loadings on the following measures: salivary output (low), percentage of solids in saliva (high), heart rate (fast), sinus arrhythmia (little), palmar and nonpalmar sweating (much), basal metabolic rate (high) and pulse pressure (low). High scores on the Nu factor indicate high activity of the ANS.

(2) A second factor—identified as Mu—that emerged from all the studies conducted by Wenger is muscular tension, regarded as a temperament factor. Mu has loadings on such characteristics as frequency of overt muscular activity, speed of movement, irritability, instability of response, and fatigability.

(3) The temperament characteristics and the physiological measures of imbalance between the two branches of the ANS are related to each other.

> Children with autonomic scores indicative of functional parasympathetic predominance were found to have a lower basal metabolic rate and a more adequate diet; to manifest more emotional inhibition, less emotional excitability, and a lower frequency of activity with less fatigue; and proved to be more patient and

---

Eppinger and Hess (1910), taking as a starting point the concept of antagonistic innervation, postulated that the two branches of the ANS act independently. Hess (1924) introduced the concept of functional polarity by showing that the ANS branches refer to one of the two functional phases: ergotropic and trophotropic. The ergotropic phase, determined by the activity of the sympathetic branch, comprises increased catabolic processes, cardiovascular activity, tension of striated muscles, and alertness. The trophotropic phase, determined by activity of the parasympathetic branch, consists of increased anabolic processes and gastrointestinal activity, and of relaxing the striated muscles and drowsiness.

neat than those children with autonomic scores indicative of functional predominance of the sympathetic system. (Wenger, 1947, pp. 308–309)

As may be concluded from this quotation based on empirical evidence, the same ANS correlates have been found for temperament traits that essentially differ from each other, for example, activity and fatigability on the one hand, and emotional excitability and emotional inhibition on the other. These data support Duffy's argument that it is not the quality (direction) of behavior, but its intensity component, that has a physiological basis in the activity of the ANS. Greater or lesser responsiveness of the ANS in interaction with the environment may, however, facilitate the development of qualitatively different temperament characteristics, for example, impulsiveness, aggression, or anxiety (Duffy, 1957, p. 272).

(4) The many experiments with the application of physiological indices as measures of ANS imbalance have shown that the correlations between the separate measures are rather low (see Wenger, 1943). This was why many important physiological correlates, for example, systolic and diastolic blood pressure, respiration rate, and dermographic scores, were not included in the composite score of the autonomic imbalance.

(5) Wenger distinguished between the phasic and chronic predominance of one of the two branches of the ANS. If relatively chronic conditions of imbalance occur, measurements of phasic imbalance may be regarded as indicators of chronic imbalance. The author was able to show that, for many of the physiological indicators, there is temporal stability as measured for different time intervals, up to 2 years (Wenger, 1941). As already mentioned, the distinction between phasic and chronic arousal has gained much attention in current research on physiological correlates of temperament traits.

Contemporary Psychophysiological Studies Based on a Multivariate Model. An extensive multivariate model with applications to studies on neuroticism as understood by H. J. Eysenck (1970) and often regarded as a synonym of emotionality has recently been developed by Fahrenberg and his coworkers. In a series of experiments, psychophysiological measures of autonomic arousal in different states and situations were compared with psychometrically diagnosed neuroticism (Andresen, 1987; Fahrenberg, 1977, 1987, 1992; Fahrenberg, Walschburger, Foerster, Myrtek, & Müller, 1983; Fahrenberg, Foerster, Schneider, Müller, & Myrtek, 1984; Myrtek, 1984). The experimental manipulation regarding psychophysiological markers of neuroticism included a broad spectrum and number of variables, such as heart rate (HR), pulse volume amplitude (PVA), EDA, EEG, respiratory irregularity, eye-blink activity, electromyography (EMG), recording during rest phase, active state (e.g., solving mental tasks), and normal state and its relation to stress. Neuroticism was measured by means of the Freiburger Persönlichkeitsinventar (FPI), an inventory widely used in Germany. The Neuroticism scale from the FPI is regarded as equivalent to Eysenck's EPI-N scale (Fahrenberg, Selg, &

TABLE 4.2. Correlations between Self-Reported Neuroticism (FPI-N) and Physiological Markers Recorded in Different Conditions

Condition	Physiological markers						
	HR	PVA	EDA	EEG	RSA	EB	EMG
Initial rest	.08	−.15	.04	−.11	.00	−.01	.06
Mental arithmetic	−.13	−.09	−.06	−.09	.16	−.11	−.11
Composite conditions	−.01	−.03	.08	.00	.19*	−.11	−.09

Note. Composite conditions refer to a score derived from the following four conditions: mental arithmetic, interview, anticipation of taking a blood sample, blood taking. HR = heart rate, PVA = pulse volume amplitude, EDA = electrodermal activity, EEG = alpha power, RSA = respiratory sinus arrhythmia, EB = eye-blink activity, EMG = electromyography. *$p < .05$. From "Psychophysiology of Neuroticism and Anxiety," by J. Fahrenberg. In A. Gale and M. W. Eysenck (Eds.), *Handbook of Individual Differences: Biological Perspectives* (1992, p. 202), Chichester, England: Wiley. Copyright 1992 by John Wiley & Sons Ltd. Adapted with permission.

Hampel, 1978). Data were aggregated taking into account such criteria as kind of physiological variables, experimental conditions, replication of measurements, and field and laboratory settings. To develop more complex physiological scores in some studies (e.g., Myrtek, 1984) factor analysis was applied.

The results of the numerous studies conducted by Fahrenberg and his coworkers are very consistent but rather pessimistic as regards psychophysiological correlates of neuroticism (emotionality). In general, they show no correlation between the different measures of autonomic arousal, on the one hand, and the measures of neuroticism, on the other. Table 4.2, which includes data collected on 125 male subjects, illustrates this state of affairs. Among the following seven markers—HR, PVA, EDA, EEG alpha power, respiratory irregularity index, eye-blink activity, and EMG—not one substantially correlated with neuroticism as measured using self-report data (Fahrenberg, 1992).

Further, a multivariate approach to anxiety shows a lack of consistency between the psychological measures of anxiety and the psychophysiological markers of this trait. For example, Van Heck (1988) conducted a study in which anxiety was measured by a self-report technique and by means of 19 observational indicators of this trait, parallel with three physiological correlates—level of skin conductance, heart rate, and forehead temperature. All these measures were recorded in eight different situations, such as threat of shock, public speaking, or accusation. The results of this study showed zero correlations between the variables under study. The lack of convergence between different indicators of trait anxiety and their physiological markers is the rule rather than the exception (see also Fahrenberg, 1992).

A multivariate approach has been applied by Kagan (1989a, 1994) and his coworkers (Kagan *et al.,* 1988) in studies on the physiological basis of inhibited versus uninhibited temperament in children (for details see Chapter 3). Assuming that inhibited children's reactions resemble the withdrawal reactions to novelty in animals, and that these reactions in animals are mediated by activity in the hypothalamus and in the limbic system (especially amygdala), the authors selected physiological indices that according to them refer to these neural structures. The following measures were related to temperament inhibition: heart rate, heart rate variability, pupillary dilation (during cognitive tests), total norepinephrine activity (from a urine sample), mean cortisol level (from saliva samples taken at home and under laboratory conditions), and skeletal muscular changes as expressed in the variability of the pitch periods of vocal utterances (under stress and under normal situations). It turned out that the correlations between the physiological variables as measured under the specific experimental conditions were rather low (ranging from $-.22$ to $+.33$; $Me = .10$), with the exception of heart rate and heart rate variability. This finding is consistent with studies on anxiety and neuroticism. When a composite index including all physiological measures of arousal was used, a significant relationship was found between the inhibited temperament and physiological arousal. Depending on the subjects' ages at which these measures were taken, the index of temperament inhibition correlated with the index of physiological arousal from .64 at 21 months, to .70 at the age of 7.5 years (Kagan *et al.*, 1988). This result is much more optimistic than findings in the domain of anxiety and neuroticism, but studies relating inhibited temperament to the physiological markers just mentioned need replication in other laboratories.

A multivariate or multimodal approach to temperament requires large laboratories in which a variety of physiological records can be taken simultaneously in different situations and with different behaviors. This is very time-consuming and expensive, which is one of the reasons why, in most of the studies, one or only a few physiological measures are related to temperament traits. As regards visceral arousal, most research refers to different characteristics of two phenomena— electrodermal activity and cardiovascular changes.

Electrodermal Activity

The number of active sweat glands is considered a basic determinant of electrodermal activity. These glands are activated by emotional arousal as well as by specific stimulation, such as auditory or visual stimuli. There are many techniques for measuring EDA as well as a large number of indices referring to different aspects of electrodermal activity (see Sosnowski, 1991). In general, it is agreed that electrodermal tonic arousal, which refers to the base level of arousal, is termed *skin conductance level* (SCL). Electrodermal phasic arousal, that is, electrodermal reaction to stimuli, is labeled *skin conductance response* (SCR). EDA has been employed as a physiological correlate of different temperament traits, such as extraversion, neuroticism, anxiety, and sensation seeking. Electrodermal responses have also been used as correlates of attention, alertness, the orienting reflex, psychopathy, and schizophrenia (Sosnowski & Zimmer, 1993; Stelmack, 1981).

EDA and Extraversion. Where EDA has been used as an indicator of the orienting reflex, most studies have shown that the orienting reaction expressed in the amplitude of EDA is larger in introverts than in extraverts. In turn, habituation to novel stimuli, as manifested in the decrease of electrodermal activity, occurs earlier in extraverts than in introverts (see H. J. Eysenck, 1990b; O'Gorman, 1977; Stelmack, 1981, 1990; Stelmack & Geen, 1992). Both findings indicate a higher phasic arousal in introverts as compared to extraverts, in line with Eysenck's theory. The results, however, are not unequivocal as shown in a detailed review by O'Gorman (1977). One of the factors that influence the intensity of the orienting reaction and the speed of habituation as expressed in EDA is the intensity of stimuli. In general, it was found that auditory stimuli of low intensity and high frequency did not differentiate extraverts from introverts in EDA orienting responses (see H. J. Eysenck, 1990b; Stelmack, 1981).

Several experiments have shown that under such conditions as high-intensity stimuli (e.g., tones at the 100 dB intensity level), large doses of caffeine, and performance of difficult tasks, EDA arousal is higher in extraverts than in introverts (see, e.g., Fowles, Roberts, & Nagel, 1977; Revelle, Amaral, & Turriff, 1976; B. D. Smith, Wilson, & Jones, 1983). This is in accord with Eysenck's hypothesis that protective inhibition develops earlier in introverts (i.e., to stimuli of lower intensity) because of their higher level of arousal.

Most of the results show that it tends to be SCR that differentiates extraverts from introverts, but some results also show differences between the two temperament types in SCL. Most spectacular in this respect is a study by G. D. Wilson (1990), who showed that introverts, in comparison to extraverts, had a higher level of tonic EDA arousal across 17 hours of continuous measurement (see Figure 4.9).

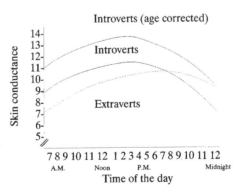

FIGURE 4.9. Relationship between extraversion and SCL. *Note.* From "Personality, Time of Day and Arousal," by G. D. Wilson, 1990, *Personality and Individual Differences, 11,* p. 165. Copyright 1990 by Elsevier Science Ltd. Reprinted with permission.

In this experiment self-recorded measures of skin conductance were taken hourly throughout one working day in 111 adult subjects. In accordance with several findings reported in the literature (see Revelle, Humphreys, Simon, & Gilliland, 1980; Revelle, Anderson, & Humphreys, 1987) it turned out that in introverts SCL was higher in the morning than in the evening, whereas in extraverts it was the reverse.

Numerous experiments have been conducted with the aim of showing relationships between extraversion and electrodermal activity, and it is impossible to present them in this chapter (for a review, see H. J. Eysenck, 1990b; H. J. Eysenck & Eysenck, 1985; B. D. Smith, 1983; Stelmack, 1981).

EDA and Negative Emotionality. It might be hypothesized that the electrodermal system, regulated by the visceral nervous system including the ANS is particularly sensitive to stimuli-generating emotions, predominantly the negative ones which are related to anxiety and neuroticism (Strelau, 1992a). During the past three decades, dozens of studies have been designed to compare levels and responses of EDA (SCL and SCR) with independent measures of state and trait anxiety as well as with neuroticism. The results are very pessimistic in that they do not allow for any reasonable conclusion to be drawn other than that there is lack of consistency in the data (see H. J. Eysenck, 1990b; Naveteur & Freixa i Baque, 1987; J. A. Stern & Janes, 1973). Naveteur and Freixa i Baque (1987) have summarized the results of 32 studies conducted since World War II on nonpathological subjects differing in state and trait anxiety. These studies were conducted under different conditions, such as rest, expositions of stimuli (tones, flashes, verbal), and physical and psychological stress. Tonic, phasic, and spontaneous electrodermal activity were measured. The conclusion to be drawn from this summary further underlines the inconsistency as regards the relationship between anxiety and electrodermal activity. The same holds true for neuroticism, often considered a synonym of anxiety (M. W. Eysenck, 1987; Zuckerman, 1991c).

EDA and Sensation Seeking. In some studies, sensation seeking has been related to electrodermal activity. Although tonic arousal as measured by EDA seems not to be related to this temperament trait (Zuckerman, 1991c), there is some evidence that EDA can be used as a marker of sensation seeking when phasic arousal is considered. Neary and Zuckerman (1976) have shown that the orienting reaction as expressed in SCR is stronger to novel stimuli in sensation seekers than in sensation avoiders. This is congruent with Zuckerman's (1984c) theory which predicts that sensation seekers are oriented toward novelty. Similar results were obtained by Feij, Orlebeke, Gazendam, and van Zuilen (1985), but in other studies this finding has not been replicated (see, e.g., Ridgeway & Hare, 1981; Zuckerman, Simons, & Como, 1988).

Summarizing the studies regarding the relationship between temperament traits and electrodermal activity, one must agree with Zuckerman's (1991c) conclusion that

[t]he research on tonic and phasic EDA suggests that differences in personality ["temperament"] interact with differences in the situation and stimulus characteristics and meanings, but the nature of the interactions is not always predictable from the theories of the personality traits. (p. 264)

Cardiovascular Activity

Both branches of the ANS have a direct influence on cardiovascular activity (CVA). Of special significance for adaptive purposes is the activity of the sympathetic nervous system. The sympathetic NS acts in such a way as to mobilize the cardiovascular system (CVS) during such states as stress, high level of mental or physical activity, energy mobilization, and, as already mentioned by Cannon (1932), in states of "fight and flight." The activity of the sympathetic NS is expressed by increased heart rate (HR) and blood pressure and in increased respiration, supplying oxygen to the blood system. Cardiovascular activity, like EDA, is under the control of higher nervous centers, especially of the hypothalamus. Regarded as an indicator of the level of arousal, CVA occurs, like EDA, in two main forms: tonic and phasic arousal. Since EDA and CVA serve different functions, there is no reason to assume that they are correlated with each other (Sosnowski, 1991). There are several indices of CVA, among which heart rate and blood pressure (systolic and diastolic) are the most commonly used.

HR as Indicator of Different Physiological States. Heart rate is taken as the index of CVA in about 90% of psychophysiological studies referring to the CVS (Ciarkowska, 1992). Heart rate, depending on the situation, kind of activity, and temporal context in which it is measured, serves as an indicator of different physiological states. Therefore some basic information is needed to understand the cardiovascular studies as related to temperament.

Taking as the point of departure the functions that heart rate serves in the organism, three different kinds of reactions can be distinguished: orienting, defense, and startle, all of them referring to phasic arousal. The cardiovascular orienting reaction occurs as a response to new stimuli and is revealed by a *deceleration* of HR. According to Sokolov (1963), who introduced the distinction between orienting and defense reflexes, the essence of the orienting reaction is the reception of cue elements of stimuli. The cardiovascular defense reaction, manifested in *acceleration* of HR, is a result of intense stimulation and strong negative emotions. The function of the defense reaction is to escape from noxious stimulation and to prepare the organism for action (Ciarkowska, 1992). The startle reaction described by F. K. Graham (1979; see also Turpin, 1986) appears in situations of surprise and unexpectancy, and manifests itself in cardiac acceleration, as is the case in defense reactions. The startle reaction has shorter latencies and habituation periods when compared with the defense reaction (F. K. Graham, 1979; Turpin, 1986).

CVA Correlates of Adult Temperament. The view that HR is a direct and simple index of anxiety (Fowles, 1992) was quite a popular one. This idea, however, has not been confirmed experimentally, nor in psychometric measures of trait anxiety (see Hodges, 1976). An extensive study on over 700 subjects by Myrtek (1984) in which several cardiovascular measures were applied in different experimental situations (rest, stress, etc.), did not lead to an unequivocal conclusion regarding the relationship between emotional lability (anxiety) and extraversion, on the one hand, and CVA measures on the other.

C. Davis (1988) conducted a study in which extreme scores (1 *SD* below or above the mean) of extraversion and neuroticism as measured by means of EPI were related to indices of basal heart rate and SCL. The physiological measures, taken from 69 adults during four consecutive sessions, showed that scores for tonic arousal refer to external stimulation rather than to strictly temperament dimensions. No correlations with neuroticism were found, and the only statistically significant relationship appeared in extraverts but not in introverts.

Other studies (Gange, Geen, & Harkins, 1979; Stelmack, Bourgeois, Chain, & Pickard, 1979) also have shown that HR scores recorded during a baseline measurement period do not distinguish extraverts from introverts. However, when HRs are recorded during task performance under low stimulative value (e.g., vigilance task), introverts show higher HR scores as compared to extraverts (see Gange *et al.,* 1979). In turn, an experiment by Geen (1984) showed that the most evident differences in HR scores between extraverts and introverts occurred when subjects were exposed to moderate intensities of auditory stimuli. Phasic arousal, expressed in HR increase, grows with intensity of stimulation; however, the differences in HR between introverts and extraverts disappeared when subjects were exposed to stimuli of low and high intensity.

In the domain of Pavlovian temperament characteristics, a study conducted by Klonowicz (1992) led to the conclusion that, of the two traits strength of excitation and mobility of NP it was strength of excitation that correlated with cardiovascular activity measured before and after task performance under stress. Both temperament traits were measured by means of Strelau's STI. Cardiovascular indices included systolic and diastolic blood pressure as well as HR. Task performance consisted of the simultaneous translation of a text from a foreign language into the native one, and the reverse. This task, considered difficult, was performed by highly qualified professional interpreters (23 Ss, 30–42 years) and by English-language students (40 Ss, 22–26 years). Taking the difference between pre- (base level) and postperformance levels of CVA as an index of physiological effort allocated to task performance, Klonowicz (1992) was able to conclude that individuals with a weak nervous system allocated more effort during task performance than "strong" individuals. This was expressed in statistically significant negative correlations between blood pressure (systolic) and HR, and strength of excitation.

In a series of experiments by Ciarkowska (1992), strength of excitation as measured by STI was related to three indices of CVA recorded during performance of easy and difficult cognitive tasks. Difficulty was determined by the number of visual elements to be recalled. The indicators of CVA used by Ciarkowska were rather sophisticated, and I refer only to heart rate scores obtained during the generation of responses in two different experiments. It turned out that, when HR was measured during this phase of task performance, a significant difference was found between individuals with strong and weak NS, but only for the complex cognitive task. In solving the difficult task, HR deceleration occurred only in individuals with strong NS; the difference between strong and weak subjects in both experiments was statistically significant. HR acceleration, which might be expected in individuals with weak NS in performance of a difficult task, did not occur in this study.

In a study conducted by Richards and Eves (1991) Eysenck's EPQ measures of extraversion, neuroticism, and psychoticism, and Strelau's STI measures of strength of excitation, strength of inhibition, and mobility of NP, were related to heart rate in response to strong (112 dB) acoustic stimuli. On the basis of experimental scores, 69 adult subjects were divided into accelerators (23 Ss) and nonaccelerators (46 subjects). Those subjects classified as accelerators showed a significant acceleration (>4 beats per minute above baseline) of long-latency HR in response to auditory stimuli. All remaining subjects were classified as nonaccelerators. The results of this study are depicted in Table 4.3. The scores on the Extraversion, Strength of Excitation, and Mobility scales were significantly lower but for Neuroticism were higher for accelerators than for nonaccelerators. This result is in accord with the theory if we consider that HR acceleration is a defense reaction to strong stimuli, to which introverts, neurotics, and individuals with a weak NS are more prone than individuals representing the opposite pole on these dimensions.

TABLE 4.3. Temperament Characteristics (Means and Standard Deviations) for Accelerators and Non-Accelerators

Scale	Accelerators ($N = 23$)	Nonaccelerators ($N = 46$)
Psychoticism	6.24 (3.87)	6.68 (3.11)
Extraversion	12.24 (5.42)	14.84 (4.08)*
Neuroticism	15.81 (5.81)	12.52 (5.20)*
Lie scale	4.29 (3.10)	4.57 (3.38)
Strength of excitation	23.50 (8.40)	27.50 (6.45)*
Strength of inhibition	27.68 (5.61)	29.50 (6.58)
Mobility of CNS properties	29.14 (6.87)	32.52 (5.55)*

Note. From "Personality, Temperament and the Cardiac Defense Response," by M. Richards and F. F. Eves, 1991, *Personality and Individual Differences, 12,* p. 1004. Copyright 1991 by Elsevier Science Ltd. Reprinted with permission.
*$p < .05$

Richards and Eves's experiment furnishes physiological support for psychometric findings which show that extraversion correlates positively with strength of excitation and mobility, while neuroticism correlates negatively with the Pavlovian temperament traits (Strelau, 1983; Strelau, Angleitner, & Ruch, 1990). The results of this study also suggest that HR acceleration is not a trait-specific physiological marker, but refers to four qualitatively different traits controlled in this study, all of which, however, refer to the concept of arousal. The nonspecificity of physiological correlates of temperament traits is the rule rather than the exception.

Studies relating sensation seeking to CVA were also conducted in the 1980s. Feij and colleagues (1985), starting with the assumption that sensation seeking is related to strength of the nervous system, hypothesized that sensation seekers, mainly those who score high on the Disinhibition scale of Zuckerman's SSS, are subjects whose nervous system can endure strong stimulation. In turn, low disinhibiters react to strong stimuli defensively (with transmarginal inhibition). In a study conducted by these authors, a series of 10 auditory stimuli (80 dB; 1000 Hz) was applied to 49 students at irregular intervals. Heart rate, measured in beats per minute (together with EDA indices), was continuously monitored. Taking into account the average of the first three trials used as indices of habituation speed, the authors calculated the mean change in phasic heart rate separately for high (14 Ss) and low disinhibiters (11 Ss). The two groups were distinguished taking as the criterion the quartile deviation from the mean on the SSS-Disinhibition scale. High disinhibiters showed an HR deceleration, an indicator of the orienting reaction, whereas low disinhibiters showed HR acceleration. As already mentioned, HR acceleration is considered an indicator of the defense reaction. The pattern of heart rates as related to the individuals' position on the Disinhibition scale is in accordance with Feij and colleagues' (1985) prediction. Similar results have been obtained by Ridgeway and Hare (1981) and by Zuckerman and colleagues (1988) for the same modality of stimuli. As concluded by Zuckerman (1991c):

> High sensation seekers, particularly of disinhibiter type, manifest a strong cardiac orienting response to auditory stimuli of low to moderate intensities whereas low sensation seekers tend to show defensive or startle reactions (cardiac acceleration) to either moderate or intense auditory stimuli. (p. 269)

CVA Correlates Applied in Studies on Child Temperament.   A variety of heart rate measures used as indices of ANS activity have also been applied in temperament studies on infants and children (see Boomsma & Plomin, 1986; Campos, 1976; Kagan, 1982b; Porges, Arnold, & Forbes, 1973). For example, Healy (1989) conducted an experiment on 45 twin pairs aged 11–35 months. Their temperament was scored by means of Fullard, McDevitt, and Carey's Toddler Temperament Scale (TTS). Tonic (baseline condition) and phasic (during a video of *Sesame Street*) cardiovascular activity was measured. Experimental and observational scores of temperament behavior were included in this study. The following three measures related to CVA were taken into account: HR (HR periods measured in ms), HR variance, and vagal tone. The last mentioned is estimated on the basis of HR variance combined with spontaneous breathing, both being vagally mediated. The vagal tone is known as the respiratory sinus arrhythmia (RSA). High RSA is associated with slow HR and high HR variance, and low RSA with fast HR and low HR variance.

The general findings of this study allowed Healy to draw some conclusions of importance for temperament studies. The correlations between ANS measures and composite measures of temperament behavior were low and statistically nonsignificant except for latency to approach. Approach latency was correlated positively (but weakly) with all three HR indices. Among the nine temperament dimensions as measured by TTS, mood and distractibility correlated positively with HR, HR variance, and RSA. The correlations, though statistically significant, were very low, varying between .18 and .33. Thus, in general, the correlations between physiological markers referring to cardiovascular activity and temperament characteristics as measured in Healy's study were low.

Summarizing, one concludes that most of the studies are equivocal as regards the relationship between CVA markers and temperament traits. This is particularly evident in respect to such traits as anxiety, neuroticism, and extraversion. Positive findings were found mainly for those CVA indices that refer to phasic arousal as related to sensation seeking.

Final Remarks

As already mentioned, EDA and CVA, used mainly in temperament studies as measures related to the visceral brain, are not the only physiological phenomena to which researchers limited the ANS markers of temperament traits. For example, the salivation output to lemon juice placed on the tongue was used as a physiological marker of extraversion (H. J. Eysenck, 1970, 1990b). Another physiological correlate applied in temperament research is critical flicker fusion. This phenomenon consists of measuring the frequency threshold at which the subject begins to perceive increasing frequency of visual stimuli as continuous light, and conversely. The frequency threshold is estimated at which the subject is able to perceive the exposed stimuli as separate flashes. Flicker fusion has been used as a physiological marker in studies on extraversion (H. J. Eysenck, 1970) and as an index of lability of the nervous system (see Chapter 2) in Teplov's laboratory (Nebylitsyn, 1972a; Strelau, 1983). In some studies pupillary dilation was used as a physiological correlate of temperament, as for extraversion (H. J. Eysenck, 1970, 1990b) or inhibited temperament (Kagan, 1989a, 1994). In many investigations temperament traits have been related to sensory thresholds for stimuli of different modalities. Some of these studies, which are more related to psychophysics than to physiology, have been mentioned in the presentation of different conceptualizations of temperament (see chapters 2 & 3).

Physiological Correlates of Temperament Referring to Cortical Arousal

It is commonly agreed that bioelectrical activity of the brain as recorded by the electroencephalogram (EEG) is a direct measure of cortical arousal (Lindsley, 1952; McGuinness & Pribram, 1980; Moruzzi & Magoun, 1949). The distinction between phasic and tonic arousal introduced in the preceding section applies also to cortical arousal. At rest, when no stimuli are exposed, spontaneous (also called background) EEG activity is recorded, and this activity reflects tonic cortical arousal. When stimuli are exposed, changes in bioelectrical activity occur which are recorded by averaging the EEG samples, resulting in waveforms known as evoked potential (EPs). Evoked potentials are considered to be measures of phasic cortical arousal. Both tonic and phasic cortical arousal have been applied to studies on temperament. Since the recognition that there is asymmetry in the functioning of the brain hemispheres, this phenomenon, as recorded by means of EEG, has also been related to temperament characteristics. The three cortical arousal approaches to studies on temperament are presented in this section.

Spontaneous EEG Activity

As early as the 1930s it had been stated (see Jasper, 1937, 1941; Lindsley, 1952) that the pattern of spontaneous EEG activity in normal adults varies widely during different states of arousal (see Figure 4.10). Generally speaking, four categories of wave forms have been distinguished: delta, theta, alpha, and beta. Delta waves are characterized by low frequency (0.5–3.5 Hz) and occur during deep sleep. Theta waves are of higher frequency (4–7.5 Hz) and are recorded during sleep states and drowsiness. Alpha waves are typical for alert states of rest and relaxation, and their frequency varies from 8 Hz to 12.5 Hz. During states of mental effort, concentration, and other kinds of activity that evoke excitation, fast, desynchronized waves occur. These are beta waves; their frequency varies from 13 Hz to 32 Hz.

As can be seen from Figure 4.10, the different categories of waves illustrating the diversity of states of arousal vary not only in frequency but also in amplitude and regularity. Frequency and amplitude characteristics, as well as their combinations (total energy), are mainly used to characterize the states of arousal. Computerization of EEG recordings has enabled the analysis of the separate frequencies—delta, theta, alpha, and beta waves—obtained from a basic recording. This is known as spectral analysis, or the power spectrum procedure. All these measures show that there are individual differences regarding EEG characteristics. As regards spontaneous EEG activity, most studies related to temperament have been conducted in states of relaxation. It was assumed that recordings of alpha activity most adequately reflect tonic arousal. As indicators of tonic cortical arousal, alpha frequency, amplitude, and the alpha index have been applied. The alpha

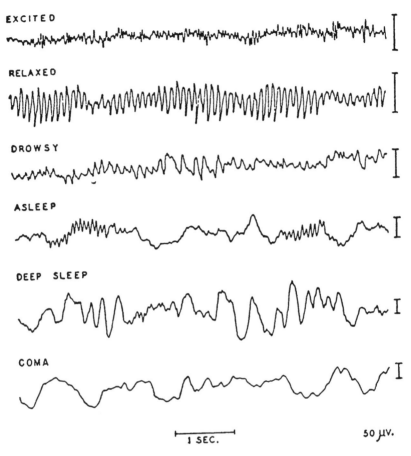

EXCITED

RELAXED

DROWSY

ASLEEP

DEEP SLEEP

COMA

1 SEC.   50 μV.

FIGURE 4.10. Range of variation in normal EEG. *Note.* From "Psychological Phenomena and the Electroencephalogram," by D. B. Lindsley, 1952, *Electroencephalography and Clinical Neurophysiology, 4,* p. 188. Copyright 1952 by Elsevier Science Ltd. Reprinted with permission.

index is usually expressed in percentage of alpha waves present in a given time unit (e.g., in 1 min). High alpha frequency, low alpha amplitude, and a low alpha index are considered indicators of a high level of tonic cortical arousal. Low cortical arousal is expressed by alpha waves of low frequency and high amplitude, a high alpha index, or both.

Even before Moruzzi and Magoun's discovery that the BSRF regulates cortical arousal, relationships between temperament characteristics and EEG activity were looked for. For example, Lemere (1936), Gottlober (1938), and Henry and Knott (1941) examined the relationship between extraversion and EEG alpha characteristics, but the results of these experiments were not unequivocal. Saul, Davis, and Davis (1937, 1949) found that passive individuals are characterized by a high alpha index and active individuals by a low alpha index.

Spontaneous EEG Characteristics as Markers of Extraversion. The most prominent temperament trait to be related to spontaneous EEG activity, especially to alpha characteristics, is extraversion. This follows from Eysenck's conceptualization regarding the physiological background of this trait. In this view individual differences in the excitation/inhibition balance (H. J. Eysenck, 1947) and, later, (H. J. Eysenck, 1967, 1970) in the chronic activation of the corticoreticular loop, are responsible for the individual's position on the extraversion–introversion dimension (for details see Chapter 2). Many studies were conducted, mainly from the 1950s until the beginning of the 1980s, in which extraversion was related to EEG measures. Different measures of extraversion have been applied, such as Eysenck's MPI, EPI, EPQ, and scales considered equivalent to Eysenck's concept of extraversion (e.g., the Sociability scale from Guilford's GZTS or Cattell's [1965] second-order Extraversion scale). In the domain of EEG activity and alpha frequencies and amplitudes, the alpha index as well as the EEG power spectrum were recorded. In line with Eysenck's theory, it was assumed that extraverts, in contrast to introverts, are characterized by lower levels of spontaneous cortical arousal, as expressed in higher alpha amplitude, lower alpha frequency, and a higher alpha index. It is impossible to cover the details of the studies which, in general, are very inconsistent and do not lead to firm conclusions regarding the EEG–extraversion relationship.

To bring some order in more than 30 studies examining the relationship between EEG activity and extraversion, Gale (1973, 1983, 1986) undertook a series of meta-analyses in which account was taken of temperament assessments, EEG scoring procedures, and the stimulative value of experimental situations. Gale's main conclusion was that the predicted relationship between alpha characteristics and extraversion occurred only in those studies conducted in experimental settings that assured a moderate level of arousal. According to Gale, experimental settings that consisted of resting conditions with eyes closed were judged as being low-arousal conditions, with repeated opening and closing of the eyes as moderate-arousal conditions, and with different task performance as high-arousal conditions.

The lack of consistency in the EEG–extraversion relationship is due to the fact that under low stimulation extraverts, by using internal stimulation (e.g., fantasy) enhance their level of arousal, thus making it equal to the level of introverts. In turn, in a situation of strong stimulative value, introverts use uncontrolled strategies to lower their high level of arousal (Gale, 1973, 1983). This results in contradictions or lack of differences in EEG measures between extraverts and introverts. According to Gale, the relationship between extraversion and EEG is not linear, as assumed in many studies. Under low task demands and high task demands the

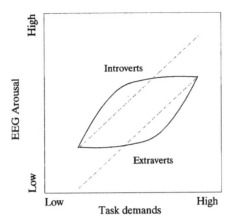

FIGURE 4.11. Arousal as a function of task demands. *Note.* From "Extraversion and the EEG: I. An Evaluation of Gale's Hypothesis," by J. G. O'Gorman, 1984, *Biological Psychology, 19,* p. 96. Copyright 1984 by Elsevier Science NL Reprinted with permission.

level of arousal between extraverts and introverts does not differ, as illustrated by Figure 4.11. Taking into account the studies in which moderate arousal was warranted by experimental conditions, most experiments have shown a relationship between EEG characteristics and extraversion scores as predicted by Eysenck's theory.

Other meta-analyses of data referring to the extraversion–EEG relationship have been conducted. O'Gorman (1984; O'Gorman & Mallise, 1984) undertook a reanalysis of Gale's comparisons, mainly by improving the clarity of criteria and methodological requirements. Studies in which extraversion was measured by invalid techniques were removed and some new studies not considered by Gale were included. Further, the stimulative value of experimental settings as described in publications was estimated by two independent judges. Using a 5-point scale, the judges scored whether the experimental setting was boring (1), interesting (5), or somewhere between these two extremes (2, 3, 4). After analyzing the data from 41 experiments, O'Gorman concluded that Gale's statement regarding the predicted EEG–extraversion relationship lacks both coherence and empirical support. However, O'Gorman (1984) also pointed out that measures of extraversion correlate significantly with estimations of the stimulative value of experimental settings in support of Eysenck (.36 to .38, depending whether the stimulative value of experimental settings was established in Gale's or in O'Gorman's analysis); this analysis was based on EEG data from 31 studies.

An independent analysis of the EEG data as related to extraversion was conducted by Bartussek (1984), who took into account some German studies, not reported in Gale's and O'Gorman's analyses. The conclusion at which Bartussek arrived after analyzing the data supports the ambiguity of the EEG–extraversion relationship. One finding, to which attention was not paid in previous analyses, shows that the relationship between extraversion and EEG characteristics occurs as predicted when, from the spectrum of EEG frequencies, beta rhythm (15–30 Hz) is taken into account in interaction with neuroticism. In subjects low in neuroticism, extraversion correlated positively with these EEG characteristics (Bartussek, 1984).

A study was conducted by O'Gorman and Malisse (1984) in which experimental settings were arranged in such a way as to produce low, moderate, and high arousal. Under moderate arousal, which according to Gale is the best experimental setting for studying the extraversion–EEG relationship, extraverts showed increased arousal expressed in lower alpha activity, contrary to Eysenck's hypothesis. Generally, relationships between alpha activity and extraversion in experimental settings differing in level of arousal showed up in this study only when extraversion was considered in interaction with neuroticism, a result similar to that reported by Bartussek. The interaction effect seems to be understandable if we consider that, on the arousal dimension, introverted neurotics and stable extraverts represent the two opposite poles.

An analysis of EEG data as related to extraversion, conducted by O'Gorman (1984), showed that the kinds of measures used to diagnose extraversion may be one of the reasons for the lack of consistency between EEG data and temperament traits. In support of this hypothesis, O'Gorman and Lloyd (1987) conducted a study on 50 undergraduates (26 female and 24 male) in which the Extraversion scale from the EPQ was used together with Eysenck's I7 inventory (see Chapter 6). Impulsivity, as measured by the I7 Impulsiveness scale, correlated significantly with alpha activity in the direction predicted by Eysenck for extraversion. By contrast, the EPQ Extraversion scale was not related to the EEG measures recorded in conditions which Gale (1973, 1983) considered to be optimal. The data furnish support for the hypothesis that it is the impulsivity rather than the sociability component of extraversion that is the major correlate of differences in EEG-defined arousal.

Spontaneous EEG Characteristics as Correlates of Different Temperament Traits. When neuroticism is considered in isolation from extraversion, no relationship has been established between this temperament dimension and EEG measures of arousal. This finding was independent of whether different scores of alpha activity were taken during a relaxed state (e.g., O'Gorman & Lloyd, 1987; Young, Lader, & Fenton, 1971) or whether EEG activity, as expressed in frequency bands, was measured in experimental settings differing in stimulative value, for example, rest, attentive listening, or emotional stress (Rosler, 1975).

A study conducted recently by Stenberg (1992) on 40 students (23 male and 17 female) also supports the relationship between impulsivity and EEG as formulated by O'Gorman and Lloyd. Stenberg's study is of special interest because of his theoretically well-grounded experimental design, and the complexity of EEG measures taken from all scalp positions and including eight separate frequency bands (from 0 to 30 Hz). As regards the personality measures, all scales from the EPI and 15 scales from the Karolinska Scales of Personality (KSP) were included. On the basis of principal component analysis, five factors were separated and two of them—anxiety and impulsivity—were related to EEG measures. The impulsivity factor had high loadings on the following scales: Extraversion, Impulsivity, Monotony Avoidance (a sensation seeking characteristic), and Social Desirability. The anxiety factor loaded highest on Neuroticism, Psychic Anxiety, and Guilt scales. EEG measures were taken in three different experimental settings: neutral condition, pleasant condition evoked by means of emotionally positive situations to be recalled by the subjects, and unpleasant condition evoked by the subject's emotional imagery of an unpleasant situation. The results, interpreted in terms of Gray's concept of temperament, showed that (1) high-impulsive individuals relative to low impulsives have EEG characteristics typical for a lower level of arousal; this was expressed in higher levels of slow activity in the theta band and higher activity in the alpha band, but the latter only when impulsivity was combined with anxiety. (2) In both situations, characterized by positive and negative emotional states, anxious individuals exhibited higher tonic arousal as compared with subjects low in trait anxiety. The increase of tonic arousal was expressed in an increase in right-sided frontal theta activity and in temporal beta activity (Stenberg, 1992).

As regards the relationship between sensation seeking and spontaneous EEG activity, Zuckerman (1991c) cited only two studies, one conducted by Golding and Richards (1985) and the other by Cox (1977; cited after Zuckerman, 1991c). Golding and Richards, taking into account alpha characteristics, did not find statistically significant relationships between sensation seeking and EEG measures, and this was also true for extraversion and neuroticism. Cox, who related frequencies in theta, alpha, and beta bands to sensation seeking, also found no links between the variables compared.

Worthy of note, because of the large number of subjects and the variety of temperamental traits measured, is a study conducted by Strelau and Terelak (1974). From a group of 762 men ages 20–40 the authors selected two extreme groups differing in alpha index scores recorded under low-arousal conditions (subjects lying relaxed with eyes closed). Taking the quartile deviation as the selection criterion, 191 subjects were classified as representing a high tonic level of arousal (low alpha index) and 190 as having a low level of tonic arousal (high alpha index). The two extreme groups were tested for temperament traits. The Maudsley Personality Inventory (MPI), Manifest Anxiety Scale (MAS), GZTS, TTS, and STI were applied (the abbreviations are explained in Chapter 6). Altogether the study comprised 24 temperament traits, of which only four showed statistically significant differences between the high- (HA) and low-arousal (LA) groups: Neuroticism from MPI (HA > LA), masculinity from GZTS (HA < LA), dominant and sociable from the TTS (for both, HA < LA). Also a tendency ($p < .10$) was found for anxiety as measured by MAS (HA > LA), strength of inhibition measured by STI (HA < LA), and GZTS sociability and objectivity (for both, HA < LA). The results demonstrated that individuals with higher tonic arousal (low alpha index) are more neurotic and anxious, lower in masculinity, objectivity, and strength of inhibition, less dominant and sociable as compared with individuals characterized by lower tonic arousal (high alpha index). However, traits like extraversion, strength of excitation, and activity did not differ between the two groups. The differences (including tendencies) obtained in this study are rather consistent.

Taking into account all the studies in which temperament characteristics have been compared with spontaneous EEG activity, no definite conclusion can be drawn. Probably more sophisticated studies, of which Stenberg's (1992) is an example, must be initiated. One can conceive such a theoretically well-grounded study in which account is taken of the whole EEG spectrum recorded from all scalp positions, under situations evoking different levels of arousal, and including a variety of temperament traits measured in an interactional paradigm. EEG experts know that this postulate is remote, for many reasons which are not discussed here.

Evoked Potentials

Under stimuli of different modalities (visual, auditory, somatosensory), changes in bioelectrical activity occur which are expressed in an increase of low-voltage and irregular EEG frequency, a phenomenon known as alpha blocking. The spontaneous EEG activity, which changes from moment to moment and is expressed in irregular EEG recordings, does not allow recording of the bioelectric response to a stimulus. Hence a series of stimuli (20–100) is applied at constant time intervals and durations. This procedure allows averaging of the shape of the numerous separate curves by means of computerization. This results in an averaged curve known as the *evoked potential* (EP), or averaged evoked response (AER, also averaged evoked potential, AEP), the last term underlining the procedure of averaging. The response to stimuli lasts over a period of 500 msec or more and is characterized by a sequence of waves with positive (P) and negative (N) peaks, as seen in Figure 4.12. The peaks are numbered according to the order of waves that appear after the stimuli are applied (N1,P1, N2,P2, etc.) or by expressing—in msec—the temporal sequence (latency) in which they occur (e.g., P100, N140, P200). The structure of the evoked potential (temporal characteristics, shapes, and amplitudes of the separate waves) is the subject of detailed studies, depending on the goal and the context in which records are obtained.

AEP Characteristics Applied in Temperament Studies. In studies on temperament the amplitude of evoked potentials has been of most interest because of

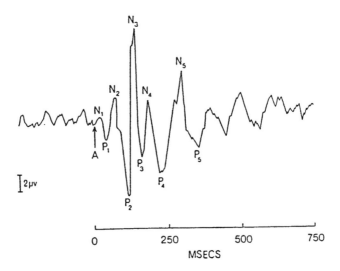

FIGURE 4.12. Diagrammatic representation of the average evoked potential. *Note.* From *Personality and Individual Differences: A Natural Science Approach* (p. 167), by H. J. Eysenck and M. W. Eysenck, 1985, New York: Plenum Press. Copyright 1985 by Plenum Press. Reprinted with permission.

its direct relation to the energetic characteristic of responses. The amplitude of EP is a function of intensity of stimuli; that is, the stronger the stimuli, the higher the amplitude, in accordance with the law of strength. When stimuli of too high intensity are applied, a decrease in the amplitude may be observed, due to protective inhibition. The relationship between intensity of stimuli and changes in response to these stimuli was used by Nebylitsyn (1960) in experiments aimed at diagnosing the strength of excitation by means of the slope of the RT curve (see Chapter 2). Buchsbaum (1976, 1978) and coworkers (Buchsbaum & Silverman, 1968; Buchsbaum, Haier, & Johnson, 1983) demonstrated that individuals differ in the way EP amplitudes change with increasing stimulus intensity. These differences, observed mainly for peaks varying from P100 to P200, are quite stable and occur in all modalities (visual, auditory, and somatosensory) of EP. Depending on whether, in response to increasing stimuli an increase or decrease in EP amplitudes occurs, Buchsbaum distinguished two types—augmenters and reducers, as illustrated in Figure 4.13. Augmenters are characterized by an increasing amplitude of EP in response to increased intensity of stimuli. In reducers the EP amplitude decreases as a function of increasing stimulation or increases to a lesser degree as compared with augmenters.

Walter, Cooper, Altridge, McCallun, and Winter (1964) have shown that, in RT experiments in which an imperative stimulus (S_2; e.g., a light to which the subject presses a button) is preceded by a warning signal (S_1; e.g., the word "attention"

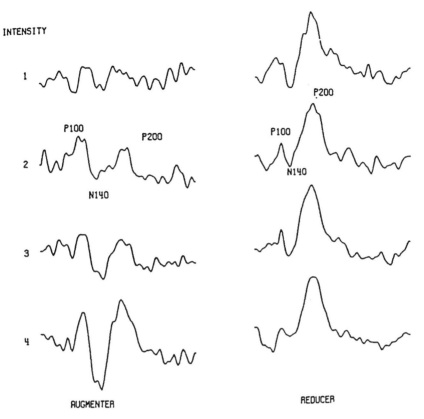

FIGURE 4.13. AEP to four intensities of light typical for augmenters and reducers. *Note.* From "Augmenting and Reducing: Individual Differences in Evoked Potentials," by M. S. Buchsbaum, R. J. Haier, and J. Johnson. In A. Gale and J. A. Edwards (Eds.), *Physiological Correlates of Human Behaviour: Individual Differences and Psychology* (1983, Vol. 3, p. 121), London: Academic Press. Copyright 1983 by Academic Press. Reprinted with permission.

or a tone), a slow upward brain wave is generated after the presentation of the warning signal (see Figure 4.14). This slow event-related potential, called contingent negative variation (CNV), occurs during a state of expectancy (readiness for reaction) and is mainly recorded in the central and frontal cortex. The CNV has two main components: the O wave reflecting an orienting response to the warning stimulus, and the E wave, which reflects expectation of the imperative stimulus. The amplitude of the slow ERP is considered the most often used indicator of CNV. Several studies report that there are differences in CNV between normal subjects, neurotics, and psychopaths (see Callaway, Tueting, & Koslow, 1978). One of the hypotheses developed in this field states that the magnitude of CNV is a result

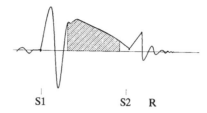

S1   S2   R

FIGURE 4.14. The contingent negative variation (CNV). *Note.* From "Neuroticism, Extraversion and Slow Brain Potentials," by F. Lolas and I. de Andraca, 1977, *Neuropsychobiology, 3,* p. 14. Copyright 1977 by S. Kanger AG, Basel. Reprinted with permission.

of interaction between the individual's actual state of arousal, contingent on the experimental situation (e.g., stress, relaxation), and his or her chronic level of arousal. This hypothesis has motivated researchers to conduct studies in which CNV is related to temperament traits.

The P300 (or P3) is another event-related potential to which attention has been devoted by some researchers interested in the relationship between cortical arousal and temperament traits. P3 is the specific positive peak of the third EP wave (see Figure 4.12) presumed to be related to cognitive activity consisting of memory and learning performance (see Donchin & Coles, 1988). "P3 amplitude reflects the amount of attention allocated to the processing of a given stimulus when memory operations are employed" (Polich & Martin, 1992, p. 534). Larger P300 components are produced by stimuli which demand allocation of greater attentional resources. It has been assumed that, depending on individual differences in the chronic level of arousal to which several temperament characteristics refer, there may be differences in the allocation of attentional resources expressed in P300 amplitude.

EP Amplitudes Related to Temperament. It is impossible to review in this chapter all the studies in which temperament characteristics have been related to the three indicators of brain activity—amplitude of EP, CNV, and P300—just described. In the domain of extraversion, which has been mostly related to the three EEG characteristics, surveys, albeit far from complete, have been published by Geen (1983), Bartussek (1984), Stelmack (1990), H. J. Eysenck, (1990b) and Zuckerman (1991c). Zuckerman has also presented a thorough review of research on sensation seeking in the context of EP and CNV (Zuckerman, 1990, 1994).

The augmenting–reducing phenomenon recorded by Buchsbaum (1976, 1978; Buchsbaum & Silverman, 1968) in the domain of evoked potentials has been proposed by Bazylevich (1974) as an indicator of strength of excitation. Taking as the point of departure the fact that strength of NS is manifested when the increasing stimulus intensity ceases to evoke increased reaction (the phenomenon of protective inhibition), Bazylevich used somatosensory EPs to measure this CNS property. A decrease of EP amplitudes in response to strong stimuli (to be observed in reducers) is diagnostic for weak NS individuals, whereas an increase of EP amplitudes to increasing intensities of stimuli is typical for individuals with a strong NS. Chuprikova (1977) proposed using the amplitude of the N1 and P2 components of the auditory EP to stimuli of different intensities for diagnosing CNS strength. Neither Bazylevich nor Chuprikova related their augmenting–reducing EP measures of strength of excitation to other diagnostic scores of this temperament dimension, which is a disadvantage of these studies. The only study in which strength of excitation, measured independently (by means of the STI-R), was related to amplitudes of EP was conducted by De Pascalis (1994), who showed that this CNS property correlates positively with N4 peak amplitude under both no-stress and stress conditions.

If the protective inhibition hypothesis is adequate for the explanation of individual differences in the relationship between intensity of stimuli and the amplitude of EP, the following may be expected. When weak and moderate stimuli are presented to individuals who have a chronically low level of arousal (in whom protective inhibition develops only under very strong stimuli) an increase of EP amplitude to increasing intensity of stimuli will be less expressed as compared to individuals having a chronically high level of arousal. This means, for example, that under such conditions for extraverts, sensation seekers, and the strong type of NS, the increase of the slope of EP amplitudes will be less pronounced than is typical for reducers. For individuals representing the opposite pole of these temperament dimensions, the slope of EP resembles that of augmenters. Under increasing intensity of stimuli, protective inhibition may occur and this will lead to a decrease of EP amplitude (typical for reducers), as observed in individuals with a chronically high level of arousal (e.g., introverts, sensation avoiders, weak type of NS). In individuals with a low level of arousal, the EP amplitude grows as a function of increasing stimuli also when the stimuli are of high intensity; hence for them the augmenting phenomenon is typical. Thus, depending on whether the exposed stimuli are in the range of low, moderate, or high intensity, both phenomena—augmenting and reducing—may occur in individuals with a chronically high, as well as chronically low, level of arousal.

The difficulty in studies considering the relationship between EP amplitudes and temperament characteristics consists in deciding what the range of intensity of stimuli is to which protective inhibition may occur in chronically high-aroused individuals. It is probable that the intensity of stimuli used in such studies is the main source of inconsistency observed in establishing the relationship between the amplitude of EP and temperament dimensions (see, e.g., Andrés Pueyo & Tous, 1992; Strelau, 1991a). Furthermore, the position from which EP are recorded (e.g., vertex versus occipital), as well as the modality of stimuli used in these studies (e.g., visual versus auditory) become sources of inconsistency when amplitudes of evoked potential are related to temperament traits (see Andrés Pueyo & Tous,

1992; De Pascalis, 1994; Lolas, Etcheberrigaray, Elgueta, & Camposano, 1989; Strelau, 1991a; Zuckerman, 1991c).

According to Eysenck's theory, introverts being chronically highly aroused are expected to respond to stimuli of weak and moderate intensity with higher EP amplitudes relative to extraverts. Such a result was obtained by Stelmack (Stelmack & Michaud-Achorn, 1985; Stelmack, Achorn, & Michaud, 1977) under conditions where tones of low frequency (500 Hz but not 1000 Hz) were applied to stimuli of intensities not higher than 80 dB. Similar results were obtained by Bruneau, Roux, Perse, and Lelord (1984). Andrés Pueyo and Tous (1992) compared 13 studies (among them 6 from their own laboratory) in which extraversion was related to the amplitude of EP. Among the 13 studies (Stelmack's included), 6 confirm the predicted relationship between extraversion and EP amplitude: the augmenting phenomenon in introverts and the reducing one in extraverts. In 4 experiments the predicted relationship was partially confirmed and in 3 the results were in contradiction.

There are also some studies, not quoted by Andrés Pueyo and Tous (1992), in which no significant relationship between extraversion and the slope of EP amplitudes was found (e.g., Ashton, Golding, Marsh, & Thompson, 1985; Maushammer, Ehmer, & Eckel, 1981; Polich & Martin, 1992) or the data were equivocal (DiTraglia & Polich, 1991). As already mentioned, the relationship between EP amplitude and given temperament characteristics may differ depending on the slope of EP for which amplitudes have been measured. For example, Lolas, Camposano, and Etcheberrigaray (1989) obtained a negative correlation between the P1N1 slope of EP amplitude to auditory stimuli and extraversion as well as neuroticism, whereas there was no correlation between these two temperament traits and amplitude of EP for slope N1P2. It was also reported in this study that augmenting–reducing, understood as a temperament dimension measured by means of Vando's RAS (see Chapter 6), does not correlate (for both slopes—P1N1 and N1P2) with amplitudes of EP. Also Stenberg, Rosen, and Risberg (1990) showed that the relationship between extraversion and amplitude of EP to visual stimuli depends on whether vertex N120, P200, or occipital N140 amplitudes are taken into account (see also De Pascalis, 1994), and that this relationship was modified depending on whether stimulus-concentrated attention was involved in the subjects' task.

A study by Stenberg, Rosen, and Risberg (1988) demonstrated that, when amplitudes of EP are measured for different kinds of stimuli, the relationship between the EP amplitude and a temperament trait does not generalize across modalities. The authors showed that the relationship between EP amplitudes and extraversion (assessed by means of EPQ) as well as disinhibition (as measured by the SSS) occurs as predicted in the domain of visual stimuli, but not when auditory stimuli are taken into account. In both modalities six different intensities of stimuli were applied.

The EP augmenting–reducing phenomenon has often been used as a physiological marker of sensation seeking. Buchsbaum (1971) and Zuckerman (1979,

1990) postulated a positive relationship between EP augmenting and sensation seeking, on an assumption that the reducing phenomenon is due to the development of protective inhibition under strong stimuli, to which individuals low on sensation seeking are more prone than sensation seekers. This assumption, however, is not very convincing if one considers that stimuli used in these experiments are indeed not as intense (e.g., 80–90 dB) or long-lasting as to develop protective inhibition.

Buchsbaum's hypothesis was first verified by Zuckerman, Murtaugh, and Siegel (1974) in a study in which visual stimuli were applied to individuals differing in sensation seeking. The predicted relationship occurred only with respect to the Disinhibition scale, one of the four scales of the SSS (see Chapter 3). Recently Zuckerman (1990) presented a table summarizing the results of 16 studies in which EP amplitudes, measured mostly in students, were related to sensation seeking, from which one may infer a general tendency in support of Buchsbaum's and Zuckerman's hypothesis; however, in most cases the correlations are very low, albeit significant. Nonetheless, when EP amplitudes to auditory and visual stimuli exposed to the same individuals are compared, there is a clear-cut inconsistency in the data (see Stenberg *et al.*, 1988; Strelau, 1991a; Zuckerman *et al.*, 1988).

As can be seen from this review, the relationship between EP amplitudes and temperament traits, as exemplified in the domain of extraversion, sensation seeking, and neuroticism, is not univocal. There are many factors that affect this relationship, and must be taken into account if any reasonable conclusion in this field is to be drawn. Research has also been conducted in relation to some other temperament traits, such as impulsivity (e.g., Barratt, Pritchard, Faulk, & Brandt, 1987), anxiety (e.g., Maushammer *et al.*, 1981), or psychoticism (e.g., Lolas, Camposano, & Etcheberrigaray, 1989). The number of studies is insufficient to come to any conclusions regarding the relationship between these traits and the slope of EP amplitudes.

CNV Correlates of Temperament. Contingent negative variation, which reflects the readiness for reaction, has also been used as one of the physiological correlates of temperament traits. These studies consist mainly of a typical RT paradigm, in which tones are used as warning signals and light flashes as imperative stimuli or the reverse (visual stimuli precede the auditory ones). The task of the subject consists of pressing a button or key as fast as possible after the occurrence of the imperative stimulus. Stimuli, especially the imperative ones, may vary in intensity. The time interval between warning signals (S1) and imperative stimuli (S2) was also varied across experiments, the foreperiod (S1-S2) lasting from 1 to several seconds. The intertrial interval may also vary in different studies from several seconds to over 1 minute. In most experiments the number of trials ranges from 20 to 50 exposures, and summation then provides an averaged CNV. In order to manipulate the individual's level of arousal, the RT task may be conducted during a normal situation, under different kinds of stress, as well as under depressant or stimulant drugs. Since CNV is strongly influenced by the interaction between excitatory and inhibitory processes (Werre, 1987), it has been proposed that subjects differing in chronic level of arousal, whether cortical (e.g., extraversion) or visceral (neuroticism, anxiety) should differ in CNV characteristics.

Most of the studies in which different components of CNV have been related to temperament traits refer to extraversion and neuroticism, as measured by Eysenck's EPI or EPQ, or to the interaction between these traits. The empirical findings are not consistent, although some interesting results have been reported. O'Connor (1980, 1982; H. J. Eysenck & O'Connor, 1979) has found that, when the level of arousal has been increased during the experimental session by means of smoking, considered as a stimulant drug, extraverts differed from introverts in the CNV characteristics. Whereas in extraverts the amplitude of the CNV-O wave decreased, no changes in the orienting phase were recorded in introverts. In turn, the amplitude of the CNV-E wave increased under smoking conditions in extraverts and decreased in introverts. This result led O'Connor to conclude that introverts are action-restrained whereas extraverts tend to be action-oriented.

Werre, Favery, and Janssen (1975) conducted an experiment on 118 students in which extraversion and neuroticism were assessed as regards temperament characteristics, and maximal CNV amplitude was regarded as a measure of CNV. The study was conducted under different conditions varying in stimulative value. Taking into account the data recorded under standard conditions and under distraction which consisted of counting numbers in addition to the RT task, the following results were obtained. Under the standard condition a positive correlation was obtained between extraversion and CNV amplitude and there was no correlation between CNV amplitude and neuroticism. Under distraction, considered as an arousal-inducing factor, no correlations were found between the temperament traits and CNV amplitude. The lack of correlation between extraversion and CNV under the exciting distraction condition was explained by the fact that in both extraverts and introverts an essential decrease of the CNV amplitude occurred. The majority of studies conducted in the domain of contingent negative variation have shown that under arousal-augmenting events a decrease of CNV occurs (see Werre, 1986, 1987). A positive correlation between CNV amplitude recorded under a standard situation and extraversion was also reported by others (see, e.g., Dincheva & Piperova-Dalbokova, 1982; Nakamura, Fukui, Kadobayashi, & Kato, 1979; Plooij-Van Gorsel & Janssen, 1978). Dincheva and Piperova-Dalbokova (1982) have stated that the difference between extraverts and introverts in CNV amplitude was expressed more strongly when tones instead of visual stimuli were used as imperative stimuli. Ritter, Rotkin, and Vaughan (1980) devoted attention to the modality specificity of CNV.

In experiments conducted by Werre and colleagues (1975), the correlation between extraversion and CNV amplitudes under standard conditions occurred only during the first session. When the standard session was repeated 90 min after initiation of the experiment, the correlation disappeared, which the authors attributed to reactive inhibition present in extraverts. The same result was obtained in another study by Janssen, Mattie, Plooij-van Gorsel, and Werre (1978). An additional finding from the latter experiment showed another interaction between extraversion and conditions under which CNV were recorded. When white noise was applied, the CNV amplitude decreased markedly in introverts as compared with the standard situation. In extraverts no difference was recorded in CNV amplitude between the two conditions. This suggests that in introverts a higher level of arousal developed during exposure to noise. In another experiment Werre, Mattie, Fortgens, Berretty, and Sluiter (1994) studied the interaction between extraversion and drug-induced conditions (administration of chlordiazepoxide and caffeine) on CNV. The results showed that for chlordiazepoxide the change in the amplitude of the O wave from baseline was positive for introverts and negative for extraverts. For caffeine the opposite relationship was found.

It should be noted that not all researchers have been able to show a correlation between extraversion and CNV amplitudes as recorded under standard conditions. For example, in an experiment by Lolas and de Andraca (1977; see also Lolas & Aguilera, 1982) it was not extraversion that correlated with the CNV amplitude, but neuroticism. In subjects high in neuroticism the amplitude was smaller as compared to low neurotics. A similar result was obtained by Nakamura and colleagues (1979), who also recorded a temperament interaction effect. In low neurotics scoring high on extraversion, the CNV amplitude was significantly higher as compared with those scoring low on extraversion. In individuals high in neuroticism, no difference in CNV amplitude between extraverts and introverts occurred.

In studies in which anxiety was related to CNV most of the findings show that, in individuals high on the anxiety dimension, the CNV amplitude is lower as compared with individuals low on this dimension (see Knott & Irwin, 1967; Low & Swift, 1971). The low amplitude in anxious individuals may be explained by reference to the ceiling effect. High-anxiety subjects have a higher baseline negativity, so that they reach the ceiling faster relative to low-anxiety subjects (Knott & Irwin, 1967). Under stress, which as a rule reduces the CNV, the amplitudes are lower in anxious than in nonanxious individuals (Glanzman & Froelich, 1984). There are, however, studies in which the foregoing relationship between anxiety and CNV amplitudes has not been confirmed (see, e.g., Low, Coats, Retting, & McSherry, 1967). Consistent with the finding regarding the CNV–anxiety relationship are the data obtained by Krijns, Gaillard, Van Heck, and Brunia (1994) in respect to sensation seeking. Results have shown that in sensation seekers the CNV amplitudes are larger than in individuals scoring low on the Sensation Seeking scale. The authors interpreted this finding by the mediating effect of emotions: approach-related in sensation seekers and avoidance-related in sensation avoiders.

Some lack of consistency of the CNV data as related to temperament may result from the fact that the relationship between the level of arousal and the amplitude of CNV is not linear but takes the shape of an inverted-U curve (see Werre, 1986, 1987). Depending whether CNV amplitudes are recorded during states of optimal arousal or under- or overarousal, the relationship between arousal-related temperament traits and CNV characteristics will differ.

P300 as a Marker of Extraversion. It has been suggested by H. J. Eysenck (1967, 1970) that (a) extraverts, due to their lower level of arousal and higher cortical inhibitory processes habituate earlier to experimental conditions under weak stimulation than do introverts; (b) under conditions consisting of solving monotonous vigilance tasks, introverts perform better than extraverts. These hypotheses, which have been verified with respect to different laboratory measures, have also stimulated interest in studies on individual differences in the P300 event-related potential. As already mentioned, the P3 reflects the required attentional resources for processing new stimuli. There is evidence that the magnitude of P3 is higher when the attentional resources needed during information processing are greater (see, e.g., Isreal, Wickens, Chesney, & Donchin, 1980; Polich, 1987). If so, it is probable that individual differences in the magnitude of P300 may be influenced by temperament characteristics, especially by extraversion, for the reasons given (a and b).

In the past few years P300 has been related to extraversion under experimental conditions that are similar across studies. The situation consists of a two-tone auditory discrimination task, in which the two stimuli differ in frequency (e.g., 1000 and 2000 Hz). The target tone to which the subject is to react (by moving the finger) is exposed in random order with different degrees of probability. The tasks may differ in duration as well as in the frequency of stimuli applied.

Daruna, Karrer, and Rosen (1985) proposed that, under experimental conditions requiring attentional resources during task performance, which consisted of predicting tones applied with different frequencies, introverts will exhibit larger P3 amplitudes than will extraverts. This is due to introverts' greater attentional resources during vigilance tasks. The hypothesis favoring introverts in respect to the magnitude of P300 amplitude was confirmed in this study.

A series of experiments in which extraversion, together with some other temperament dimensions, was related to P3 ERP, were carried out by Polich and his coworkers (Cahill & Polich, 1992; DiTraglia & Polich, 1991; Polich & Martin, 1992). The data of these studies, all conducted on undergraduate students, again show inconsistency regarding the relationship under discussion. In a study (DiTraglia & Polich, 1991) in which extreme groups of introverts and extraverts were selected, it was noted that the P300 amplitude to the target stimuli (2000 Hz, 60 dB, exposed with a probability of .20) does not differentiate extraverts and introverts. However, a decline of the P300 amplitude during the experimental session was observed for extraverts, whereas no change in the amplitude occurred in introverts. DiTraglia and Polich explained this finding by referring to higher habituation rate in extraverts than in introverts, as already shown in H. J. Eysenck's

(1967, 1970) laboratory. Another experiment (Cahill & Polich, 1992) consisted in exposure of the same kind of target stimuli with different degrees of probability (.20, .40, .60, .80). Individuals were also selected to represent extreme scores on the extraversion dimension. It emerged that P300 was generally smaller for introverts than for extraverts, suggesting that the P300–extraversion relationship reflects the amount of attentional resources required by introverts and extraverts.

A third study (Polich & Martin, 1992), in which subjects (54 undergraduates balanced for sex) were not selected for temperament traits and in which, besides extraversion (as measured by EPQ and the Myers–Briggs Type Indicator; MBTI), neuroticism and psychoticism were also measured did not support the previous findings. P300 amplitudes, measured during a standard auditory discrimination task, did not correlate with either measure of extraversion in the total sample. No correlation was found either for neuroticism or for psychoticism. The same result was found when these temperament dimensions were related to P3 latency. However, when results were considered separately for males and females, a negative correlation of over .40 (for both measures) was obtained for males. It follows that for males P3 amplitudes are lower in extraverts and higher in introverts, a result consistent with those of Daruna and colleagues (1985), but in contradiction with the data of Cahill and Polich (1992).

Stenberg (1994) applied pictorial stimuli for studying the amplitude difference in the P300 component of visual event-related potentials between extraverts and introverts. The subjects were required to solve tasks related to color, semantic, and color–semantic aspects of the pictures. Higher P300 amplitude was shown in extraverts as compared to introverts. Impulsivity, controlled in this experiment by means of scores obtained from the EPI Impulsivity subscale, was responsible for the extraversion–P300 amplitude relationship.

Studies in which extraversion was related to the P300 ERP are too scanty to come to any general conclusion. But even the experiments just reported suggest that one may hardly expect an unequivocal conclusion regarding the relationship under discussion. As suggested by Polich and Martin (1992), differences in sample characteristics, in P300 recordings, and other factors may account for the variety of findings.

Cerebral Asymmetry

Individual differences in the asymmetry of cortical activation have been recorded in several studies (e.g., Glass, 1987; Rusalov, 1979), with some evidence that they are stable over time (see Amochaev & Samaly, 1979). There is now good evidence that hemispheric asymmetry is related to the emotions, especially to the frontal and anterior temporal regions which have broad connections with the limbic system (see R. J. Davidson, 1984; Kinsbourne & Bemporad, 1984; R. E. Myers, 1972; Tucker & Frederick, 1989). The findings that hemispheric asymmetry shows more or less stable differentiation across individuals, and is related to the emotions, gives a good starting point for examining the relationship between temperament characteristics and cerebral asymmetry. Studies examining this relationship are very scanty.

Golu (1987), who assumed that norepinephrine–serotonin activity is better represented in the right hemisphere and dopamine–cholinergic activity in the left hemisphere, hypothesized specific relationships between temperament traits and cerebral asymmetry. According to him the dominance of the right hemisphere coincides with such characteristics as lower level of arousal and higher emotional tonus. Activity, as understood by Strelau (see Chapter 3), is related to the dominance of the left hemisphere (Golu, 1987). In the neo-Pavlovian research, Rusalov (1979) postulated that the polarity–amplitude asymmetry of AEPs, as recorded from the frontal, occipital, and central brain areas, may be considered an index of a general property of the CNS, besides the well-known Pavlovian NS properties.

Cerebral Asymmetry and Emotional States. R. J. Davidson (1987) has put forward a hypothesis that the approach–withdrawal reactions, as expressed in positive and negative emotions, are determined by lateralized cortical activity. The left anterior hemisphere region supervises the approach system and the right region controls the withdrawal system.

A study conducted by R. J. Davidson, Ekman, Saron, Senulis, and Friesen (1990) examined whether the asymmetry phenomenon, as measured by alpha and beta power used as indices of cortical arousal, occurs under conditions in which withdrawal-related negative emotion (disgust) and approach-related positive emotion (happiness) are elicited. The study was conducted on 11 adult females (after a thorough selection from 37 right-handed women) by taking into account the methodological requirements for evoking and controlling emotions with parallel EEG recordings from left and right frontal, central, anterior temporal, and parietal regions. Emotions were generated by four 1-min film trials, two of which were intended to evoke positive emotions and two negative ones. Among the emotions being evoked, happiness and disgust, as the ones that occurred most often under these experimental conditions, were related to EEG recordings. Face-rating of emotions, based on video recordings and self-rating of happiness and disgust were taken into account. The findings, largely in accord with the authors' hypotheses, showed that negative affect is associated with cortical right-sided anterior activation. This was expressed in lower alpha powers in the right frontal and anterior temporal regions under the state of disgust as compared with the state of happiness. It was also found that, in the anterior temporal region, the state of happiness is accompanied by more left-sided activation, measured by alpha power, as compared with disgust.

A finding, reported in several studies on adults, that the two cerebral hemispheres are differentially lateralized for positive and negative emotions, has also been replicated for infants. R. J. Davidson and Fox (1982) conducted two experiments on 10-month-old female infants (18 and 20 subjects) in which positive and negative affects were elicited by showing a videotaped actress generating either happy or sad facial expressions. The EEG data recorded from the left and right frontal and parietal regions during the video sessions in both experiments demonstrated a greater left frontal activation in response to stimuli evoking the state of happiness than to those evoking the state of sadness. As a measure of cortical activation, raw data and laterality ratio scores were filtered from spontaneous EEG activity for frequencies of 1–12 Hz. From these results the authors concluded that "the observed frontal activation asymmetry may reflect the differential tendency of the affective stimuli to elicit approach or avoidance behavior" (R. J. Davidson & Fox, 1982, p.218.).

In both studies, which serve here as examples of research in which emotional states are related to hemispheric asymmetry, temperament characteristics were not taken into account. Approach–withdrawal was measured not as a tendency (trait) but as an actual state. To bring these studies closer to considerations on temperament, the emotions of happiness, sadness, and disgust, as measured in the reported experiments, could be considered expressions of temperament dimensions, that is, as tendencies to experience happiness, sadness, or disgust. If so, then they have to be treated, according to the temperament tradition, as characteristics separate from approach–withdrawal. This does not mean that they do not correlate with each other (Goldsmith & Campos, 1990; Rothbart, 1989a; A. Thomas & Chess, 1977).

Cerebral Asymmetry as Marker of Temperament. There are very few studies, at least known to me, in which temperament traits have been related to hemispheric asymmetry. Collin and Lolas (1985), taking the amplitude of evoked potential as defined by Buchsbaum (1976, 1978) as the basis for assessing the augmenting–reducing dimension, examined the extent to which this phenomenon is hemisphere-specific. Auditory evoked potentials were recorded at the vertex in 40 male adult subjects responding to clicks of three intensities exposed with an interstimulus interval (ISI) of 1.5 s. Taking as a criterion the slope of EP amplitude across the three intensities of stimuli, the subjects were assessed as augmenters (positivity of the slope) or reducers (negativity of the slope). Records taken from both hemispheres showed that in augmenters there is a higher involvement of the left hemisphere, whereas the negative slope of reducers is more strongly expressed in the right hemisphere. The difference, however, does not refer to absolute EP amplitudes but to changes in amplitudes as a response to stimuli of different intensity. Considering the EP augmenting–reducing as a phenomenon that refers to individual differences in the "intensive aspect of attention," Collin and Lolas interpret their finding as reflecting a hemispheric specificity.

Extraversion and neuroticism as measured in 22 adult males were related to hemispheric asymmetry by Lolas (1987). On the basis of EPI, subjects were selected for extreme scores on the extraversion dimension. They were further divided into two groups representing low and average scores on the Neuroticism scale. The EEG study consisted of measuring CNV in a standard RT experiment in which tones were used as warning signals and light flashes served as imperative stimuli. Two ISI were randomly presented: 1,000 ms and 4,000 ms. ERP records were taken from both hemispheres at central leads. The results, based on laterality ratio scores and only in respect to 1,000 ms ISI, allowed for the following conclusion: In more neurotic subjects, right hemispheric activation, as expressed by CNV amplitudes, was higher as compared to individuals who scored lower on the neuroticism dimension. In this study extraversion was not related to hemispheric asymmetry. This result is partially consistent with the studies that show that negative emotions (to which neuroticism refers) tend to be related to right-sided activation, though in studies on emotions EEG has been significantly related to emotions in the frontal and not in the central brain regions.

A recent study conducted by De Pascalis (1993) on 60 female university students contains a broad spectrum of measures on both sides: hemispheric asymmetry and temperament characteristics. Regarding the latter account was taken of extraversion, neuroticism, and psychoticism, as assessed by EPQ, and strength of excitation, strength of inhibition, and mobility of NP, as diagnosed by PTS. Hemispheric reactivity was measured in the domain of auditory and visual event-related potentials (ERP) during performance of simple (identification of target stimulus exposed in a predictable sequence) and difficult RT tasks (the same stimulus exposed in an unpredictable sequence). Hemispheric activity was measured taking into account the most reliable and consistent peaks of the ERPs, which were N1, P2, N2, and P3. So-called hemispheric reactivity indices were derived as ERP changes between states during which difficult and easy tasks were applied. Asymmetry was measured by a number of interhemispheric reactivity indices, based on asymmetry ratio scores from the left and right anterior and posterior sites. A positive score indicated the dominance of the right hemisphere over the left; a negative ratio was an indicator of dominant activity in the left hemisphere. The many variables included in this study were factor analyzed separately for ERP characteristics, as well as combined for ERP and temperament traits.

The most important findings regarding the temperament–hemispheric asymmetry relationship, as shown by means of correlation and factor analysis, may be summarized as follows: (1) Neuroticism correlated positively with right hemispheric anterior and posterior activity, but only for auditory ERPs; the link between neuroticism and right hemispheric activity is consistent with Lolas's (1987) data. (2) Psychoticism was associated with the dominance of the right hemisphere in the posterior area for visual ERPs. (3) Extraversion is positively related to increase of activity in the posterior right hemisphere and anterior left hemisphere; however, both correlations refer to the auditory modality only. (4) Strength of excitation is associated with right-hemisphere dominance in the posterior area for visual stimuli and with left-hemisphere dominance also in the posterior area, but only for auditory stimuli. (5) A low score of inhibition accompanied right-hemisphere dominance for auditory modality. (6) Mobility, which in most studies is highly correlated with strength of excitation as well as with extraversion (see Strelau, 1983; Strelau, Angleitner, & Ruch, 1990), did not show any relationship to hemispheric asymmetry.

The findings based on De Pascalis's experiment need to be replicated in order to allow any conclusion regarding the links between specific temperament traits and hemisphere asymmetry. Nevertheless, some general conclusions may be derived from this study. They most probably also refer to other investigations on cerebral laterality as related to temperament. The hemispheric asymmetry–temperament relationship is contingent on (a) the specific region from which EEG recordings are taken, (b) the specific wave of the ERP being analyzed, (3) the modality of the stimuli applied to evoke ERPs, and (4) the kinds of conditions under which cortical activity is measured. This multifold relationship hinders explorations in this field of study. If we consider that (a) ontogenetically the right hemisphere matures earlier than the left (see Crowell, Jones, Kapuniani, & Nakagawa, 1973; Thatcher, Walker, & Giudice, 1987) and (b) there are developmentally specific temperament characteristics such as the dominance of negative emotions and lack of control in early infancy (Gunnar, 1990; Kinsbourne & Bemporad, 1984; Rothbart, 1989a), then the importance of studies in which hemisphere asymmetry is related to temperament is obvious.

Biochemical Correlates of Temperament

Studies in which biochemical measures have been related to temperament characteristics refer to two basic categories. The first category refers to the activity of the hormonal system under the control of the hypothalamic–pituitary–adrenal axis. Under activation of the sympathetic branch of the ANS, the medulla of the adrenal gland secretes adrenaline (epinephrine). In turn, the pituitary gland, under the control of the hypothalamus, activates the adrenal cortex which secretes cortisol. The two hormones—adrenaline and cortisol—are especially active under states of emotional tension and stress requiring increased mobilization, effort, and activity of the organism. One may hypothesize that both hormones are related to those temperament traits that mediate behavior under states of stress.

The second category refers to neurotransmitters, which became an intensive subject of studies after the discovery that interneuronal transmission of excitatory processes is possibly due only to transmitters located in the neuron's presynaptic vesicles. The fact that neurotransmitters mediate the energetic (intensity) component of transmitted information may serve as a good starting point for the hypothesis that arousal-oriented temperament characteristics are associated with activity of given neurotransmitters.

In a condensed review by Janke and Kallus (1995) biochemical correlates (hormones and neurotransmitters) of such temperament characteristics as neuroticism, anxiety, extraversion, sensation seeking, impulsivity, and psychoticism were described. The purpose of this section is to present some empirical findings in which both hormones and neurotransmitters have been related to temperament traits. As regards hormones, the presentation is limited to studies reported mainly in the temperament literature. They consist of comparing cortisol measures with temperament characteristics.

Cortisol: The Hormone That Gained Highest Popularity in Temperament Studies

Cortisol, one of the corticostereoid hormones, is an example of a hormone the activity of which is a result of interaction between the ANS, the CNS (hypothalamus), and the endocrinological system. The level of cortisol is often regarded as one of the indicators of visceral arousal (Dabbs & Hopper, 1990; Kagan, Reznick, & Snidman, 1987). Cortisol is present in saliva, urine, and serum, and the fact that the level of cortisol can be measured without inconvenience to subjects, whether adults or children (especially from saliva samples), has contributed to the popularity of such studies in temperament research.

Studies on Children

Among studies in which temperament characteristics were related to cortisol measures, those conducted by Kagan and colleagues (1987, 1988) on infants and children with inhibited and uninhibited temperament are the best known. Experiments conducted on 21-month-old infants and on children at the age of 5½ have consistently shown that inhibited children have significantly higher levels of cortisol as compared to uninhibited children. The correlation between inhibited behavior and level of cortisol varied at the different ages from .30 to over .40. This finding emerged independently of whether measures of salivary cortisol were taken in normal conditions (morning samples taken at home) or in laboratory settings (more or less stressful conditions).

The authors suggested that in inhibited children the hypothalamic–pituitary–adrenal axis has a tonically higher level of activity as compared with uninhibited children. In the studies of Kagan and colleagues the cortisol level allowed prediction of a child's belonging in the inhibited or uninhibited group more precisely than has been the case with any other physiological measure used in these studies (e.g., heart rate indices, pupillary dilation, muscle tension, norepinephrine level from urine samples). Omitting the details presented elsewhere (see Chapter 3), the authors assumed that children differ in ease of excitability in those regions of the central nervous system (probably located in the limbic structures) that contribute, on the one hand, to behavioral reactions to unfamiliar and cognitive challenging events, and, on the other, to physiological arousal.

The finding that baseline cortisol activity allows predictions of temperament characteristics comparable to inhibited and uninhibited behavior did not gain support from Gunnar and her coworkers (Gunnar, 1990; Gunnar, Mangelsdorf, Larson, & Hertsgaard, 1989; Gunnar, Larson, Hertsgaard, Harris, & Brodersen, 1992) in their studies conducted on 9- and 13-month-old infants.

In the 1989 study 9-month-old infants' emotional temperament was measured by means of the Louisville temperament assessment procedure. At the age of 13 months temperament was assessed on the Fullard, McDevitt, and Carey's Toddler Temperament Scale, taking into account the scores for approach, adaptability, and mood. On the basis of factor analysis, one temperament score—Emotional Temperament—was extracted and related to basal measures of cortisol activity for infants at both ages. It was found that basal cortisol activity correlated with emotional temperament (.33) only at the age of 13 months. This correlation was, however, in the direction opposite to that predicted by Kagan's data if we assume that negative emotional responses resemble inhibited temperament. In the 1992 study, conducted on 9-month-old infants, Rothbart's IBQ was applied, and the two scales—Fear and Distress to limitations—which are most closely linked to inhibited behavior did not show significant correlations with cortisol level from saliva samples.

In both studies (Gunnar et al., 1989; Gunnar et al., 1992), separation of infant from the mother was used as the stress-inducing factor. It is known from experiments conducted on nonhuman primates that separation from the mother activates high levels of cortisol (e.g., Levine, Wiener, Coe, Bayart, & Hayashi, 1987). The experiments conducted by Gunnar and coworkers showed that, when the social context of mother separation was threatening, infants with negative emotional tone and high scores on the Distress to Limits scale exhibited a significant increase in cortisol activity not present in infants scoring low on these temperament dimensions. These data suggest that cortisol activity per se should not be considered a physiological correlate of temperament characteristics; it is the emotional state evoked by a stress-inducing factor that triggers the differences in cortisol level. However, temperament traits most probably mediate the emotional state during conditions of stress.

Studies on Adults

Studies in which cortisol measures have been related to temperament traits in adults have a more pessimistic inference. When scores of basal cortisol level are taken into account, most of the results show that cortisol level cannot be considered a biochemical correlate of temperament traits hitherto under study, as exemplified by most of the studies conducted during the past decade.

Ballenger and colleagues (1983) conducted a study of 43 adults in whom, among several biochemical measures mostly referring to neurotransmitters, basal cortisol level was taken from cerebrospinal fluid (CSF), serum, and urine samples. These measures were associated with temperament scores, including extraversion, neuroticism, and psychoticism, as measured by EPQ, and sensation seeking assessed by means of SSS-IV. Correlations in which age, height, and weight of the subjects were controlled showed that the basal cortisol levels from urine samples did not correlate with any of the temperament traits compared. However, CSF cortisol correlated negatively with SSS-disinhibition (−.48) and with psychoticism (−.35). Since cortisol measures across different samples are highly correlated with each other (see e.g., Kahn, Rubinow, Davis, Kling, & Post, 1988), the inconsistency of the cortisol–temperament data of Ballenger and colleagues (1983) is difficult to explain.

Dabbs and Hopper (1990) selected two extreme samples representing 10% of the lowest and 10% of the highest salivary cortisol levels from two separate groups: 102 male college students and 4462 male military veterans. Individual characteristics in students were measured by means of the NEO PI and in veterans by using the MMPI. While these inventories do not directly relate to temperament characteristics, some conclusions interesting for our review may be drawn from this study. High-cortisol students were higher on anxiety and depression (as measured by the Neuroticism NEO scale) and lower on extraversion (the gregarious facet of the Extraversion NEO scale) as compared with low-cortisol students. Similarly, high-cortisol veterans were higher on anxiety and introversion as compared with low-cortisol veterans. These differences, however, lose their significance if we take into account correlational measures comprising the whole group. For the more than 4,000 veterans, the correlation between MMPI introversion and basal cortisol level was practically zero (.06), and the same was true for anxiety (.04). A reanalysis of the veteran data was conducted by Windle (1994). He applied a fourfold taxonomy for the MMPI characteristics among which behavior inhibition and behavior activation categories were distinguished. Relationships between these catetories and cortisol levels were statistically nonsignificant. Lack of correlation between trait anxiety and basal cortisol level has also been found in other studies (Bohnen, Nicolson, Sulon, & Jolles, 1991; Brandtstadter, Baltes-Gotz, Kirschbaum, & Hellhammer, 1991; W. Hubert & De Jong-Meyer, 1989).

As regards the temperament–cortisol relationship in normal adults, a significant investigation was recently conducted by Kirschbaum, Bartussek, and Strasburger (1992). In two separate studies salivary cortisol was measured in college students (50 and 37 subjects) of both sexes under two conditions: normal situation and psychological stress. Stress consisted of public speaking and performance of mental arithmetic in front of an audience. Salivary samples were obtained at 10 min intervals before and after task performance. Temperament measures included extraversion, neuroticism, psychoticism, sensation seeking (all four subtraits), strength of excitation, strength of inhibition, and mobility, these traits being measured by EPQ-E, SSS, and PTS successively. As expected, salivary cortisol levels increased markedly in response to psychological stress in both groups. Striking, however, are the results regarding the temperament–cortisol relationship. Neither basal cortisol scores nor cortisol response levels (changes under stress) correlated with the ten temperament traits under study. A study by Bossert and colleagues (1988) on 12 male college students also showed that stress-induced cortisol measures do not correlate with such temperament characteristics as anxiety, impulsiveness, neuroticism, and extraversion as measured by STAI and the FPI. On the basis of their own data, and other reported studies, Kirschbaum and colleagues (1992) arrived at the following conclusion:

> If one agrees that psychobiological research should consider correlations of at least medium effect sizes (i.e. $r = 0.30$ or higher by conventional definition), the available literature seems to indicate that no further research is needed in personality psychology in conjunction with cortisol measures. (p. 1355)

Although the authors agree that this conclusion is too far-reaching, their statement illustrates the state of affairs in studies on adults' temperament in relation to cortisol measures, which does not appear as promising as one may have expected from the findings of Kagan and colleagues (1987, 1988) in studies on child temperament.

Temperament–Neurotransmitter Relationship

Studies on the relationship between neurotransmitters and temperament characteristics have recently gained popularity for reasons some of which have already been mentioned. The following seem to be the most important: (a) No interneuronal transmission of excitation is possible without neurotransmitters; (b) neurotransmitters participate in mediating the energetic component of transmitted information; (c) information on the activity of specific neurotransmitters allows for approximate identification of the neural structures being activated; (d) by means of drugs that facilitate activity of neurotransmitters (agonistic effect) or repress their activity (antagonistic effect), it is possible to manipulate the level of neurotransmitters; (e) peripheral measures of neurotransmitters, such as plasma and urine samples, are relatively easy to take, although they hardly reflect CNS activity. For CSF samples, considered as the most reliable (Zuckerman, 1991c), a lumbar puncture procedure is required.

There are few studies in which temperament traits, as measured by inventories or in laboratory settings, have been related to neurotransmitters. Most of the research in this area consists of speculation about a hypothesized relationship between temperament characteristics and neurotransmitters, regarded as their biochemical roots. Such conceptualizations are based mainly on studies in which animal behavior has been related to different neurotransmitters or their enzymes (see, e.g., Gray, 1982a, 1982b; Panksepp, 1982; Soubrie, 1986; Stein, 1983), or in which neurotransmitters have been studied in relation to different states of disease or deviations in behavior as, for example, in schizophrenics, Parkinson patients, alcoholics, criminals, or psychopaths (Cloninger, von Knorring, & Oreland, 1985; Murphy, 1977; Schalling, Asberg, Edman, & Oreland, 1987; Stein, 1974).

Monaminergic Neurotransmitters and Their Enzymes Related to Temperament

The discussion regarding the relationship between monaminergic neurotransmitters (norepinephrine, dopamine, and serotonin) or their enzymes, and aspects of temperament behavior or mechanisms underlying this behavior (reward and punishment systems as understood by Gray, 1982a), has been summarized by Zuckerman (1984b, 1991c). Table 4.4 adapted from this author (Zuckerman, 1991c, p. 184), gives some idea about the different hypotheses regarding the relationship between the monaminergic functions and temperament characteristics.

As can be seen from Table 4.4, most authors agree about the function of serotonin as regulating behavioral inhibition, and of dopamine as related to approach and behavior directed to rewards. Much less agreement prevails regarding the function of norepinephrine. Some authors associate NE with behaviors based on punishment (e.g., anxiety); others hypothesize in the opposite direction, relating NE to behavior based on reward functions. The empirical evidence regarding the temperament–neurotransmitter relationship in humans is still too scanty to provide unequivocal support for any of these hypotheses.

The most comprehensive study in which temperament traits have been related to monoamine neurotransmitters and their enzymes is that of Ballenger and colleagues (1983). From 43 normal adult subjects (26 male and 17 female, aged 19–64 years) a broad range of biochemical measures was obtained in a clinical center. They included CSF norepinephrine; the norepinephrine metabolite, MHPG (in CSF, plasma, and urine samples); DBH, the enzyme that catalyzes the conversion of DA to NE (taken from CSF and plasma samples); blood platelet monoamine oxidase (MAO); and plasma regarded as an index of central MAO activity. Cortisol measures were also taken, as already mentioned in the previous section. The psychological measures comprised traits assessed by means of EPQ, MMPI, and SSS-IV. For our purpose the EPQ and SSS temperament scales are of particular significance. Table 4.5 summarizes the data reflecting the relationship between biochemical measures and such temperament traits as extraversion, neuroticism, psychoticism, and sensation seeking (General and the Disinhibition scale). Age, height, and weight of the subjects were controlled.

It may be concluded from Table 4.5 that extraversion did not show any significant correlation with any of the biochemical measures. On the basis of theo-

TABLE 4.4. Hypotheses Regarding the Relationship between Monaminergic Neurotransmitters and Temperament Characteristics

Author	Serotonin	Norepinephrine	Dopamine
Gray (1982a)	Anxiety: high levels = inhibition of behavior; low levels = disinhibition of aggression	Anxiety: sensitization by novel stimuli & stimuli associated with punishment	Approach: stimuli associated with reward; positive affect
Redmond (1985)		Anxiety: low levels = novelty detection, alarm system	
Mason (1984)		Focuses attention on significant environmental stimuli; screens out irrelevant stimuli	Orienting, interest in environment
Crow (1977) & Stein (1978)	General inhibition of behavior; sensitivity to punishment or signals of punishment	Reward: guides response selection in line with previously rewarded responses	Energizes and activates behavior directed to primary biological rewards
Panksepp (1982)	General inhibition of all emotive systems	General arousal of all emotive systems	Foraging, exploration, intrinsic reward; hope, desire, joy (in humans)
Soubrie (1986)	General inhibition of behavior in conflict situations. Low levels = impulsivity, aggression self or other directed (humans)		
Cloninger (1986)	Harm avoidance: behavioral inhibition, caution, indecision, anxiety	Reward sensitivity, dependence, emotional warmth, social attachment, sociability. Low levels = nonconformity, social detachment	Novelty seeking
Zuckerman (1991c)	Inhibition of all emotional systems (positive and negative)	Amplifies reward and punishment effects	Novelty seeking and sensation seeking

Note. From *Psychobiology of Personality* (p. 184), by M. Zuckerman, 1991, New York: Cambridge University Press. Copyright 1991 by Cambridge University Press. Adapted with permission.

TABLE 4.5. Relationship between Biochemical Measures and Temperament Traits

Biochemicals	EPQ-E	EPQ-N	EPQ-P	SSS-Gen	SSS-Dis
CSF NE	−.01	−.15	−.23	−.49**	−.22
CSF MHPG	.21	−.20	−.23	.09	.15
Plasma MHPG	−.25	−.44*	−.26	.24	.05
Urine MHPG	.12	−.07	−.04	−.06	.13
CSF DBH	.25	−.20	−.06	−.12	.20
Plasma DBH	.33	−.26	.00	−.60**	−.33
Platelet MAO	−.15	−.04	.17	−.13	−.09
Plasma AO	.08	−.19	−.07	−.33*	−.22

Note. Age, height and weight controlled. For abbreviations of biochemicals see Appendix. From "Biochemical Correlates of Personality Traits in Normals: An Exploratory Study," by J. C. Ballenger, R. M. Post, D. C. Jimerson, C. R. Lake, D. Murphy, M. Zuckerman, and C. Cronin, 1983, *Personality and Individual Differences, 4,* p. 621. Copyright 1983 by Elsevier Science Ltd. Adapted with permission.
*$p < .10$; **$p < .05$.

retical considerations abstracted in Table 4.4, it could have been hypothesized that extraversion is related to noradrenergic activity. Neither is psychoticism related to any of the biochemical measures relating to different aspects of NE activity. It emerged, however, that neuroticism and sensation seeking, which did not correlate with each other in this study, nor in most of the studies in which these temperament traits have been compared, showed a configuration similar to indicators of NE activity. Neuroticism correlated negatively with plasma MHPG, the central metabolite of NE; sensation seeking correlated, also negatively, with CSF, NE, and DBH, the enzyme that is released for the conversion of DA to NE. Apart from some speculations, including those of Ballenger and colleagues (1983), there is as yet no satisfactory interpretation for these data.

Kagan and colleagues (1987, 1988) have also shown that inhibited behavior in 4- and 5½-year-old children, which might be compared to neuroticism, correlated (between .31 and.34) with NE activity as measured by means of MHPG scores. The correlation, however, was in the opposite direction. Kagan and colleagues explained this finding by referring to higher sympathetic activity among the inhibited children as compared to the uninhibited ones.

It is worth noting that the correlations between sensation seeking (general) and indicators of NE activity are very consistent, all of them showing a negative relationship between noradrenergic activity and sensation seeking, a result contrary to the authors' expectation (Ballenger *et al.,* 1983). This expectation was based on a hypothesis (Stein, 1978; Zuckerman, 1979) that the NE system mediates reward-oriented behavior which is typical for sensation seekers.

As has been illustrated in Figure 4.3, for the three monoamine neurotransmitters—NE, DA, and 5-HT—specific metabolites have been identified: MHPG for norepinephrine, HVA for dopamine, and 5-HIAA for serotonin. Hence values of these metabolites, which may be taken from different media (CS, plasma, urine) give indirect information about the activity of the specific monoamine systems. It might be expected that in the future these measures will be used in studies aimed at relating temperament or personality characteristics to the activity of neurotransmitters. Some preliminary attempts of this kind have been reported by Zuckerman (1991c).

Referring to two studies conducted by Schalling, Asberg, and Edman (1984, unpublished data cited by Zuckerman, 1991c) and by Schalling and colleagues (1990, unpublished data cited by Zuckerman, 1991c), which I have not found in published form, Zuckerman presents data on the relationship between the neurotransmitter metabolites (5-HIAA, HVA, and MHPG) and some temperament characteristics. When these metabolites were related in a study by Schalling and colleagues (1984) to extraversion, neuroticism, and psychoticism (measured by EPQ) in normal adult subjects, it was noted that extraversion and neuroticism did not correlate with any of the three metabolites. Psychoticism correlated negatively with 5-HIAA (−.43) and HVA (−.42), both coefficients being statistically significant.

The negative correlation between psychoticism and the serotonin metabolite (5-HIAA), seems to be theoretically grounded if we consider that serotonin mediates inhibitory control. It is known that individuals high in psychoticism have a rather low position on temperament dimensions that are related to control of behavior (Ruch, Angleitner, & Strelau, 1991; Zuckerman, 1991c). The negative correlation with the dopamine metabolite (HVA) is theoretically less clear. Also, impulsivity and monotony avoidance (a measure of sensation seeking), as assessed by means of the Karolinska Personality Inventory, did not show any significant relationship with the three metabolites. Results from Schalling and colleagues (1990) did not support the 1984 data and pointed to some other findings. It was found that 5-HIAA did not correlate with psychoticism but did with extraversion. These studies, as well as others not mentioned here (Kulcsar, Kutor, & Arato, 1984; Redmond et al., 1986) are susceptible of various interpretations and replete with confusion. They allow us to conclude only that we are still far from establishing the relationship between the activity of the monoamine systems and temperament characteristics.

MAO Activity Applied as a Biochemical Correlate of Temperament Characteristics

In most studies examining the relationship between neurotransmitters and temperament, researchers have concentrated on measuring the activity of monoamine oxidase. As already mentioned (see Figure 4.3), MAO is an enzyme that degrades all three monoamine neurotransmitters and occurs in two forms, A and B. MAO-A is primarily involved in the degradation of NE and serotonin, MAO-B in the breakdown of dopamine. MAO-B, which is dominant in the human brain, is also localized in serotonin-rich areas (Zuckerman, 1991c). MAO type B occurs in blood platelets. Platelet MAO scores, for which there is some evidence of a relationship to brain MAO (Zuckerman, 1984b, 1991c), have been mainly used in temperament studies as indicators of MAO activity.

A study conducted by Sostek, A. J. Sostek, Murphy, Martin, and Born (1981) in infants, whose temperament was measured by means of the Brazelton Neonatal Behavioral Assessment Scale demonstrated the existence of a significant relationship between temperament behavior and level of MAO. Higher levels of MAO were found in infants characterized as having a higher level of chronic arousal. Indicators of arousal were temperament measures referring to motor behavior and sleep–awake characteristics.

Most of the MAO studies related to temperament were conducted on adults, and most data have been reported for sensation seeking and related traits, such as monotony avoidance and impulsivity. Zuckerman (1991c) has summarized 11 studies conducted between 1977 and 1989 in which platelet MAO was correlated with Zuckerman's sensation seeking scales (Form IV and V). Among the 11 samples 7 comprised college students, the remainder other adults; 5 were male, 3 female, and 3 mixed (F & M) samples; the number of subjects varied from 13 to 65. Meta-analysis of the data obtained from the 11 samples has given the following results: (1) All but one of the coefficients of correlation between the SS scales and platelet MAO were negative; (2) the negative correlations, seven of which were statistically significant, varied from −.15 to −.66, the median being −.25; (3) among the four SSS scales, Dis, ES, and TAS correlated more or less equally often with platelet MAO, whereas BS correlated with MAO only in one sample.

A review of eight studies in which monotony avoidance, a Swedish equivalent of sensation seeking (Schalling, Edman, & Asberg, 1983), was related to platelet MAO, has given a similar result. In all eight samples compared by Zuckerman (1991c) monotony avoidance correlated negatively with platelet MAO, the median being −.215, a result almost equivalent to the one for sensation seeking.

There are many other studies not reported in Zuckerman's comparison tables (e.g., A. L. von Knorring, Bohman, von Knorring, & Oreland, 1985; L. von Knorring, Oreland, & Winblad, 1984; Zuckerman, Buchsbaum, & Murphy, 1980) which support the finding that sensation seeking, especially the Disinhibition scale, and with more consistent data in male samples, correlates negatively with platelet MAO. According to Schalling (Schalling & Asberg, 1985; Schalling et al., 1983; Schalling, Edman, Asberg, & Oreland, 1988) and Zuckerman (1979, 1991c), the negative correlation between sensation seeking and monotony avoidance on the one hand, and platelet MAO on the other, may be explained by the fact that MAO-A values obtained in these studies refer to serotonin activity which controls inhibitory behavior. The negative correlation should be interpreted in such a way that subjects with low MAO levels are characterized by various disinhibitory and impulsive behaviors, typical for sensation seekers. A study conducted by Schalling and colleagues (1988), and briefly reported in the following paragraphs, gives some empirical support for this hypothesis.

Fifty-eight adult male subjects, ages 23–42, were divided on the basis of their platelet MAO scores into three groups: high- MAO (12 Ss), low-MAO (12 Ss) and intermediate-MAO (34 Ss). To all subjects the following inventories were given: EPQ, KSP, and the Impulsiveness–Venturesomeness–Empathy (IVE) scales (S. B. G. Eysenck & Eysenck, 1978). The results permitted the following conclusions: (1) No difference between the three MAO subgroups was found for any of the EPQ scales; (2) low-MAO subjects had higher IVE impulsivity scores as compared with the other two MAO subgroups; (3) a correlational analysis including the 58 subjects showed that MAO values were not highly but significantly correlated with both measures (from IVE and KSP) of impulsivity (–.32 and –.25). This study gives some limited support for the hypothesis that MAO activity is related to impulsivity; however, no support was found for the repeatedly reported relationship between monotony avoidance and platelet MAO.

The negative correlation between platelet MAO and the different kinds of impulsivity scores has also been reported in several other studies conducted on adults and children (e.g., Schalling et al., 1983; Shekim et al., 1984). The lack of correlation between MAO values and extraversion, neuroticism, and psychoticism had been found earlier by Ballenger and colleagues (1983) and also has been reported in other investigations (e.g., Schalling et al., 1983; L. von Knorring et al., 1984). Some studies, however, support a negative relationship between extraversion and platelet MAO activity (e.g., Demisch, Georgi, Patzke, Demisch, & Bochnik, 1982; Gattaz & Beckman, 1981), consistent with the sensation seeking and impulsivity data, if we consider that extraversion is positively correlated with these temperament traits (Ruch et al., 1991; Zuckerman, 1991c). In a recent study Mezzich and colleagues (1994) showed that platelet MAO activity is negatively related to the syndrome of difficult temperament as measured by DOTS-R; this finding occurred, however, in the substance abuse group of females but not in the control group.

On the basis of the data regarding the relationship between neurotransmitters and their enzymes, and temperament characteristics in normal subjects, not many constructive conclusions can yet be drawn. The only statement that seems to have empirical support is that sensation seeking and traits closely related to this temperament characteristic are negatively correlated with platelet MAO activity.

General Remarks

The biochemical approach to temperament is in its infancy and one may assume that in the next decade hundreds of studies will be undertaken to bring us closer to an understanding of the biological nature of temperament by examining the biochemical markers of this behavior characteristic. A good starting point may be the suggested relationship between selected temperament dimensions and several biochemical components, as proposed by Netter (1991). In Table 4.6 the tem-

TABLE 4.6. Possible Biochemical Indicators of Aspects of Temperament Described in Different Theories

Dimension of temperament	T&C	B&P	S	R	Biochemical variables	Parameters
Approach/withdrawal	+				Catecholamines (plasma)	Level, response
Sociability		+			ACTH, cortisol	relationship between
Ergonicity, social				+	ACTH, cortisol	the two systems
Activity level		+			NA, A (plasma) any	Ratio, level, ampli-
Ergonicity, object-related				+	indicators of sym- pathetic arousal	tude, duration, number of variables
Intensity	+					
Strength of excitation			+		NA, DA (CNS)	Level, turnover
Strength of inhibition			+		NA, DA (CNS)	Level, turnover
Plasticity				+	DA (CNS)	Level
Mobility			+		DA (CNS)	Return to baseline
Adaptation	+				Any (plasma)	No ISR, no SSR =
Flexibility/rigidity	+				Any (plasma)	bad adaptation, SSR-pattern = flexible, good adap- tation; ISR = rigid
Rhythmicity	+				Cortisol, ACTH, 5-HT	Regularity of chrono- biological pattern
Impulsivity		+			5-HT	Level, receptor sensitivity
Distractibility	+				NA, DA, ACh (CNS)	Level?, turnover?
Persistence	+				NA?	Level?, turnover?
Speed				+	Any (plasma)	Latency
Lability			+		NA, DA, 5-HT (CNS)	Turnover
Emotionality		+			Catecholamines (plasma, CNS)	Threshold
Emotional reactivity			+	+	Catecholamines, ACTH,	Levels, ratios or con-
Mood	+				cortisol (plasma), NA, DA, opioids (CNS)	figurations of NA & A level, turnover

Note. NA = noradrenaline, A = adrenaline, 5-HT = serotonin, DA, ACh = acetylcholine, dopamine, ACTH = adreno-corticotropic hormone, CNS = central nervous system, ISR = individual-specific response, SSR = stimulus-specific response. T&C = Thomas & Chess, B&P = Buss & Plomin, S = Strelau, R = Rusalov. From "Biochemical Variables in the Study of Temperament: Purposes, Approaches, and Selected Findings," by P. Netter. In J. Strelau and A. Angleitner (Eds.), *Explorations in Temperament: International Perspectives on Theory and Measurement* (1991, p. 158), New York: Plenum Press. Copyright 1991 by Plenum Press. Adapted with permission.

perament dimensions according to Thomas and Chess, Buss and Plomin, Pavlov, and Rusalov have been hypothetically related to such biochemical components as cortisol, adrenaline, acetylcholine, adrenocorticotropic hormone, and monoamine neurotransmitters (NE, DA, and 5-HT).

In the domain of psychophysiology Gale and Edwards (1983b), H. J. Eysenck (1990b), and Strelau (1991a) have drawn attention to several methodological difficulties confronting researchers on individual differences when studying the relationship between personality or temperament traits and their physiological correlates. In a similar way Netter (1991) pointed out numerous weak points of the biochemical approach to studies concerned with individual differences, some of which are worth mentioning here:

(1) When comparing temperament traits with biochemical components:

> It must be kept in mind, however, that one transmitter or hormone is involved in many functions, and conversely, one type of behavior is mediated by a variety of transmitters and peripheral biochemical variables. Most approaches . . . do not easily provide hypotheses as to which psychological variables are expected to be associated with the biochemical measure. The reason is that biochemical responses have a much lower specificity for a certain stimulus than psychological ones (Netter, 1991, pp. 152, 156).

(2) We do not have direct access to neurotransmitters in the brain. The peripheral measures taken in temperament studies, such as plasma or urine samples, reflect only about 5% of the brain's biochemical activity.

(3) Because of the many compensatory feedback loops between release of a neurotransmitter and inhibition of its release, the levels of metabolites measured in a sample can be indicators of different stages of the biochemical turnover; they may be indicators of high release in one instance or of high inhibition of a transforming enzyme in another.

The biochemical approach along with physiological, neurophysiological, and behavior-genetic studies is needed to examine the complex biological background of temperament traits. The scanty, and hitherto inconsistent, information about the biochemical nature of these traits does not as yet allow for optimistic conclusions. This does not imply, however, that further studies regarding the biochemical components of temperament characteristics are useless.

5

Behavior-Genetic Research
on Temperament

The data and considerations on psychobiological aspects of temperament are greatly varied and may be viewed with a very broad perspective. Whereas Chapter 4 refers to biological phenomena which can be studied in laboratories and characterized by means of strong quantitative measures, the psychobiological phenomena presented in this chapter refer to theoretical constructs and conceptualizations, although often based on empirical data. The chapter concentrates on behavior-genetic studies on temperament. Together with the information presented in Chapter 4, the behavior-genetic approach brings us closer to the understanding of the biological nature of temperament.

As already mentioned in the "Introduction" to Chapter 4, data that show that individual differences in temperament characteristics are codetermined by the genetic factor speak in favor of biological backgrounds of temperament. It is not behavior itself that is genetically determined but rather the physiological and biochemical mechanisms that underlie behavior. Therefore, evidence that demonstrates the existence of physiological and biochemical correlates of temperament traits justifies the search for genetic determinants of individual differences in temperament. However, one can equally well argue the other way around. If differences in temperament characteristics have a genetic basis, there must be some genetically determined carriers in the individual's body (anatomical, physiological, or biochemical, or a combination) that are the causes of this differentiation. Whatever the starting point of the biological approach, the importance of behavior-genetic studies is undeniable.

It has been emphasized (see Chapter 4) that the behavior-genetic approach allows only for the statement "yes" or "no" regarding the biological determination of the variety of temperaments. This statement is, however, only partially true, for at least three reasons. First, as will be shown, behavior genetics allows for the search for more specific genetic components underlying individual differences, thus giving more detailed information about the biological backgrounds of temperament. Second, behavior genetics furnishes some of the strongest evidence regarding the role of environment in determining individual differences, a fact usually not recognized by environmentally oriented researchers. Third, behavior genetics allows for a quantitative evaluation of the extent to which each of the two factors—genes and environment—contributes to individual differences in behavior characteristics.

It is not the purpose of this chapter to describe in detail the behavior-genetic approach to individual differences, on which comprehensive information can be found in many textbooks and monographs (e.g., Fuller & Thompson, 1978; Hay, 1985; Plomin, 1986; Plomin, DeFries, McClearn, & Rutter, 1997). Only some basic information will be given (mainly for the reader who is not well advanced in behavior genetics) to avoid misunderstanding and confusion when presenting and interpreting the empirical data. Further, the behavior-genetic evidence based on empirical research regarding temperament characteristics in children and adults has become so abundant (for review, see Borkenau, 1992; Eaves, Eysenck, & Martin, 1989; Goldsmith, 1989; Loehlin, 1992; Loehlin & Nichols, 1976; Zuckerman, 1991c) that it is impossible here to give a systematic review of these studies. Thus some selected data is presented to illustrate the state of affairs in this domain of research.

Theoretical Issues of Behavior Genetics as Related to Temperament Research in Humans

The behavior-genetic approach applied to studies on individual differences, whether they relate to intelligence, abilities, personality, or temperament, examines the extent to which individual differences in given behaviors and traits depend on genetic (and environmental) factors. Irrespective of the domain in which we study the contribution of the genetic factors to the variance of behavior (and traits), there are some common denominators typical for the behavior-genetic approach discussed here.

With few exceptions, which refer to pathology, it has been commonly accepted that individual differences in behavior known to have biological roots, whether in man or animals, have a polygenic determination. The very fact that not single genes, but interactions among many genes, determine individual differences in behavior requires the application of behavior genetics instead of the conventional (Mendelian) genetics. Whereas the latter refers to single genes and specific genotypes, the former is based on quantitative statistics, and therefore is also known as quantitative genetics. The individual differences approach based on quantitative genetics has far-reaching consequences for conclusions regarding the genetic determination of behavior, including temperament characteristics. Two of these consequences, which make us aware of some limitations on behavior-genetic studies, seem most important for our considerations: (1) Data based on the behavior-genetic approach allow *only* for conclusions about the contribution of genes to the variance, that is, to individual differences in behavior or traits. (2) Any finding or conclusion concerning the genetic determination of individual differences refers not to individuals but *only* to samples from which the data are recorded or to populations of which the samples are representative.

As regards the theoretical aspect of behavior-genetic studies on temperament the following issues are now discussed: (a) ways in which the genetic contribution to the variance of temperament traits is estimated, (b) methods of collecting data on the basis of which conclusions regarding the "nature–nurture" contribution to individual differences in temperament have been drawn, (c) hypothesized relationships between genes and environment, and the contribution of behavior genetics to an understanding of the developmental nature of temperament traits.

Heritability as a Measure of the Contribution of Genetic Factors to Individual Differences in Behavior Characteristics

Individual differences are usually expressed as the phenotypic variance of behavior characteristics. This variance can be divided into a number of variance components which refer to different aspects of heredity and environment, and which are additive. In the simplest way the phenotypic variance (V_P) of behavior is regarded as a total sum of two variance components (Hirsch, 1962): genes (V_G) and environment (V_E). This may be expressed as follows:

$$V_P = V_G + V_E$$

The Genetic Components Contributing to the Phenotypic Variance

The estimation of heritability of a given behavior (trait) is based on the assumption that the phenotypic variance can be partitioned into separate variance components. Let us assume for a moment that the additive model of the phenotypic variance (V_P) can be partitioned into two components only: genetic variance (V_G) and environmental variance (V_E). *Heritability* (h^2) is defined as the proportion of the phenotypic (total) variance that is attributable to the genetic variance (see Fuller & Thompson, 1978; Plomin *et al.*, 1997), thus:

$$h^2 = \frac{V_G}{V_G + V_E}; \qquad h^2 = \frac{V_G}{V_P}$$

Heritability as estimated in the equation is known as broad-sense heritability (h^2_B) because it comprises all the sources of genetic variance. It refers to the total proportion of the variation of behavior characteristics that is due to the genes, regardless of whether they have an additive or nonadditive effect.

The genetic variance (V_G) can be partitioned into two basic components: additive genetic variance (V_A) and nonadditive genetic variance (V_{NA}). Additive genetic variance refers to the part of the genetic endowment that "breeds true." This is the genetic dosage that accounts for the resemblance between parent and offspring, because they share one half of their genes. Heritability which takes into account only additive genetic variance is known as narrow-sense heritability (h^2_N). The latter must be understood as the proportion of phenotypic variance due to additive genetic variance, and may be expressed as follows:

$$h^2_N = \frac{V_A}{V_P}$$

Since narrow-sense heritability refers to the part of genetic variation that is transmissible across generations, it gained especially high popularity in behavior-genetic animal studies in which selective breeding has been used as the main method for studying the genetic contribution to the phenotypic variance of behavior. Personality and temperament researchers, like those in the domain of intelligence trying to understand the genetic determinants of individual differences, are more interested in broad-sense heritability (Loehlin, 1992), which comprises not only the additive but also the nonadditive genetic variance. The nonadditive genetic variance may be partitioned into genetic variance due to dominance (V_D) and to epistasis (V_{EP}), thus heritability in the broad sense has the following formula:

$$h^2_B = \frac{V_A + V_D + V_{EP}}{V_P}; \qquad h^2_B = \frac{V_A + V_{NA}}{V_P}$$

Dominance refers to the interaction between two alleles at a given, single chromosomal locus. The variance due to dominance (V_D) depends on the proportion of dominant and recessive alleles that account for the genotype of a particular trait. Since the offspring cannot receive both of these alleles from the parent, this means that the genotypic values do not add up (genetic endowment which does not "breed true"). In effect, the offspring will be different from the parent (Plomin et al., 1997). Epistasis refers to interaction across alleles at different chromosomal loci. Different kinds of epistatic interactions may essentially influence the phenotype. Epistatic effects contribute to the genetic variation, but they are not transmitted from parent to offspring.

The Environmental Components Contributing to the Phenotypic Variance

For a proper understanding of the contribution of genes and environment as well as their interaction in determining the phenotypic variance, environment as well as the genetic factor has been partitioned into more detailed components. A dichotomy of shared (E_s) and nonshared environment (E_{ns}), also used synonymously as between- and within-family environment, has become the most popular (Hay, 1985; Loehlin, 1992; Plomin *et al.*, 1997). The shared (between-family) environment refers to the environmental influences that render members of the same family similar to one another, and different from individuals belonging to other families. For example, it is assumed that such factors as rearing practices, home furnishings, and the parents' SES are common (shared) among members of the same family. In contrast, a nonshared (within-family) environment refers to those environmental influences that create differences among members of the same family, as for example, birth order, parental differential attitude toward separate children, and interaction with schools and peers not shared by other siblings.

Since environment as understood in the broadest sense comprises all phenomena which are not inherited, it often happens that random errors, mainly related to different shortcomings of measurement technique are included in environment variance. This procedure artificially increases the contribution of nonshared environment to the variance of phenotypic behavior.

Heritability Estimation

Depending on the method applied for collecting data, and on the kind of data available, different formulae have been used to estimate heritability. The most popular formula was elaborated by Falconer (1960), one of the founders of quantitative genetics. Falconer's heritability index refers to broad-sense heritability and is calculated on the basis of data collected on monozygotic (MZ, identical) twins and dizygotic (DZ, fraternal) twins reared together. The index is estimated as twice the difference between MZ and DZ intraclass correlations as presented in the following formula:

$$h^2 = 2(r_{MZ} - r_{DZ})$$

For a proper understanding of the contribution of the different genetic and environment components to individual differences in behavior characteristics, path models and model-fitting programs have recently been applied (for a detailed description see Boomsma, Martin, & Neale, 1989; Neale & Cardon, 1992; Loehlin, 1992; Plomin, 1986; Plomin *et al.*, 1997). One of the most typical path models serving for model-fitting procedures based on structural equations to which mostly LISREL programs were applied is presented in the next section when discussing the design of MZ versus DZ twins reared together.

Basic Behavior-Genetic Methods Used in Temperament Studies

Behavior-genetic methods used in human studies are based on the assumption that, if individual differences in a given behavior or trait have a genetic determination, then the degree of similarity in this behavior or trait should be a linear function of genetic similarity (degree of kinship). This means the more genes are shared by a pair of compared individuals the more similar they will be in respect to the trait or behavior that has a genetic background. According to the polygenetic theory, parents and offspring, as well as siblings (ordinary and dizygotic twins), share on the average 50% of their genes. Monozygotic twins, who result from a single zygote (fertilization of a single ovum by a single sperm), share 100% of genes, thus they are genetically identical. Grandparent and grandchild share 25%, and first cousins 12.5% of genes. Unrelated individuals have no genes in common.

Since environment cannot be ignored as a determinant of individual differences in behavior, behavior-genetic methods refer to such configurations of individuals that differ not only in respect to genetic similarity but also in environmental influences, that is, who share or do not share the same environment. Among the many behavior-genetic methods used in studies on individual differences, the following three methods are of special significance in temperament studies: MZ and DZ twins reared together, adoption studies, and the adoption/twin design. For a proper interpretation of the empirical data it is worth knowing the basic assumptions underlying these methods.

MZ and DZ Twins Reared Together

The design of MZ versus DZ twins reared together is the most often used method in human behavior genetics, and this is also true for temperament research. The conclusions regarding the contribution of heredity and environment to individual differences in behavior characteristics are based in the twin design on the following assumptions:

1. Any differences in behavior characteristics observed in MZ twins are due to environmental effects.
2. The variance in behavior characteristics in DZ twins, who are genetically like siblings, must be attributed to both environmental and genetic effects.
3. There is no difference in environmental effects between identical and fraternal twins reared together.
4. If individual differences in observed behavior are, to a given extent, determined by heredity, the intrapair coefficient of correlation for MZ twins should be larger as compared with intracorrelation for DZ twins. An in-

trapair DZ correlation coefficient that is about half of the MZ intrapair correlation is interpreted in terms of the additive genetic variance.

Each of these assumptions has been subjected to criticism, particularly assumption (3) concerning the equivalence of environments for MZ and DZ twins (see, e.g., Goldsmith, 1988; Hoffman, 1991; Plomin *et al.,* 1997; Wachs, 1983; Wachs, 1992). Notwithstanding the criticism, in most of behavior-genetic studies on temperament the assumptions just listed are treated as legitimate.

Over 90% of behavior-genetic studies refer to twins reared together. Among them those in which model-fitting programs have been applied are mostly based on the following assumptions: (1) the shared environment (C) which produces differences among twin pairs does not differ for MZ and DZ twins, (2) the nonshared environment (E) is individual-specific and unique to each member of a twin pair and it also includes measurement errors that are uncorrelated between members of a twin pair, (3) the additive genetic factor (A) does not differ among MZ twins whereas DZ twins share one half of their genes, and (4) the nonadditive genetic factor (D), which comprises dominance and epistasis, is the same for MZ twins who share all their genetic material whereas DZ twins share 25% of the nonadditive genetic components due to dominance. (5) There is no assortative mating in respect to the traits under study. Figure 5.1 depicts a path diagram that describes the relationship between the factors determining the phenotype (P), in our case temperament traits, of two twins, separately for MZ and DZ twins.

The phenotype may be expressed as a sum of the four factors, A, D, C, and E which are unobserved (latent) variables. The paths indicated by corresponding lower-case letters (a, d, c, and e), known as path coefficients, refer to the effects of the latent variables on the trait being measured. In terms of a structural equation

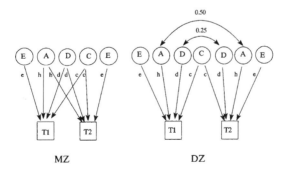

FIGURE 5.1. Path models of MZ and DZ twin correlations. *Note.* T1, T2 = twins of a pair; A = additive genetic component; D = nonadditive genetic component; C = shared environment; E = nonshared environment; Paths a, d, c, and e = effects of A, D, C, and E on trait. For MZ twins intraclass correlations for A, C, and D are 1.00. The same holds true in respect to C for DZ twins.

that serves mostly as the basis for statistical analysis the relationships between variables under discussion may be expressed as follows:

$$P = aA + dD + cC + eE$$

The Adoption Design

Adoption generates a unique situation, where genetically unrelated adoptive parents and child live together, and genetically related biological parents and child live apart. Adoption often creates a situation in which biological and adoptive siblings live in the same family. In these studies conclusions about the significance of heredity and environment as causes of individual differences in temperament are based on the following assumptions:

1. A significant correlation in behavior characteristics between biological parent and child accounts for heredity as an important factor in determining individual differences.
2. An evident correlation between adoptive parent and child (who are genetically unrelated) supports the conclusion that individual differences in the trait under study are affected by environment.
3. The predominance of the biological parent–child correlation over the adoptive parent–child one is evidence that the genetic factor plays a more important role than environment in determining the individual differences under study. The superiority of the adoptive parent–child correlation over the biological parent–child one is used as an argument for the environment as the dominant component responsible for the phenotypic variance.
4. Significant correlations in behavior characteristics between adoptive and biological siblings argue in favor of the environmental contribution, whereas lack of correlation speaks in favor of the biological contribution to the variance of traits under study.

Path models which illustrate the contribution of genetic and environmental components to the phenotypic temperament variance of biological and adoptive child together with adequate equations have been presented in detail by Loehlin (1992). Adoption studies are regarded as providing the best evidence for the contribution of both factors, heredity and environment, in determining individual differences (Bouchard & McGue, 1990; Plomin & DeFries, 1985). There are also some doubts regarding adoption studies, the main objection referring to selective placement. This is due to the practice of adoption agencies who used to match adoptive and biological parents in respect to certain features. As a rule, adoptive parents are older and have a higher SES as compared with biological parents. The similarity of adoptive parents in many traits and behavior to biological parents may influence the genetic and environmental effects (Goldsmith, 1988; Plomin *et al.,*

1997); however, this criticism refers more to intellectual characteristics, such as intelligence, than to personality and temperament.

The Adoption–Twin Design

This design, regarded as the most powerful, combines the advantages of twins and adoption methods (Plomin, Pedersen, McClearn, Nesselroade, & Bergeman, 1988). The adoption–twin design consists in studying MZ and DZ twins reared together and apart. The comparison of MZ twins reared apart with MZ twins reared together, as well as the same comparison for DZ twins, and especially the difference between these comparisons allows for more detailed information about the contribution of both shared and nonshared environment to individual differences under study. One of the main shortcomings of this design is the very small number available of twins reared apart.

Relationships between Genes and Environment and the Genetic Regulation of Development

The possible relationships between genes and environment may be expressed in two main forms: interaction and correlation. These relationships, as well as developmental issues related to genetic regulation, most extensively discussed by Plomin (1986; see also Loehlin, 1992), are briefly presented here.

Genotype–Environment Interaction

The term *interaction* has different meanings, two of which need to be distinguished for our purposes. In a theoretical sense, interaction between genotype and environment means that the genotype interacts from the moment of conception with the environment in a multidirectional manner. There is a feedback interrelation in genes–environment interactions, and the individual's activity plays an essential role in regulating this process (Magnusson, 1988; L. Pervin, 1978). This somewhat abstract understanding of the term "interaction" can hardly be subject to behavior-genetic study, even if possible.

In a statistical sense, genotype–environment interaction means that genotypes may respond differently to different environments. This is due to the fact that a genotype has a range of possible phenotypic expressions, known as the range of reaction. Genotypes may differ in reaction range. "If reaction ranges are similar for all genotypes, no genotype–environment interaction occurs regardless of the magnitude of the 'range of action'" (Plomin, 1986, p. 95). The interaction between genotype and environment can be measured by estimating the genetic and environmental components of variance from relationships that differ in genetic or environmental similarity. The ways of assessing the genotype–environment interaction have been described in detail by Plomin (1986). There is not as yet much empirical evidence to show the existence of genes–environment interaction in the temperament domain, and the data collected so far in studies on child temperament have not shown any significant effect of the genes–environment interaction (see Plomin & DeFries, 1985).

Genotype–Environment Correlation

The extent to which individuals are exposed to environment on the basis of their genetic predispositions can be described by means of genotype–environment correlations, three types of which have been distinguished by Plomin, DeFries, and Loehlin (1977). Their importance for understanding the contribution of genotype and environment to the process of human development has been demonstrated in a theory developed by Scarr and McCartney (1983; see also Scarr, 1992). The three types of genotype–environment correlations are the following: passive, reactive, and active.

Passive genotype–environment correlation occurs between genetically related individuals. Children who have genotypes similar to those of their parents are exposed to an environment (the behavior of parents and the surroundings arranged by parents) that correlates with their genetic predispositions. A sensation seeking child has parents who are also sensation seekers and lives in an environment that reinforces this kind of behavior.

Reactive genotype–environment correlation occurs when parents or other significant persons react to the individual's genetically determined behavior in such a way as to strengthen or weaken this behavior. Children with high sensation seeking characteristics may be stimulated by others to develop this trait (positive correlation) or restrained in this behavior in order to decrease the tendency of sensation seeking (negative correlation).

Active genotype–environment correlation refers to a situation in which individuals actively search, select, or create their own environment according to genetically determined behavior tendencies. A sensation seeker seeks situations, performs activities, or joins sensation seeking peers in order to satisfy his or her need for stimulation. This is an example of a positive correlation but the active genotype–environment correlation may also be expressed in a negative form. A highly anxious individual may organize the environment in such a way as to decrease his or her level of anxiety.

According to Scarr and McCartney (1983), the three types of genotype–environment correlation are developmentally specific and their importance changes with age. The passive type, on which the child does not have any influence, occurs in early infancy and declines with age. The active type can develop only when the child is able to organize his or her own experience. "Children select and build niches that are correlated with their talents, interests, and personality characteristics" (p. 433).

Genetic Regulation of Development

One of the most often expressed views regarding the biological bases of behavior, also shared among many psychologists, claims that, if individual differences in behavior characteristics are genetically determined, they should be present from early infancy and remain rather stable across the life span. Developmental behavior genetics provides evidence, some of which is described in the next section, that to a large extent contradicts this opinion. The evidence regarding the genetic regulation of development is based on data derived from two different approaches, both based on the concept of *genetic change*. The term "genetic change," as used in behavior genetics, is a population concept. It does not refer to changes in molecular mechanisms, but to "changes in the effects of genes on behavioral differences among individuals" (Plomin, 1986, p. 43).

The first approach consists of measuring changes in the contribution of genetic and environmental variance for a given behavior characteristic across the life span. The main question in this approach from our point of view is whether there exist developmental changes in the heritability of a given temperament characteristic. More specifically, one may ask, for example, whether temperament traits are more heritable in infancy, in childhood, or in adolescence. Depending on developmental stage, the variance of a given temperament trait may be due more to environmental variance or genetic variance may be the more crucial. Cross-sectional studies are needed to provide the answer to this issue.

The second approach referring to genetic change consists of measuring changes in genetic covariance during development. Longitudinal data are required for estimating at two different periods of development (Age 1 and Age 2) the extent to which differences in the phenotypic variance of a given behavior characteristic, as measured at Age 1 and Age 2, can be interpreted by differences in the genetic as well as the environmental variance between the two ages. This approach enables us to answer the question whether the contribution of genetic and environmental variance to the phenotypic variance at Age 1 predicts the contribution of both genes and environment to the phenotypic variance at Age 2. In other words, to what extent are developmental changes mediated by genes and to what extent by environment? If there is no genetic change from Age 1 to Age 2, the genetic correlation will be 1.0. High genetic correlation does not mean, however, high heritability. It means rather that the genetic variance has contributed to the phenotypic variance of a given trait at Age 1 to the same extent as at Age 2. But at each age the contribution of the genetic variance may be different; if low, for example, it will be expressed in a low heritability index. In turn, the difference in environmental variance between Age 1 and Age 2 indicates to what extent the difference in the phenotypic variance between the two ages is correlated with environmental effects.

> Genetic and environmental correlations are critical concepts in developmental behavioral genetics because they indicate the extent to which developmental change and continuity are mediated genetically or environmentally (Plomin, 1986, p. 51).

Longitudinal and cross-sectional studies conducted on twins and based on adoption designs can provide answers to these questions.

Behavior-Genetic Studies on Temperament: Selected Empirical Data

As already mentioned in Chapter 1, one of the first studies regarding the genetic determination of temperament traits was conducted in the first decade of the 20th century by Heymans and Wiersma. Since methods developed by behavior geneticists were at that time unavailable, the authors' rather naive analysis of data collected from parents and their offspring did not allow for any reasonable conclusion with respect to the genetic determination of individual differences in temperament.

Studies on Animals as the First Step in Searching for the Genetic Determination of Individual Differences in Temperament

By the 1920s, sufficient evidence had been collected to examine the genetic determination of temperament traits in animals. Such behavior-genetic methods as selective breeding were applied mainly to rats and mice, and comparison of genetically different strains yielded information regarding the narrow-sense heritability of several traits, among which emotionality, aggression, and activity were the most common. Studies on emotionality in rats, initiated by Hall (1941) and continued to the present (e.g., P. L. Broadhurst & Levine, 1963; Gabbay, 1992; van der Staay, Kerbusch, & Raaijmakers, 1990), in spite of differences in indicators used as measures of this trait, have shown that selective breeding results in strains that are evidently different with respect to emotionality. A spectacular result is that of Rundquist (1933) in studies of motor activity in rats as measured in running wheels. Selecting from a random sample of white rats the most active and most inactive ones, he was able to breed after several generations two strains of rats who differed essentially in activity, as illustrated in Figure 5.2. In addition, studies in which an activity cage instead of the activity wheel was used as an indicator of activity, supported the conclusion that there are strongly expressed individual differences in rats (Hunt & Schlosberg, 1939). Results supporting the hypothesis regarding the contribution of heredity to individual differences in rodents' temperament were also demonstrated in the domain of aggressiveness (see, e.g., F. C. Davis, 1935; Lagerspetz & Lagerspetz, 1971).

A series of experiments conducted on different strains of dogs enabled Fuller and Thompson (1978) to conclude that there are clear-cut differences in temperament behavior among the canine strains compared. This kind of study, often conducted with the aim of breeding dogs with given temperament characteristics

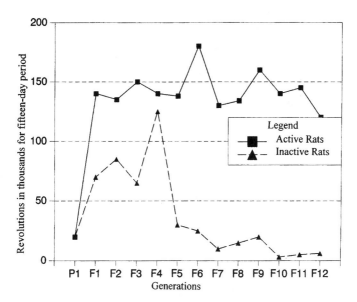

FIGURE 5.2. Activity in active and passive rats as measured in a running wheel. *Note.* From "Inheritance of Spontaneous Activity in Rats," by E. A. Rundquist, 1933, *Journal of Comparative Psychology, 16,* 421.

important for working purposes (e.g., in military service or guiding service for the blind), demonstrates the significance of temperament traits for behavior in specific situations (e.g., Goddard & Beilharz, 1982; Mackenzie, Oltenacu, & Leighton, 1985).

The development of human behavior genetics over the past three decades has accelerated the collection of data with direct reference to human temperament. Some of the data are presented here to illustrate the state of this domain of research rather than to give a comprehensive review.

Extraversion and Neuroticism: The Two Temperament Traits Most Often Explored in Behavior-Genetic Studies

Among the many temperament traits extraversion and neuroticism became the ones on which most of the behavior-genetic studies have been conducted. These studies, initiated in the beginning of the 1950s by Eysenck and his coworkers, suggested a strong contribution of the genetic factor to individual differences on both extraversion (H. J. Eysenck & Prell, 1956) and neuroticism (H. J. Eysenck & Prell, 1951). From a series of studies conducted by Eysenck's group in the 1970s on samples comprising more than 800 pairs of adult twins, the conclusion was drawn that individual differences in extraversion are to be explained by referring to the additive genetic variance and to the nonshared environment (Eaves & Eysenck, 1975). The same was true for neuroticism, with some evidence showing that the genetic component for the variance in neuroticism becomes operative later in life (Eaves & Eysenck, 1976a, 1976b). These studies and some others were summarized by Eaves and colleagues (1989).

Heritability of Extraversion

The findings by Eysenck and his coworkers stimulated dozens of researchers to examine the genetic determination of extraversion. Among the many studies of special importance are those conducted in the 1980s on thousands of twin pairs in Sweden (Floderus-Myrhed, Pedersen, & Rasmuson, 1980), Australia (N. G. Martin & Jardine, 1986), and Finland (Rose, Koskenvuo, Kaprio, Sarna, & Langinvainio, 1988). Loehlin (1989, 1992) summarized these data (see Tables 5.1. and 5.2), including also British pairs (Eaves *et al.,* 1989) and his own results (U.S. pairs; Loehlin & Nichols, 1976).

In analyzing the data presented in Table 5.1 we can see that the heritability index calculated according to Falconer's formula varies between .54 and .80 for males, and between .56 and .70 for females. At first glance, we may conclude that the genetic components (broad-sense heritability) contribute over 50% to the variance of extraversion. However, if we remember that according to the additive genetic variance the intrapair correlation of DZ twins should be about one half of the

TABLE 5.1. The Genetic and Environmental Contribution to Individual Differences in Extraversion

Twins	Britain		U.S.		Sweden		Australia		Finland	
	r	Pairs	r	Pairs	r	Pairs	r	Pairs	r	Pairs
Male twins										
MZ pairs	.65	70	.57	197	.47	2,274	.50	566	.46	1,027
DZ pairs	.25	47	.20	122	.20	3,660	.13	351	.15	2,304
h^2	.80		.74		.54		.74		.62	
c^2	−.15		−.17		−.07		−.24		−.16	
Female twins										
MZ pairs	.46	233	.62	284	.54	2,713	.53	1,233	.49	1,293
DZ pairs	.18	125	.28	190	.21	4,130	.19	751	.14	2,520
h^2	.56		.68		.66		.68		.70	
c^2	−.10		−.06		−.12		−.15		−.21	

Note. Sources: Britain—Eaves, Eysenck, and Martin (1989); U.S.—Loehlin and Nichols (1976); Sweden—Floderus-Myrhed, Pedersen, and Rasmuson (1980); Australia—Martin and Jardine (1986), correlations calculated from mean squares; Finland—Rose, Koskenvuo, Kaprio, Sarna, and Langinvainio (1988). h^2 = broad heritability, c^2 = variance of nonshared environment. From *Genes and Environment in Personality Development* (p. 15), by J. C. Loehlin, 1992, Newbury Park, CA: Sage. Copyright 1992 by Sage Publications. Reprinted with permission.

MZ intrapair correlation, we can easily see that in most of the cases, especially in the Australian and Finnish studies, the DZ correlations are lower than expected from the additive genetic model. This may be interpreted at least in the following ways: (1) Nonadditive genetic factors (dominance and epistasis), which are identical for MZ twins, contribute to the higher similarity of MZ twins; (2) nonadditive genetic factors, especially epistasis, contribute to dissimilarity between DZ twins; (3) MZ twins and DZ twins have unequal environments, for example, DZ twins are treated more differently (contrast effect) whereas MZ twins are treated more equally (similarity effect).

Having at our disposal the intracorrelations for MZ and DZ twins we are also able to calculate the contribution of the shared environment to the variance of extraversion by using the following formula (Loehlin, 1992):

$$E_s^2 = r_{MZ} - h^2$$

The logic behind this formula says that the part of the variance for MZ twins reared together that cannot be explained by the genetic variance must be accounted for by shared environment. As can be seen from Table 5.1, the variance of E_s has in all five studies (for men and women) a negative value, which is impossible, and speaks against the simplified heritability model as expressed by Falconer's formula.

This type of argument was taken into account by Loehlin (1992) in his meta-analysis of the extraversion and neuroticism data. Using a goodness-of-fit model and alternative MZ–DZ path analyses, he showed that the Falconer formula, which takes into account only the global contribution of genes and unshared environment, is not sufficient to draw conclusions about the contribution of the genetic-specific and environmental-specific effects on individual differences in extraversion.

In order to obtain an adequate answer regarding the contribution of genetic and environmental effects to the variance of extraversion, Loehlin conducted a detailed analysis of a whole range of behavior-genetic data based on different designs but all referring to extraversion. The analysis of data from three adoption studies (Eaves *et al.,* 1989; Loehlin, Willerman, & Horn, 1985; Scarr, Webber, Weinberg, & Wittig, 1981), two twin-family (twins and their own children) studies (Loehlin, 1986; Price, Vandenberg, Iyer, & Williams, 1982), four adoption–twin design studies (Langinvainio, Kaprio, Koskenvuo, & Lonnqvist, 1984; Pedersen, Plomin, Mc-Clearn, and Frisberg, 1988; Shields, 1962; Tellegen *et al.,* 1988), and a combined model-fitting analysis that included all behavior-genetic designs enabled Loehlin (1992) to arrive at the following conclusion:

> The genes accounted for 35% to 39% of the individual variation in Extraversion, depending on the particular model, with shared environment accounting for 0% to 19%—values above 4% being found only for MZ twins. Remaining factors, including environmental influences not shared by family members, possible

gene–environment interactions, and errors of measurement, account collectively for 46% to 63%. (p. 46)

Because of the thorough analysis conducted by Loehlin and the many studies included in this analysis which took into account different behavior-genetic designs, this conclusion regarding heritability of extraversion is considered among the most adequate ones.

Heritability of Neuroticism

The five large-scale studies based on the "twins reared together" design which have been reported in relation to extraversion refer also to neuroticism. The data collected in these studies are summarized in Table 5.2.

From a general examination of the table the conclusion can be drawn that the data regarding neuroticism are more heterogeneous as compared with extraversion. The heritability scores vary for men from .42 to .98, and for women from .50 to .72. The negative scores for shared environment are also more pronounced in comparison with extraversion (from 0 to −.47). These data, again, speak against the application of a simple heritability coefficient for estimating the genetic and environmental contribution to individual differences in neuroticism. Loehlin's (1992) complex analysis which comprised, as in investigations on extraversion, not only the same studies on twins reared together, but also the same three adoption studies, two twin family studies and four twin–adoption design studies, allowed for the following two alternative conclusions (p. 55): (1) For a model excluding nonadditive genetic variance, heritability for neuroticism is estimated as .31; shared environment accounts for 15% in MZ males and 21% for MZ females, and 5% and 9%

TABLE 5.2. The Genetic and Environmental Contribution to Individual Differences in Neuroticism

	Britain		U.S.		Sweden		Australia		Finland	
Twins	r	Pairs	r	Pairs	r	Pairs	r	Pairs	r	Pairs
Male twins										
MZ pairs	.51	70	.58	197	.46	2,279	.46	566	.33	1,027
DZ pairs	.02	47	.26	122	.21	3,670	.18	351	.12	2,304
h^2	.98		.64		.50		.56		.42	
c^2	−.47		−.06		−.04		−.10		−.09	
Female twins										
MZ pairs	.45	233	.48	284	.54	2,720	.52	1,233	.43	1,293
DZ pairs	.09	125	.23	190	.25	4,143	.26	751	.18	2,520
h^2	.72		.50		.58		.52		.50	
c^2	−.27		−.02		−.04		.00		−.07	

Note. For explanation see Table 5.1. From *Genes and Environment in Personality Development* (p. 53), by J. C. Loehlin, 1992, Newbury Park, CA: Sage. Copyright 1992 by Sage Publications. Reprinted with permission.

for male and female DZ twins or siblings respectively. (2) According to a model with an equal environment assumption narrow-sense heritability of neuroticism is .30 and epistatic variance is .12; broad-sense heritability for neuroticism is .42 with 5% shared environment for males and 10% for females.

Recent Australian studies were conducted by Heath, Cloninger, and Martin (1994) on a sample of 2,680 adult (25–89 years old) twin pairs and by Macaskill, Hopper, White, and Hill (1994) on a sample of 1,400 twin pairs aged 11 to 18, in which model-fitting programs were applied for estimating the genetic and environmental contribution to the phenotypic variance of extraversion and neuroticism. The conclusions of these studies are close to Loehlin's findings. In both studies the data showed that the contribution of the genetic and environmental components is sex-specific, and in the sample composed of children and adolescents contribution of these components is age-dependent (Macaskill *et al.,* 1994).

Heritability of Selected Temperament Traits

Behavior-genetic studies on human temperaments are not limited to extraversion and neuroticism. Several other traits, more or less related to the two Eysenckian superfactors, have been examined with the aim of establishing the extent to which genes and environment contribute to individual differences in these traits. Some results which refer to traits most interesting from the temperament perspective are presented in the following sections.

Emotionality–Activity–Sociability

As mentioned in Chapter 3, according to Buss and Plomin's (1984) theory, temperament traits have, by definition, a strong genetic determination. During the past two decades several studies have been conducted in which the EASI or EAS Temperament Survery (EAS-TS) in self-rating (adults) and parent-rating (children) forms were applied, by using different behavior genetic designs (see Buss, Plomin, & Willerman, 1973; Plomin *et al.,* 1988; Plomin, Coon, Carey, DeFries, & Fulker, 1991). To delineate the results regarding heritability of emotionality (distress, fear, and anger), activity, and sociability, as measured by means of the EAS-TS, I refer to a study by Plomin and colleagues (1988) on twins reared apart and twins reared together (adoption–twin design). This study illustrates the kind of information that may be obtained regarding the contribution of genes and environment from an approach based on the adoption–twin design.

The study embraced results obtained from 99 MZ and 229 DZ twin pairs reared apart and from 160 MZ and 212 DZ twin pairs reared together. The average age was 58.6 years (27–80+ years), and 60% of the twins were women. The

TABLE 5.3. Intraclass Correlations for MZ and DZ Twins Reared Apart (A) and Reared Together (T) in SATSA

EAS traits	MZA	MZT	DZA	DZT
Emotionality-distress	.30	.52	.26	.16
Emotionality-fear	.37	.49	.04	.08
Emotionality-anger	.33	.37	.09	.17
Activity level	.27	.38	.00	.18
Sociability	.20	.35	.19	.19
n of twin pairs	92–94	135–141	199–204	187–198

Note. SATSA = Swedish Adoption/Twin Study of Aging; EAS = emotionality, activity level, sociability. From "EAS Temperaments during the Last Half of the Life Span: Twins Reared Apart and Twins Reared Together," by R. Plomin, N. L. Pedersen, G. E. McClearn, J. R. Nesselroade, and C. S. Bergeman, 1988, *Psychology and Aging, 3*, p. 47. Copyright 1988 by American Psychological Association. Reprinted with permission.

average age of separation was 2.8 years (more than 80% of the twins reared apart were separated at the age of 5 years). The EAS-TS questionnaire was included in a battery of inventories mailed to the subjects. The intraclass correlations obtained in this study are depicted in Table 5.3.

On the basis of these results Plomin and colleagues (1988) calculated several heritability indices as summarized in Table 5.4. The intraclass correlations for MZ twins reared apart are considered to be direct measures of broad-sense heritability (column 1). As can be seen, h^2_B varies from .20 (activity) to .37 (emotionality-fear). The Falconer formula (column 2) gives the highest heritability scores, varying from .32 (activity) to .82 (emotionality-fear). Two other measures of heritability applied in this study differ essentially from the two already mentioned. The range of these heritability indices is larger, and their scores seem at first glance to be contradictory. The third heritability index (column 3) consists of doubling the correlation between DZ twins reared apart. Assuming that nonadditive genetic variance contributes to the difference between DZ twins, this index underestimates heritability. As can be seen from Table 5.4 in the cases of emotionality-fear, emotionality-anger and activity, for which very low or zero heritability scores were obtained (.08, .18, and .00, respectively), nonadditive genetic variance (V_{NA}) indeed contributed to the variance of these temperament traits. V_{NA} was estimated by comparing the intraclass correlations for MZ twins with the intraclass correlation for DZ twins (average score from both reared together and apart). The fourth heritability index (see column 4) consisted of doubling the difference between correlations for MZ and DZ twins reared apart (Falconer formula applied to twins reared apart). By using this measure the lowest heritability was found for emotionality-distress (.08) and sociability (.02). Assuming that nonadditive genetic variance accounts for the three temperament traits just mentioned, the essentially higher heritability scores for emotionality-fear (.58), emotionality-anger (.48), and activity (. 54) are due to the fact that MZ twins are genetically identical, which

TABLE 5.4. Heritability Estimates and Shared Environment Calculated from the Plomin *et al.*, 1988 Study on MZ and DZ Twins Reared Apart and Reared Together

EAS traits	Heritability estimates					Contribution of	
	(1)	(2)	(3)	(4)	(5)	V_{NA}	E_s
Emotionality-distress	.30	.72	.52	.08	.40	no	.06
Emotionality-fear	.37	.82	.08	.58	.46	yes	.07
Emotionality-anger	.33	.40	.18	.48	.35	yes	.06
Activity level	.27	.40	.00	.54	.30	yes	.14
Sociability	.20	.32	.38	.02	.23	no	.07

Note. (1) = Intraclass correlations for MZ twins reared apart (direct measure of broad-sense heritability; (2) = Falconer formula; (3) = doubling the correlation between DZ twins reared apart; (4) = doubling the difference between correlations for MZ and DZ twins reared apart (Falconer formula applied to twins reared apart); (5) average heritability estimate including indices (1), (2), (3) and (4); V_{NA} = nonadditive genetic variance; E_s = shared environment.

means they also do not differ in V_{NA}. Finally, an average heritability estimate (column 5) was calculated which includes all four indices.

Taking into account the average heritability index, one may conclude that the contribution of genetic variance to individual differences in temperament characteristics as measured by EAS is an essential one, however different for each trait. The highest heritability score was obtained for emotionality-fear (.46) and the lowest for sociability (.23). The contribution of shared environment is not essential for the traits under study, with the exception of activity. For this trait 14% of the variance was due to E_s. The results obtained by Plomin and colleagues (1988) by using model-fitting techniques did not differ basically from those just presented.

Temperamental Traits as Measured by the Thurstone Temperament Schedule

Loehlin (1986) conducted a thorough analysis of four studies aimed at examining the heritability of temperament traits as measured by the Thurstone Temperament Schedule (TTS). The TTS comprises seven scales, which allow measurement of the following traits, described in terms of adjectives: active, vigorous, impulsive, dominant, emotionally stable, sociable, and reflective (see Chapter 6). The TTS was applied in the following four studies: (1) 45 MZ and 34 DZ high-school twin pairs from Michigan State (Vandenberg, 1962), (2) 102 MZ and 119 DZ twin pairs from a World War II Veterans sample (Rosenman, Rahe, Borhani, & Feinleib, 1976), (3) 220 family members with at least one adopted child not younger than 14 years (Loehlin *et al.,* 1985), and (4) 44 MZ twins from the Veterans sample and their children aged at least 18 years (unpublished data). The data, which include the two studies that refer to MZ and DZ twins reared together (Michigan and Veterans samples) are presented in Table 5.5.

As can be seen from this table the distribution of MZ intraclass correlations across the seven traits is significant and varies for the two samples from .19 (stable,

TABLE 5.5. Intraclass Correlations of Temperament Traits Measured by TTS for MZ and DZ Twins Reared Together

Scale	Michigan			Veterans		
	MZ	DZ	h^2	MZ	DZ	h^2
Active	.59	−.01	1.16 (?)	.49	−.05	1.08 (?)
Vigorous	.67	.37	.60	.44	.23	.42
Impulsive	.39	−.11	1.00 (?)	.52	.02	1.00 (?)
Dominant	.56	.27	.58	.58	.03	1.10 (?)
Stable	.19	−.02	.42	.19	−.04	.46
Sociable	.47	.00	.94	.45	.08	.74
Reflective	.35	.27	.16	.52	.15	.74

Note. From "Heredity, Environment, and the Thurstone Temperament Schedule," by J. C. Loehlin, 1986, *Behaviour Genetics, 16,* p. 65. Copyright 1986 by Plenum Press. Reprinted with permission.

in both samples) to .67 (vigorous in the Michigan sample), the average intraclass correlation across traits and samples being for MZ twins .46. The scores for DZ twin pairs are, with five exceptions, below .10, and among them five intraclass correlations are with minus scores. The intraclass correlations suggest that the heritability scores of the seven compared traits are different, probably the highest for active, vigorous, impulsive, dominant, and sociable. They also suggest that, for such traits as active, impulsive, stable, and sociable, the nonadditive genetic variance plays an essential role. As can be seen from Table 5.5, in both twin studies (1 and 2) the DZ intraclass correlations for these four traits are very low and far from half of the intraclass correlation obtained for MZ twins. The minus scores obtained for five intraclass DZ correlations suggest that a contrast effect might have contributed to the results. If DZ twins behave in such a way as to differentiate themselves, it may result in negative DZ correlations (Loehlin, 1986).

The strange configuration of intraclass correlations, as illustrated in Table 5.5, does not allow for an estimation of heritability on the basis of the Falconer formula. In several cases, h^2 estimated in such a way would score 1.0 (impulsive in both samples) or even >1.0 (active, also for both samples), which indicates the absurdity of this procedure. Heritability cannot be higher than 1.0, and in fact never reaches the value of 1.0 for behavior characteristics.

Loehlin (1986), who took into account the data obtained in all four studies, as well as model-fitting procedures, was able to conclude that the additive genetic variance (h^2_N) contributes to the temperament traits as follows: active (.55), vigorous (.43), stable (.13), reflective (−.06), and extraverted (.46). The extraverted characteristic resulted from factor analysis of the TTS scales. This analysis applied by Loehlin has shown that the three scales, Impulsive, Dominant, and Sociable have high loadings on one factor which Loehlin identified as extraversion.

Sensation Seeking

In respect to sensation seeking there is rather scanty information regarding the contribution of the genetic factor to individual differences on this temperament trait. In a study conducted on 233 MZ and 189 DZ pairs of adult twins Fulker, Eysenck, and Zuckerman (1980) were able to conclude that 58% of the variance of sensation seeking may be attributed to broad-sense heritability. Pedersen and colleagues (1988) in a study based on an adoption–twin design conducted on adult twins whose average age was 58.6 years have shown that monotony avoidance, which is a Swedish scale of sensation seeking, has a broad-sense heritability of .23, a score markedly lower than the Fulker and colleagues (1980) result. Nonshared environment contributed 73% to the phenotypic variance of this temperament trait. Impulsivity, which has much in common with the sensation seeking trait (Zuckerman, 1991c), attained in Pedersen and colleagues' study a value of $h^2_B = .45$, comparable to the result obtained by Eaves, Martin, and Eysenck (1977).

Temperament Traits Subject to Study in the Bielefeld–Warsaw Twin Project

Angleitner and colleagues (1995) in Germany, and Strelau, Oniszczenko, and Zawadzki (1994) in Poland, conducted parallel studies on twins reared together in which to all subjects five temperament inventories were administered both in self-report and peer-report forms. In the temperament domain the study is unique because of the large number of traits measured (27 temperament characteristics); the fact that apart from self-rating, peer-rating scores were obtained; the same kind of measures and procedures were applied to twins representing two different cultures.

The statistical analysis of the results obtained in this study is still in progress; thus I limit the presentation of data to the Polish sample. The sample consisted of 546 pairs. Among them were 317 MZ and 229 DZ twin pairs, 322 were female pairs and 224 male pairs. The age of twins ranged from 17 to 64 years ($M = 34.63$; $SD = 10.76$). Zygosity was identified by means of the Questionnaire of Twins Physical Resemblance (Oniszczenko & Rogucka, 1996; QTPR), in which subjects were asked to describe and compare themselves with their cotwin on a number of physical characteristics and to judge the extent of twin confusion by parents, relatives, peers, and strangers. The QRPR allows for diagnosing zygosity with probability over 96%. Each set of twins was assessed by two peers, the peers being different for twin and cotwin. Altogether we were able to collect data from 2,014 peers, 1,282 females and 716 males (age characteristics: $M = 36.40$; $SD = 13.59$). For 16, peer gender was not identified. Mostly peers were recruited among spouses, good friends, relatives, and coworkers. On a 5-point rating scale (1—very good, 5—very little) the degree of the twin's acquaintance with peer was judged between very good and good ($M = 1.63$; $SD = .72$).

The following temperament inventories were administered to all twins: Formal Characteristics of Behavior—Temperament Inventory (FCB-TI), Pavlovian Temperament Survey (PTS), Revised Dimensions of Temperament Survey (DOTS-R), Emotionality–Activity–Sociability Temperament Survey (EAS-TS), and the Eysenck Personality Questionnaire—Revised (EPQ-R). Detailed information regarding these questionnaires is given in Chapter 6. The peer-report version of the five temperament inventories was identical to the self-report version, except that the first-person form had been changed to the third-person form.

The statistical analysis of data consisted of structural equation modeling by means of the LISREL8 program (Joreskog & Sorbom, 1993), a procedure used in most contemporary behavior-genetic studies. Self- and peer-report data were corrected for age and sex and analyses were based on aggregated scale scores. Peer reports were averaged across two raters per target.

Taking as a point of departure the equation $P = aA + dD + cC + eE$, we compared the fit of the following univariate models: additive genetic models (ACE, AE), a nonadditive genetic model (DE), a full genetic model—additive and nonadditive components (ADE), and nongenetic models (CE, E).

Models were fitted to twin pair covariance matrices by the method of maximum likelihood (see Heath, Neale, Hewitt, Eaves, & Fulker, 1989; Neale, Heath, Hewitt, Eaves, & Fulker, 1989). Chi-square was used as a background goodness-of-fit test. Models that showed unsatisfactory fit were rejected. Additionally two other criteria were applied: the goodness-of-fit index (GFI) and the Akaike (1987) information criterion (AIC). Models with the highest GFI scores were selected, but when models were competitive AIC served as the basis for selection. AIC equals the chi-square minus twice the degree of freedom. The lowest value of AIC indicates the combination of goodness of fit and parsimony.

To exemplify the procedure based on structural equation modeling the outcome of fitting univariate genetic models in respect to the temperament traits as proposed by the regulative theory of temperament and measured by means of FCB-TI (self-report data) is presented in Table 5.6. All possible models—additive genetic models (ACE, AE), a nonadditive genetic model (DE), a full genetic model (ADE), and nongenetic models (CE, E)—were taken into account.

The same procedure was applied with respect to scales from the four remaining temperament inventories (PTS, EAS-TS, DOTS-R, and EPQ-R) in both self-report and peer-report versions. After selecting the best-fitting model for each temperament trait and for both assessment procedures separately, the variance scores for all 27 temperament traits were also calculated separately for self-rating and peer-rating data. The results are presented in Table 5.7.

In general, it should be stated that the best-fitting models are trait-specific, a finding replicated in most of the studies concerned with temperament and personality traits. The best-fitting models differ also dependent on whether self- or peer-report data are taken into account, thus the results must be discussed separately for the two assessment procedures.

TABLE 5.6. Results of Univariate Model-Fitting Analyses in Respect to Temperament Characteristics Measured by FCB-TI

Model	Goodness of fit				
	Chi-square	df	p	GFI	AIC
Briskness					
1. ACE	7.14	3	.07	.981	1.14
2. ADE	6.43	3	.09	.983	.43
3. AE	7.14	4	.13	.981	−.86
4. DE	7.62	4	.11	.978	−.38
5. CE	22.12	4	.00	.954	14.12
6. E	83.09	5	.00	.945	73.09
Perseveration					
1. ACE	1.24	3	.74	.996	−4.76
2. ADE	.43	3	.93	.999	−5.57
3. AE	1.24	4	.87	.996	−6.76
4. DE	.75	4	.95	.997	−7.25
5. CE	11.65	4	.02	.972	3.65
6. E	60.24	5	.00	.981	50.24
Sensory sensitivity					
1. ACE	8.74	3	.04	.986	2.74
2. ADE	8.76	3	.03	.986	2.76
3. AE	8.76	4	.07	.997	.76
4. DE	12.13	4	.02	.972	4.13
5. CE	15.32	4	.00	.974	7.32
6. E	66.10	5	.00	.935	56.10
Emotional reactivity					
1. ACE	.37	3	.95	.999	−5.63
2. ADE	.23	3	.97	.999	−5.77
3. AE	.37	4	.98	.999	−7.63
4. DE	2.62	4	.62	.989	−5.38
5. CE	15.84	4	.00	.965	7.84
6. E	104.92	5	.00	.952	94.92
Endurance					
1. ACE	2.03	3	.57	.998	−3.97
2. ADE	2.03	3	.57	.998	−3.97
3. AE	2.03	4	.73	.998	−5.57
4. DE	4.59	4	.33	.996	−3.41
5. CE	10.40	4	.03	.979	2.40
6. E	74.32	5	.00	.956	64.32
Activity					
1. ACE	4.01	3	.26	.994	−1.89
2. ADE	3.06	3	.38	.997	−2.94
3. AE	4.01	4	.40	.994	−3.99
4. DE	3.81	4	.43	.994	−4.19
5. CE	20.05	4	.00	.961	12.05
6. E	88.04	5	.00	.967	78.04

Note. A = additive genetic factor, D = nonadditive genetic factor (dominance and epistasis), C = shared environment, E = nonshared environment; ACE and AE = additive genetic models, DE = nonadditive genetic model, ADE = full genetic model, CE and E = environmental models, GFI = goodness-of-fit index, AIC = Akaike information criterion.

TABLE 5.7. Estimates of Genetic and Environmental Variance Components under the Best-Fitting Models for 27 Temperament Characteristics

Temperament scale	Self-report data						Peer-report data					
	Chi^2	p	A	D	C	E	Chi^2	p	A	D	C	E
FCB-TI												
BR	6.43	.09	26	21		53	8.79	.07		33		67
PE	.43	.93	15	25		60	5.65	.23		31		69
SS	8.76	.07	40			60	3.01	.56		28		72
ER	.37	.98	50			50	1.79	.77	31			69
EN	2.03	.73	42			58	1.42	.84	34			66
AC	3.06	.38	22	25		53	6.60	.16		35		65
M			44			56			32			68
PTS												
SE	.59	.96	39			61	.02	.99	8		10	82
SI	3.16	.53		32		68	2.14	.54	24		3	73
MO	2.19	.54	15		22	63	4.67	.32	22			78
M			29			64			18			78
EAS-TS												
SOC	2.77	.60		37		63	9.02	.06		36		64
ACT	2.24	.69		29		71	1.67	.80		28		72
FE	1.69	.79		42		58	2.74	.60		28		72
DS	3.02	.55		40		60	3.04	.55		28		72
AN	2.40	.66		27		73	4.06	.25	14	15		71
M			35			65			30			70
DOTS-R												
A-G	2.80	.59		34		66	2.61	.62		28		72
A-S	.31	.99	23			67	6.6118	.05				
A-W	1.97	.57	15	15		70	1.475	n.s.				
F-R	1.33	.72	22		13	64	1.156	n.s.				
MQ	.67	.95	23			77	0.507	n.s.				
R-S	2.73	.60	40			60	4.013	.05				
R-E	1.96	.57	18		15	67	1.337	n.s.				
R-H	.88	.93	34			66	11.923	.001				
DIS	.47	.98		32		68	3.444	n.s.				
PER	4.93	.21		20		80	1.230	n.s.				
M			28			69		.32				
EPQ-R												
E	3.40	.33	6	30		64	4.789	.05				
N	3.04	.38	16	25		59	8.993	.01				
P	6.03	.20		41		59	19.923	.001				
M			39			61		.54				

Note. The variance scores are expressed in percentages. The abbrevations of scales are as follows: Formal Characteristics of Behavior—Temperament Inventory (FCB-TI): Briskness (BR), Perseveration (PE), Sensory Sensitivity (SS), Emotional Reactivity (ER), Endurance (EN), Activity (AC); Pavlovian Temperament Survey (PTS): Strength of Excitation (SE), Strength of Inhibition (SI), Mobility of Nervous Processes (MO); EAS Temperament Survey (EAS-TS): Activity (ACT), Sociability (SOC), Fear (FE), Distress (DS), and Anger (AN); Revised Dimensions of Temperament Survey (DOTS-R): Activity-General (A-G), Activity-Sleep (A-S), Approach–Withdrawal (A-W), Flexibility–Rigidity (F-R), Mood Quality (MQ), Rhythmicity-Sleep (R-S), Rhythmicity-Eating (R-E), Rhythmicity-Daily Habits (R-H), Distractibility (DIS), Persistence (PER); Eysenck Personality Questionnaire–Revised (EPQ-R): Extraversion (E), Neuroticism (N), Psychoticism (P).

Self-report data show that the genetic contribution is evident for all temperament traits, although for some of them (mobility of nervous processes, rhythmicity-sleep, persistency) broad heritability varies only from 15% to 20%. Only for emotional reactivity did the genetic component reach the score of 50%. Taking into account both genetic components (A and D) separately for each of the five inventories we conclude that for the FCB-TI traits 44% of the variance can be explained by referring to genes. For the remaining inventories the scores are as follows: PTS (29%), EAS-TS (35%), DOTS-R (28%) and EPQ-R (39%). On the average 35% of the phenotypic variance of temperament traits can be explained by the genetic factor. The fact that for many temperament traits (especially for EAS-TS, DOTS-R, and EPQ-R) the best fitting was obtained for the nonadditive genetic model is not exceptional when both additive and nonadditive genetic models are included in the structural equation modeling procedure (see Heath *et al.,* 1994; Plomin *et al.,* 1988).

As can be seen from the self-report data presented in Table 5.7 the nonshared environment has a significant contribution to the phenotypic variance of all temperament traits. The contribution varies across the five inventories from 56% (FCB-TI) to 69% (DOTS-R) of the total variance, with an average score of 63%. Since nonshared environment includes measurement errors a more adequate picture emerges if we extract from this score the percentage of variance due to unreliability of the temperament scales applied in this study (the average Cronbach's alpha score for the five inventories was in cases of self-reports .74—see Table 6.3). The nonshared environment when corrected for unreliability accounts on average for about 37% of the total variance of temperament traits. The results of our study allow us to conclude that the contribution of the factors—genes (35%) and nonshared environment (37%)—to the phenotypic variance of temperament traits is almost equal. This result is very close to the findings based on a meta-analysis of personality (temperament) data conducted by Loehlin (1992).

A different picture emerges regarding the contribution of the genetic and environmental factors to the phenotypic variance of temperament traits if we take into account peer-rating data. In respect to the FCB-TI, PTS, and DOTS-R scales the contribution of the genetic factor (AD) to the total variance is at least 10% lower as compared with self-rating data and only for the EPQ-R scales are the self-report and peer-report data consistent (39% vs. 40% of the genotypic variance). On the average the genetic factor explains 28% of the total variance of temperament traits when peer reports are taken into account. In turn, in respect to nonshared environment the average score across the five temperament inventories is higher for peer reports. E contributes 70% to the variance of temperament traits, and when corrected for reliability (for peer reports the mean of Cronbach's alpha scores was .77—see Table 6.3) nonshared environment accounts for about 47% of the total variance of temperament traits. As seen, peer-report data show an increased contribution of nonshared environment what may be due to the specificity of the assessment procedure.

As already mentioned the best-fitting models are not only trait-specific but they differ also depending on whether self- or peer-report data are taken into account. Whereas for self-reports only genetic models were chosen as showing the best fit, peer-report data did not replicate these models in respect to three DOTS-R characteristics: activity-sleep, flexibility–rigidity, and rhythmicity–daily habits. For these traits the nongenetic model (CE) has shown the best fit. If we consider that the presence of the genetic contribution to the variance of temperament traits is one of the definitional criteria for classifying a trait as belonging to the domain of temperament then the peer-report data may be regarded as critical for the three DOTS-R characteristics just mentioned. To some extent the peer-report data for strength of excitation also question the temperament nature of this trait. Although an additive genetic model (AE) has shown the best fit for this Pavlovian trait, the contribution of the genetic factor to the variance of strength of excitation, 8%, is very marginal.

Twin studies on temperament based on peer-report data, with different peers for twin and cotwin involved in the assessment procedure, are rather specific for the Bielefeld–Warsaw Twin Project, thus replications are needed to explain the inconsistencies regarding the contribution of genetic and environmental factors to the total variance of temperamental traits when measured by means of self-report and peer-report questionnaires.

Developmental Changes in the Contribution of Genes and Environment to Individual Differences in Temperament

Empirical evidence supports the assumption that there are age- and trait-specific dynamics in the proportion of genetic and environmental contribution to individual differences in temperament characteristics.

A Behavior-Genetic Study on Neonatal Twins

Despite the common view that in early development individual differences in temperament should be attributed to the genetic factor, the data show that in newborn twins it is environment that plays the key role in determining individual differences in temperament traits. A study conducted by Riese (1990) suggests that individual differences in neonatal temperament may be determined by intrauterine and perinatal factors. In this study temperament of 316 newborn twins (MZ and DZ of same and opposite sex) was assessed in the first week of life by means of an observation technique developed by the author (Riese, 1983). The following five categories of temperament characteristics were distinguished: irritability, resistance to soothing, reactivity, reinforcement value (effect of infant's behavior on the attitude of the examiner toward the infant), and activity. Heritability estimates for neonatal temperament characteristics were not significantly different from zero, and MZ twins were not more like each other than DZ twins. Also, the same-sex DZ twins did not differ in temperament traits from opposite-sex twins. A model-fitting analysis showed that for such traits as irritability, resistance to soothing, and rein-forcement value, shared environment played an important role in determining in-dividual differences. Further analysis showed that such perinatal indicators of risk as lower birth weight, lower 1-min Apgar scores, more days spent in isolette, and more days spent in hospital essentially influenced differences in temperament characteristics. This was evident for such traits as activity, reinforcement value, and irritability. The results of this study led to the following conclusion:

> Behavioral patterns might be genetically influenced but not necessarily present at birth to be heritable. Rather, environment appears to account for most of the known variance for the neonatal temperament variables. (Riese, 1990, p. 1236)

Longitudinal Studies Demonstrating Changes in the Proportion of Genetic and Environmental Contribution to Individual Differences in Temperament

The importance of genes in determining individual differences in tempera-ment becomes evident at successive developmental stages, and the data suggest that, for some temperament traits, the genetic influence increases in childhood with age (Goldsmith, 1983; Loehlin, 1992; Loehlin, Horn, & Willerman, 1990; Matheny, 1989; 1990; Plomin & Nesselroade, 1990; Torgersen, 1985).

A longitudinal study conducted by Braungart, Plomin, DeFries, and Fulker (1992) on 1- and 2-year-old infants provides evidence for the significance of ge-netic influence on temperament characteristics during infancy. Two samples were included in this comparative study. From the Colorado Adoption Project 95 pairs of nonadoptive siblings and 80 pairs of adoptive siblings at ages of 1 and 2 years were compared and from the Louisville Twin Study 85 MZ and 50 DZ twin pairs at the same ages were compared. The two samples were combined in maximum-likelihood model-fitting analyses for the following three temperamental traits: af-fect-extraversion, activity, and task orientation. These traits were assessed by means of the Infant Behavior Record (IBR; Bayley, 1969). In the analysis four pa-rameters were taken into account: additive and nonadditive genetic variance, shared and nonshared environmental variance. The results based on model-fitting estimates are depicted on Figure 5.3.

As can be seen, the genetic factor contributes essentially to the variance of all three temperament traits. Taking into account the average scores from ages 1 and 2, the broad-sense heritability accounted for 42% of the variance for affect-extraver-sion, 47% for activity, and 44% for task orientation. Whereas for activity and task orientation additive genetic variance contributed to phenotypic individual differ-ences, in the case of affect-extraversion nonadditive genetic variance was of impor-tance. The figure demonstrates the nonsignificance of shared environment (except

12 Months   24 Months

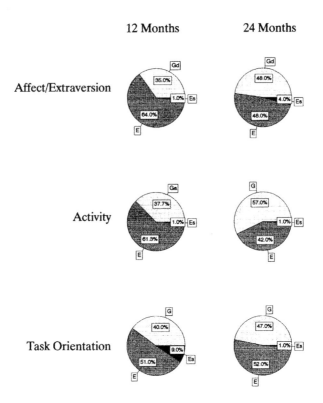

FIGURE 5.3 Genetic and environmental variance contributing to individual differences in temperament traits as measured by means of IBR at ages 1 and 2 years. *Note.* From "Genetic Influence on Tester-Rated Infant Temperament as Assessed by Bayley's Infant Behavior Record: Nonadoptive and Adoptive Siblings and Twins," by J. M. Braungart, R. Plomin, J. C. DeFries, and D. W. Fulker, 1992, *Developmental Psychology, 28,* p. 44. Copyright 1992 by American Psychological Association. Reprinted with permission.

task orientation at the age of 12 months) and the significant contribution of non-shared environment (over 50% of the variance on average, including error variance) to the three temperament traits under study. Figure 5.3 also suggests that the magnitude of genetic influence increased with age, which is especially evident for activity. The differences in the genetic variance between 12 and 24 months are, however, statistically nonsignificant, possibly due to the relatively small samples under study.

In this study temperament traits were assessed not by means of parents' reports but by an examiner during behavior in a structured situation. A study in which the same temperament traits were assessed by using parental ratings in respect to the same sample from the Colorado Adoption Project has not given support for an essential contribution of the genetic factor to the variance of temperament characteristics (Plomin *et al.,* 1991).

Matheny (1989), who studied behavior inhibition in twins from the Louisville Twin Study by means of three assessment techniques—laboratory measures, tests, and parental rating—obtained consistent results regarding the heritability of this temperament trait. Behavior inhibition was estimated in 33 MZ twin pairs and 32 DZ twin pairs at the ages of 12, 18, 24 and 30 months. As measures of behavior inhibition the following indicators were used: (1) emotional tone assessed during behavior in a standardized laboratory playroom, (2) the scale Fearfulness from the IBR during test performance, and (3) 12 items from the Toddler Temperament Scale (see Chapter 6) which pertain to approach–withdrawal (completed by the mother). It turned out that, for all three measures, at all four developmental stages (12, 18, 24, and 30 months), the intrapair correlations for MZ twins were higher than for DZ twins (among the 12 MZ–DZ comparisons, 9 were significantly different). This result suggests that individual differences in behavior inhibition, whether measured under laboratory conditions, in a test situation, or by means of parent rating, have a strong genetic determination.

Matheny's study also revealed that the dynamics in the proportion between the genetic and environmental factors contributing to the variance of behavior inhibition changes with age. Taking into account the composite standardized scores of behavior inhibition for all four developmental stages, Matheny calculated the age-to-age correlations. The results showed that the measure of heritability at 12 months scarcely permits prediction of heritability of this trait when the child is 30 months old (.18). Heritability measured at 18 months may be adequately used as a predictor of heritability at 24 (.61) and 30 (.53) months. A recent longitudinal study by Cherny, Fulker, Corley, Plomin, and DeFries (1994) on 163 MZ and 138 same-sex DZ twin pairs aged from 14 (first measure) to 20 months (second measure) in respect to shyness, which is similar on the operational level to the inhibited temperament, resulted in similar findings.

Taking into account the data as presented, for example, in the Matheny (1989) study which show that there are developmental changes in heritability, Plomin and Nesselroade (1990) put forward a hypothesis that "when developmental changes in heritability are found, heritability tends to increase" (p. 191). A longitudinal study conducted by Torgersen (1987) in which temperament traits in MZ and DZ twins were measured at the ages of 2 months, 9 months, 6 years, and 15 years gives support for this hypothesis.

In the Torgersen study seven temperament categories, according to A. Thomas and Chess (1977), were assessed by means of semistructured interviews with the mothers for 44 same-sex twin pairs (29 MZ and 15 DZ). The separated categories were the following: activity, approach–withdrawal, adaptability, intensity, threshold, mood, and attention span with persistence. Whereas at the age of 2 months the within-pair variances in the two zygosity groups were significantly different only for intensity and threshold (Torgersen, 1985); for all the remaining stages of development (9 months, 6 and 15 years) these variances were

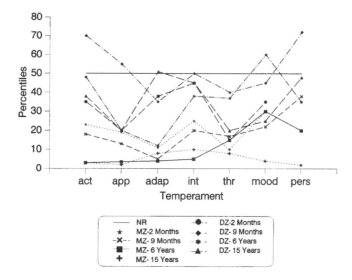

FIGURE 5.4. Developmental changes in MZ and DZ similarity in temperament. *Note.* From "Longitudinal Research on Temperament in Twins," by A. M. Torgersen, 1987, *Acta Geneticae Medicae et Gemellologiae, 36,* p. 148. Copyright 1987 by Luigi Gedda. Reprinted with permission.

significantly different for all seven temperament categories, showing that MZ twins were more similar within pairs than the DZ twins. In order to demonstrate the developmental changes in within-pair temperament similarity for MZ and DZ twins, Torgersen calculated the median within-pair difference for both MZ and DZ twins and for each of the seven temperament categories separately. These medians were related to the distribution of differences within nonrelative pairs which served as a frame of reference (the common norm being 50 on a percentile scale). The lower the percentile score the lower the median within-pair differences in temperament characteristics. As can be seen from Figure 5.4 for several temperament categories (activity, approach–withdrawal, persistence) MZ similarity increases with age, thus supporting Plomin and Nesselroade's hypothesis. However, the small number of twin pairs in this study as well as lack of more sophisticated biometric analysis of data permits treatment of this study not as an argument but only as an exemplification of developmental changes in temperament traits.

Meta-Analysis of Developmental Changes in Heritability of Temperament

A developmental meta-analysis of twin data by McCartney, Harris, and Bernieri (1990) which comprised 103 studies conducted in the period between 1967 and 1985 allows for further conclusions regarding developmental changes in twin similarity in temperament, including adults. In this study, which embraced subjects aged approximately from 1 to 50 years, intelligence as well as personality–temperament variables were taken into account. The personality–temperament variables included the following categories: activity-impulsivity, aggression, anxiety, dominance, emotionality, masculinity–femininity, sociability, and task orientation. Analysis of the data has shown that, for all 8 temperament–personality traits MZ, intrapair correlations are greater than DZ correlations (from .42 to .59 for MZ and from .16 to 33 for DZ). The difference between MZ and DZ intrapair correlations for a combined score (including all eight categories) was .29. An important finding, which seems to be in contradiction to Plomin and Nesselroade's (1990) hypothesis, shows that as twins (MZ and DZ) get older the similarity between them decreases, as illustrated on Table 5.8. For all temperament–personality categories but one (dominance), the correlations between age of twins and intrapair correlations are negative. This is especially evident for such characteristics as masculinity–femininity, task orientation, and activity-impulsivity. Only aggression and emotionality show little association with age. The developmentally decreasing concordance between the compared twins demonstrates, according to the authors, the importance of nonshared experience.

Goldsmith (1983), after analyzing dozens of studies in which the genetic influence on temperament and personality from infancy to adulthood was examined, arrived at a conclusion which seems to be adequate at the current state of knowledge regarding developmental behavior-genetic studies on temperament:

> The genetic evidence is perhaps weakest in three areas: at young ages (the first half of life in twin studies, childhood in adoption studies), for personality traits bordering on social attitudes, and when variables are relatively "unprocessed" recordings of discrete behaviors. (p. 349)

TABLE 5.8. Correlations between Intraclass *r*s and Age of Twins (from Independent Studies) for Personality-Temperament Variables

Personality/ temperament trait	Number of studies	MZ twins	DZ twins	Median age	Age range in years
Activity-impulsivity	14[a]	−.48	−.33	7.6	1–50
Aggression	8	−.09	−.06	11.5	7–49
Anxiety	5	−.34	−.49	20.4	7–30
Dominance	5	.67	.07	30.0	7–50
Emotionality	8[a]	−.11	.30	6.3	1–50
Masculinity–femininity	7	−.81	−.74	16.0	7–50
Sociability	20[a]	−.24	.26	16.5	3–50
Task orientation	5	−.69	−.89	28.0	1–50
M^b		−.30	−.32		

Note. [a]DZ results are based on 1 fewer study.
[b]Arithmetic mean calculated on Fisher's *z*–transformed *r*s.
From "Growing Up and Growing Apart: A Developmental Meta-Analysis of Twin Studies," by K. McCartney, M. J. Harris, and J. Bernieri, 1990, *Psychological Bulletin, 107,* p. 229. Copyright 1990 by American Psychological Association. Adapted with permission.

From Quantitative Genetics to Molecular Genetics

Behavior genetic studies based on quantitative genetics allow us to conclude that among the many traits and behaviors being investigated some of them seem to have a stronger genetic background than others. This fact has provoked researchers to go deeper into the genetic mechanisms of those human characteristics to the variance of which the genetic factor contributes especially strongly. Molecular genetics, which gained high popularity in the last decade in studies aimed at identifying genes for several diseases and disorders, has made its first steps also in attempts to identify the genetic background of normal human behavior and traits.

Since normal human behavior and traits have a polygenic determination there is no rationale to study them by using the "one gene, one disorder" (OGOD) approach which has been applied quite successfully by molecular geneticists in the domain of pathology. To identify the genetic background of psychological traits the quantitative trait loci (QTL) approach has been applied in several studies. This approach is based on the assumption that traits are distributed quantitatively and that multiple-gene effects contribute additively and interchangeably to the genetic variance of these traits. What QTL is has been well explained by Plomin, Owen, and McGuffin (1994), who wrote:

> Genes that contribute to genetic variance in quantitative traits are called quantitative trait loci (QTL). One implication of a multigene system is that genotypes are distributed quantitatively (dimensionally) even when traits are assessed phenotypically by dichotomous diagnoses. . . . The term QTL replaces the word "polygenic," which literally means "multiple genes" but has come to connote many genes of such infinitesimal effect size that they are unidentifiable. QTL denote multiple genes of varying effect size. (p. 1736)

In studies aimed at identifying genes for specific personality–temperament dimensions the best candidate for QTL is allelic association expressed in correlation between a phenotype and a particular allele. Allelic association is "usually assessed as an allelic or genotypic frequency difference between cases and controls" (Plomin *et al.,* 1994, p. 1733). When studied in large samples it allows detection of small QTL effects.

As mentioned in Chapter 4 psychological traits are not inherited as such. The genetic transmission refers to physiological and biochemical mechanisms underlying specific traits. Genetic variability in these mechanisms contributes to individual differences in these traits. Therefore the best candidates among temperament dimensions to search for allelic association are the ones for which some specific physiological or biochemical mechanisms have been discovered or at least postulated. Several studies already have been conducted that exemplify this thinking.

Ebstein and colleagues (1996) conducted a study in which novelty seeking as measured by Cloninger's Tridimentional Personality Questionnaire (TPQ) was associated with a functional polymorphism in the D4 dopamine receptor gene (D4DR). The point of departure of this study was Cloninger's theory which postulates that novelty seeking is mediated by dopamine transmission, as well as evidence that stems from animal experiments showing that novelty seeking behavior is related to dopamine. The study conducted on 124 adult subjects (males and females) has shown that D4DR genotype is related to novelty seeking, as predicted, and shows no relationship with the remaining TPQ dimensions (reward dependence, persistence, and harm avoidance).

Very recently a study was conducted by Lesch and colleagues (1996) who demonstrated an association between a functional polymorphism in the serotonin transporter gene (5-HTT) and neuroticism as well as symptoms of depression and anxiety. The authors stated that functional polymorphism accounts for 3% to 4% of the total variance of these temperament traits. Data were collected on 505 adult subjects (more than 90% males). Neuroticism was measured by means of the NEO PI–R and anxiety with Cattell's 16PF inventory. The finding that neuroticism, anxiety, and depression are mediated by serotonin transmission was essential for investigating this allelic association.

Ball and colleagues (1997) replicated Lesch and coworkers' study on two extreme samples (high neuroticism group vs. low neuroticism group, 50 subjects each) selected from 2,085 adult subjects taking part in the Bielefeld–Warsaw Twin Project. A peer-report form of the German version of the NEO-FFI administered to two peers for each target served to assess neuroticism. The result of this study is negative. No association was found between peer-rated neuroticism and the serotonin transporter gene and the same negative result occurred when self-report NEO-FFI data were taken into account.

As seen, there is a discrepancy in results regarding the allelic association between the particular temperament dimensions and QTL candidates. The inconsistency in data and the fact that the genetic variance of temperament dimensions is not determined by a single gene but by an unknown number of genes, suggests that the way that leads to the identification of genes underlying biological mechanisms of particular temperament dimensions is very long if not endless.

Final Remarks

Researchers on temperament for whom the genetic determination of individual differences in temperament traits is regarded as a definitional component of the construct "temperament" are confronted with some difficulties. There is growing evidence that the genetic factor contributes to the phenotypic variance not only in the domain of temperament (and intelligence), but also in respect to phenomena considered not to have biological backgrounds, such as social attitudes and values (see Bouchard & McGue, 1990; Bouchard, Lykken, McGue, Segal, & Tellegen, 1990; N. G. Martin *et al.,* 1986). One of the most spectacular studies regarding heritability of social attitudes and values was conducted by Waller, Kojetin, Bouchard, Lykken, and Tellegen (1990). By using different assessment techniques the authors measured religious values, attitudes, and interests in two twin samples: (1) 53 MZ and 31 DZ adult twin pairs, both reared apart, and (2) 1,642 adult twins (MZ and DZ) reared together. Without going into the details of this study in which model-fitting designs were used for calculating the data it was found that, for all seven measures of religious values and interests applied in this project, the MZ intracorrelations were higher than the corresponding DZ correlations. The findings of this study led the authors to conclude:

> Individual differences in religious attitudes, interests, and values arise from both genetic and environmental influences. More specifically, genetic factors account for approximately 50% of the observed variance on our measures. (Waller *et al.,* 1990, p. 140)

There is as yet no satisfactory explanation for the significance of the genetic factor in determining individual differences in social attitudes and values. Probably several more or less competitive hypotheses could be developed. One of them suggests that temperament traits present from infancy may be regarded as one of the mediators in molding social attitudes and values. Probably a more specific comprehension of the concept of environment could lead to a better differentiation of the variance components contributing to individual differences in social and religious attitudes. Such a proposal, for example, was made by Wachs (1992), who introduced the construct of environmental system with a hierarchical structure of multiple levels playing specific roles at different developmental stages, and covarying with a variety of nonenvironmental factors.

The finding that a broad range of personality traits, whether regarded as biologically or as socially determined, do not differ in heritability has already been reported by Loehlin and Nichols (1976). In the context of this finding and of the data obtained in other studies it is difficult if not impossible to demonstrate that the variance of temperament traits has a larger genetic determination than attitudes and personality traits outside the domain of temperament. To detect differential heritability huge samples are needed. As described by Plomin (1986, pp. 243–244) over 500 pairs of each type of twin are needed to demonstrate a significant difference between a heritability of .40 and a heritability of .60, and over 2,000 pairs of MZ and DZ twins are needed to show significant differential heritability, when the heritabilities differ by .10.

In behavior-genetic studies on temperament, especially those conducted on infants and children at preschool and school ages, the samples are too small to permit any conclusions regarding differential heritability of the traits under study.

Furthermore, large-scale research is lacking in which temperament traits are studied together with social attitudes in order to show whether the categories of individual characteristics differ in heritability estimates.

Although the contribution of the genetic factor to individual differences in temperament is regarded by many researchers as a criterion for classifying a trait as being of temperament, this criterion is not sufficient. Presence in early ontogenesis and occurrence of equivalent characteristics in animals, are, besides heritability, inseparable criteria ascribed to temperament traits.

6

Assessment of Temperament: Diagnosis and Methodological Issues

The fate of a theory in psychology depends to a large extent on whether the postulates and conceptual problems formulated by the theory are susceptible to verification. This holds true also in the domain of temperament. Questions regarding the biological nature of temperament, its structure and developmental specificity, the role temperament plays in everyday behavior, and many other issues can be answered only if at least the following two requirements are met: (1) it is known what temperament is, and (2) there is adequate operationalization of this construct in terms of assessment procedures that allow measurement of temperament. Consequently, one may conclude that a temperament theory, no matter how interesting, has no chance of survival if it does not offer instruments (experimental, observational, or inventory measures) that allow us to operationalize and to assess the basic concepts of the theory.

The 12 theories of temperament presented in chapters 2 and 3 clearly demonstrate that there is no consensus among researchers as to what temperament is; hence there is no commonly accepted view on *how* to measure temperament, and *what* must be measured. These issues become more complicated if we consider that temperament is one of the phenomena present in animals, infants, and adults. Thus, depending on *who* is the subject of study, the methodological requirements for measuring temperament will differ.

The three basic inquiries—how to measure temperament, what must be measured, and who is the subject of temperament assessment—are inseparable. They are regarded as landmarks for the construction of this chapter.

Methods of Temperament Assessment

From a historical perspective the first method used to assess temperament was observation of behavior in natural settings. The persistent popularity of the Hippocrates–Galen typology of temperament (see Ruch, 1992; Stelmack & Stalikas, 1991), developed on the basis of observational data, suggests that this method is a valuable source of information regarding temperament characteristics. In contemporary research, observation of behavior under natural or seminatural conditions arranged in laboratory settings has gained increasing popularity.

Among physicians who were pioneers in studying temperament, introspective data in the form of anamnesis and interviews were often applied to assess temperament in children (A. Thomas, Chess, Birch, Hertzig, & Korn, 1963) and adults (Birman, 1951; Kretschmer, 1944). This method, requiring individual contacts with patients or clients, can be used with only a limited number of persons; this led to a decrease in its popularity.

The need for assessing the temperament of many individuals representing different populations, and at the same time more precisely and under standardized conditions contributed to the development of inventories, which have attained during the past three decades the greatest popularity in temperament research. In view of the fact that questionnaires are the most frequently used methods for assessing temperament, issues regarding these assessment instruments are presented in a separate section. Observations, interviews, inventories, and occasionally psychophysical and psychophysiological measures have been the basic methods for assessing temperament.

Assessment of Temperament Based on Observational Data

The observational method for assessing temperament developed independently in both hemispheres—in Russia and in the United States—and almost exclusively in research on children. The method varies in such aspects as degree of control over the child's behavior, the extent to which natural environment is arranged, and the manner of recording behavior. Some of these approaches are described in the following sections.

Games as Procedures Used to Assess Temperament in Natural Settings

In spite of the dominant psychophysiological approach to assess Pavlovian or neo-Pavlovian temperament characteristics, developmentally oriented Russian psychologists (e.g., Basan, 1960; Davydova, 1954; Gorbacheva, 1954; Leites, 1956; Merlin, 1955) elaborated procedures that allow an assessment of children's temperament on the basis of behavior characteristics expressed in natural settings. Particularly popular were various games labeled "Block-Building" (Samarin, 1954), "Signalman" (Umansky, 1958), or "Driver" (Chudnovsky, 1963). Essentially these games exposed the children to standardized natural situations that are provocative of behaviors in which temperament characteristics occur. Controls over the situation and the stimuli exposed during games give these observations the status of natural experiments.

The game situation arranged in controlled settings allows for quantitative assessment of such characteristics as frequency of given behaviors, their duration, and their intensity. These characteristics are regarded as expressions of children's temperament. In general, games arranged by Russian psychologists were based on the assumption that the child's CNS properties (strength of excitation, strength of inhibition, and mobility of nervous processes) are revealed in motor reactions, during the process of elaborating and transforming habits, and in the intensity and duration of emotions. To illustrate this kind of temperament assessment a short description of the game "Signalman" is given.

Children aged 3–7 years took part in a game in which the investigator plays the role of "captain" and the child "signalman" on a vessel on which six other "sailors" (6 chairs) are on board. The task of the signalman is to keep in contact with other "vessels" by using a special flag, and to pass commands from the captain to the sailors. As "commands," colored blocks, located on the back of the child's hand, were used. The task of the child consisted of acting as precisely and quickly as possible until the whole game is performed correctly. The captain, seated at a table during the game, carries on continuous observation, recording the speed and duration of the child's motor reactions, and the number and kind of mistakes. The game has four parts: contact of the child with the investigator and introduction to the game, training sessions, sessions during which different situations are arranged (e.g., extension of playing time, delay in giving commands, requirements to speed up, different distractors), and a control game. The whole procedure required dozens of 5–20-min sessions and lasted several months. Different indices were used to assess the separate CNS properties. For example, strength of excitation was diagnosed by taking into account the behavior of children in response to such variables as (a) distractors (b) command "quicker," (c) strong stimuli (sounds) exposed before starting the game, and (d) competition among children.

Observation as a method for studying temperament, also in natural settings such as home and school environments (Leites, 1956; Merlin, 1973), gained some popularity in Russia in the 1950s and 1960s. But the methodological postulates formulated by Teplov (1964) and Nebylitsyn (1972a), according to which CNS properties are most clearly manifested in involuntary movements (see Chapter 2), led to the virtual disappearance of observational methods from Russian temperament research.

The most critical shortcoming of temperament assessment by the observational procedures developed by Russian researchers was the lack of reliability and validity measures. The belief that these procedures permit the measurement of CNS properties as proposed by Pavlov was not grounded on empirical evidence.

Home Observations

One of the methods for assessing temperament, applied mainly to infants and children not exceeding kindergarten age, is observation of behavior in natural settings, most typically the home environment. Observational assessments of temperament were successfully conducted on 1-week-old and even 1-day-old infants (e.g., Ricciuti & Breitmayer, 1988; Riese, 1990). Home observations are based on the assumption that home is the most natural and influential environment for children until they reach school age. Parent–child interactions, with the distinctive role of the mother, are essential for the behavioral expression of the child's temperament and for the way it is perceived by parents (Bates, 1987; Olson, Bates, & Bayles, 1990; Rothbart, 1989c).

In the literature on temperament a variety of studies are reported in which home observation was conducted with the aim of assessing children's temperament (see, e.g., Bates, Freeland, & Lounsbury, 1979; Billman & McDevitt, 1980; Hagekull & Boehlin, 1986; Hinde & Tobin, 1986; Olson *et al.,* 1990; Rothbart, 1986; St James-Roberts & Wolke, 1986; Vaughn, Taraldson, Crichton, & Egeland, 1981). Depending on the goal of the study, home observation procedures differed, but there are some common denominators worth noting.

Observations were conducted usually for periods not exceeding 3 hr, and in two or more sessions. The child's behavior was recorded by trained observers and frequently scores from several observers were collected. Observations centered on specific situations (e.g., feeding, dressing, play) and on behaviors expected to be expressions of temperament characteristics. To eliminate subjectivity, situations were often structuralized and behaviors videotyped.

Several studies showed high interrater agreement depending on the kind of behavior being assessed. Rothbart (1986) reported that interrater agreement between three observers in a study conducted on 52 infants varied from .56 (for behaviors indicating fear and distress) to .90 (behavioral expressions of activity). On the average, interrater agreement on temperament characteristics based on home observation is about .80 (Bates *et al.,* 1979; Frankel & Bates, 1990; Vaughn *et al.,* 1981). Intersession stability and split-half reliability of temperament measures based on observational data were usually much lower, probably not exceeding average scores between .20 and .30 (Billman & McDevitt, 1980; Ricciuti & Breitmayer, 1988; Rothbart, 1986). When specific behaviors such as activity were assessed on the basis of mechanical measures of activity recorded from children's limbs by means of an actometer, internal consistency increased appreciably. Eaton (1983) and coworkers

(Eaton & Dureski, 1986; Saudino & Eaton, 1995), in a series of studies conducted during free play in home settings, found that composite actometer measures of motor activity are very reliable, with Cronbach's alpha between .80s and .90s.

Observation was rarely employed in isolation from other methods of assessing temperament. In several studies this method has been used to test the concurrent validity of diverse diagnostic instruments, especially inventories assessing temperament in infants and preschool children (e.g., Bates *et al.,* 1979; Billman & McDevitt, 1980; Rothbart, 1986; Vaughn *et al.,* 1981).

The fact that home observation is conducted in the most natural environment has its price, mainly diminished control of the situation in which children's behavior is recorded. Coding behavior during observation on the whole is imprecise and is biased by the observer's limited capacity to grasp the whole range of relevant behavior (see Rothbart & Goldsmith, 1985). Observation under laboratory conditions is devoid of these problems.

Observations Based on Rating Scales

For diagnosing reactivity in terms of Strelau's (1983) RTT, Friedensberg (1985; Friedensberg & Strelau, 1982) developed three Reactivity Rating Scales (RRS), intended to assess this temperament trait by means of the observation method applied to preschool children (RRS_1), primary school children (RRS_2), and secondary school pupils (RRS_3). The rating scales, constructed in a way that allows comparison of assessments across ages, are composed of 9 (RRS_1) to 11 (RRS_3) items, rated on a 5-point scale. This instrument is intended for teachers and refers to samples of behaviors and situations typical for the preschool and school environments. An item sample from RRS_1 illustrates the composition of the scales (for a full description, see Strelau, 1983).

Item 2. IS RESISTANT TO SET-BACKS

1	2	3	4	5
Under the influence of failure (criticism etc.) discontinues current activity (drawing, cut-outs, etc.), has to be encouraged to complete it.		Under the influence of failure may just as often become discouraged in his/her work, as he/she is willing to pass on the next tasks assigned to him/her		Failure does not discourage him/her in work. Willingly passes to next tasks, which are carried out more carefully.

Retest reliabilities (with a 1-month interval between measures) varied for the samples from .89 to .98 for the RRS_1, from .67 to .98 for the RRS_2, and from .69 to .94 for the RRS_3. The interrater agreement of two teachers (preschool and school) varied across the three rating scales. Among the 16 correlations illustrating interrater agreement, 11 reached the score of .70 or more. They were mainly obtained from teachers who had known the assessed child longer than 6 months.

The shortcomings of the RRS instruments lie in their addressing only male subjects and in their lack of extensive validity measures. Chipperfield and Eaton (1992) in a study in which actometer measures were compared with RRS scores of school-age children ($N = 127$) showed that high-reactive children (RRS measure) supressed their activity (actometer scores) when exposed to a high level of environmental stimulation. This result holds promise regarding predictive validity of the RRS scales.

Observation in Laboratory Settings

Observation under conditions that allow for control not only of behavior but also of the specific stimuli and situations expected to provoke behavior in which temperament characteristics reveal themselves has recently gained considerable popularity among child-oriented temperament researchers. Among the attempts to measure children's temperament by controlling behavior characteristics under laboratory conditions, three lines of research deserve attention: (1) the Louisville Twin Study, in which Matheny and his coworkers have researched children's temperament for about 20 years, (2) Kagan's study on inhibited children which started over a decade ago, and (3) Goldsmith and Rothbart's current attempts to elaborate standardized laboratory methods for assessing infant and toddler temperament.

The Louisville Longitudinal Twin Project. One of the methods used in the Louisville Longitudinal Study for assessing infant and toddler temperament were structured age-specific tasks organized in a series of episodes called vignettes (for a full description, see Matheny, 1991; Matheny & Wilson, 1981). The vignettes were standardized situations in which different kinds of interactions with caregivers, age-related challenges, and different games were arranged in a way that enabled the recording of children's behavior and emotional reactions provoked by these situations. Depending on age, vignettes varied in number from 9 (for 3-month-old infants) to 15 (for ages 24 and 30 months), each episode lasting 2–10 min, typically the shorter time. Infant and toddler behavior was videotaped and a temperament profile was assessed by an independent rater. The vignettes were scheduled in a sequence duplicated for each child of the given age. Rating scales were adapted from Bayley's (1969) Infant Behavior Record. A single summary score derived from ratings of behavior recorded during the standardized episodes served for assessing temperament. This laboratory method enabled assessment of such dimensions as emotional tone, activity, attentiveness, social orientation to staff, and resistance to restraint.

For illustration, two vignettes are described, the first one for 3-month-old infants, the second one for 18- to 30-month-old toddlers.

(1) *Chewey, rattle* (2 minutes): The infant is lying supine in a crib and the *chewey* (a toy that can safely be chewed by the infant) is waved or shaken in front of the

infant's face and then placed in one of the infant's hands. When about 30 seconds have elapsed or when the infant releases the chewey, the object is placed in the infant's other hand. The same sequence is then carried out for a rattle. (Matheny, 1991, p. 44)

(2) *Slinky* (2 minutes): The coiled spring toy called "Slinky" is shown to the infant, and the changeable properties of the toy are demonstrated. The infant is given the toy, and no further assistance is provided by *E* [examiner-interactionist] unless the infant solicits participation by *E*. (Matheny, 1991, p. 50)

Studies conducted on infants 6–12 months of age (Riese, Wilson, & Matheny, 1985; R. S. Wilson & Matheny, 1983) and on toddlers ages 18–24 months (Matheny, 1991; Matheny, Wilson, & Nuss, 1984) have shown a satisfactory agreement between raters, interrater reliabilities varying in 12-month infants from .65 (social orientation to staff) to .92 (emotional tone), and in 18–24-month-old toddlers from .72 (social orientation to staff) to .94 (resistance to restraint).

A factor labeled *tractability* representing a temperament cluster composed of emotional tone, attentiveness, social orientation to staff, and reaction to restraint as measured in laboratory settings has shown satisfactory age-to-age stability (Matheny, 1991). The highest correlations were obtained when tractability was measured at 6-month intervals between ages 18–24 months (.59), and 24–30 months (.54).

Kagan's Laboratory Settings. The laboratory settings in which inhibited and uninhibited temperaments, as proposed by Kagan, were assessed are described in Chapter 2 (see "Assessment Procedures Used in Kagan's Laboratory"). As with the Louisville project, episodes were arranged according to the child's age and the goal of the study. One of the main differences between the two approaches concerns the laboratory measures. Laboratory studies by Matheny and coworkers were always accompanied by inventory measures of temperament; Kagan (1994) and associates combined the behavioral indices of inhibited versus uninhibited temperament with psychophysiological markers of these temperament characteristics.

The Laboratory Temperament Assessment Battery. Goldsmith and Rothbart recently developed a Laboratory Temperament Assessment Battery (LAB-TAB), which has two versions: a prelocomotor version for 6-month-olds (Goldsmith & Rothbart, 1992b), and a locomotor version for 12- to 18-month-olds (Goldsmith & Rothbart, 1992a). The LAB-TAB (which is still undergoing verification, especially in respect to validity data) is intended only for research purposes.

The LAB-TAB enables assessment of the following five temperament characteristics, called *dimensions:* activity level, fearfulness, anger proneness, interest/persistence, and joy/pleasure. In the prelocomotor version each dimension is assessed on the basis of three settings, called *episodes;* in the locomotor version four episodes form the context for measuring each of the temperament dimensions. The LAB-TAB for 6-month-olds is composed of 15 episodes, and for 12- to

18-month-olds, of 20 episodes carried out by at least two experimenters. Episodes are divided into *epoches* (trials) during which infant *responses* (e.g., smiling, crying) are recorded taking account of their formal features such as latency, duration, and intensity, termed *parameters.*

The assessment procedure is conducted in a typical developmental research laboratory with standard settings and equipment fully described and illustrated by photographs. The LAB-TAB manual outlines the guidelines for scoring and analyzing the data. During a single visit not more than eight episodes can be run. Each episode is outlined in detail, taking into account the rationale, physical setting, procedure, camera instructions, and an elaborated instruction regarding scoring criteria. It is impossible to describe here the consecutive episodes aimed at assessing temperament dimensions. For example, in the prelocomotor version, fear is assessed on the basis of such episodes as Parasol Opening, Masks, and Unpredictable Mechanical Toy; anger is assessed from such episodes as Gentle Arm Restraint, Toy Retraction, and Barrier. Some of the episodes occur in both LAB-TAB versions; examples are Masks (for fear episodes) and Gentle Arm Restraint and Barrier (for anger episodes).

The Laboratory Temperament Assessment Battery is the most standardized laboratory procedure ever elaborated for diagnosing temperament in children. The shortcomings of LAB-TAB are the lack of validity data and the scanty reliability measures. As mentioned by the authors (Goldsmith & Rothbart, 1991), interrater agreement for composite measures based on several behavioral events for most episodes is high, ranging from 87% to 100%. Preliminary data reported by Goldsmith and Rothbart (1991) in respect to the joy/pleasure temperament dimension suggest that intercorrelations across epoches and cross-modal correlations within the same episode, which reached scores over .60, are promising measures of internal consistency.

Observation in the laboratory setting, although regarded as the most objective method yet devised, has several shortcomings (see Rothbart & Goldsmith, 1985). For the child, a laboratory setting is a new environment that may evoke avoidance behavior or inhibit typical reactions. Some parents are reluctant to agree to laboratory assessment, and this results in selected samples of children for study. Individual-specific experimenter–child interactions also influence the assessment procedure.

Critical Remarks

Observational methods, regardless of procedures applied, whether at home or in the laboratory, are based on the premise that temperament characteristics are revealed in behavior typical for natural or seminatural settings. This assumption is only partially supported. As underlined by Haynes (1978; Haynes & Horn, 1982), behavioral observation is biased by so-called reactivity effects which occur when the observing process alters the behavior of individuals observed, at home or in the laboratory. The presence of an observer, who as a rule is strange to the child, may lead to such changes in behavior as increase or decrease in behavior rates, orientation toward observers, deficits in task performance, and other behavior modifications. What is more, there are individual differences in proneness to reactivity effects.

There are other drawbacks of all forms of observation. First, observation is a time-consuming procedure. It requires usually more than one session (visit), requires individual contacts between observer and subject and, because of its specificity, it can be applied only to a limited number (possibly a score or so) of individuals. Second, the variety of behaviors available for assessment during observation is very limited as compared with the enormous number and diversity of behaviors that occur in everyday life. This poses the question as to what extent the behavior measured during observation can be regarded as representative of the child's typical behavioral style. Third, reliability estimation can be properly done only when more than one observer takes part in the assessment procedure; this increases the costs of observation and the time needed for its accomplishment. Fourth, to conduct an observation that allows for a proper temperament assessment, the observer must be trained. A list of sources of variation in the child's temperament assessment based on home and laboratory observations has been drawn up by Rothbart and Goldsmith (1985; see also Goldsmith & Rieser-Danner, 1990).

Psychophysical and Psychophysiological Indicators of Temperament Characteristics

The tradition of measuring temperament by experimental procedures and recording changes in the organism during response to stimuli stems from Pavlov (1951–1952) and his students. Speed of conditioning, intensity of conditioned reflexes (CRs), efficiency of extinction of CRs, and other indicators of this type served in Pavlov's laboratory as methods for assessing nervous system properties (see Chapter 1). Neo-Pavlovian psychologists used experimental procedures to measure psychophysiological and psychophysical behaviors and these procedures became dominant methods for assessing CNS properties. In the West, too, some attempts have also been made to use such methods for assessing temperament characteristics. This tendency was most evident in research on the reducing–augmenting dimension.

Invasion of Psychophysiological and Psychophysical Procedures Aimed at Assessing CNS Properties

The methodological credo developed by Teplov and Nebylitsyn (1963b; see Chapter 2) assumed basically that CNS properties are disguised by environmental influences and therefore must be studied by means of involuntary reactions. This belief was essential for developing psychophysiological and psychophysical procedures aimed at assessing these properties. Some of the methods developed in Teplov's laboratory for assessing CNS properties have been described in Chapter 2. More detailed reports were presented by Gray (1964a), Nebylitsyn (1972a), Mangan (1982), and Strelau (1983).

To illustrate the sophistication of the experimental procedures used in Teplov's laboratory (see Chapter 2), a list of methods (exhaustively described by Strelau, 1983) for assessing strength of excitation is given below:

1. Extinction with reinforcement (see Figure 2.6)
2. Induction method based on Pavlov's law of induction
3. Sensitivity threshold in different modalities
4. Slope of reaction time (RT) curve (see Figure 2.7)
5. Change of simple RT under repeatedly applied stimuli
6. Photic driving reaction (PDR) to stimuli of low frequency
7. Total power value of PDR
8. Evoked potential amplitude to stimuli of different intensity

Researchers from the Teplov–Nebylitsyn school used almost exclusively psychophysiological and psychophysical measures for assessing CNS properties. These procedures, especially in the domain of EEG activity, are also applied in current research focused on constructs stemming from Pavlovian typology (e.g., Aminov, 1988; Golubeva, 1993; Guseva, 1989; Ravich-Shcherbo, 1988).

As already mentioned in Chapter 2, the main criticism to be addressed in respect to these methods is the lack of evidence regarding cross-temporal stability and cross-situational consistency. I have not found convincing reliability estimates of the Pavlovian constructs as assessed in psychophysiological laboratories. Concurrent validity of these measures collected in small samples, which consisted of comparing the experimental indices of CNS properties with each other, is questionable (see Strelau, 1983).

Laboratory Measures of Reducing–Augmenting

Petrie's (1967) observations that clinical patients differ in sensitivity to pain led her to the idea that individual differences in sensory sensitivity that occur in all modalities are due to a biologically determined tendency which she identified as the reducing–augmenting dimension. This dimension has much in common with the construct of extraversion. H. J. Eysenck's (1955) study, which showed that the figural aftereffect is more strongly expressed in extraverts than in introverts, influenced Petrie's way of studying the reducing–augmenting dimension.

The Kinesthetic Figural Aftereffect. A special apparatus for measuring reduction and augmentation was constructed. The experiment with Petrie's equipment consisted of two tests administered to a blindfolded subject: a large-block stimulation test and a small-block stimulation test administered with a 48-hr interval. In the first test, a wooden block 2.5 inches wide was used for stimulation and a 1.5-inch block for measurement. In the second test, the blocks were presented in reverse order: the 1.5-inch block was used for stimulation and the 2.5-inch block for measurement. The blocks are held between the subject's thumb and forefinger of the dominant hand. After rubbing the stimulating block for 90 s the subject assessed the width of the test block. For this purpose the subject moved the thumb and forefinger of the other hand along a tapered bar and determined the width perceived as equal to the measuring (test) block. According to Petrie there were clear individual differences in the perception of the width of the test block after the period of rubbing. Individuals who perceived the test block as increased in size in comparison with the stimulating block were called augmenters and those who perceived the measuring block as decreased in size were called reducers. In extreme cases, increase or decrease reached 50% as compared with the test block.

The psychophysical measure that consists of developing a kinesthetic figural aftereffect was used by Petrie as the basic method for assessing an individual's position on the reducing–augmenting dimension. Petrie (1967) assumed that stimulus intensity modulation as expressed in the kinesthetic figural aftereffect generalizes across several sensory modalities; this assumption has not been confirmed (e.g., A. Broadhurst & Millard, 1969; Hilgard, Morgan, & Prytulak, 1968; Schooler & Silverman, 1971). The lack of confirmation has led to developing questionnaire methods for assessing the reducing–augmenting dimension (Barnes, 1985; Kohn, Hunt, Cowles, & Davis, 1986), and to searching for individual differences in stimulus intensity modulation on a more basic, neurological level.

Amplitude of Evoked Potentials. Buchsbaum (1976, 1978) and coworkers (Buchsbaum, Haier, & Johnson, 1983) developed the idea that individual differences in the perception of stimulation intensity can be conceptualized in terms of the energetic characteristics of brain activity. Buchsbaum and his associates showed that the amplitude of evoked potentials (EP) to sensory stimuli, which is a function of the intensity of stimuli, is moderated by an individual-specific tendency to reduce or to augment this amplitude. Buchsbaum (1976, 1978), referring to Petrie's temperament construct, identified this tendency as the reducing–augmenting dimension.

The experiment aimed at assessing an individual's position on the reducing–augmenting dimension consists of exposing stimuli of different intensities, usually four (e.g., light flash at 2-, 30-, 80-, and 240-foot lamberts), and recording EPs to these stimuli. To define the reducing–augmenting dimension the usual measure is the peak-to-trough from P100 to N120 components (the amplitude length between the components). Reducers are characterized by decreasing EP amplitude to increasing intensity of stimuli; for augmenters, increase of EP amplitude in response to increasing intensity of stimuli is typical (see Figure 4.14 in Chapter 4).

For Buchsbaum (1976, 1978), the size of changes in EP amplitudes is the critical measure for locating an individual on the reducing–augmenting dimension. Thus, assessment of this temperament trait is based exclusively on a psycho(neuro)physiological measure, as distinct from other studies on temperament in which the EP measures of reducing–augmenting are treated as markers of given temperament characteristics, such as sensation seeking (Zuckerman, 1991a), extraversion (Stelmack & Geen, 1992) or impulsivity (Barratt, Pritchard, Faulk, & Brandt, 1987).

Instead of studying selected samples of behavior in a limited number of situations and occasions, which happens when temperament is assessed by observation methods and by recording psychophysical reactions or psychophysiological changes treated as indicators of temperament characteristics, one may assess temperament on the basis of the individual's experience. To measure temperament a retrospective procedure can be used, which refers to experience accumulated over a lengthy period of time, across situations, and across the whole diversity of behaviors.

Interview as a Source of Information Regarding Temperament

The retrospective procedure, which requires given memory capacities on which individuals differ, is applicable for assessing temperament in two ways: (1) by reference to the individual's own experience expressed in introspective reports and (2) by reference to the accumulated experience of someone who has had close contact with that individual. Both approaches, expressed in the form of self-rating and rating by others, are typical for interviews and inventories.

The interview, along with observation, has been used by physicians since ancient times and has an old tradition in clinical practice. It is a method for collecting information about the patient's health status, well-being, family, environmental settings, and so on. As distinct from observation, which permits only the recording of overt behavior, an interview can reveal information about covert (internal) reactions and states. Whether applied directly to individuals or to partners, parents, and teachers assessing others (mostly children) an interview is always based on retrospective data which are essentially subjective.

The interview method for diagnosis of temperament has been preferred by psychiatrists and pediatricians (Garrison, 1991). In temperament studies questions asked by the interviewer refer to behaviors and situations considered to be relevant for assessment of temperament characteristics. Interview questions, mostly face-to-face, are often unstructured. Even when structured and answered in terms of quantitative rating they do not have the psychometric properties typical for questionnaires.

At the beginning of the 1950s the interview method was applied, mainly in Russia, to assess the type of nervous system in adult patients (Bakulev & Busalov, 1957; Birman, 1951; Cytawa, 1959; Lang-Belonogova & Kok, 1952). In these interviews questions were asked concerning behavior in different life situations in which CNS properties could be revealed. They referred, for example, to such aspects of behavior as endurance of strong or long-lasting stimuli, resistance to external inhibition, and behavior in highly stimulating social situations. As a result, qualitative characteristics were obtained that permitted classification of individuals according to type of higher nervous activity. There were virtually no attempts to quantitatively characterize the nervous system properties.

In the domain of child temperament, Thomas and Chess (A. Thomas *et al.,* 1963; A. Thomas, Chess, & Birch, 1968) introduced the interview method in the New York Longitudinal Study (NYLS), initiated in 1956. Parents' interview protocols based on a 3-point rating scale were used as the basis for distinguishing the well-known nine temperament categories (see Chapter 2). The first clinical interviews conducted with parents of 3-month-old infants were relatively unstructured. However, under the influence of accumulated experience, the authors developed guidelines for interviewers in clinical practice (A. Thomas & Chess, 1977; A. Thomas *et al.,* 1968), including a list of questions related to each of the nine temperament categories and suggestions of ways to assess temperament.

In a series of studies the interview method was used to assess children's temperament in the tradition of the Thomas–Chess NYLS approach. Some modifications were introduced to this method applied largely to parents (mainly mothers). These consisted of further structuring and standardizing the interview procedure, as well as reducing the number of temperament categories or introducing new temperament constructs (Garside *et al.,* 1975; Graham, Rutter, & George, 1973; Stevenson-Hinde & Hinde, 1986; Torgersen, 1985; R. S. Wilson, Brown, & Matheny, 1971).

Interviews may be regarded as an important source of information about temperament characteristics when personal contact with individuals (patients, parents, teachers) is possible.

> Structured questions about temperament and parental perceptions in the face-to-face interview allow for more in-depth probing of responses and the elicitation of information not captured through paper-and-pencil techniques alone (Garrison, 1991, p. 202).

Because this procedure requires much time from the interviewer, the number of interviewed persons is, as a rule, small, rarely exceeding several dozen individuals. The interview as a method for assessing temperament should be regarded as a prelude to the methodologically more advanced questionnaires. Questions formulated during interviews often generated questionnaire items, as was the case in the A. Thomas and Chess (1977; Thomas *et al.,* 1968) NYLS project.

Temperament Questionnaires

At first glance it seems paradoxical that temperament as a phenomenon with evident biological background, present in human infants and animals, can be studied by means of "paper-and-pencil" techniques. As generally accepted, temperament, whatever the mechanisms underlying this phenomenon, reveals itself in behavior and emotional reactions. If so, then it seems reasonable to measure these behaviors and reactions by answering written questions or statements presumed to be indicators of temperament expressions present in these behaviors and reactions that occurred in the past (the past week, month, or year). This retrospective procedure is typical for questionnaires or inventories (terms used as synonyms) constructed for assessing personality traits to which temperament characteristics also belong.

Before concentrating on temperament inventories, it is pertinent to inquire whether temperament questionnaires differ from this kind of instrument used in other areas of personality. Angleitner and Riemann (1991, pp. 194–195), taking as their point of departure Strelau's (1987a) criteria for distinguishing temperament from other personality characteristics (see Chapter 1), showed that temperament inventories have some specific features. The items of temperament inventories focus on (1) behaviors that have a biological background rather than those based on learned reactions, (2) the *how* of reactions and behavior instead of the content of behavior, (3) behavior that shows some stability over a person's life span, (4) behavior that is already present in infancy, (5) behavior and reactions that can be judged reliably by observers, instead of nonobservable (covert) behavior, and (6) certain types of activities and environmental settings instead of cognitive aspects of behavior, attitudes, values, and goals.

In the Angleitner–Riemann study, three raters conducted an analysis of items taken from four temperament inventories (PTS, STQ, DOTS-R, and EASI-III—full names are presented in Table 6.2) and compared them with items taken from Cattell's 16PF and the MMPI. Although a slightly different classification for judging the items was used, as compared with the six criteria previously mentioned, the result of this study, in which rater agreement was 60%, confirmed to a large extent the distinguishing features of temperament items as compared with nontemperament personality inventories.

It is not the purpose of this chapter to discuss methodological and psychometric requirements in constructing temperament inventories. This topic has been extensively treated in the literature (see Angleitner & Wiggins, 1986; Brzeziński, 1996; Burisch, 1984; D. T. Campbell & Fiske, 1959; Cheek, 1982; Edwards, 1957; Epstein, 1979; Goldsmith & Rieser-Danner, 1990; Jackson, 1975; Mischel, 1968; Reynolds & Willson, 1985, Tuma & Elbert, 1990; Wiggins, 1973; Windle, 1988). Many of these requirements are common for all kinds of personality inventories, especially the criteria regarding itemmetric analysis (Angleitner, John,

& Loehr, 1986) and measures of reliability and validity (Barnett & Macmann, 1990).

As mentioned in the introduction to this chapter, depending on *who* will be subject to study, some methodological requirements for assessing temperament differ, and this holds true also for questionnaires in the domain of temperament. The questionnaire method used for assessing children's temperament is based on information given by parents, other caregivers, and teachers. In the case of adolescents and adults, questionnaires refer to self-report, although rating by others (partners, peers) is possible. Taking the *who* criterion as the point of departure, issues relating to questionnaire assessment of children's and adult's temperament are presented separately.

Questionnaire Approach to the Study of Temperament in Infants and Children[1]

The semistructuralized NYLS interview procedure that referred to behavior regarded as expressions of infant temperament was a good starting point for constructing inventories. Since W. B. Carey (1970)[2] developed what was most likely the first questionnaire designed for assessing temperament in infants, the number of inventories for diagnosing infants' and children's temperament has grown to more than 50. N. C. Hubert, Wachs, Peters-Martin, and Gandour (1982), in their analysis of the psychometric properties of temperament instruments designed for infants and children, listed 26 such instruments of which only a few are not inventories. An updated review made from a similar point of view 9 years later (Slabach, Morrow, & Wachs, 1991) added 7 new questionnaires. This illustrates not only the number of inventories used in the domain of infant and child temperament research, but also the continuing dynamics in constructing this type of instrument, mainly in the United States.

Table 6.1 presents an updated review of 21 inventories that are the most often used and are significant instruments in recent studies on infant and child temperament. The list comprises exclusively those inventories constructed for English-language populations, although there are interesting and recognized inventories in other than English-speaking countries. Mention here can be made of the Swedish

---

[1] In distinguishing between infants and children in this chapter the term *child* or *children* refers to children older than infants and comprises, depending on the context, toddlers, preschool, and school-age children.

[2] The Bayley (1969) Infant Behavior Record (IBR) was constructed prior to Carey's Infant Temperament Questionnaire (ITQ). The IBR, although used as an instrument for assessing infant temperament, is primarily aimed at measuring infants' level of development. Temperament can be measured indirectly, by referring to the examiner's observation during test performance; hence I agree with Slabach, Morrow, and Wachs (1991) that the ITQ cannot be considered a temperament inventory.

TABLE 6.1. Questionnaires Aimed at Assessing Temperament in Infants and Children

Inventory and References	Scale	Format
Behavioral Style Questionnaire (BSQ) McDevitt & Carey, 1978	Activity Rhythmicity Adaptability Approach–Withdrawal Threshold level Intensity of reaction Mood quality Distractibility Persistence	3–7 years 100 items 6-point scale for parents
Children's Behavior Questionnaire (CBQ) Rothbart *et al.,* 1995	Approach HiPleasure Smiling Activity Impulsivity Shyness Discomfort Fear Anger Sadness Soothability InhibitoryControl Attention LoPleasure PerceptualSensitivity	4–7 years 195 items 7-point scale for parents
Colorado Childhood Temperament Inventory (CCTI) Rowe & Plomin, 1977	Sociability Emotionality Activity Attention span-persistence Reaction to food Soothability	1–6 years 74 items 5-point scale for parents
Early Infancy Temperament Questionnaire (EITQ) Medoff-Cooper *et al.,* 1993	All BSQ scales	1–4 months 76 items 6-point scale for parents
EAS Temperament Survey (EAS-TS)—for children Buss & Plomin, 1984	Emotionality Shyness Distress Fearfulness Anger Activity Sociability	1–12(?) years 20 items 5-point scale for parents
Eysenck Personality Questionnaire (Junior) (JEPQ)	Psychoticism Extraversion Neuroticism	7–15 years 90 items Yes/No format

TABLE 6.1. (*Continued*)

Inventory and References	Scale	Format
H. J. Eysenck & Eysenck, 1975	Lie scales	self-rating
Infant Behavior Questionnaire (IBQ) Rothbart, 1981	Activity level Smiling and laughter Fear Distress to limitations Soothability Duration of orienting	3–12 months 87 items 7-point scale for parents
Infant Characteristics Questionnaire (ICQ) Bates *et al.*, 1979	Changeability Soothability Fussiness Sociability	4–6 months 24 items 7-point scale for parents
Junior 16 (16) S. B. G. Eysenck *et al.*, 1984	Impulsiveness Venturesomeness Empathy	7–15 years 77 items Yes/No format self-rating
Middle Childhood Temperament Questionaire (MCTQ) Hegvik *et al.*, 1982; McClowry et al., 1993	All BSQ scales	8–12 years 99 items 6-point scale for parents
Parent Temperament Questionnaire (PTQ) A. Thomas & Chess, 1977	Activity level Rhythmicity Adaptability Approach–Withdrawal Threshold level Intensity of reaction Quality of mood Distractibility Persistence and attention span	3–7 years 72 items 7-point scale for parents
Revised Dimensions of Temperament Survey (DOTS-R) Windle & Lerner, 1986; for DOTS see R. M. Lerner *et al.*, 1982	Activity level-general Activity level-sleep Approach–Withdrawal Flexibility–Rigidity Mood Rhythmicity-sleep Rhythmicity-eating Rhythmicity-daily habits Task orientation	preschool and elementary school 54 items 4-point scale preschool form for parents school form: self-rating
Revised Infant Temperament Questionnaire (RITQ) W. B. Carey & McDevitt, 1978	All BSQ scales	4–8 months 95 items 6-point scale for parents

(*continued*)

TABLE 6.1. (*Continued*)

Inventory and References	Scale	Format
Revised Infant Temperament Questionnaire—short form (SITQ) Sanson *et al.*, 1987	Approach Rhythmicity Cooperation-manageability Activity–Reactivity Irritability	4–8 months 30 items 6-point scale for parents
School-Age Temperament Inventory (SATI) McClowry, 1995	Negative reactivity Task persistence Approach–Withdrawal Activity	8–11 years 38 items 5-point scale for parents
Sensation Seeking Scale for Children (SSSC) Russo *et al.*, 1993	Thrill and adventure seeking Drug and alcohol attitudes Social disinhibition	9–14 years 26 items forced-choice items (A & B) self-rating
Teacher Temperament Questionnaire (TTQ) A. Thomas & Chess, 1977	All PTQ scales except Rhythmicity	3–7 years 64 items 7-point scale for teachers
Teacher Temperament Questionnaire—short form (TTQ-S) Keogh *et al.*, 1982; Pullis & Cadwell, 1982	Task orientation Adaptability Reactivity	3–7 years 23 items 6-point scale for teachers
Temperament Assessment Battery (TAB) R. P. Martin, 1988b	Activity Adaptability Approach–Withdrawal Emotional intensity Distractibility Persistence	3–7 years 48 items: parents and teachers 24 items: clinicians 7-point scale
Toddler Behavior Assessment Questionnaire (TBAQ) Goldsmith *et al.*, 1986; Goldsmith, 1996	Activity level Social Fearfulness Anger proneness Pleasure Interest/persistence	16–36 months 106 items 7-point scale for parents
Toddler Temperament Scale (TTS) Fullard *et al.*, 1984	All BSQ scales	1–3 years 97 items 6-point scale for parents

temperament inventories (which refer to the NYLS approach) such as the Baby Behavior Questionnaire (BBQ; Bohlin, Hagekull, & Lindhagen, 1981), the Swedish 6-month Temperament Questionnaire (STQ-6; Persson-Blennow & Mc-

Neil, 1979) and the Swedish Temperament Questionnaire for 12- and 24-month-old toddlers (STQ-12 & STQ-24; Persson-Blennow & McNeil, 1980).

The inventories presented in Table 6.1 illustrate the diversity of approaches in the construction of questionnaires in terms of such criteria as theory underlying the instrument, population of respondents being addressed, age of infants and children for whom these instruments are designed, strategies used in constructing inventories, the answering format, and the number and kind of traits being measured.

Temperament Theory Guiding Inventory Construction

Thomas and Chess's clinical approach, as represented in the NYLS study on infant and child temperament (see Chapter 2), influenced not only the development of theories and conceptualizations that emerged in this domain of research during the past quarter of a century, but was also most influential regarding the construction of questionnaires referring to the NYLS theory. A series of inventories has been developed for measuring the nine temperament categories as proposed by A. Thomas and Chess (1977; Thomas *et al.,* 1968). The authors themselves (A. Thomas & Chess, 1977) constructed two questionnaires which made possible assessments of these temperament categories in 3- to 7-year-old children (Parent Temperament Questionnaire—PTQ, and Teacher Temperament Questionnaire—TTQ).

Carey and McDevitt, who represent the most orthodox NYLS approach, in cooperation with others have developed a set of inventories to measure temperament as a construct composed of the nine Thomas–Chess categories (see Table 6.1). A content analysis of the NYLS interview protocols was the starting point for constructing these inventories. In addition, by referring to a composite of temperament categories, the inventories make it possible to assess the three basic NYLS clusters: easy, slow-to-warm-up, and difficult temperament.

Five temperament inventories have been constructed by these authors for assessing temperament during the following developmental stages:

1. 1- to 4-month-old infants: Early Infancy Temperament Questionnaire (EITQ; Medoff-Cooper, Carey, & McDevitt, 1993)
2. 4- to 8-month-old infants: Revised Infant Temperament Questionnaire (RITQ; W. B. Carey & McDevitt, 1978)
3. 1- to 3-year-old toddlers: Toddler Temperament Scale (TTS; Fullard, McDevitt, & Carey, 1984)
4. 3- to 7-year-old preschool children: Behavioral Style Questionnaire (BSQ; McDevitt & Carey, 1978)
5. 8- to 12-year-old school children: Middle Childhood Temperament Questionnaire (MCTQ; Hegvik, McDevitt, & Carey, 1982; see also McClowry, Hegvik, & Teglasi, 1993)

The five inventories are based on A. Thomas and Chess's (1977; see Chapter 2) assumption that the structure of temperament is invariant across age, allowing for definitional identity over time. Changes refer to the behavioral expressions of temperament due to the developmental changes in range and quality of behaviors. Because of these changes the items in the consecutive inventories are age-specific.

A series of inventories based on the Thomas–Chess temperament theory were modified in conceptualization on temperament and/or psychometric procedures applied in their construction, and the authors arrived at different solutions regarding the assessment of temperament (see Bates, 1989; Rothbart and Mauro, 1990; Windle, 1988). Some examples illustrate this.

The Colorado Childhood Temperament Inventory (CCTI) developed by Rowe and Plomin (1977) is the result of a combined approach which takes into account Buss and Plomin's (1975) EASI theory and the conceptualizations of A. Thomas and colleagues (1968). In turn, Bates and colleagues (1979), concentrating mainly on Thomas and Chess's conceptualization regarding the construct of difficult temperament, developed an inventory that allowed for measurement of difficultness (fussiness) as a separate dimension along with other temperament characteristics.

Thomas and Chess's idea concerning goodness of fit served Windle and Lerner (1986) as a starting point for developing the Revised Dimensions of Temperament Survey (DOTS-R) which measures temperament traits recalling those proposed by the two New Yorkers. At the same time, however, the DOTS-R is constructed in a way that allows for the assessment of the contextual demands (in terms of parents' or teachers' expectancies) and for obtaining a fit score or index indicating the discrepancy between the individual's temperament as perceived by a rater, and the expected temperament.

An Australian adaptation of W. B. Carey and McDevitt's (1978) RITQ, conducted on a large sample and with detailed factor analysis for processing the data, enabled Sanson, Prior, Garino, Oberklaid, and Sewell (1987) to construct the Revised Infant Temperament Questionnaire—short form (SITQ) with scales differing from the NYLS categories as the starting point. The School-Age Temperament Inventory (SATI), recently constructed by McClowry (1995) and containing only four scales, also belongs to the family of inventories based on the Thomas–Chess theory of temperament.

Additional questionnaires, derived from temperament theories that differ from the NYLS approach, gained significant attention in research on children. The EAS Temperament Survey (EAS-TS) makes possible the measurement of children's temperaments according to the behavior-genetic theory of temperament developed by Buss and Plomin (1984; see Chapter 3). The construction of the EAS-TS is, to some extent, based on the Thomas–Chess assumption which states that after reaching preschool age the structure of temperament is invariant across age, and that developmental changes refer to the behavioral expressions of temperament. On this assumption the authors constructed the EAS-TS, which is almost identical for children and adults.

Two temperament questionnaires—Infant Behavior Questionnaire (IBQ; Rothbart,1981), and Children's Behavior Questionnaire (CBQ; Ahadi, Rothbart, & Ye, 1993; Rothbart, Ahadi, Hershey, & Fisher, 1995)—have been developed by Rothbart and her coworkers, based on her developmental model of temperament (see Rothbart, 1989b, 1991; also Chapter 3). As a consequence, the scales included in both inventories refer mainly to different aspects of reactivity and self-regulation, and cover all kinds of behavior, with strong emphasis on emotional reactions; the scales of both questionnaires are age-specific. The different number and quality of scales in the two inventories—IBQ and CBQ—are grounded on Rothbart's (1989c) postulate that the structure of temperament, in terms of quality and number of temperament characteristics, changes across age due to biological maturation, environmental influences, and child–parent (and other) interactions.

Goldsmith (1996; Goldsmith, Elliot, & Jaco, 1986) constructed an inventory which was considered a developmental continuation of Rothbart's IBQ. His Toddler Behavior Assessment Questionnaire (TBAQ) is strongly oriented to measuring the intensity and temporal characteristics of negative and positive emotions, a consequence of the Goldsmith–Campos theory of temperament (see Chapter 3).

The great majority of inventories designed to measure temperament in infants and children were constructed by researchers who concentrated their study on early developmental stages not extending beyond school age. Among child temperament questionnaires there are also some that are secondary to inventories developed for adults. Some examples are the Junior Eysenck Personality Questionnaire (EPQ; H. J. Eysenck & Eysenck, 1975), the Junior Impulsivity Questionnaire (I6; S.B.G. Eysenck, Easting, & Pearson, 1984), and the Sensation Seeking Scale for Children (SSSC; Russo et al., 1993). The first two inventories were developed as a consequence of H. J. Eysenck's (1970; see Chapter 2) theory of extraversion and neuroticism; the third resulted from Zuckerman's (1979) sensation-seeking theory (see Chapter 3). Whereas the majority of child-oriented temperament questionnaires are meant for parents or teachers, these questionnaires have a self-rating format. The I6 and SSSC also illustrate another tendency rather typical for adult-oriented temperament researchers: the concentration on one temperament dimension (eventually with subcategories) instead of taking into account the whole structure of temperament.

Respondents Assessing Infant and Child Temperament, and Interrater Agreement

The foregoing review referred to inventories that are addressed to parents, especially mothers, as the basic informants regarding behavioral expressions of infant and child temperament. Questionnaires designed for parents refer mainly to child behavior observable at home or in surroundings where parents are with their child. After age 3, children spend a large part of the day in kindergarten and school—a surrounding that demands from the child new activities and situation-specific adaptation.

To study the functional significance of children's temperament in kindergarten and school activity, inventories have been developed for teachers. They are composed of items that refer to behaviors observable in the school environment. Probably the first temperament inventory constructed for teachers was the Teacher Temperament Questionnaire (TTQ) developed by A. Thomas and Chess (1977). The TTQ fully corresponds with the NYLS approach, and the only difference between this inventory and Thomas–Chess's PTQ for parents consists of item content relating to the specific situations in which the child is assessed.

The TTQ began the construction of other questionnaires assessing children's temperament using teachers as informants on pupil behavior. Keogh, Pullis, and Cadwell (1982), after factor analysis of the Thomas–Chess TTQ scales, arrived at a three-factor solution concerning the specificity of temperament traits expressed in school behavior situations: task orientation, adaptability, and reactivity. The Teacher Temperament Questionnaire—Short Form (TTQ-S) measures these traits (Keogh *et al.*, 1982).

R. P. Martin's (1988b) Temperament Assessment Battery (TAB), also based on the Thomas–Chess approach, allows teachers to diagnose the NYLS characteristics, with rhythmicity and quality of mood omitted from the seven TAB scales. Martin's battery is unique among temperament instruments in that it allows measurement in 3- to 7-year-old children of the same traits by parents, teachers, and clinicians.

Assessment of the same child by different persons: mother-father, mother-caretaker, parent-teacher makes possible comparisons yielding results in some studies concordant but in others discordant. This fact provoked a discussion of the reliability and validity of temperament inventories (see Garrison, 1991; Goldsmith & Rieser-Danner, 1990; Rothbart & Mauro, 1990; Windle, 1988). Two questions were critical in this discussion: (1) to what extent the assessment of a child's temperament depends on who the rater is (mother, father, or teacher; interscorer reliability), and (2) what is measured by means of inventories—the child's real temperament or the perception of temperament by mother, father, and teacher (validity issue).

Interrater Agreement. Numerous studies have shown that the correlations between mother and father temperament ratings are only moderate, at best in the range between .40 and .60, depending on the scale taken into account (see, e.g., Bates *et al.,* 1979; Field, Vega-Lahr, Scafidi, & Goldstein, 1987; Goldsmith & Campos, 1986; Lyon & Plomin, 1981; Marcovitch, Goldberg, MacGregor, & Lojkasek, 1986; Martin & Halverson, 1991; McClowry, 1995). N. C. Hubert and colleagues (1982) presented interparent agreement for nine studies in which eight different temperament inventories for infants and children were applied. Considering the average (or median) scores derived from these studies, interparent agreement varied from .08 (Pfeffer & Martin, 1983; TAB applied to 48 children) to .60 (Rothbart & Derryberry, 1981; IBQ applied to 22 children). After calculating the median from the average (median) scores obtained in these nine studies, I got a value of .41. However, most samples were small, varying in size from 16 to 203 children. When Martin and Halverson (1991) summarized interparent agreement from four studies (one of them already included in Hubert and colleagues' analysis) in which the TAB was applied, the scores varied from –.21 to .66. After additional analysis which consisted of averaging the coefficients of correlation from the four studies, in which temperaments were measured by six TAB scales, I got a score of .36. This result does not differ essentially from the median score obtained from the nine studies just presented. A very recent study conducted by Rothbart and colleagues (1995) on three samples (altogether 308 mothers and fathers) where the CBQ was applied also corresponds with the interparent reliability scores obtained in earlier studies. The average that I calculated from 45 scores (3 samples and 15 CBQ scales) is .43, with the highest scores for Shyness (.65) and Impulsivity scales (.60) and the lowest for Smiling (.25) and Perceptual Sensitivity (.29) scales.

Considering these moderate, or even less than moderate, correlations in mother–father ratings from a reliability perspective, presumably the same measure is not the same for mothers and fathers. There are several variables that contribute to the reliability of parents' temperament assessment (see N. C. Hubert *et al.*, 1982; Rothbart & Goldsmith, 1985; Slabach *et al.*, 1991). For example, parents use different criteria in judging the inventory items, and to mother and father for whom different behaviors of the assessed infant and child are available, they ascribe different weights to the behaviors, and so on. Also the social desirability factor contributes differently to temperament assessment by mother and father.

In some inventory studies, parent (mostly mother) rating was compared with teacher rating (e.g., Field & Greenberg, 1982; Goldsmith & Rieser-Danner, 1986, 1990; Victor, Halverson, & Wampler, 1988). Assuming that parental agreement does not on the average extend much above .40, one might expect that parent–teacher agreement would be even lower, since children's behavior and the situations in which this behavior occurs differ essentially for the informants—parent and teacher.

Goldsmith and Rieser-Danner (1986) summarized correlations for mother and teacher agreement taking into account nine studies from the Austin Day Care Project, in which eight temperament inventories were applied (IBQ, ITQ, ICQ, TTS, EASI-III, TBAQ, BSQ and DOTS). No average scores were given, only the ranges of correlations in mother–teacher ratings with respect to the dozens of scales of which the eight inventories are composed. The ranges varied from –.49 to .55, with negative correlations representing the extreme scores in six studies. Taking into account only the highest correlations obtained in the nine studies, the average score is .38, which raises question as to the generalizability of temperament assessment (Bates, 1987).

An illustrative study was conducted by Field and Greenberg (1982), who took into account all possible comparisons in temperament rating by mothers, fathers, and teachers. Temperament was assessed in infants (N = 16) by means of the RITQ and in toddlers (N = 33) by using the TTS, both inventories composed of the nine Thomas–Chess scales. From the correlations presented by the authors, I have taken the average from the nine scales with respect to all possible comparisons, and the results are as follows: mother–father: .36 (infants [I]) and .46 (toddlers [T]), mother–teacher: .20 (I) and .35 (T), father–teacher: .33 (I) and .39 (T), teacher–teacher: .31 (I) and .37 (T). These results, although based on a small number of subjects, suggest that agreement is highest when parent rating is taken into account, and lowest between mother and teacher. Most likely, in inventory studies one should not expect the parent–teacher correlation to exceed .40.

Because parents and teachers assess children's temperament on the basis of inventory items that differ as concerns behaviors and situations assumed to be expressions of child temperament, the degree of agreement in parent–teacher rating should be considered in terms of concurrent validity.

Inventories as a Measure of Real or Perceived Temperament. The moderate agreement between parent ratings, and even poorer agreement of parent–teacher ratings, prompted researchers to ask whether the phenomenon to be measured can indeed be identified as children's temperament. Two most radical positions have been taken by A. Thomas and Chess (1977; A. Thomas, Chess, & Korn, 1982) and by Bates (1980, 1983, 1989) (see "The Concept of Difficult Temperament," in Chapter 7). According to the first, inventories allow for measurement of real temperament modified by parents' attitudes and behavior. In contrast, Bates postulates that questionnaires measure only the perception of children's temperament by parents and other raters. Both views influenced the thinking about assessment in the temperament domain. Researchers using inventories in the Thomas and Chess tradition are, in general, closer to the view that real temperament is the object of measurement, whereas followers of Bates's line of research represent the perceptual approach in diagnosing temperament (e.g. Cardell & Parmar, 1988; B. N. Gordon, 1983; Huitt & Ashton, 1982; Shwalb, Shwalb, & Shoij, 1994).

Without denying the fact that temperament is a reality that can be measured in infants and children by means of inventories, several authors (Goldsmith & Rieser-Danner, 1986, 1990; R. M. Lerner & Lerner, 1987; Rothbart & Mauro, 1990; Windle, 1988) postulate that assessment of temperament is an outcome of a variety of interactions between the assessed child and the rater, including the social context, the actual situation, accumulated experience, and the raters' own personality-temperament characteristics. This approach to assessing children's temperament favors a view according to which validity criteria applied in temperament assessment should be considered in the context of the purpose of that measurement.

Reliability and Validity Measures

As already mentioned, interrater agreement, depending on the context, may be used as a measure of reliability or validity of temperament inventories. The most representative information regarding measures of the reliability and validity of these instruments for assessing temperament in infants and children may be found in N. C. Hubert and colleagues (1982) and Slabach and colleagues (1991; see also Bates, 1987; Goldsmith & Rieser-Danner, 1990; Rothbart & Goldsmith, 1985; Rothbart & Mauro, 1990; Windle, 1988). It is not possible to summarize here the hundred and more studies on reliability scores for all kinds of temperament inventories, taking into account especially such measures as Cronbach's alpha (internal reliability) and stability scores (test–retest coefficient). The number of validity studies is much lower. Some of these, with respect to construct validity and predictive validity, are presented in the next chapter where the functional significance of temperament is discussed.

Summarizing their review nine years after the first presentation of reliability and validity data, Slabach and colleagues (1991) arrived at several conclusions, some of which are worthy of mention. First, the 1991 review confirms that moderate internal consistency is the norm for most temperament inventories, with some scales from CCTI, MCTQ, IBQ, TBAQ, DOTS-R, TAB, and TTQ-S demonstrating levels of internal consistency higher than .80, or at least .75. The recently developed SATI shows reliabilities in the range of .85–.90 (McClowry, 1995). Second, most temperament questionnaires for assessment of infants and children show, in general, satisfactory short test–retest reliability and moderate cross-time stability. Third, several instruments, for example, TTQ-S, RITQ, IBQ, TTS, and BSQ, show satisfactory external or convergent validity, or both, measured by such criteria as behavior disorders, behavior in the classroom, behavior at home, and relationship with attachment.

Such elements of temperament questionnaires as strategies used for constructing the instrument and number and kind of traits being measured are common to all kinds of inventories, regardless of whether temperament is assessed in children or adults; hence these issues are discussed after presenting the inventories designed for the assessment of temperament in adolescents and adults.

Temperament Questionnaires for Adolescents and Adults

The use of inventories for diagnosing temperament in adolescents and adults[3] dates from the beginning of the 20th century. Heymans and Wiersma (1906–1918; for details, see Chapter 1) constructed a 90-item questionnaire for assessing three basic temperament characteristics: activity, emotionality, and primary and sec-

---

[3] When using the term *adult* or *adults* in the context of temperament questionnaires the reference includes adolescents as well, unless the difference is noted.

ondary function. However, the way this instrument was constructed makes it similar to a well-structured interview.

It is about 50 years since the first inventories were introduced for assessing temperament in adults. In 1949 the Guilford–Zimmerman Temperament Survey (GZTS; Guilford, Zimmerman, & Guilford, 1976) was published, and two years later Thurstone (1951, 1953) constructed the Thurstone Temperament Schedule (TTS), which is a modified (reduced in number of factors) version of the GZTS. The GZTS, which is the result of factor analysis of hundreds of items, although labeled a temperament instrument, was intended for measuring personality as a broader construct, including also traits which are beyond the temperament domain (e.g., objectivity, personal relations).

It was in the 1950s, too, that H. J. Eysenck (1956) published the Maudsley Personality Inventory (MPI) for the measurement of extraversion and neuroticism. This instrument, together with the earlier Maudsley Medical Questionnaire (MMQ; H. J. Eysenck, 1947), was the starting point for constructing the widely used Eysenck Personality Inventory (EPI; H. J. Eysenck & Eysenck, 1964), and the Eysenck Personality Questionnaires (EPQ; H. J. Eysenck & Eysenck, 1975; EPQ-R; S. B. G. Eysenck, Eysenck, & Barrett, 1985; for details, see Chapter 2). The temperament questionnaires published in the 1950s were influential in further developments in constructing adult temperament inventories. There are several dozen questionnaires in use in current studies for assessing temperament in adults (see Strelau, 1991b). Table 6.2 presents selected questionnaires that have been constructed or adapted for English-speaking populations and which are currently among the most popular.

Referring to the instruments included in Table 6.2, I discuss several issues, such as theoretical background, self- versus peer-rating agreement, construction strategies, and status of traits for measurement.

Theoretical Background

Among the 17 questionnaires presented in Table 6.2 there are three instruments originally constructed for children. Two of them—the Early Adult Temperament Questionnaire (EATQ; A. Thomas, Mittelman, Chess, Korn, & Cohen, 1982), and the DOTS-R (Windle & Lerner, 1986) have their background in the NYLS approach. Inventories based on the Thomas–Chess theory have already been discussed in the previous section, together with Buss and Plomin's (1984) EAS-TS, which is the third inventory with roots in child research.

The Thurstone Temperament Schedule, constructed more than 40 years ago (Thurstone, 1953) and still in use among researchers (e.g., Loehlin, 1986; Loehlin, Willerman, & Horn, 1985; Rosenman, Rahe, Borhani, & Feinleib, 1976), may serve as an example of a purely atheoretical approach to assessing temperament. The only criterion for constructing the inventory was the factor analytical solution. Taking 13 personality factors distinguished by Guilford as a starting point, Thurstone (1951)

TABLE 6.2. Questionnaires Aimed at Assessing Temperament in Adolescents and Adults

Inventory and References	Scale	Format
Affect Intensity Measure (AIM) Larsen & Diener, 1987	Affect intensity	40 items 6-point scale
Arousal Predisposition Scale (APS) Coren, 1988, 1990	Arousability	12 items 5-point scale
Barratt Impulsiveness Scale (BIS-10) Barratt, 1985	Motor impulsiveness Cognitive impulsiveness Non-planning impulsiveness	34 items 4-point scale
Early Adult Temperament Questionnaire (EATQ) A. Thomas *et al.*, 1982	Activity level Rhythmicity Adaptability Approach–Withdrawal Intensity Sensory threshold Mood quality Distractibility Persistence/attention span	140 items 7-point scale
EAS Temperament Survey (EAS-TS)—for adults Buss & Plomin, 1984	Distress Fearfulness Anger Activity Sociability	20 items 5-point scale
Eysenck Personality Questionnaire–Revised (EPQ-R) S. B. G. Eysenck *et al.*, 1985; for EPQ, see H. J. Eysenck & Eysenck, 1975	Psychoticism Extraversion Neuroticism Lie scale	100 items Short-scale EPQ-R—48 items Yes/No format
Formal Characteristics of Behaviour–Temperament Inventory (FCB-TI) Strelau & Zawadzki, 1993, 1995	Briskness Perseveration Sensory sensitivity Emotional reactivity Endurance Activity	120 items Yes/No format
I7 Impulsiveness Questionnaire (I7) S. B. G. Eysenck *et al.*, 1985	Impulsiveness Venturesomeness Empathy	54 items Yes/No format
Pavlovian Temperament Survey (PTS) Strelau & Angleitner, 1994; Newberry *et al.*, 1997	Strength of excitation Strength of inhibition Mobility of nervous processes	66 items 4-point scale

(continued)

TABLE 6.2. *(Continued)*

Inventory and References	Scale	Format
Pleasure-Arousal-Dominance scales (PAD) Mehrabian, 1978b, 1995a	Trait-pleasure Trait-arousal Trait-dominance	47 pairs of adjectives 9-point scale
Reactivity Scale (RS) Kohn, 1985	Reactivity	24 items 5-point scale
Reducer–Augmenter Scale (RAS) Barnes, 1985; Kohn *et al.,* 1986; for revised RAS (RRAS), see Clapper, 1990	Reducing–augmenting	54 items RRAS: 34 items forced choice items (A & B)
Revised Dimensions of Temperament Survey (DOTS-R) Windle & Lerner, 1986; for DOTS, see R. M. Lerner *et al.,* 1982	Activity level-general Activity level-sleep Approach–Withdrawal Flexibility–Rigidity Mood Rhythmicity-sleep Rhythmicity-eating Rhythmicity-daily habits Distractibility Persistence	54 items 4-point scale
Sensation Seeking Scale (SSS)—form IV & V Zuckerman, 1979, 1994	Thrill and adventure seeking Experience seeking Disinhibition Boredom susceptibility Sensation seeking (general—IV, total—V)	SSS-IV: 72 items SSS-V: 40 items forced-choice items (A & B)
Structure of Temperament Questionnaire (STQ) Rusalov, 1989c	Ergonicity, object-related Ergonicity, social Plasticity, object-related Plasticity, social Tempo, object-related Tempo, social Emotionality, object-related Emotionality, social	105 items Yes/No format
Thurstone Temperament Schedule (TTS) Thurstone, 1953	Active Vigorous Impulsive Dominant Emotionally stable Sociable Reflective	140 items 3-point scale
Trait Arousability Scale (TAS) Mehrabian, 1977a, 1977b	Stimulus screening– arousability	40 items 9-point scale

rotated the orthogonal factor matrix to oblique simple structures. This procedure resulted in a solution proposing 7 factors—active, vigorous, impulsive, dominant, stable, sociable, and reflective—from which the TTS scales were composed.

The theoretical background of the Eysenck Personality Questionnaire–Revised (EPQ-R; S. B. G. Eysenck, Eysenck, & Barrett, 1985) was discussed in Chapter 2. The theories underlying the Formal Characteristics of Behavior—Temperament Inventory (FCB-TI; Strelau & Zawadzki, 1993, 1995), the Pleasure–Arousal–Dominance Scales (PAD); Mehrabian, 1995a), and the Structure of Temperament Questionnaire (STQ; Rusalov, 1989c) have been presented in Chapter 3. The Pavlovian Temperament Survey (PTS; Strelau & Angleitner, 1994; Strelau, Angleitner, Bantelmann, & Ruch, 1990; see also Newberry *et al.,* 1997), which is a modified version of the Strelau Temperament Inventory (STI; Strelau, 1983) has its background in Pavlov's typology (see Chapter 2). The PTS is based on the assumption that the CNS properties—strength of excitation, strength of inhibition, and mobility of nervous processes—which also constitute the scales of this inventory, are explanatory concepts. The PTS measures the behavioral expressions of these constructs extricated from Pavlov's conceptual nervous system theory (Windholz, 1987).

There are at least two common denominators of the EPQ-R, FCB-TI, STQ, and PTS inventories. First, all of them refer to theories in which the construct of arousal, although differently understood, plays an essential role. This has been a good reason for studying the convergence across scales comprised by these questionnaires (e.g., Ruch, Angleitner, & Strelau, 1991; Strelau & Zawadzki, 1995). Second, these inventories, including also the PAD, are intended to grasp the whole temperament structure, although the solution regarding the structure differs across inventories, due to the particular temperament theory guiding the construction of a given questionnaire.

On the list of temperament inventories for adolescents and adults (Table 6.2), there are quite a number aimed at assessing a single temperament trait, sometimes composed of subtraits, or first-order factors. The Affect Intensity Measure (AIM; Larsen & Diener, 1987), Arousal Predisposition Scale (APS; Coren, 1988, 1990), Reactivity Scale (RS; Kohn, 1985), Reducer–Augmenter Scale (RAS; Barnes, 1985), and the Trait Arousability Scale (TAS; Mehrabian, 1977a, 1977b) are examples of questionnaires that focus on assessing single traits, not composed of subtraits. All of them refer to the energetic characteristic of behavior mainly expressed in emotional reactions, and in all of them, referring to their theoretical backgrounds, the construct of arousal (again differently understood) plays a crucial role.

In contrast, such instruments as the Barratt Impulsiveness Scale (BIS-10; Barratt, 1985), the I7 Impulsiveness questionnaire (I7; S. B. G. Eysenck, Pearson, *et al.,* 1985), and the Sensation Seeking Scale (SSS–form IV & V; Zuckerman, 1979, 1994) belong to the category of inventories that measure traits composed of subtraits. Among these questionnaires Zuckerman's Sensation Seeking Scales, the theory of which has been presented in Chapter 3, has won greatest popularity. The I7 questionnaire was developed as a consequence of the PEN theory. Since impulsivity scored high on all three Eysenckian factors—PEN, S. B. G. Eysenck, Pearson, and colleagues (1985) developed a scale that allows for measurement of different aspects of impulsivity. Barratt's Impulsiveness Scale, which measures impulsiveness expressed in different kinds of behavior, including cognitive activity, is based on an eclectic approach that combines the construct of arousal and Eysenck's PEN theory with information-processing conceptualizations.

Assessment of Temperament Based on Self- and Peer Rating

Temperament questionnaires for adults are based on self-rating, which is one of the features discriminating them from temperament inventories for children. Through retrospection the subject refers to his or her own experience stored in memory, and reports on the frequency, preference, and intensity of given behaviors and reactions regarded as expressions of temperament characteristics. The subject's answers in the format of Yes/No, True/False, Likert rating scales, or choices of alternative statements, are the basis for assessing temperament by means of questionnaires, whether applied to children or to adults.

One of the methods for validating temperament inventories in adult populations is the comparison of self-rating with peer rating; in the latter, the same questionnaire items are reformulated in the third person singular (Angleitner & Wiggins, 1986). This procedure is based on the assumption that a peer, who is a friend, partner, or family member, is well acquainted with the subject, and has had opportunities to observe the subject's behavior in different situations over time.

Hofstee (1991, 1994), discussing issues on personality assessment, including temperament, has argued for the priority of peer rating. His main argument is that in self-judgments there is only one "me," thus judgment errors cannot be averaged out. By the peer-rating procedure the number of independent judges may be increased. As known from the Spearman–Brown formula, the reliability of averaged judgment is a function of the number of judges: the more of them the higher the reliability. This is in accordance with the principle of aggregation (Rushton, Brainerd, & Pressley, 1983).

In spite of the advantages for reliability and validity of estimations derived from supplementing self-rating by peer-rating data, not many studies have been conducted in which temperament inventories were administered in both self- and peer-rating forms. Most of the data referring to self- and peer-rating inventory comparisons have been collected by researchers interested in the Big Five issue (e.g., McCrae & Costa, 1985c, 1987; Ostendorf & Angleitner, 1992).

As concerns questionnaires, the richest evidence of self- and peer-rating comparisons in temperament characteristics has been collected by Angleitner, Strelau, and their coworkers (Angleitner *et al.,* 1995; Strelau, Oniszczenko, Zawadzki, Bodunov, & Angleitner, 1995) in the Bielefeld–Warsaw Twin Project (BWTP). The following temperament inventories were applied to German and Polish samples of MZ and DZ twins (adolescents and adults): PTS, FCB-TI, EAS-TS, DOTS-R, and EPQ-R. These inventories are representative of the most popular conceptualizations in the adult temperament area. In light of the issues raised in this chapter, the uniqueness of the BWTP study consists of having measures from the same subjects from five questionnaires, regarding PK reliability scores for both self- and peer-rating, agreement between raters (two peers), and agreement between self-report and peer-report.

In presenting the data I refer to both German (G) and Polish (P) samples of the BWTP (Angleitner *et al.,* 1995; Strelau, Oniszczenko, & Zawadzki, 1994) composed of 14- to 80-year-old subjects in Germany, and 16- to 63-year-old subjects in Poland (females and males) to whom inventories were administered. In the German sample questionnaires were administered in two waves (wave I [N = 2,087]: PTS, FCB-TI; wave II [N = 1,303]: EAS-TS, DOTS-R, EPQ-R). To subjects in the Polish sample (N = 1,092) all questionnaires were given simultaneously. Table 6.3 summarizes the findings.

Internal Consistency. Reliability of temperament scales measured by Cronbach's alphas is high, or at least satisfactory. In the G sample only four scales in self-report data (EAS-TS Activity and Sociability, DOTS-R Rhythmicity-daily habits, and EPQ-R Psychoticism) show Cronbach's alpha <.70. In the Polish study there are 10 scales among the 27 presented in Table 6.3 that show alphas below .70. They refer to EAS-TS (4 scales), DOTS-R (5 scales), and to the EPQ-R Psychoticism scale.

For peer rating the same DOTS-R and EPQ-R scales, and EAS-TS Sociability, did not reach .70 in the G sample. In the P sample, the EAS-TS (2 scales) and DOTS-R (5 scales) reached the lowest alpha coefficients.

Taking into account the mean alpha scores for self- and peer rating, we see that PTS and FCB-TI (in the P sample also EPQ-R in peer-rating form) reached reliabilities .80 or higher. For both samples the lowest internal consistency for self- and peer-rating forms occurred for EAS-TS (G sample: .70 and .71; P sample: .64 and 68). The small number of items (5 per scale) explains the low alpha scores of the EAS-TS.

In general, it is clear that temperament inventories for adolescents and adults, as represented by five questionnaires (PTS, FCB-TI, EAS-TS, DOTS-R, and EPQ-R), which altogether include 27 scales, exhibit satisfactory reliability. This statement holds true for both German and Polish samples and for both forms—self-report (G = .78, P = .74) and peer report (G = .79, P = .77).

Agreement between Raters. The peer sample involved in assessing temperament in the BWTP was double the number of twins. This was due to the fact that each twin was assessed by two peers who differed for each twin. On average the age of peers was comparable to the age of assessed subjects. The majority of raters

TABLE 6.3. Reliability Scores and Rater Agreement on Temperament Scales: Self(S)- and Peer(P)-Rating Data from German (G) and Polish (P) Samples

| Scales | Alpha Cronbach | | | | Agreement between raters[b] | | S–P reports[c] | |
| | S-report | | P-report[a] | | | | | |
	G	P	G	P	G	P	G	P
PTS (N = 2,087, 1,092)[d]								
Strength of excitation	.85	.82	.85	.83	.61	.51	.52	.46
Strength of inhibition	.81	.72	.81	.76	.51	.47	.37	.38
Mobility of NP	.89	.83	.90	.84	.59	.52	.53	.46
Mean	**.85**	**.79**	**.86**	**.81**	**.57**	**.50**	**.48**	**.43**
FCB-TI (N = 2,087, 1,092)								
Briskness	.79	.78	.80	.85	.55	.62	.50	.48
Perseveration	.79	.80	.79	.78	.48	.58	.42	.46
Sensory sensitivity	.79	.73	.84	.80	.42	.47	.40	.40
Emotional reactivity	.85	.85	.85	.83	.66	.63	.54	.56
Endurance	.84	.86	.86	.87	.53	.58	.46	.53
Activity	.75	.84	.77	.86	.66	.71	.57	.65
Mean	**.80**	**.81**	**.82**	**.83**	**.56**	**.60**	**.49**	**.51**
EAS-TS (N = 1,303, 1,092)								
Distress	.74	.77	.72	.76	.54	.54	.46	.47
Fearfulness	.73	.68	.72	.67	.57	.59	.39	.54
Anger	.72	.62	.74	.70	.60	.50	.47	.46
Activity	.64	.66	.71	.70	.58	.59	.53	.52
Sociability	.66	.48	.67	.56	.61	.53	.60	.46
Mean	**.70**	**.64**	**.71**	**.68**	**.58**	**.55**	**.49**	**.49**
DOTS-R (N = 1,303, 1,092)								
Activity level-general	.70	.71	.71	.77	.54	.50	.41	.47
Activity level-sleep	.82	.83	.76	.77	.27	.45	.29	.44
Approach–withdrawal	.79	.72	.81	.76	.55	.53	.48	.49
Flexibility–rigidity	.72	.64	.72	.61	.38	.44	.36	.38
Mood	.90	.81	.87	.82	.52	.56	.46	.54
Rhythmicity-sleep	.78	.66	.75	.65	.54	.47	.52	.43
Rhythmicity-eating	.82	.78	.83	.80	.39	.35	.34	.32
Rhythmicity-daily hab.	.69	.64	.61	.60	.44	.40	.45	.35
Distractibility	.82	.48	.82	.55	.38	.31	.32	.23
Persistence	.76	.49	.75	.57	.46	.44	.41	.27
Mean	**.79**	**.68**	**.77**	**.69**	**.45**	**.45**	**.41**	**.39**
EPQ-R (N = 1,303, 1,092)								
Psychoticism	.59	.64	.67	.79	.59	.53	.52	.50
Extraversion	.84	.84	.86	.86	.72	.69	.69	.66
Neuroticism	.79	.88	.75	.87	.59	.66	.48	.57
Lie scale	.70	.80	.76	.84	.49	.48	.37	.46
Mean	**.74**	**.79**	**.77**	**.84**	**.60**	**.59**	**.53**	**.55**
Mean for 5 inventories	.78	.74	.79	.77	.55	.54	.48	.47

Note. [a]For peer report the number of subjects is double because each twin was rated by two peers.
[b]Intraclass-correlations (ICC 1.2 including Spearman–Brown correction for 2 raters) for rater agreement (rater 1 and rater 2 per target).
[c]Correlations between self-report and averaged peer report; in the German sample the number of subjects for EAS-TS, DOTS-R, and EPQ-R was $N = 1,156$.
[d]The number of subjects in the German sample is given first, in the Polish sample next.

were good friends having frequent contacts with the subjects. Occasionally, when friends were not available or were unwilling to take part in the project, relatives served as raters.

Agreement between raters was based on intraclass correlation, corrected for attenuation by means of the Spearman–Brown formula. As can be seen from Table 6.3, the only interrater agreement below .40 was obtained in both German and Polish samples for the DOTS-R scales: in both samples for Rhythmicity-eating and Distractibility, and also in the G sample for Activity level-general and Flexibility–rigidity. In contrast, the Extraversion scale and the FCB-TI Activity scale showed the highest interrater agreement (G = .72, P = .69, and G = .66, P = .71, respectively).

In general, interrater agreement was very consistent across inventories, and varied from .45 (DOTS-R in both samples) to .60 (EPQ-R in the G sample, and FCB-TI in the P sample). On average, interrater agreement for the five inventories was .55 for the German sample, and .54 for the Polish one. This result, showing high consistency across samples, is a value somewhat higher than that based on inventory studies in infants and children.

Agreement between Self-Report and Peer Report. As an indicator of agreement between self-report and peer report, their correlation coefficient (with averaged peer reports) was taken into account. The DOTS-R scales showed the lowest agreement between self- and peer reports. The coefficients of correlation for Flexibility–rigidity, Rhythmicity-eating, and Distractibility were below .40 for both samples. In addition, the correlation for four other DOTS-R scales in both samples was <.40. For both samples a similar result was obtained for the Strength of inhibition scale. In contrast, the highest agreement between self- and peer report was obtained in both samples for Extraversion (G = .69, P = .66), and in addition for the Endurance (P = .65) and Sociability (G = 60) scales.

Overall, the data on agreement between self- and peer rating are very consistent across the samples. The agreement is the highest for the EPQ-R scales (G = .53, P = .55) and the lowest for the DOTS-R scales (G = .41, P = .39). Taking into account the mean score calculated from means for all five inventories, agreement between self-report and peer report is at best moderate (G =.48, P = .47). Data from the BWTP suggest that self-report–peer-report agreement (not corrected for attenuation) is comparable with agreement between peers.

Strategies for Constructing Temperament Inventories, and Traits Measured by These Instruments

The construction of temperament inventories, which belong to the family of personality questionnaires broadly understood, is guided by rules typical for measuring phenomena to which the status of trait is ascribed (Amelang & Borkenau,

1986; Fiske, 1986), on condition that the trait does not belong to the domain of intelligence (H. J. Eysenck & M. W. Eysenck, 1985; H. J. Eysenck & S. B. G. Eysenck, 1975; Kagan, 1994; Strelau, 1983). Specific strategies have been developed for constructing instruments aimed at assessing intellectual capacities.

Construction Strategies on Which Temperament Inventories Are Based

This section does not deal with the question as to how to construct a personality inventory, an issue broadly discussed in the literature (e.g., Angleitner & Wiggins, 1986; Brzeziński, 1996; Burisch, 1984; Edwards, 1970; Fiske, 1971; Jackson & Paunonen, 1985; Reynolds & Willson, 1985; Wiggins, 1973). Here we ask, What are the strategies on the basis of which temperament inventories are constructed?

Windle (1988), discussing the psychometric strategies of recently developed temperament inventories, mentioned the following six strategies: clinical research measures (the NYLS and followers approach), personality theory measures (Buss and Plomin's strategy), neo-Pavlovian measures (Strelau's attempt), the psychobiological approach (Rothbart and Derryberry), and the developmental-contextual approach represented by Lerner and Windle. This classification took as its starting point the particular theory represented by the questionnaire constructor. However, from a psychometric perspective, inventories in each of these theories can be constructed differently. Moreover, the neo-Pavlovian approach, which is also psychobiologically oriented, is focused on adults, whereas Windle's classification of strategies refers to diagnostic instruments with roots in research on infants and children. Most questionnaires that have developed in studies on adults have not been affected by Windle's strategic categories.

In a methodological perspective on temperament inventories for assessment of children and adults, reference can be made to three basic strategies used in constructing personality inventories: deductive strategy, inductive strategy, and external strategy (Burisch, 1984, 1986). These strategies may be characterized as follows:

a. *Deductive strategy*—a theoretical concept (construct) underlying a scale is selected first, and then items are chosen, taking into account the explicit or implicit understanding of the construct.

b. *Inductive strategy*—items are written or chosen first, and on the basis of clusters of correlating items a scale is constructed, followed by a proposed parallel personality (temperament) concept.

c. *External strategy*—a concept, not necessarily theoretically grounded, and mainly stemming from psychological practice (e.g., clinical or educational), is initially chosen; items correlating with the external criterion (e.g., neurotics, aggressive individuals) are grouped into a scale.

In light of these three strategies, it should be noted that most temperament inventories, whether for children or adults, were constructed using the deductive strategy (described later), with major modifications in this approach (see Goldsmith & Rieser-Danner, 1990; Rothbart & Goldsmith, 1985; Windle, 1988).

The inductive strategy of which Cattell's (Cattell, Eber, & Tatsuoka, 1970) construction of the Sixteen Personality Factor Questionnaire (16 PF) is most representative, and which has become the dominant strategy in assessing personality in the Big Five approach, did not become popular among temperament researchers. Thurstone's (1953) TTS is probably the only one that took items (from Guilford's temperament inventory) as the starting point for developing scales, without postulating in advance the constructs of which temperament is composed. As we see later, some authors have used a mixed, deductive–inductive strategy for constructing their temperament inventories.

To my knowledge, there is no temperament inventory published in English that has roots in the external strategy of constructing questionnaires. However, reference to external criteria, for example, groups at the extreme poles of proposed temperament dimensions, such as neurotic patients or psychopaths, was a very influential procedure for eliminating or adding items to already constructed scales. Eysenck's MPI, EPI, and EPQ(R) are the best examples here.

The Deductive Strategy. As mentioned earlier, the majority of temperament inventories were constructed using the deductive strategy. Temperament researchers, however, differing in their understanding of what temperament is and what its structure is, took their conceptualizations with respect to these issues as a starting point for constructing questionnaires. In spite of essential distinctions between temperament inventories, this statement can be generalized across all 37 questionnaires (Thurstone's TTS is an exception) presented in Tables 6.1 and 6.2. Differences in construction strategies refer mainly to the psychometric and itemmetric advances. From this point of view several categories of temperament inventories can be distinguished.

(1) *Inventories developed on the basis of interview items, which are similar to a well-structured interview with scales corresponding with the theoretical concepts.* Grouping items into scales was done arbitrarily, without any psychometric procedure to support it. The PTQ and TTQ questionnaires developed by A. Thomas and Chess (1977) fall into this category. Also Strelau's Temperament Inventory (STI), constructed in the 1960s (Strelau, 1972a) from items taken from Strelau's observation chart, can be classified as devoid of basic psychometric characteristics.

(2) *Questionnaires in which theoretical constructs have been operationalized in scales composed of items having content validity, and internal consistency with the scale to which they have been ascribed.* Most representative of this category of inventories are those developed in the Thomas–Chess tradition by Carey, McDevitt, and their coworkers (BSQ, EITQ, MCTQ, RITQ, TTS). The EATQ

constructed by A. Thomas, Mittelman, and colleagues (1982) has this kind of status as well. Other inventories based on different temperament theories may also be classified in this category. Rothbart's (1981; Rothbart *et al.*, 1995) inventories (IBQ and CBQ), Rusalov's (1989c) STQ, the RAS inventory (Barnes, 1985), Kohn's (1985) RS inventory, Barratt's (1985) BIS-10 inventory, the Mehrabian Temperament Scale (Mehrabian, 1978b) and his TAS inventory (Mehrabian, 1977b), and the APS (Coren, 1988) fall into this category.

(3) *Questionnaires that have been constructed by thorough psychometric analysis, including content validity, internal consistency, convergent and divergent validity, and detailed itemmetric characteristics.* The PTS developed by Strelau and Angleitner (1994; Strelau, Angleitner, & Ruch, 1990), the FCB-TI by Strelau and Zawadzki (1993), and Goldsmith's (1996) TBAQ are typical examples of this kind of construction strategy.

(4) *Questionnaires based on theoretical constructs to which, by means of factor analytic procedures, scales have been developed mainly in the attempt to obtain as much orthogonality between scales as possible.* This strategy focuses on scale construction with less attention to itemmetric analysis. Several temperament questionnaires have been constructed by use of this strategy, such as the EAS-TS (Buss & Plomin, 1984), the Junior I6 (S. B. G. Eysenck *et al.*, 1984), EPQ-Junior (H. J. Eysenck & Eysenck, 1975), EPQ-R (S. B. G. Eysenck, Eysenck, & Barrett, 1985), the AIM scale (Larsen & Diener, 1987), the Impulsiveness Questionnaire—I7 (S. B. G. Eysenck, Pearson, *et al.*, 1985), and both forms of Zuckerman's (1979) sensation seeking scales.

The Deductive–Inductive Strategy. The Sensation Seeking Scale developed by Zuckerman exemplifies the deductive–inductive strategy. The deductive strategy was taken as a starting point. His conceptualization, derived from experiments on sensory deprivation, that individuals differ in need for stimulation, led him to develop the sensation seeking scale (deductive strategy). But, taking items as the basis for factor analysis, he arrived at the conclusion that sensation seeking is composed of four subtraits (see Chapter 3 and Table 6.2). Thus, items became the basis for developing more detailed scales and concepts (inductive strategy).[4]

There are a number of questionnaires that resulted from a mixture of the deductive and inductive strategies of scale construction. These are instruments for

---

[4]Zuckerman (Zuckerman, Kuhlman, Thornquist, & Kiers, 1991; Zuckerman, Kuhlman, Teta, Joireman, & Carroccia, 1992), using a "let us see what comes out" procedure, constructed an inventory known as the ZKPQ (probably Zuckeraman–Kuhlman Personality Questionnaire; not presented in Table 6.2). Items taken from 33 different personality–temperament scales became the basis for constructing five scales, and in parallel, five basic personality constructs, which, according to his understanding (Zuckerman, 1991c), have the status of temperament traits. The five scales (and personality constructs) that resulted from a purely inductive strategy are the following: Impulsive Sensation Seeking, Neuroticism-Anxiety, Aggression-Hostility, Activity, and Sociability.

the construction of which items and/or scales of existing inventories were taken as a starting point, and that are composed of scales that are a result of different factor analytic procedures. Most typical of this family of inventories are the ones which have taken the Thomas–Chess theory and the Carey–McDevitt inventories as a point of departure. Questionnaire constructors representing this approach arrived at different scale solutions, mostly (with the exception of DOTS-R) with a reduced number of scales as compared with the nine categories and nine scales proposed by Thomas–Chess and Carey–McDevitt. The following inventories are good examples: ICQ, DOTS-R, SITQ, SATI, TTQ-S, TAB, and CCTI. The final scale solution regarding quality and number of scales was on the whole not guided by prior theory, but resulted from factor analysis of items or scales. Although items were based on a given concept—the Thomas–Chess approach (deductive strategy), the items served as a starting point for developing scales and constructs (inductive strategy). The SSSC inventory developed by Russo and colleagues (1993), based on Zuckerman's (1979) sensation scale, also belongs to this category.

Remarks. The approaches to the construction of temperament inventories illustrate the diversity of solutions in this domain. The answer to the question as to which of these approaches is the best one depends on the criteria applied (N. C. Hubert *et al.,* 1982; Slabach *et al.,* 1991). These criteria are, for example, the purpose for which the inventory is to be used, the context of temperament assessment, the evaluative judgment of factor analysis as a tool for constructing scales, and the degree to which orthogonality is expected. Most important is that users of temperament inventories be conscious of the construction strategy of the assessment instrument that they are applying. However, independently of their specificity, every temperament questionnaire, to be acceptable, must fulfill the basic psychometric criteria regarding reliability, long-term stability, and validity (Bates, 1989; Brzeziński, 1996; Goldsmith & Rieser-Danner, 1990; Slabach *et al.,* 1991; Windle, 1988).

Traits Assessed by Temperament Inventories

The statement that research on temperament concentrates on an enormous number of traits, together with the diversity of inventories for their measurement, should be regarded, at first sight, in terms of positive evaluations. It reflects a concern to embrace the whole richness of human behavior, an aspiration to study temperament from many different perspectives, and a high level of research activity in this field. In the context of efforts to reduce the whole personality, including temperament, to three superdimensions, as proposed by H. J. Eysenck (1970), to the Big Five factors as suggested many years ago by Norman (1963), or even to the sixteen advanced by Cattell (1965), one must ask whether the increasing multiplication of temperament traits is the path to follow.

On the basis of available psychometric tools for diagnosing temperament in adults, Strelau (1991b) prepared a list of more than 80 traits (dimensions, factors). Since the number of paper-and-pencil temperament measures seems far from being exhausted, it may be expected that the quantity of temperament traits under study far exceeds a hundred. Table 6.4 presents a list of 71 traits that can be measured by means of one or more of the 38 inventories listed in Tables 6.1 and 6.2. The variety of traits renders them subject to analysis from many points of view (see Strelau, 1991b), some of which are presented in the following sections.

Traits Measured by Temperament Inventories Refer to Different Levels of Behavior Organization. The traits depicted in Table 6.4 represent differing levels of generality. For example, extraversion or activity seem to be traits that refer to a broad range of behavior characteristics, whereas such temperament characteristics as activity level-sleep, cognitive impulsiveness, or smiling are examples of very narrow concepts.

Some traits, although regarded by some authors as sharing the level in the structure of temperament, should be regarded as subcomponents of more general traits (factors). This is, for example, the case with rhythmicity, which assumes more specific shapes, such as rhythmicity-daily habits, rhythmicity-eating, or rhythmicity-sleep (Windle & Lerner, 1986). The question arises, however, as to whether such specific traits, considered habits (see H. J. Eysenck, 1970), should appear on the temperament list at all. Several studies (see Angleitner & Ostendorf, 1994; Ruch et al., 1991; Strelau & Zawadzki, 1996) have shown that these three specific rhythmicity characteristics constitute one factor: rhythmicity. Viewing the traits listed in Table 6.4 factorially, it should be clear which of the traits are components of first-order factors (e.g., rhythmicity-eating), and which are first-order factors (e.g., rhythmicity). The most reasonable way to compare traits measured by temperament inventories is to compare those on the same structural level.

Temperamental Traits Are Not so Diverse as the Names Suggest. Many of the traits (and scales by which they are measured) bearing different labels refer to similar aspects of behavior, which suggests that factor analytic studies that include these traits should reduce their number. One example includes the following dimensions: activity, approach, arousability, ergonicity, extraversion, sensation seeking, impulsivity, intensity, reactivity, reducing–augmenting, sociability, and strength of the nervous system. Evidence for links between some of the aforementioned traits already exists. For example, we now know a good deal about the relationships among extraversion, sensation seeking, reducing–augmenting, strength of the NS, and impulsivity (see Angleitner & Ostendorf, 1994; Kohn, Cowles, & Lafreniere, 1987; Ruch et al., 1991; Strelau & Zawadzki, 1996, 1997; Windle 1989b; Zuckerman, Kuhlman, Thornquist, & Kiers, 1991). Factor analysis shows unambiguously that these traits in many cases are not orthogonal to each other. The many links ac-

TABLE 6.4. Temperamental Traits to Be Measured by Means of Inventories

Trait	Inventory	
	Infants and children	Adolescents and adults
Activity (general)	BSQ, CBQ, CCTI, EITQ, EAS-TS, IBQ, MCTQ, PTQ, DOTS-R, RITQ, SATI, TTQ, TAB, TBAQ, TTS	EATQ, EAS-TS, FCB-TI, DOTS-R, TTS
Activity level-sleep	DOTS-R	DOTS-R
Activity-reactivity	SITQ	
Adaptability	BSQ, EITQ, MCTQ, PTQ, RITQ, TTQ, TTQ-S, TAB, TTS,	EATQ
Affect intensity		AIM
Anger	CBQ, TBAQ,	EAS-TS
Approach–withdrawal	BSQ, CBQ, EITQ, MCTQ, PTQ, DOTS-R, RITQ, SITQ, SATI, TTQ, TTS	EATQ, DOTS-R
Arousability		APS, PAD, TAS
Boredom susceptibility		SSS-IV, SSS-V
Briskness		FCB-TI
Changeability	ICQ	
Cognitive impulsiveness		BIS-10
Cooperation-manageability	SITQ	
Discomfort	CBQ	
Disinhibition		SSS-IV, SSS-V
Distractibility	BSQ, EITQ, MCTQ, PTQ, RITQ, TTQ, TAB, TTS	EATQ, DOTS-R
Distress		EAS-TS
Distress to limitations	IBQ	
Dominance		PAD, TTS
Drug and alcohol attitudes	SSSC	
Duration of orienting	IBQ	
Emotional reactivity Emotionality)	CCTI, TAB	FCB-TI, STQ, TTS, EAS-TS
Empathy	I_6	I_7
Endurance		FCB-TI
Ergonicity (object and social related)		STQ
Experience seeking		SSS-IV, SSS-V
Extraversion		EPQ-R, EPQ (Junior and Adult)

(continued)

TABLE 6.4. (*Continued*)

Trait	Inventory	
	Infants and children	Adolescents and adults
Fearfulness (Fear)	CBQ, IBQ,	EAS-TS
Flexibility–rigidity	DOTS-R	DOTS-R
Fussiness	ICQ	
Impulsiveness (Impulsivity)	CBQ, I_6	I_7, TTS
Inhibitory control	CBQ	
Intensity of reaction	BSQ, EITQ, MCTQ, PTQ, RITQ, TTQ	EATQ
Interest/persistence	TBAQ	
Irritability	SITQ	
Mobility of nervous processes		PTS
Mood quality	BSQ, EITQ, MCTQ, PTQ, DOTS-R, RITQ, TTQ, TTS	EATQ, DOTS-R
Motor impulsiveness		BIS-10
Negative reactivity	SATI	
Neuroticism		EPQ-R, EPQ (Junior and Adult)
Nonplanning impulsiveness		BIS-10
Perseveration		FCB-TI
Persistence (and attention span)	BSQ, CBQ, CCTI, EITQ, MCTQ, PTQ, RITQ, TTQ, TAB, TTS	EATQ, DOTS-R
Plasticity (object and social related)		STQ
Pleasure	CBQ, TBAQ	PAD
Psychoticism		EPQ-R, EPQ (Junior and Adult)
Reaction to food	CCTI	
Reactivity	TTQ-S	RS
Reducing–augmenting		RAS, RRAS
Reflective		TTS
Rhythmicity	BSQ, EITQ, MCTQ, PTQ, RITQ, SITQ	EATQ
Rhythmicity-daily habits	DOTS-R	DOTS-R
Rhythmicity-eating	DOTS-S	DOTS-R
Rhythmicity-sleep	DOTS-R	DOTS-R
Sadness	CBQ	
Sensation seeking		SSS-IV, SSS-V
Shyness	CBQ, EAS-TS	
Smiling (and laughter)	CBQ, IBQ	
Sociability	CCTI, EAS-TS, ICQ	EAS-TS, TTS

TABLE 6.4. (*Continued*)

Trait	Inventory	
	Infants and children	Adolescents and adults
Social disinhibition	SSSC	
Social fearfulness	TBAQ	
Soothability	CBQ, CCTI, IBQ, ICQ	
Strength of excitation		PTS
Strength of inhibition	PTS	
Task orientation	DOTS-R, TTQ-S	
Task persistence	SATI	
Tempo (object and social related)		STQ
Threshold level (Sensory-perceptual sensitivity)	BSQ, CBQ, EITQ, MCTQ, PTQ, RITQ, TTQ, TTS	EATQ, FCB-TI
Thrill and adventure seeking	SSSC	SSS-IV, SSS-V
Venturesomeness	I_6	I_7
Vigor		TTS

tually found (see, e.g., Table 1.6 in Chapter 1) are food for thought about the close relationships between the different temperament scales and concepts.

Rothbart and Mauro (1990), after a content analysis of scales derived from six temperament inventories in infant studies, arrived at the conclusion that the following six dimensions, under different labels, can be identified: reaction to novelty, distress proneness, susceptibility to positive affect, activity level, rhythmicity, and attention span/persistence. Their rational analysis exemplifies another approach to integrating research on temperament assessment.

Traits and Scales under the Same Labels May Differ in Content. Some of the traits listed in Table 6.4 are specific for given theories or conceptualizations, for example, strength of the nervous system, ergonicity, duration of orienting, extraversion, or briskness. In these cases we know approximately what the traits signify and how they can be measured. Nevertheless, there are traits which, despite bearing the same label, stem from different theoretical approaches. Activity, anger, emotionality, and impulsivity are good examples here. Referring to these traits without the specific theoretical context in which they occur leads to many misunderstandings. Activity is an example. In scales based on the A. Thomas and Chess (1977) tradition, activity refers to the motor component of the child's reactions and behavior; for Buss and Plomin (1984), activity is composed of speed and tempo; for Thurstone (1951), general activity is a factor composed of activity, cooperativeness, and, to a lesser degree, objectivity and ascendance. In contrast, Strelau (1995a; Strelau & Zawadzki, 1995) defined activity in terms of the tendency to undertake behavior (not limited to the motor components) of high stimulative value. Thus, in using scales with the same label, but from different inventories, we are in fact assessing different phenomena.

It also happens that the same author, when elaborating new versions of his or her inventory, uses the same scale labels, although the scale content essentially has been changed. The construction of the personality (temperament) inventories by Eysenck is the best example. As already mentioned in Chapter 2, the Eysenck Personality Inventory (EPI; H. J. Eysenck & Eysenck, 1964) was composed of three scales: Extraversion, Neuroticism, and the Lie scale. In the EPI the Extraversion scale was constructed from a theoretical concept according to which extraversion has two components: impulsivity and sociability. The next questionnaire, the EPQ (H. J. Eysenck & Eysenck, 1975) consisted of four scales: Psychoticism, Extraversion, Neuroticism, and the Lie scale. This suggests that the Extraversion scale taken from both inventories measures the same phenomenon. This, however, is not the case. Whereas extraversion, as measured by means of the EPI, is composed of impulsivity and sociability, the EPQ and the EPQ-R allow for measurement of extraversion reduced to sociability. As shown in several studies, the construct of arousal, so important in H. J. Eysenck's (1970; H. J. Eysenck & Eysenck, 1985) theory of extraversion, refers mainly to the impulsivity component of extraversion but not to sociability (see Anderson & Revelle, 1994; Revelle, Anderson, & Humphreys, 1987; Zuckerman, 1991c). This means that Eysenck's statements in his theory of extraversion formulated on the basis of inventory data collected during the first two decades of his research are based on an understanding of extraversion assessed by a scale with two subcomponents—impulsivity and sociability. In contrast, findings from the past two decades refer mainly to data based on an understanding of extraversion as a more narrow construct when compared with Eysenck's former conceptualization.

Selected Issues Related to Temperament Assessment

From the review and discussion presented earlier it is clear that every method aimed at assessing temperament has some limits. Observation, even though conducted in natural settings, does not allow for full control of behavior; laboratory measures, while ensuring control over the situation, are not devoid of artificiality; further, both methods grasp only selected samples of behavior relevant to temperament. Interview, albeit enabling face-to-face contact with the respondent, can be used only for small samples. Questionnaires, applicable for assessing temperament in thousands of individuals, are limited to retrospective reports.

To avoid these limitations one of the solutions in assessing temperament is to use more than one method with the same individual, an assessment strategy recommended by several temperament researchers. The multimethod approach, the best way to produce a manifold characterization of a temperament trait, brings to light the discrepancies in temperament assessment of the different methods.

Most constructors of temperament questionnaires share the view that this retrospective procedure makes possible the assessment of temperament understood as a phenomenon that has a biological background as postulated by their theory. In order to test this assumption, research was conducted using psychophysiological and biochemical measures, considered as markers of a given trait, as criteria for construct validity of questionnaire scales. These investigations, although advancing our knowledge on the biological background of temperament, have raised fresh problems. They have shown that there is a considerable discrepancy among biological measures taken as validity criteria of questionnaire scales.

It is no exaggeration to state that at least 90% of temperament research is based on questionnaire assessment procedures. This method for diagnosing temperament is attractive for many reasons, some of which already have been presented. One is the possibility of conducting cross-cultural comparisons without much investment. In many countries researchers have taken advantage of the already constructed inventories and adapted certain of them to their (language and culture) populations. And temperament assessment from a cross-cultural perspective has brought to light new issues as yet undiscussed.

The problems just indicated, though far from exhausting the whole domain of methodological and diagnostic issues in respect to temperament, are the topic of the following sections.

The Manifold Approach to Temperament Assessment

In view of the limits of each assessment instrument, attempts have been made, especially by child-oriented temperament researchers, to make use of a complex of methods. This line of research, advocated by several authors (e.g., Bates, 1986; Garrison, 1991; Goldsmith & Rieser-Danner, 1990; Goldsmith & Rothbart, 1992b; A. Thomas & Chess, 1977), is best represented by Matheny and Kagan.

The Multimethod Approach

In the longitudinal Louisville Twin Study conducted by Matheny (1981, 1984, 1991) and his coworkers (Matheny & Wilson, 1981; Matheny, Wilson, & Thoben, 1987; R. S. Wilson & Matheny, 1983), assessment of infant and toddler temperament was always complex. The previously described structured observations in laboratory settings that consisted of a series of episodes were combined with other methods. Parental ratings from temperament questionnaires (RITQ, TTS), and ratings on the Bayley Infant Behavior Record made during mental testing provided additional information about children's temperament.

Laboratory measures and questionnaire data when compared for the same temperament dimension correlated with each other at best in the range from about .30 to .50, although not all correlations were significant. Matheny and coworkers, who advocated the multimethod approach, considered the discrepancies in temperament assessment as perspectives throwing different light on the nature of child temperament.

In one of their studies R. S. Wilson and Matheny (1983) factor analyzed data separately from laboratory observations and from the TTS measures taken from 84 infant twins. The first factors from both measures (laboratory and questionnaire) represented by such categories as adaptability, approach, attention and persistence, and positive mood, correlated .52 with each other. R. S. Wilson and Matheny (1983) concluded that "the results supported the argument that aggregate, rather than single, measures are more likely to yield a coherent picture of stable individual differences" (p. 181). This statement is in line with Epstein's (1979, 1980) view strongly supporting the power of aggregated data for personality assessment.

Child temperament assessment conducted in Kagan's laboratory was, as a rule, based on the assumption that the nature of temperament, as any other object, can be understood only when studied from different perspectives.

> Each way of gathering information is limited and can inform us about only a part of the phenomenon we wish to understand. That flaw is applicable to the EEG and to positron emission tomography (PET) as it is to questionnaires. Therefore, the more varied the source of evidence, the clearer the vision of the secret that nature is holding in her closed hand. (Kagan, 1994, p. 67)

According to Kagan (1994), questionnaire methods for assessing children's temperament are strongly biased by subjective factors. In his laboratory, structured observation in combination with physiological measures, accompanied by parental interview, was the basic strategy for assessing temperament in infants and children (Kagan, 1994; Kagan & Reznick, 1986; Kagan & Snidman, 1991; Kagan, Reznick, & Gibbons, 1989).

A complete diagnosis of children's temperament, which Kagan restricted to the inhibited or uninhibited categories, consisted of two basic measures: behavioral and physiological characteristics (see Chapter 3). In contrast to most questionnaire-oriented temperament researchers who consider physiological indices as markers of a given trait, Kagan and his coworkers used these measures for diagnosing the inhibited–uninhibited temperament.[5]

Only when the behavioral characteristics, such as shyness, emotional reservation, and timidity in response to unfamiliar events, were consistently paralleled by physiological measures of high reactivity in the limbic system was a child classified with confidence as having an inhibited temperament.

---

[5] As already mentioned, physiological measures, but not in conjunction with behavior characteristics, were also used in the Teplov–Nebylitsyn laboratory for assessing temperament.

One of the problems Kagan and his coworkers were confronted with in using up to eight physiological measures (e.g., heart rate, heart rate variability, pupillary dilation, blood pressure) was the lack of consistency between them. To overcome the discrepancy in physiological characteristics of limbic arousal, an aggregate score was used as an indicator of physiological excitability. The diagnostic issue was solved, but the problem of lack of consistency between the physiological measures remained (see Strelau, 1995d).

Convergence between Methods: Concurrent Validity

In most temperament studies, especially of children, if more than one method is applied for assessing temperament, the main purpose of the multimethod approach is to confirm the validity of a given diagnostic instrument. As previously mentioned, comparisons between raters or respondents using the same method (questionnaire or observation) show that agreement in diagnosing temperament traits rarely extends the correlation beyond .50. This finding suggests that no more agreement can be expected when different methods are applied to distinct kinds of behavior and to divergent situations.

Studies on infants have shown that, in general, correlations between parental reports in the form of inventory data and observer ratings of infant behavior account, on the whole, for less than 15% of the variance (Bates, 1987; Goldsmith & Rieser-Danner, 1990). There may be many reasons for the lack of agreement in temperament assessment between questionnaire data and scores based on observations. These include the following: differences in parent and observer experience with the child, dissimilarity between inventory items and infant behavior under observation, differences in sampled situations across the two measures, global behavior rated by parents and molecular behavior subject to observation, unreliable inventory measures on the one hand and observations of irrelevant behavior for temperament characteristics on the other (see Goldsmith & Rieser-Danner, 1990).

As emphasized by Bates (1987), there are some objective reasons for disagreement between parental report and observer rating, even between reports by father and mother by either interview or inventory. Such reasons consist of ontogenetically developed and individual-specific child–parent interactions determined by genetic and environmental factors.

The numbers of studies comparing questionnaire reports by parents or teachers with home or laboratory observations runs into the scores (see Bates, 1986, 1987; Goldsmith & Rieser-Danner, 1990; Rothbart & Goldsmith, 1985). I limit my review to selected reports that allow for modest optimism regarding agreement between methods of temperament assessment.

In a longitudinal study conducted by Rothbart (1986) on 46 infants at the ages of 3, 6, and 9 months, home observations were compared with IBQ measures taken from mothers. Three home observations, 30–45 min in length, were made at each age by three different coders. Interrater correlations varied from .56 (distress to limitations) to .90 (activity level).

Correlations between the IBQ scales and aggregated observational data varied depending on the scale and age taken into account. Most interesting are the comparisons between the ages of 3 and 9 months. For 3-month-old infants, only four of the eight correlations were significant. They varied from .15 (activity level and positive reactivity) to .44 (fear; .43—overall reactivity). On the average the correlation between observational data and IBQ scales was .27. When the infants were 9 months old, the convergence between the two assessment procedures increased. Except for distress to limitation (.09) the correlations varied from .32 (negative reactivity) to .50 (smiling and laughter) with seven coefficients being statistically significant. The average agreement between the two methods was .39. Hence, it can be concluded that agreement between the two methods increased with the infants' age, which is related to the fact that in younger infants observable temperament characteristics are not so strongly expressed as in older ones. The so-called reactivity effect (see critical remarks in reference to observation) and method-specific features listed earlier contributed to the divergence of the two assessment procedures applied by Rothbart (1986).

As a rule, in studies where questionnaire data were compared with assessment based on observation, the observation was limited to selected behaviors and situations far less complex than the ones to which inventory items refer (e.g., Rothbart, 1986; Rothbart & Derryberry, 1981; Vaughn et al., 1981).

Hagekull, Bohlin, and Lindhagen (1984) conducted a unique study in which questionnaire data were related to observations representing a full range of behaviors and situations covered by inventory items. In three samples of infants varying in number from 18 to 24, and in age from 13 to 48 weeks, the Baby Behavior Questionnaire (BBQ), completed by parents, was related to direct observations. Depending on the sample, observations were conducted by observers, by parents, or by both observers and parents. In sample 1, a trained observer spent approximately 8 hr in the home with the infant; in sample 2, infants were observed simultaneously by observer and parent on two occasions lasting about 4 hr each; in sample 3, parents recorded five times the infant's behavior in situations expected to express four temperament characteristics measured by the BBQ—approach–withdrawal, sensory sensitivity, attentiveness, and manageability. In sample 3, observational records were taken during a period of 1 to 2 months. The observation was structured in all three samples in such a way as to cover all kinds of behavior and situations comprised by the BBQ items. Altogether the observational procedure included 36 items rated on a 5-point scale. These items were common for both the BBQ scales and direct observation.

The results of this study, in which many correlations were obtained, depending on the conduct of the observation, showed that in general similarity between questionnaire and observation items enhances the degree of agreement between assessment based on these two methods. Taking into account scores from samples 2 and 3,[6] agreement between trained observer observation and BBQ was on the average .43 and between parent observation and BBQ, .48. Coefficients of correlation between the four BBQ scales and observational scores in sample 3 (parent observation), when corrected for measurement errors, increased significantly up to an average score of .66. This result suggests that when different methods for temperament assessment are matched so that similar behaviors are recorded, a significant degree of multimethod agreement can be obtained.

For the majority of studies, direct observations served as criterion measures for validating retrospective reports in the form of questionnaire data. Reverse patterns also were applied in which inventory scales served as reference methods for validating observational data. Studies addressed to measuring motor activity illustrate this approach.

Eaton (1983, 1994; Eaton & Dureski, 1986), defining temperament activity as customary energy expenditure through movement, devoted many years to the study of this temperament trait by means of an instrument consisting of mechanical measures of movements, known as an actometer. This is a self-winding watch (motion recorder) that records movements of the individual's limbs to which it is fixed (arms or legs or both). Actometer scores (mostly composite ones) are taken as the index of gross motor activity. The reliability of actometer measures is high (up to .90) and increases as a function of the number of actometers worn by the subject (e.g., one per limb) and time during which gross motor activity is recorded. By means of this instrument motor activity was measured in young infants as well as in school-age children. Validity of actometer activity was assessed by several methods, such as free play (Butcher & Eaton, 1989; Halverson & Waldrop, 1973), home observation (Rothbart, 1986), and teacher judgments (Buss, Block, & Block, 1980), but most frequently by activity scales taken from questionnaires.

Eaton (1983) studied a sample of 27 children (3.5- to 5-year-olds), by measuring their activity with actometers and on the Activity scale from the CCTI. He found that the two methods correlate with each other from .75 to .78, depending on the way actometer measures were calculated. Further, a composite measure of children's activity based on observations taken by seven observers in the classroom correlated from .59 to .69 with actometer scores and .73 with CCTI activity.

Another study conducted by Eaton and Dureski (1986), but on two younger samples (46 and 50 infants ages 12–22 weeks), did not replicate the findings indicated in the 1983 study. For measuring activity, Rothbart's IBQ was applied. The main differences between the two samples consisted in the way parents had to respond to items of the Activity scale. Whereas under standard conditions items referred to the infant's behavior during the previous week (sample 1), responses for sample 2 took into account behavior during the previous 24 hours. Although com-

[6]Results from sample 1, for which skewed distributions for the scale score were obtained, are omitted.

posite actometer scores as well as IBQ data reached satisfactory reliability, the two measures of activity did not correlate with each other. The correlation between actometer scores and the IBQ Activity scale was zero. In view of the fact that items from the IBQ scales are situation-specific, the authors correlated actometer scores separately with five facets of the Activity scale: dressing and bathing, supine and held, sleeping, feeding, and seated. Correlations varied between .24 and −.20 but no one coefficient was statistically significant. In more detail, the separate items from the Activity scale were correlated with the actometer scores. None of the 16 items correlated with actometer activity. This result suggests that the two assessment instruments refer to different kinds of activity, at least when measured at the age of about 3 months. An essential question arises that goes beyond this specific study: Which of the two methods should be regarded as a criterion measure for validating other methods aimed at assessing activity?

The multitude of studies aimed at assessing temperament show that, whatever the method for measuring the same temperament trait, comparisons between different methods show that only rarely does agreement reach a correlation of .50. This finding has far-reaching consequences for assessing temperament. It illustrates that the limits of our diagnosis are determined by the specific features of the method we apply. Such questions as who makes the assessment, who is being assessed, what is the range and kind of behavior being assessed, and under what conditions measures are taken, must be answered before reasonable conclusions can be drawn regarding the individual's temperament characteristics.

Construct Validity of Temperament Inventories Based on Psychophysiological and Psychophysical Measures

Cattell (1965) and H. J. Eysenck (1970) are among the pioneers who used inventories along with psychophysiological and psychophysical measures of personality, including temperament. For Eysenck, these measures were considered to be indices of the biological components of extraversion and neuroticism that have a genetic determination. Cattell regarded these measures as being equivalent to questionnaire data. This idea is expressed in the statement "that the same factor can often be measured equally well by either paper-and-pencil or physiological measures" (Cattell & Warburton, 1967, p. 112). Temperament researchers, for whom the construct of arousal plays an essential role in explaining individual differences in temperament (Strelau, 1994a), have used psychophysiological or psychophysical measures in two ways: (1) as indicators of temperament dimensions, and (2) as validity measures of psychometrically diagnosed temperament traits.

The first approach, already discussed in this chapter, is typical of the Teplov–Nebylitsyn school. It can be found in studies on the reducing–augmenting dimension as represented by Petrie and Buchsbaum, and it is also present in

Kagan's laboratory where integrative attempts have been made to assess children's temperament in terms of the inhibited and uninhibited categories.

When psychophysiological or psychophysical measures correspond with expectations predicted from the theory underlying the trait under examination, they are taken as an argument in favor of the construct validity of the questionnaire scale aimed at measuring this trait. Among the indicators of arousal and arousability to which many temperament constructs refer, the following have been the major ones used as measures demonstrating construct validity: spontaneous electroencephalographic (EEG) activity (e.g., Bartussek, 1984; Gale, 1983), amplitude of evoked potentials (EP) (e.g., Zuckerman, 1984c), reaction time (RT), and intensity of motor reactions (e.g., Kohn, 1987), sensitivity thresholds (e.g., Stelmack & Campbell, 1974), and speed of conditioning (e.g., H. J. Eysenck & Levey, 1972).

In Chapter 4 a detailed discussion regarding the biological markers of temperament characteristics was presented. In many studies in which psychophysiological and psychophysical measures were taken to prove construct validity of temperament inventories, researchers were confronted with a lack of agreement between inventory scores and the biological marker or markers of a given trait, as well as between the biological indices themselves when more than one marker was used. I presented a broad discussion of these issues a few years ago (Strelau, 1991a).

Selected Studies Demonstrating Lack of Agreement between Inventory Assessment and Biological Markers of Temperament Characteristics

The majority of studies in which psychophysiological and psychophysical measures were taken in order to demonstrate construct validity of inventories refer to such arousal-oriented temperament dimensions as extraversion, neuroticism, sensation seeking, and strength of the nervous system. Some findings showing the relationships between psychometrically measured temperament characteristics and their physiological markers, including data demonstrating inconsistencies in these relationships, were presented in Chapter 4.

Extraversion. As known from H. J. Eysenck's (1967, 1970) theory, conditioning should be more efficient in introverts when stimuli of low intensity are used, whereas in extraverts the efficiency of conditioning is higher when more intense stimuli are applied. Speed of conditioning is used as one of the main measures of construct validity of the extraversion scale. In many studies the relationship between speed of conditioning and extraversion–introversion, as hypothesized by Eysenck, has not been proved, this being an argument against construct validity of the psychometric measures of extraversion. In response to these data, H. J. Eysenck and Levey (1972), referring to their own study, offered a "prescription" of the precise conditions which should be fulfilled for eyelid conditioning to prove the construct validity of the extraversion scale. Introverts favor a 67% reinforcement schedule, a 400-ms CS–UCS interval, and a UCS strength of 3 lb/in^2. In contrast, extraverts prefer a 100% reinforcement schedule, 800-ms CS–UCS intervals, and a UCS strength of 6 lb/in^2. Not much imagination is needed to realize that, among just these three variables when manipulated (UCS intensity, CS–UCS interval, and reinforcement schedule), hundreds, if not thousands, of possibilities exist. The question then arises as to which of the theoretically possible conditions can be accepted as fulfilling Eysenck's criteria for good measures of construct validity. It is impossible to answer this question on empirical grounds.

Amelang and Ullwer (1991) conducted a laboratory study on 181 adult subjects in which five different markers of extraversion were compared with inventory data—EPI and EPQ. On the basis of EPI data, the two components of extraversion—impulsivity and sociability—were separated. Measures taken in laboratory settings included psychophysiological and psychophysical tests recognized by Eysenck and his coworkers as valid markers of extraversion; for example, salivation test, pain threshold and pain tolerance, flicker fusion, eyelid conditioning, and tapping under different conditions.

The results of Amelang and Ullwer's study showed that, among the 200 correlation coefficients between psychometric data and laboratory indices, only 19 correlations reached statistical significance and all coefficients for females were contrary to expectations. Only one correlation occurred for flicker fusion and no correlations with eyelid conditioning were recorded. As the authors concluded: "the psychophysiological and the experimental variables do not correlate in any significant degree with the various questionnaire-based indices of extraversion" (Amelang & Ullwer, 1991, p. 311), although reliability and consistency across the varied conditions were acceptable.

A more optimistic picture regarding the relationship between extraversion and its physiological markers emerges from findings presented by Stelmack (1990). These derive from his own studies as well as from studies conducted by others. However, the extensive data recorded in research on extraversion show that electrodermal as well as EEG indicators of the base level of arousal do not provide evidence for differences between introverts and extraverts as assessed by the Eysenckian inventories.

Discrepancies in EEG indices related to extraversion already have been discussed in Chapter 4 (see also Bartussek, 1984). During the past decade or so a series of studies have been conducted in which brainstem auditory evoked responses (BAER), taken as a measure of arousal in the ARAS structures, were related to extraversion–introversion (Bullock & Gilliland, 1993; K. B. Campbell, Baribeau-Braun, & Braun, 1981; Stelmack & Wilson, 1982). The results showed lack of consistency between ARAS markers of extraversion as psychometrically assessed. Different intensities of stimuli, different BAER waves (I–VI), and different wave latencies have been regarded as characteristic for extraverts and introverts.

Neuroticism. The most extensive studies comparing psychophysiological measures of neuroticism in different states and situations with psychometrically diagnosed neuroticism have been conducted by Fahrenberg (1977, 1987, 1992) and his coworkers. They were presented in Chapter 4 (see "A Multivariate Approach").

Fahrenberg, reviewing the extensive data collected in his laboratory during a period of more than a decade, arrived at the conclusion that research on physiological correlates of neuroticism has come to a standstill. Objectively measured physiological parameters in large-scale, methodologically well-controlled and replicated investigations have not substantiated the hypothesis that physiological measures, indicating level of arousal in the visceral brain, can be regarded as markers of psychometrically measured neuroticism (Fahrenberg, 1987, p. 117). There is as yet no unequivocal answer to the question which of the psychophysiological scores, and under what conditions, can be accepted as validity measures of psychometrically diagnosed neuroticism (Fahrenberg, 1992).

Sensation Seeking. Zuckerman, Simons, and Como (1988, p. 363), reviewing the studies in which the SSS was used together with psychophysiological markers of the sensation seeking trait, came to the conclusion that until that time the psychophysiology of sensation seeking had been explored in piecemeal fashion, with each study typically examining one system (cortical, electrodermal, or cardiovascular), and with one type of stimulus (visual or auditory).

Taking this statement as a starting point, Zuckerman and colleagues (1988) conducted an experiment in which different psychophysiological markers of sensation seeking were used in different laboratory settings. In two groups of subjects, differing in one of the sensation seeking traits (30 high-disinhibitors and 24 low-disinhibitors), three pychophysiological measures were recorded: EP amplitude with short (2-s) and long (17-s) interstimulus intervals (ISI), HR, and EDA. For all three psychophysiological measures, stimuli of different intensities were exposed in two modalities (visual and auditory). Whereas the EP amplitude was regarded as an indicator of augmenting–reducing, HR and EDA were used as measures of the orienting response (OR). As often stated by Zuckerman (see, e.g., 1984c), both augmenting–reducing and OR are among the best measures of the construct validity of the Sensation Seeking Scale.

The results obtained in this study are probably more pessimistic than the authors (Zuckerman *et al.,* 1988) expected them to be. The following findings were reported. First, OR as measured by EDA does not differentiate between the two sensation seeking groups (high- vs. low-disinhibitors), and this holds true for both modalities (visual and auditory). Second, cross-modality correlations of EP amplitude measures of augmenting–reducing show, in general, lack of correlations among the six possible coefficients of correlation (auditory vs. visual and short vs. long ISI), and only one reached statistical significance. Third, among the eight possible correlations for auditory stimuli between HR and EP, only one was statistically significant—in the opposite direction from that expected. Finally, no statistically significant correlation was found between EP slope and HR measure in the visual modality.

There is little doubt that this diversity in psychophysiological versus psychometric comparisons would grow if the three other SSS scales (TAS, ES, and BS) were taken into account. A further increase in diversity may be expected if more experimental variables are included, for example, kinesthetic stimulation, some other ISIs, or different states of the subjects (rest vs. active states).

In the context of these data the basic question arises as to which of the psychophysiological markers and which of the specific experimental conditions (e.g., visual or auditory) should be regarded as a satisfactory measure of construct validity of one of the specific SSS scales (Disinhibition). Zuckerman and colleagues' study (1988), was expected to bring us closer to the answers, but has instead increased the doubts regarding the utility of psychophysiological scores as measures of construct validity of psychometrically measured traits.

An analysis of studies in which Zuckerman (1990) compared sensation seeking with augmenting and reducing of the evoked potential, considered as the physiological marker of this trait, appears to lead to more optimistic conclusions, but is still far from satisfactory. For example, among the 16 studies reviewed by the author, there are only 2 in which visual and auditory stimuli were used for measuring augmenting–reducing on the basis of averaged evoked potential (AEP) slopes. When results for both modalities were compared with SSS measures, opposite findings occurred. Carrillo-de-la-Pena (1992), reviewing studies in which psychometrically measured sensation seeking was related to EP amplitudes, suggested that stimulus intensities and ISI contribute essentially to the inconsistencies in findings regarding the EP augmenting–reducing and sensation seeking relationship. However, no prescription was given by the author in terms of intensities of stimuli and ISI regarded as optimal for considering EP amplitudes as markers of sensation seeking.

Strength of Excitation. Many studies by Russian differential psychophysiologists (e.g., Nebylitsyn, 1972c; Rusalov, 1977) and in Strelau's (1972b, 1983, 1991a) laboratory, have documented that discrepancies exist in assessing the CNS properties depending on modality of stimuli, type of reinforcement, and kind of physiological measures applied in laboratory settings. Inconsistency is also evident when psychophysiological and psychophysical measures are contrasted with questionnaire scores of CNS properties. This is illustrated by a study conducted by Kohn (1987).

With a view to comparing different constructs that refer to the concept of arousability, Kohn used several psychometric and experimental measures. The psychometric measures included the following traits: extraversion (EPI), reactivity (Kohn's Reactivity Scale), augmenting–reducing (Vando's RAS), and strength of excitation (STI). The laboratory score of strength of excitation included the slope of the reaction time curve—auditory and visual versions. As mentioned in Chapter 2, this was one of the robust methods used in Teplov's laboratory for assessing strength of excitation.

The results obtained from 53 college students showed statistically significant correlations among all the psychometric scores, the sign of the correlations being in all cases in the theoretically predicted direction (Kohn, 1987; Strelau, 1983). From Kohn's (1987) data it emerged that strength of excitation as measured by STI correlated negatively with reactivity (–.45), and positively with extraversion (.30) and augmenting–reducing (.29). However, no correlation occurred between strength of excitation scored by the slope of RT curve and psychometrically assessed reactivity, extraversion, and augmenting–reducing. Likewise, there was no correlation between the two laboratory measures of strength of excitation (visual vs. auditory stimuli), or between the two modality versions of the slope of RT curve and strength of excitation as measured by the STI.

Two studies were conducted by De Pascalis (1993, 1994) in which the Strength of Excitation scale (from STI and PTS) was related to energetic and temporal characteristics of visual and auditory event-related potentials (ERP) under stress and no-stress conditions. The results of these studies do not allow for unequivocal conclusions regarding these electrophysiological measures as markers of strength of excitation, although theoretically such a relationship, especially under stress conditions, is reasonable.

Remarks. The data reported in the literature and selectively presented in the previous sections suggest that psychophysiological–physical measures are candidates for estimating construct validity of temperament inventories, but only in limited circumstances, some of which are listed here.

a. When laboratory settings are used to measure phasic but not base (tonic) level of arousal, in other words, only when physiological responses or psychophysical reactions to given stimuli are recorded;

b. when cross-modality agreement occurs among compared measures, that is, when comparison of visual, auditory, and other modalities of stimuli lead to consistent results;

c. when reciprocal studies with the same experimental settings (e.g., kind of stimuli, quality of reaction, temporal parameters, technical standards) replicate the findings on the relationship between psychometric and psychophysiological–physical measures;

d. when intensity of exposed stimuli and the stimulative value of experimental settings are not below or beyond the "average level," although this level, because it is estimated, is difficult to define.

Assuming these requirements are fulfilled (see also Gale & Edwards, 1983b), results reflecting the relationship between psychophysiological–psychophysical measures and questionnaire data still do not allow for generalization beyond the stimuli, reactions, and kind of measurement techniques used in laboratory settings.

Categorical Differences between Questionnaire and Psychophysiological–Physical Measures as Sources of Discrepancy in Validity Studies

The lack of concordance between psychometric measures of temperament and psychophysiological–physical scores arises not only from methodological and theoretical deficiencies of the measures to be compared but primarily from the categorical differences between them. For an understanding of the failure of concordance, the fundamental differences between psychometric and psychophysiological–physical measures used in this type of research require elucidation, taking into account several perspectives (see Strelau, 1991a), some of which are presented here.

1. Temperament questionnaires refer to multiple-occasion measures, whereas psychophysiological–physical scores are mostly based on one-occasion measures (Olweus, 1980a).
2. Generalizability constitutes one of the main features of temperament inventories, whereas psychophysical as well as psychophysiological measures are very limited in this respect.
3. Even a single inventory item refers to cross-temporal, and, to some degree, to cross-situational behavior, whereas psychophysiological–physical measures, also when aggregated, are mostly time- and situation-specific.
4. Temperament inventories are addressed to goal-directed, molar, or macro behavior; psychophysiological and psychophysical methods tend to measure reactive responses, micro behavior, and molecular reactions.
5. Temperament questionnaires, due to their aggregation features, are aimed at measuring traits, whereas psychophysiological and psychophysical scores are expressions of states, processes, or specific responses (O'Connor, 1983).
6. In questionnaire research the behavior to be assessed or self-assessed refers to natural settings and real-life situations. This is not the case with psychophysiological and psychophysical measures. They are recorded under artificial conditions, for the most part unfamiliar to the subject (Olweus, 1980a; West, 1986).
7. Psychometrically measured behavior is guided by social rules and by demands and expectancies of the social environment; in psychophysiological (psychophysical) experiments the reactions or behaviors under study are mainly regulated by the experimenter's instruction.

In the comparisons mentioned in the preceding list the extreme characteristics tend to be exposed. In fact, we have to do with a dominating tendency. For example, in stating that the behavior measured by psychometric tools is guided by social rules, I do not mean that the social factor plays no role in laboratory settings, but that, in behavior as measured by inventories, the social environment plays the decisive role.

As stressed by Jackson and Paunonen (1985), there are two reasons why construct validity fails: (a) The instrument does not measure the construct, or (b) the theory on which the measure was constructed is inadequate. It appears that, when the construct validity of questionnaires is tested by psychophysiological or psychophysical measures, there is a third reason: Measures are from two qualitatively different levels of behavior organization, although both psychophysiological (psychophysical) reactions and macro behavior measured by the inventories refer to the same phenomenon—temperament, characterized from different perspectives.

Temperament Assessment from a Cross-Cultural Perspective

In most cross-cultural studies on temperament the meaning of culture has rarely been described (see Super & Harkness, 1986). There is no agreement among scientists as to what culture is. Soudijn, Hutschemaekers, and van de Vijver (1990) analyzed 128 definitions with the objective of elaborating a taxonomy of culture definitions. For the purpose of this chapter I refer to one of the descriptive definitions, regarded as a classic one, by which culture is "that complex whole which includes knowledge, belief, art, law, morals, custom, and any other capabilities and habits acquired by man as a member of society" (Kroeber & Kluckhohn, 1963, p. 81).

In cross-cultural studies viewed from the perspective of temperament assessment two questions seem to be crucial: (1) What inclines researchers on temperament to take a cross-cultural approach in their studies (Strelau & Angleitner, 1994); and (2) how to construct and, as a consequence, also adapt to other cultures assessment instruments that take into account criteria of conceptual, metrical, and scalar equivalence. The latter issue has been broadly discussed in several publications (see Brislin, 1976; Brzeziński, 1996; Drwal, 1990; Poortinga, 1989), hence I concentrate on the state of affairs concerning temperament questionnaires already in use in cross-cultural studies.

Arguments for Studying Temperament in a Cross-Cultural Context

The view that temperament refers to primary (fundamental) personality traits present in early childhood, which have a biological background and may also be observed in animals (see Chapter 1), is a strong argument for the assumption that temperament traits belong among those psychological characteristics that are common (universal) for human beings regardless of their specific cultural environment. Further, if we consider that temperament characteristics refer mainly to the *how* of behavior and to the formal aspects rather than to the content of human activity, then again the assumption that the same temperament characteristics may be expressed in different, culturally specific, behaviors speaks for the universality of temperament traits. It is highly probable that universality refers not only to particular traits but also to their configuration, that is, to the structure of temperament as postulated and supported by the enormously rich empirical evidence in the domain of Eysenck's three superfactors of personality (P. Barrett & Eysenck, 1984; H. J. Eysenck, 1970; H. J. Eysenck & Eysenck, 1985).

Whereas the search for universality in the temperament domain represents the etic approach,[7] there are also studies aimed at demonstrating the importance of the specific culture for the development of temperament, thus concentrating on the emic approach. Most temperament researchers accept that temperament traits serve adaptive functions. Depending on interaction with the culture-specific environment, different developmental and behavioral effects can occur. This idea has been broadly elaborated by Super and Harkness (1986) in their concept of the "developmental niche" which "consists of the physical and social setting children are found in" (p. 133). The interaction between individual temperament traits and developmental niche results in different forms of adaptation and different values of temperament dispositions for individual development. Depending on cultural specificity, the same temperament trait may reveal itself in different situations and behaviors, and may have different adaptive values (Strelau & Angleitner, 1994). The concepts of goodness of fit, difficult child, and temperament risk factor (broadly discussed in Chapter 7), are examples.

Temperament inventories, just as assessment instruments in other domains of psychology, are often adapted to a given country or language. The aim is not so much for cross-cultural comparisons but for studying temperament in a culturally different population. Although comparisons between the constructed and the adapted inventories serve mainly validation of the latter, the fact that presumably the same temperament inventories are used in different cultures contributes directly or indirectly to cross-cultural comparisons (Kohnstamm, 1989b). There is also a reverse relationship. Studies on temperament with a cross-cultural perspective are legitimate only if equivalent temperament instruments are used. But in the literal sense identical temperament inventories across cultures do not exist. When supposedly adapting the same questionnaires to different language versions, we

---

[7]There are two basic approaches typical for cross-cultural studies in psychology (Berry, 1969), also present in assessment of temperament across cultures, nations, or ethnic groups: (1) the *emic* approach aimed at describing the specificity of psychological phenomena, behavior, or both, depending on the cultural conditions in which compared individuals or groups live, and (2) the *etic* approach which consists of grasping similarities or identities (universals) of given psychological phenomena or behaviors across different cultures (nations, ethnic groups).

use strategies that differ in degree and range of equivalence, and this also holds true for temperament questionnaires.

Strategies Applied for the Construction (Adaptation) of Temperament Inventories Used in Cross-Cultural Studies

Cross-cultural research in the area of child and adult temperament has gained increasing popularity during the past decade (Kohnstamm, 1989b; Strelau & Angleitner, 1994), especially in assessment based on inventories. Some researchers who construct temperament questionnaires have developed strategies that allow for their adaptation to different countries or language-specific populations (e.g., H. J. Eysenck & Eysenck, 1982; S. B. G. Eysenck, 1983; Strelau & Angleitner, 1994), whereas others have developed inventories to assess temperament primarily in the population for which they were constructed and, only secondarily, these inventories have been adapted to other culture-specific populations. The way questionnaires are constructed influences the process of adaptation. Depending on the criterion of cross-cultural equivalence three strategies briefly discussed in the following paragraphs are probably typical for adapting temperament questionnaires to other cultures. These strategies postulate (1) cross-cultural equivalence of items, (2) cross-cultural equivalence of scales, and (3) culture-specific items and cross-cultural equivalent definitional scale components.

Strategies Based on Cross-Cultural Equivalence of Items. The common denominator of this strategy for adaptation of temperament questionnaires consists of taking the same items as they occur in the original inventory as the basis for adaptation. Translations of items vary from literal, as for most items, to making a travesty of them in trying to adapt them to a culture-specific population (see Drwal, 1990; Hulin, 1987), as for example in the adaptation of the IBQ to assess temperament of Chinese infants (Ahadi *et al.,* 1993), or of Zuckerman's (1979) SSS which overflows with culturally biased items (e.g., Andresen, 1986; Oleszkiewicz, 1982). By means of internal consistency measures (mostly Cronbach's alpha) and discriminant analyses, authors of adapted questionnaires have tried to replicate the original scales. With few exceptions, the number of items in the adapted scales is the same as in the original version, which allows for cross-cultural comparisons. This strategy is the most popular among child-oriented investigators. It is illustrated in the adaptations of W. B. Carey and McDevitt's (1978) RITQ or its former version, Infant Temperament Questionnaire (ITQ), to East African tribes living in Kenya (De Vries & Sameroff, 1984), Taiwanese babies (Hsu, Soong, Stigler, Hong, & Liang, 1981), the French-speaking Canadian population (Maziade, Boudreault, Thivierge, Caperaa, & Cote, 1984), Malay infants (Banks, 1989), and Australian, Chinese, and Greek babies (Prior, Kyrios, & Oberklaid, 1986; Prior, Garino, Sanson, & Oberklaid, 1987). The adaptation of

Bates and colleagues' (1979) ICQ to Dutch infants by Kohnstamm (1989b), Fullard and colleagues' (1984) TTS to Italian toddlers by Axia, Prior, and Carelli (1992), and recently Rothbart's CBQ to Chinese children by Ahadi and colleagues (1993) also illustrates this approach. The psychometric limitation to internal consistency measures and discriminant analysis typical for adapting these infant and child inventories is due to the fact that the scales of the original inventories are for the most part not orthogonal to each other, so factor analysis would not allow for replicating these scales in adapted inventories.

The aim of these studies using the strategy of item equivalence (and as a consequence scale equivalence), was to answer the question whether infants and children from different countries and cultures differ on the temperament dimensions being assessed. Differences served as arguments for the influence of culture on child temperament or on the perception of temperament. In these studies the American samples served as references. Figure 6.1. gives selected results from the largest cross-cultural study (in terms of number of countries compared) conducted on infants by Prior, Kyrios, and Oberklaid (1986). Temperament characteristics from

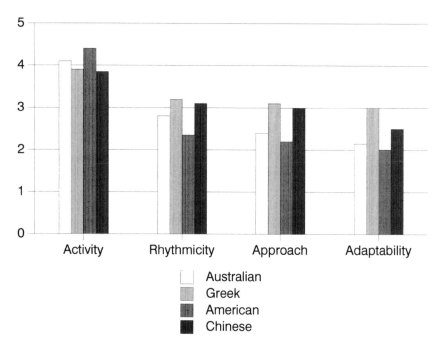

FIGURE 6.1. Selected infant temperament characteristics from four country samples. *Note.* From "Temperament in Australian, Chinese, and Greek Infants: Some Issues and Directions for Future Research," by M. R. Prior, M. Kyrios, and F. Oberklaid, 1986, *Journal of Cross-Cultural Psychology, 17,* p. 462. Copyright 1986 by Sage Publications. Adapted with permission.

four country samples were compared in respect to nine temperament dimensions measured by RITQ (four of them are presented in Figure 6.1). The same number of items in the four country versions allowed the authors to draw conclusions about infant temperament in terms of cross-cultural specificity of given temperament traits as well as configuration of traits (e.g., the pattern of difficult temperament).

In a critical review of cross-cultural studies on infants and children by means of inventories, with reference to the Thomas–Chess tradition and on the basis of item equivalence strategy, Kohnstamm (1989b) drew attention to several weaknesses. First, the samples for comparisons were mostly small and unrepresentative of the population for which the inventories were adapted. Second, the original questionnaires, such as Carey and McDevitt's set of inventories, are not proper instruments for cross-cultural adaptation because of weak psychometric characteristics. Among the temperament inventories for children and adolescents the DOTS-R, constructed for the American population by using statistics such as exploratory and confirmatory factor analysis, and adapted to Japanese culture by Windle, Iwawaki, and Lerner (1987, 1988), serves as an example of satisfactory contemporary psychometric requirements.

The infant and child inventories have been constructed almost exclusively in the United States for the purpose of assessing temperament of American children. As a consequence they are loaded by a country-specific ethnocentrism. Although the probability is high that behavioral and situational expressions of infant's and young children's temperament are more universal than that of adolescents and adults, there are culture-specific child-rearing practices, demands, and situations not embraced by items constructed by Americans (see Persson-Blennow & McNeil, 1979). Difficulties occur especially when adapting inventories that are based on behavior-specific and situation-specific items such as Rothbart's CBQ (Ahadi *et al.*, 1993; Rothbart *et al.*, 1995) or, in the area of adults, Zuckerman's (1979) SSS. Inventories constructed of items that are not behavior- and situation-specific, and that are core items, such as Buss and Plomin's (1984) EAS-TS, are free, or almost free, from the ethnocentric objection.

Strategy Based on Cross-Cultural Equivalence of Scales. Inventory constructions that take the strategy of cross-cultural equivalence of scales as their starting point are based on the assumption that temperament traits are universal. Not only the traits, but also the structure of traits, is assumed to be cross-culturally common. Most representative of this strategy are the cross-cultural studies conducted by H. J. Eysenck and Eysenck (1982; S. B. G. Eysenck, 1983) and their coworkers (P. Barrett & Eysenck, 1984; Hanin, Eysenck, Eysenck, & Barrett, 1991) designed to examine universality of the three superfactors (PEN) by means of EPQ or EPQ-R (Junior and Adults).

The adaptational procedure of EPQ(R) consists of translating items (verbatim translation, making a travesty of items) and, when required, adding new, culture-specific items. Principal component analysis and internal consistency of scales are the main criteria for inclusion of items in a given scale. The adaptation of the EPQ to a given country is regarded as being equivalent to the reference (British) questionnaire when the three postulated scales—Psychoticism, Extraversion, and Neuroticism—emerge, and when the factors are orthogonal, or almost orthogonal, to each other as postulated by Eysenck's PEN theory. Further, the scales must show internal consistency (Cronbach's alpha) usually not less than .70. The number (sometimes also the content) of items that fulfill these criteria, and of which the separate scales are composed, differs across countries. In order to assure cross-country comparisons, not only with respect to the structure of factors but also on the scale level, transformation of scale means is conducted such that each scale is composed of 30 items. The strategy of adapting the EPQ described by the Eysencks in detail (e.g., P. Barrett & Eysenck, 1984; H. J. Eysenck & Eysenck, 1982; S. B. G. Eysenck, 1983) allowed for demonstration of universality of the three temperament factors across dozens of countries covering nearly all continents.

Strategy Based on Selection of Items from a Universal Item Pool Representing Cross-Culturally Equivalent Definitional Scale Components. This strategy applied by Strelau and Angleitner (1994; Strelau, Angleitner, Bantelman, & Ruch, 1990) for the construction of the PTS differs from the previously described procedures in two ways. First, more emphasis was given to the operationalization of a construct and the item generation process. Second, from the very beginning of scale construction attention was paid to the etic and emic aspects in a way allowing for construction of cross-culturally equivalent PTS inventories, which refer, in contrast to the EPQ-R scales, to nonorthogonal constructs. This strategy incorporates basic ideas formulated by Loevinger (1957) as well as some ideas taken from D. T. Campbell and Fiske's (1959) conceptualization of convergent and divergent validation by the multitrait-multimethod matrix.

Constructing the PTS began with operationalization of the theoretical constructs—strength of excitation (SE), strength of inhibition (SI), and mobility of nervous processes (MO), on which the scales were built. These constructs are assumed to be etic, that is, common across cultures.

The operationalization of the constructs involved the generation of their definitional components. Altogether 17 components were generated: seven for the SE scale (i.e., the individual is able to react adequately under strong emotional tension) and five for each of the remaining two scales—SI and MO (for description see Strelau & Angleitner, 1994; Strelau, Angleitner, & Newberry, in press). These components (facets) are also supposed to be cross-culturally comparable (etic). The definitional components of the PTS scales constituted the basis for generating items. Since temperament traits reveal themselves in behaviors that may be culturally specific, a broad list of items was generated. The item pool, consisting of

252 items assessed by judges as being prototypical for the 17 PTS components, is considered the universe of items. The items are common for all language versions and they refer to as many as possible kinds of behavior and situations in which temperament traits can be expressed.

The emic approach in constructing the PTS for a given country or language consisted of selecting from the 252-item pool, by means of elaborated psychometric procedures, those items which for the given culture (language version) are most representative for the etic constructs (i.e., the 17 facets). For each language (culture) version the number and kind of items was, or might have been, different. Scores expressed in average per-item responses allow for comparisons between different language versions of the same scales (Newberry *et al.,* 1997). Due to the fact that the theoretical constructs and their definitional components are etic, cross-cultural comparison between the three scale constructs (SE, SI, and MO) is possible.

The strategy just described was applied in the construction of more than a dozen of PTS language versions, in Europe, Asia, Australia, and in the United States (Newberry *et al.,* 1997; Strelau & Angleitner, 1994; Strelau *et al.,* in press). In a recent study conducted on a South Korean sample, new items were generated for the 17 definitional components in order to verify that the 252-item pool is not eurocentric biased (Strelau, Kang, & Angleitner, 1996). A study conducted on a Korean sample to which both versions of the PTS were administered—one based on the 252-item pool and the other constructed on the basis of items generated by Koreans—resulted in comparable PTS characteristics.

Another inventory, based on the same construction strategy, is Strelau and Zawadzki's (1993, 1995) FCB-TI, for which a 381-item pool is the starting point for constructing cross-culturally equivalent questionnaires. The FCB-TI recently has been adapted to the German, Italian, Russian, and U.S. populations.

7

The Functional Significance of Temperament

The ancient Greek typology of temperament developed as a result of observations that inappropriate activity, and amount and mixture of the four humors that constituted the physiological basis of temperament, led to different kinds of illnesses. Hippocrates and his follower, Galen, were the first to show that temperament plays an important role in human functioning. The significance of temperament as a factor that accelerates or is conducive to psychiatric disorders has been strongly emphasized by constitutionally oriented researchers such as Kretschmer and Sheldon (see Chapter 1), who, however, entirely ignored the contribution of environment to the origin of these disorders.

Pavlov was probably one of the first to show that temperament traits, when in interaction with an adverse environment, result in behavior disorders. His experiments conducted on dogs demonstrated the functional significance of temperament traits, especially strength of the CNS, in the individual's adaptation to environmental demands, such as strong stimulation, deprivation, and radical changes in the surroundings.

As was shown in chapters 2 and 3, research on temperament conducted in the second half of the 20th century followed different paths depending on whether it was focused on infants and children or on adults. To some extent studies examining the role temperament plays in human functioning under different circumstances and in different environments are also age-specific. For example, in children, the functional significance of temperament is mainly expressed in social interactions with parents and other caregivers and in behavior under all types of school demands, from nursery to college level. In adults the role of temperament is evident in professional activity, in the pursuit of leisure-time activity, in social interactions, or in partner relationships.

Independently of age-specific activity and situations, many researchers agree (e.g., Chess & Thomas, 1989; Kagan, 1983; Nebylitsyn, 1972a; Strelau, 1983; A. Thomas & Chess, 1977; Zuckerman, 1991c) that the functional significance of temperament traits comes to the fore when the individual is confronted with difficult situations and extreme demands. From this point of view, as well, specific approaches have developed, depending on whether these situations and demands refer to children or to adults. In research on children, specific concepts, such as "difficult temperament" and "goodness of fit," have been developed, whereas in studies on adults concepts referring to different aspects of stress have gained widest popularity. This distinction, while not exclusive since both approaches are taken in studies of children and adults, constitutes the structural basis for this chapter.

The Contribution of Temperament to Child Behavior and Adjustment in Adverse Situations

The NYLS project on temperament undertaken in the mid-1950s by A. Thomas and Chess (1977; A. Thomas, Chess, & Birch, 1968) has shown that temperament traits and their specific configurations, in interaction with adverse environments, can result in behavior disorders in children. Under the influence of these eminent psychiatrists hundreds of studies have been conducted to examine the functional significance of temperament at different stages of child development, in different situations, and in respect to various activities. The concepts difficult temperament, introduced almost at the beginning of NYLS (A. Thomas, Chess, Birch, Hertzig, & Korn, 1963), and goodness of fit, developed under the influence of subsequent research (A. Thomas & Chess, 1977; Chess & Thomas, 1986, 1991) became landmarks referred to by most studies concerning the functional significance of children's temperament.

The Concept of Difficult Temperament

As already mentioned in Chapter 2, where Thomas and Chess's interactional theory of temperament is described in detail, the concept of difficult temperament emerged as a result of clinical observations. These led to the conclusion that extremes of one or another temperament trait, or a configuration of these traits found in a normal population, are regarded by parents or caregivers as causal factors for the child's inappropriate behavior and maladjustment. They may result in behavior disorders, especially when in interaction with an adverse environment.

The NYLS Approach

According to A. Thomas and Chess (1977; Chess & Thomas, 1984, 1986) a configuration of such temperament traits as (1) biological irregularity, (2) withdrawal responses to new stimuli, (3) slow or nonadaptability to change, (4) negative mood expressions, and (5) high intensity of emotional reactions constitute the most typical pattern of difficult temperament. A difficult temperament score has been developed. The scores for the five categories of temperament are added separately for each individual, resulting in a single number as the quantitative indicator of a difficult temperament. In A. Thomas, Chess, and Korn's (1982) view:

> Difficult temperament, as well as temperament in general, represents an actual attribute of the individual as does motivation or cognition. Parental characteristics and other environmental factors may modify or intensify the child's difficult temperament just as the child's temperament may influence the parent's attitudes and behavior. (p. 3).

The constellation of traits composing the difficult temperament, replicated in factor analytic studies, was present in about 10% of children from the NYLS sample representing the American middle-class population. The temperament inventories developed by Carey and McDevitt (W. B. Carey, 1985a), assessing children's temperament from parents' reports as proposed by Thomas and Chess, allow for a quantitative measure of difficultness understood as a pattern of the temperament characteristics mentioned earlier.

Clinical evaluations, systematic observations, and statistical measures of behavior characteristics and environmental conditions, with special attention to the family environment, were conducted by the eminent New York psychiatrists on 133 subjects from early infancy to adulthood. This work led to the conclusion that difficult temperament encountered at the age of at least 3 years, when in interaction with an inappropriate or adverse environment, can predict adjustment disorders in young adults (Chess & Thomas, 1984, 1986; A. Thomas & Chess, 1984). The variables taken into account as potential predictors of behavior disorders in later developmental stages were not limited to temperament characteristics. Using multiple regression analysis the authors showed that, among many antecedent variables such as adjustment scores at ages 3 and 5, easy versus difficult temperament at 3 years, and parental attitudes, accounted for 34% of the variance in early adult behavior disorders. Similar results were reported by Cameron (1977, 1978), who reanalyzed the NYLS data, taking into account temperament traits and parental characteristics. Only in the 4th year of life did the temperament data significantly predict mild disturbances in behavior.

The Extension of the Concept Difficult Temperament

In other studies in which the Thomas–Chess theory of temperament was taken as a starting point, the pattern of difficult temperament has been replicated, but with the number and quality of temperament characteristics slightly different from the NYLS approach. For example, Maziade and coworkers (Maziade, Cote, Boudreault, Thivierge, & Caperaa, 1984; Maziade, Boutin, Cote, & Thivierge, 1986), on the basis of several studies conducted on thousands of normal children from Quebec City aged 7 to 12 years, obtained a consistent structure of temperament in which the first factor based on principal component analysis was regarded as a pattern typical for the easy–difficult temperament. This factor comprised activity, predictability, adaptability, intensity, mood, and persistence. Children judged by parents as difficult to manage were characterized by high activity, low predictability, low adaptability, high intensity, negative mood, and low persistence. A study conducted by Maziade, Boudreault, Thivierge, Caperaa, and Cote (1984) on more than 700 infants aged from 4 to 8 months resulted in a different pattern of difficult temperament composed of withdrawal, low adaptability, high intensity, and high distractibility. The latter study demonstrates that the pattern of difficult temperament may be age-specific, an issue not considered by Thomas and Chess.

Windle (1991), whose concept of temperament developed within the Thomas–Chess tradition, based the construct of difficult temperament on a risk factor approach. Risk of behavior disorders increases with the number of factors involved. In his view any temperament dimension that has an extreme value constitutes a difficult temperament. Since, according to Windle, the structure of temperament is composed of 10 traits, the number of traits that constitute the difficult temperament may vary from 1 to 10. The more traits are of extreme value, the more difficult is the temperament.

As will be shown in this chapter other authors also used the category of difficult temperament with configuration of traits differing from that proposed by Thomas and Chess. One of the reasons for the discrepancy between the number and quality of temperament traits constituting the difficult temperament is the fact that many authors did not succeed in replicating the temperament structure composed of nine traits as proposed by Thomas and Chess. Factor analysis largely reduced the number of the NYLS traits.

Most unlike the NYLS approach was the concept of difficult temperament proposed by Bates (1980, 1987). Bates, Freeland, and Lounsbury (1979) developed an inventory, The Infant Characteristics Questionnaire (ICQ), aimed at measuring difficultness understood as a single factor called by them fussy-difficult and regarded as a score of parents' perception of difficultness. This view became a starting point for a critique of Thomas and Chess's concept of difficult temperament. A special issue of the journal *Merrill-Palmer Quarterly* was devoted to a discussion of the concept of difficult temperament.

Critical Remarks Related to Difficult Temperament

According to Bates (1980, 1983), who opened the discussion, difficult temperament understood as a characteristic of the child, and regarded by A. Thomas and Chess (1977) as a constitutional/biological concept, is unacceptable. The construct difficult temperament has an inescapably social and perceptual core. "We can regard parent perceptions as an integral part of the social reality, and we need to understand them in order to understand the meaning of difficult temperament" (Bates, 1983, p. 94).

Rothbart (1982) argued for lack of consistency of the quality of difficult temperament over age, especially during the period of infancy. Apart from the developmental specificity of difficultness, the construct in itself has a relative meaning. A temperament characteristic that is undesirable in one situation may prove to be desirable in another situation. There are benefits and costs associated with any temperament characteristic (Rothbart, 1982).

According to Plomin (1982) there is no need to encumber the domain of temperament with Bates's view that traits are constructed in the mind of the observer as postulated by attribution theory. Since "parental perception" has several meanings, it seems more appropriate to use such terms as parental ratings or parental interviews. These procedures, at least, can be judged in terms of reliability and validity.

Kagan (1982a), who tended to sympathize with the position of Thomas and Chess, argued that there are objective characteristics of extreme temperament that are not totally a construction of the parents, for example, fearfulness. Such temperament characteristics no doubt affect the mood and behavior of parents as well as other socializing agents, thus providing Thomas and Chess with a rationale for using the label "difficult."

As I have argued (Strelau, 1989a, 1991b), the unfortunate construct difficult temperament has an evaluative component that emphasizes the significance of temperament traits (the personological context) in determining difficulty in behavior or education. We should learn from the experience accumulated in intelligence studies that evaluative labels concerning traits remove from parents and educators the responsibility for inefficient teaching and upbringing. This is true as well when the child's temperament is described as difficult.

A. Thomas, Chess, and Korn (1982), in replying to this critique, especially to Bates's perceptual approach to the difficult temperament, maintained their view according to which difficult temperament is not a social perception but a within-the-individual characteristic. In their words (A. Thomas, Chess, & Korn, 1982): "we believe, that difficult temperament is a reality independent of the mother's perception" (p. 16). This statement has to be understood that it is not difficulty per se that is a reality, but it is the constellation of temperament traits labeled as difficult temperament that exists as a personological characteristic of the child. Despite the criticism regarding the understanding of difficult temperament, many studies have taken the Thomas–Chess approach as their starting point.

Probably the common denominators of the concept difficult temperament accepted by the majority of researchers who use this construct are the following: (a) Difficult temperament refers to extreme values in temperament characteristics, (b) they can be met in a normal human population from infancy to adolescence and, (c) under given conditions they increase the probability of behavior disorders.

Temperament and Goodness of Fit

Thomas and Chess, partially in response to the criticism surrounding the construct of difficult temperament (sometimes labeled by them as "difficult child"), but mainly under the influence of their own clinical experience, introduced in their studies the concept of goodness of fit already described in Chapter 2.

The NYLS Approach

The construct *goodness of fit,* which implies that the adequacy of the individual's functioning is dependent on the degree to which environmental demands are in accord with the individual's own characteristics, was applied by the New Yorkers mainly in respect to temperament. The numerous case studies described by A. Thomas and Chess (1977; Chess & Thomas, 1986, 1991; A. Thomas *et al.,* 1968) showed that, when there is an adequate interaction (goodness of fit) between the child's difficult temperament and parental or other caregiver practices and demands, behavior disorders may not occur. Thus there is no direct relationship between difficult temperament and behavior disorders or maladjustment. Poorness of fit between the child's temperament characteristics and parental (caretaker's) practices or other environmental demands enhances the risk that difficult temperament could lead to behavior disturbances.

Several studies reported in the literature have shown that, depending on the kind of demands and social expectancies, different temperament patterns may be regarded as difficult or the reverse, and the NYLS difficult temperament pattern may have, under specific conditions, a positive adaptive value. As already shown by A. Thomas and Chess (1977), for a working-class Puerto Rican sample living in New York high activity became a temperament trait that resulted in some individuals in behavioral disorders expressed in excessive motor activity that was almost absent in the NYLS sample, which consisted of children living in upper-middle-class families. Puerto Rican children, in contrast to the NYLS sample, lived in small, overcrowded flats—a microenvironment that did not allow the children with high-activity temperament to accommodate to their environment. In another example, lack of rhythmicity, which in the NYLS sample often led to sleeping disturbances, did not result in such disorders in Puerto Rican preschool children. These differences are due to the fact that Puerto Rican parents, unlike the NYLS parents, took no care of the children's time schedule for going to bed and getting up.

The Cultural Context as a Codeterminant
of the Functional Significance of Temperament

A study conducted by de Vries (1984, 1987) on Masai families living in Southern Kenya may serve as the most illustrative example of how cultural specificity can change the functional significance of temperament characteristics. Among forty-eight 4- to 5-month-old Masai infants diagnosed by means of the Infant Temperament Questionnaire, two extreme groups were selected: 10 infants with highest scores on the five Thomas–Chess temperament characteristics composing the difficult temperament, and 10 infants with lowest scores—the easy temperament. After 3 months a follow-up study was conducted. In the meantime, however, a tragic event occurred. A sub-Saharan drought disrupted the life of the Masai people. Food stores were depleted and grazing land was reduced. This situation forced the Masai families to migrate in search of better conditions for survival. The tragic event resulted in increased infant mortality. Because of the migration only 13 families among the 20 selected for further study were found— 7 with an easy and 6 with a difficult infant as diagnosed 3 months earlier. Among the 7 easy children 5 died, whereas only 2 died among the 6 difficult children. The difference in mortality between easy and difficult infants, which approached statistical significance ($p = .07$), is striking. The higher mortality of easy Masai infants was explained by de Vries (1987) by means of the "squeaky wheel" hypothesis. "The difficult, more fussy infant acts as a greater stimulus in the demand feeding situation, thereby spending more time suckling" (p. 180). The easy infant, who is quieter and more manageable, provides an attenuated feeding stimulus and, as a result, gets less milk and food.

The number of subjects who were examined by de Vries does not allow for a definite conclusion. However, this study demonstrates that the functional significance of temperament traits depends on the specific interaction with environmental factors, such as culture and physical conditions. The physical demands under conditions of sub-Saharan drought, in interaction with Masai maternal attitudes toward infants, were in dissonance with the structure of easy temperament as postulated by Thomas and Chess. Poorness of fit resulted in higher mortality among Masai easy infants. De Vries (1994) described case studies of developmental outcome of difficult infants living in different East African societies that illustrate that risk at any point in early development is not a function of difficult temperament alone, but a result of goodness of fit between temperament and physical, social, cultural, and family environments.

Super and Harkness (1986, 1994), taking as their point of departure Thomas and Chess's concept of goodness of fit, and findings that showed cultural differences in temperament, including their own comparative study conducted on infants living in Kenya and in the United States (Super & Harkness, 1982), arrived at the conclusion that organization of environments influences the expression and function of temperament. They developed the concept of *developmental niche.*

> The niche consists of the physical and social setting children are found in; the culturally regulated customs for child care, socialization, and behavior management; and the psychology of the caretakers, including beliefs and values about the nature of development. (Super & Harkness, 1986, p. 133)

The concept of difficult temperament may be properly solved only when culture-specific developmental niches in which children grow up are taken into account. In different contexts there are different ethnotheories of difficult temperament.

Attempts to Operationalize the Construct Goodness of Fit

Making use of both constructs, goodness of fit as developed by Thomas and Chess, and developmental niche as proposed by Super and Harkness, J. V. Lerner (1984, 1993) together with R. M. Lerner (J. V. Lerner & Lerner, 1994; R. M. Lerner & Lerner, 1987; R. M. Lerner *et al.,* 1986; Talwar, Nitz, Lerner, & Lerner, 1991) undertook to operationalize the concept of goodness of fit as applied to studies on temperament.

The assumption was made by Lerner and coworkers that there are a variety of demands placed on children and adolescents (among others on their temperament) by the social and physical environment, such as (1) attitudes, values, or stereotypes held by others, especially parents and other caregivers (expectational demands), (2) demands imposed by the temperaments of significant others, and (3) demands on temperament imposed by physical settings. In children whose temperament characteristics are incongruent with one or more of the demands mentioned (mismatched children), risk of maladaptive behavioral and cognitive development occurs.

Centering their research interests on expectational demands about children's and adolescents' temperament imposed by significant others, Lerner's group adapted the Revised Dimensions of Temperament Survey (DOTS-R) to allow for measuring these demands. All items of DOTS-R were reformulated in terms of preferences held by parents, teachers, or peers. All items are expressed in four response alternatives of which the two extreme ones are most wanted and therefore *not difficult* and do not want at all and therefore *very difficult.* DOTS-R, with items formulated in this way, is known as the "DOTS-R: Ethnotheory" questionnaire (Windle & Lerner, 1986). On the basis of two temperament scores, one, the individual's characteristics obtained by means of self-report or, in children, by means of parental (caretaker) report, and the other, the ethnotheory report which reports the extent to which a given temperament characteristic is wanted or unwanted by parents (caretakers, teachers, or peers), a fit score may be obtained (Talwar *et al.,* 1991). This score indicates the size of the discrepancy between the individual's temperament (based on self-report or rating by others) and parents' (teachers', peers') expectations of temperament difficulty. A series of studies was conducted by means of the ethnotheory of temperament (see Ballantine & Klein, 1990; Doelling & Johnson, 1990; H. A. Klein & Ballantine, 1988; J. V. Lerner, 1984, 1993) that demonstrated the usefulness of the goodness of fit approach as operationalized by Lerner's group.

The literature on research related to the construct of difficult temperament, especially in a variety of clinical settings, is enormous (cf., e.g., W. B. Carey & McDevitt, 1989, 1994; Chess & Thomas, 1986; Garrison & Earls, 1987; Kohnstamm, Bates, & Rothbart, 1989). I discuss some of the most representative directions or tendencies in this field. These refer to studies looking at the relationship between difficult temperament and (1) psychiatric disorders, (2) behavioral disorders, (3) clinical issues, and (4) functioning in the school environment.

Difficult Temperament and Psychiatric Disorders

Overview

Rutter, Birch, Thomas, and Chess (1964) based their work on the NYLS data which was from a group of children studied longitudinally from infancy to 7 years. They showed that children with psychiatric cases (21 Ss), as compared with children without clinical experience (71 Ss), were more irregular, nonadaptable, intense, and negative in mood. This relationship was influenced by parent–child interaction.

In a different population of children, all of whom had a mentally ill parent, which was considered a high risk factor for child psychiatric disorder, Graham, Rutter, and George (1973) studied the relationship between temperament characteristics and psychiatric disorders. In a group of sixty 3- to 7-year-old children, such temperamental traits as low habit regularity and low fastidiousness were predictive of psychiatric disorders 1 year after the temperament diagnosis was established. This was one of the first studies conducted on a sample not related to NYLS that supported Thomas and Chess's concept of difficult temperament.

A study by Malhorta, Varma, and Verma (1986) on 100 children aged 5–10 years who attended a child guidance clinic and were diagnosed with neuroses, adjustment reactions, conduct disorders, emotional disorders, and a hyperkinetic syndrome showed that different temperament characteristics based on the Thomas and Chess theory are related to different disorders. For example, low intelligence with behavior problems was significantly related to emotionality, conduct disorders to energy, and the somatization factor to attentivity, a temperament characteristic similar to distractibility. On the basis of these data the authors concluded that temperament cannot be viewed as a general risk factor.

The Contribution of the Quebec Group

The largest amount of data has been collected in a most systematic way by Maziade and his coworkers. In one of the studies (Maziade *et al.,* 1985) among 980 7-year-old children from a general population 24 were selected as the most difficult and 16 as the most easy by means of the NYLS Parent Temperament Questionnaire. Five years later they were compared for clinical status according to *DSM-III* criteria. Medical history, developmental data, and history of stressful events were obtained. Standard measures of child behavior and family functioning were also applied. Among the 24 difficult children 12 were qualified 5 years later for a *DSM-III* diagnosis, whereas only 1 among the 16 easy temperaments qualified. A multivariate analysis showed that there was no association between temperament and family functioning, nor between family functioning and clinical disorders, but the relationship temperament–clinical disorders remained significant. The association between temperament and clinical disorders was mainly found in the dysfunctional families. Although the number of subjects was low, the data are illustrative.

A study conducted by the Quebec group (Maziade, Caron, Cote, Boutin, & Thivierge, 1990) on more than five hundred 3–7-year-old children and more than three hundred 8–12-year-olds with psychiatric problems demonstrated that it is not the structure of temperament but the larger number of cases with difficult temperament that distinguished these two groups from the general population, as shown in Table 7.1. In this study two factors of difficult temperament were distinguished. Factor I was composed of five traits typical for the easy–difficult temperament, and Factor II was composed of low persistence, high sensory threshold, and high activity level. Only extreme scores on both factors were taken into account. The authors distinguished four types of disorder: internalized disorders (neurotic and emotional symptoms), externalized disorders (conduct problems, overactivity, etc.), developmental delay (disorders in specific areas of development) and mental retardation (IQ < 70). Factor I occurred mainly in children with external disorders and Factor II occurred in children with developmental delay. The study has also shown that difficult temperament is not the only factor that predicts psychiatric disorders.

The studies by Maziade and co-workers (Maziade, Cote, Bernier, Boutin, & Thivierge, 1989), conducted from infancy, give strong evidence that the relationship between psychiatric disorders and difficult temperament comes out most clearly when considered in interaction with other factors. A 9-year follow-up study by Maziade, Caron, Cote, Merette, and colleagues (1990) showed that the diagno-

TABLE 7.1. Comparison of Proportions of Extremely Difficult Temperaments (EDT) in the Child Psychiatric Population with Those in the General Population According to Age Levels

| | Proportions in population, No (%) | | | | | |
| | Child psychiatric | | | General | | |
Type of EDT	Total	Boys	Girls	Total	Boys	Girls
Factor 1[a]						
3–7 y	112/477 (24)	80/324 (25)	32/153 (21)	78/879 (9)	53/453 (12)	25/426 (6)
8–12 y	42/271 (16)	34/207 (16)	8/64 (13)	37/514 (7)	20/245 (8)	17/269 (6)
Factor 2[b]						
3–7 y	54/477 (11)	42/324 (13)	12/153 (8)	35/879 (4)	26/453 (6)	9/426 (2)
8–12 y	43/271 (16)	37/207 (18)	6/64 (9)	22/514 (4)	16/245 (7)	6/269 (2)

[a]The adverse pole of Factor 1 was composed of at least four of the following five temperament categories: low adaptability, very withdrawing, negative mood, very intense, and low distractibility.
[b]The adverse pole of Factor 2 was composed of low persistence, high sensory threshold, and high activity level.
Note. From "Extreme Temperament and Diagnosis," by M. Maziade, C. Caron, R. Cote, P. Boutin, and J. Thivierge, 1990, *Archives of General Psychiatry, 47,* p. 480. Copyright 1990 by American Medical Association. Reprinted with permission.

sis of temperament at the age of 7 years was not a good predictor of psychiatric disorders 9 years later when only temperament was taken into account. However, a statistically significant relationship was found between temperament and psychiatric disorders at the age of 16 in children who lived in dysfunctional families. In contrast, for children in families with superior behavior control functioning there was no difference in psychiatric outcome between children with easy and difficult temperament. The studies of the Quebec group deserve particular attention because of the well-controlled empirical settings, clearly defined variables, and the thorough demographic characterization of the samples under investigation.

Difficult Temperament and Adjustment

Behavior disorders, defined mostly in terms of extreme scores on adjustment or behavior disorder dimensions (as measured by different kinds of inventories), in a series of studies were related to measures of difficult temperament. These psychometrically established relationships were often studied in interaction with environmental factors and parental characteristics.

The Australian Study

One of the most comprehensive approaches to this kind of research is the longitudinal study conducted by Kyrios and Prior (1990) from La Trobe University in

Bundoora on 3–4-year-old children, and based on a "stress resilience" model of temperament. The study showed the moderating role of high reactivity–low manageability and low self-regulation in behavioral adjustment under family stressors. These two temperament characteristics influenced behavior disturbances both directly and indirectly, by moderating parental maladjustment, a family stressor that was causally related to children's behavior disturbances.

A group of 120 children (balanced for gender, with initial mean age 3.8 years) and their mothers were followed at 1-year intervals. Most of the measures were taken in phase 1. Behavioral adjustment was assessed in both phases. Child and environmental variables were controlled. Child variables comprised behavioral adjustment, development history, fine and gross motor coordination, health history, facility attendance, word knowledge, stress, and temperament. Environmental variables consisted of marital adjustment, parental psychological functioning, child-rearing practices, parental employment, and social status.

Using a broad statistical approach that comprised factor analysis, correlational procedures, multiple regression, and path analysis, the authors arrived at the conclusion that the interaction of many variables contributes to behavior disturbances at the age of 4–5 years as depicted by a path diagram in Figure 7.1. However, temperament characteristics are the most predictive variables of child

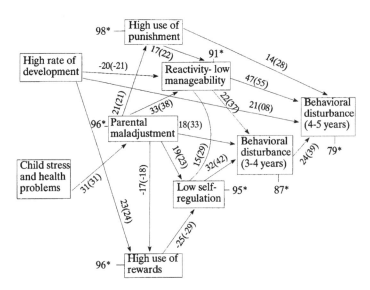

FIGURE 7.1. Path diagram of a causal model for behavioral disturbance in 3- to 5-year-old children. *Note.* From "Temperament, Stress and Family Factors in Behavioural Adjustment of 3–5-Year-Old Children," by M. Kyrios and M. Prior, 1990, *International Journal of Behavioral Development, 13,* p. 84. Copyright 1990 by International Society of Behavioral Development. Reprinted with permission.

behavioral adjustment. Low self-regulation and high reactivity–low manageability contributed the most to the variance of behavior disturbances at the age of 3–4 years, and high reactivity–low manageability was the strongest predictor of behavioral maladjustment at the age of 4–5 years. High reactivity–low manageability, composed of such traits as unmanageable, irritable, highly active and intense, and low temperament self-regulation, comprising high distractibility, low rhythmicity, and low persistence, are considered to be traits composing the difficult temperament. In this study "parental dysfunction was also seen as contributing to difficult temperament and early childhood behavioural dysfunction" (Kyrios & Prior, 1990, p. 88).

Over the past twenty years other studies conducted also have shown the contribution of different configurations of traits constituting difficult temperament, mainly in interaction with other variables referring to family functioning, parental characteristics, and environmental changes, and to children's and adolescents' adaptation and behavior disorders (e.g., Barron & Earls, 1984; Cowen, Wyman, & Work, 1992; Gordon, 1981, 1983; Olweus, 1980b; Prior, Garino, Sanson, & Oberklaid, 1987; Simonds & Simonds, 1982; Ventura & Stevenson, 1986; Windle, 1989a).

Studies Highlighting Different Aspects of Temperamental Influence on Behavior Disorders

I refer only to those studies that throw new light on the difficult temperament issue. Earls and Jung (1987) followed 95 children of both sexes in two waves with a 1-year interval at the ages of 2 and 3. Children's temperament, adjustment scores, and family characteristics were taken into account. A correlational analysis of temperament and home environment data taken at age 2 and behavior problems at age 3 indicated that only temperament characteristics, that is, high activity, low adaptability, high intensity, and negative mood, were significantly related to behavior problems. Multiple regression analysis led to the conclusion that low adaptability and high intensity were the two temperament variables that accounted for unique variance in child behavior problems from age 2 to 3.

Taking as their point of departure a conceptual model of child maladjustment, McClowry and colleagues (1994) studied 89 mothers with children between ages 8 and 11 years with the objective of ascertaining the interactional influence of a variety of variables on child maladjustment. Maladjustment, with a distinction made between two factors—externalizing and internalizing—was the dependent variable, the independent variables being parental distress, maternal psychiatric syndromes, temperament of the child, temperament of the mother, major life events, maternal daily hassles, and SES. Causal modeling with residual analysis indicated that the strongest predictors of child maladjustment were two temperament dimensions— negative reactivity and low task persistence—and maternal hassles. These variables explained 56% of child externalizing behavior. Maternal temperament (intensity), major life events, and maternal psychiatric symptoms influenced maternal hassles directly, thus having an indirect influence on child externalizing behavior.

Brody, Stoneman, and Burke (1988) demonstrated that, in families consisting of two children of the same gender (brother pairs and sister pairs), one 4.5 to 6.5 years old, and the other 7 to 9 years old, fathers and mothers perceived a consistent relationship between difficult temperament and level of adjustment. Children assessed as having a high level of persistence, activity, and emotional intensity were perceived as less well adjusted in comparison to children with low scores on these dimensions. This also resulted when temperament was measured by one of the parents, and adjustment by the other one.

A rather sophisticated reanalysis of the NYLS project which consisted of a cluster analysis of the data in order to construct longitudinal group profiles of easy–difficult temperament was conducted by Tubman, Lerner, Lerner, and von Eye (1992). The aim of the study was to show the dynamics of the relationship between temperament and adjustment across time, characterized by four different clusters. For 129 subjects, three measures of temperament difficulty composed of the five NYLS temperament characteristics were taken into account when the subjects were ages 16–17 years, 18–23 years, and 25–31 years. Cluster 1 had the most difficult temperament with increasing scores across time, Cluster 2 showed an increase from easy to difficult temperament, Cluster 3 a decrease from moderate level of easy–difficult to more easy temperament, and Cluster 4 curvilinear changes in difficultness across age. Negative emotional–behavioral states were measured retrospectively for ages 1 through 6 and age 7 through 12. During young adulthood psychological adjustment was measured in the following nine areas: self-evaluation, family relationships, school functioning, social functioning, sexual functioning, goals and implementation of goals, coping styles, functioning at work, communication, emotional expressiveness, and routines. The results showed that members of the highest difficult temperament score group (Cluster 1) had significantly lower adjustment scores as compared to the remaining clusters, and this finding was consistent for all the separate adjustment scores except for family relations as well as for the global adjustment score.

Critical Approaches to the Relationship
Difficult Temperament–Behavior Disorders

The relationship between difficult temperament and behavior disorders, assuming the latter are measured by different kinds of psychometric techniques, is not so obvious as it seems at first glance. There is strong contamination of items from both types of scales. Some temperament characteristics at their extremes refer to behaviors that are judged to be behavior problems.

Sanson, Prior, and Kyrios (1990a, 1990b) conducted a study in which 20 items taken from the Short Toddlers Temperament Scale were randomly mixed with 20 items taken from two commonly used behavior problem inventories—Behaviour Checklist (Richman & Graham, 1971) and Preschool Behavior Questionnaire (Behar & Stringfield, 1974). This mixed-item pool was given to 36 clinical child psychologists who judged on a 5-point Likert scale the extent to which items from both temperament and behavior problem questionnnaires constituted indices for both temperament dimensions and behavior problems. The results of this judgment yielded an overlap of .88 on a 0–1 scale. The overlap was particularly evident concerning internalizing problems such as anxiety, fearfulness, shyness, and phobias. As the authors conclude, "an internalizing problem might be seen as little more than an extreme position on a continuum of intrinsic behavioral style dimensions, that is, as nothing but an extreme temperamental characteristic" (Sanson *et al.,* 1990a, p. 188). The data from this study show that externalizing problems, which refer to behaviors known as aggressiveness, tantrum, and hyperactivity, are more distinct from temperament characteristics. On the basis of their findings the authors concluded that in many studies in which overlap occurs between these two constructs (difficult temperament and behavior problems) the statement that "temperament predicts behavior problems" is too far-reaching (Sanson *et al.,* 1990b).

Lee and Bates (1985) demonstrated the absence of a direct relationship between a child's difficult temperament as perceived by the mother when the child is at the age of 6, 12, and 24 months and behavioral disorders as measured by home observations when the child is 24 months of age. However, temperament-specific interactions were found between the child's trouble behavior, the mother's control responses, and the child's response to the mother's control.

A study that took a multimethod approach to assessing a single temperament characteristic, that is, activity, was conducted by Schaughency and Fagot (1993). Activity was measured by means of inventory scores, home observation, play sessions under laboratory conditions, and with an actometer, on 192 children (96 boys and 96 girls) at the age of 5 years. Adjustment was assessed 2 years later by means of the Child Behavior Checklist (Achenbach & Edelbrock, 1981), the Conners Parent Rating Scale (Goyette, Conners, & Ulrich, 1978), and a self-report adjustment measure. The data are not as positive as several other studies suggest. The results showed, however, that the relationship between temperament activity and adjustment scores was strongest when both variables were measured by parents, that is, by means of inventory techniques. Activity at age 5 was related to parents' ratings of aggression and hyperactivity, and to learning problems (but only in girls) at age 7.

During the past decade several findings have argued against the difficult temperament–behavior disorder relationship. Vaughn, Bradley, Joffe, Seifer, and Barglow (1987) reanalyzed several studies in which difficult temperament was assessed by means of the Infant Temperament Questionnaire (W. B. Carey & McDevitt, 1978). Two studies were also conducted by these authors, applying the same inventory in combination with a variety of personality measures taken from mothers prenatally. The results, based on several analyses, allowed them to conclude that prenatally assessed personality characteristics, especially anxiety, significantly distinguished mothers who diagnosed their infants' temperament as difficult from those who diagnosed their infants as easy during the first 8 months of life. Hormonal measures taken during different stages of pregnancy and postpartum did not show relationships with infant temperament characteristics. These findings may suggest that the assessment of a child's difficult temperament is the result of mother–child interaction in which the mother's own personality plays a crucial role.

A thorough study was conducted by Daniels, Plomin, and Greenhalgh (1984) with the aim of relating parental report of infants' difficult temperament, based on the Thomas–Chess concept, to three basic areas: infant functioning (in terms of adjustment scores), parental personality, and home environment. Data were collected from families consisting of 152 adopted and 120 nonadopted infants tested in their homes at the ages of 12 and 24 months. The findings from this study are very pessimistic. No significant relationship was found between difficult temperament and any other of the variables under study, and interactions with difficult temperament were not recorded. The same results emerged when only 10% of each of the two extremes of the difficult dimension were taken into account.

Difficult Temperament and Adjustment Expressed in Functioning
under Environmental Changes

In discussing the relationship between difficult temperament and adjustment, mention should be made of a line of research in which the focus of examination was not behavior disorders but functioning under changes in the surroundings or in new situations. A series of studies was conducted by Klein, who demonstrated that temperament activity in 2- to 5-year-old children predicted adjustment to group care centers (H. A. Klein, 1980; for another study, see Scholom, Zucker, & Stollak, 1979), and that high threshold of responsiveness, low persistence, and withdrawal from new situations were good predictors for maladjustment to kindergarden settings (H. A. Klein, 1982; see also Billman & McDevitt, 1980). Furthermore, adjustment of adolescents to new settings in postsecondary education (H. A. Klein, 1987), and to college residence (H. A. Klein & Rennie, 1985) was related to temperament. Approach and positive mood predicted positive adaptation to starting postsecondary education; high adaptability, low motoric activity, and high attention were good predictors of adjustment to college residence.

Other studies regarding the relationship between temperament characteristics and adjustment under changes in the surroundings refer to children's functioning after hospitalization. McClowry (1990) showed that in 8- to 12-year-old children such temperament variables as mood, approach, and predictability were consistent predictors of behavior after hospitalization. A study conducted by Carson, Council, and Gravley (1991) on children ages 4 to 12 years indicated that children with such a pattern of difficult temperament as low rhythmicity, withdrawal, low adaptability, and negative mood showed poor adaptation after hospitalization.

Difficult Temperament in Clinical Samples

Overview

There are a large number of investigations in which child or adolescent temperament characteristics, in particular, patterns of difficult temperament, have been related to clinical issues that are not related to psychiatric disorders. I specify some lines of research addressed to these relationships. Children's and adolescents' temperament characteristics have been related to such issues as alcoholism and other substance abuse (e.g., af Klinteberg, Andersson, Magnusson, & Stattin, 1993; Andersson & Magnusson, 1990; Blackson, Tarter, Martin, & Moss, 1994; Mezzich et al., 1994; Osborne, Hinz, Rappaport, Williams, & Tuma, 1988; Simon, Stacy, Sussman, & Dent, 1994; Tarter, Laird, Kabene, Bukstein, & Kaminer, 1990; L. von Knorring, Oreland, & von Knorring, 1987; Windle, 1991), eating disorders, especially predisposition to obesity (Bulik, Sullivan, Weltzin, & Kaye, 1995; W. B. Carey, 1985b; W. B. Carey, Hegvik, & McDevitt, 1988; Mehrabian & Riccioni, 1986; Mehrabian, Nahum, & Duke, 1985–1986), accidental injuries and injury liability (L. L. Davidson, 1987; Manheimer & Mellinger, 1967; Matheny, 1986, 1987, 1988), and allergic symptoms (Bell, Jasnoski, Kagan, & King, 1990; Kagan, Snidman, Julia-Sellers, & Johnson, 1991; Priel, Henik, Dekel, & Tal, 1990).

Probably the most common denominator of these studies is the conclusion that temperament, when considered only in interaction with other variables such as family functioning, physical and social demands, and all kinds of stressors, may be regarded as a factor that contributes to the clinical cases mentioned. Generally, the causal relationship between temperament and clinical issues is equivocal and age-specific. The fact that, almost without exception, studies have been conducted on small samples and by use of different temperament measures impedes generalization of the conclusions.

Difficult Temperament and the Down Syndrome

The numerous studies conducted on the relationship between temperament characteristics and disabilities associated with nervous system deficits, especially in children with Down's syndrome (DS), demonstrate that despite the diversity of the findings some more or less clear conclusions are to be drawn. In order to make comparisons across studies, S. Goldberg and Marcovitch (1989) overviewed a number of them conducted on young children with Down's syndrome in whom temperament was measured in the Thomas–Chess tradition or by comparable inventories. The handicapped children were compared with normally developing children. Table 7.2 presents the results of this overview, to which I have added two recent studies (Huntington & Simeonsson, 1993; Pueschel & Myers, 1994).

All the studies show that, for some age groups, there are at least two temperament dimensions (Huntington & Simeonsson, 1993; Rothbart & Hanson, 1983), and usually three or more (Bridges & Cicchetti, 1982; Gunn & Berry, 1985a, 1985b; Hefferman, Black, & Poche, 1982; Marcovitch, Goldberg, MacGregor, & Lojkasek, 1986; Pueschel & Myers, 1994) in which DS children differ from normally developing ones. The only consistent result across ages (from 10 months to 16 years) is that the handicapped children have lower levels of persistence as compared with the control groups. From Table 7.2 another finding clearly emerges, namely, the DS–temperament relationship shows a developmentally de-

TABLE 7.2. Temperament Characteristics of Children with Down's Syndrome as Compared with Normally Developing Children

Study (number of subjects)	Means age of sample	Temperament dimensions								
		PE	AP	TH	PM	AL	RH	IN	DI	AD
Rothbart & Hanson, 1983 (n = 15)	6 m									
	9 m		<		<					
	12 m									
Bridges & Cicchetti, 1982 (n = 74)	10 m									
	16 m	<	<	<						
Hefferman, Black, & Poche, 1982 (n = 57)	21 m	<	<	>		<				
Gunn & Berry, 1985a, (n = 23)	30 m vs. CA^a match	<	<	>				<		
	30 m vs. MA^b match	<	>	<	>		>	<		>
Huntington & Simeonsson, 1993 (n = 40)	24–36 m	<		>						
Marcovitch, Goldberg, MacGregor, & Lojkasek, 1986 (n = 96)	39 m	<	>	>						
Gunn & Berry, 1985b (n = 23)	57 m	<			>	>	>		>	
Pueschel & Myers, 1994 (n = 40)	4–16 y	<	>							<

Note. PE = persistence, AP = approach, TH = threshold, PM = positive mood, AL = activity level, RH = rhythmicity, IN = intensity, DI = distractibility, AD = adaptability.
^aCA = chronological age
^bMA = mental age
< = children with DS rated lower as normally developing children, > = children with DS rated higher; lack of < or > means that no difference was recorded or the trait was not measured. From "Temperament in Developmentally Disabled Children," by S. Goldberg and S. Marcovitch. In G. A. Kohnstamm, J. E. Bates, and M. K. Rothbart (Eds.), *Temperament in Childhood* (1989, p. 394), Chichester, England: Wiley. Copyright 1989 by John Wiley & Sons Ltd. Adapted with permission.

termined specificity. If DS children differ in temperament from normally developing ones, they are, up to the age of about 30 months, lower in approach, positive mood, and activity level, and higher in adaptability. In turn, both groups (DS and control) show a reverse relationship at ages above 30 months. Handicapped children are higher in approach, positive mood, and activity level, and lower in adaptability. Most inconsistent are the results in respect to threshold where all possible relationships, including lack of relationship with DS, occur.

The relationship between the Down syndrome and temperament characteristics may essentially change if temperament characteristics other than the Thomas–Chess ones are taken into account. For example, Rothbart and Hanson (1983) measured temperament characteristics of 6- to 12-month-old infants by means of the Infant Behavior Questionnaire which is based on Rothbart's theory of temperament (see Chapter 3). It emerged from this study that DS infants were lower on Smiling and Laughter scales and higher on Duration of Orienting, Fear, and Startle scales. They were also lower in motor and vocal activity when compared with a control sample.

Rothbart and Hanson's (1983) study, conducted on 15 DS infants, together with the seven other studies presented in Table 7.2, comprise a total of 372 subjects (from 15 to 96 in a sample). This exemplifies the paucity of clinical samples and their limited sizes, hardly acceptable for questionnaire measures by which temperament was assessed. The causal relationship between temperament characteristics and the Down syndrome is not clear. Probably the most acceptable conclusion drawn by most researchers dealing with the DS–temperament relationship is that temperament may act as a moderator in the DS child's interaction with the social environment, especially with parents and other caretakers (see S. Goldberg & Markovitch 1989; Huntington & Simeonsson, 1993). The typical Down syndrome characteristics, in particular the neurologically determined intellectual deficit, is an important factor in codetermining the specific DS child–social environment interaction.

Temperament and Schooling

Functioning in the school environment must take into account aspects of the child's cognitive characteristics directly or indirectly related to schooling. Thus, the temperament–schooling relationship is discussed with respect to such specific issues as cognitive functioning in early childhood, level of intelligence, teachability, academic achievement, scholastic abilities, and general educational outcomes.

Temperament and Cognitive Functioning in Infants

The research hitherto conducted on early infancy shows certain relationships between temperament and cognitive functioning (e.g., Field *et al.,* 1978; Ross, 1987; Roth, Eisenberg, & Sell, 1984; A. M. Sostek & Anders, 1977). In the

majority of these studies the Bayley Mental Scales were used for measuring efficiency of performance, and temperament was assessed according to the
Thomas–Chess tradition. In general, the studies showed that decrease in infants'
cognitive performance was significantly associated with such temperament characteristics as low adaptability, low persistence, withdrawal from new stimulation,
and low rhythmicity. These data did not allow any conclusions regarding a causal
relationship between temperament characteristics and cognitive functioning.

A more complex study was conducted by Wachs and Gandour (1983) on one
hundred 6-month-old infants in which the temperament–cognitive development relationship was examined by taking into account the interaction with the physical
and social environment. Three measures served as predictor variables: the infant's
pattern of difficult and easy temperament (as postulated by Thomas and Chess),
the infant's social environment as measured by observations on home environment
and mother–infant interaction (the Yarrow scale), and the physical environment for
which the Purdue Home Stimulation Inventory was used. The criterion variable
was the infant's performance level on the Infant Psychological Development Scale
(IPDS; Uzgiris & Hunt, 1975), which is a Piagetian measure of sensorimotor intelligence. On the basis of canonical and univariate analyses, Wachs and Gandour
demonstrated a direct relation between temperament and several aspects of sensorimotor intelligence. High activity, withdrawal, and intensity predicted an advanced level of gestural imitation but a low level of uses of objects as means.
Infants with easy temperament were more sensitive to both physical and social environment than infants with a pattern of difficult temperament. A significant
canonical relationship between sensorimotor intelligence and both environments
was found for babies with easy, but not with difficult, temperament. Wachs and
Gandour suggest that kinesthetic stimulation and exploratory freedom, to which
easy babies are more responsive than are difficult infants, are particularly salient
for intellectual development in the first months of life.

The relationship between temperament and cognitive functioning has been of
special interest in studies in different kinds of school settings. The findings of the
past two decades suggest that the conclusions regarding the contribution of temperament differ depending on the specific aspect related to schooling.

Temperament and Intelligence

A series of studies have been conducted with the aim of ascertaining whether
there is a relationship between children's intelligence, as measured by various intelligence tests, and temperament characteristics. The results are not unequivocal.
A. Thomas and Chess (1977) did not find a relationship between temperament and
IQ measured in a group of more than 500 children in grades 3 through 6. Also,
studies conducted by Keogh (1986) on normally developing preschool children
and on learning-disabled pupils yielded no relationship between temperament

characteristics, as understood by Thomas and Chess, and IQ measures (see also Sewell, Thurman, & Hutchins, 1981).

More recently, Czeschlik (1993) compared the temperament characteristics of a group of more than 150 ten-year-old children of very high intelligence (top 2% of more than 7,000 children) with a group of 134 children of average intelligence. The groups were matched for age, gender, and SES. Temperament was measured by parents' and teachers' ratings. The Middle Childhood Temperament Questionnaire (MCTQ; Hegvik, McDevitt, & Carey, 1982) and the Short Form of the Teacher Temperament Questionnaire (TTQ-S; Keogh, Pullis, & Cadwell, 1982) were used. The data show that high-intelligence pupils differed from average-intelligence pupils in lower distractibility and intensity (MCTQ scores) and higher task orientation and personal–social flexibility (TTQ scores).

If we consider that the Keogh and colleagues (1982) Task Orientation scale is composed of persistence, distractibility, and activity and the Personal–Social Flexibility scale of adaptability, approach–withdrawal, and mood, then Czeschlik's results correpond with the data reported by R. P. Martin (1988a) from two doctoral studies. In one of these (Matthews-Morgan's Ph.D. thesis), in which high-IQ pupils (IQ > 130) were compared with average-IQ pupils in respect to temperament measures, persistence was higher for high-IQ children. In the other study (Burk's Ph.D thesis) the high-IQ group was higher on approach, adaptability, positive mood, and persistence, and lower on distractibility. Also, R. P. Martin and Holbrook (1985) reported significant relationships between IQ and such temperament dimensions as adaptability, approach, and persistence in more than 100 first-grade pupils.

Several hypotheses have been developed to explain the temperament–intelligence and the temperament–scholastic ability relationship. For example, R. P. Martin (1988a) suggested that genetically determined attention span and distractibility may influence learning rates. Another temperament characteristic—the tendency to approach in novel situations—leads to contacts with a greater variety of environmental stimuli, which, in turn, affects the rate of learning. After reviewing studies in which children's and adolescents' temperament was related to giftedness, I concluded that such temperament traits as, for example, sensation seeking, approach, and activity may be preconditions for an interaction between the individual's genetically determined intellectual potential and the environment, resulting in a higher development of intelligence (Strelau, 1992b). Individuals who are sensation seekers and approachers, and who are active, especially in the cognitive domain, have more possibilities and opportunities to make contact with the surrounding world, with unknown and ambiguous stimulation, as against persons closed to experience, avoiding sensations, and remaining passive. Studies reported by Zuckerman (1994) illustrate the temperament–cognitive abilities relationship in respect to sensation seeking (see Table 7.3).

Certain temperament traits also may influence the increase or decrease of the individual's cognitive development in a more indirect way, because of changes in

TABLE 7.3. **Correlations between IQ as Measured by the Wechsler Adult Intelligence Scale (WAIS) and Scholastic Aptitudes (SAT) and Sensation Seeking (SSS)**

	WAIS	SAT	
	High school	College students	
SSS	students ($n = 138$)	males ($n = 200$)	females ($n = 200$)
General/Total	.22*	.19*	.19*
TAS	.11	.13	.16*
ES	.34**	.18**	.02
Dis	.19*	−.07	−.14*
BS	.21*	.20**	.10

Note. From *Behavioral Expressions and Biosocial Bases of Sensation Seeking* (p. 367), by M. Zuckerman, 1994, New York: Cambridge University Press. Copyright 1994 by Cambridge University Press. Adapted with permission.
*$p < .05$, **$p < .01$.

the surroundings caused by these traits. A longitudinal study conducted by Maziade, Cote, Boutin, Bernier, and Thivierge (1987) on temperament and intellectual development from infancy to 5 years demonstrated the indirect temperament–IQ relationship, but with results that are contradictory to the findings already cited.

From 358 infants three groups were selected on the basis of temperament measures (Infant Temperament Questionnaire): difficult, easy, and average temperament. Each group included 29 infants matched for sex and SES. At the age of 4.5 years the children's intelligence was assessed on the Wechsler scale. To obtain information about certain aspects of family functioning, the McMaster's Model of Family Functioning was applied; with this assessment instrument family communication and family behavior control was scored. The authors found that temperament and intelligence correlated significantly at age 4;7 years in the middle and upper social classes. The same held true when family communication was taken into account. In both cases children characterized by the difficult temperament syndrome had higher IQs. The authors interpreted their results in terms of the stimulative value of the social environment. In order to calm the child, or to shape the child's style in a more desirable way, parents would pay greater attention, talk more, or interact more with their children. Such parents would stimulate the difficult infant more than the extremely easy infant, who is more readily left to him- or herself.

There are at least two research centers conducting intensive studies on the relationship temperament–schooling, with special attention to the pattern of difficult temperament, one group at the University of California headed by Barbara Keogh, and the other group led by Roy P. Martin at the University of Georgia. The difference between the groups in approaching the temperament–schooling relationship consists mainly in the way temperament is assessed and different issues of schooling approached.

Temperament and Teachability

Keogh (1982, 1986, 1989) and her coworkers (Keogh & Burstein, 1988; Keogh & Pullis, 1980; Kornblau & Keogh, 1980; Pullis & Cadwell, 1982) introduced the concept of teachability, which reflects the teacher's view about the attributes of a model pupil. Teachability is a teacher-generated description of pupils clustered into three primary dimensions: cognitive autonomous behavior, school-related behavior, and personal–social characteristics. Several studies showed that pupils judged by teachers to be low-teachable were characterized by a temperament pattern considered to be difficult temperament. In these studies temperament was diagnosed by a short version of the Teacher Temperament Questionnaire (TTQ) (Keogh *et al.,* 1982). After factor analysis of the eight dimensions measured by means of TTQ, Keogh and colleagues separated three factors: Task Orientation (composed of persistence, distractibility, and activity), Personal–Social Flexibility (approach, positive mood, and adaptability), and Reactivity (negative mood, threshold of response, and intensity of response). Teachers' judgments of pupil's low teachability were significantly related to such temperament characteristics as low task orientation, low flexibility, and high reactivity, a pattern considered by the California group to mean difficult temperament.

Temperament and Academic Achievement

Studies conducted by R. P. Martin (1988a; 1989) and his associates (R. P. Martin & Holbrook, 1985; R. P. Martin, Nagle, & Paget, 1983; R. P. Martin, Drew, Gaddis, & Moseley, 1988; Paget, Nagle, & Martin, 1984) refer to different educational outcomes. I concentrate on academic achievement and scholastic abilities, as rated by standardized methods and by teachers, in relationship to temperament. Temperament was assessed by means of the Temperament Assessment Battery for Children (TABC) developed by R. P. Martin (1988b; for a detailed discussion, see Chapter 6). Depending on the specificity of the study, different measures were used by the Georgia group for estimating scholastic achievement; examples were the Stanford Achievement Test, the Peabody Individual Achievement Test, and the Metropolitan Achievement Test. In addition, teachers' grades were taken from cumulative records.

The real importance of Martin's studies consists not only in the use of different measures of scholastic achievements, but also in the use of different intervals (from 6 months to 4 years) between the predictor (temperament measures assigned by teachers) and the criterion variables (scholastic achievement scores). Most of the studies (see R. P. Martin, 1988a, 1989; R. P. Martin *et al.,* 1988) showed that three of the six temperament dimensions—activity, distractibility, and persistence—that compose one factor labeled by R. P. Martin (1989) Task Attention

TABLE 7.4. Relationship between Activity, Distractibility, and Persistence, and Academic Achievement

	Time span[a] (years)	Achievement			
		Grades		Standardized tests	
Temperament trait		Reading	Math	Reading	Math
Activity					
Study 1 ($n = 104$)	1/2	−.43	−.42	−.45	−.24
Study 2 ($n = 80$)	1/2	−.29	n.s.	−.25	−.36
Study 3 ($n = 117$)	1	−.58	−.49	−.51	−.34
Study 4 ($n = 22$)	2	−.40	−.42	n.s.	n.s.
Study 5 ($n = 63$)	4	−.39	−.30	−.42	−.26
Distractibility					
Study 1	1/2	−.56	−.52	−.45	−.39
Study 2	1/2	−.63	−.52	−.55	−.59
Study 3	1	−.41	−.43	−.49	−.45
Study 4	2	−.61	−.59	n.s.	n.s.
Study 5	4	−.30	−.35	−.48	−.48
Persistence					
Study 1	1/2	.65	.60	.49	.48
Study 2	1/2	.69	.61	.63	.50
Study 3	1	.48	.60	.62	.60
Study 4	2	.64	.72	n.s.	n.s.
Study 5	4	n.s.	.37	.45	.43
Median[b]		**.48**	**.49**	**.45**	**.39**

[a] Time between measurement of temperament and measurement of achievement. Study 1: R. P. Martin & Holbrook (1985); temperament and achievement measured in first grade. Study 2: R. P. Martin, Nagle, & Paget (1983); temperament and achievement measured in first grade. Study 3: R. P. Martin, Drew, Gaddis, & Moseley (1988); temperament measured in kindergarten. Study 4: R. P. Martin *et al.* (1988); temperament measured in preschool. Study 5: R. P. Martin *et al.* (1988); temperament measured in first grade.

[b] The median reflects the strength of relationship between temperament and achievement without taking into account the sign of correlation.

Note. From Study 1: "Relationship of Temperament Characteristics to the Academic Achievement of First Grade Children," by R. P. Martin and J. Holbrook, 1985, *Psychoeducational Assessment, 3,* 131–140. Study 2: "Relationship between Temperament and Classroom Behavior, Teacher Attitudes, and Academic Achievement," by R. P. Martin, R. Nagel, and K. Paget, 1983, *Psychoeducational Assessment, 1,* 377–386. Study 3: "Prediction of Elementary School Achievement from Preschool Temperament: Three Studies," by R. P. Martin, D. Drew, L. Gaddis, and M. Moseley, 1988, *School Psychology Review, 17,* 125–137. Study 4: "Prediction of Elementary School Achievement from Preschool Temperament: Three Studies," by R. P. Martin, D. Drew, L. Gaddis, and M. Moseley, 1988, *School Psychology Review, 17,* 125–137. Study 5: "Prediction of Elementary School Achievement from Preschool Temperament: Three Studies," by R. P. Martin, D. Drew, L. Gaddis, and M. Moseley, 1988, *School Psychology Review, 17,* 125–137. "Activity Level, Distractibility and Persistence: Critical Characteristics in Early Schooling," by R. P. Martin. In G. A. Kohnstamm, J. E. Bates, and M. K. Rothbart (Eds.), *Temperament in Childhood* (1989, p. 456), Chichester, England: Wiley. Copyright 1989 by John Wiley & Sons Ltd. Adapted with permission.

(equivalent to Keogh's Task Orientation) permits prediction of scholastic achievement as measured by standardized methods and teachers' grades. Table 7.4 summarizes the results of five studies on the temperament–scholastic achievement relationship conducted by Martin and his coworkers.

As is clear from Table 7.4, with only a few exceptions, the correlations are statistically significant and vary from .24 to .72 depending on the achievement criterion taken into account. If we leave out the sign of relationship, positive for persistence, and negative for distractibility and activity, the median correlation between temperament characteristics and scholastic achievement as rated by teachers is .48 for reading and .49 for mathematics. In the case of standardized scholastic achievement tests the coefficients, albeit lower, are not essentially different, that is, .45 for reading and .39 for mathematics.

A recent longitudinal investigation by R. P. Martin, Olejnik, and Gaddis (1994) on more than 100 pupils from first to fifth grades confirmed the findings reported earlier. In addition, LISREL analysis showed that the factor Task Orientation (tendency to be active, distractible, and nonpersistent) had a stronger impact on mathematics and reading performance than did scholastic ability. The result is not so surprising as the authors suggest if we consider that at least one third of the variance in academic achievement depends on the temperament-personality factors (see Cattell, 1971). A study conducted by Lewowicki (see Strelau, 1992b) on 1,820 pupils from fifth to eighth grades has shown that school achievement correlated better with temperament traits, such as strength of excitation (.52) and mobility of nervous processes (.42), than with intelligence (.37). Temperament was measured by the Strelau Temperament Rating Scale and intelligence by Raven's Progressive Matrices. Psychologically, the strength of excitation may be interpreted in terms of endurance and persistence. Since school achievement was probably measured under some kind of stress (examination situation), it seems reasonable to assume that "strong" and mobile pupils, being more resistant to stress, performed better than "weak" and slow children (Strelau, 1992b).

Temperament and Scholastic Abilities

Furthermore, studies summarized by R. P. Martin (1988a, 1989) on the relationship between temperament characteristics and scholastic abilities, as measured by standardized cognitive ability tests, show that the three temperament dimensions—activity, distractibility, and persistence—are related to scholastic abilities in the same way as they are to scholastic achievements.

Among the possible interpretations of the links between temperament on the one hand and scholastic abilities and achievements on the other, the claim that activity level, distractibility, and persistence composing the Task Attention factor are related to cognitive abilities, because "attention is in all probability a part of general intellectual ability" (R. P. Martin, 1989, p. 459) deserves special mention. This hypothesis, however, does not support the position that traits that refer to attention, especially distractibility, should be regarded as temperament characteristics (see Chapter 3).

Referring the data obtained by Martin and his coworkers to the concept of difficult temperament, one could say that such traits as high activity and distractibility, combined with low persistence, might be regarded as difficult temperament, but only under conditions typical for school demands, again supporting the idea of goodness of fit.

> Persistence and distractibility do not play a major role in most conceptions of the easy or difficult child as seen in the context of the family. The reasons for this are clear. The demand for sustained attention to difficult learning tasks is not a dominant feature of home life for most families; it is the central demand characteristic of the school. Mood and emotional intensity rarely are seen as major correlates of academic outcomes, but are often the best predictors of adjustment in the home. (R. P. Martin, 1988a, p. 202)

The number of studies in which temperament characteristics have been related to different educational outcomes extends beyond the scope of this chapter (see, e.g., W. B. Carey, Fox, & McDevitt, 1977; E. M. Gordon & Thomas, 1967; J. V. Lerner, Lerner, & Zabski, 1985; for review, see Keogh, 1986; R. P. Martin, 1988a, 1889). However, a methodologically specific line of research represented by Barclay deserves some attention.

Typology of Temperament Appplied to Educational Outcomes

On the basis of a series of studies, Barclay (1983b, 1991, 1992) developed a typology of temperament that underlines the functional significance of a pupil's temperament by taking into account the variety of interactions between temperament and educational treatment. This typology was based on a statistical procedure known as the Barclay Classroom Assessment System (BCAS; Barclay, 1983a) that integrates self-report, peer judgment, and teacher evaluation, in conjunction with conceptualizations derived from the mainstream of temperament theories, with special reference to Strelau's (1983) regulative theory of temperament.

The four temperament types distinguished by Barclay (1991, 1992) may be briefly described as follows:

- *Thinkers:* highly reactive students, often strongly stimulated by their thought processes, and low in their endurance of a continued bombardment of stimuli from the classroom;
- *Leaders:* low reactive, tending toward extraversion, with tolerance for social ambiguity, enjoying social stimulation, with a high threshold of stimulation and endurance;
- *Followers:* tend to be more passive in classroom stimulation, highly reactive in their overall temperament approach, do not manifest a high order of energy and activity;
- *Agitators:* low reactive, with fluctuating energy level, high need for great stimulation, together with low endurance.

Studies by Barclay (1992) showed that in junior high school (male and female) students' temperament is responsible for as much as 20% of the total variance of the predicted standardized achievement scores. The author (Barclay, 1991) emphasized that temperament is an essential variable for school adaptation in the social as well as in the intellectual (achievement) domain.

Temperament as a Moderator of Stress Phenomena

In several temperament theories the assumption that temperament plays an important role in moderating stress is one of the most important postulates. For example, Kagan (1983) considered the two types of temperament distinguished by him—inhibited and uninhibited temperaments—as representing different vulnerabilities to stress in situations of unexpected or unpredictable events. In his initial research on sensation seeking, Zuckerman (1964) came to the conclusion that some individuals are resistant to sensory deprivation, whereas others react under such conditions in a way that suggests that perceptual isolation for them is stressful. His definition of sensation seeking underlines the willingness to take physical and social risks as an attribute of sensation seekers (Zuckerman, 1979, 1994). According to Nebylitsyn (1972a) and Strelau (1983) the functional significance of temperament is evident when individuals are confronted with extreme situations or demands.

In arousal-oriented theories of temperament, which refer to the concepts of optimal level of arousal or stimulation, temperament characteristics are regarded as moderators in experiencing stress at extreme levels of stimulation, as exemplified in the domain of extraversion (H. J. Eysenck, 1970; H. J. Eysenck & Eysenck, 1985), stimulus screening (Mehrabian, 1977b), reactivity (Strelau, 1983, 1988), or sensation seeking (Zuckerman, 1994).

The question arises as to why temperament traits should be regarded as important variables moderating stress phenomena. Temperament traits are *moderators,* by which I mean, after Folkman and Lazarus (1988), that they constitute antecedent conditions that influence other conditions. The individual has a given temperament since birth and it is present before stressors and states of stress occur. If so, one may expect that temperament traits modify all kinds of stress phenomena (Strelau, 1995c).

Temperament traits, as general, formal characteristics, penetrate all kinds of behavior, whatever the content or direction of this behavior. In so doing they contribute to a variety of stress phenomena. Connected mainly with energetic and temporal characteristics of behavior, they act as moderators in all stress phenomena that are characterized by energy and time.

Many temperament characteristics are directly related to emotions. They tend to generate emotional processes as exemplified by emotionality (Strelau, 1987b).

As commonly accepted (see, e.g., Lazarus, 1991, 1993), emotions are one of the core constructs in the state of stress.

There is no agreement on an understanding of stress and related phenomena; therefore, before considering the temperament–stress relationship some explanations are needed regarding the different conceptualizations in the domain of stress as understood in this chapter.

The Understanding of Stress Phenomena

Studies on temperament as related to stress take into account different aspects of stress, such as (1) the impact of temperament in determining the intensity of stressors, (2) the role of temperament as a codeterminant of stress, (3) the moderating effect of temperament in coping with stress, and (4) the contribution of temperament traits to the psychophysiological–psychological costs of stress.

Stressors and Psychological Stress

Psychological stress is understood here as a state characterized by strong negative emotions, such as fear, anxiety, anger, hostility, or other emotional states evoking distress, accompanied by physiological and biochemical changes that exceed the baseline level of arousal. Neuroendocrine changes are inherent attributes of emotions and they cannot be ignored as components of psychological stress. This statement is based on strong empirical evidence of which the most representative are the findings of Frankenhaeuser (1979, 1986; see also Magnusson, Klinteberg, & Stattin, 1991) in respect to adrenal-medullary and adrenal-cortical changes as a reaction to stressors. Such an understanding of stress, which underlines the importance of emotions and arousal as inseparable components of stress, with expressed modifications regarding the concept of arousal and the nature of emotions, is encountered among many researchers in the domain of stress.

Most researchers on stress differ, however, with regard to the causes of stress. In my own view (Strelau, 1988, 1995c), the stress is caused by the lack of equilibrium (occurrence of discrepancy) between demands and the individual's capability (capacity) to cope with them. This conceptualization of stress can also be found elsewhere (see Krohne & Laux, 1982; McGrath, 1970; Schulz & Schönpflug, 1982). The magnitude of stress is a function of the degree of discrepancy between the demands and capacities, assuming the individual is motivated to cope with the demands with which he or she is confronted.

The demands are regarded as *stressors* or *stress-inducing situations.* The following factors may be considered as demands: unpredictable and uncontrollable life events, hassles, significant life changes, situations of extreme high or extreme low stimulative value, and internalized values and standards of behavior. Demands exist in two forms: objective and subjective; the latter is a result of individual-specific appraisal. Appraisal of threat, harm, and challenge, whether conscious or unconscious, which is the cause of stress according to Lazarus (1966, 1991), is subject to study only in man.

Demands that exist objectively act as such independently of the individual's perception. This refers to traumatic or extreme life changes, such as death, bereavement, disaster, and war. As shown by Holmes and Rahe (1967), there is a very high degree of consensus between groups and among individuals about the significance of life events. The fact that there are high correlations (about .9) across age, sex, marital status, and education in the intensity and time necessary to accommodate to specific life events speaks in favor of the existence of objective, universal stressors (see Aldwin, Levenson, Spiro, & Bosse, 1989; Freedy, Kilpatrick, & Resnick, 1993; Pellegrini, 1990).

The individual's capability to cope with demands depends on the following characteristics: intelligence, special abilities, skills, knowledge, personality and temperament traits, features of the physical makeup, experience with stress-inducing situations, coping strategies, and the actual (physical and psychic) state of the individual.

Depending on the specificity of the demands, different individual characteristics influence an individual's capability. Capabilities, too, may occur in two forms. They exist objectively, and as such they may be subject to measurement. But they may also be subjectively experienced, this being the result of individual-specific appraisal. The *state of stress* is the outcome of interaction between real or perceived demands and the individual's response capability as it really exists or is perceived by the given individual.

Also, if we define stress in terms of resources, a view that has recently gained popularity (see Hobfoll, 1988, 1991; Schönpflug, 1983, 1986; Schönpflug & Battmann, 1988), the effect of potential or actual loss of valued resources, regarded here as causes of stress, can be understood only if we take account of the interaction between invested and gained resources. "*Resources* are defined as those objects, personal characteristics, conditions, or energies that are valued by the individual or that serve as a means for attainment of these objects, personal characteristics, conditions, or energies" (Hobfoll, 1989). Important in conceptualizations defining stress in terms of resources is the fact that not only perceived, but also *actual* (objectively), loss or lack of gain is regarded as a source of stress. This is especially evident in the theory of conservation of resources developed by Hobfoll (1989).

Coping with Stress

The state of stress is inseparable from coping. *Coping* with stress is understood in this chapter as a regulatory function that consists of maintaining an adequate balance between demands and capacities, or of reducing the discrepancy between demands and capacities (Strelau, 1996b). Efficient coping, which results in a match or goodness of fit between demands and capacities, reduces the state of stress whereas inefficient coping leads to an increase in the state of stress (see Vitaliano, DeWolfe, Maiuro, Russo, & Katon, 1990). As emphasized by Lazarus (1993; Lazarus & Folkman, 1984) as concerns subjectively experienced stressors, coping is a process that consists of managing specific demands appraised as overwhelming or taxing. "Coping is highly *contextual*, since to be effective it must change over time and across different stressful conditions" (Lazarus, 1993, p. 8).

Coping that leads to resolving the state of stress may also be considered from the angle of a resource management process in terms of gains and loss (Schönpflug & Battmann, 1988). The benefits of coping consist of gains in, or savings of, resources, whereas the costs of coping incorporate allocation, loss, and consumption of resources. The individual copes with stress by means of replacement, substitution, or investment of resources (Hobfoll, 1989). The intensity, extent, and persistence with which coping attempts are applied refer to effort expenditure, a construct broadly discussed by Schönpflug (1986) with account taken of the individual differences approach.

Consequences of Stress

A low discrepancy between demands and capacities, assuming it is not a chronic state, may result in positive changes as measured by efficiency of performance or developmental shifts. According to Chess and Thomas (1986), absence of stress may constitute a poorness of fit. "New demands and stresses, when consonant with developmental potentials, are constructive in their consequences" (p. 158; see also Chess & Thomas, 1989, 1991). As the authors point out, it is excessive stress resulting from a demand the individual is unable to cope with that leads to maladaptive functioning. Maladaptive functioning and behavior disorders, including pathology resulting from excessive or chronic stress are regarded in this chapter as *consequences* or *costs* of stress. *Excessive stress* consists of extremely strong negative affects accompanied by unusually high elevation of the level of arousal. *Chronic stress* is regarded as a state of stress not necessarily excessive but experienced permanently or frequently. As a consequence of both excessive and chronic stress, changes in the organism occur that may result in psychological malfunctioning, such as an increased level of anxiety and depression, or in physiological or biochemical disturbances expressed in psychosomatic diseases or other health problems.

Not all excessive or chronic states of stress lead to the negative consequences just described. Stress should be regarded as one of the many risk factors (external and internal) contributing to maladaptive functioning and disorders. When the state of stress interacts with other factors that decrease or dampen the consequences of stress, maladjustment or behavioral disturbances may not occur.

Temperament and Stress: Hypothesized Relationships and Empirical Findings

I concentrate on the relationship between temperament and stress, referring to such aspects of the latter as stressors, the state of stress, coping with stress, and consequences of stress.

The Impact of Temperament in the Regulation of the Demand–Capability Interaction

Temperament may contribute significantly to determining the state of stress from at least the following three perspectives: (1) intensity characteristics (stimulative value) of demands, (2) optimal level of arousal as a standard for normal functioning, and (3) emotion-oriented temperament traits as expressed in tendencies to elicit emotions, especially negative ones.

Temperamental Traits as Moderators of the Intensity Characteristics of the Demand–Capability Relationship. As postulated by Selye (1975) "deprivation of stimuli and excessive stimulation are both accompanied by an increase in stress, sometimes to the point of distress" (p. 21). Lundberg (1982), McGrath (1970), Strelau (1988), and Weick (1970) also considered intensity of demands as stressors.

All life events that can be interpreted in terms of intensity of stimulation and, as a consequence, in terms of arousal effects, as assumed by Rahe (1987), may be regarded as factors subject to moderation by temperament traits. Which of the specific temperament characteristics plays the role of moderator, by elevating or reducing the stimulative value of life events, depends on the kind of event.

Ursin (1980) pointed out that, under a high level of arousal, the tolerability for life events of high intensity is lowered. This is caused by the process of augmentation of acting stimuli. Under a low level of arousal there is a decrease in tolerability for life events of low stimulative value (e.g., deprivation, isolation), this resulting from suppression processes in relation to acting stimuli.

In several publications (Strelau, 1983, 1988, 1994a) I have developed the idea that arousal-oriented temperament dimensions are based on the assumption that there are stable individual differences in the level of arousal. According to Gray (1964c), the chronic level of arousal in which individuals differ is described by the term *arousability*. There are at least a dozen temperament traits for which the construct of arousal has been used when referring to their biological background (Strelau, 1994a).

Without going into the specificity of the different arousal-oriented temperament traits, one may predict that temperament traits that refer to low arousability, for example extraversion, high sensation seeking, or strong type of nervous sys-

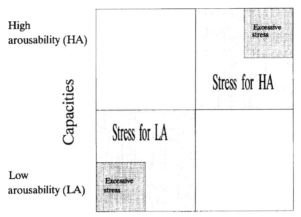

FIGURE 7.2. Arousability and the state of stress. *Note.* From "Temperament and Stress: Temperament as a Moderator of Stressors, Emotional States, Coping, and Costs," by J. Strelau. In C. D. Spielberger and I. G. Sarason (Eds.), *Stress and Emotion: Anxiety, Anger, and Curiosity* (1995, Vol. 15, p. 225), Washington, DC: Hemisphere. Copyright 1995 by Taylor & Francis. Reprinted with permission.

tem, when in interaction with life events characterized as demands of low stimulative value, such as deprivation or isolation, act as moderators that increase the state of stress, leading in extreme cases to excessive stress. In contrast, temperament traits characterized by high arousability, such as introversion, low sensation seeking, or weak type of nervous system, interacting with life events characterized as demands of high stimulation value, for example, death, disaster, or traumatic stressors, act as moderators to increase the state of stress, again leading in extreme cases to excessive stress as illustrated in Figure 7.2.

As can be seen from Figure 7.2 the same temperament trait, depending on the kind of environment (demand), may or may not operate as a moderator of stress. Furthermore, opposite poles of the same trait may be considered as moderators of stress, depending on the specificity of the demands with which they interact. For example, highly reactive individuals or introverts (both characterized by high arousability), when confronted with high stimulation, experience a state of stress not present under such conditions in extraverts or low reactive individuals. In turn, for individuals characterized by low arousability (e.g., extraverts or low reactives), low stimulation (e.g., deprivation, isolation) leads to a state of stress.

A good example is neuroticism, one of the most representative temperament traits based on the construct of activation. H. J. Eysenck (1983b) postulated "that *ceteris paribus* high N individuals live a more stressful life, not in the sense that they necessarily encounter more stressful stimuli (although that may be so) but because identical stressful stimuli produce a greater amount of strain in them" (p. 126). Strain, according to Eysenck, corresponds to the state of stress. Figure 7.3, taken from H. J. Eysenck (1983b) in a modified form, illustrates the relation-

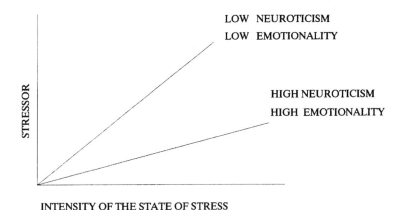

LOW NEUROTICISM
LOW EMOTIONALITY

HIGH NEUROTICISM
HIGH EMOTIONALITY

STRESSOR

INTENSITY OF THE STATE OF STRESS

FIGURE 7.3. The relationship between intensity of stressors and the state of stress moderated by temperamental traits. *Note.* From "Stress, Disease, and Personality: The 'Inoculation Effect,'" by H. J. Eysenck. In C. L. Cooper (Ed.), *Stress Research* (1983, p. 122), London: Wiley. Copyright 1983 by John Wiley & Sons Ltd. Adapted with permission.

ships between the intensity of stressors and state of stress as moderated by temperament traits, such as neuroticism or emotionality.

Figure 7.3 shows that a life event that develops a state of stress of low intensity may be moderated by emotionality or other temperament traits in such a way as to increase the state of stress and vice versa. The same state of stress, in terms of intensity, may result from low-intensity life events interacting with high emotionality and from high-intensity life events interacting with low emotionality.

The Deviation from Optimal Level of Arousal, Moderated by Temperament, as a Source of Stress. As shown more than a century ago by Wundt (1887), the sign of emotion depends on the strength of sensory stimuli and this relationship has an inverted U-shape (see also Schneirla, 1959). The fact that intensity of stimuli is a source of positive or negative hedonic tones has been applied to the concept of optimal level of arousal (Berlyne, 1960), where the hedonic tone plays the role of the affective–motivational process regulating the need for stimulation. Low level of arousal, the result of weak stimulation, as well as very high level of arousal, the result of stimulation of high intensity, are regarded as sources of a negative hedonic tone, the increase of which results in the state of stress. An intermediate level of arousal, evoked by stimuli of average intensity, is a source of positive hedonic tone. Life events, objectively of the same intensity, may be a source of a positive or negative hedonic tone, hence, nonstressing or stressing, depending on the position an individual holds on a given temperament dimension. This relationship can be attributed without much simplification to such dimensions as extraversion (H. J.

Eysenck, 1970; H. J. Eysenck & Eysenck, 1985), sensation seeking (Zuckerman, 1979, 1994), and reactivity (Strelau, 1983, 1988). It can be generalized that, under high-intensity stressors, individuals characterized by high arousability experience a negative hedonic tone (state of stress). On the other hand, in response to the same stressors, low-arousability individuals may not experience distress; in fact, they may even experience a positive hedonic tone, as exemplified by sensation seekers.

Temperament Determined Tendency to Express Negative Emotions in Stress-Inducing Situations. Temperament traits moderate the state of stress not only by regulating the intensity (arousal) component of stress or by sharing in the regulation of optimal level of arousal regarded as a source of hedonic tone. Certain temperament dimensions, such as neuroticism, emotionality, and emotional reactivity, defined independently of their specificity in terms of a tendency (disposition) to generate given emotions, operate as moderators of the state of stress. They do this by increasing or decreasing the emotional response to stressors, depending on the position an individual occupies on the emotion-oriented temperament dimension (see Strelau, 1987b). This is especially evident in relation to temperament traits that refer to negative emotions. As vividly expressed by Buss and Plomin (1984), "Emotionality equals distress, the tendency to become upset easily and intensely" (p. 54).

From another point of view it could be said that a given neurophysiological basis predisposes the individual to experience more negative emotions than others. For example, Gray (1994) argued that a high level of reactivity in the BIS predisposes the individual to experience anxiety even when stressors are absent. As a consequence of chronically high reactive BIS, individuals are more prone to develop personality disorders under traumatic life events than are individuals with low-reactive BIS.

Selected Evidence Illustrating the Moderating Effect
of Temperament on the State of Stress

The possible interactions between demands and capacities in which temperament plays a moderating role in determining the state of stress are exemplified in some selected studies.

Aldwin and coworkers (1989), in a study conducted on more than 1,000 men aged 40 to 88 showed that emotionality, as measured by means of items from the Neuroticism scale of Eysenck's EPI, contributed to the number of stress events reported. High-emotional individuals (neurotics) reported both more life events and more hassles than did low-emotional (emotionally stable) individuals. Bolger and Schilling (in press) studied 166 married couples who, for a period of 6 weeks, judged their experience of distress to daily stressors by diary method. Neuroticism was found to be strongly related to distress experienced to daily stressors. In interpreting their data, the authors suggested that the results support Watson and Clark's (1984) conclusion that neuroticism is to be regarded as a tendency to experience distress even in the absence of stressors, due to a disposition to experience negative emotional states. However, McLennan and Bates (1993), comparing individual characteristics of two groups of subjects, those who experienced psychological distress and those who did not, stated that, while neuroticism was a discriminator between the two groups, negative affect as measured on the Positive and Negative Affect Scale (Watson, Clark, & Tellegen, 1988) was not. They hypothesized that neuroticism, as a factor influencing vulnerability to psychological distress, taps additional factors over those tapped by negative affect.

Kohn, Lafreniere, and Gurevich (1991) demonstrated that trait anxiety and hassles contribute to perceived stress, accounting for over 50% of the variance in stress reactions. Anxiety in this study was measured in more than 200 undergraduate students by means of Spielberger's STAI (Spielberger, Gorsuch, & Lushene, 1970).

As already mentioned, sensation seeking is a trait the definition of which incorporates risky behavior as a need of high sensation seekers (Zuckerman, 1979). In other words, one could say that sensation seekers function in such a way as to raise the stimulative value of the situation or behavior in order to increase the level of arousal which assures optimal functioning. Interpreting this statement in terms of stress, it may be said that situations and behaviors that, for low sensation seekers (risk avoiders), are already stressors, are not so for high sensation seekers. Empirical findings support the sensation seeking–risk relationship (for a review see Zuckerman, 1994). For example, Horvath and Zuckerman (1993), in a study carried out on almost 500 undergraduate students, showed that sensation seeking, as measured on the SSS–Form V, is a good predictor of risky behaviors as assessed by the General Risk Appraisal Scale (GRAS), which permits separate measurements of risk appraisal and risky activities.

Duckitt and Broll (1982) demonstrated in a study conducted on 139 students that, among the six factors derived from Cattell's 16 PF, it was extraversion that moderated the impact of recent life changes on psychological strain (state of stress) as measured by the Langner Inventory.

If we treat the state of stress as a deviation from the optimal level of arousal (accompanied by negative emotions) and a decrease in performance as an indicator of this state, then dozens of studies could be cited to show that temperament characteristics, in particular extraversion and neuroticism (H. J. Eysenck, 1970; H. J. Eysenck & Eysenck, 1985; Goh & Farley, 1977), strength of the nervous system, or (using my term) reactivity (Klonowicz, 1987a, 1987b, 1992; Strelau, 1983, 1988; Zawadzki, 1991), play an important role as moderators of performance.

To give one example, Żmudzki (1986; see also Strelau, 1988), showed that, during starts in national and international competitions, efficiency of performance of weight lifters representing the Polish national team differed depending on the level of reactivity. These competitions were regarded as highly stressful demands. Reactivity was measured by means of the Strelau Temperament Inventory (Strelau, 1983). Taking the quartile devation as a criterion for separating subjects differing in the level of reactivity, the author distinguished among 75 weight lifters, 19 low-reactive (LR) and 18 high-reactive (HR) individuals. The efficiency of performance during 10 national and international competitions was estimated on a 7-point scale. As can be seen in Figure 7.4, efficiency of performance in the stressful situation was significantly higher in LR individuals than for HR weight lifters. This study is of particular interest because it provides aggregated data collected in natural settings. Performance efficiency was measured in real competitions and the results expressed in Figure 7.4 as a single number are outcomes of studies conducted in 10 situations, all of the same kind and characterized as highly demanding.

In all probability, temperament dimensions that not only differ in terms of arousal components and emotion-oriented tendencies, but that represent a whole spectrum of qualitatively different behavior characteristics, play a different role in regulating the demand–capability balance, depending on the kind of stress taken into account. Presumably the moderatory role of temperament could be specific, depending on whether we take into account stress at work, community stress, natural or technical disasters, acculturative stress, or stress resulting from everyday life events.

In studies on stress, the main research focus has been not on the state of stress itself but on coping with stress and on the consequences of this state.

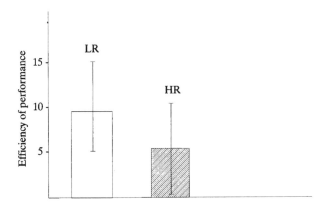

FIGURE 7.4. Efficiency of performance under highly stressful competition in high- (HR) and low-reactive (LR) weight lifters expressed in average scores and in standard deviations. *Note.* From "Temperamental Dimensions as Co-determinants of Resistance to Stress," by J. Strelau. In M. P. Janisse (Ed.), *Individual Differences, Stress, and Health Psychology* (1988, p. 158), New York: Springer. Copyright 1988 by Springer Verlag. Reprinted with permission.

The Role of Temperament in Coping with Stress

Despite numerous studies addressed to coping since Lazarus (1966) published his fundamental monograph *Psychological Stress and the Coping Process,* little attention has been paid to the role of personality, in particular to its specific component, temperament, as a moderator of coping.

To show the role temperament plays in coping with stress I concentrate on two different approaches to coping: (1) Lazarus's (1991; Folkman & Lazarus, 1988) view, according to which coping is a process that shapes emotions, and (2) the resource-oriented approach, which treats coping in terms of resource management processes (Hobfoll, 1989; Schönpflug 1986; Schönpflug & Battmann, 1988).

Temperament and Coping as a Process That Shapes Emotions. The individual differences approach incorporated in Lazarus's coping theory was expressed mainly in the assumption that the process of appraisal is individual-specific and that there are situation-specific (contextual) coping processes, apart from individual differences in coping styles (Folkman & Lazarus, 1988; Lazarus, 1993).

If we treat coping as a process that shapes emotions (Lazarus, 1991), temperament characteristics may be considered as moderators taking part in the regulation of emotional processes. Looking at temperament in terms of a tendency to experience negative emotions, it may be assumed that such temperament traits as neuroticism, emotionality, or emotional reactivity cannot be neutral in the ongoing effort to manage specific demands appraised as taxing or overwhelming (Lazarus, 1993, p. 8). Kagan (1983), for instance, has shown the role played by inhibited temperament in children in moderating coping as a reaction to negative emotions.

As Folkman and Lazarus (1985) suggest, some strategies of coping, distinguished between the two basic coping styles (action- and emotion-oriented), depend on personality, and here the authors refer to the tendency to experience positive or negative mood. But, if we consider coping also in terms of styles the individual applies in order to change the unfavorable person–environment relationship (Folkman & Lazarus, 1985, 1988), it can be hypothesized that whether problem-focused coping or emotion-focused coping develops depends to some extent on the moderating role of temperament characteristics. One may assume that action-oriented traits, such as extraversion, sensation seeking, strength of the nervous system, or activity should facilitate the problem-focused coping style. This style consists of making attempts to change the unfavorable person–environment relationship through coping actions. In contrast, the emotion-oriented temperament traits, for example, withdrawal tendency, inhibited temperament, neuroticism, emotionality, or emotional reactivity, contribute to the development of the emotion-focused coping style.

A study that gives some support for the two hypotheses just presented was conducted by Parkes (1986). This author studied coping in stressful episodes experienced by 135 female first-year student nurses, using an interactional para-digm. Parkes took into account such variables as environmental factors, situational characteristics, temperament traits, and coping styles. She found that extraversion and neuroticism, together with environmental and situational factors, predicted coping styles. Whereas direct coping was rather typical for extraversion, suppres-sion occurred with neuroticism. These relationships were further modified by the environment and situation.

Additional studies, not necessarily following the Lazarus paradigm, support the hypothesis relating action-oriented coping styles to action-oriented tempera-ment traits. Similarly, emotion-centered temperament characteristics appear to be related to emotion-centered coping styles.

Bolger (1990), who defined coping as personality in action under stress, has shown in a study on medical college students that neuroticism influences the cop-ing strategies people select, and increases daily anxiety under examination stress. Baum, Calesnick, Davis, and Gatchel (1982) took a temperament characteristic, in this case screening as measured by Mehrabian's Stimulus Screening scale, as part of a coping style. In their study, embracing more than 200 residents of long- and short-corridor dormitories, coping referred to students' responses to high-density dormitory settings. Residents who displayed the stimulus-screening coping style were more successful in adapting to the crowded environment. According to Mehrabian (1977b), screeners are able to screen out irrelevant stimuli. In so doing they reduce the random character of the stimuli; this, in turn, leads to a lower level of arousal and more rapid decrease of arousal in comparison with nonscreeners.

In a study that controlled, apart from personality variables, the Pavlovian tem-perament traits, Vingerhoets, Van den Berg, Kortekaas, Van Heck, and Croon (1993) demonstrated that weeping in women, considered as emotion-focused cop-ing, was negatively related to strength of excitation and strength of inhibition. Women occupying a high position on the weeping dimension were characterized by both weak excitation and weak inhibition of the nervous system. The Pavlov-ian properties were measured by using the Pavlovian Temperament Survey. In our laboratory (Strelau, 1996b) we found that task-oriented coping style correlates with action-oriented temperament characteristics (e.g., briskness), whereas emo-tion-oriented coping style was related to emotion-centered temperament charac-teristics (e.g., emotional reactivity). Coping style was measured by means of the CISS (Endler & Parker, 1990) and the FCB-TI (Strelau & Zawadzki, 1993) was used to assess temperament traits.

The Place of Temperament in the Resource-Oriented Approach to Coping. The view of coping as a resource management process proposes replacing coping as a regulator that shapes emotions with coping treated as replacement, substitu-tion, and investment of resources (Hobfoll, 1989; Schönpflug & Battmann, 1988; Szczepaniak, Strelau, & Wrzeźniewski, 1996). The degree to which an individual is engaged in coping with stress can be characterized by the extent, intensity, and persistence with which resources are allocated and consumed. This approach, which offers a different view on coping, also enables us to look at temperament as a moderator of coping from a different perspective.

In his effort regulation theory, Schönpflug (1986) stressed how temperament traits, as understood by Strelau (1983), may contribute to effort expenditure. This is a core concept in Schönpflug's regulation theory which he considered as a quantitative dimension of coping involvement. Effort expenditure comprises the three formal characteristics of allocation and consumption of resources—intensity, extent, and persistence. Schönpflug gave salience to the place of temperament in effort regulation in the following two contexts:

(1) *Temperament traits as codeterminants of the amount of effort allocated in task performance.* Here effort is expressed in terms of subjective ratings, behavioral involvement, and level of arousal or biochemical changes. For example, highly anxious individuals invest more effort as compared with low-anxiety persons to attain a comparable level of performance in highly demanding conditions.

(2) *Temperament as a regulator of the stimulative value of the conditions or activity under which coping occurs moderates the conservation of resources.* To exemplify this statement Schönpflug refers to the concept of *style of action* which was developed by Strelau (1983) on the basis of Tomaszewski's (1978) distinction between basic and auxiliary actions. Auxiliary actions, by means of preventive acts and checking operations, constitute supplementary portions of behavior and consume extra resources but "under conditions of high risk and possibility of failures, the involvement in auxiliary activities may help in maintaining a high level of productivity and thus conserve resources" (Schönpflug, 1986, p. 277).

The idea of considering style of action as strategies to cope with stress has been developed by Strelau (1988). Style of action, understood as the typical manner in which an action is performed by the individual, develops under environmental influences on the basis of the temperament endowment, especially reactivity. According to the regulative theory of temperament (Strelau, 1983), style of action is considered one of the regulators of stimulation need. If we divide auxiliary actions into orienting, preparatory, corrective, controlling, and protective activities, as proposed by Tomaszewski (1978), it becomes clear that auxiliary actions lower the risk of failure in task performance under stressors. Using Hobfoll's (1989) and Schönpflug's (1986) terminology, it follows that auxiliary actions contribute to the conservation of resources. Activities that lead directly to the attainment of a certain goal should be regarded as basic. "Considering the relation between auxiliary and basic actions from the point of view of intensity of stimulation means that auxiliary actions, by safeguarding, facilitating, or simplifying the basic ones, lower the stimulative value of activity or the situation in which the activity is performed" (Strelau, 1988, p. 157). Strelau (1983) hypothesized that in high-reactive individuals, characterized by a high level of arousability, auxiliary actions (AA) will dominate over basic ones (BA). I have labeled this style of action the *adjunctive style*. In low-reactive individuals, for whom a low level of arousability is typical, there will be more of a balance between the two types of actions, or a predominance of basic over auxiliary actions. This I have called the *straightforward style* of action. The relationship between reactivity and style of action may be expressed as follows:

> High reactives: adjunctive style (BA $<$ AA)
> Low reactives: straightforward style (BA $\geqslant$ AA)

Thus, coping strategies defined in terms of style of action, and strongly related to temperament, may be considered moderators of resource conservation aimed at avoiding or reducing the state of stress.

Selected Data Illustrating the Role of Temperament in Coping Viewed as a Resource Management Process

In my laboratory a series of experiments were designed to examine the importance of temperament in human functioning under stress. Most of these experiments deal with effort when coping with demands, as measured by psychological and psychophysiological changes, and with style of action as a coping strategy (see Strelau, 1983, 1988).

Effort Expenditure and Temperament. Several studies relating to effort expenditure during coping with demands of different kinds have been carried out by Klonowicz (1974, 1985, 1987a, 1987b). In her experiments, reactivity and mobility, as proposed by the regulative theory of temperament (Strelau, 1983), and measured by means of the Strelau Temperament Inventory, were considered to be moderators of effort expenditure. The psychological indicators of effort expenditure, depending on the specific experiment, were expressed in changes in level of anxiety and fatigue, the latter measured by the number of mistakes during performance, or by reaction time. The psychophysiological indicators comprised electrodermal activity (EDA) changes and self-reported level of activation as measured by means of Thayer's Activation–Deactivation Adjective Check List.

The most general finding from Klonowicz's data suggests that high-reactive individuals, as compared with low-reactive individuals, when coping with demands characterized by stressors of high stimulative value (difficult task, stimuli of high intensity), allocate more effort in terms of psychological and psychophysiological changes. In situations of lower stimulative value there is no evident difference between high- and low-reactive individuals. When the demand–capability balance is threatened because of very low stimulative value of demands, effort expenditure may be higher in low-reactive individuals. In most of Klonowicz's experiments an interactional effect was obtained, which illustrated the contribution of mobility operating as an enhancer of reactivity effects.

In one of her most recent experiments, Klonowicz (1990, 1992) studied effort expenditure as measured by heart rate (HR) changes during coping under different degrees of task difficulty in highly skilled simultaneous interpreters. The tasks consisted of listening, listening combined with simultaneous speech reproduction, and listening with simultaneous translation and speech production, the first task being the easiest one and the last the most difficult. Individual characteristics comprised reactivity as measured by Strelau's STI, and anxiety, anger, and curiosity traits assessed by means of Spielberger's STPI. Limiting the presentation to individual characteristics, the data "indicate that reactivity temperament, trait-anxiety, and trait-curiosity influence cardiac activity during the anticipatory periods, task periods, and after-task recovery" (Klonowicz, 1990, p. 46). However, this finding holds true only for the more difficult tasks—shadowing and interpreting. The changes in resource demands monitored by HR were positively correlated with reactivity, thus showing the moderating effect of this temperament trait on coping.

Temperament-Related Style of Action as a Coping Strategy. The role of temperament-determined style of action in coping with stress was shown in several studies in which reactivity (in Pavlovian terminology the reverse of strength of excitation) was the temperament variable (Strelau, 1983, 1988). Reactivity has never been viewed, however, from the perspective of effort regulation as proposed by Schönpflug (1986). Using constructs belonging to this approach one may say that high-reactive individuals, by means of the auxiliary style, perform more actions as compared with low-reactive subjects, thus they allocate more resources in order to cope with stress. On the other hand, by allocating more resources in auxiliary actions, they avoid failures and maintain an adequate level of efficiency in task performance under highly stimulative situations. This, in turn, may be considered to be a gain of resources. Hence, temperament-determined style of action, when viewed from the perspective of resource management, can be characterized in terms of gains and loss, where the benefits of auxiliary actions, which are dominant in high-reactive individuals, extend their costs when coping with stress.

In almost all our studies, independent of the population (e.g., children, adolescents, adults) and type of task under investigation (e.g., mental load, motor performance), the results showed that, under demands of high stimulative value for high-reactive individuals, the dominance of the adjunctive style assures efficient functioning. For low-reactive individuals, by contrast, the prevalence of the straightforward style results in better functioning under stress (Strelau, 1983).

An investigation that illustrates the role of auxiliary actions in high- and low-reactive individuals coping with stress under long-lasting and demanding mental load was also carried out in Schönpflug's laboratory. Mündelein (1982) arranged seminatural experimental settings in which adult subjects were instructed to work for a period of 3 hr as an insurance agent operating with a computer system. The task was to calculate the amount of compensation for clients suffering loss. During this demanding work performance, signals of possible computer overloadings and disturbances were monitored. In order to avoid them, subjects were allowed to press special buttons, which in fact did not influence the computer system and were purely auxiliary actions. The function of pressing them was to protect the basic actions (collecting and processing information and decision making) against possible disturbances. Results obtained in this study showed that, in relation to the number and time of pressing protection buttons, high-reactive subjects obtained significantly higher scores than did low-reactive subjects. Reactivity was measured by two procedures—Strelau's STI and the slope of reaction time (for description, see Strelau, 1983).

Temperament as a Moderator of Stress Consequences: The Temperament Risk Factor

As mentioned, it is excessive or chronic stress that leads to behavior disorders, maladaptive functioning, and pathology regarded here as consequences (costs) of stress. A. Thomas and Chess (1977; Chess & Thomas, 1984, 1986; A. Thomas et al., 1968) are the pioneers who showed that behavior disorders in children cannot be explained only by unfavorable environmental factors (stressors), and that an essential part of the variance in behavior disorders concerns a given configuration of temperament traits that they called difficult temperament.

The Construct Temperament Risk Factor

To underline the fact that disturbances of behavior and pathology in children occur only when temperament characteristics predisposing a child to poor fit interact with an unfavorable environment, W. B. Carey (1986, 1989), introduced the concept of temperament risk factor. However, he limited this concept to excessive interactional stress experienced by children. To give the temperament risk factor a more universal meaning, extending this concept to the entire human population, its definition was modified (Strelau 1989a; 1995b; Strelau & Eliasz, 1994). By *temperament risk factor* (TRF) I mean any temperament trait, or configuration of traits, that in interaction with other factors acting excessively, persistently, or recurrently (e.g., physical and social environment, educational treatment, situations, the individual's characteristics) increases the risk of developing behavior disorders or pathology, or that favors the shaping of a maladjusted personality.

Assessing temperament traits as risky or not risky is meaningful only under conditions in which given temperament traits, or configurations of traits, are considered within the context of other variables with which they interact. This means that a particular configuration of temperament traits considered as a TRF in one situation or for a given environment may not be a TRF in other situations or for other environments. Using the concepts of absolute and relative risk behaviors as understood by Jeffery (1989), one might say that TRF belongs to the category of relative risk. TRF can be assessed as the probability of behavior disorders as consequences of exposure to stressors in individuals with given temperament traits, compared to the risk of behavior disorders in response to the same stressors in individuals without these temperament traits.

In studying the contribution of temperament to unfavorable consequences of the state of stress it is important to consider the existence of many risk factors contributing to behavior disorders and psychopathology. The epidemiological aspects of these disorders and pathology, account taken of temperament as one of many risk factors, have been broadly discussed from a theoretical and methodological perspective by W. B. Carey and McDevitt (1989, 1994), Chess and Thomas (1984), Garrison and Earls (1987), Maziade (1988), Pellegrini (1990), and Rutter (1991). Kyrios and Prior (1990; see also J. Smith & Prior, 1995) postulated a theoretical model for the development of early childhood behavior disturbances, in which, among other risk factors, the role of temperament in codetermining behavior disorders has been placed in evidence.

Joint Temperament and Environment Effect on Vulnerability to Behavior Disorders. Maziade (1988) postulated that children with an adverse temperament, the equivalent to difficult temperament, when in interaction with adverse environmental factors, present special vulnerability (liability) to clinical disorders. Developing an additive and synergistic model of adverse temperament–adverse environment interaction, Maziade referred to Kendler and Eaves's (1986) models for the joint effect of genotype and environment on liability to psychiatric illness. The authors proposed that the etiology of psychiatric disorders lies in the interactional effect of genes and environment. The joint effect of genes and environment on liability to psychiatric disorders may comprise three basic models: (1) additive effects of genotype and environment, (2) genetic control of sensitivity to the environment, and (3) genetic control of exposure to the environment.

Taking the three basic models introduced by Kendler and Eaves (1986), and Maziade (1988) as a starting point, I have adapted these models to the construct of temperament risk factor. Instead of limiting the consequences of stress to liability to illness, they have been extended to behavior disorders that can be met in a normal population exposed to stress-inducing environments. Genotype has been replaced in the models by temperament. As postulated by many temperament researchers (see Buss & Plomin, 1984; H. J. Eysenck, 1970; Strelau, 1994a; Zuckerman, 1991c), the genetic endowment plays an essential role in determining the variance of temperament traits. Furthermore, Kendler and Eaves (1986), in exemplifying the contribution of genes to psychiatric disorder liability, referred to such traits as impassivity and emotional instability as being influenced by genes, thus contributing, in interaction with a predisposing environment, to illness.

Without specifying the temperament traits or combination of traits that constitute the TRF, which traits can be different for different environments, a distinction should be made between the presence and absence of temperament risk factors. *TRF present* means that, given the presence of temperament traits or configuration of traits, vulnerability to behavior disorders will be evidenced. *TRF absent* implies that temperament traits or configurations of traits are different from those typical for TRF present, and do not constitute a risk factor for behavior disorders.

As concerns environment, the distinction has been made (according to Kendler and Eaves, 1986) between protective and predisposing environments. *Protective environment* refers, in this context, to a lack of excessive or chronic stressors; this diminishes the probability of behavior disorders and pathology. In contrast, *predisposing environment,* which may be characterized in terms of chronic or excessive stress-inducing environments, increases the probability of behavior disorders and pathology. Further, when using the term *behavior disorders,* pathology is also meant as a possible cost of stress, although this would imply an extreme consequence of poorness of fit between temperament and environmental demands.

Models of Temperament–Environment Interactions Producing the Risk of Behavior Disorders. In line with Kendler and Eaves's (1986) considerations, five models for joint temperament and environment effect on vulnerability to behavior disorders or pathology are presented in the following paragraphs, for the purpose of indicating the different ways in which temperament and environment may interact with each other to produce the risk of behavior disorders.

(1) *Behavior disorders as a summary effect of two independent factors—temperamental and environmental.* This model, depicted in Figure 7.5, postulates that vulnerability to behavior disorders is a function of temperament and environment with additive effects of both. Individuals in whom the TRF is present show, by comparison with individuals in whom the TRF is absent, higher vulnerability to behavior disorders and pathology. This tendency is independent of the kind of environment, whether protective or predisposing to vulnerability. In turn, the effect of exposure to protective or predisposing environment is the same, regardless of the individual's temperament characteristics. This model underlines the significance of temperament itself as predisposing the individual to poor fit, hence, as a predisposition to develop behavioral disorders. As exemplified by H. J. Eysenck's (1992a) understanding of psychoticism, this temperament trait, expressed in its extreme form, is directly related to pathology and behavior disorders. The same is to be said about neuroticism when this dimension is regarded as a tendency to experience distress even in the absence of stressors (Watson & Clark, 1984).

(2) *Behavior disorders as an effect of temperament which modifies sensitivity to the environment.* This model proposes (see Figure 7.6) that vulnerability to

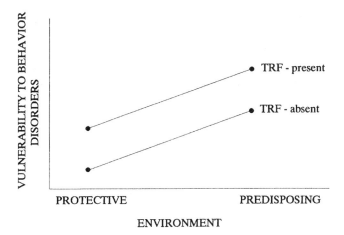

FIGURE 7.5. Vulnerability to behavior disorders as a function of temperament and environment with additive effects of both. *Note.* From "Temperament Risk Factor: The Contribution of Temperament to the Consequences of the State of Stress," by J. Strelau. In S. E. Hobfoll and M. W. de Vries (Eds.), *Extreme Stress and Communities: Impact and Intervention* (1995, p. 70), Dordrecht, The Netherlands: Kluwer Academic Publishers. Copyright 1995 by Kluwer Academic Publishers. Reprinted with permission.

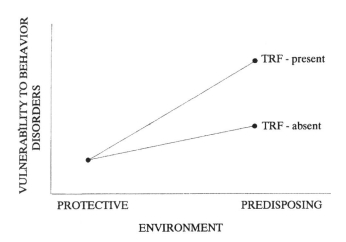

FIGURE 7.6. Vulnerability to behavior disorders as a function of temperament and environment with temperament control of sensitivity to the environment. *Note.* From "Temperament Risk Factor: The Contribution of Temperament to the Consequences of the State of Stress," by J. Strelau. In S. E. Hobfoll and M. W. de Vries (Eds.), *Extreme Stress and Communities: Impact and Intervention* (1995, p. 71), Dordrecht, The Netherlands: Kluwer Academic Publishers. Copyright 1995 by Kluwer Academic Publishers. Reprinted with permission.

behavior disorders is a function of temperament and environment, with temperament influencing sensitivity to the environment. Given temperament traits or configuration of traits, regarded here as TRF, moderate the intensity of stressors by heightening sensitivity to stress-inducing situations. As a consequence of increased sensitivity to the predisposing environment, vulnerability to behavior disorders is greater in individuals in whom the TRF is present. Such temperament traits as high anxiety, emotionality, intensity of reaction, and reactivity increase the tendency to experience negative affects in terms of their frequency and intensity.

(3) *Behavior disorders as an effect of temperament that moderates the exposure to the environment.* Temperament may influence the vulnerability to behavior disorders via the individual's behavior which consists of selecting, creating, or approaching such environments that are predisposing or protective with respect to vulnerability to behavior disorders (see Figure 7.7). TRF is composed of those temperament traits that expose the individual to excessive or chronic stressors predisposing to behavior disorders. Sensation seeking, characterized by undertaking risky activities and approaching risky environments (Stacy, Newcomb, & Bentler, 1993; Zuckerman, 1994), best exemplifies temperament-determined exposure to predisposing environment. Temperament activity, tendency to approach, or uninhibited temperament may also serve as examples of temperament traits that raise the risk of exposure to stressors.

The remaining two models are secondary to the three already described. Probably they are closer to real-life situations in which the interactions between

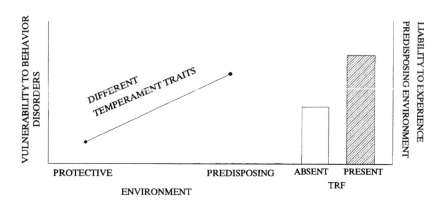

FIGURE 7.7. Vulnerability to behavior disorders as a function of temperament and environment with temperament control of exposure to the environment. *Note.* From "Temperament Risk Factor: The Contribution of Temperament to the Consequences of the State of Stress," by J. Strelau. In S. E. Hobfoll and M. W. de Vries (Eds.), *Extreme Stress and Communities: Impact and Intervention* (1995, p. 72), Dordrecht, The Netherlands: Kluwer Academic Publishers. Copyright 1995 by Kluwer Academic Publishers. Reprinted with permission.

temperament and environment are more complex in producing the risk of behavior disorders or pathology as a consequence of chronic or excessive stress.

(4) *Temperament control of behavior disorders and sensitivity to the environment.* This model is a combination of model (1) and model (2). As depicted by Figure 7.8, it postulates a synergistic effect of temperament with environment. TRF makes the individual more vulnerable to behavior disorders in a predisposing environment, whereas the absence of TRF protects the individual from negative consequences of the predisposing environment. In other words, TRF increases the risk of behavior disorders when in interaction with a predisposing environment.

(5) *Temperament control of behavior disorders and exposure to the environment.* This model (see Figure 7.9) is a combination of models (1) and (3). On the one hand, temperament by itself predisposes to behavior disorder vulnerability. On the other hand, temperament controls exposure to predisposing environment. Hence, there is a cumulative effect of the temperament risk factor on vulnerability to behavior disorders. First, the effect results from temperament traits that contribute to the risk of behavior disorders. Second, due to these temperament traits, the risk of exposure to predisposing environment increases, thus elevating the vulnerability to behavior disorders and pathology.

The models presented in the preceding paragraphs reflect the approaches that have been, or can be, employed to pinpoint the significance of temperament in

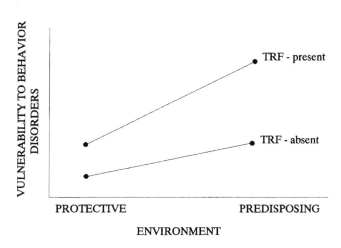

FIGURE 7.8. Vulnerability to behavior disorders as a function of temperament and environment with temperament control of vulnerability to behavior disorders and sensitivity to the environment. *Note.* From "Temperament Risk Factor: The Contribution of Temperament to the Consequences of the State of Stress," by J. Strelau. In S. E. Hobfoll and M. W. de Vries (Eds.), *Extreme Stress and Communities: Impact and Intervention* (1995, p. 73), Dordrecht, The Netherlands: Kluwer Academic Publishers. Copyright 1995 by Kluwer Academic Publishers. Reprinted with permission.

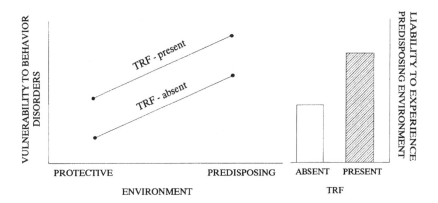

FIGURE 7.9. Vulnerability to behavior disorders as a function of temperament and environment with temperament control of vulnerability to disorders and exposure to the environment. *Note.* From "Temperament Risk Factor: The Contribution of Temperament to the Consequences of the State of Stress," by J. Strelau. In S. E. Hobfoll and M. W. de Vries (Eds.), *Extreme Stress and Communities: Impact and Intervention* (1995, p. 74), Dordrecht, The Netherlands: Kluwer Academic Publishers. Copyright 1995 by Kluwer Academic Publishers. Reprinted with permission.

producing the consequences of stress. They may also serve as a starting point for formulating hypotheses regarding the role of temperament as a moderator of the behavior and health consequences of chronic or excessive states of stress.

The Temperament Risk Factor: Selected Findings

Several books (e.g., Chess & Thomas, 1984, 1986; Garrison and Earls, 1987; A. Thomas *et al.,* 1968) and many papers have described the role of temperament traits in interaction with adverse environments to produce maladjusted personality, behavior disorders, and pathology. A selective review is given in the following paragraphs.

Windle (1989a) showed that, among five temperament factors (extraversion, emotional stability, activity, adaptability, and task orientation) in late adolescents and early adults, it was mainly emotional instability and introversion that were the strongest predictors of mental health; these traits were composed of such factors as anxiety, depression, loss of control, and emotional ties. Kohn and colleagues (1991), studying undergraduate students, demonstrated the moderating effect of temperament not only on the state of stress but also on consequences of stress. Hassles and trait anxiety both contributed to perceived stress, hassles and temperament reactivity both had significant impact on minor ailments, and hassles and trait anxiety had a significant effect on psychiatric symptomathology. Another study carrried out by Mehrabian and Ross (1977), also on university students, demonstrated that high arousability (the opposite pole of stimulus screening), when in interaction with long-lasting arousal states caused by life changes, may be regarded as a TRF for incidence of illness, as judged by subjective ratings. Feij, Doorn, van Kampen, van den Berg, and Resing (1992) studied the relationship between life events and physical illness in adult subjects and concluded that this relationship was moderated by thrill and adventure seeking, one of the sensation seeking dimensions. The influence of temperament on somatic symptoms became particularly evident with controllable life events. Type A behavior pattern in adolescents, regarded as an activity of high stimulative value, when in interaction with high reactivity regarded in this study as a TRF, increases, in comparison with low reactivity, the probability of developing a high level of anxiety (Strelau & Eliasz, 1994).

In some of the studies just listed, multivariate analysis was applied to show some semicausal relationships between controlled variables. Causal modeling became the most fruitful approach in examining the contribution of temperament, in interaction with other risk factors, to behavior disorders and pathology. Several additional detailed examples are given in order to reveal the diversity and complexity of approaches to the issue of the temperament risk factor.

A study that shows the role of one temperament trait, emotionality, in moderating the effect of stressors on vulnerability to behavior disorders is that of Aldwin and coworkers (1989). As already mentioned, this study showed that individuals characterized by high emotionality report more stressors as compared with low-emotional persons. Most important, however, is that a high level of this temperament dimension permitted prediction of mental health symptoms. Thus, high emotionality, under the conditions studied by Aldwin and colleagues (1989), may be regarded as a temperament risk factor.

The foregoing study was conducted on over 1,000 men aged 40 to 88 years. Emotionality was assessed 10 years prior to measurements of stress by means of items from the Eysenck Personality Inventory. The authors distinguished between objective and subjective stressors. As a measure of objective stressors, life events were assessed with the aid of a scale constructed by the senior author. For measuring subjective stressors the Hassles Scale developed by DeLongis, Folkman, and Lazarus (1988) was used. Mental health was assessed by means of the Hopkins Symptom Checklist SCL-90 (Derogatis, 1983).

Using multivariate analysis of the data, the authors showed that emotionality had a stronger effect on mental health than did hassles and life events, but, when taken together, emotionality, life events, and hassles accounted for almost 40% of the variance on the Global Severity Index. The interactional effect of emotionality and hassles on psychological symptoms is illustrated by Figure 7.10. The results depicted in this figure have much in common with Model (4), which shows the synergistic effect of temperament and environment on psychological consequences of stress.

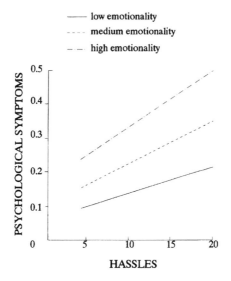

——— low emotionality

- - - - medium emotionality

– – high emotionality

FIGURE 7.10. Effect of the interaction between emotionality and hassles on psychological symptoms. *Note.* From "Does Emotionality Predict Stress? Findings from the Normative Aging Study," by C. M. Aldwin, M. R. Levenson, A. Spiro, III, and R. Bosse, 1989, *Journal of Personality and Social Psychology, 56,* p. 622. Copyright 1989 by American Psychological Association. Reprinted with permission.

As regards adults, a series of studies examined the relationship between the Eysenckian temperament dimensions, especially neuroticism and extraversion, and physical illnesses, such as cancer and coronary heart disease (see H. J. Eysenck, 1983b; 1985; Kissen, 1967; Kissen & Eysenck, 1962). Among the determinants of these diseases, which may be interpreted as consequences of interactions between a variety of factors, such as immune system regulation, neuroendocrine and biochemical factors, genetically determined vulnerability, and environmental risk factors, an important role was found for temperament and personality dimensions.

The majority of studies support the view that cancer patients, as compared with control groups, are significantly lower on the neuroticism and psychoticism dimensions, and tend to be extraverts. Low neuroticism and also extraversion, typical for cancer patients, are explained by the fact that these patients tend to suppress negative emotions (H. J. Eysenck, 1994b). This explanation differs from the one introduced by H. J. Eysenck (1983b, 1985) as the "inoculation effect" hypothesis which says that high neurotic scorers and introverts under conditions of chronic state of stress (strain) are protected to some extent from stressors through the experience of previous high strain. In other words, in neurotic and introverted individuals under long-lasting stressors, a desensitization effect of strain takes

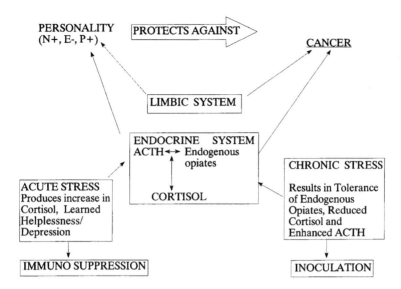

FIGURE 7.11. Personality–cancer relationship as mediated by stress factors and the endocrine system. *Note.* From "Personality, Cancer and Cardiovascular Disease: A Causal Analysis," by H. J. Eysenck, 1985, *Personality and Individual Differences, 6,* p. 552. Copyright 1985 by Elsevier Science Ltd. Reprinted with permission.

place, thus lowering the risk of cancer. The complex personality–cancer relationship, as hypothesized by H. J. Eysenck (1985) in a causal theory linking personality (temperament) and disease, is illustrated by Figure 7.11.

The literature also reports a great deal of research in which coronary heart disease (CHD) has been related to the Eysenckian temperament dimensions. Findings from several studies (see H. J. Eysenck, 1983b, 1985, 1988; C. B. Thomas & Greenstreet, 1973; for a review, see Booth-Kewley & Friedman, 1987; Friedman & Booth-Kewley, 1987) suggest that high neuroticism and high psychoticism (in terms of hostility and aggressiveness) interact with stressors to raise the risk of developing CHD. However, the personality-temperament–coronary-prone behaviors relationship differs, depending on whether patients with coronary heart disease or coronary artery disease (CAD) are taken into account. In patients with CAD no relationship with neuroticism was found (see, e.g., Costa, 1986; Costa, Fleg, McCrae, & Lakatta, 1982; Keehn, Goldberg, & Beebe, 1974).

The most impressive studies on the relationship between personality variables (which most probably included temperament characteristics), stress, and physical illness, that is, cancer and coronary heart disease, are these of Grossarth-Maticek and coworkers (Grossarth-Maticek, 1980; Grossarth-Maticek & Eysenck, 1991; Grossarth-Maticek, Bastiaans, & Kanazir, 1985). Three independent prospective studies were conducted over a 10-year period, one in Yugoslavia (both genders, 60 years of age on average) and two in Heidelberg (both genders, about 10 years younger). In all of them, healthy individuals varying in number from 800 to more than 1,300 were randomly selected. The two Heidelberg samples differed in that one was composed of persons judged by relatives and friends as living permanently under stress. Subjects in all three samples were categorized by means of inventories into four personality types: Type I (equivalent to Type C)—cancer-prone, overcooperative, unassertive, unexpressive of negative emotions, avoiding conflicts, overpatient and defensive in response to stress; Type II (equivalent to Type A)—CHD-prone, chronically irritated and angry, failing to establish stable emotional relations, showing aggression and hostility reponses; Type III—hysterical, oscillating between inadequacy and anger; Type IV (equivalent to Type B)—mentally healthy. At the end of the 10-year period, mortality and cause of death were recorded. The results disclosed that, in all three samples, cancer mortality was highest in Type I and CHD mortality in Type II. In Types III and IV cancer and CHD mortality were significantly lower. There was also a significant difference between the two Heidelberg samples, in that the sample diagnosed by relatives and friends as being permanently stressed showed significantly higher mortality rates (cancer and CHD) as compared with the nonselected (normal) group (see Figure 7.12).

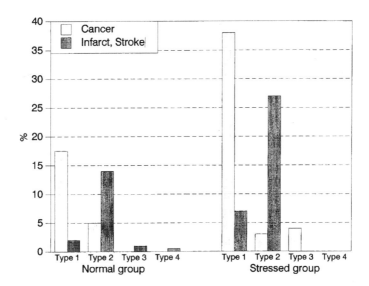

FIGURE 7.12. Cancer and CHD mortality and causes of deaths by personality type in both normal and stressed Heidelberg samples. *Note.* From "Personality type, smoking habit, and their interaction on predictions of cancer and coronary heart disease," by R. Grossarth-Maticek, H.J. Eysenck, & H. Vetter, 1988. *Personality and Individual Differences, 9*, p. 487. Copyright by Elsevier Science Ltd. Adapted with permission.

A replication of the Grossarth-Maticek studies conducted by Smedslund (1995) on more than 5,000 persons (mean age: 42.2) in Norway, in which only Type I (cancer-prone), Type II (CHD-prone), and Type IV (healthy) were distinguished, showed that individuals representing Type IV reported significantly less heart disease as compared with types I and II. There were no significant differences between the three types on cancer. The relationship between heart disease and personality type was confounded by such variables as age, smoking, diet, and exercise. Types I and II were older and smoked more, and Type IV persons had a healthier diet and exercised more.

The Grossarth-Maticek studies, described in detail by H. J. Eysenck (1991c, 1994b), and criticized by several authors (Fox, 1989; Fox & Temoshok, 1988; Zonderman, Costa, & McCrae, 1989), mainly for being "too good to be true," go far beyond temperament characteristics as regards the personal variables contributing to risk of cancer and CHD. For example, Grossarth-Maticek, Kanazir, Schmidt, and Vetter (1982) in a path analysis with standardized partial regression coefficients in which cancer was regarded as the dependent variable and psychosocial characteristics as independent variables, showed that such reactions to stressors as chronic hopelessness, lack of rational behavior, chronic excitement, lack of emotions, lack of harmonic social relationship, and hypochondric behavior were the strongest predictors of cancer mortality. Among these individual characteristics, only chronic excitement and antiemotional behavior can be regarded as belonging to the domain of temperament. Schmitz (1992, 1993), in a study in which students and subjects with psychosomatic complaints were assessed by means of the Personality-Stress-Inventory developed by Grossarth-Maticek and Eysenck (1990), and Eysenck's EPQ-R, found that the Grossarth-Maticek personality types can be described in terms of neuroticism, extraversion, and psychoticism.

Final Remarks

My aim has been to show the place of temperament in studies on stress phenomena, including stressors, state of stress, coping with stress, and consequences of stress. In general, the possible relationships between temperament and the different aspects of stress discussed in this chapter may be depicted as in Figure 7.13.

Upon reading this chapter, one may be left with the impression that temperament is the sole, or the most important, individual characteristic moderating different aspects of stress. In many studies the significance of such personological constructs as hardiness (e.g., Kobasa, 1979; Kobasa & Puccetti, 1983), repression-sensitization (e.g., Krohne, 1986), self-esteem (e.g., Chan, 1977; Ormel & Schaufeli, 1991), locus of control (e.g., Ormel & Schaufeli, 1991: Parkes, 1984), self-confidence (e.g., Holohan & Moos, 1986), sense of coherence (Antonovsky, 1987), and several other personality variables has been brought out. However, my

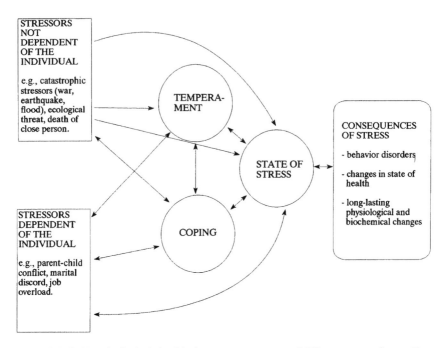

FIGURE 7.13. Hypothesized relationships between temperament and different aspects of stress. *Note.* From "The Regulative Theory of Temperament: Current Status" by J. Strelau, 1996, *Personality and Individual Differences, 20,* p. 135. Copyright 1996 by Elsevier Science. Reprinted with permission.

intention has been to demonstrate that temperament, as one of the many personal variables, cannot be ignored for a proper understanding of human functioning under stress. In other words, stress has been viewed here from a temperament perspective to demonstrate the functional significance temperament has in human life.

A special position in studies centered on the stress–temperament relationship must be assigned to the temperament risk factor because of the far-reaching consequences for individuals resulting from excessive or chronic stress to which temperament contributes in different ways. Among the many risk factors regarded as causes of behavior disorders and pathology, temperament plays a specific role because of its low susceptibility to modification. Whereas some risk factors, acting as stressors, can be avoided or diminished by the individual alone (e.g., noise, crowd, job overload, parent–child conflict), others are not prone to modification or cannot be avoided at all. As Pellegrini (1990) emphasized, "some risk factors are more likely to be preventable or modifiable once they occur (e.g., marital discord), others simply are not (e.g., gender) or are less likely to be so (e.g., difficult temperament)" (pp. 206–207).

One of the senior researchers on child temperament, Rutter (1979), who studied protective factors in children's responses to stress, has shown the powerful influence of increasing numbers of risk factors for the epidemiology of behavior disorders. The probability of behavior disorders increases with the number of risk factors taken into account. The rate of behavior disorders was, in practice, the same for an individual with only one risk factor as for an individual free of this risk factor. But when the number of jointly acting risk factors extended to four or more, the rate of behavior disorders increased to 20%. This finding is a strong argument for taking temperament into account as one of the many possible risk factors contributing to psychological, psychophysiological, and pathological consequences of stress.

Appendix

Abbreviations used in Temperament:
A Psychological Perspective

ACh	Acetylcholine
ACTH	Adrenocorticotropic hormone
AEP	Averaged evoked potential
AER	Averaged evoked response
AIC	Akaike information criterion
ANS	Autonomic nervous system
AO	Amine oxidase
ARAS	Ascending reticular activating system
ARP	Event related potential
BAS	Behavioral approach (activation) system
BIS	Behavioral inhibition system
BA	Balance of nervous processes
BAER	Brainstem auditory evoked responses
BSRF	Brain stem reticular formation
CAD	Coronary artery disease
CHD	Coronary heart disease
C.N.S.	Conceptual nervous system
CNS	Central nervous system
CNV	Contingent negative variation
COMT	Catechol-O-methyltransferase
CR	Conditioned reflex (reaction)
CS	Conditioned stimulus
CSA	Catecholamine systems activity

CSF	Cerebrospinal fluid
CVA	Cardiovascular activity
CVS	Cardiovascular system
D4DR	D4 dopamine receptor gene
DA	Dopamine
DBH	Dopamine beta-hydroxylase
DNA	Deoxyribonucleic acid
DOPA	Dihydroxyphenylaline
DS	Down's syndrome
DTPS	Diffuse thalamic projection system
DTS	Diffuse thalamocortical system
ZD	Dizygotic (fraternal)
E	Epinephrine
EDA	Electrodermal activity
EEG	Electroencephalography (electroencephalogram)
EMG	Electromyography
EP	Evoked potential
EPSP	Excitatory postsynaptic potential
ERP	Event-related potential
E_s	Shared environment
E_{ns}	Nonshared environment
F/FLS	Fight/flight system
GABA	Gamma-aminobutyric acid
GFI	Goodness-of-fit index
GTH	Gonadotropic hormones
5-HIAA	5-hydroxyindoleacetic acid
5-HT	5-hydroxytryptamine (serotonin)
h^2_B	Broad-sense heritability
h^2_N	Narrow-sense heritability
HNA	Higher nervous activity
HR	Heart rate
HVA	Homovanillic acid
IPSP	Inhibitory postsynaptic potential
isi	Interstimulus interval
MAO	Monoamine oxidase
MHPG	3-methoxy-4-hydroxyphenylglycol
MO	Mobility of nervous processes
MZ	Monozygotic (identical)
NE	Norepinephrine (noradrenaline)
NP	Nervous processes
NS	Nervous system
OR	Orienting reflex (reaction)

PDR	Photic driving reaction
PNS	Peripheral nervous system
PSP	Postsynaptic potential
PVA	Pulse volume amplitude
QTL	Quantitative trait loci
RAS	Reticular activating system
RMSR	Root-mean square residual
RNA	Ribonucleic acid
RSA	Respiratory sinus arrhythmia
RT	Reaction time
SCL	Skin conductance level
SCR	Skin conductance response
SE	Strength of excitation
SEP	Somatosensory evoked potential
SES	Socioeconomic status
SI	Strength of inhibition
TNS	Type of nervous system
TRF	Temperament risk factor
TSH	Thyrotropic hormone
UCR	Unconditioned reflex (reaction)
UCS	Unconditioned stimulus
V_A	Additive genetic variance
V_D	Variance due to dominance
V_E	Environmental variance
V_{EP}	Variance due to epistasis
V_G	Genetic variance
V_I	Variance of interaction between genes and environment
V_{NA}	Nonadditive genetic variance
V_P	Phenotypic variance

References

Ach, ᴛ N. (1910). *Über den Willensakt und das Temperament: Eine experimentelle Untersuchung* [On the act of will and temperament: An experimental study]. Leipzig, Germany: Verlag von Quelle.

Achenbach, T. M., & Edelbrock, C. S. (1981). Behavioral problems and competencies reported by parents of normal and disturbed children aged four through sixteen. *Monographs of the Society for Research in Child Development, 46* (No. 188).

Adams, D. B. (1979). Brain mechanisms for offence, defense, and submission. *Behavioral and Brain Sciences, 2,* 201–241.

Adcock, C. (1948). A factorial examination of Sheldon's types. *Journal of Personality, 16,* 312–319.

Adcock, C. J. (1957). The differentiation of temperament from personality. *Journal of General Psychology, 57,* 103–112.

af Klinteberg, B., Andersson, T., Magnusson, D., & Stattin, H. (1993). Hyperactive behavior in childhood as related to subsequent alcohol problems and violent offending: A longitudinal study of male subjects. *Personality and Individual Differences, 15,* 381–388.

Aggleton, J. P., & Mishkin, M. (1986). The amygdala: Sensory gateway to the emotions. In R. Plutchik & H. Kellerman (Eds.), *Emotions: Theory, research, and experience* (Vol. 3, pp. 281–299). New York: Academic Press.

Ahadi, S. A., & Rothbart, M. K. (1994). Temperament, development, and the Big Five. In C. F. Halverson, Jr., G. A. Kohnstamm, & R. P. Martin (Eds.), *The developing structure of temperament and personality from infancy to adulthood* (pp. 189–207). Hillsdale, NJ: Erlbaum.

Ahadi, S. A., Rothbart, M. K., & Ye, R. (1993). Children's temperament in the US and China: Similarities and differences. *European Journal of Personality, 7,* 359–377.

Akaike, H. (1987). Factor analysis and AIC. *Psychometrika, 52,* 317–332.

Aldwin, C. M., Levenson, M. R., Spiro, A., III, & Bosse, R. (1989). Does emotionality predict stress? Findings from the normative aging study. *Journal of Personality and Social Psychology, 56,* 618–624.

Allport, F. H. (1924). *Social psychology.* Boston: Houghton Mifflin.

Allport, F. H., & Allport, G. W. (1921/1922). Personality traits: Their classification and measurement. *Journal of Abnormal and Social Psychology, 16,* 6–40.

Allport, G. W. (1937). *Personality: A psychological interpretation.* New York: Holt.

Allport, G. W., & Vernon, P. E. (1930). The field of personality. *Psychological Bulletin, 27,* 677–730.

Amelang, M., & Bartussek, D. (1990). *Differentielle Psychologie und Persönlichkeitsforschung* [Differential psychology and research on personality] (3rd ed.). Stuttgart, Germany: Verlag W. Kohlhammer.

Amelang, M., & Borkenau, P. (1986). The trait concept: Current theoretical considerations, empirical facts, and implications for personality inventory construction. In A. Angleitner & J. S. Wiggins (Eds.), *Personality assessment via questionnaires* (pp. 7–34). Berlin, Germany: Springer.

Amelang, M., & Ullwer, U. (1991). Correlations between psychometric measures and psychophysiological as well as experimental variables in studies on extraversion and neuroticism. In J. Strelau & A. Angleitner (Eds.), *Explorations in temperament: International perspectives on theory and measurement* (pp. 287–315). New York: Plenum.

Aminov, N. A. (1988). Psychophysiological and psychological prerequisites of pedagogical abilities. *Voprosy Psikhologii, 5,* 71–77. (in Russian)

Amochaev, A., & Samaly, A. (1979). Stability of EEG laterality effects. *Psychophysiology, 16,* 242–246.

Amsel, A. (1962). Frustrative nonreward in partial reinforcement and discrimination learning: Some recent history and a theoretical extension. *Psychological Review, 69,* 306–328.

Anderson, K. J., & Revelle, W. (1994). Impulsivity and time of day: Is rate of change in arousal a function of impulsivity? *Journal of Personality and Social Psychology, 67,* 334–344.

Andersson, T., & Magnusson, D. (1990). Biological maturation in adolescence and the development of drinking habits and alcohol abuse among young males: A prospective longitudinal study. *Journal of Youth and Adolsecence, 19,* 33–41.

Andrés Pueyo, A., & Tous, J. M. (1992). Potenciales evocados cerebrales y dimensiones de personalidad [Cerebral evoked potentials and dimensions of personality]. *Psicothema, 4,* 209–220.

Andresen, B. (1986). Reizsuche- und Erlebnismotive I: Eine psychometrische Reanalyse der SSS V Zuckermans im Kontext der MISAP-Entwicklung [Sensation seeking and the experience motive I: A psychometric reanalysis of Zuckerman's SSS–Form V in the context of the MISAP development]. *Zeitschrift für Differentielle und Diagnostische Psychologie, 7,* 177–203.

Andresen, B. (1987). *Differentielle Psychophysiologie valenzkontrarer Aktivierungsdimensionen* [Differential psychophysiology of activation dimensions characterized by contrary valency]. Frankfurt am Main, Germany: Peter Land.

Angleitner, A. (1991). Personality psychology: Trends and developments. *European Journal of Personality, 5,* 185–197.

Angleitner, A., & Ostendorf, F. (1994). Temperament and the Big Five factors of personality. In C. F. Halverson, Jr., G. A. Kohnstamm, & R. P. Martin (Eds.), *The developing structure of temperament and personality from infancy to adulthood* (pp. 69–90). Hillsdale, NJ: Erlbaum.

Angleitner, A., & Riemann, R. (1991). What can we learn from the discussion of personality questionnaires for the construction of temperament inventories? In J. Strelau & A. Angleitner (Eds.), *Explorations in temperament: International perspectives on theory and measurement* (pp. 191–204). New York: Plenum.

Angleitner, A., & Wiggins, J. S. (Eds.). (1986). *Personality assessment via questionnaires.* Berlin, Germany: Springer.

Angleitner, A., John, O. P., & Lohr, F-J. (1986). It's *what* you ask and *how* you ask it: An itemmetric analysis of personality questionnaires. In A. Angleitner & J. S. Wiggins (Eds.), *Personality assessment via questionnaires* (pp. 61–107). Berlin, Germany: Springer.

Angleitner, A., & Ostendorf, F., & John, O. P. (1990). Towards a taxonomy of personality descriptors in German: A psycho-lexical study. *European Journal of Personality, 4,* 89–118.

Angleitner, A., Riemann, R. Spinath, F. M., Hempel, S., Thiel, W., & Strelau, J. (1995, July). *The Bielefeld–Warsaw Twin Project: First report on the Bielefeld samples.* Workshop on Genetic Studies on Temperament and Personality, Pułtusk, Poland.

Anokhin, P. K. (1978). *Collected works: Philosophical aspects of the functional system theory.* Moscow, Russia: Nauka. (in Russian)

Antonovsky, A. (1987). *Unraveling the mystery of health: How people manage stress and stay well.* San Francisco: Jossey-Bass.

Asendorpf, J. B., & Van Aken, M. A. G. (1991). Correlations of the temporal consistency of personality patterns in childhood. *Journal of Personality, 59,* 689–703.

Ashmun, M. (1908). A study of temperaments as illustrated in literature. *American Journal of Psychology, 19,* 519–535.

Ashton, C. H., Golding, J. F., Marsh, V. R., & Thompson, J. W. (1985). Somatosensory evoked potentials and personality. *Personality and Individual Differences, 6,* 141–143.

Attili, G. (1989). The psychology of character and temperament in Italy: A historical review and recent trents. In G. A. Kohnstamm, J. E. Bates & M. K. Rothbart (Eds.), *Temperament in childhood* (pp. 581–596). Chichester, England: Wiley.

Axia, G., Prior, M., & Carelli, M. G. (1992). Cultural influences on temperament: A comparison of Italian, Italo-Australian and Anglo-Italian toddlers. *Australian Psychologist, 27,* 52–56.

Bakulev, A. N., & Busalov, A. A. (1957). The significance of I. P. Pavlov's theory on types of higher nervous activity for applied surgery. In *Problems of physiology of the central nervous system* (pp. 40–49). Leningrad, Russia: SSSR Academy of Sciences. (in Russian)

Ball, D., Hill, L., Freeman, B., Eley, T. C., Strelau, J., Riemann, R., Spinath, F. M., Angleitner, A., & Plomin, R. (1997) The serotonin transporter gene and peer-rated neuroticism. *NeuroReport, 8,* 1301–1304.

Ball, S. A., & Zuckerman, M. (1990). Sensation seeking, Eysenck's personality dimensions and reinforcement sensitivity in concept formation. *Personality and Individual Differences, 11,* 343–353.

Ballantine, J. H., & Klein, H. A. (1990). The relationship of temperament and adjustment in Japanese schools. *Journal of Psychology, 124,* 299–309.

Ballenger, J. C., Post, R. M., Jimerson, D. C., Lake, C. R., Murphy, D., Zuckerman, M., & Cronin, C. (1983). Biochemical correlates of personality traits in normals: An exploratory study. *Personality and Individual Differences, 4,* 615–625.

Balleyguier, G. (1989). Temperament and character: The French school. In G. A. Kohnstamm, J. E. Bates, & M. K. Rothbart (Eds.), *Temperament in childhood* (pp. 597–606). Chichester, England: Wiley.

Bandura, A., & Walters, R. H. (1963). *Social learning and personality development.* New York: Holt.

Banks, E. (1989). Temperament and individuality: A study of Malay children. *American Journal of Orthopsychiatry, 59,* 390–397.

Barclay, J. R. (1983a). *Manual of the Barclay Classroom Assessment System.* Los Angeles: Western Psychological Services.

Barclay, J. R. (1983b). A meta-analysis of temperament–treatment interactions with alternative learning and counseling treatments. *Developmental Review, 3,* 410–443.

Barclay, J. R. (1991). *Psychological assessment: A theory and systems approach.* Malabar, FL: Krieger.

Barclay, J. R. (1992). *Technical report on the assessment of the gifted child.* Unpublished manuscript, University of Kentucky, Lexington.

Barnes, G. E. (1985). The Vando R-A Scale as a measure of stimulus reducing–augmenting. In J. Strelau, F. H. Farley, & A. Gale (Eds.), *The biological bases of personality and behavior: Theories, measurement techniques, and development* (Vol. 1, pp. 171–180). Washington, DC: Hemisphere.

Barnett, D. W., & Macmann, G. M. (1990). Personality assessment: Critical issues for research and practice. In C. R. Reynolds & R. W. Kamphaus (Eds.), *Handbook of psychological and educational assessment of children: Personality, behavior, and context* (pp. 30–51). New York: Guilford.

Barratt, E. S. (1985). Impulsiveness subtraits: Arousal, and information processing. In J. T. Spence & C. E. Izard (Eds.), *Motivation, emotion, and personality* (pp. 137–146). Amsterdam: North Holland.

Barratt, E. S., & Patton. J. H. (1983). Impulsivity: Cognitive, behavioral, and psychophysiological correlates. In M. Zuckerman (Ed.), *Biological bases of sensation seeking, impulsivity, and anxiety* (pp. 77–116). Hillsdale, NJ: Erlbaum.

Barratt, E. S., Pritchard, W. S., Faulk, D. M., & Brandt, M. E. (1987). The relationship between impulsiveness subtraits, trait anxiety, and visual N100-augmenting–reducing: A topographic analysis. *Personality and Individual Differences, 8,* 43–51.

Barrett, P., & Eysenck, S. B. G. (1984). The assessment of personality factors across 25 countries. *Personality and Individual Differences, 5,* 615–632.

Barron, A. P., & Earls, F. (1984). The relation of temperament and social factors to behavior problems in three-year-old children. *Journal of Child Psychology and Psychiatry and Allied Disciplines, 25,* 23–33.

Bartussek, D. (1984). Extraversion und EEG: Ein Forschungsparadigma in der Sackgasse? [Extraversion and EEG: A research paradigm in a blind alley]. In M. Amelang & H. J. Ahrens (Eds.), *Brennpunkte der Persönlichkeitsforschung* (pp. 157–189). Göttingen, Germany: Hogrefe.

Basan, L. I. (1960). Technique of investigation of higher nervous activity in children in natural settings. *Zhurnal Vysshei Nervnoi Deyatelnosti, 10,* 800–803. (in Russian)

Bates, J. E. (1980). The concept of difficult temperament. *Merrill-Palmer Quarterly, 26,* 299–319.

Bates, J. E. (1983). Issues in the assessment of difficult temperament: A reply to Thomas, Chess, and Korn. *Merrill-Palmer Quarterly, 29,* 89–97.

Bates, J. E. (1986). The measurement of temperament: In R. Plomin & J. Dunn (Eds.), *The study of temperament: Changes, continuities and challenges* (pp. 1–11). Hillsdale, NJ: Erlbaum.

Bates, J. E. (1987). Temperament in infancy. In J. D. Osofsky (Ed.), *Handbook of infant development* (2nd ed., pp. 1101–1149). New York: Wiley.

Bates, J. E. (1989). Concepts and measures of temperament. In G. A. Kohnstamm, J. E. Bates, & M. K. Rothbart (1989). *Temperament in childhood* (pp. 3–26). Chichester, England: Wiley.

Bates, J. E., Freeland, C. A. B., & Lounsbury, M. L. (1979). Measurement of infant difficultness. *Child Development, 50,* 794–803.

Baum, A., Calesnick, L. E., Davis, G. E., & Gatchel, R. J. (1982). Individual differences in coping with crowding: Stimulus screening and social overload. *Journal of Personality and Social Psychology, 43,* 821–830.

Bayley, N. (1969). *Bayley scales of infant development.* New York: Psychological Corporation.

Bazylevich, T. F. (1974). The expression of strength of the regulative brain system in the dynamics of the somatosensory evoked potential. In V. D. Nebylitsyn (Ed.), *Problems of differential psychophysiology: Electrophysiological studies on the fundamental properties of the nervous system* (pp. 77–92). Moscow, Russia: Nauka. (in Russian)

Bazylevich, T. F. (1983). *Somatosensory evoked potentials in differential psychophysiology.* Moscow, Russia: Nauka. (in Russian)

Behar, L., & Stringfield, S. (1974). A behavior rating scale for the preschool child. *Developmental Psychology, 10,* 601–610.

Bell, I. R., Jasnoski, M. L., Kagan, J., & King, D. S. (1990). Is allergic rhinitis more frequent in young adults with extreme shyness?. *Psychosomatic Medicine, 52,* 517–525.

Berlyne, D. E. (1960). *Conflict, arousal, curiosity.* New York: McGraw-Hill.

Berry, J. W. (1969). On cross-cultural comparability. *International Journal of Psychology, 4,* 119–128.

Betz, B. J., & Thomas, C. B. (1979). Individual temperament as a predictor of health or premature disease. *Johns Hopkins Medical Journal, 144,* 81–89.

Billman, J., & McDevitt, S. C. (1980). Convergence of parent and observer ratings of temperament with observations of peer interaction in nursery school. *Child Development, 51,* 395–400.

Birman, B. N. (1951). An attempt for a clinical-physiological assessment of types of higher nervous activity. *Zhurnal Vysshei Nervnoi Deyatelnosti, 1,* 879–888. (in Russian)

Bishop. D., Jacks, H., & Tandy, S. B. (1993). The Structure of Temperament Questionnaire (STQ): Results from a U.S. sample. *Personality and Individual Differences, 14,* 485–487.

Bishop, D. V. M. (1977). The P scale and psychosis. *Journal of Abnormal Psychology, 86,* 127–134.

Blackson, T. C., Tarter, R. E., Martin, C. S., & Moss, H. B. (1994). Temperament mediates the effects of family history of substance abuse on externalizing and internalizing child behavior. *American Journal of Addictions, 3,* 58–66.

Block, J. (1977). The Eysencks and psychoticism. *Journal of Abnormal Psychology, 86,* 653–654.

Block, J. (1995). A contrarian view of the five-factor approach to personality description. *Psychological Bulletin, 117,* 187–215.

Boddy, J. (1983a). Information processing and functional systems in the brain. In A. Gale & J. A. Edwards (Eds.), *Physiological correlates of human behaviour: Basic issues* (Vol. 1, pp. 49–77). London: Academic Press.

Boddy, J. (1983b). The nervous system: Structure and fundamental processes. In A. Gale & J. A. Edwards (Eds.), *Physiological correlates of human behaviour: Basic issues* (Vol. 1, pp. 21–47). London: Academic Press.

Boddy, J., Carver, A., & Rowley, K. (1986). Effects of positive and negative verbal reinforcement on performance as a function of extraversion–introversion: Some tests of Gray's theory. *Personality and Individual Differences, 7,* 81–88.

Bodunov, M. V. (1986). Typology of mental activity as a temperamental trait and the level of activation of the nervous system. In J. Strelau, F. H. Farley, & A. Gale (Eds.), *The biological bases of personality and behavior: Psychophysiology, performance, and application* (Vol. 2, pp. 43–57). Washington, DC: Hemisphere.

Bodunov, M. V. (1993). Studies on temperament in Russia: After Teplov and Nebylitsyn. *European Journal of Personality, 7,* 299–311.

Bohlin, G., Hagekull, B., & Lindhagen, K. (1981). Dimensions of infant behavior. *Infant Behavior and Development, 4,* 83–96.

Bohnen, N., Nicolson, N., Sulon, J., & Jolles, J. (1991). Coping style, trait anxiety and cortisol reactivity during mental stress. *Journal of Psychosomatic Research, 35,* 141–147.

Bolger, N. (1990). Coping as a personality process: A prospective study. *Journal of Personality and Social Psychology, 59,* 525–537.

Bolger, N., & Schilling, E. A. (in press). Personality and the problems of everyday life: The role of neuroticism in exposure and reactivity to daily stressors. *Journal of Personality.*

Boomsma, D. I., & Plomin, R. (1986). Heart rate and behavior of twins. *Merrill-Palmer Quarterly, 26,* 299–319.

Boomsma, D. I., Martin, N. G., & Neale, M. C. (Eds.). (1989). Genetic analysis of twin and family data: Structural modeling using LISREL. *Behavior Genetics, 19* (Special issue).

Booth-Kewley, S., & Friedman, H. S. (1987). Psychological predictors of heart disease: A quantitative review. *Psychological Bulletin, 101,* 343–362.

Borisova, M. N. (1959). Determination of discrimination threshold and elaboration of fine sensory differentiations as a means of studying the concentration of excitation. In B. M. Teplov (Ed.), *Typological features of higher nervous activity in man* (Vol. 2, pp. 199–219). Moscow, Russia: RSFSR Academy of Pedagogical Sciences. (in Russian)

Borisova, M. N. (1972). Concentration of nervous processes as an individual typological feature of higher nervous activity. In V. D. Nebylitsyn & J. A. Gray (Eds.), *Biological bases of individual behavior* (pp. 29–42). New York: Academic Press.

Borisova, M. N., Gurevich, K. M., Yermolayeva-Tomina, L. B., Kolodnaya, A Ya., Ravich-Shcherbo, I. V., & Shvarts, L. A. (1963). Materials for comparative studies of various indices of mobility of the nervous system in man. In B. M. Teplov (Ed.), *Typological features of higher nervous activity in man* (Vol. 3, pp. 180–201). Moscow, Russia: RSFSR Academy of Pedagogical Sciences. (in Russian)

Borisova, M. N., Golubeva, E. A., Leites, N. S., Olshannikova, A. E., Ravich-Shcherbo, I. V., Rozhdestvenskaya, V. I., & Rusalov, V. M. (Eds.). (1977). *Problems of differential psychophysiology* (Vol. 9). Moscow, Russia: Pedagogika. (in Russian)

Borkenau, P. (1992). *Wörauf beruhen Personlichkeitsunderschiede? Eine Einführung in die Anlage-Umwelt Forschung* [What are the bases for personality differences? An introduction to the nature–nurture research]. Göttingen, Germany: Hogrefe.

Bornstein, M. H., Gaughran, J. M., & Homel, P. (1986). Infant temperament: Theory, tradition. critique, and new assessments. In C. E. Izard & P. B. Read (Eds.), *Measuring emotions in infants and children* (Vol. 2, pp. 172–199). New York: Cambridge University Press.

Bossert, S., Berger, M., Krieg, J. C., Schreiber, W., Junker, M., & von Zerssen, D. (1988). Cortisol response to various stressful situations: Relationship to personality variables and coping styles. *Neuropsychobiology, 20,* 36–42.

Bouchard, T. J., Jr., & McGue, M. (1990). Genetic and rearing environmental influences on adult personality: An analysis of adopted twins reared apart. *Journal of Personality, 58,* 263–292.

Bouchard, T. J., Lykken, D. T., McGue, M., Segal, N. L., & Tellegen, A. (1990). Sources of human psychological differences: The Minnesota study of twins reared apart. *Science, 250,* 223–228.

Brandtstadter, J., Baltes-Gotz, B., Kirschbaum, C., & Hellhammer, D. (1991). Developmental and personality correlates of adrenocortical activity as indexed by salivary cortisol: Obwervations in the age range of 35 to 65 years. *Journal of Psychosomatic Research, 35,* 173–185.

Braungart, J. M., Plomin, R., DeFries, J. C., & Fulker, D. W. (1992). Genetic influence on tester-rated infant temperament as assessed by Bayley's Infant Behavior Record: Nonadoptive and adoptive siblings and twins. *Developmental Psychology, 28,* 40–47.

Brazelton, T. B. (1973). *Neonatal Behavioral Assessment Scale.* London: Spastics International Medical Publications.

Brazelton, T. B., Nugent, J. K., & Lester, B. M. (1987). Neonatal Behavioral Assessment Scale. In J. D. Osofsky (Ed.), *Handbook of infant development* (pp. 780–817). New York: Wiley.

Brebner, J., & Stough, C. (1993). The relationship between the structure of temperament and extraversion and neuroticism. *Personality and Individual Differences, 14,* 623–626.

Brengelmann, J. C. (1952). Kretschmer's zyklothymer und schizothymer Typus im Bereich der normalen Persönlichkeit [Kretschmer's cyclotymic and schizotymic types in the domain of normal personality]. *Psychologische Rundschau, 3,* 31–38.

Bridges, F. A., & Cicchetti, D. (1982). Mother's ratings of the temperament characteristics of Down's syndrome infants. *Developmental Psychology, 18,* 238–244.

Brislin, R. W. (1976). Comparative research methodology: Cross-cultural studies. *International Journal of Psychology, 11,* 215–229.

Broadhurst, A., & Millard, D. W. (1969). Augmenters and reducers: A note on a replication failure. *Acta Psychologica, 29,* 290–296.

Broadhurst, P. L. (1975). The Maudsley reactive and non-reactive strains of rats: A survey. *Behavior Genetics, 5,* 299–319.

Broadhurst, P. L., & Levine, S. (1963). Behavioral consistency in strains of rats selectively bred for emotional elimination. *British Journal of Psychology, 56,* 121–125.

Brody, G. H., Stoneman, Z., & Burke, M. (1988). Child temperament and parental perceptions of individual child adjustment: An intrafamilial analysis. *American Journal of Orthopsychiatry, 58,* 532–542.

Bruneau, W., Roux, S. Perse, J., & Lelord, G. (1984). Frontal evoked responses, stimulus intensity control, and the extraversion dimension. In R. Karrer, J. Cohen, & P. Teuting (Eds.), *Brain and information: Event-related potentials. Annals of the New York Academy of Sciences, 425,* 546–550.

Brzeziński, J. (1996). *Metodologia badań psychologicznych* [Methodology of psychological research]. Warsaw, Poland: Wydawnictwo Naukowe PWN.

Buchsbaum, M. S. (1971). Neural events and the psychophysical law. *Science, 172,* 502.

Buchsbaum, M. S. (1976). Self-regulation of stimulus intensity: Augmenting/reducing and the average evoked response. In G. E. Schwartz & D. Shapiro (Eds.), *Consciousness and self-regulation* (Vol. 1, pp. 101–135). New York: Plenum.

Buchsbaum, M. S. (1978). Neurophysiological studies of reduction and augmentation. In A. Petrie, *Individuality in pain and suffering* (pp. 141–157). Chicago: University of Chicago Press.

Buchsbaum, M. S., & Silverman, J. (1968). Stimulus intensity control and the cortical evoked response. *Psychosomatic Medicine, 30,* 12–22.

Buchsbaum, M. S., Haier, R. J., & Johnson, J. (1983). Augmenting and reducing: Individual differences in evoked potentials. In A. Gale & J. A. Edwards (Eds.), *Physiological correlates of human behavior: Individual differences and psychopathology* (Vol. 3, pp. 120–138). London: Academic Press.

Bulik, C. M., Sullivan, P. F., Weltzin, T. E., & Kaye, W. H. (1995). Temperament and eating disorders. *International Journal of Eating Disorders, 17,* 251–261.

Bullock, W. A., & Gilliland, K. (1993). Eysenck's arousal theory of introversion–extraversion: A converging measures investigation. *Journal of Personality and Social Psychology, 64,* 113–123.

Burchard, E. M. L. (1936). Physique and psychosis: An analysis of the postulated relationship between constitution and mental disease syndrome. *Comparative Psychology Monographs, 13* (No. 1).

Burisch, M. (1984). Approaches to personality inventory construction: A comparison of merits. *American Psychologist, 39,* 214–227.

Burisch, M. (1986). Methods of personality inventory development—A comparative analysis. In A. Angleitner & J. S. Wiggins (Eds.), *Personality assessment via questionnaires* (pp. 109–120). Berlin, Germany: Springer.

Buss, A. H. (1961). *The psychology of aggression.* New York: Wiley.

Buss, A. H. (1981). Predicting parent–child interactions from children's activity level. *Developmental Psychology, 17,* 598–605.

Buss, A. H. (1988). *Personality: Evolutionary heritage and human distinctiveness.* Hillsdale, NJ: Erlbaum.

Buss, A. H. (1989a). Personality as traits. *American Psychologist, 44,* 1378–1388.

Buss, A. H. (1989b). Temperaments as personality traits. In G. A. Kohnstamm, J. E. Bates, & M. K. Rothbart (Eds.), *Temperament in childhood* (pp. 49–58). Chichester, England: Wiley.

Buss, A. H. (1991). The EAS theory of temperament. In J. Strelau & A. Angleitner (Eds.), *Explorations in temperament: International perspectives on theory and measurement* (pp. 43–60). New York: Plenum.

Buss, A. H., & Finn, S. E. (1987). Classification of personality traits. *Journal of Personality and Social Psychology, 52,* 432–444.

Buss, A. H., & Plomin, R. (1975). *A temperament theory of personality development.* New York: Wiley.

Buss, A. H., & Plomin, R. (1984). *Temperament: Early developing personality traits.* Hillsdale, NJ: Erlbaum.

Buss, A. H., & Plomin, R. (1986). The EAS approach to temperament. In R. Plomin & J. Dunn (Eds.), *The study of temperament: Changes, continuities and challenges* (pp. 67–79). Hillsdale, NJ: Erlbaum.

Buss, A. H., Plomin, R., & Willerman, L. (1973). The inheritance of temperament. *Journal of Personality, 41,* 513–524.

Buss, D. M., Block, J. H., & Block, J. (1980). Preschool activity level: Personality correlates and developmental implications. *Child Development, 51,* 401–408.

Butcher, J. E., & Eaton, W. O. (1989). Gross and fine motor proficiency in preschoolers: Relationships with free play behavior and activity level. *Journal of Human Movement Studies, 16,* 27–36.

Cahill, J. M., & Polich, J. (1992). P300, probability, and introverted/extroverted personality types. *Biological Psychology, 33,* 23–35.

Callaway, E., Tueting, P., & Koslow, S. H. (Eds.). (1978). *Event-related brain potentials in man.* New York: Academic Press.

Cameron, J. R. (1977) Parental treatment, children's temperament, and the risk of childhood behavioral problems: 1. Relationships between parental characteristics and changes in children's temperament over time. *American Journal of Orthopsychiatry, 47,* 568–576.

Cameron, J. R. (1978). Parental treatment, children's temperament and the risk of childhood behavioral problems: 2. Initial temperament, parental attitudes, and the incidence and form of behavioral problems. *American Journal of Orthopsychiatry, 48,* 140–147.

Campbell, D. T., & Fiske, D. W. (1959). Convergent and discriminant validation by the multitrait–multimethod matrix. *Psychological Bulletin, 56,* 81–105.

Campbell, K. B., Baribeau-Braun, J., & Braun, C. (1981). Neuroanatomical and physiological foundations of extraversion. *Psychophysiology, 18,* 263–267.

Campos, J. J. (1976). Heart rate: A sensitive tool for the study of emotional development in the infant. In L. Lipsitt (Ed.), *Developmental psychobiology: The significance of infancy* (pp. 1–34). Hillsdale, NJ: Erlbaum.

Campos, J. J., & Stenberg, C. (1981). Perception, appraisal, and emotion: The onset of social referencing. In M. E. Lamb & L. R. Sherrod (Eds.), *Infant social cognition: Empirical and theoretical considerations* (pp. 273–314). Hillsdale, NJ: Erlbaum.

Campos, J. J., Barrett, K. C., Lamb, M. E., Goldsmith, H. H., & Stenberg, C. (1983). Socioemiotional development. In M. M. Haith & J. J. Campos (Eds.), *Handbook of child psychology: Infancy and developmental psychobiology* (Vol. 2, pp. 783–915). New York: Wiley.

Cannon, W. B., (1932). *The wisdom of the body.* New York: Norton.

Cantor, N., & Zirkel, S. (1990). Personality, cognition, and purposive behavior. In L. A. Pervin (Ed.), *Handbook of personality: Theory and research* (pp. 135–163). New York: Guilford.

Caprara, G. V., & Van Heck, G. L. (Eds.) (1992). *Modern personality psychology: Critical reviews and new directions.* Hertfordshire, England: Harvester Wheatsheaf.

Cardell, C. D., & Parmar, R. S. (1988). Teacher perceptions of temperament characteristics of children classified as learning disabled. *Journal of Learning Disabilities, 21,* 497–502.

Carey, G., Goldsmith, H. H., Tellegen, A., & Gottesman, I. I. (1978). Genetics and personality inventories: The limits of replication with twin data. *Behavior Genetics, 8,* 299–313.

Carey, W. B. (1970). A simplified method for measuring infant temperament. *Journal of Pediatrics, 77,* 188–194.

Carey, W. B. (1983). Some pitfalls in infant temperament research. *Infant Behavior and Development, 6,* 247–254.

Carey, W. B. (1985a). Clinical use of temperament data in pediatrics. *Developmental and Behavioral Pediatrics, 6,* 137–142.

Carey, W. B. (1985b). Temperament and increased weight gain in infants. *Developmental and Behavioral Pediatrics, 6,* 128–131.

Carey, W. B. (1986). The difficult child. *Pediatrics in Review, 8,* 39–45.

Carey, W. B. (1989). Introduction: Basic issues. In W. B. Carey & S. C. McDevitt (Eds.), *Clinical and educational applications of temperament research* (pp. 11–20). Lisse, The Netherlands: Swets & Zeitlinger.

Carey, W. B., & McDevitt, S. C. (1978). Revision of the Infant Temperament Questionniare. *Pediatrics, 61,* 735–739.

Carey, W. B., & McDevitt, S. C. (Eds.). (1989). *Clinical and educational applications of temperament research.* Lisse, The Netherlands: Swets & Zeitlinger.

Carey, W. B., & McDevitt, S. C. (Eds.). (1994). *Prevention and early intervention: Individual differences as risk factors for the mental health of children.* New York: Brunner/Mazel.

Carey, W. B., Fox, M., & McDevitt, S. C. (1977). Temperament as a factor in early school adjustment. *Pediatrics, 60,* 621–624.

Carey, W. B., Hegvik, R. L., & McDevitt, S. C. (1988). Temperament factors associated with rapid weight gain and obesity in middle childhood. *Journal of Developmental and Behavioral Pediatrics, 9,* 194–198.

Carrillo-de-la-Pena, M. T. (1992). ERP augmenting/reducing and sensation seeking: A critical review. *International Journal of Psychophysiology, 12,* 211–220.

Carrol, E. N., Zuckerman, M., & Vogel, W. H. (1982). A test of the optimal level of arousal theory of sensation seeking. *Journal of Personality and Social Psychology, 42,* 572–575.

Carson, D. K., Council, J. R., & Gravley, J. E. (1991). Temperament and family characteristics as predictors of children's reactions to hospitalization. *Developmental and Behavioral Pediatrics, 12,* 141–147.

Cattell, R. B. (1934–1935). Friends and enemies: A psychological study of character and temperament. *Character and Personality, 3,* 54–63.

Cattell, R. B. (1950). *Personality: A systematical theoretical and factual study.* New York: McGraw-Hill.

Cattell, R. B. (1957). *Personality and motivation: Structure and measurement.* New York: World Book.

Cattell, R. B. (1965). *The scientific analysis of personality.* Harmondsworth, England: Penguin Books.

Cattell, R. B. (1971). *Abilities: Their structure, growth, and action.* New York: Houghton Mifflin.

Cattell, R. B., & Warburton, F. W. (1967). *Objective personality & motivation tests: A theoretical introduction and practical compendium.* Urbana: University of Illinois Press.

Cattell, R. B., Eber, H. W., & Tatsuoka, M. M. (1970). *Handbook for the Sixteen Personality Factor Questionnaire (16PF) in clinical, educational, industrial and research psychology.* Champaign, IL: Institute for Personality and Ability Testing.

Chan, K. B. (1977). Individual differences in reactions to stress and their personality and situational determinants: Some implications for community mental health. *Social Science and Medicine, 11,* 89–103.

Cheek, J. M. (1982). Aggregation, moderator variables, and the validity of personality tests: A peer rating study. *Journal of Personality and Social Psychology, 43,* 1254–1269.

Cherny, S. S., Fulker, D. W., Corley, R. P., Plomin, R., & DeFries, J. C. (1994). Continuity and change in infant shyness from 14 to 20 months. *Behavior Genetics, 24,* 365–379.

Chess, S., & Thomas, A. (1984). *Origins and evolution of behavior disorders: From infancy to early adult life.* New York: Brunner/Mazel.

Chess, S., & Thomas, A. (1986). *Temperament in clinical practice.* New York: Guilford.

Chess, S., & Thomas, A. (1989). Temperament and its functional significance. In S. I. Greenspan & G. H. Pollock (Eds.), *The course of life* (Vol. 2, pp. 163–227). Madison, CT: International Universities Press.

Chess, S., & Thomas, A. (1991). Temperament and the concept of goodness of fit. In J. Strelau & A. Angleitner (Eds.), *Explorations in temperament: International perspectives on theory and measurement* (pp. 15–28). New York: Plenum.

Chess, S., Korn, S., & Fernandez, P. (1971). *Psychiatric disorders of children with congenital rubella.* New York: Brunner/Mazel.

Chipperfield, J. G., & Eaton, W. O. (1992). Reactivity and environmental stimulation as predictors of motor activity level in children. *Personality and Individual Differences, 13,* 591–601.

Chudnovsky, V. E. (1963). Concerning the age approach to typological features. *Voprosy Psikhologii, 9,* 23–34. (in Russian)

Chuprikova, N. I. (1977). The analysis of psychological structure and physiological mechanisms of activity as a condition of the diagnosis of nervous system properties. In A. A. Simrnov (Ed.), *Psychology and psychophysiology of individual differences* (pp. 131–141). Moscow, Russia: Pedagogika. (in Russian)

Ciarkowska, W. (1992). *Psychofizjologiczna analiza aktywności poznawczej* [Psychophysiological analysis of cognitive activity]. Wrocław, Poland: Ossolineum.

Clapper, R. L. (1990). Adult and adolescent arousal preferences: The Revised Reducer–Augmenter Scale. *Personality and Individual Differences, 11,* 1115–1122.

Claridge, G. (1985). *Origins of mental illness: Temperament, deviance and disorder.* New York: Blackwell.

Claridge, G. (1987). Psychoticism and arousal. In J. Strelau & H. J. Eysenck (Eds.), *Personality dimensions and arousal* (pp. 133–150). New York: Plenum.

Cloninger, C. R. (1986). A unified biosocial theory of personality and its role in the development of anxiety states. *Psychiatric Developments, 3,* 167–226.

Cloninger, C. R., von Knorring, L., & Oreland, L. (1985). Parametric distribution of platelet monoamine oxidase activity. *Psychiatry Research, 15,* 133–143.

Cloninger, C. R., Svrakic, D. M., & Przybeck, T. R. (1991). The Tridimensional Personality Questionnaire: US normative data. *Psychological Reports, 69,* 1047–157.

Cloninger, C. R., Svrakic, D. M., & Przybeck T. R. (1993). A psychobiological model of temperament and character. *Archives of General Psychiatry, 50,* 975–990.

Collin, C., & Lolas, F. (1985). Hemispheric contribution to vertex augmentation/reduction of the auditory evoked potential. *Arquivos de Neuro-Psiquiatria, 43,* 347–354.

Conrad, K. (1941). *Der Konstitutionstypus: Theoretische Grundlegung und praktische Bestimmung* [The constitutional type: Theoretical foundation and practical significance]. Berlin, Germany: Springer.

Coren, S. (1988). Prediction of insomnia from arousability predisposition scores: Scale development and cross-validation. *Behaviour Research and Therapy, 26,* 415–420.

Coren, S. (1990). The Arousal Predisposition Scale: Normative data. *Bulletin of the Psychonomic Society, 28,* 551–552.

Costa, P. T., Jr. (1986) Is neuroticism a risk factor for CAD? Is Type A a measure of neuroticism? In T. H. Schmidt, T. M. Dembroski, & G. Blumchen (Eds.), *Biological and psychological factors in cardiovascular disease* (pp. 85–95). New York: Springer.

Costa, P. T., Jr., & McCrae, R. R. (1988). Personality in adulthood: A six-year longitudinal study of self-reports and spouse ratings on the NEO Personality Inventory. *Journal of Personality and Social Psychology, 54,* 853–863.

Costa, P. T., Jr., & McCrae, R. R. (1989). *NEO PI/FFI manual supplement.* Odessa, FL: Psychological Assessment Recources.

Costa, P. T., Jr., & McCrae, R. R. (1992a). Four ways five factors are basic. *Personality and Individual Differences, 13,* 653–665.

Costa, P. T., Jr., & McCrae, R. R. (1992b). *Revised NEO Personality Inventory (NEO PI–R) and NEO Five Factor Inventory (NEO-FFI): Professional manual.* Odessa, FL: Psychological Assessment Recources.

Costa, P. T., Jr., Fleg, J. L., McCrae, R. R., & Lakatta, E. G. (1982). Neuroticism, coronary artery disease, and chest pain complaints: Cross-sectional and longitudinal studies. *Explorations in Aging Research, 8,* 37–44.

Cowen, E. I., Wyman, P. A., & Work, W. C. (1992). The relationship between retrospective reports of early child temperament and adjustment at ages 10–12. *Journal of Abnormal Child Psychology, 20,* 39–50.

Cox, D. N. (1977). *Psychophysiological correlates of sensation seeking and socialization during reduced stimulation.* Unpublished doctoral dissertation, University of British Columbia, Vancouver, Canada.

Crow, T. J. (1977). Neurotransmitter related pathways: The structure and function of central monoamine neurons. In A. N. Davison (Ed.), *Biochemical correlates of brain structure and function* (pp. 137–174). New York: Academic Press.

Crowell, D. H., Jones, R. H., Kapuniani, L. E., & Nakagawa, J. K. (1973). Unilateral cortical activity in newborn humans: An early index of cerebral dominance? *Science, 180,* 205–208.

Cytawa, J. (1959). Badanie typu układu nerwowego człowieka na podstawie wywiadu [Assessment of the human type of nervous system by means of interview]. *Annales Universitatis Mariae Curie-Skłodowska, 14,* 137–156.

Czeschlik, T. (1993). General intelligence, temperament, and the Matching Familiar Figures Test. *European Journal of Personality, 7,* 379–386.

Dabbs, J. M., Jr., & Hopper, C. H. (1990). Cortisol, arousal, and personality in two groups of normal men. *Personality and Individual Differences, 11,* 931–935.

Daitzman, R. J., & Zuckerman, M. (1980). Disinhibitory sensation seeking personality, and gonadal hormones. *Personality and Individual Differences, 1,* 103–110.

Daniels, D., Plomin, R., & Greenhalgh, J. (1984). Correlates of difficult temperament in infancy. *Child Development, 55,* 1184–1194.

Danilova, N. N. (1986). Dynamics of AEP and heart rate as indicators of individual arousal level and learning. In J. Strelau, F. H. Farley, & A. Gale (Eds.), *The biological bases of personality and be-*

havior: Psychophysiology, performance, and application (Vol. 2, pp. 91–96). Washington, DC: Hemiphere.

Daruna, J. H., Karrer, R., & Rosen, A. J. (1985). Introversion, attention, and the late positive component of event-related potentials. *Biological Psychology, 20,* 249–259.

Davidson, L. L. (1987). Hyperactivity, antisocial behavior, and childhood injury: A critical analysis of the literature. *Developmental and Behavioral Pediatrics, 8,* 335–340.

Davidson, R. J. (1984). Hemispheric asymmetry and emotion. In K. Scherer & P. Ekman (Eds.), *Approaches to emotion* (pp. 39–57). Hillsdale, NJ: Erlbaum.

Davidson, R. J. (1987). Cerebral asymmetry and the nature of emotion: Implications for the study of individual differences and psychopathology. In R. Takahashi, P. Flor-Henry, J. Gruzelier, & S. Niwa (Eds.), *Cerebral dynamics, laterality and psychopathology* (pp. 71–83). New York: Elsevier.

Davidson, R. J., & Fox, N. A. (1982). Asymmetrical brain activity discriminates between positive and negative affective stimuli in human infants. *Science, 218,* 1235–1236.

Davidson, R. J., Ekman, P., Saron, C. D., Senulis, J. A., & Friesen, W. V. (1990). Approach–withdrawal and cerebral asymmetry: Emotional expression and brain physiology I. *Journal of Personality and Social Psychology, 58,* 330–341.

Davis, C. (1988). Reliability of psychophysiological assessment within temperament groups. *International Journal of Psychophysiology, 6,* 299–305.

Davis, F. C. (1935). The measurement of aggressive behavior in laboratory rats. *Journal of Genetic Psychology, 43,* 213–217.

Davis, H. (1898). The psychology of temperament and its epistemological applications. *Philosophical Review, 7,* 162–180.

Davydova, A. N. (1954). Monographic study of children with features of various types of nervous system. *Izvestiya Academii Pedagogicheskikh Nauk RSFSR, 52,* 141–183. (in Russian)

DeFries, J. C., & Plomin, R. (1978). Behavioral genetics. *Annual Review of Psychology, 29,* 473–515.

De Giovanni, A. (1891). *Morfologia del corpo umano* [Morphology of the human body]. Milan, Italy: U. Hoepli.

DeLongis, A., Folkman, S., & Lazarus, R. S. (1988). The impact of daily stressors on health and mood: Psychological and social measures as mediators. *Journal of Personality and Social Psychology, 54,* 486–495.

Demisch, L., Georgi, K., Patzke, B., Demisch, K., & Bochnik, H. J. (1982). Correlation of platelet MAO activity with introversion: A study on a German rural population. *Psychiatry Research, 6,* 303–311.

De Pascalis, V. (1993). Hemispheric asymmetry, personality and temperament. *Personality and Individual Differences, 14,* 825–834.

De Pascalis, V. (1994). Personality and temperament in the event-related potentials during stimulus recognition tasks. *Personality and Individual Differences, 16,* 877–889.

De Pascalis, V., Strelau, J., & Zawadzki, B. (in press). Event-related potentials, heart rate and reaction time correlates of temperamental traits. *Personality and Individual Differences, 25.*

Derogatis, L. R. (1983). *SCL-90–R revised manual.* Baltimore: Johns Hopkins University School of Medicine.

Derryberry, D. (1987). Incentive and feedback effects on target detection: A chronometric analysis of Gray's model of temperament. *Personality and Individual Differences, 8,* 855–865.

Derryberry, D., & Rothbart, M. K. (1984). Emotion, attention, and temperament. In C. E. Izard, J. Kagan, & R. Zajonc (Eds.), *Emotion, cognition and behavior* (pp. 132–166). Cambridge, England: Cambridge University Press.

Derryberry, D., & Rothbart, M. K. (1988). Arousal, affect, and attention as components of temperament. *Journal of Personality and Social Psychology, 55,* 958–966.

de Vries, M. W. (1984). Temperament and infant mortality among the Masai of East Africa. *American Journal of Psychiatry, 141,* 1189–1194.

de Vries, M. W. (1987). Cry babies, culture, and catastrophe: Infant temperament among the Masai. In N. Scheper-Hughes (Ed.), *Child survival* (pp. 165–185). Dordrecht, The Netherlands: D. Reidel.

de Vries, M. W. (1994). Kids in context: Temperament in cross-cultural perspective. In W. B. Carey & S. C. McDevitt (Eds.), *Prevention and early intervention: Individual differences as risk factors for the mental health of children* (pp. 126–148). New York: Brunner/Mazel.

de Vries, M. W., & Sameroff, A. J. (1984). Culture and temperament: Influences on infant temperament in three East African cultures. *American Journal of Orthopsychiatry, 54,* 83–96.

Diamond, S. (1957). *Personality and temperament.* New York: Harper.

Digman, J. M. (1990). Personality structure: Emergence of the five-factor model. *Annual Review of Psychology, 41,* 417–440.

Digman, J. M., & Takemoto-Chock, N. K. (1981). Factors in the natural language of personality: Reanalysis, comparison, and interpretation of six major studies. *Multivariate Behavioral Research, 16,* 149–170.

Dincheva, E. G., & Piperova-Dalbokova, D. L. (1982). Differences in contingent negative variation (CNV) related to extraversion–introversion. *Personality and Individual Differences, 3,* 447–451.

DiTraglia, G. M., & Polich, J. (1991). P300 and introverted/extraverted personality types. *Psychophysiology, 28,* 177–184.

Doelling, J. L., & Johnson, J. H. (1990). Predicting success in foster placement: The contribution of parent–child temperament characteristics. *American Journal of Orthopsychiatry, 60,* 585–593.

Dollard, J., & Miller, N. E. (1950). *Personality and psychotherapy.* New York: McGraw-Hill.

Donchin, E., & Coles, M. G. H. (1988). Is the P300 component a manifestation of context updating? *Behavioral and Brain Sciences, 11,* 357–374.

Downey, J. E. (1923). *The will–temperament and its testing.* New York: World Book.

Drwal, R. L. (1990). Problemy kulturowej adaptacji kwestionariuszy osobowości [Problems in the cultural adaptation of personality questionnaires]. In A. Ciechanowicz (Ed.), *Kulturowa adaptacja testów* [Cultural adaptation of tests] (pp. 115–138). Warsaw, Poland: Polish Psychological Society.

Dubos, R. (1965). *Man adapting.* New Haven, CT: Yale University Press.

Duckitt, J., & Broll, T. (1982). Personality factors as moderators of the psychological impact of life stress. *South African Journal of Psychology, 12,* 76–80.

Duffy, E. (1957). The psychological significance of the concept of "arousal" or "activation." *Psychological Review, 64,* 265–275.

Earls, F., & Jung, K. G. (1987). Temperament and home environment characteristics as causal factors in the early development of childhood psychopathology. *Journal of the American Academy of Child and Adolescent Psychiatry, 26,* 491–498.

Eaton, W. O. (1983). Measuring activity level with actometers: Reliability, validity, and arm length. *Child Development, 54,* 720–726.

Eaton, W. O. (1994). Temperament, development, and the five-factor model: Lessons from activity level. In C. F. Halverson, Jr., G. A. Kohnstamm, & R. P. Martin (Eds.), *The developing structure of temperament and personality from infancy to adulthood* (pp. 173–187). Hillsdale, NJ: Erlbaum.

Eaton, W. O., & Dureski, C. M. (1986). Parent and actometer measures of motor activity level in the young infant. *Infant Behavior and Development, 9,* 383–393.

Eaton, W. O., & Saudino, K. J. (1992). Prenatal activity level as a temperament dimension? Individual differences and developmental functions in fetal movement. *Infant Behavior and Development, 15,* 57–70.

Eaves, L. J., & Eysenck, H. J. (1975). The nature of extraversion: A genetical analysis. *Journal of Personality and Social Psychology, 32,* 102–112.

Eaves, L. J., & Eysenck, H. J. (1976a). Genetical and environmental components of inconsistency and unrepeatability in twins' responses to a neuroticism questionnaire. *Behavior Genetics, 6,* 145–160.

Eaves, L. J., & Eysenck, H. J. (1976b). Genotype x age interaction for neuroticism. *Behavior Genetics, 6,* 359–362.

Eaves, L. J., & Eysenck, H. J. (1977). A genotype-environmental model for psychoticism. *Advances in Behaviour Research and Therapy, 1,* 5–26.

Eaves, L. J., Martin, N. G., & Eysenck, S. B. G. (1977). An application of the analysis of covariance structures to the psychogenetical study of impulsiveness. *British Journal of Mathematical and Statistical Psychology, 30,* 185–197.

Eaves, L. J., Eysenck, H. J., & Martin, N. G. (1989). *Genes, culture and personality: An empirical approach.* New York: Academic Press.

Ebstein, R. P., Novick, O., Umansky, R., Priel, B., Osher, Y., Blaine, D., Bennett, E. R., Nemanov, L., Katz, M., & Belmaker, R. H. (1996). Dopamine D4 receptor (D4DR) exon III polymorphism associated with the human personality trait of novelty seeking. *Nature Genetics, 12,* 78–80.

Edwards, A. L. (1957). *The social desirability variable in personality assessment and research.* New York: Dryden.

Edwards, A. L. (1970). *The measurement of personality traits by scales and inventories.* New York: Holt, Rinehart & Winston.

Ekman, G. (1951). On the number and definition of dimensions in Kretschmer's and Sheldon's constitutions systems. In G. Ekman (Ed.), *Essays in psychology dedicated to David Katz* (pp. 72–103). Uppsala, Sweden: Almquist and Wiksells.

Ekman, P. (1992). An argument for basic emotions. *Congition and Emotion, 6,* 169–200.

Eliasz, A. (1981). *Temperament a system regulacji stymulacji* [Temperament and system of regulation of stimulation]. Warsaw: Państwowe Wydawnictwo Naukowe.

Eliasz, A. (1985). Transactional model of temperament. In J. Strelau (Ed.), *Temperamental bases of behavior: Warsaw studies on individual differences* (pp. 41–78). Lisse, The Netherlands: Swets & Zeitlinger.

Eliasz, A. (1990). Broadening the concept of temperament: From disposition to hypothetical construct. *European Journal of Personality, 4,* 287–302.

Eliasz, A., & Wrześniewski, K. (1986). Type A behavior resulting from internal or external reinforcements. *Polish Psychological Bulletin, 17,* 39–53.

Ellis, M. V., & Robbins, E. (1990). In celebration of nature: A dialogue with Jerome Kagan. *Journal of Counseling & Development, 68,* 623–627.

Emde, R. N., Plomin, R., Robinson, J. Corley, R., DeFries, J., Fulker, D. W., Reznick, J. S., Campos, J., Kagan, J., & Zahn-Waxler, C. (1992). Temperament, emotion, and cognition at fourteen months: The MacArthur Longitudinal Twin Study. *Child Development, 63,* 1437–1455.

Emmons, R. A., Diener, E., & Larsen, R. J. (1986). Choice and avoidance of everyday situations and affect congruence: Two models of reciprocal interactionism. *Journal of Personality and Social Psychology, 51,* 815–826.

Endler, N. S. (1989) The temperamental nature of personality. *European Journal of Personality, 3,* 151–165.

Endler, N. S., & Parker, J. D. A. (1990). *Coping Inventory for Stressful Situations (CISS): Manual.* Toronto, Ontario, Canada: Multi-Health Systems.

Enke, W. (1930). Die Psychomotorik der Konstitutionstypen [The psycho-motor of constitutional types]. *Zeitschrift für angewandte Psychologie, 36,* 237–287.

Eppinger, H., & Hess, L. (1910). *Die Vagotonie* [Vagotonia]. Berlin, Germany: Springer.

Epstein, S. (1979). The stability of behavior: On predicting most of the people much of the time. *Journal of Personality and Social Psychology, 37,* 1097–1126.

Epstein, S. (1980). The stability of behavior: II. Implications for psychological research. *American Psychologist, 35,* 790–806.

Epstein, S. (1990). Cognitive-experiental self-theory. In L. A. Pervin (Ed.), *Handbook of personality: Theory and research* (pp. 165–192). New York: Guilford.

Escalona, S. K. (1968). *The roots of individuality: Normal patterns of development in infancy.* Chicago: Aldine.

Ewald, G. (1924). *Temperament und Charakter* [Temperament and character]. Berlin, Germany: Springer.

Eysenck, H. J. (1944). Types of personality—A factorial study of 700 neurotics. *Journal of Mental Science, 90,* 851–861.

Eysenck, H. J. (1947). *Dimensions of personality.* London: Routledge & Kegan Paul.

Eysenck, H. J. (1952). *The scientific study of personality.* London: Routledge & Kegan Paul.

Eysenck, H. J. (1955). Cortical inhibition, figural aftereffects, and theory of personality. *Journal of Abnormal and Social Psychology, 51,* 94–106.

Eysenck, H. J. (1956). The questionnaire measurement of neuroticism and extraversion. *Revista de Psicologica, 54,* 113–140.

Eysenck, H. J. (1957). *The dynamics of anxiety and hysteria.* London: Routledge & Kegan Paul.

Eysenck, H. J. (1959). *A manual of the Maudsley Personality Inventory.* London: University of London Press.

Eysenck, H. J. (Ed.). (1963). *Experiments with drugs.* London: Pergamon.

Eysenck, H. J. (1964). The biological basis of criminal behavior. *Nature, 203,* 952–953.

Eysenck, H. J. (Ed.). (1965). *Experiments in motivation.* Oxford, England: Pergamon.

Eysenck, H. J. (1967). *The biological basis of personality.* Springfield, IL: Thomas.

Eysenck, H. J. (1970). *The structure of human personality* (3rd ed.). London: Methuen.

Eysenck, H. J. (1976). *Sex and personality.* London: Open Books.

Eysenck, H. J. (1977). *Crime and personality* (3rd ed.). London: Routledge & Kegan Paul.

Eysenck, H. J. (1978). Superfactors P, E, and N in a comprehensive factor space. *Multivariate Behavioral Research, 13,* 475–482.

Eysenck, H. J. (1981). General features of the model. In H. J. Eysenck (Ed.), *A model for personality* (pp. 1–37). Berlin, Germany: Springer.

Eysenck, H. J. (1982). The biological basis of cross-cultural differences in personality: Blood group antigens. *Psychological Reports, 51,* 531–540.

Eysenck, H. J. (1983a). A biometrical-genetical analysis of impulsive and sensation seeking behavior. In M. Zuckerman (Ed.), *Biological bases of sensation seeking, impulsivity, and anxiety* (pp. 1–36). Hillsdale, NJ: Erlbaum.

Eysenck, H. J. (1983b). Stress, disease, and personality: The "inoculation effect." In C. L. Cooper (Ed.), *Stress research* (pp. 121–131). London: Wiley.

Eysenck, H. J. (1985). Personality, cancer and cardiovascular disease: A causal analysis. *Personality and Individual Differences, 6,* 535–556.

Eysenck, H. J. (1986). Models and paradigms in personality research. In A. Angleitner, A. Furnham, & G. Van Heck (Eds.), *Personality psychology in Europe: Current trends and controversies* (Vol. 2, pp. 213–223). Lisse, The Netherlands: Swets & Zeitlinger.

Eysenck, H. J. (1988). The respective importance of personality, cigarette smoking and interaction effects for the genesis of cancer and coronary heart disease. *Personality and Individual Differences, 9,* 453–464.

Eysenck, H. J. (1990a). Biological dimensions of personality. In L. A. Pervin (Ed.), *Handbook of personality: Theory and research* (pp. 244–276). New York: Guilford.

Eysenck, H. J. (1990b). Genetic and environmental contributions to individual differences: The three major dimensions of personality. *Journal of Personality, 58,* 245–261.

Eysenck, H. J. (1991a). Biological dimensions of personality. In L. A. Pervin (Ed.), *Handbook of personality* (pp. 244–276). New York: Guilford.

Eysenck, H. J. (1991b). Dimensions of personality: The biosocial approach to personality. In J. Strelau & A. Angleitner (Eds.), *Explorations in temperament: International perspectives on theory and measurement* (pp. 87–103). New York: Plenum.

Eysenck, H. J. (1991c). *Smoking, personality and stress: Psychosocial factors in the prevention of cancer and coronary heart disease.* New York: Springer.

Eysenck, H. J. (1992a). The definition and measurement of psychoticism. *Personality and Individual Differences, 13,* 757–785.

Eysenck, H. J. (1992b). Four ways five factors are not basic. *Personality and Individual Differences, 13,* 667–673.

Eysenck, H. J. (1992c). *A hundred years of personality research, from Heymans to modern times.* Twelfth Duijker Lecture. Houten, The Netherlands: Bohn Stafleu Van Loghum.

Eysenck, H. J. (1993). From DNA to social behaviour: Conditions for a paradigm of personality research. In J. Hettema & I. J. Deary (Eds.), *Foundations of personality* (pp. 55–66). Dordrecht, The Netherlands: Kluwer Academic Publishers.

Eysenck, H. J. (1994a). The Big Five or Giant Three: Criteria for a paradigm. In C. F. Halverson, Jr., G. A. Kohnstamm, & R. P. Martin (Eds.), *The developing structure of temperament and personality from infancy to adulthood* (pp. 37–51). Hillsdale, NJ: Erlbaum.

Eysenck, H. J. (1994b). Cancer, personality and stress: Prediction and prevention. *Advances in Behaviour Research and Therapy, 16,* 167–215.

Eysenck, H. J., & Eysenck, M. W. (1985). *Personality and individual differences: A natural science approach.* New York: Plenum.

Eysenck, H. J., & Eysenck, S. B. G. (1964). *The Eysenck Personality Inventory.* London: University of London Press.

Eysenck, H. J., & Eysenck, S. B. G. (1975). *Manual of the Eysenck Personality Questionnaire (Junior & Adult).* London: Hodder & Stoughton.

Eysenck, H. J., & Eysenck, S. B. G. (1976). *Psychoticism as a dimension of personality.* London: Hodder & Stoughton.

Eysenck, H. J., & Eysenck, S. B. G. (1982). Recent advances in the cross-cultural study of personality. In C. D. Spielberger & J. N. Butscher (Eds.), *Advances in personality assessment* (Vol. 2, pp. 41–69). Hillsdale, NJ: Erlbaum.

Eysenck, H. J., & Gudjonsson, G. (1990). *The causes and cures of criminality.* New York: Plenum.

Eysenck, H. J., & Levey, A. (1972). Conditioning, introversion–extraversion and the strength of the nervous system. In V. D. Nebylitsyn & J. A. Gray (Eds.), *Biological bases of individual behavior* (pp. 206–220). New York: Academic Press.

Eysenck, H. J., & O'Connor, K. P. (1979). Smoking, arousal and personality. In A. J. Remond & J. Tizard (Eds.), *Electrophysiological effects of nicotine* (pp. 115–128). Amsterdam, The Netherlands: Elsevier.

Eysenck, H. J., & Prell, D. B. (1951). The inheritance of neuroticism: An experimental study. *Journal of Mental Science, 97,* 441–465.

Eysenck, H. J., & Prell, D. B. (1956). The inheritance of introversion–extraversion. *Acta Psychologica, 12,* 95–110.

Eysenck, H. J., Wilson, G., & Jackson, C. (1996). *EPP: Eysenck Personality Profiler.* London: Psi-Press.

Eysenck, M. W. (1987). Trait theories of anxiety. In J. Strelau & H. J. Eysenck (Eds.), *Personality dimensions and arousal* (pp. 79–97). New York: Plenum.

Eysenck, S. B. G. (1965). *The Junior Eysenck Personality Inventory.* London: University of London Press.

Eysenck, S. B. G. (1983). One aproach to cross-cultural studies of personality. *Australian Journal of Psychology, 35,* 381–391.

Eysenck, S. B. G., & Eysenck, H. J. (1978). Impulsiveness and venturesomeness: Their position in a dimensional system of personality description. *Psychological Reports, 43,* 1247–1255.

Eysenck, S. B. G., & Eysenck, H. J. (1980). Impulsiveness and venturesomeness in children. *Personality and Individual Differences, 1,* 73–78.

Eysenck, S. B. G., Easting, G., & Pearson, P. R. (1984). Age norms for impulsiveness, venturesomeness and empathy in children. *Personality and Individual Differences, 5,* 315–321.

Eysenck, S. B. G., Eysenck, H. J., & Barrett, P. (1985). A revised version of the Psychoticism scale. *Personality and Individual Differences, 6,* 21–29.

Eysenck, S. B. G., Pearson, P. R., Easting, G, & Allsopp, J. F. (1985). Age norms for impulsiveness, venturesomeness and empathy in adults. *Personality and Individual Differences, 6,* 613–619.

Fahrenberg, J. (1977). Physiological concepts in personality research. In R. B. Cattell & R. M. Dreger (Eds.), *Handbook of modern personality theory* (pp. 585–611). Washington, DC: Hemisphere.

Fahrenberg, J. (1987). Concepts of activation and arousal in the theory of emotionality (neuroticism): A multivariate conceptualization. In J. Strelau & H. J. Eysenck (Eds.), *Personality dimensions and arousal* (pp. 99–120). New York: Plenum.

Fahrenberg, J. (1992). Psychophysiology of neuroticism and anxiety. In A. Gale & M. W. Eysenck (Eds.), *Handbook of individual differences: Biological perspectives* (pp. 179–226). Chichester, England: Wiley.

Fahrenberg, J., Selg, H., & Hampel, R. (1978). *Das Freiburger Personlichkeitsinventar (FPI). Handanweisung* [The Freiburger Personality Inventory (FPI). Manual] (3rd ed.). Göttingen, Germany: Hogrefe.

Fahrenberg, J., Walschburger, P, Foerster, F., Myrtek, M., & Müller, W. (1983). An evaluation of trait, state, and reaction aspects of activation processes. *Psychophysiology, 20,* 188–195.

Fahrenberg, J., Foerster, F., Schneider, H. J., Muller, W., & Myrtek, M. (1984). *Aktivierungsforschung im Labor-Feld-Vergleich* [Research on arousal in laboratory-field comparisons]. Munich, Germany: Minerva-Publitation.

Falconer, D. S. (1960). *Introduction to quantitative genetics.* New York: Ronald.

Falkiewicz, L. (1874). *O poznawaniu temperamentów dzieci* [The study on temperament in children]. Kraków, Poland: Czytelnia Ludowa.

Feij, J. A. (1984). Heymans' temperament model [Heymans' model of temperament]. *Nederlands Tijdschrift voor de Psychologie, 39,* 127–145.

Feij, J. A., & Orlebeke, J. F. (1974). Spiral after-effect duration as a correlate of impulsiveness. *Journal of Research in Personality, 8,* 189–197.

Feij, J. A., Orlebeke, J. F., Gazendam, A., & van Zuilen, R. W. (1985). In J. Strelau, F. H. Farley, & A. Gale (Eds.), *The biological bases of behavior: Theories, measurement techniques, and development* (Vol. 1, pp. 195–210). Washington, DC: Hemisphere.

Feij, J. A., Doorn, C. D., van Kampen, D., van den Berg, P. T., & Resing, W. C. M. (1992). Sensation seeking and social support as moderators of the relationship between life events and physical illness. In J. A. M. Winnubst & S. Maes (Eds.), *Life styles, stress and health: New developments in health psychology* (pp. 285–302). Leiden, The Netherlands: Leiden University Press.

Festinger, L. (1957). *A theory of cognitive dissonance.* Stanford, CA: Stanford University Press.

Field, T., & Greenberg, R. (1982). Temperament ratings by parents and teachers of infants, toddlers, and preschool children. *Child Development, 53,* 160–163.

Field, T., Hallock, N., Ting, G., Dempsey, J., Dabira, C., & Shuman, H. (1978). A first year follow-up of high risk infants: Formulating a cumulative risk index. *Child Development, 53,* 160–163.

Field, T., Vega-Lahr, N., Scafidi, F., & Goldstein, S. (1987). Reliability, stability, and relationships between infant and parent temperament. *Infant Behavior and Development, 10,* 117–122.

Fiske, D. W. (1971). *Measuring the concepts of personality.* Chicago: Aldine.

Fiske, D. W. (1986). The trait concept and the personality questionnaire. In A. Angleitner & J. S. Wiggins (Eds.), *Personality assessment via questionnaires* (pp. 35–46). Berlin, Germany: Springer.

Fiske, D. W., & Maddi. S. R. (1961). *Functions of varied experience.* Homewood, IL: Dorsey.

Floderus-Myrhed, B., Pedersen, N., & Rasmuson, I. (1980). Assessment of heritability for personality, based on a short-form of the Eysenck Personality Inventory: A study of 12,898 twin pairs. *Behavior Genetics, 10,* 153–162.

Folkman, S., & Lazarus, R. S. (1985). If it changes it must be a process: Study of emotion and coping during three stages of a college examination. *Journal of Personality and Social Psychology, 48,* 150–170.

Folkman, S., & Lazarus, R. S. (1988). Coping as a mediator of emotion. *Journal of Personality and Social Psychology, 54,* 466–475.

Fouillée, A. (1895). *Le tempérament et le caractére selon les individus, les sexes et les ages* [Temperament and character in individuals differing in sex and age]. Paris: Felix Alcan.

Fowles, D. C. (1980). The three arousal model: Implications of Gray's two-factor learning theory for heart rate, electrodermal activity and psychopathy. *Psychophysiology, 17,* 87–104.

Fowles, D. C. (1992). Motivational approach to anxiety disorders. In D. G. Forgays, T. Sosnowski, & K. Wrzeźniewski (Eds.), *Anxiety: Recent developments in cognitive, psychophysiological, and health research* (pp. 181–192). Washington, DC: Hemisphere.

Fowles, D. C., Roberts, R., & Nagel, K. (1977). The influence of introversion/extraversion on the skin conductance response to stress and stimulus intensity. *Journal of Research in Personality, 11,* 129–146.

Fox, B. (1989). Depressive symptoms and risk of cancer. *Journal of the American Medical Association, 262,* 1231.

Fox, B., & Temoshok, L. (1988). Mind–body and behavior in cancer incidence. *Advances, Institute for the Advancement of Health, 5,* 41–56.

Frankel, K. A., & Bates, J. E. (1990). Mother–toddler problem solving: Antecedents in attachment, home behavior, and temperament. *Child Development, 61,* 810–819.

Frankenhaeuser, M. (1979). Psychoneuroendocrine approaches to the study of emotion as related to stress and coping. In H. E. Howe & R. A. Dienstbier (Eds.), *Nebraska Symposion on Motivation, 1978* (pp. 123–161). Lincoln: University of Nebraska Press.

Frankenhaeuser, M. (1986). A psychobiological framework for research on human stress and coping. In M. H. Appley & R. Trumbull (Eds.), *Dynamics of stress: Physiological, psychological, and social perspectives* (pp. 101–116). New York: Plenum.

Freedy, J. R., Kilpatrick, D. G., & Resnick, H. S. (1993). Natural disasters and mental health: Theory, assessment, and intervention. *Journal of Social Behavior and Personality, 8,* 49–103.

Friedensberg, E. (1985). Reactivity and individual style of work exemplified by constructional-type task performance: A developmental study. In J. Strelau, F. H. Farley, & A. Gale (1985). *The biological bases of personality and behavior: Theories, measurement techniques, and development* (Vol. 1, pp. 241–253). Washington, DC: Hemisphere.

Friedensberg, E., & Strelau, J. (1982). The Reactivity Rating Scale (RRS): Reliability and validity. *Polish Psychological Bulletin, 13,* 223–237.

Friedman, H. S., & Booth-Kewley, S. (1987). The "disease-prone personality": A meta-analytic view of the construct. *American Psychologist, 42,* 539–555.

Fulker, D. W., Eysenck, S. B. G., & Zuckerman, M. (1980). A genetic and environmental analysis of sensation seeking. *Journal of Research in Personality, 14,* 261–281.

Fullard, W., McDevitt, S. C., & Carey, W. B. (1984). Assessing temperament in one-to-three-year-old children. *Journal of Pediatric Psychology, 9,* 205–216.

Fuller, J. L., & Thompson, W. R. (1978). *Foundations of behavior genetics.* St. Louis, MO: Mosby.

Furnham, A. (1981). Personality and activity preference. *British Journal of Social Psychology, 20,* 57–68.

Gabbay, F. H. (1992). Behavior-genetic strategies in the study of emotion. *Psychological Science, 3,* 50–55.

Gacsaly, S. A., & Borges, C. A. (1979). The male physique and behavioral expectancies. *Journal of Psychology, 101,* 97–102.

Gale, A. (1973). The psychophysiology of individual differences: Studies of extraversion and the EEG. In P. Kline (Ed.), *New approaches in psychological measurement* (pp. 211–256). London: Wiley.

Gale, A. (1983). Electroencephalographic studies of extraversion–introversion: A case study in the psychophysiology of individual differences. *Personality and Individual Differences, 4,* 371–380.

Gale, A. (1986). Extraversion–introversion and spontaneous rhythms of the brain: Retrospect and prospect. In J. Strelau, F. H. Farley, & A. Gale (Eds.), *The biological bases of personality and behavior: Psychophysiology, performance, and applications* (Vol. 2, pp. 25–42). Washington, DC: Hemisphere.

Gale, A., & Edwards, J. A. (Eds.). (1983a). *Physiological correlates of human behavior: Basic issues* (Vol. 1). London: Academic Press.

Gale, A., & Edwards, J. A. (1983b). Psychophysiology and individual differences: Theory, research procedures, and the interpretation of data. *Australian Journal of Psychology, 35,* 361–379.

Gale, A., & Eysenck, M. W. (Eds.). (1992). *Handbook of individual differences: Biological perspective.* Chichester, England: Wiley.

Gange, J. J., Geen, R. G., & Harkins, S. G. (1979). Autonomic differences between extraverts and introverts during vigilance. *Psychophysiology, 16,* 392–397.

Garau, A., & Garcia-Sevilla, L. (1985). Drug postulate of Eysenck in the rat. *Personality and Individual Differences, 6,* 189–194.

Garcia-Coll, C., Kagan, J., & Reznick, J. S. (1984). Behavioral inhibition in young children. *Child Development, 55,* 1005–1019.

Garrison, W. T. (1991). Assessment of temperament and behavioral style. In J. H. Johnson & J. Goldman (Eds.), *Developmental assessment in clinical child psychology: A handbook* (pp. 197–218). New York: Pergamon.

Garrison, W. T., & Earls, F. J. (1987). *Temperament and child psychopathology.* Newbury Park, CA: Sage.

Garside, R. F., Birch, H., Scott, D. M., Chambers, S., Kolvin, I., Tweedle, E. G., & Barber, L. M. (1975). Dimensions of temperament in infant school children. *Journal of Child Psychology and Psychiatry, 16,* 219–231.

Gattaz, W. F., & Beckmann, H. (1981). Platelet MAO activity and personality characteristics: A study in schizophrenic patients and normal individuals. *Acta Psychiatrica Scandinavica, 63,* 479–485.

Geen, R. G. (1983). The psychophysiology of extraversion–introversion. In J. T. Cacioppo & R. E. Petty (Eds.), *Social psychophysiology: A sourcebook* (pp. 391–416). New York: Guilford.

Geen, R. G. (1984). Preferred stimulation levels in introverts and extraverts: Effects on arousal and performance. *Journal of Personality and Social Psychology, 46,* 1303–1312.

Gesell, A., & Ames, L. B. (1937). Early evidence on individuality in the human infant. *Scientific Monthly, 45,* 217–225.

Gibbs, M. V., Reeves, D., & Cunningham, C. C. (1987). The application of temperament questionnaires to a British sample: Issues of reliability and validity. *Journal of Child Psychology and Psychiatry, 28,* 61–77.

Giese, H., & Schmidt, A. (1968). *Studenten Sexualität* [The sexuality of students]. Hamburg, Germany: Rowohlt.

Glanzman, P., & Froelich, W. D. (1984). Anxiety, stress and the contingent negative variation reconsidered. *Annals of the New York Academy of Sciences, 425,* 578–584.

Glass, A. (Ed.). (1987). *Individual differences in hemispheric specialization.* New York: Plenum.

Goddard, M. E., & Beilharz, R. G. (1982). Genetic and environmental factors affecting suitability of dogs as guide dogs for the blind. *Theoretical and Applied Genetics, 62,* 97–102.

Goh, D. S., & Farley, F. H. (1977). Personality effects on cognitive test performance. *Journal of Psychology, 96,* 111–122.

Goldberg, L. R. (1990). An alternative "description of personality": The Big-Five factor structure. *Journal of Personality and Social Psychology, 59,* 1216–1229.

Goldberg, L. R., & Rosolack, T. K. (1994). The big five factor structure as an integrative framework: An empirical comparison with Eysenck's P-E-N model. In C. F. Halverson, Jr., G. A. Kohnstamm, & R. P. Martin (Eds.), *The developing structure of temperament and personality from infancy to adulthood* (pp. 7–35). Hillsdale, NJ: Erlbaum.

Goldberg, S., & Marcovitch, S. (1989). Temperament in developmentally disabled children. In G. A. Kohnstamm, J. E. Bates, & M. K. Rothbart (Eds.), *Temperament in childhood* (pp. 387–403). Chichester, England: Wiley.

Golding, J. F., & Richards, M. (1985). EEG spectral analysis, visual evoked potential and photic-driving correlates of personality and memory. *Personality and Individual Differences, 6,* 67–76.

Goldsmith, H. H. (1983). Genetic influences on personality from infancy to adulthood. *Child Development, 54,* 331–355.

Goldsmith, H. H. (1988). Human developmental behavioral genetics: Mapping the effects of genes and environments. *Annals of Child Development, 5,* 187–227.

Goldsmith, H. H. (1989). Behavior-genetic approaches to temperament. In G. A. Kohnstamm, J. E. Bates, & M. K. Rothbart (Eds.), *Temperament in childhood* (pp. 111–132). Chichester, England: Wiley.

Goldsmith, H. H. (1993). Temperament: Variability in developing emotion systems. In M. Lewis & J. M. Haviland (Eds.), *Handbook of emotions* (pp. 353–364). New York: Guilford.

Goldsmith, H. H. (1994). Genetics and emotional development. In N. Frijda (Ed.), *Proceeding of the International Society for Research on Emotion* (pp. 252–256). Storrs, CT: ISRE Publications.

Goldsmith, H. H. (1996). Studying temperament via construction of the Toddler Behavior Assessment Questionnaire. *Child Development, 67,* 218–225.

Goldsmith, H. H., & Campos, J. J. (1982). Toward a theory of infant temperament. In R. N. Emde & R. J. Harmon (Eds.), *The development of attachment and affiliative systems* (pp. 161–193). New York: Plenum.

Goldsmith, H. H., & Campos, J. J. (1986). Fundamental issues in the study of early temperament: The Denver Twin Temperamental Study. In M. E. Lamb, A. L. Brown, & B. Rogoff (Eds.), *Advances in developmental psychology* (Vol. 4, pp. 231–283). Hillsdale, NJ: Erlbaum.

Goldsmith, H. H., & Campos, J. J. (1990). The structure of temperamental fear and pleasure in infants: A psychometric perspective. *Child Development, 61,* 1944–1964.

Goldsmith, H. H., & Gottesman, I. I. (1981). Origins of variation in behavioral style: A longitudinal study of temperament in young twins. *Child Development, 52,* 91–103.

Goldsmith, H. H., & Harman, C. (1994). Temperament and attachment; Individuals and relationships. *Current Directions in Psychological Science, 3,* 53–57.

Goldsmith, H. H., Rieser-Danner, L. A. (1986). Variation among temperament theories and validation studies of temperament assessment. In G. A. Kohnstamm (Ed.), *Temperament discussed* (pp. 1–9). Lisse, The Netherlands: Swets & Zeitlinger.

Goldsmith, H. H., & Rieser-Danner, L. A. (1990). Assessing early temperament. In C. R. Reynolds & R. W. Kamphaus, (Eds.), *Handbook of psychological and educational assessment of children: Personality, behavior, and context* (pp. 245–278). New York: Guilford.

Goldsmith, H. H., & Rothbart, M. K. (1991). Contemporary instruments for assessing early temperament by questionnaire and in the laboratory. In J. Strelau & A. Angleitner (Eds.). *Explorations in temperament: International perspectives on theory and measurement* (pp. 249–272). New York: Plenum.

Goldsmith, H. H., & Rothbart, M. K. (1992a). *Laboratory Temperament Assessment Battery (LAB-TAB): Locomotor version 2.01.* Unpublished manuscript, Universtiy of Oregon, Department of Psychology, Eugene.

Goldsmith, H. H., & Rothbart, M. K. (1992b). *Laboratory Temperament Assessment Battery (LAB-TAB): Prelocomotor version 2.0.* Unpublished manuscript, University of Oregon, Department of Psychology, Eugene.

Goldsmith, H. H., Bradshaw, D. L., & Rieser-Danner, L. A. (1986). Temperament as a potential developmental influence on attachment. In J. V. Lerner & R. M. Lerner (Eds.), *Temperament and social interaction during infancy and childhood* (pp. 5–34). San Francisco: Jossey-Bass.

Goldsmith, H. H., Elliot, T. K., & Jaco, K. L. (1986). Construction and initial validation of a new temperament questionnaire. *Infant Behavior and Development, 9,* 144.

Goldsmith, H. H., Buss, A. H., Plomin, R., Rothbart, M. K., Thomas, A., Chess, S., Hinde, R. A., & McCall, R. B. (1987). Roundtable: What is temperament? Four approaches. *Child Development, 58,* 505–529.

Goldsmith, H. H., Losoya, S. H., Bradshaw, D. L., & Campos, J. J. (1994). Genetics of personality: A twin study of the five-factor model and parent–offspring analyses. In C. F. Halverson, Jr., G. A.

Kohnstamm, & R. P. Martin (Eds.), *The developing structure of temperament and personality from infancy to adulthood* (pp. 241–265). Hillsdale, NJ: Erlbaum.

Golu, M. (1987). Neurophysiological mechanisms of the typology of behavior. *Revue Roumaine des Sciences Sociales: Serie de Psychologie, 31,* 57–63.

Golubeva, E. A. (1972a). The driving reaction as a method of study in differential psychophysiology. In V. D. Nebylitsyn & J. A. Gray (Eds.), *Biological bases of individual behavior* (pp. 11–28). New York: Academic Press.

Golubeva, E. A. (1972b). On the study of bioelectrical correlates of memory in differential psychophysiology. *Voprosy Psikhologii, 18,* 25–36. (in Russian)

Golubeva, E. A. (1975). Unconditioned- and conditioned-reflex characteristics of individual differences and the problem of nervous system properties splitting. In B. A. Nikityuk (Ed.), *Differential psychophysiology and its genetic aspects* (pp. 39–41). Moscow, Russia: SSSR Academy of Pedagogical Sciences. (in Russian)

Golubeva, E. A. (1980). *Individual properties of human memory: Psychophysiological study.* Moscow, Russia: Pedagogika. (in Russian)

Golubeva, E. A. (1993). *Abilities and individuality.* Moscow, Russia: Prometey. (in Russian)

Golubeva, E. A., & Ravich-Shcherbo, I. V. (Eds.). (1981). *Problems of differential psychophysiology* (Vol. 10). Moscow, Russia: Pedagogika. (in Russian)

Golubeva, E. A., & Rozhdestvenskaya, V. I. (1976). On the psychological manifestations of the properties of the nervous system. *Voprosy Psikhologii, 22,* 37–44. (in Russian)

Golubeva, E. A., & Rozhdestvenskaya, V. I. (1978). Psychological manifestation of the strength of the nervous system. In V. V. Davydov (Ed.), *Problems of general, developmental and pedagogical psychology* (pp. 22–37). Moscow, Russia: Pedagogika. (in Russian)

Gorbacheva, V. A. (1954). An attempt to study individual and typological features of three-year-old children. *Izvestiya Academii Pedagogicheskikh Nauk RSFSR, 52,* 6–39. (in Russian)

Gordon, B. N. (1981). Child temperament and adult behavior: An exploration of "goodness of fit." *Child Psychiatry and Human Development, 11,* 167–178.

Gordon, B. N. (1983). Maternal perception of child temperament and observed mother–child interaction. *Child Psychiatry and Human Development, 13,* 153–167.

Gordon, E. M., & Thomas, A. (1967). Children's behavioral style and the teacher's appraisal of their intelligence. *Journal of School Psychology, 5,* 292–300.

Goryńska, E., & Strelau, J. (1979). Basic traits of the temporal characteristics of behavior and their measurement by an inventory technique. *Polish Psychological Bulletin, 10,* 199–207.

Gottlober, A. B. (1938). The relationship between brain potentials and personality. *Journal of Experimental Psychology, 22,* 67–74.

Goyette, C. H., Conners, C. K., & Ulrich, R. F. (1978). Normative data on revised Conners parent and teacher rating scales. *Journal of Abnormal Child Psychology, 6,* 221–236.

Graham, F. K. (1979). Distinguishing among orienting, defense, and startle reflexes. In H. D. Kimmer, G. H. van Olst, & J. F. Orlebeke (Eds.), *The orienting reflex in humans* (pp. 137–169). Hillsdale, NJ: Erlbaum.

Graham, P., Rutter, M., & George, S. (1973). Temperamental characteristics as predictors of behavior disorders in children. *American Journal of Othopsychiatry, 43,* 328–339.

Gray, J. A. (Ed.). (1964a). *Pavlov's typology: Recent theoretical and experimental developments from the Laboratory of B. M. Teplov.* Oxford, England: Pergamon.

Gray, J. A. (1964b). Strength of the nervous system as a dimension of personality in man. In J. A. Gray (Ed.), *Pavlov's typology* (pp. 157–287). Oxford, England: Pergamon.

Gray, J. A. (1964c). Strength of the nervous system and levels of arousal: A reinterpretation. In J. A. Gray (Ed.), *Pavlov's typology* (pp. 289–364). Oxford, England: Pergamon.

Gray, J. A. (1967). Disappointment and drugs in the rat. *The Advancement of Science, 24,* 293–305.

Gray, J. A. (1968). *Level of arousal and length of rest as determinants of pursuit rotor performance.* Unpublished doctoral dissertation,University of London.

Gray, J. A. (1970). The psychophysiological basis of introversion–extraversion. *Behaviour Research and Therapy, 8,* 249–266.

Gray, J. A. (1972). The psychophysiological nature of introversion–extraversion: A modification of Eysenck's theory. In V. D. Nebylitsyn & J. A. Gray (Eds.), *Biological bases of individual behavior* (pp. 182–205). New York: Academic Press.

Gray, J. A. (1973). Causal theories of personality and how to test them. In J. R. Royce (Ed.), *Multivariate analysis and psychological theory* (pp. 409–463). New York: Academic Press.

Gray, J. A. (1975). *Elements of a two-process theory of learning.* London: Academic Press.

Gray, J. A. (1978). The neuropsychology of anxiety. *British Journal of Psychology, 69,* 417–437.

Gray, J. A. (1981). A critique of Eysenck's theory of personality. In H. J. Eysenck (Ed.), *A model for personality* (pp. 246–276). Berlin, Germany: Springer.

Gray, J. A. (1982a). *The neuropsychology of anxiety: An inquiry into the functions of the septo-hippocampal system.* Oxford, England: Oxford University Press.

Gray, J. A. (1982b). Precis of The neuropsychology of anxiety: An inquiry into the functions of the septo-hippocampal system. *Behavioral and Brain Sciences, 5,* 469–534.

Gray, J. A. (1983). Where should we search for biologically based dimensions of personality? *Zeitschrift für Differentielle und Diagnostische Psychologie, 4,* 165–176.

Gray, J. A. (1987). Perspectives on anxiety and impulsivity: A commentary. *Journal of Research in Personality, 21,* 493–509.

Gray, J. A. (1991). The neuropsychology of temperament. In J. Strelau & A. Angleitner (Eds.), *Explorations in temperament: International perspectives on theory and measurement* (pp. 105–128). New York: Plenum.

Gray, J. A. (1994). Framework for a taxonomy of psychiatric disorder. In S. H. M. van Goozen, N. E. Van de Poll, & J. A. Sergeant (Eds.), *Emotions: Essays on emotion theory* (pp. 29–59). Hillsdale, NJ: Erlbaum.

Gray, J. A., & Smith, P. T. (1969). An arousal-decision model for partial reinforcement and discrimination learning. In R. M. Gilbert & N. S. Sutherland (Eds.), *Animal discrimination learning* (pp. 243–272). London: Academic Press.

Gray, J. A., Owen, S., Davis, N., & Tsaltas, E. (1983). Psychological and physiological relations between anxiety and impulsivity. In M. Zuckerman (Ed.), *Biological bases of sensation seeking, impulsivity, and anxiety* (pp. 181–217). Hillsdale, NJ: Erlbaum.

Gray, J. A., Feldon, J., Rawlins, J. N. P., Hemsley, D. R., & Smith, A. D. (1991). The neuropsychology of schizophrenia. *Behavioral and Brain Sciences, 14,* 1–84.

Graziano, W. G. (1994). The development of agreeableness as a dimension of personality. In C. F. Halverson, Jr., G. A. Kohnstamm, & R. P. Martin (Eds.), *The developing structure of temperament and personality from infancy to adulthood* (pp. 339–354). Hillsdale, NJ: Erlbaum.

Gross, O. (1902). *Die cerebrale Sekundärfunktion* [The cerebral secondary function]. Leipzig, Germany: Verlag von F. C. W. Vogel.

Grossarth-Maticek, R. (1980). Social psychotherapy and course of the disease. *Psychotherapy and Psychosomatics, 33,* 129–138.

Grossarth-Maticek, R., Eysenck, H. J., & Vetter, H. (1988). Personality type, smoking habit and their interaction on predictors of cancer and coronary heart disease. *Personality and Individual Differences, 9,* 479–495.

Grossarth-Maticek, R., & Eysenck, H. J. (1990). Personality, stress and disease: Description and validation of a new inventory. *Psychological Reports, 66,* 355–373.

Grossarth-Maticek, R., & Eysenck, H. J. (1991). Personality, stress, and motivational factors in drinking as determinants of risk for cancer and coronary heart disease. *Psychological Reports, 69,* 1027–1093.

Grossarth-Maticek, R., Kanazir, D., Schmidt, P., & Vetter, H. (1982). Psychosomatic factors in the process of cancerogenesis. *Psychotherapy and Psychosomatics, 38,* 282–302.

Grossarth-Maticek, R., Bastiaans, J., & Kanazir, D. T. (1985). Psychosocial factors as strong predictors of mortality from cancer, ischaemic heart disease and stroke: The Yugoslav prospective study. *Journal of Psychosomatic Research, 29,* 167–176.

Guilford, J. P. (1959). *Personality.* New York: McGraw-Hill.

Guilford, J. P. (1975). Factors and factors of personality. *Psychological Bulletin, 82,* 802–814.

Guilford, J. P., & Zimmerman, W. S. (1950). Fourteen dimensions of temperament. *Psychological Monographs: General and Applied, 70* (10, whole No. 417).

Guilford, J. S., Zimmerman, W. S., & Guilford, J. P. (1976). *The Guilford–Zimmerman Temperament Survey handbook: Twenty-five years of research and application.* San Diego, CA: Edits.

Gunn, P., & Berry, P. (1985a). Down's syndrome, temperament and maternal response to descriptions of child behavior. *Developmental Psychology, 21,* 842–847.

Gunn, P., & Berry, P. (1985b). The temperament of Down's syndrome toddlers and their siblings. *Journal of Child Psychology and Psychiatry, 6,* 973–979.

Gunnar, M. R. (1990). The psychobiology of infant temperament. In J. Colombo & J. Fagen (Eds.), *Individual differences in infancy: Reliability, stability, prediction* (pp. 387–409). Hillsdale, NJ: Erlbaum.

Gunnar, M. R., Mangelsdorf, S., Larson, M., & Hertsgaard, L. (1989). Attachment, temperament, and adrenocortical activity in infancy: A study of psychoendocrine regulation. *Developmental Psychology, 25,* 355–363.

Gunnar, M. R., Larson, M. C., Hertsgaard, L., Harris, M. L., & Brodersen, L. (1992). The stressfulness of separation among nine-month-old infants: Effects of social context variables and infant temperament. *Child Development, 63,* 290–303.

Gurevich, K. M. (1970). *Professional fitness and basic nervous system properties.* Moscow, Russia: Nauka. (in Russian)

Gurevich, K. M., & Matveyev, V. F. (1966). On the professional fitness of operators and methods of assessment. In B. M. Teplov & K. M. Gurevich (Eds.), *Problems of professional fitness of power plants operation section staff* (pp. 3–96). Moscow, Russia: Prosveshcheniye. (in Russian)

Guseva, E. P. (1989). The relationship between developmental and typological prerequisites of abilities. In E. A. Golubeva (Ed.), *Abilities and dispositions* (pp. 33–56). Moscow, Russia: Pedagogika. (in Russian)

Hagekull, B. (1989). Longitudinal stability of temperament within a behavioral style framework. In G. A. Kohnstamm, J. E. Bates, & M. K. Rothbart (Eds.), *Temperament in childhood* (pp. 283–297). Chichester, England: Wiley.

Hagekull, B. (1994). Infant temperament and early childhood functioning: Possible relations to the five-factor model. In C. F. Halverson, Jr., G. A. Kohnstamm, & R. P. Martin (Eds.), *The developing structure of temperament and personality from infancy to adulthood* (pp. 227–240). Hillsdale, NJ: Erlbaum.

Hagekull, B., & Bohlin,, G. (1986). Mother–infant interaction and perceived infant temperament. *International Journal of Behavioral Development, 9,* 297–313.

Hagekull, B., Bohlin, G., & Lindhagen, K. (1984). Validity of parental reports. *Infant Behavior and Development, 7,* 77–92.

Haier, R. J., Sokolski, K., Katz, M., & Buchsbaum, M. S. (1987). The study of personality with positron emission. In J. Strelau & H. J. Eysenck (Eds.), *Personality dimensions and arousal* (pp. 251–267). New York: Plenum.

Hall, C. S. (1941). Temperament: A survey of animal studies. *Psychological Bulletin, 38,* 909–943.

Hall, C. S., & Lindzey, G. (1978). *Theories of personality* (3rd ed.). New York: Wiley.

Halmiova, O., & Sebova, E. (1986). Nervous system properties and coding processes. In J. Strelau, F. H. Farley, & A. Gale (Eds.), *The biological bases of personality: Psychophysiology, performance, and application* (Vol. 2, pp. 127–134). Washington, DC: Hemisphere.

Halverson, C. F., Jr., & Waldrop, M. F. (1973). The relations of mechanically recorded activity level to varieties of preschool play behavior. *Child Development, 44,* 678–681.

Halverson, C. F., Jr., Kohnstamm, G. A., & Martin R. P. (Eds.). (1994). *The developing structure of temperament and personality from infancy to adulthood*. Hillsdale, NJ: Erlbaum.

Hanin, Y., Eysenck, S. B. G., Eysenck, H. J., & Barrett, P. (1991). A cross-cultural study of personality: Russia and England. *Personality and Individual Differences, 12*, 265–271.

Hare, R. D. (1982). Psychopathy and the personality dimensions of psychoticism, extraversion and neuroticism. *Personality and Individual Differences, 3*, 35–42.

Hay, D. A. (1985). *Essentials of behaviour genetics*. Oxford, England: Blackwell.

Haynes, S. N. (1978). *Principles of behavioral assessment*. New York: Gardner.

Haynes, S. N., & Horn, W. F. (1982). Reactivity in behavioral observation: A review. *Behavioral Assessment, 4*, 369–385.

Healy, B. T. (1989). Autonomic nervous system correlates of temperament. *Infant Behavior and Development, 12*, 289–304.

Heath, A. C., & Martin, N. G. (1990). Psychoticism as a dimension of personality: A multivariate genetic test of Eysenck and Eysenck's psychoticism construct. *Journal of Personality and Social Psychology, 58*, 111–121.

Heath, A. C., Neale, M. C., Hewitt, J. K., Eaves, L. J., & Fulker, D. W. (1989). Testing structural equation models for twin data using LISREL. *Behavior Genetics, 19*, 9–35.

Heath, A. C., Cloninger, C. R., & Martin, N. G. (1994). Testing a model for the genetic structure of personality: A comparison of the personality systems of Cloninger and Eysenck. *Journal of Personality and Social Psychology, 66*, 762–775.

Hebb, D. O. (1955). Drives and the C.N.S. (conceptual nervous system). *Psychological Review, 62*, 243–254.

Hefferman, L., Black, F. W., & Poche, P. (1982). Temperament patterns in young neurologically impaired children. *Journal of Pediatric Psychology, 22*, 189–194.

Hegvik, R., McDevitt, S., & Carey, W. (1982). The Middle Childhood Temperament Questionnaire. *Developmental and Behavioral Pediatrics, 3*, 197–200.

Hellwig, B. (1872). *Die vier Temperamente bei Kindern* [The four temperaments in children]. Paderborn, Germany: Esser.

Hellwig, B. (1888). *Die vier Temperamente bei Erwachsenen* [The four temperaments in adults]. Paderborn, Germany: Esser.

Henderson, L. J. (1913). *The fitness of the environment*. New York: Macmillan.

Henry, C. T., & Knott, J. R. (1941). A note on the relationship between "personality" and the alpha rhythm of the electroencephalogram. *Journal of Experimental Psychology, 28*, 362–366.

Hess, W. R. (1924). Über die Wechselbeziehungen zwischen psychischen und vegetativen Funtionen [On reciprocal relationships between psychic and vegetative functions]. *Archiv für Neurologie und Psychiatrie, 15*, 260–277.

Heymans, G. (1899–1909). Untersuchungen über psychische Hemmung [Studies on psychic inhibition]. *Zeitschrift für Psychologie und Physiologie der Sinnesorgane, 21* (321–359), *26* (305–382), *34* (15–28), *41* (28–37), *53* (401–415).

Heymans, G. (1908). Über einige psychische Korrelationen [About some psychological correlations]. *Zeitschrift für angewandte Psychologie, 1*, 313–381.

Heymans, G., & Wiersma, E. (1906–1918). Beiträge zur speziellen Psychologie auf Grund einer Massenuntersuchung [Contribution to special psychology based on large-scale investigation]. *Zeitschrift für Psychologie* (1906a), *42*, 81–127; (1906b), *42*, 258–301; (1906c), *43*, 321–373; (1907), *45*, 1–42; (1908a), *46*, 321–333; (1908b), *49*, 414–439; (1909), *51*, 1–72; (1912), *62*, 1–59; (1918), *80*, 76–89.

Hilgard, E. R., Morgan, A. H., & Prytulak, S. (1968). The psychophysics of the kinesthetic aftereffect in the Petrie block experiment. *Perception and Psychophysics, 4*, 129–132.

Hinde, R. A. (1989). Temperament as an intervening variable. In G. A. Kohnstamm, J. E. Bates, & M. K. Rothbart (Eds.), *Temperament in childhood* (pp. 27–33). Chichester, England: Wiley.

Hinde, R. A., & Stevenson-Hinde, J. (1987). Interpersonal relationships and child development. *Developmental Review, 7,* 1–21.

Hinde, R. A., & Tobin, C. (1986). Temperament at home and behaviour at preschool. In G. A. Kohnstamm (Ed.), *Temperament discussed* (pp. 123–132). Lisse, The Netherlands: Swets & Zeitlinger.

Hines, M., & Mehrabian, A. (1979). Approach–avoidance behaviors as a function of pleasantness and arousing quality of settings and individual differences in stimulus screening. *Social Behavior and Personality, 7,* 223–233.

Hippokrates (1895). *Samtliche Werke* [Complete works]. Munich, Germany: H. Luneburg Verlag.

Hirsch, J. (1962). Individual differences in behavior and their genetic basis. In E. L. Bliss (Ed.), *Roots of behavior* (pp. 3–23). New York: Hoeber–Harper.

Hirt, E. (1905). *Die Temperamente, ihr Wesen, ihre Bedeutung für das seelische Erleben und ihre besondere Gestaltungen* [Temperaments, their nature, their significance for psychic experience and their specific molding]. Wiesbaden, Germany: Verlag von J. F. Bergmann.

Hobfoll, S. E. (1988). *The ecology of stress.* Washington, DC: Hemisphere.

Hobfoll, S. E. (1989). Conservation of resources: A new attempt at conceptualizing stress. *American Psychologist, 44,* 513–524.

Hobfoll, S. E. (1991). Conservation of resources in community intervention. *American Journal of Community Psychology, 19,* 111–121.

Hodges, W. F. (1976). The psychophysiology of anxiety. In M. Zuckerman & C. D. Spielberger (Eds.), *Emotions and anxiety: New concepts, methods and applications* (pp. 176–194). Hillsdale, NJ: Erlbaum.

Hodgkin, A. L. (1951). The ionic basis of electrical activity in nerve and muscle. *Biological Review, 26,* 339.

Hoffman, L. W. (1991). The influence of the family environment on personality: Accounting for sibling differences. *Psychological Bulletin, 110,* 187–203.

Hofstee, W. K. B. (1991). The concepts of personality and temperament. In J. Strelau & A. Angleitner (Eds.), *Explorations in temperament: International perspectives on theory and measurement* (pp. 177–188). New York: Plenum.

Hofstee W. K. B. (1994). Who should own the definition of personality?, *European Journal of Personality, 8,* 149–162.

Holden, C. (1987). The genetics of personality. *Science, 237,* 598–601.

Holmes, T. H., & Rahe, R. H. (1967). The Social Readjustment Rating Scale. *Journal of Psychosomatic Research, 11,* 213–218.

Holohan, C. J., & Moos, R. H. (1986). Personality, coping, and family resources in stress resistance: A longitudinal analysis. *Journal of Personality and Social Psychology, 51,* 389–395.

Homburger, A. (1926). *Vorlesungen über Psychopathologie des Kindesalters* [Lectures on psychopathology in childhood]. Berlin, Germany: Springer.

Horvath, P., & Zuckerman, M. (1993). Sensation seeking, risk appraisal, and risky behavior. *Personality and Individual Differences, 14,* 41–52.

Howarth, E. (1988). Mood differences between the four Galen personality types. *Personality and Individual Differences, 9,* 439–440.

Howells, W. W. (1952). A factorial study of constitutional type. *American Journal of Physiological Anthropology, 9,* 159–191.

Hsu, C. C., Soong, W. T., Stigler, J. W., Hong, C. C., & Liang, C. C. (1981). The temperamental characteristics of Chinese babies. *Child Development, 52,* 1337–1340.

Hubert, N. C., Wachs, T. D., Peters-Martin, P., & Gandour, M. J. (1982). The study of early temperament: Measurement and conceptual issues. *Child Development, 53,* 571–600.

Hubert, W., & de Jong-Meyer, R. (1989). Emotional stress and saliva cortisol response. *Journal of Clinical Chemistry and Clinical Biochemistry, 27,* 235–237.

Huitt, W. G., & Ashton, P. T. (1982). Parents' perception of infant temperament: A psychometric study. *Merrill-Palmer Quarterly, 28,* 95–109.

Hulin, C. L. (1987). A psychometric theory of evaluation of item and scale translations. Fidelity across languages. *Journal of Cross-Cultural Psychology, 18,* 115–142.

Hull, C. L. (1943). *Principles of behavior: An introduction to behavior theory.* New York: Appleton-Century-Crofts.

Hull, C. L. (1952). *A behavior system.* New Haven, CT: Yale University Press.

Humphreys, L. G. (1957). Characteristics of type concepts with special reference to Sheldon's typology. *Psychological Bulletin, 54,* 218–228.

Hunt, J. M., & Schlosberg, H. (1939). General activity in the male white rat. *Journal of Comperative Psychology, 28,* 23–38.

Huntington, G. S., & Simeonsson, R. J. (1993). Temperament and adaptation in infants and young children with disabilities. *Infant Mental Health Journal, 14,* 49–60.

Ilin, E. P. (1978). *A study of nervous system properties.* Yaroslavl, Russia: Yaroslavl University Press. (in Russian)

Isreal, J. B., Wickens, C. D., Chesney, G. L., & Donchin, E. (1980). The event-related brain potential as an index of display-monitoring workload. *Human Factors, 22,* 211–224.

Ivanov-Smolensky, A. G. (1935). The experimental investigation of higher nervous activity in children. *Fiziologicheskii Zhurnal SSSR, 19,* 133–140. (in Russian)

Ivanov-Smolensky, A. G. (1953). The study of types of higher nervous activity in animals and man. *Zhurnal Vysshei Nervnoi Deyatelnosti, 3,* 36–54. (in Russian)

Izard, C. E. (1977). *Human emotions.* New York: Plenum.

Izard, C. E. (1993). *The psychology of emotions.* New York: Plenum.

Jackson, D. N. (1975). The relative validity of scales prepared by naive item writers and those based on empirical methods of personality scale construction. *Educational and Psychological Measurement, 35,* 361–370.

Jackson, D. N., & Paunonen, S. V. (1985). Construct validity and the predictability of behavior. *Journal of Personality and Social Psychology, 49,* 554–570.

Janke, W. (Ed.). (1983). *Response variability to psychotropic drugs.* Oxford, England: Pergamon.

Janke , W., & Kallus, K. W. (1995). Reaktivität [Reactivity]. In M. Amelang (Ed.) *Enzyklopädie der Psychologie: Verhaltens- und Leistungsunterschiede: Vol. 2. Differentielle Psychologie und Persönlichkeitsforschung* [Encyclopedia of psychology: Differences in behavior and performance: Vol. 2. Differential psychology and personality research] (pp. 1–89). Göttingen, Germany: Hogrefe.

Janke, W., & Netter, P. (Eds.). (1986). *Angst und Psychopharmaka* [Anxiety and drugs]. Stuttgart, Germany: Kohlhammer.

Janoff, I. Z., Beck, L. H., & Child, I. L. (1950). The relation of somatotype to reaction time, resistance to pain, and expressive movement. *Journal of Personality, 18,* 454–460.

Janssen, R. H. C., Mattie, H., Plooij-van Gorsel, P. C., & Werre, P. F. (1978). The effects of a depressant and a stimulant drug on the contingent negative variation. *Biological Psychology, 6,* 209–218.

Jasper, H. H. (1937). Electrical signs of cortical activity. *Psychological Bulletin, 34,* 411–481.

Jasper, H. H. (1941). Electroencephalography. In W. Penfield & T. C. Erickson (Eds.), *Epilepsy and cerebral localization* (pp. 14–25). Springfield, IL: Thomas.

Jeffery, R. W. (1989). Risk behaviors and health: Contrasting individual and population perspectives. *American Psychologist, 44,* 1194–1202.

John, O. P. (1990). The "Big Five" factor taxonomy: Dimensions of personality in the natural language and in questionnaires. In L. A. Pervin (Ed.), *Handbook of personality: Theory and research* (pp. 66–100). New York: Guilford.

John, O. P., Angleitner, A., & Ostendorf, R. (1988). The lexical approach to personality: A historical review of trait taxonomic research. *European Journal of Personality, 2,* 171–203.

Joreskog, K. G., & Sorbom, D. (1993). *LISREL8: User's reference guide.* Chicago: SPSS.

Joyce, P. R., Mulder, R. T., & Cloninger, C. B. (1994). Temperament and hypercortisolemia in depression. *American Journal of Psychiatry, 151,* 195–198.

Jung, C. G. (1923). *Psychological types.* London: Routledge & Kegan Paul.

Kagan, J. (1974). Discrepancy, temperament, and infant distress. In M. Lewis & L. A. Rosenblum (Eds.), *The origins of fear* (pp. 229–248). New York: Wiley.

Kagan, J. (1982a). The construct of difficult temperament: A reply to Thomas, Chess, and Korn. *Merrill-Palmer Quarterly, 28,* 21–24.

Kagan, J. (1982b). Heart rate and heart rate variability as signs of a temperamental dimension in infants. In C. E. Izard (Ed.), *Measuring emotions in infants and children* (pp. 38–66). Cambridge, England: Cambridge University Press.

Kagan, J. (1983). Stress and coping in early development. In N. Garmezy & M. Rutter (Eds.), *Stress, coping and development in children* (pp. 191–216). New York: McGraw-Hill.

Kagan, J. (1989a). Temperamental contributions to social behavior. *American Psychologist, 44,* 668–674.

Kagan, J. (1989b). *Unstable ideas: Temperament, cognition, and self.* Cambridge, MA: Harvard University Press.

Kagan, J. (1994). *Galen's prophecy: Temperament in human nature.* New York: Basic Books.

Kagan, J., & Moss, H. A. (1962). *Birth to maturity.* New York: Wiley.

Kagan, J., & Reznick, J. S. (1986). Shyness and temperament. In W. H. Jones, J. M. Cheek, & S. R. Briggs (Eds.), *Shyness* (pp. 81–90). New York: Plenum.

Kagan, J., & Snidman, N. (1991). Infant predictors of inhibited and uninhibited profiles. *Psychological Science, 2,* 40–44.

Kagan, J., Kearsley, R. B., & Zelazo, P. R. (1978). *Infancy: Its place in human development.* Cambridge, MA: Harvard University Press.

Kagan, J., Reznick, J. S., & Snidman, N. (1987). The physiology and psychology of behavioral inhibition in children. *Child Development, 58,* 1459–1473.

Kagan, J., Reznick, J. S., & Snidman, N. (1988). Biological bases of childhood shyness. *Science, 240,* 167–171.

Kagan, J., Reznick, J. S., & Gibbons, J. (1989). Inhibited and uninhibited types of children. *Child Development, 60,* 838–845.

Kagan, J., Snidman, N., Julia-Sellers, M., & Johnson, M. O. (1991). Temperament and allergic symptoms. *Psychosomatic Medicine, 53,* 332–340.

Kahn, J. P., Rubinow, D. R., Davis, C. L., Kling, M., & Post, R. M. (1988). Salivary cortisol: A practical method for evaluation of adrenal function. *Biological Psychiatry, 23,* 235–249.

Kant, I. (1912). *Anthropologie in pragmatischer Hinsicht* [Anthropology from a pragmatic point of view] (5th ed.). Leipzig, Germany: Verlag von Felix Meiner.

Keehn, R. J., Goldberg, I. P., & Beebe, G. W. (1974). Twenty-four year mortality follow-up of army veterans with disability separation for psychoneurosis in 1944. *Psychosomatic Medicine, 36,* 27–76.

Kelly, G. A. (1955). *The psychology of personal constructs* (Vols. 1 & 2). New York: Norton.

Kendler, K. S., & Eaves, L. J. (1986). Model for the joint effect of genotype and environment on liability to psychiatric illness. *American Journal of Psychiatry, 143,* 279–289.

Keogh, B. K. (1982). Children's temperament and teachers' decisions. In R. Porter & G. M. Collins (Eds.), *Temperamental differences in infants and young children* (pp. 269–285). London: Pitman.

Keogh, B. K. (1986). Temperament and schooling: Meaning of "goodness of fit"? In J. V. Lerner & R. M. Lerner (Eds.), *Temperament and social interaction in infants and children* (pp. 89–108). San Francisco: Jossey-Bass.

Keogh, B. K. (1989). Applying temperament research to school. In G. A. Kohnstamm, J. E. Bates, & M. K. Rothbart (Eds.), *Temperament in childhood* (pp. 437–450). Chichester, England: Wiley.

Keogh, B. K., & Burstein, N. D. (1988). Relationship of temperament to preschoolers' interaction with peers and teachers. *Exceptional Children, 54,* 69–74.

Keogh, B. K., & Pullis, M. (1980). Temperament influences on the development of exceptional children. In B. K. Keogh (Ed.), *Advances in special education: Basic construct and theoretical orientation* (Vol. 1, pp. 239–276). Greenwich, CT: JAI.

Keogh, B. K., Pullis, M. E., & Cadwell, J. (1982). A short form of the Teacher Temperament Questionnaire. *Journal of Educational Measurement, 19,* 323–329.

Kinsbourne, M., & Bemporad, B. (1984). Lateralization of emotion: A model and the evidence. In N. A. Fox & R. J. Davidson (Eds.), *The psychobiology of affective development* (pp. 259–291). Hillsdale, NJ: Erlbaum.

Kirschbaum, C., Bartussek, D., & Strasburger, C. J. (1992). Cortisol responses to psychological stress and correlations with personality traits. *Personality and Individual Differences, 13,* 1353–1357.

Kissen, D. M. (1967). Psychological factors, personality and lung cancer in men aged 55–64. *British Journal of Medical Psychology, 40,* 29–34.

Kissen, D. M., & Eysenck, H. J. (1962). Personality in male lung cancer patients. *Journal of Psychosomatic Research, 6,* 123–137.

Klein, H. A. (1980). Early childhood group care: Predicting adjustment from individual temperament. *Journal of Genetic Psychology, 137,* 125–131.

Klein, H. A. (1982). The relationship between children's temperament and adjustment to kindergarten and Head Start settings. *Journal of Psychology, 112,* 259–268.

Klein, H. A. (1987). The relationship of temperament scores to the way young adults adapt to change. *Journal of Psychology, 121,* 119–135.

Klein, H. A., & Ballantine, J. H. (1988). The relationship of temperament to adjustment in British infant schools. *Journal of Social Psychology, 128,* 585–595.

Klein, H. A., & Rennie, S. E. (1985). Temperament as a factor in initial adjustment to college residence. *Journal of College Student Personnel, 26,* 58–62.

Klein, P. S. (1984). Behavior of Israeli mothers toward infants in relation to infants' perceived temperament. *Child Development, 55,* 1212–1218.

Klineberg, O., Asch, S. E., & Block, H. (1934). An experimental study of constitutional types. *Genetic Psychology Monographs, 16,* 140–221.

Klonowicz, T. (1974). Reactivity and fitness for the occupation of operator. *Polish Psychological Bulletin, 5,* 129–136.

Klonowicz, T. (1985). Temperament and performance. In J. Strelau (Ed.), *Temperamental bases of behavior: Warsaw studies on individual differences* (pp. 79–115). Lisse, The Netherlands: Swets & Zeitlinger.

Klonowicz, T. (1986). Reactivity and performance: The third side of the coin. In J. Strelau, F. H. Farley, & A. Gale (Eds.), *The biological bases of personality and behavior: Psychophysiology, performance, and application* (Vol. 2, pp. 119–126). Washington, DC: Hemisphere.

Klonowicz, T. (1987a). Reactivity and the control of arousal. In J. Strelau & H. J. Eysenck (Eds.), *Personality dimensions and arousal* (pp. 183–196). New York: Plenum.

Klonowicz, T. (1987b). *Reactivity, experience, and capacity.* Warsaw, Poland: Warsaw University Press.

Klonowicz, T. (1990). A psychophysiological assessment of simultaneous interpreting: The interaction of individual differences and mental workload. *Polish Psychological Bulletin, 21,* 37–48.

Klonowicz, T. (1992). *Stres w Wieży Babel: Różnice indywidualne a wysiłek inwestowany w trudną pracę umysłową* [Stress in the Bable Tower: Individual differences and allocation of effort during difficult mental work]. Wrocław, Poland: Ossolineum.

Klyagin, V. S. (1974). Diagnostic relevance of individual stability of the total power EEG activity. In K. M. Gurevich (Ed.), *Psychophysiological problems of higher level professional experience* (Vol. 1, pp. 116–140). Moscow, Russia: Sovetskayja Rossiya. (in Russian)

Knott, J. R., & Irwin, D. A. (1967). Anxiety, stress, and the contingent negative variation. *Electroencephalography and Clinical Neurophysiology, 22,* 188.

Kobasa, S. C. (1979). Stressful life events, personality and health: An inquiry into hardiness. *Journal of Personality and Social Psychology, 37,* 1–11.

Kobasa, S. C., & Puccetti, M. C. (1983). Personality and social resources in stress resistance. *Journal of Personality and Social Psychology, 45,* 839–850.

Kohn, P. M. (1985). Sensation seeking, augmenting–reducing, and strength of the nervous system. In J. T. Spence & C. E. Izard (Eds.), *Motivation, emotion, and personality* (pp. 167–173). Amsterdam, The Netherlands: North-Holland.

Kohn, P. M. (1987). Issues in the measurement of arousability. In J. Strelau & H. J. Eysenck (Eds.), *Personality dimensions and arousal* (pp. 233–250). New York: Plenum.

Kohn, P. M., Hunt, R. W., Cowles, M. P., & Davis, C. (1986). Factor structure and construct validity of the Vando Reducer–Augmenter Scale. *Personality and Individual Differences, 7,* 57–64.

Kohn, P. M., Cowles, M. P., & Lafreniere, K. (1987). Relationships between psychometric and experimental measures of arousability. *Personality and Individual Differences, 8,* 225–231.

Kohn, P. M., Lafreniere, K., & Gurevich, M. (1991). Hassles, health, and personality. *Journal of Personality and Social Psychology, 61,* 478–482.

Kohnstamm, G. A. (1989a). Historical and international perspectives. In G. A. Kohnstamm, J. E. Bates, & M. K. Rothbart (Eds.), *Temperament in childhood* (pp. 557–566). Chichester, England: Wiley.

Kohnstamm, G. A. (1989b). Temperament in childhood: Cross-cultural and sex differences. In G. A. Kohnstamm, J. E. Bates, & M. K. Rothbart (Eds.), *Temperament in childhood* (pp. 483–508). Chichester, England: Wiley.

Kohnstamm, G. A., Bates, J. E., & Rothbart, M. K. (Eds.). (1989). *Temperament in childhood.* Chichester, England: Wiley.

Koopmans, J. S., Boomsma, D. I., Heath, A. C., & van Doornen, L. J. P. (1995). A multivariate genetic analysis of sensation seeking. *Behavior Genetics, 25,* 349–356.

Kornblau, B. W., & Keogh, B. K. (1980). Teachers' perceptions and educational decisions. In J. J. Gallagher (Ed.) *New directions for exceptional children: The ecology of exeptional children* (pp. 87–101). San Francisco: Jossey-Bass.

Krasnogorsky, N. I. (1939). *Development of studies on the physiological activity of the brain in children.* Leningrad, Russia: Biomedgiz. (in Russian)

Krasnogorsky, N. I. (1953). Typological properties of higher nervous activity in children. *Zhurnal Vysshei Nervnoi Deyatelnosti, 3,* 169–183. (in Russian)

Kretschmer, E. (1944). *Körperbau und Charakter: Untersuchungen zum Konstitutionsproblem und zur Lehre von den Temperamenten* [Physique and character: Research concerning problems of constitution and knowledge on temperaments] (17th–18th ed.). Berlin, Germany: Springer.

Krijns, P. W., Gaillard, A. W. K., Van Heck, G. L., & Brunia, C. H. M. (1994). Personality effects on brain potentials in an S1–S2 paradigm. *Personality and Individual Differences, 16,* 561–570.

Kroeber, A. L., & Kluckhohn, C. (1963). *Culture: A critical review of concepts and definitions.* Cambridge, MA: Harvard University Press.

Krohne, H. W. (1986). Coping with stress: Dispositions, strategies, and the problem of measurement. In M. H. Appley & R. Trumbull (Eds.), *Dynamics of stress: Physiological, psychological, and social perspectives* (pp. 209–234). New York: Plenum.

Krohne, H. W., & Laux, L. (Eds.). (1982). *Achievement, stress, and anxiety.* New York: Hemisphere/McGraw-Hill.

Kuhn, T. S. (1970). Logic of discovery or psychological research. In I. Lakatos & A. Musgrave (Eds.), *Criticism and the growth of knowledge* (pp. 1–22). Cambridge, England: Cambridge University Press.

Kulcsar, Z., Kutor, L., & Arato, M. (1984). Sensation seeking, its biochemical correlates, and its relation to vestibo-ocular functions. In H. Bonarius, G. van Heck, & N. Smid (Eds.), *Personality psychology in Europe: Theoretical and empirical developments* (pp. 327–346). Lisse, The Netherlands: Swets & Zeitlinger.

Kyrios. M., & Prior, M. (1990). Temperament, stress and family factors in behavioural adjustment of 3–5-year-old children. *International Journal of Behavioral Development, 13,* 67–93.

Lagerspetz, K. M. J., & Lagerspetz, K. Y. H. (1971). Changes in the aggressiveness of mice resulting from selective breedings, learning and social isolation. *Scandinavian Journal of Psychology, 12,* 241–248.

Lang-Belonogova, N. S., & Kok, E. P. (1952). The significance of the study of anamnesis in patients for the assessment of their types of higher nervous activity and for the eludication of the functional state of the central nervous system prior to illness. *Trudy Instituta Fiziologii im. I. P. Pavlova, 1,* 493–506. (in Russian)

Langinvainio. H., Kaprio, J. Koskenvuo, M., & Lonnqvist, J. (1984). Finnish twins reared apart: III. Personality factors. *Acta Geneticae Medicae et Gemellologiae, 33,* 259–264.

Larsen, R. J., & Diener, E. (1985). A multitrait–multimethod examination of affect structure: Hedonic level and emotional intensity. *Personality and Individual Differences, 6,* 631–636.

Larsen, R. J., & Diener, E. (1987). Affect intensity as an individual difference characteristics: A review. *Journal of Research in Personality, 21,* 1–39.

Larsen, R. J., & Ketelaar, T. (1991). Personality and susceptibility to positive and negative emotional states. *Journal of Personality and Social Psychology, 61,* 132–140.

Larsen, R. J., & Zarate, M. A. (1991). Extending reducer/augmenter theory into the emotion domain: The role of affect in regulating stimulation level. *Personality and Individual Differences, 12,* 713–723.

Lazarus, R. S. (1966). *Psychological stress and the coping process.* New York: McGraw-Hill.

Lazarus, R. S. (1991). *Emotion and adaptation.* New York: Oxford University Press.

Lazarus, R. S. (1993). From psychological stress to the emotions: A history of changing outlooks. *Annual Review of Psychology, 44,* 1–21.

Lazarus, R. S., & Folkman, S. (1984). *Stress, appraisal, and coping.* New York: Springer.

Le Gall, R. (1950). *Caractérologie des enfants et des adolescents* [Characterology of children and adolescents]. Paris: Presses Universitaires de France.

Le Senne, R. (1945). *Traité de caractérologie* [Traits of characterology]. Paris: Presses Universitaires de France.

Lee, C. L., & Bates, J. E. (1985). Mother–child interaction at age two years and perceived difficult temperament. *Child Development, 56,* 1314–1325.

Leites, N. S. (1956). An attempt to give a psychological description of temperament. In B. M. Teplov (Ed.), *Typological features of higher nervous activity in man* (Vol. 1, pp. 267–303). Moscow, Russia: RSFSR Academy of Pedagogical Sciences. (in Russian)

Leites, N. S. (1972). Problems of interrelationship between typological features and age. In V. D. Nebylitsyn & J. A. Gray (Eds.), *Biological bases of individual behavior* (pp. 74–85). New York: Academic Press.

Lemere, F. (1936). The significance of individual differences in the Berger rhythm. *Brain, 59,* 366–375.

Leontev, A. N. (1978). *Activity, consciousness and personality.* Englewood Cliffs, NJ: Prentice-Hall.

Lerner, J. V. (1984). The import of temperament for psychosocial functioning: Tests of a "goodness of fit" model. *Merrill-Palmer Quarterly, 30,* 177–188.

Lerner, J. V. (1993). The influence of child temperamental characteristics on parent behaviors. In T. Luster & L. Okagaki (Eds.), *Parenting: An ecological perspective* (pp. 101–120). Hillsdale, NJ: Erlbaum.

Lerner, J. V., & Lerner, R. M. (1983). Temperament and adaptation across life: Theoretical and empirical issues. *Life-Span Development and Behavior, 9,* 197–231.

Lerner, J. V., & Lerner, R. M. (1994). Explorations of the goodness-of-fit model in early adolescence. In W. B. Carey & S. C. McDevitt (Eds.), *Prevention and early intervention: Individual differences as risk factors for the mental health of children* (pp. 161–169). New York: Brunner/Mazel.

Lerner, J. V., Lerner, R. M., & Zabski, S. (1985). Temperament and elementary school children's actual and rated academic performance: A test of a "goodness-of-fit" model. *Journal of Child Psychology and Psychiatry, 26,* 125–136.

Lerner, J. V., Nitz, K., Talwar, R., & Lerner, R. M. (1989). On the functional significance of temperamental individuality: A developmental contextual view of the concept of goodness of fit. In G. A. Kohnstamm, J. E. Bates, & M. K. Rothbart (Eds.), *Temperament in childhood* (pp. 509–522). Chichester, England: Wiley.

Lerner, R. M., & Lerner, J. V. (1987). Children in their contexts: A goodness of fit model. In J. B. Lancaster, J. Altmann, A. S. Rossi, & L. R. Sherrod (Eds.), *Parenting across the life span: Biosocial dimensions* (pp. 377–404). Chicago: Aldine.

Lerner, R. M., Palermo, M, Spiro, A., III, & Nesselroade, J. R. (1982). Assessing the dimensions of temperamental individuality across the life span: The Dimensions of Temperament Survey (DOTS). *Child Development, 53,* 149–159.

Lerner, R. M., Lerner, J. V., Windle, M., Hooker, K., Lenerz, K., & East, P. L. (1986). Children and adolescents in their contexts: Tests of a goodness of fit model. In R. Plomin & J. Dunn (Eds.), *The study of temperament: Changes, continuities and challenges* (pp. 99–114). Hillsdale, NJ: Erlbaum.

Lesch, K-P., Bengel, D., Heils, A., Sabol, S. Z., Greenberg, B. D., Petri, S., Benjamin, J., Muller, C. R., Hamer, D. H., & Murphy, D. L. (1996). Association of anxiety-related traits with a polymorphism in the serotonin transporter gene regulatory region. *Science, 274,* 1527–1531.

Leshner, A. I. (1978). *An introduction to behavioural endocrinology.* Oxford, England: Oxford University Press.

Lester, D. (1990). Galen's four temperaments and four-factor theories of personality: A comment on "Toward a four-factor theory of temperament and/or personality." *Journal of Personality Assessment, 54,* 423–426.

Leuba, C. (1955). Toward some integration of learning theories: The concept of optimal stimulation. *Psychological Reports, 1,* 27–33.

Levine, S., Wiener, S. G., Coe, C., Bayart, F. S., & Hayashi, K. T. (1987). Primate vocalization: A psychobiological approach. *Child Development, 58,* 1408–1419.

Lindsley, D. B. (1952). Psychological phenomena and the electroencephalogram. *Electroencephalography and Clinical Neurophysiology, 4,* 443–456.

Lindzey, G. (1967). Behavior and morphological variation. In J. N. Spuhler (Ed.), *Genetic diversity and human behavior* (pp. 227–240). Chicago: Aldine.

Loehlin, J. C. (1986) Heredity, environment, and the Thurstone Temperament Schedule. *Behavior Genetics, 16,* 61–73.

Loehlin, J. C. (1989). Partitioning environmental and genetic contributions to behavioral development. *American Psychologist, 44,* 1285–1292.

Loehlin, J. C. (1992). *Genes and environment in personality development.* Newbury Park, CA: Sage.

Loehlin, J. C., & Nichols, R. C. (1976). *Heredity, environment, and personality.* Austin: University of Texas Press.

Loehlin, J. C., Willerman, L., & Horn, J. M. (1985). Personality resemblances in adoptive families when the children are late-adolescent or adult. *Journal of Personality and Social Psychology, 48,* 376–392.

Loehlin, J. C., Horn, J. M., & Willerman, L. (1990). Heredity, environment, and personality change: Evidence from the Texas Adoption Project. *Journal of Personality, 58,* 221–243.

Loevinger, J. (1957). Objective tests as instruments of psychological theory. *Psychological Reports, 3,* 635–694.

Lolas, F. (1987). Hemispheric asymmetry of slow brain potentials in relation to neuroticism. *Personality and Individual Differences, 8,* 969–971.

Lolas, F., & Aguilera, N. (1982). Extraversion and inhibition. *Biological Psychiatry, 17,* 963–969.

Lolas, F., & de Andraca, I. (1977). Neuroticism, extraversion and slow brain potentials. *Neuropsychobiology, 3,* 12–22.

Lolas, F., Etcheberrigaray, R., Elgueta, D., & Camposano, S. (1989). Visual evoked potential (VEP) reducing: A vertex feature of late components. *Research Communications in Psychology, Psychiatry and Behavior, 14,* 173–176.

Lolas, R., Camposano, S., & Etcheberrigaray, R. (1989). Augmenting/reducing and personality: A psychometric and evoked potential study in a Chilean sample. *Personality and Individual Differences, 10,* 1173–1176.

Low, M. D., & Swift, S. J. (1971). The contingent negative variation and the "resting" D.C. potential of the human brain: Effect of situational anxiety. *Neuropsychologia, 9,* 203–208.

Low, M. D., Coats, A. C., Retting, G. M., & McSherry, J. W. (1967). Anxiety, attentiveness-alertness: A phenomenological study of the CNV. *Neuropsychologia, 5,* 379–384.

Lundberg, U. (1982). Psychophysiological aspects of performance and adjustment to stress. In H. W. Krohne & L. Laux (Eds.), *Achievement, stress, and anxiety* (pp. 75–91). Washington, DC: Hemisphere.

Lyon, M. E., & Plomin, R. (1981). The measurement of temperament using parental ratings. *Journal of Child Psychology and Psychiatry, 22,* 47–53.

Łukaszewski, W. (1974). *Osobowźs: struktura i funkcje regulacyjne* [Personality: Structure and regulatory functions]. Warsaw, Poland: Państwowe Wydawnictwo Naukowe.

MacAndrew C., & Steele T. (1991). Gray's behavioral inhibition system: A psychometric examination. *Personality and Individual Differences, 12,* 157–171.

Macaskill, G. T., Hopper, J. L., White, V., & Hill, D. J. (1994) Genetic and environmental variation in Eysenck Personality Questionnaire scales measured on Australian adolescent twins, *Behavior Genetics, 24,* 481–491.

Mackenzie, S. A., Oltenacu, E. A. B., & Leighton, E. (1985). Heritability estimate for temperament scores in German shepherd dogs and its genetic correlation with hip dysplasia. *Behavior Genetics, 15,* 475–482.

MacKinnon, D. W. (1944). The structure of personality. In J. M. Hunt (Ed.), *Personality and the behavior disorders* (Vol. 1, pp. 1–48). New York: Ronald.

Magnusson, D. (1988). *Individual development from an interactional perspective: A longitudinal study.* Hillsdale, NJ: Erlbaum.

Magnusson, D., Klinteberg, B., & Stattin, H. (1991). *Autonomic activity/reactivity, behavior and crime in a longitudinal perspective.* Reports from the Department of Psychology, No. 738. Stockholm: Stockholm University.

Malhorta, S., Varma, V. K., & Verma, S. G. (1986). Temperament as determinant of phenomenology of childhood psychiatric disorders. *Indian Journal of Psychiatry, 28,* 263–276.

Maltzman, I., & Raskin D. C. (1965). Effects of individual differences in the orienting reflex on conditioning and complex processes. *Journal of Experimental Research in Personality, 1,* 1–16.

Mangan, G. (1982). *The biology of human conduct: East–West models of temperament and personality.* Oxford, England: Pergamon.

Manheimer, D. A., & Mellinger, G. D. (1967). Personality characteristics of the child accident repeater. *Child Development, 38,* 491–513.

Marcovitch, S., Goldberg, S., MacGregor, D., & Lojkasek, M. (1986). Patterns of temperament variation in three groups of developmentally delayed preschool children: Mother and father ratings. *Developmental and Behavioral Pediatrics, 7,* 247–252.

Martin, N. G., & Jardine, R. (1986). Eysenck's contributions to behaviour genetics. In S. Modgil & C. Modgil (Eds.), *Hans Eysenck: Consensus and controversy* (pp. 13–47). Sussex, England: Falmer.

Martin, N. G., Eaves, L. J., Heath, A. C., Jardine, R., Feingold, L. M., & Eysenck, H. J. (1986). Transmittion of social attitudes. *Proceedings of the National Academy of Sciences, USA, 83,* 4364–4368.

Martin, R. P. (1988a). Child temperament and educational outcomes. In A. D. Pellegrini (Ed.), *Psychological bases for early education* (pp. 185–205). Chichester, England: Wiley.

Martin, R. P. (1988b). *The Temperament Assessment Battery for Children: Manual.* Brandon, VT: Clinical Psychology Press.

Martin, R. P. (1989). Activity level, distractibility and persistence: Critical characteristics in early schooling. In G. A. Kohnstamm, J. E. Bates, & M. K. Rothbart (Eds.), *Temperament in childhood* (pp. 451–461). Chichester, England: Wiley.

Martin, R. P., & Halverson, C. F., Jr. (1991). Mother–father agreement in temperament ratings: A preliminary investigation. In J. Strelau & A. Angleitner (Eds.), *Explorations in temperament: International perspectives on theory and measurement* (pp. 235–248). New York: Plenum.

Martin, R. P., & Holbrook, J. (1985). Relationship of temperament characteristics to the academic achievement of first grade children. *Psychoeducational Assessment, 3,* 131–140.

Martin, R. P., Nagel, R., & Paget, K. (1983). Relationship between temperament and classroom behavior, teacher attitudes, and academic achievement. *Psychoeducational Assessment, 1,* 377–386.

Martin, R. P., Drew, D., Gaddis, L., & Moseley, M. (1988). Prediction of elementary school achievement from preschool temperament: Three studies. *School Psychology Review, 17,* 125–137.

Martin, R. P., Olejnik, S., & Gaddis, L. (1994). Is temperament an important contributor to schooling outcomes in elementary school? Modeling effects of temperament and scholastic ability on academic achievement. In W. B. Carey & S. C. McDevitt (Eds.), *Prevention and early intervention: Individual differences as risk factors for the mental health of children* (pp. 59–68). New York: Brunner/Mazel.

Martin, R. P., Wisenbaker, J., & Huttenen, M. (1994). Review of factor analytic studies of temperament measures based on the Thomas–Chess structural model: Implications for the Big Five. In C. F. Halverson, Jr., G. A. Kohnstamm, & R. P. Martin (Eds.), *The developing structure of temperament and personality from infancy to adulthood* (pp. 157–172). Hillsdale, NJ: Erlbaum.

Mason, S. T. (1984). *Catecholamines and behaviour.* Cambridge, England: Cambridge University Press.

Matheny, A. P., Jr. (1981). Assessment of temperament in twin children: A reconciliation between structured and naturalistic observations. In L. Gedda, P. Parisi, & W. E. Nance (Eds.), *Progress in clinical and biological research: (Vol. 69B). Twin research 3: Intelligence, personality and development* (pp. 279–282). New York: Liss.

Matheny, A. P., Jr. (1984). Twin similarity in the developmental transformations of infant temperament as measured in a multi-method, longitudinal study. *Acta Geneticae Medicae Gemmellologiae, 33,* 181–189.

Matheny, A. P., Jr. (1986). Injuries among toddlers: Contributions from child, mother, and family. *Journal of Pediatric Psychology, 11,* 163–176.

Matheny, A. P., Jr. (1987). Psychological characteristics of childhood accidents. *Journal of Social Issues, 43,* 45–60.

Matheny, A. P., Jr. (1988). Accidental injuries. In D. K. Routh (Ed.), *Handbook of pediatric psychology* (pp. 108–134). New York: Guilford.

Matheny, A. P., Jr. (1989). Children's behavioral inhibition over age and across situations: Genetic similarity for a trait during change. *Journal of Personality, 57,* 215–235.

Matheny, A. P., Jr. (1990). Developmental behavior genetics: Contributions from the Louisville Twin Study. In M. E. Hahn, J. K. Hewitt, N. D. Henderson, & R. H. Benno (Eds.), *Developmental behavior genetics: Neural, biometrical, and evolutionary approaches* (pp. 25–39). New York: Oxford University Press.

Matheny, A. P., Jr. (1991). Play assessment of infant temperament. In C. E. Schaefer, K. Gitlin, & A. Sandgrund (Eds.), *Play diagnosis and assessment* (pp. 39–63). New York: Wiley.

Matheny, A. P., Jr., & Brown-Dolan, A. (1980). A twin study of personality and temperament during middle childhood. *Journal of Research in Personality, 14,* 224–234.

Matheny, A. P., Jr., & Wilson, R. S. (1981). Developmental tasks and rating scales for the laboratory assessment of infant temperament. *JSAS Catalog of Selected Documents in Psychology, 11,* 81 (MS #2367).

Matheny, A. P., Jr., Wilson, R. S., & Nuss, S. M. (1984). Toddler temperament: Stability across settings and over ages. *Child Development, 55,* 1200–1211.

Matheny, A. P., Jr., Wilson, R. S., & Thoben, A. S. (1987). Home and mother: Relations with infant temperament. *Developmental Psychology, 23,* 323–331.

Matysiak, J. (1985). Need for sensory stimulation: Affects on activity. In J. Strelau (Ed.), *Temperamental bases of behavior: Warsaw studies on individual differences* (pp. 141–180). Lisse, The Netherlands: Swets & Zeitlinger.

Matysiak, J. (1993). *Gżód stymulacji* [Need for stimulation]. Warsaw, Poland: University of Warsaw, Faculty of Psychology Press.

Maushammer, C., Ehmer, G., & Eckel, K. (1981). Pain, personality and individual differences in sensory evoked potentials. *Personality and Individual Differences, 2,* 335–336.

Maziade, M. (1988). Child temperament as a developmental or an epidemiological concept: A methodological point of view. *Psychiatric Developments, 3,* 195–211.

Maziade, M., Boudreault, M., Thivierge, J. Caperaa, P., & Cote, R. (1984). Infant temperament: SES and gender differences and reliability of measurement in a large Quebeck sample. *Merrill-Palmer Quarterly, 30,* 213–226.

Maziade, M. Cote, R., Boudreault, M., Thivierge, J., & Caperaa, P. (1984). The New York Longitudinal Studies Model of temperament: Gender differences and demographic correlates in a French-speaking population. *Journal of the American Academy of Child Psychiatry, 23,* 582–587.

Maziade, M., Caperaa, P., Laplante, B., Boudreault, M., Thivierge, J., Cote, R., & Boutin P. (1985). Value of difficult temperament among 7-year olds in the general population for predicting psychiatric diagnosis at age 12. *American Journal of Psychiatry, 142,* 943–946.

Maziade, M., Boutin, P., Cote, R., & Thivierge, J. (1986). Empirical characteristics of the NYLS temperament in middle childhood: Congruities and incongruities with other studies. *Child Psychiatry and Human Development, 17,* 38–52.

Maziade, M., Cote, R., Boutin, P., Bernier, H., & Thivierge, J. (1987). Temperament and intellectual development: A longitudinal study from infancy to four years. *American Journal of Psychiatry, 144,* 144–150.

Maziade, M., Cote, R., Bernier, H., Boutin, P, & Thivierge, J. (1989). Singificance of extreme temperament in infancy for clinical status in pre-school years: 1. Value of extreme temperament at 4–8 months for predicting diagnosis at 4.7 years. *British Journal of Psychiatry, 154,* 535–543.

Maziade, M., Caron, C., Cote, R., Boutin, P., & Thivierge, J. (1990). Extreme temperament and diagnosis. *Archives of General Psychiatry, 47,* 447–484.

Maziade, M., Caron, C., Cote, R., Merette, C., Bernier, H., Laplante, B., Boutin. P., & Thivierge, J. (1990). Psychiatric status of adolescents who had extreme temperaments at age 7. *American Journal of Psychiatry, 147,* 1531–1536.

McCartney, K., Harris, M. J., & Bernieri, F. (1990). Growing up and growing apart: A developmental meta-analysis of twin studies. *Psychological Bulletin, 107,* 226–237.

McCaulley, M. H. (1990). The Myers–Briggs Type Indicator: A measure for individuals and groups. *Measurement and Evaluation in Counseling and Development, 22,* 181–195.

McCleary, R. A. (1966). Response-modulating functions of the limbic system: Initiation and suppression. In E. Stellar & J. M. Sprague (Eds.), *Progress in physiological psychology* (Vol. 1, pp. 209–272). New York: Academic Press.

McClowry, S. G. (1990). The relationship of temperament to pre- and posthospitalization behavioral responses of school-age children. *Nursing Research, 39,* 30–35.

McClowry, S. G. (1995). The development of the School-Age Temperament Inventory. *Merrill-Palmer Quarterly, 41,* 271–285.

McClowry, S. G., Hegvik, R. L., & Teglasi, H. (1993). An examination of the construct validity of the Middle Childhood Temperament Questionnaire. *Merrill-Palmer Quarterly, 39,* 279–293.

McClowry, S. G., Giangrande, S. K., Tommasini, N. R., Clinton, W., Foreman, N. S., Lynch, K., & Ferketich, S. L. (1994). The effects of child temperament, maternal characteristics, and family circumstances on the maladjustment of school-age children. *Research in Nursing & Health, 17,* 25–35.

McCrae, R. R. (1987). Creativity, divergent thinking, and openness to experience. *Journal of Personality and Social Psychology, 52,* 1258–1265.

McCrae, R. R. (1989). Why I advocate the five-factor model: Joint analyses of the NEO-PI and other instruments. In D. M. Buss & N. Cantor (Eds.), *Personality psychology: Recent trends and emerging directions* (pp. 237–245). New York: Springer.

McCrae, R. R., & Costa, P. T., Jr. (1985a). Comparison of EPI and psychoticism scales with measures of the five-factor model of personality. *Personality and Individual Differences, 6,* 587–597.

McCrae, R. R., & Costa, P. T., Jr. (1985b). Openness to experience. In R. Hogan & W. H. Jones (Eds.), *Perspectives in personality* (Vol. 1, pp. 145–172). Greenwich, CT: JAI.

McCrae, R. R., & Costa, P. T., Jr. (1985c). Updating Norman's adequate taxonomy: Intelligence and personality dimensions in natural language and in questionnaires. *Journal of Personality and Social Psychology, 49,* 710–721.

McCrae, R. R., & Costa, P. T., Jr. (1987). Validation of the five-factor model of personality across instruments and observers. *Journal of Personality and Social Psychology, 52,* 81–90.

McCrae, R. R., & Costa, P. T., Jr. (1989). Reinterpreting the Myers–Briggs Type Indicator from the perspective of the five-factor model of personality. *Journal of Personality, 57,* 17–40.

McDevitt, S. C., & Carey, W. B. (1978). The measurement of temperament in 3–7 year old children. *Journal of Child Psychology and Psychiatry and Allied Disciplines, 19,* 245–253.

McDougall, W. (1923). *Outline of psychology.* New York: Scribner's.

McGrath, J. E. (Ed.). (1970). *Social and psychological factors in stress.* New York: Holt, Rinehart and Winston.

McGuinness, D., & Pribram, K. (1980). The neuropsychology of attention: Emotional and motivational controls. In M. C. Wittrock (Ed.), *The brain and psychology* (pp. 95–109). New York: Academic Press.

McLennan, J., & Bates, G. W. (1993). Vulnerability to psychological distress: Empirical and conceptual distinctions between measures of neuroticism and negative affect. *Psychological Reports, 73,* 1315–1323.

Medoff-Cooper, B., Carey, W. B., & McDevitt, S. C. (1993). The Early Infancy Temperament Questionnaire. *Journal of Developmental and Behavioral Pediatrics, 14,* 230–235.

Meehl, P. E. (1992). Factors and taxa, traits and types, differences of degree and differences in kind. *Journal of Personality, 60,* 117–174.

Mehrabian, A. (1965). Communication length as an index of communicator attitude. *Psychological Reports, 17,* 519–522.

Mehrabian, A. (1968). Inference of attitudes from the posture, orientation, and distance of a communicator. *Journal of Consulting and Clinical Psychology, 32,* 296–308.

Mehrabian, A. (1969). Measures of achieving tendency. *Educational and Psychological Measurement, 29,* 445–451.

Mehrabian, A. (1972). *Nonverbal communication.* Chicago: Aldine–Atherton.

Mehrabian, A. (1976a). *Manual for the Questionnaire Measure of Stimulus Screening and Arousability.* Unpublished manuscript, University of California, Los Angeles.

Mehrabian, A. (1976b). *Public places and private spaces: The psychology of work, play, and living environments.* New York: Basic Books.

Mehrabian, A. (1977a). Individual differences in stimulus screening and arousability. *Journal of Personality, 45,* 237–250.

Mehrabian, A. (1977b). A questionnaire measure of individual differences in stimulus screening and associated differences in arousability. *Environmental Psychology and Nonverbal Behavior, 1,* 89–103.

Mehrabian, A. (1978a). Characteristic individual reactions to preferred and unpreferred environments. *Journal of Personality, 46,* 717–731.

Mehrabian, A. (1978b). Measures of individual differences in temperament. *Educational and Psychological Measurement, 38,* 1105–1117.

Mehrabian, A. (1980). *Basic dimensions for a general psychological theory: Implications for personality, social, environmental, and developmental studies.* Cambridge, MA: Oelgeschlager, Gunn & Hain.

Mehrabian, A. (1986). Arousal-reducing effects of chronic stimulant use. *Motivation and Emotion, 10,* 1–10.

Mehrabian, A. (1987). *Eating characteristics and temperament: General measures and interrelationships.* New York: Springer.

Mehrabian, A. (1991). Outline of a general emotion-based theory of temperament. In J. Strelau & A. Angleitner (Eds.), *Explorations in temperament: International perspectives on theory and measurement* (pp. 75–86). New York: Plenum.

Mehrabian, A. (1995a). Framework for a comprehensive description and measurement of emotional states. *Genetic, Social, and General Psychology Monographs, 121,* 339–361.

Mehrabian, A. (1995b). Theory and evidence bearing on a scale of trait arousability. *Current Psychology: Development, Learning, Personality, 14,* 3–28.

Mehrabian, A. (1995–1996). Distinguishing depression and trait anxiety in terms of basic dimensions of temperament. *Imagination, Cognition and Personality, 15,* 133–143.

Mehrabian, A., & Bernath, M. S. (1991). Factorial composition of commonly used self-report depression inventories: Relationships with basic dimensions of temperament. *Journal of Research in Personality, 25,* 262–275.

Mehrabian, A., & Falender C. A. (1978). A questionnaire measure of individual differences in child stimulus screening. *Educational and Psychological Measurement, 38,* 1119–1127.

Mehrabian, A., & Hines, M. (1978). A questionnaire measure of individual differences in dominance–submissiveness. *Educational and Psychological Measurement, 38,* 479–484.

Mehrabian, A., & Ksionzky, S. (1972). Some determiners of social interaction. *Sociometry,* 588–609.

Mehrabian, A., & Ksionzky, S. (1974). *A theory of affiliation.* Lexington, MA: Heath.

Mehrabian, A., & O'Reilly E. (1980). Analysis of personality measures in terms of basic dimensions of temperament. *Journal of Personality and Social Psychology, 38,* 492–503.

Mehrabian, A., & Riccioni, M. (1986). Measures of eating-related characteristics for the general population: Relationships with temperament. *Journal of Personality Assessment, 50,* 610–629.

Mehrabian, A., & Ross, M. (1977). Quality of life change and individual differences in stimulus screening in relation to incidence of illness. *Psychological Reports, 41,* 267–278.

Mehrabian, A., & Russell, J. A. (1974a). *An approach to environmental psychology.* Cambridge, MA: MIT Press.

Mehrabian, A., & Russell, J. A. (1974b). The basic emotional impact of environments. *Perceptual and Motor Skills, 38,* 283–301.

Mehrabian, A., & Stanton-Mohr, L. (1985). Effects of emotional state on sexual desire and sexual dysfunction. *Motivation and Emotion, 4,* 315–330.

Mehrabian, A., Nahum, I. V., & Duke, V. (1985–1986). Individual difference correlates and measures of predisposition to obesity and to anorexia. *Imagination, Cognition and Personality, 5,* 339–355.

Mehrabian, A., Young, A. L., & Sato, S. (1988). Emotional empathy and associated individual differences. *Current Psychology: Research & Reviews, 7,* 221–240.

Merenda, P. F. (1987). Toward a four-factor theory of temperament and/or personality. *Journal of Personality Assessment, 51,* 367–374.

Merlin, V. S. (1955). The role of temperament in emotional reaction to school mark. *Voprosy Psikhologii, 1,* 62–71. (in Russian)

Merlin, V. S. (1970). The relationship between type and individual features of temperament. *Voprosy Psikhologii, 16,* 21–27. (in Russian)

Merlin, V. S. (Ed.). (1973). *Outline of the theory of temperament* (2nd ed.). Perm, Russia: Permskoye Knizhnoye Izdatelstvo. (in Russian)

Merlin, V. S. (1986). *Outline of integral research on individuality.* Moscow, Russia: Pedagogika. (in Russian)

Meyer, H. J. (1988). Temperament. In A. R. Asanger & G. Wenninger (Eds.), *Handwörterbuch der Psychologie* (4th ed., pp. 777–782). Munich, Germany: Psychologie Verlagsunion.

Mezzich, A. C., Tarter, R. E., Moss, H. B., Yao, J. K., Hsieh, Y., & Kirisci, L. (1994). Platelet monoamine oxidase activity and temperament and personality in adolescent female substance abusers. *Personality and Individual Differences, 16*, 417–424.

Miller, G. A., Galanter, E., & Pribram, K. H. (1960). *Plans and the structure of behavior.* New York: Holt.

Miller, N. E. (1951). Learnable drives and rewards. In S. S. Stevens (Ed.), *Handbook of experimental psychology* (pp. 435–472). New York: Wiley.

Mischel, W. (1968). *Personality and assessment.* New York: Wiley.

Morris, L. W. (1979). *Extraversion and introversion: An interactional perspective.* Washington, DC: Hemisphere.

Moruzzi, G., & Magoun, H. W. (1949). Brain stem reticular formation and activation of the EEG. *Electroencephalography and Clinical Neurophysiology, 1*, 455–473.

Mowrer, O. H. (1960). *Learning theory and behavior.* New York: Wiley.

Mündelein, H. (1982) *Simulierte Arbeitssituation an Bildschirmterminals: Ein Beitrag zu einer okologisch orientierten Psychologie* [Simulated job situation at computer terminals: A contribution to ecological-oriented psychology]. Frankfurt am Main, Germany: Fischer Verlag.

Murphy, D. L. (1977). The behavioral toxicity of monoamine oxidase–inhibiting antidepressants. In A. Goldin, F. Hawking, & I. J. Kodin (Eds.), *Advances in pharmacology and chemotherapy* (pp. 71–105). New York: Academic Press.

Murphy, G. (1947). *Personality.* New York: Harper.

Myers, I. B., & McCaulley, M. H. (1985). *Manual: A guide to the development and use of the Myers–Type Indicator.* Palo Alto, CA: Consulting Psychologists Press.

Myers, R. E. (1972). Role of prefrontal and anterior temporal cortex in social behavior and affect in monkeys. *Acta Neurobiologica Experimentalis, 32*, 567–579.

Myrtek, M. (1984). *Constitutional psychophysiology.* New York: Academic Press.

Nakamura, M., Fukui, Y., Kadobayashi, I., & Kato, N. (1979). A comparison of the CNV in young and old subjects: Its relation to memory and personality. *Electroencephalography and Clinical Neurophysiology, 46*, 337–344.

Naveteur, L. J., & Freixa i Baque, E. F. (1987). Individual differences in the electrodermal activity as a function of subjects' anxiety. *Personality and Individual Differences, 8*, 615–626.

Neale M. C., Cardon L. R. (1992). *Methodology for Genetic Studies of Twins and Families.* Dordrecht, The Netherlands: Kluwer Academic Publishers.

Neale, M. C., & Stevenson, J. (1989). Rater bias in the EASI temperament scales: A twin study. *Journal of Personality and Social Psychology, 56*, 446–455.

Neale, M. C., Heath, A. C., Hewitt, J. K., Eaves, L. J., & Fulker, D. W. (1989). Fitting genetic models with LISREL: Hypothesis testing. *Behavior Genetics, 19*, 37–49.

Neary, R. S., & Zuckerman, M. (1976). Sensation seeking, trait and state anxiety, and the electrodermal orienting reflex. *Psychophysiology, 13*, 205–211.

Nebylitsyn, V. D. (1957). Individual differences in strength-sensitivity in the visual and auditory analyzers. *Voprosy Psikhologii, 3*, 53–69. (in Russian)

Nebylitsyn, V. D. (1960). Reaction time and strength of nervous system. *Doklady Akademii Pedagogicheskikh Nauk RSFSR, 4*, 93–100; *5*, 71–74. (in Russian)

Nebylitsyn, V. D. (1963). The structure of the basic properties of the nervous system. *Voprosy Psikhologii, 9*, 21–34. (in Russian)

Nebylitsyn, V. D. (1964). The photic driving reaction as a function of the intensity of the pulsing light. *Zhurnal Vysshei Nervnoi Deyatelnosti, 14*, 569–576. (in Russian)

Nebylitsyn, V. D. (1965). Dynamism of nervous processes and individual differences in resting EEG in man. In B. M. Teplov (Ed.), *Typological features of higher nervous activity in man* (Vol. 4, pp. 105–110). Moscow, Russia: Prosveshcheniye. (in Russian)

Nebylitsyn, V. D. (Ed.). (1969–1974). *Problems of differential psychophysiology* (Vol. 6, 1969),

Moscow: Prosveshcheniye; (Vol. 7, 1972b), Moscow, Russia: Pedagogika; (Vol. 8, 1974), Moscow, Russia: Nauka. (in Russian)

Nebylitsyn, V. D. (1972a). *Fundamental properties of the human nervous system*. New York: Plenum.

Nebylitsyn, V. D. (1972c). The problem of general and partial properties of the nervous system. In V. D. Nebylitsyn & J. A. Gray (Eds.), *Biological bases of individual behavior* (pp. 400–418). New York: Academic Press.

Nebylitsyn, V. D. (1976). *Psychophysiological studies on individual differences*. Moscow, Russia: Nauka. (in Russian)

Nebylitsyn, V. D., & Gray, J. A. (Eds.). (1972). *Biological bases of individual behavior*. New York: Academic Press.

Netter, P. (1991). Biochemical variables in the study of temperament: Purposes, approaches, and selected findings. In J. Strelau & A. Angleitner (Eds.), *Explorations in temperament: International perspectives on theory and measurement* (pp. 147–161). New York: Plenum.

Newberry, B. H., Clark, W. B., Crawford, R. L., Strelau, J., Angleitner, A., Jones, J. H., & Eliasz, A. (1997). An American English version of the Pavlovian Temperament Survey. *Personality and Individual Differences, 22,* 105–114.

Nikiforovsky, P. M. (1952). *The pharmacology of conditioned reflexes as a method for their study.* Moscow, Russia: SSSR Academy of Medical Sciences. (in Russian)

Norman, W. T. (1963). Toward an adequate taxonomy of personality attributes: Replicated factor structure in peer nomination personality ratings. *Journal of Abnormal and Social Psychology, 66,* 574–583.

Nyborg, H. (1994). *Hormones, sex, and society: The science of physiology.* Westport, CT: Praeger.

Nyborg, H. (Ed.). (1997). *The scientific study of human nature: Tribute to Hans J. Eysenck at eighty.* Oxford, England: Pergamon.

O'Connor, K. P. (1980). The contingent negative variation and individual differences in smoking behavior. *Personality and Individual Differences, 1,* 57–72.

O'Connor, K. P. (1982). Individual differences in the effect of smoking on frontal-central distribution of the CNV: Some observations on smoker's control of attentional behavior. *Personality and Individual Differences, 3,* 271–285.

O'Connor, K. P. (1983). The authors' reply to Gale and Edwards. *Personality and Individual Differences, 4,* 437–438.

O'Gorman, J. G. (1977). Individual differences in habituation of human physiological responses: A review of theory, method and findings in the study of personality correlates in non-clinical populations. *Biological Psychology, 5,* 257–318.

O'Gorman, J. G. (1984). Extraversion and the EEG: I. An evaluation of Gale's hypothesis. *Biological Psychology, 19,* 95–112.

O'Gorman, J. G., & Lloyd, J. E. M. (1987). Extraversion, impulsiveness, and EEG alpha activity. *Personality and Individual Differences, 8,* 169–174.

O'Gorman, J. G., & Mallise, L. R. (1984). Extraversion and the EEG. II: A test of Gale's hypothesis. *Biological Psychology, 19,* 113–127.

Olds, J., & Olds, M. (1965). Drives, rewards and the brain. In F. Barron, W. C. Dement, W. Edwards, H. Lindmann, L. D. Phillips, J. Olds, & M. Olds (Eds.), *New directions in psychology* (Vol. 2, pp. 329–410). New York: Holt, Rinehart and Winston.

Oleszkiewicz, Z. (1982). Demand for stimulation and vocational preferences. *Polish Psychological Bulletin, 13,* 185–195.

Olson, S. L., Bates, J. E., & Bayles, K. (1990). Early antecedents of childhood impulsivity: The role of parent–child interaction, cognitive competence, and temperament. *Journal of Abnormal Child Psychology, 18,* 317–334.

Olweus, D. (1980a). The consistency issue in personality psychology revisited—with special reference to aggression. *British Journal of Social and Clinical Psychology, 19,* 377–390.

Olweus, D. (1980b). Familial and temperamental determinants of aggressive behavior in adolescent boys: A causal analysis. *Developmental Psychology, 16,* 644–660.

Oniszczenko W. (1997). *Genetyczne podstawy temperamentu* [The genetic foundations of temperament]. Warsaw, Poland: Wydziaż Psychologii UW.

Oniszczenko W., Rogucka E. (1996) Diagnoza zygotycznoźci bliźniąt na podstawie Kwestionariusza Fizycznego Podobieństwa Bliźniąt [The diagnosis of zygosity in twins based on the Questionnaire of Twins' Physical Resemblance]. *Przegląd Psychologiczny, 39,* 151–160.

Ormel, J., & Schaufeli, W. B. (1991). Stability and change in psychological distress and their relationship with self-esteem and locus of control: A dynamic equilibrium model. *Personality and Social Psychology, 60,* 288–299.

Osborne, Y. H., Hinz, L. D., Rappaport, N. B., Williams, H. S., & Tuma, J. M. (1988). Parent social attractiveness, parent sex, child temperament, and socioeconomic status as predictors of tendency to report child abuse. *Journal of Social and Clinical Psychology, 6,* 69–76.

Ostendorf, F., & Angleitner, A. (1992). On the generality and comprehensiveness of the five-factor model of personality: Evidence for five robust factors in questionnaire data. In G. V. Caprara & G. L. Van Heck (Eds.), *Modern personality psychology: Critical reviews and new directions* (pp.73–109). Hertfordshire, England: Harvester Wheatsheaf.

Paget, K. D., Nagle, R. J., & Martin, R. P. (1984). Interrelationships between temperament characteristics and first-grade teacher–student interaction. *Journal of Abnormal Child Psychology, 12,* 547–560.

Panksepp, J. (1982). Toward a general psychobiological theory of emotions. *Behavioral and Brain Sciences, 5,* 407–467.

Parkes, K. R. (1984). Locus of control, cognitive appraisal, and coping in stressful episodes. *Journal of Personality and Social Psychology, 46,* 655–668.

Parkes, K. R. (1986). Coping in stressful episodes: The role of individual differences, environmental factors, and situational characteristics. *Journal of Personality and Social Psychology, 51,* 1277–1292.

Pavlov, I. P. (1951–1952). *Complete works* (2nd ed.). Moscow, Russia: SSSR Academy of Sciences. (in Russian)

Pawłow, I. P. (1952). *Dwadzieźcia lat badań wyższej czynnoźci nerwowej (zachowania się) zwierząt* [Twenty years' experience in objective studies of higher nervous activity (behavior) of animals]. Warsaw, Poland: Państwowy Zakżad Wydawnictw Lekarskich.

Pedersen, N. L., Plomin, R., McClearn, G. E., & Frisberg, L. (1988). Neuroticism, extraversion, and related traits in adult twins reared apart and reared together. *Journal of Personality and Social Psychology, 55,* 950–957.

Pellegrini, D. S. (1990). Psychosocial risk and protective factors in childhood. *Journal of Developmental and Behavioral Pediatrics, 11,* 201–209.

Persson-Blennow, I., & McNeil, T. (1979). A questionnaire for measurement of temperament in six-month-old infants: Development and standardization. *Journal of Child Psychology and Psychiatry and Allied Disciplines, 20,* 1–13.

Persson-Blennow, I., & McNeil, T. (1980). Questionnaire for measurement of temperament in one and two year old children. *Journal of Child Psychology and Psychiatry, 21,* 37–46.

Persson-Blennow, I., McNeil, T. F., & Blennow, G. (1988). Temperament in children delivered by vacuum extraction. *American Journal of Orthopsychiatry, 58,* 304–309.

Pervin, L. A. (1978). Theoretical approaches to the analysis of individual–environment interaction. In L. A. Pervin, & M. Lewis (Eds.), *Perspectives in interactional psychology* (pp. 67–85). New York: Plenum.

Pervin, L. A. (Ed.). (1990). *Handbook of personality: Theory and research.* New York: Guilford.

Pervin, L. A. (1996). *The science of personality.* New York: Wiley.

Petrie, A. (1967). *Individuality in pain and suffering.* Chicago: University of Chicago Press.

Pfeffer, J., & Martin, R. P. (1983). Comparison of mothers' and fathers' temperament ratings of referred and nonreferred preschool children. *Journal of Clinical Psychology, 39,* 1013–1020.

Pickering, A. D. (1997). The conceptual nervous system and personality: From Pavlov to neural networks. *European Psychologist, 2,* 139–163.

Plomin, R. (1976). A twin and family study of personality in young children. *Journal of Psychology, 94,* 233–235.

Plomin, R. (1982). The difficult concept of temperament: A response to Thomas, Chess, and Korn. *Merrill-Palmer Quarterly, 28,* 25–33.

Plomin, R. (1986). *Development, genetics, and psychology.* Hillsdale, NJ: Erlbaum.

Plomin, R., & DeFries, J. C. (1985). *Origins of individual differences in infancy: The Colorado Adoption Project.* New York: Academic Press.

Plomin, R. & Dunn, J. (Eds.). (1986). *The study of temperament: Changes, continuities and challenges.* Hillsdale, NJ: Erlbaum.

Plomin, R., & Nesselroade, J. R. (1990). Behavioral genetics and personality change. *Journal of Personality, 58,* 191–220.

Plomin, R., & Rowe, D. C. (1977). A twin study of temperament in young children. *Journal of Psychology, 97,* 107–113.

Plomin, R., DeFries, J. C., & Loehlin, J. C. (1977). Genotype–environment interaction and correlation in the analysis of human behavior. *Psychological Bulletin, 84,* 309–322.

Plomin, R., Owen, M. J., & McGuffin, P. (1994). The genetic basis of complex human behaviors. *Science, 264,* 1733–1739.

Plomin, R., Pedersen, N. L., McClearn, G. E., Nesselroade, J. R., & Bergeman, C. S. (1988). EAS temperaments during the last half of the life span: Twins reared apart and twins reared together. *Psychology and Aging, 3,* 43–50.

Plomin, R., DeFries, J. C., McClearn, G. E. & Rutter, M. (1997). *Behavioral genetics: A primer* (3rd ed.). New York: Freeman.

Plomin, R., Coon, H., Carey, G., DeFries, J. C., & Fulker, D. W. (1991). Parent–offspring and sibling adoption analyses of parental ratings of temperament in infancy and childhood. *Journal of Personality, 59,* 705–732.

Plooij-van Gorsel, P. C., & Janssen, R. H. C. (1978). Contingent negative variation (CNV) and extraversion in a psychiatric population. In C. Barber (Ed.), *Evoked potentials: Proceedings of an international evoked potentials symposium* (pp. 505–514). Lancaster, England: Medical and Technical Publications.

Plutchik, R. (1980). *Emotion: A psychoevolutionary synthesis.* New York: Harper and Row.

Polich, J. (1987). Task difficulty, probability and inter-stimulus interval as determinants of P300 from auditory stimuli. *Electroencephalography and Clinical Neurophysiology, 68,* 311–320.

Polich, J., & Martin, S. (1992). P300, cognitive capability, and personality: A correlational study of university undergraduates. *Personality and Individual Differences, 13,* 533–543.

Poortinga, Y. H. (1989). Equivalence of cross-cultural data: An overview of basic issues. *International Journal of Psychology, 24,* 737–756.

Popper, K. R. (1959). *The logic of scientific discovery.* London: Hutchinson.

Porges, S. W., Arnold, W. R., & Forbes, E. V. (1973). Heart rate variability: An index of attentional responsivity in human newborns. *Developmental Psychology, 3,* 85–92.

Powell, G. E. (1979). *Brain and personality.* Farnborough, England: Saxon House.

Price, R. A., Vandenberg, S. G., Iyer, H., & Williams, J. S. (1982). Components of variation in normal personality. *Journal of Personality and Social Psychology, 43,* 328–340.

Priel, B., Henik, A., Dekel, A., & Tal A. (1990). Perceived temperamental characteristics and regulation of physiological stress: A study of wheezy babies. *Journal of Pediatric Psychology, 15,* 197–209.

Prior, M. R. (1992). Childhood temperament. *Journal of Child Psychology and Psychiatry, 33,* 249–279.

Prior, M. R., Crook, G., Stripp, A., Power, M., & Joseph, M. (1986). The relationship between temperament and personality: An exploratory study. *Personality and Individual Differences, 7,* 875–881.

Prior, M. R., Kyrios, M., & Oberklaid, F. (1986). Temperament in Australian, Chinese, and Greek infants: Some issues and directions for future research. *Journal of Cross-Cultural Psychology, 17,* 455–474.

Prior, M. R., Garino, E., Sanson, A., & Oberklaid, F. (1987). Ethnic influences on "difficult" temperament and behavioral problems in infants. *Australian Journal of Psychology, 39,* 163–171.

Prior, M. R., Sanson, A. V., & Oberklaid, F. (1989). The Australian Temperament Project. In G. A. Kohnstamm, J. E. Bates, & M. K. Rothbart (Eds.), *Temperament in childhood* (pp. 537–554). Chichester, England: Wiley.

Pueschel, S. M., & Myers, B. A. (1994). Environmental and temperament assessments of children with Down's syndrome. *Journal of Intellectual Disability Research, 38,* 195–202.

Pullis, M., & Cadwell, J. (1982). The influence of children's temperament characteristics on teachers' decision strategies. *American Educational Research Journal, 19,* 165–181.

Putnins, A. L. (1982). The Eysenck Personality Questionnaire and delinquency prediction. *Personality and Individual Differences, 3,* 339–340.

Rahe, R. H. (1987). Recent life changes, emotions, and behaviors in coronary heart disease. In A. Baum & J. E. Singer (Eds.), *Handbook of psychology and health* (Vol. 5, pp. 229–254). Hillsdale, NJ: Erlbaum.

Ravich-Shcherbo, I. V. (1956). Study of typological differences in mobility of the nervous processes in the visual analyzer. In B. M. Teplov (Ed.), *Typological features of higher nervous actvity in man* (Vol. 1, pp. 153–176). Moscow, Russia: RSFSR Academy of Pedagogical Sciences. (in Russian)

Ravich-Shcherbo, I. V. (1977). Preliminary results of investigation of nervous system properties based on the twin method. In A. A. Smirnov (Ed.), *Psychology and psychophysiology of individual differences* (pp. 89–99). Moscow, Russia: Pedagogika. (in Russian)

Ravich-Shcherbo, I. V. (Ed.). (1988). *The role of nurture and nature in molding the individuality in man.* Moscow, Russia: Pedagogika. (in Russian)

Ravich-Shcherbo, I. V., Shlakhta, N. F., & Shibarovskaya, G. A. (1969). A study of some typological indices in twins. In V. D. Nebylitsyn (Ed.), *Problems of differential psychophysiology* (Vol. 6, pp. 174–196). Moscow, Russia: Prosveshcheniye. (in Russian)

Redmond, D. E., Jr. (1985). Neurochemical basis for anxiety and anxiety disorders: Evidence from drugs which decrease human fear or anxiety. In A. H. Tuma & J. D. Maser (Eds.), *Anxiety and the anxiety disorders* (pp. 533–555). Hillsdale, NJ: Erlbaum.

Redmond, D. E., Jr., Katz, M. M., Maas, J. W., Swann, A., Casper, R., & Davis, J. M. (1986). Cerebrospinal fluid amine metabolites: Relationships with behavioral measurements in depressed, manic, and healthy controls. *Archives of General Psychiatry, 43,* 938–947.

Reed, M. A., Pien, D. L., & Rothbart, M. K. (1984). Inhibitory self-control in preschool children. *Merrill-Palmer Quarterly, 30,* 131–147.

Revelle, W., Amaral, P., & Turriff, S. (1976). Introversion–extraversion, time stress, and caffeine: Effect on verbal performance. *Science, 192,* 149–150.

Revelle, W., Humphreys, M. S., Simon, L., & Gilliland, K. (1980). The interactive effect of personality, time of day, and caffeine: A test of the arousal model. *Journal of Experimental Psychology: General, 109,* 1–31.

Revelle, W., Anderson, K. J., & Humphreys, M. S. (1987). Empirical tests and theoretical extensions of arousal-based theories of personality. In J. Strelau & H. J. Eysenck (Eds.), *Personality dimensions and arousal* (pp. 17–36). New York: Plenum.

Reykowski, J. (1975). Osobowoźś jako centralny system regulacji i integracji czynnoźci [Personality as the central regulation and integration system of actions]. In T. Tomaszewski (Ed.), *Psychologia* (pp. 762–825). Warsaw, Poland: Państwowe Wydawnictwo Naukowe.

Reykowski, J. (1979) *Motywacja, postawy spożeczne a osobowożs* [Motivation, prosocial attitudes and personality]. Warsaw, Poland: Państwowe Wydawnictwo Naukowe.

Reynolds, C. R., & Willson, V. L. (1985). *Methodological and statistical advances in the study of individual differences.* New York: Plenum.

Reznick, J. S., Kagan, J., Snidman, N., Gersten, M., Baak, K., & Rosenberg, A. (1986). Inhibited and uninhibited children: A follow-up study. *Child Development, 57,* 660–680.

Ribot, T. (1887). *L'hérédité psychologique* [Psychological heredity]. Paris: Librairie Felix Alcan.

Ricciuti, H. N., & Breitmayer, B. J. (1988). Observational assessments of infant temperament in the natural setting of the newborn nursery: Stability and relationship to perinatal status. *Merrill-Palmer Quarterly, 34,* 281–299.

Richards, M., & Eves, F. F. (1991). Personality, temperament and the cardiac defense response. *Personality and Individual Differences, 12,* 999–1007.

Richman, N., & Graham P. J. (1971). A behavioural screening questionnaire for use with 3-year-old children: Preliminary findings. *Journal of Child Psychology and Psychiatry, 12,* 5–33.

Richmond, J. B., & Lustman, L. Q. (1955). Individual differences in the neonate. *Psychosomatic Medicine, 17,* 269–280.

Ridgeway, D., & Hare, R. D. (1981). Sensation seeking and psychophysiological responses to auditory stimulation. *Psychophysiology, 18,* 613–618.

Riese, M. L. (1983) Assessment of behavioral patterns in neonates. *Infant Behavior and Development, 6,* 241–246.

Riese, M. L. (1990). Neonatal temperament in monozygotic and dizygotic twin pairs. *Child Development, 61,* 1230–1237.

Riese, M. L., Wilson, R. S., & Matheny, A. P., Jr. (1985). Multimethod assessment of temperament in twins: Birth to six months. *Acta Geneticae Medicae et Gemellologiae, 34,* 15–31.

Ritter, W. Rotkin, L, & Vaughan, J. G., Jr. (1980). The modality specificity of the slow negative wave. *Psychophysiology, 17,* 222–227.

Roback, A. A. (1931). *The psychology of character: With a survey of temperament* (3rd ed.) London: Kegan Paul, Trench & Trubner.

Robinson, D. L. (1986). A commentary on Gray's critique of Eysenck's theory. *Personality and Individual Differences, 7,* 461–468.

Rocklin, T., & Revelle, W. (1981). The measurement of extraversion: A comparison of the Eysenck Personality Inventory and the Eysenck Personality Questionnaire. *British Journal of Social Psychology, 20,* 279–284.

Rose, R. J., Koskenvuo, M., Kaprio, J., Sarna, S., & Langinvainio, H. (1988). Shared genes, shared experiences, and similarity of personality: Data from 14,288 adult Finnish co-twins. *Journal of Personality and Social Psychology, 54,* 161–171.

Rosenman, R. H., Rahe, R. H., Borhani, N. O., & Feinleib, M. (1976). Heritability of personality and behavior pattern. *Acta Geneticae Medicae et Gemellologiae, 25,* 221–224.

Rösler, F. (1975). Die Abhängigkeit des Elektroencephalogramms von den Persönlichkeitsdimensionen E und N sensu Eysenck and unterschiedlich aktivierenden Situationen [The dependency of the electroencephalogram from Eysenck's E and N personality dimensions and from situations which differ in arousal]. *Zeitschrift für experimentelle und angewandte Psychologie, 22,* 630–667.

Ross, G. (1987). Temperament of preterm infants: Its relationship to perinatal factors and one-year outcome. *Journal of Developmental and Behavioral Pediatrics, 8,* 106–110.

Rostan, L. (1824). *Cours élémentaire d'hygiène* [Lectures on rudimentary hygienics] (2nd ed.). Paris: Bechet Jeune.

Roth, K., Eisenberg, N., & Sell, E. R. (1984). The relationship of preterm and full-term infants' temperament to test-taking behaviors and developmental status. *Infant Behavior & Development, 7,* 495–505.

Rothbart, M. K. (1981). Measurement of temperament in infancy. *Child Development, 52,* 569–578.

Rothbart, M. K. (1982). The concept of difficult temperament: A critical analysis of Thomas, Chess, and Korn. *Merrill-Palmer Quarterly, 28,* 35–40.

Rothbart, M. K. (1986). Longitudinal observation of infant temperament. *Developmental Psychology, 22,* 356–365.

Rothbart, M. K. (1988). Temperament and the development of inhibited approach. *Child Development, 59,* 1241–1250.

Rothbart, M. K. (1989a). Biological processes in temperament. In G. A. Kohnstamm, J. E. Bates, & M. K. Rothbart (Eds.), *Temperament in childhood* (pp. 77–110). Chichester, England: Wiley.

Rothbart, M. K. (1989b). Temperament in childhood: A framework. In G. A. Kohnstamm, J. E. Bates, & M. K. Rothbart (Eds.), *Temperament in childhood* (pp. 59–73). Chichester, England: Wiley.

Rothbart, M. K. (1989c). Temperament and development. In G. A. Kohnstamm, J. E. Bates, & M. K. Rothbart (Eds.), *Temperament in childhood* (pp. 187–247). Chichester, England: Wiley.

Rothbart, M. K. (1991). Temperament: A developmental framework. In J. Strelau & A. Angleitner (Eds.), *Explorations in temperament: International perspectives on theory and measurement* (pp. 61–74). New York: Plenum.

Rothbart, M. K., & Ahadi, S. A. (1994). Temperament and the development of personality. *Journal of Abnormal Psychology, 103,* 55–66.

Rothbart, M. K., & Derryberry, D. (1981). Development of individual differences in temperament. In M. E. Lamb & A. L. Brown (Eds.), *Advances in developmental psychology* (Vol. 1. pp. 37–86). Hillsdale, NJ: Erlbaum.

Rothbart, M. K., & Goldsmith, H. H. (1985). Three approaches to the study of infant temperament. *Developmental Review, 5,* 237–260.

Rothbart, M. K., & Hanson, M. J. (1983). A caregiver report comparison of temperamental characteristics of Down syndrome and normal infants. *Developmental Psychology, 19,* 766–769.

Rothbart, M. K., & Mauro, J. A. (1990). Questionnaire approaches to the study of infant temperament. In J. Colombo & J. Fagen (Eds.), *Individual differences in infancy: Reliability, stability, prediction* (pp.411–429). Hillsdale, NJ: Erlbaum.

Rothbart, M. K., & Posner, M. I. (1985). Temperament and the development of self-regulation. In L. C. Hartlage & C. F. Telzrow (Eds.), *The neuropsychology of individual differences: A developmental perspective* (pp. 93–123). New York: Plenum.

Rothbart, M. K., Derryberry, D., & Posner, M. I. (1994). A psychobiological approach to the development of temperament. In J. E. Bates & T. D. Wachs (Eds.), *Temperament: Individual differences at the interface of biology and behavior* (pp. 83–116). Washington, DC: American Psychological Association.

Rothbart, M. K., Posner, M. I., & Rosicky, J. (1994). Orienting in normal and pathological development. *Developmental and Psychopathology, 6,* 635–652.

Rothbart, M. K., Ahadi, S. A., Hershey, K. L., & Fisher, P. (1995). *Temperament in children 4–7 years as assessed in the Children's Behavior Questionnaire.* Unpublished manuscript, University of Oregon, Eugene.

Rotter, J. B. (1972). *Applications of a social learning theory of personality.* New York: Holt, Rinehart and Winston.

Rowe, D. C., & Plomin, R. (1977). Temperament in early childhood. *Journal of Personality Assessment, 41,* 150–156.

Royce, J. R. (1955). A factorial study of emotionality in the dog. *Psychological Monographs, 69,* whole No. 22.

Royce, J. R., & Powell, A. (1983). *Theory of personality and individual differences: Factors, systems, and processes.* Englewood Cliffs, NJ: Prentice-Hall.

Rozhdestvenskaya, I. V. (1955). An attempt to measure the strength of the excitatory process through aspects of its irradiation and concentration in the visual analyser. *Voprosy Psikhologii, 1,* 90–98. (in Russian)

Rozhdestvenskaya, V. I. (1980). *Individual differences in work efficiency.* Moscow, Russia: Pedagogika. (in Russian)

Rozhdestvenskaya, V. I., Golubeva, E. A., & Yermolayeva-Tomina, L. B. (1969). The role of strength of the nervous system in the dynamics of mental capacity for work in different kinds of activity. In V. D. Nebylitsyn (Ed.), *Problems of differential psychophysiology* (Vol. 6, pp. 138–148). Moscow, Russia: Prosveshcheniye. (in Russian)

Rubinstein, S. L. (1946). *Fundamentals of psychology* (2nd ed.). Moscow, Russia: Institute of Philosophy of SSSR Academy of Sciences. (in Russian)

Ruch, W. (1992). Pavlov's types of nervous system, Eysenck's typology and the Hippocrates–Galen temperaments: An empirical examination of the asserted correspondence of three temperament typologies. *Personality and Individual Differences, 12,* 1259–1271.

Ruch, W., Angleitner, A., & Strelau, J. (1991). The Strelau Temperament Inventory–Revised (STI-R): Validity studies. *European Journal of Personality, 5,* 287–308.

Rumelin, G. (1890). Über die Temperamente [On temperaments]. *Deutsche Rundschau, 64,* 397–412.

Rundquist, E. A. (1933). Inheritance of spontaneous activity in rats. *Journal of Comparative Psychology, 16,* 415–438.

Rusalov, V. M. (1967). On inter-analyser differences in sensory sensitivity. *Novye Issledovaniya v Pedagogicheskikh Naukakh, 11,* 76–81. (in Russian)

Rusalov, V. M. (1972). Absolute sensitivity of the analysers and somatotype in man. In V. D. Nebylitsyn & J. A. Gray (Eds.), *Biological bases of individual behavior* (pp. 128–140). New York: Academic Press.

Rusalov, V. M. (1974). Polar-amplitudinal asymmetry of evoked potentials. In V. D. Nebylitsyn (Ed.), *Problems of differential psychophysiology: Electrophysiological investigations of the fundamental properties of the nervous system* (Vol. 8, pp. 34–53). Moscow, Russia: Nauka. (in Russian)

Rusalov, V. M. (1977). On the nature of general and partial properties of the nervous system in man. In A. A. Smirnov (Ed.), *Psychology and psychophysiology of individual differences* (pp. 108–116). Moscow, Russia: Pedagogika. (in Russian)

Rusalov, V. M. (1979). *Biological bases of individual-psychological differences.* Moscow, Russia: Nauka. (in Russian)

Rusalov, V. M. (1982). The interrelationship between temperamental traits and efficiency of individual and shared activity. *Psikhologicheskii Zhurnal, 6,* 50–59. (in Russian)

Rusalov, V. M. (1985). On the nature of temperament and its place in the structure of human individual differences. *Voprosy Psikhologii, 1,* 19–32. (in Russian)

Rusalov, V. M. (1986). Theoretical problems regarding the construction of a special theory of human individuality. *Psikhologicheskii Zhurnal, 7,* 23–35. (in Russian)

Rusalov, V. M. (1989a). The natural prerequisites of development of human individuality. *Studia Psychologica, 31,* 53–67.

Rusalov, V. M. (1989b). Object-related and communicative aspects of human temperament. *Psikhologicheskii Zhurnal, 10,* 10–21. (in Russian)

Rusalov, V. M. (1989c). Object-related and communicative aspects of human temperament: A new questionnaire of the structure of temperament. *Personality and Individual Differences, 10,* 817–827.

Rusalov, V. M., Parilis, S. E. (1991) Temperament and the self-concept of the cognitive system of personality. *Psikhologicheskii Zhurnal, 12,* 118–123. (in Russian)

Rushton, J. P., Brainerd, C. J., & Pressley, M. (1983). Behavioral development and construct validity: The principle of aggregation. *Psychological Bulletin, 94,* 18–38.

Russell, J. A., & Mehrabian, A. (1977). Evidence for a three-factor theory of emotions. *Journal of Research in Personality, 11,* 273–294.

Russo, M. F., Stokes, G. S., Lahey, B., Christ, M. A. G., McBurnett, K., Loeber, R., Stouthammer-Loeber, M., & Green, S. M. (1993). A Sensation Seeking Scale for Children: Further refinement and psychometric development. *Journal of Psychopathology and Behavioral Assessment, 15,* 69–86.

Rutter, M. (1979). Protective factors in children's responses to stress and disadvantage. In M. W. Kent & J. E. Rolf (Eds.), *Primary prevention of psychopathology* (Vol. 3, pp. 49–74). Hanover, NH: University Press of New England.

Rutter, M. (1982). Temperament: Concepts, issues and problems. In R. Porter & G. M. Collins (Eds.), *Temperamental differences in infants and young children. Ciba Foundation Symposium 89* (pp. 1–19). London: Pitman.

Rutter, M. (1987). Temperament, personality and personality disorder. *British Journal of Psychiatry, 150,* 443–458.

Rutter, M. (1991). Nature, nurture, and pschopathology: A new look at an old topic. *Development and Psychopathology, 3,* 125–136.

Rutter, M., Birch, H. G., Thomas, A., & Chess, S. (1964). Temperamental characteristics in infancy and the later development of behavioural disorders. *British Journal of Psychiatry, 110,* 651–661.

Samarin, Y. A. (1954). An attempt at the experimental psychological study of typological features of the nervous system in children. *Izvestiya Akademii Pedagogicheskikh Nauk RSFSR, 52,* 81–140. (in Russian)

Sameroff, A. J., Seifer, R., & Elias, P. K. (1982). Sociocultural variability in infant temperament ratings. *Child Development, 53,* 164–173.

Sanson, A., Prior, M., Garino, E. Oberklaid, F., & Sewell, J. (1987). The structure of infant temperament. Factor analysis of the Revised Infant Temperament Questionnarie. *Infant Behavior and Development, 10,* 97–104.

Sanson, A., Prior, M., & Kyrios. M. (1990a). Contamination of measures in temperament research. *Merrill-Palmer Quarterly, 36,* 179–192.

Sanson, A., Prior, M., & Kyrios, M. (1990b). Further exploration of the link between temperament and behavior problems: A reply to Bates. *Merrill-Palmer Quarterly, 36,* 573–576.

Saudino, K. J., & Eaton. W. O. (1995). Continuity and change in objectively assessed temperament: A longitudinal twin study of activity level. *British Journal of Developmental Psychology, 13,* 81–95.

Saul, L. J., Davis, H., & Davis, P. A. (1937). Correlation between electroencephalograms and the psychological organization of the individual. *Transactions of the American Neurolgical Association, 63,* 167–169.

Saul, L. J., Davis, H., & Davis, P. A. (1949). Psychologic correlations with the electroencephalogram. *Psychosomatic Medicine, 11,* 361–376.

Scarr, S. (1992). Developmental theories for the 1990s: Development and individual differences. *Child Development, 63,* 1–19.

Scarr, S., & McCartney, K. (1983). How people make their own environments: A theory of genotype→environment effects. *Child Development, 54,* 424–435.

Scarr, S., Webber, P. L., Weinberg, R. A., & Wittig, M. A. (1981). Personality resemblance among adolescents and their parents in biologically related and adoptive families. *Journal of Personality and Social Psychology, 40,* 885–898.

Schalling, D., & Asberg, M. (1985). Biological and psychological correlates of impulsiveness and monotony avoidance. In J. Strelau, F. H. Farley, & A. Gale (Eds.), *The biological bases of behavior: Theories, measurement techniques, and development* (Vol. 1, pp. 181–194). Washington, DC: Hemisphere.

Schalling, D., Edman, G., & Asberg, M. (1983). Impulsive cognitive style and inability to tolerate boredom: Psychobiological studies of temperamental vulnerability. In M. Zuckerman (Ed.), *Biological bases of sensation seeking, impulsivity, and anxiety* (pp. 123–145). Hillsdale, NJ: Erlbaum.

Schalling, D., Asberg, M., Edman, G., & Oreland, L. (1987). Markers for vulnerability to psychopathology: Temperament traits associated with platelet MAO activity. *Acta Psychiatrica Scandinavica, 76,* 172–182.

Schalling, D., Edman, G., Asberg, M., & Oreland, L. (1988). Platelet MAO activity associated with impulsivity and aggressivity. *Personality and Individual Differences, 9,* 597–605.

Schaughency, E. A., & Fagot, B. I. (1993). The prediction of adjustment at age 7 from activity at age 5. *Journal of Abnormal Child Psychology, 21*, 29–50.

Scherer, K. R., & Ekman, P. (Eds.). (1982). *Handbook of methods in nonverbal behavior research.* Cambridge, England: Cambridge University Press.

Schmitz, P. G. (1992). Personality, stress-reactions and disease. *Personality and Individual Differences, 13*, 683–691.

Schmitz, P. G. (1993). Personality, stress-reactions, and psychosomatic complaints. In G. L. Van Heck, P. Bonaiuto, I. J. Deary, & W. Nowack (Eds.), *Personality psychology in Europe* (Vol. 4, pp. 321–343). Tilburg, The Netherlands: Tilburg University Press.

Schneirla, T. C. (1957). The concept of development in comparative psychology. In D. B. Harris (Ed.), *The concept of development* (pp. 78–108). Minneapolis: University of Minnesota Press.

Schneirla, T. C. (1959). An evolutionary and developmental theory of biphasic processes underlying approach and withdrawal. In M. J. Jones, (Ed.), *Nebraska Symposion on Motivation* (Vol. 7, pp. 1–42). Lincoln: University of Nebraska Press.

Schneirla, T. C. (1965). Aspects of stimulation and organization in approach–withdrawal processes underlying vertebrate development. In D. S. Lehrman, R. A. Hinde, & E. Show (Eds.), *Advances in the study of behavior* (Vol. 1, pp. 1–74). New York: Academic Press.

Scholom, A., Zucker, R. A., & Stollak. G. E. (1979). Relating early child adjustment to infant and parent temperament. *Journal of Abnormal Child Psychology, 7*, 297–308.

Schönfeld, K. (1962). *Die Temperamentlehre in deutschsprachigen Handschriften des 15. Jahrhunderts* [The temperament knowledge in German-language manuscripts of the 15th century]. Heidelberg, Germany: A. Grosch.

Schönpflug, W. (1983). Coping efficiency and situational demands. In G. R. J. Hockey (Ed.), *Stress and fatigue in human performance* (pp. 299–329). Chichester, England: Wiley.

Schönpflug, W. (1986). Effort regulation and individual differences in effort expenditure. In G. R. J. Hockey, A. W. K. Gaillard, & M. G. H. Coles (Eds.), *Energetics and human information processing* (pp. 271–283). Dordrecht, The Netherlands: Martinus Nijhoff.

Schönpflug, W., & Battmann, W. (1988). The costs and benefits of coping. In S. Fisher & J. Reason (Eds.), *Handbook of life stress, cognition and health* (pp. 699–713). Chichester, England: Wiley.

Schooler, C., & Silverman, J. (1971). Differences between correlates of perceptual style and Petrie task performance in chronic and acute schizophrenics. *Perceptual and Motor Skills, 32*, 595–601.

Schulz, P., & Schönpflug, W. (1982). Regulatory activity during states of stress. In H. W. Krohne & L. Laux (Eds.), *Achievement, stress, and anxiety* (pp. 51–73). Washington, DC: Hemisphere.

Schwartz, M. (1978). *Physiological psychology.* Englewood Cliffs, NJ: Prentice-Hall.

Scott, J. P., & Fuller, J. L. (1965). *Genetics and the social behavior of the dog.* Chicago: Chicago University Press.

Segal, N. L. (1990). The importance of twin studies for individual differences research. *Journal of Counseling and Development, 68*, 612–622.

Selye, H. (1956). *The stress of life.* New York: McGraw-Hill.

Selye, H. (1975). *Stress without distress.* New York: New American Library.

Sewell, T. E., Thurman, S. K., & Hutchins, D. (1981, April). *Temperament and cognitive styles in academic achievement of low-income Black preschool children.* Paper presented at the annual meeting of the American Educational Research Association, Los Angeles.

Shekim, W. O., Hodges, K., Horowitz, E., Glaser, R. D., Davis, L., & Bylund, D. B. (1984). Psychoeducational and impulsivity correlates of platelet MAO in normal children. *Psychiatry Research, 11*, 99–106.

Sheldon, W. H., & Stevens, S. S. (1942). *The varieties of temperament: A psychology of constitutional differences.* New York: Harper & Brothers.

Sheldon, W. H., Stevens, S. S., & Tucker, W. B. (1940). *The varieties of human physique.* New York: Harper & Brothers.

Shields, J. (1962). *Monozygotic twins: Brought up apart and brought up together.* London: Oxford University Press.

Shvarts, L. A. (1965). Speed of restoration of visual sensitivity after visual fatigue and after light exposure as indices of lability of nervous processes. In B. M. Teplov (Ed.), *Typological features of higher nervous activity in man* (Vol. 4, pp. 141–146). Moscow, Russia: Prosveshcheniye. (in Russian)

Shwalb, B. J., Shwalb, D. W., & Shoji, J. (1994). Structure and dimensions of maternal perceptions of Japanese infant temperament. *Developmental Psychology, 30,* 131–141.

Sigaud, C. (1914). *La forme humain* [Human physique]. Paris: A. Maloine.

Simon, T. R., Stacy, A. W., Sussman, S., & Dent, C. W. (1994). Sensation seeking and drug use among high risk Latino and Anglo adolescents. *Personality and Individual Differences, 17,* 665–672.

Simonds, J. F., & Simonds, M. P. (1982). Nursery school children's temperament related to sex, birth position, and socioeconomic status. *Journal of Pediatric Psychology, 7,* 49–59.

Simonov, P. V. (1984). The need-informational theory of emotions. *International Journal of Psychophysiology, 1,* 277–289.

Simonov, P. V. (1987). Individual characteristics of brain limbic structures interactions as the basis of Pavlovian/Eysenckian typology. In J. Strelau & H. J. Eysenck (Eds.), *Personality dimensions and arousal* (pp. 123–132). New York: Plenum.

Slabach, E. H., Morrow, J., & Wachs, T. (1991). Questionnaire measurement of infant and child temperament. In J. Strelau & A. Angleitner (Eds.), *Explorations in temperament: International perspectives on theory and measurement* (pp. 205–234). New York: Plenum.

Smedslund, G. (1995). Personality and vulnerability to cancer and heart disease: Relations to demographic and life-style variables. *Personality and Individual Differences, 19,* 691–697.

Smith, B. D. (1983). Extraversion and electrodermal activity: Arousability and the inverted-U. *Personality and Individual Differences, 4,* 411–420.

Smith, B. D., Wilson, R. J., & Jones, B. E. (1983). Extraversion and multiple levels of caffeine-induced arousal: Effects of overhabituation and dishabituation. *Psychophysiology, 15,* 29–34.

Smith, H. C. (1949). Psychometric checks on hypotheses derived from Sheldon's work on physique and temperament. *Journal of Personality, 17,* 310–320.

Smith, J., & Prior, M. (1995). Temperament and stress resilience in school-age children: A within-families study. *Journal of American Academy of Child and Adolescent Psychiatry, 34,* 168–179.

Snider, J. G., & Osgood, C. E. (Eds.). (1969). *Semantic differential technique.* Chicago: Aldine.

Sokolov, E. N. (1963). *Perception and the conditioned reflex.* New York: Macmillan.

Sosnowski, T. (1991). *Wzorce aktywności psychofizjologicznej w warunkach krótkotrwałego stresu antycypacyjnego* [Patterns of psychophysiological activity under conditions of short-lived anticipatory stress]. Wrocław, Poland: Ossolineum.

Sosnowski, T., & Bialski, Y. (1992). *Strive and retreat: Gray's theory of personality in questionnaire examination.* Unpublished manuscript, University of Warsaw, Faculty of Psychology, Warsaw, Poland.

Sostek, A. J., Sostek, A. M., Murphy, D. L., Martin, E. B., & Born, W. S. (1981). Cord blood amine oxidase activities relate to arousal and motor functioning in human newborns. *Life Science, 28,* 2561–2568.

Sostek, A. M., & Anders, T. F. (1977) Relationships among the Brazelton Neonatal Scale and the Baley Infant Scale, and early temperament. *Child Development, 48,* 320–323.

Soubrie, P. (1986). Reconciling the role of central serotonin neurons in animal and human behavior. *Behavioral and Brain Sciences, 9,* 319–364.

Soudijn, K. A., Hutschemaekers, G. J. M., & van de Vijver, F. J. R. (1990). Culture conceptualisations. In F. J. R. van de Vijver, & G. J. M. Hutschemaekers (Eds.), *The investigation of culture: Current issues in cultural psychology* (pp. 19–39). Tilburg, The Netherlands: Tilburg University Press.

Spence, J. T., & Spence, K. W. (1966). The motivational components of manifest anxiety: Drive and drive stimuli. In C. D. Spielberger (Ed.), *Anxiety and behavior* (pp. 291–326). London: Academic Press.

Spielberger, C. D., Gorsuch, R. L., & Lushene, R. E. (1970). *Manual for the State-Trait Anxiety Inventory*. Palo Alto, CA: Consulting Psychologists Press.

Stacy, A. W., Newcomb, M. D., & Bentler, P. M. (1993). Cognitive motivations and sensation seeking as long-term predictors of drinking problems. *Journal of Social and Clinical Psychology, 12,* 1–24.

Stein, L. (1974). Norepinephrine reward pathways: Role in self-stimulation, memory consolidation and schizophrenia. In J. K. Cole & T. B. Sonderegger (Eds.), *Nebraska Symposium on Motivation* (Vol. 31, pp. 113–161). Lincoln: University of Nebraska Press.

Stein, L. (1978). Catecholamines and opioid peptides. In M. A. Lipton, D. Mascio, & K. F. Killman (Eds.), *Psychopharmacology: A generation of progress* (pp. 569–581). New York: Raven.

Stein, L. (1983). The chemistry of positive reinforcement. In M. Zuckerman (Ed.), *Biological bases of sensation seeking, impulsivity, and anxiety* (pp. 151–175). Hillsdale, NJ: Erlbaum.

Stelmack, R. M. (1981). The psychophysiology of extraversion and neuroticism. In H. J. Eysenck (Ed.), *A model for personality* (pp. 38–64). Berlin, Germany: Springer.

Stelmack, R. M. (1990). Biological bases of extraversion: Psychophysiological evidence. *Journal of Personality, 58,* 293–311.

Stelmack, R. M., & Campbell, K. B. (1974). Extraversion and auditory sensitivity to high and low frequency. *Perceptual and Motor Skills, 38,* 875–879.

Stelmack, R. M., & Geen, R. G. (1992). The psychophysiology of extraversion. In A. Gale & M. W. Eysenck (Eds.), *Handbook of individual differences: Biological perspectives* (pp. 227–254). Chichester, England: Wiley.

Stelmack, R. M., & Michaud-Achorn, A. (1985). Extraversion, attention, and habituation of the auditory evoked response. *Journal of Research in Personality, 19,* 416–428.

Stelmack, R. M., & Stalikas, A. (1991). Galen and the humour theory of temperament. *Personality and Individual Differences, 12,* 255–263.

Stelmack, R. M., & Wilson, K. (1982). Extraversion and the effects of frequency and intensity on the auditory brainstem evoked response. *Personality and Individual Differences, 3,* 373–380.

Stelmack, R. M., Achorn, E., & Michaud, A. (1977). Extraversion and individual differences in auditory evoked response. *Psychophysiology, 14,* 368–374.

Stelmack, R. M., Bourgeois, R. P., Chain, J., & Pickard, C. W. (1979). Extraversion and the orienting reaction habituation rate to visual stimuli. *Journal of Research in Personality, 13,* 49–58.

Stenberg, G. (1992). Personality and the EEG: Arousal and emotional arousability. *Personality and Individual Differences, 13,* 1097–1113.

Stenberg, G. (1994). Extraversion and the P300 in a visual classification task. *Personality and Individual Differences, 16,* 543–560.

Stenberg, G., Rosen, I., & Risberg, J. (1988). Personality and augmenting/reducing in visual and auditory evoked potentials. *Personality and Individual Differences, 9,* 571–579.

Stenberg, G., Rosen, I., & Risberg, J. (1990). Attention and personality in augmenting/reducing of visual evoked potentials. *Personality and Individual Differences, 11,* 1243–1254.

Stern, J. A. (1964). Towards a definition of psychophysiology. *Psychophysiology, 1,* 90–91.

Stern, J. A., & Janes, C. L. (1973). Personality and psychophathology. In W. F. Prokasy & D. C. Raskin (Eds.), *Electrodermal activity in psychological research* (pp. 284–337). New York: Academic Press.

Stern, W. (1921). *Differentielle Psychologie* [Differential psychology] (3rd ed.). Leipzig, Germany: Johann Ambrosius Barth.

Sternberg, J. (Ed.). (1982). *Handbook of human intelligence*. Cambridge, England: Cambridge University Press.

Stevenson, J., & Graham, P. (1982). Temperament: A consideration of concepts and methods. In R. Porter & G. M. Collins (Eds.), *Temperamental differences in infants and young children. Ciba Foundation Symposium 89* (pp. 36–50). London: Pitman.

Stevenson-Hinde, J., & Hinde, R. (1986). Changes in associations between characteristics and interactions. In R. Plomin & J. Dunn (Eds.), *The study of temperament: Changes, continuities and challenges* (pp. 115–129). Hillsdale, NJ: Erlbaum.

Stevenson-Hinde, J., Stillwell-Barnes, R., & Zunz, M. (1980). Subjective assessment of rhesus monkeys over four successive years. *Primates, 21,* 66–82.

St James-Roberts, I., & Wolke, D. (1986). Bases for a socially referenced approach to temperament. In G. A. Kohnstamm (Ed.), *Temperament discussed* (pp. 17–26). Lisse, The Netherlands: Swets & Zeitlinger.

Stough, C. Brebner, J., & Cooper, C. J. (1991). The Rusalov Structure of Temperament Questionnaire (STQ): Results from Australian sample. *Personality and Individual Differences, 12,* 1355–1357.

Strelau, J. (1958). Problem parcjalnych typów wyższej czynności nerwowej [Problems of partial types of higher nervous activity]. *Psychologia Wychowawcza, 1,* 244–251.

Strelau, J. (1960). Przewaga ruchliwoźci analizatora wzrokowego nad słuchowym u człowieka [The prevalence of mobility of the visual analyzer over the auditory one in man]. *Studia Psychologiczne, 3,* 181–198.

Strelau, J. (1965). *Problemy i metody badań typów układu nerwowego człowieka* [Problems and methods of research into types of nervous system in man]. Wrocław, Poland: Ossolineum.

Strelau, J. (1969). *Temperament i typ układu nerwowego* [Temperament and type of nervous system]. Warsaw, Poland: Państwowe Wydawnictwo Naukowe.

Strelau, J. (1972a). A diagnosis of temperament by nonexperimental techniques. *Polish Psychological Bulletin, 3,* 97–105.

Strelau, J. (1972b). The general and partial nervous system types—Data and theory. In V. D. Nebylitsyn & J. A. Gray (Eds.), *Biological bases of individual behavior* (pp. 62–73). London: Academic Press.

Strelau, J. (1974). Temperament as an expression of energy level and temporal features of behavior. *Polish Psychological Bulletin, 5,* 119–127.

Strelau, J. (1983). *Temperament, personality, activity.* London: Academic Press.

Strelau, J. (Ed.). (1985). *Temperamental bases of behavior: Warsaw studies on individual differences.* Lisse, The Netherlands: Swets & Zeitlinger.

Strelau, J. (1986). Stability does not mean stability. In G. A. Kohnstamm (Ed.), *Temperament discussed: Temperament and development in infancy and childhood* (pp. 59–62). Lisse, The Netherlands: Swets & Zeitlinger.

Strelau, J. (1987a). The concept of temperament in personality research. *European Journal of Personality, 1,* 107–117.

Strelau, J. (1987b). Emotion as a key concept in temperament research. *Journal of Research in Personality, 21,* 510–528.

Strelau, J. (1988). Temperamental dimensions as co-determinants of resistance to stress. In M. P. Janisse (Ed.), *Individual differences, stress, and health psychology* (pp. 146–169). New York: Springer.

Strelau, J. (1989a). Individual differences in tolerance to stress: The role of reactivity. In C. D. Spielberger, I. G. Sarason, & J. Strelau (Eds.), *Stress and anxiety* (Vol. 12, pp. 155–166). New York: Hemisphere.

Strelau, J. (1989b). The regulative theory of temperament as a result of East–West influences. In G. A. Kohnstamm, J. E. Bates, & M. K. Rothbart (Eds.), *Temperament in childhood* (pp. 35–48). Chichester, England: Wiley.

Strelau, J. (1989c). Temperament risk factors in children and adolescents as studied in Eastern Europe. In W. B. Carey & S. C. McDevitt (Eds.), *Clinical and educational applications of temperament research* (pp. 65–77). Lisse, The Netherlands: Swets & Zeitlinger.

Strelau, J. (1991a). Are psychophysiological/psychophysical scores good candidates for diagnosing temperament/personality traits and for a demonstration of the construct validity of psychometrically measured traits? *European Journal of Personality, 5,* 323–342.

Strelau, J. (1991b). Renaissance in research on temperament: *Where to?* In J. Strelau & A. Angleitner

(Eds.), *Explorations in temperament: International perspectives on theory and measurement* (pp. 337–358). New York: Plenum.

Strelau, J. (1992a). Introduction: Current studies on anxiety from the perspective of research conducted during the last three decades. In D. G. Forgays, T. Sosnowski, & K. Wrześniewski (Eds.), *Anxiety: Recent developments in cognitive, psychophysiological, and health research* (pp. 1–10). Washington, DC: Hemisphere.

Strelau, J. (1992b). Temperament and giftedness in children and adolescents. In F. Monks & W. Peters (Eds.), *Talent for the future: Social and personality development of gifted children* (pp. 73–86). Assen/Maastricht, The Netherlands: Van Gorcum.

Strelau, J. (1993). The location of the regulative theory of temperament (RTT) among other temperament theories. In J. Hettema & I. J. Deary (Eds.), *Foundations of personality* (pp. 113–132). Dordrecht, The Netherlands: Kluver Academic Publishers.

Strelau, J. (1994a). The concepts of arousal and arousability as used in temperament studies. In J. E. Bates & T. D. Wachs (Eds.), *Temperament: Individual differences at the interface of biology and behavior* (pp. 117–141). Washington, DC: American Psychological Association.

Strelau, J. (1994b). Gerhard Heymans—The pioneer of empirical studies on temperament. In B. De Raad, W. K. B. Hofstee, & G. L. Van Heck (Eds.), *Personality psychology in Europe* (Vol. 5, pp. 84–103). Tilburg, The Netherlands: Tilburg University Press.

Strelau, J. (1995a). The regulative theory of temperament: Current status. *Personality and Individual Differences, 20,* 131–142.

Strelau, J. (1995b). Temperament risk factor: The contribution of temperament to the consequences of the state of stress. In S. E. Hobfoll & M. W. de Vries (Eds.), *Extreme stress and communities: Impact and intervention* (pp. 63–81). Dordrecht, The Netherlands: Kluwer Academic Publishers.

Strelau, J. (1995c). Temperament and stress: Temperament as a moderator of stressors, emotional states, coping, and costs. In C. D. Spielberger & I. G. Sarason (Eds.), *Stress and emotion: Anxiety, anger, and curiosity* (Vol. 15, pp. 215–254). Washington, DC: Hemisphere.

Strelau, J. (1995d). Theory and research on inhibited and uninhibited temperaments as a unique approach to children's temperament. *Psychological Inquiry, 6,* 339–343.

Strelau, J. (1996a). The regulative theory of temperament: Current status. *Personality and Individual Differences, 20,* 131–142.

Strelau, J. (1996b). Temperament as a moderator of coping with stress. In W. Battmann & S. Dutke (Eds.), *Processes of the molar regulation of behavior* (pp. 205–217). Lengerich, Germany: Pabst Science Publishers.

Strelau, J., & Angleitner, A. (1991). Temperament research: Some divergences and similarities. In J. Strelau & A. Angleitner (Eds.), *Explorations in temperament: International perspectives on theory and measurement* (pp. 1–12). New York: Plenum.

Strelau, J., & Angleitner, A. (1994). Cross-cultural studies on temperament: Theoretical considerations and empirical studies based on the Pavlovian Temperament Survey. *Personality and Individual Differences, 16,* 331–342.

Strelau, J., & Eliasz, A. (1994). Temperament risk factors for Type A behavior patterns in adolescents. In W. B. Carey & S. C. McDevitt (Eds.), *Prevention and early intervention: Individual differences as risk factors for the mental health of children* (pp. 42–49). New York: Brunner/Mazel.

Strelau, J., & Eysenck, H. J. (Eds.). (1987). *Personality dimensions and arousal.* New York: Plenum.

Strelau, J., & Plomin, R. (1992). A tale of two theories of temperament. In G. V. Caprara & G. L. Van Heck (Eds.), *Modern personality psychology: Critical reviews and new directions* (pp. 327–351). Hertfordshire, England: Harvester Wheatsheaf.

Strelau, J., & Terelak, J. (1974). The alpha index in relation to temperamental traits. *Studia Psychologica, 16,* 40–50.

Strelau, J., & Zawadzki, B. (1993). The Formal Characteristics of Behaviour—Temperament Inventory (FCB-TI): Theoretical assumptions and scale construction. *European Journal of Personality, 7,* 313–336.

Strelau, J., & Zawadzki, B. (1995). The Formal Characteristics of Behavior—Temperament Inventory (FCB-TI): Validity studies. *European Journal of Personality, 9,* 207–229.

Strelau, J., & Zawadzki, B. (1996). Temperament dimensions as related to the Giant Three and the Big Five factors: A psychometric approach. In A. V. Brushlinsky & T. N. Ushakova (Eds.), *V. D. Nebylitsyn: Life and scientific creativity* (pp. 260–281). Moscow, Russia: Ladomir.

Strelau, J., & Zawadzki, B. (1997). Temperament and personality: Eysenck's superfactors as related to temperamental dimensions. In H. Nyborg (Ed.), *The scientific study of human nature: Tribute to Hans J. Eysenck at eighty* (pp. 68–91). Oxford, England: Pergamon.

Strelau, J., Angleitner, A., Bantelmann, J., & Ruch, W. (1990). The Strelau Temperament Inventory–Revised (STI-R): Theoretical considerations and scale development. *European Journal of Personality, 4,* 209–235.

Strelau, J., Angleitner, A., & Ruch, W. (1990). Strelau Temperament Inventory (STI): General review and studies based on German samples. In J. N. Butcher & C. D. Spielberger (Eds.), *Advances in personality assessment* (Vol., 8, pp. 187–241). Hillsdale, NJ: Erlbaum.

Strelau, J., Oniszczenko, W., & Zawadzki, B. (1994). *Genetyczne uwarunkowanie i struktura temperamentu młodzieży i dorosłych* [Genetic determination and the structure of temperament in adolescents and adults] (KBN Report No 1.1108.91.02). Warsaw, Poland: University of Warsaw, Department of Psychology.

Strelau, J., Oniszczenko, W., Zawadzki, B., Bodunov, M., & Angleitner, A. (1995, July). *Genetic determination and the structure of temperament and personality in adults: Cross-cultural study based on German and Polish samples: Report from the Polish part of the German–Polish project.* Workshop on Genetic Studies on Temperament and Personality, Pułtusk, Poland.

Strelau, J., Kang, I. S., & Angleitner, A. (1996). *Cross-cultural studies on temperament: Theoretical basis and empirical data.* Unpublished manuscript, University of Warsaw, Warsaw, Poland.

Strelau, J., Angleitner, A., & Newberry, B. H. (in press). *The Pavlovian Temperament Survey (PTS): An international handbook.* Göettingen, Germany: Hogrefe.

Suomi, S. J. (1987). Genetic and maternal contributions to individual differences in rhesus monkey biobehavioral development. In N. A. Krasnegor, E. M. Blass, M. A. Hofer, & W. P. Smotherman (Eds.), *Perinatal development: A psychobiological perspective* (pp. 397–420). New York: Academic Press.

Super, C. M., & Harkness, S. (1982). The infant's niche in rural Kenya and metropolitan America. In L. L. Adler (Ed.), *Cross-cultural research at issue* (pp. 47–55). New York: Academic Press.

Super, C. M., & Harkness, S. (1986). Temperament, development, and culture. In R. Plomin & J. Dunn (Eds.), *The study of temperament: Changes, continuities and challenges* (pp. 131–149). Hillsdale, NJ: Erlbaum.

Super, C. M., & Harkness, S. (1994). Temperament and the developmental niche. In W. B. Carey & S. C. McDevitt (Eds.), *Prevention and early intervention: Individual differences as risk factors for the mental health of children* (pp. 115–125). New York: Brunner/Mazel.

Svrakic, D. M., Whitehead, C., Przybeck, T. R., & Cloninger, R. (1993). Differential diagnosis of personality disorders by the seven-factor model of temperament and character. *Archives of General Psychiatry, 50,* 991–999.

Szczepaniak, P., Strelau, J., Wrześniewski, K. (1996). Diagnoza stylów radzenia sobie ze stresem za pomocą polskiej wersji kwestionariusza CISS Endlera i Parkera [Assessment of styles of coping with stress by means of Endler and Parker's CISS: Polish version]. *Przegląd Psychologiczny, 39,* 187–210.

Talwar, R., Nitz, K., Lerner, J. V., & Lerner, R. M. (1991). The functional significance of organismic individuality: The sample case of temperament. In J. Strelau & A. Angleitner (Eds.), *Explorations in temperament: International perspectives on theory and measurement* (pp. 29–42). New York: Plenum.

Tarter, R. E., Laird, S. B., Kabene, M., Bukstein, O., & Kaminer, Y. (1990). Drug abuse severity in adolescents is assosiated with a deviation in temperament traits. *British Journal of Addiction, 85,* 1501–1504.

Tellegen, A. (1985). Structure of mood and personality and their relevance to assessing anxiety with an emphasis on self-report. In A. H. Tuma & J. D. Maser (Eds.), *Anxiety and the anxiety disorders* (pp. 681–706). Hilsdale, NJ: Erlbaum.

Tellegen, A., Lykken, D. T., Bouchard, T. J., Jr., Wilcox, K. J., Segal, N. L., & Rich, S. (1988). Personality similarity in twins reared apart and together. *Journal of Personality and Social Psychology, 54,* 1031–1039.

Teplov, B. M. (1936). The dependence of the absolute visual threshold on the presence of an additional stimulus in the field of vision. *Journal of General Psychology, 15,* 3–12.

Teplov, B. M. (1954). An attempt to elaborate methods for investigating typological features of higher activity in man. *Proceedings of a conference on psychology (July 3–8, 1953)* (pp. 284–293). Moscow, Russia: RSFSR Academy of Pedagogical Sciences. (in Russian)

Teplov, B. M. (1955). The study on types of higher nervous activity and psychology. *Voprosy Psikhologii, 1,* 36–41. (in Russian)

Teplov, B. M. (Ed.). (1956–1967). *Typological features of higher nervous activity in man* (Vol. 1, 1956; Vol. 2, 1959; Vol. 3, 1963a), Moscow: RSFSR Academy of Pedagogical Sciences; (Vol. 4, 1965; Vol. 5, 1967), Moscow, Russia: Prosveshcheniye. (in Russian)

Teplov, B. M. (1963b). New data for the study of nervous system properties in man. In B. M. Teplov (Ed.), *Typological features of higher nervous activity in man* (Vol. 3, pp. 3–46). Moscow, Russia: RSFSR Academy of Pedagogical Sciences. (in Russian)

Teplov, B. M. (1964). Problems in the study of general types of higher nervous activity in man and animals. In J. A. Gray (Ed.), *Pavlov's typology: Recent theoretical and experimental developments from the Laboratory of B. M. Teplov* (pp. 3–153). Oxford, England: Pergamon.

Teplov, B. M. (1972). The problem of types of human higher nervous activity and methods of determining them. In V. D. Nebylitsyn & J. A. Gray (Eds.), *Biological bases of individual behavior* (pp. 1–10). New York: Academic Press.

Teplov, B. M. (1985). *Selected works* (Vol. 1 & 2). Moscow, Russia: Pedagogika. (in Russian)

Teplov, B. M., & Nebylitsyn, V. D. (1963a). Experimental study of properties of the nervous system in man. *Zhurnal Vysshei Nervnoi Deyatelnosti, 13,* 789–797.

Teplov, B. M., & Nebylitsyn, V. D. (1963b). The study of basic properties of the nervous system and their significance in psychology of individual differences. *Voprosy Psikhologii, 9,* 38–47. (in Russian)

Thatcher, R. W., Walker, R. A., & Giudice (1987). Human cerebral hemispheres develop at different rates and ages. *Science, 236,* 1110–1113.

Thomas, A., & Chess, S. (1957). An approach to the study of sources of individual differences in child behavior. *Journal of Clinical and Experimental Psychopathology and Quarterly Review of Psychiatry and Neurology, 18,* 347–357.

Thomas, A., & Chess, S. (1977). *Temperament and development.* New York: Brunner/Mazel.

Thomas, A., & Chess, S. (1984). Genesis and evolution of behavioral disorders: From infancy to early adult life. *American Journal of Psychiatry, 141,* 1–9.

Thomas, A., & Chess, S. (1985). The behavioral study of temperament. In J. Strelau, F. H. Farley, & A. Gale (1985). *The biological bases of personality and behavior: Theories, measurement techniques, and development* (Vol. 1, pp. 213–225). Washington, DC: Hemisphere.

Thomas, A., & Chess, S. (1986). The New York Longitudinal Study: From infancy to early adult life. In R. Plomin & J. Dunn (Eds.), *The study of temperament: Changes, continuities and challenges* (pp. 39–52). Hillsdale, NJ: Erlbaum.

Thomas, A., Chess, S., Birch, H. G., Hertzig, M. E., & Korn, S. (1963). *Behavioral individuality in early childhood.* New York: New York University Press.

Thomas, A., Chess, S., & Birch, H. G. (1968). *Temperament and behavior disorders in children.* New York: New York University Press.

Thomas, A., Chess, S., & Korn, S. J. (1982). The reality of difficult temperament. *Merrill-Palmer Quarterly, 28,* 1–20.

Thomas, A., Mittelman, M., Chess, S., Korn, S. J., & Cohen, J. (1982). A temperament questionnaire for early adult. *Educational and Psychological Measurement, 42,* 593–600.

Thomas, C. B., & Greenstreet, R. L. (1973). Psychological characteristics in youth as predictors of five disease states: Suicide, mental illness, hypertension, coronary heart disease and tumour. *Johns Hopkins Medical Journal, 132,* 16–43.

Thompson, R. F., Berger, T. W., & Berry, S. D. (1980). Introduction to the anatomy, physiology and chemistry of the brain. In M. C. Wittrock (Ed.), *The brain and psychology* (pp. 3–32). New York: Academic Press.

Thurstone, L. L. (1951). The dimensions of temperament. *Psychometrica, 16,* 11–20.

Thurstone, L. L. (1953). *Examiner manual for the Thurstone Temperament Schedule* (2nd ed.) Chicago: Science Research Associates.

Tomaszewski, T. (1963). *Wstęp do psychologii* [Introduction to psychology]. Warsaw, Poland: Państwowe Wydawnictwo Naukowe.

Tomaszewski, T. (1978). *Tätigkeit und Bewusstsein: Beiträge zur Einfuhrung in die polnische Tätigkeitspsychologie* [Action and consciousness: Contribution to the introduction to Polish theory of action]. Weinheim, Germany: Beltz Verlag.

Tomkins, S. (1982). Affect theory. In P. Ekman (Ed.), *Emotion in the human face* (pp. 112–141). New York: Cambridge University Press.

Tooby, J., & Cosmides, L. (1990). On the universality of human nature and the uniqueness of the individual: The role of genetics and adaptation. *Journal of Personality, 51,* 17–67.

Torgersen, A. M. (1985). Temperamental differences in infants and 6-year-old children: A follow-up study of twins. In J. Strelau, F. H. Farley, & A. Gale (Eds.), *The biological bases of behavior: Theories, measurement techniques, and development* (Vol. 1, pp. 227–239). Washington, DC: Hemisphere.

Torgersen, A. M. (1987). Longitudinal research on temperament in twins. *Acta Geneticae Medicae et Gemellologiae, 36,* 145–154.

Triandis, H. C. (1978). Some universals of social behavior. *Personality and Social Psychology Bulletin, 4,* 1–16.

Triandis, H. C., Lambert, W., Berry, J., Lonner, W., Heron, A., Brislin, R., & Draguns, J. (Eds.). (1980–1981). *Handbook of cross-cultural psychology* (Vol. 106). Boston: Allyn & Bacon.

Tubman, J. G., Lerner, R. M., Lerner, J. V., & von Eye, A. (1992). Temperament and adjustment in young adulthood: A 15-year longitudinal analysis. *American Journal of Orthopsychiatry, 62,* 564–574.

Tucker, D. M., & Frederick, S. L. (1989). Emotion and brain lateralization. In H. Wagner & T. Manstead (Eds.), *Handbook of psychophysiology: Emotion and social behaviour* (pp. 27–70). London: Wiley.

Tuma, J. M., & Elbert, J. C. (1990). Critical issues and current practice in personality assessment of children. In C. R. Reynolds & R. W. Kamphaus (Eds.), *Handbook of psychological and educational assessment of children: Personality, behavior, and context* (pp. 3–29). New York: Guilford.

Turpin, G. (1986). Effects of stimulus intensity on autonomic responding: The problem of differentiating orienting and defense reflexes. *Psychophysiology, 23,* 1–14.

Tyler, L. E. (1965). *The psychology of human differences* (3rd ed.). New York: Appleton-Century-Crofts.

Tzeng, O. C. S., Ware, R., & Bharadwaj, N. (1991). Comparison between continuous bipolar and unipolar ratings of the Myers–Briggs Type Indicator. *Educational and Psychological Measurement, 51,* 681–690.

Umansky, L. I. (1958). Experimental study of typological features of children's nervous system (using play material). *Voprosy Psikhologii, 4,* 184–190. (in Russian)

Ursin, H. (1980). Personality, activation and somatic health: A new psychosomatic theory. In S. Levine & H. Ursin (Eds.), *Coping and health* (pp. 259–279). New York: Plenum.

Uzgiris, I., & Hunt, J. M. (1975) *Assessment in infancy*. Urbana: University of Illinois Press.

Van der Staay, F. J., Kerbusch, S., & Raaijmakers, W. (1990). Genetic correlation in validating emotionality. *Behavior Genetics, 20,* 51–62.

Van der Werff, J. J. (1985). Heymans' temperamental dimensions in personality research. *Journal of Research in Personality, 19,* 279–287.

Van der Werff, J. J., & Verster, J. (1987). Heymans' temperamental dimensions recomputed. *Personality and Individual Differences, 8,* 271–276.

Van Heck, G. L. (1988). Modes and models in anxiety. *Anxiety Research, 1,* 199–214.

Vandenberg, S. G. (1962). The hereditary abilities study: Hereditary components in a psychological test battery. *American Journal of Human Genetics, 14,* 220–237.

Vaughn, B. E., Taraldson, B. J., Crichton, L., & Egeland, B. (1981). The assessment of infant temperament: A critique of the Carey Infant Temperament Questionnaire. *Infant Behavior and Development, 4,* 1–17.

Vaughn, B. E., Bradley, C. F., Joffe, L. S., Seifer, R., & Barglow, P. (1987). Maternal characteristics measured prenatally are predictive of ratings of temperament "difficulty" on the Carey Infant Temperament Questionnaire. *Developmental Psychology, 23,* 152–161.

Ventura, J. N., & Stevenson, M. B. (1986). Relations of mothers' and fathers' reports of infant temperament, parents' psychological functioning, and family characteristics. *Merrill-Palmer Quarterly, 32,* 275–289.

Vernon, P. E. (1979). *Intelligence, heredity and environments*. San Francisco: Freeman.

Victor, J. B., Halverson, C. F., Jr., & Wampler, K. S. (1988). Family–school context: Parent and teacher agreement on child temperament. *Journal of Consulting and Clinical Psychology, 56,* 573–577.

Vingerhoets, A. J. J. M., Van den Berg, M. P., Kortekaas, R. T. J., Van Heck, G. L., & Croon, M. A. (1993). Weeping: Associations with personality, coping, and subjective health status. *Personality and Individual Differences, 14,* 185–190.

Viola, M. (1906). *L'antropometria come base di classificazione delle constituzioni individuali* [Anthropometrics as the basis for the classification of the individual's constitution]. Torino, Italy: Bocca.

Vitaliano, P. P., DeWolfe, D. J., Maiuro, R. D., Russo, J., & Katon, W. (1990). Appraised changeability of a stressor as a modifier of the relationship between coping and depression: A test of the hypothesis of fit. *Journal of Personality and Social Psychology, 59,* 582–592.

von Knorring, A. L., Bohman, M., von Knorring, L., & Oreland, L. (1985). Platelet MAO activity as a biological marker in subgroups of alcoholism. *Acta Psychiatrica Scandinavica, 72,* 51–58.

von Knorring, L. (1984). The biochemical basis of sensation-seeking behavior. *Behavioral and Brain Sciences, 7,* 443–445.

von Knorring, L., Oreland, L., & Winblad, B. (1984). Personality traits related to monoamine oxidase activity in platelets. *Psychiatry Research, 12,* 11–26.

von Knorring, L., Oreland, L., & von Knorring, A. L. (1987). Personality traits and platelet MAO activity in alcohol and drug abusing teenage boys. *Acta Psychiatrica Scandinavica, 75,* 307–314.

Wachs, T. D. (1983). The use and abuse of environment in behavior-genetic research. *Child Development, 54,* 396–407.

Wachs, T. D. (1992). *The nature of nurture*. Newbury Park, CA: Sage.

Wachs, T. D. (1994). Fit, context, and the transition between temperament and personality. In C. F. Halverson, Jr., G. A. Kohnstamm, & R. P. Martin (Eds.), *The developing structure of temperament and personality from infancy to adulthood* (pp. 209–220). Hillsdale, NJ: Erlbaum.

Wachs, T. D., & Gandour, M. J. (1983). Temperament, environment, and six-month cognitive-intellectual developments: A test of the organismic specificity hypothesis. *International Journal of Behavioral Development, 6,* 135–152.

Waller, N. G., Kojetin, B. A., Bouchard, T. J., Jr, Lykken, D. T., & Tellegen, A. (1990). Genetic and environmental influences on religious interests, attitudes, and values: A study of twins reared apart and together. *Psychological Science, 1,* 138–142.

Walter, W. G., Cooper, R., Aldridge, V. J., McCallun, W. G., & Winter, A. L. (1964). Contingent negative variation: An electric signs of sensorimotor association and expectancy in the human brain. *Nature, 203,* 380–384.

Watson, D., & Clark, L. A. (1984). Negative affectivity: The disposition to experience negative emotional states. *Psychological Bulletin, 96,* 465–490.

Watson, D., & Tellegen, A. (1985). Toward a consensual structure of mood. *Psychological Bulletin, 98,* 219–235.

Watson, D., Clark, L. A., & Tellegen, A. (1988). Development and validation of brief measures of positive and negative affect: The PANAS scales. *Journal of Personality and Social Psychology, 54,* 1063–1070.

Weick, K. E. (1970). The "ess" in stress. Some conceptual and methodological problems. In J. E. McGrath (Ed.), *Social and psychological factors in stress* (pp. 287–347). New York: Holt, Rinehart and Winston.

Wells, W. D., & Siegel, B. (1961). Stereotyped somatotypes. *Psychological Reports, 8,* 77–78.

Wenger, M. A. (1938). Some relationships between muscular processes and personality and their factorial analysis. *Child Development, 9,* 261–276.

Wenger, M. A. (1941). The measurement of individual differences in autonomic balance. *Psychosomatic Medicine, 3,* 427–434.

Wenger, M. A. (1943). An attempt to appraise individual differences in level of muscular tension. *Journal of Experimental Psychology, 32,* 213–225.

Wenger, M. A. (1947). Preliminary study of the significance of measures of autonomic balance. *Psychosomatic Medicine, 9,* 301–309.

Wenger, M. A. (1966). Studies in autonomic balance: A summary. *Psychophysiology, 2,* 173–186.

Werre, P. F. (1986). Contingent negative variation: Relation to personality and modification by stimulation and sedation. In J. Strelau, F. H. Farley, & A. Gale (Eds.), *The biological bases of personality and behavior: Psychophysiology, performance, and applications* (Vol. 2, pp. 77–90). Washington, DC: Hemisphere.

Werre, P. F. (1987). Extraversion–introversion, contingent negative variation, and arousal. In J. Strelau & H. J. Eysenck (Eds.), *Personality dimensions and arousal* (pp. 59–76). New York: Plenum.

Werre, P. F., Faverey, H. A., & Janssen, R. H. C. (1975). Contingent negative variation and personality. *Nederlands Tijdschrift foor de Psychologie, 30,* 277–299.

Werre. P. F., Mattie, H., Fortgens, C., Berretty, E. W., & Sluiter, W. (1994). Interaction between extraversion and drug-induced conditions as indicated by the contingent negative variation. *Biological Psychology, 39,* 45–56.

West, S. G. (1986). Methodological developments in personality research: An introduction. *Journal of Personality, 54,* 1–17.

Wiersma, E. (1906–1907). Die Sekundarfunktion bei Psychosen [The secondary functions in psychosis]. *Journal für Psychologie und Neurologie, 8,* 1–24.

Wiggins, J. S. (1968). Personality structure. *Annual Review of Psychology, 19,* 293–350.

Wiggins, J. S. (1973). *Personality and prediction: Principles of personality assessment.* Reading, MA: Addison-Wesley.

Wiggins, J. S., & Pincus, A. L. (1992). Personality: Structure and assessment. *Annual Review of Psychology, 43,* 473–504.

Wiggins, J. S., Renner, K. E., Clore, G. L., & Rose, R. J. (1971). *The psychology of personality.* Reading, MA: Addison-Wesley.

Williams, R. V. (1956). *Biochemical individuality.* New York: Wiley.

Wilson, G. D. (1981). Personality and social behaviour. In H. J. Eysenck (Ed.), *A model for personality* (pp. 210–245). Berlin, Germany: Springer.

Wilson, G. D. (1990). Personality, time of day and arousal. *Personality and Individual Differences, 11,* 153–168.

Wilson, G. D., Barrett, P. T., & Gray, J. A. (1989). Human reactions to reward and punishment: A questionnaire examination of Gray's personality theory. *British Journal of Psychology, 80,* 509–515.

Wilson, R. S., & Matheny A. P., Jr. (1983). Assessment of temperament in infant twins. *Developmental Psychology, 19,* 172–183.

Wilson, R. S., & Matheny, A. P., Jr. (1986). Behavior-genetics research in infant temperament: The Louisville twin study. In R. Plomin & J. Dunn (Eds.), *The study of temperament: Changes, continuities and challenges* (pp. 81–97). Hillsdale, NJ: Erlbaum.

Wilson, R. S., Brown, A. M., & Matheny, A. P., Jr. (1971). Emergence and persistence of behavioral differences in twins. *Child Development, 42,* 1381–1398.

Windholz, G. (1987). Pavlov as a psychologist: A reappraisal. *Pavlovian Journal of Biological Science, 22,* 103–112.

Windle, M. (1988). Psychometric strategies of measure of temperament: A methodological critique. *International Journal of Behavioral Development, 11,* 171–201.

Windle, M. (1989a). Predicting temperament–mental health relationships: A covariance structure latent variable analysis. *Journal of Research in Personality, 23,* 118–144.

Windle, M. (1989b). Temperament and personality: An exploratory interinventory study of the DOTS-R, EASI-II, and EPI. *Journal of Personality Assessment, 53,* 487–501.

Windle, M. (1991). The difficult temperament in adolescence: Associations with substance use, family support, and problem behaviors. *Journal of Clinical Psychology, 47,* 310–315.

Windle, M. (1992). Temperament and social support in adolescence: Interrelations with depressive symptoms and delinquent behaviors. *Journal of Youth and Adolescence, 21,* 1–21.

Windle, M. (1994). Temperamental inhibition and activation: Hormonal and psychosocial correlates and associated psychiatric disorders. *Personality and Individual Differences, 17,* 61–70.

Windle, M., & Lerner, R. M. (1986). Reassessing the dimensions of temperamental individuality across the life-span: The Revised Dimensions of Temperament Survey (DOTS-R). *Journal of Adolescent Research, 1,* 213–230.

Windle, M., Iwawaki, S., & Lerner, R. M. (1987). Cross-cultural comparability of temperament among Japanese and American early- and late-adolescents. *Journal of Adolescent Research, 2,* 423–446.

Windle, M., Iwawaki, S., & Lerner, R. M. (1988). Cross-cultural comparability of temperament among Japanese and American preschool children. *International Journal of Psychology, 23,* 547–567.

Wittman, P., Sheldon, W. H., & Katz, C. J. (1948). A study of the relationship between constitutional variations and fundamental psychotic behavior reactions. *Journal of Nervous and Mental Disease, 108,* 470–476.

Wittrock, M. C. (Ed.). (1980). *The brain and psychology.* New York: Academic Press.

Wright, J. C., & Mischel, W. (1987). A conditional approach to dispositional constructs: The local predictability of social behavior. *Journal of Personality and Social Psychology, 53,* 1159–1177.

Wundt, W. (1887). *Grundzüge der physiologischen Psychologie* [Outlines of physiological psychology] (3rd ed., Vol. 2). Leipzig, Germany: Verlag von Wilhelm Engelmann.

Yerkes, R. M., & Dodson, J. D. (1908). The relation of strength of stimulus to rapidity of habit-formation. *Journal of Comparative Neurology and Psychology, 18,* 459–582.

Young, J. P. R., Lader, M. H., & Fenton, G. W. (1971). The relationship of extraversion and neuroticism to the EEG. *British Journal of Psychiatry, 119,* 667–670.

Zapan, G. (1974). The temperament system and its diagnosis. *Revue Roumaine des Sciences Sociales. Serie de Psychologie, 18,* 109–117.

Zawadzki, B. (1991). Temperament: Selekcja czy kompensacja? [Temperament: Selection or compensation?]. In T. Tyszka (Ed.), *Psychologia i sport* (pp. 85–112). Warsaw, Poland: Academy of Sports Education Publisher.

Zawadzki, B., & Strelau, J. (in press). Społeczno-przedmiotowe zróżnicowanie temperamentu: polska adaptacja "Kwestionariusza Struktury Temperamentu" Rusałowa [Social-object differentiation of temperament: Polish adaptation of the "Structure of Temperament Questionnaire"]. *Przegląd Psychologiczny, 41.*

Zonderman, A. B., Costa, P. T., Jr., & McCrae, R. R. (1989). Depression as a risk factor for cancer morbidity and mortality in a nationally representative sample. *Journal of the American Medical Association, 262,* 1191–1195.

Zubek, J. P. (Ed.). (1969). *Sensory deprivation: Fifteen years of research.* New York: Appleton-Century-Crofts.

Zuckerman, M. (1960). The development of an Affect Adjective Check List for the measurement of anxiety. *Journal of Consulting Psychology, 24,* 457–462.

Zuckerman, M. (1964). Perceptual isolation as a stress situation: A review. *Archives of General Psychiatry, 11,* 225–276.

Zuckerman, M. (1969). Theoretical formulations. In J. P. Zubek (Ed.), *Sensory deprivation: Fifteen years of research* (pp. 407–432). New York: Appleton-Century-Crofts.

Zuckerman, M. (1971). Dimensions of sensation seeking. *Journal of Consulting and Clinical Psychology, 36,* 45–52.

Zuckerman, M. (1974). The sensation seeking motive. In B. A. Mahler (Ed.), *Progress in experimental personality research* (Vol. 7, pp. 80–148). New York: Academic Press.

Zuckerman, M. (1979). *Sensation seeking: Beyond the optimal level of arousal.* Hillsdale, NJ: Erlbaum.

Zuckerman, M. (Ed.). (1983a). *Biological bases of sensation seeking, impulsivity, and anxiety.* Hillsdale, NJ: Erlbaum.

Zuckerman, M. (1983b). A biological theory of sensation seeking. In M. Zuckerman (Ed.), *Biological bases of sensation seeking, impulsivity, and anxiety* (pp. 37–76). Hillsdale, NJ: Erlbaum.

Zuckerman, M. (1984a). Experience and desire: A new format for sensation seeking scales. *Journal of Behavioral Assessment, 6,* 101–114.

Zuckerman, M. (1984b). The neurobiology of some dimensions of personality. *International Review of Neurobiology, 25,* 391–436.

Zuckerman, M. (1984c). Sensation seeking: A comparative approach to a human trait. *Behavioral and Brain Sciences, 7,* 413–471.

Zuckerman, M. (1985). Biological foundations of sensation-seeking temperament. In J. Strelau, F. H. Farley, & A. Gale (Eds.), *The biological bases of personality and behavior: Theories, measurement techniques, and development* (Vol. 1, pp. 97–112). Washington, DC: Hemisphere.

Zuckerman, M. (1987a). Brain monoamine systems and personality. In D. Hellhammer, I. Florin, & H. Weiner (Eds.), *Neurobiological approaches to brain disease* (pp. 5–14). Toronto, Ontario, Canada: Hans Huber.

Zuckerman, M. (1987b). Is sensation seeking a predisposing trait for alcoholism? In E. Gotheil, K. A. Druley, S. Pashkey, & S. P. Weinstein (Eds.), *Stress and addiction* (pp. 283–301). New York: Brunner/Mazel.

Zuckerman, M. (1990). The psychophysiology of sensation seeking. *Journal of Personality, 58,* 313–345.

Zuckerman, M. (1991a). Biotypes for basic personality dimensions? "The twilight zone" between genotype and social phenotype. In J. Strelau & A. Angleitner (Eds.), *Explorations in temperament: International perspectives on theory and measurement* (pp. 129–146). New York: Plenum.

Zuckerman, M. (1991b). One person's stress is another person's pleasure. In C. D. Spielberger, I. G. Sarason, Z. Kulcsar, & G. L. Van Heck (Eds.), *Stress and emotion: Anxiety, anger, and curiosity* (Vol. 14, pp. 31–45). Washington, DC: Hemisphere.

Zuckerman, M. (1991c). *Psychobiology of personality.* New York: Cambridge University Press.

Zuckerman, M. (1992). What is a basic factor and which factors are basic? Turtles all the way down. *Personality and Individual Differences, 13,* 675–681.

Zuckerman, M. (1993). Personality from top (traits) to bottom (genetics) with stops at each level between. In J. Hettema & I. J. Deary (Eds.), *Foundations of personality* (pp. 73–100). Dordrecht, The Netherlands: Kluwer Academic Publishers.

Zuckerman, M. (1994). *Behavioral expressions and biosocial bases of sensation seeking.* New York: Cambridge University Press.

Zuckerman, M., Kolin, E. A., Price, L., & Zoob, I. (1964). Development of a Sensation-Seeking Scale. *Journal of Consulting Psychology, 28,* 477–482.

Zuckerman, M., Murtaugh, T., & Siegel, J. (1974). Sensation seeking and cortical augmenting–reducing. *Psychophysiology, 11,* 535–542.

Zuckerman, M., Eysenck, S. B. G., & Eysenck H. J. (1978). Sensation seeking in England and America: Cross-cultural, age and sex comparisons. *Journal of Consulting and Clinical Psychology, 46,* 139–149.

Zuckerman, M., Buchsbaum, M. S., & Murphy, D. L. (1980). Sensation seeking and its biological correlates. *Psychological Bulletin, 88,* 187–214.

Zuckerman, M., Simons, R. F., & Como, P. G. (1988). Sensation seeking and stimulus intensity as modulators of cortical, cardiovascular, and electrodermal response: A cross-modality study. *Personality and Individual Differences, 9,* 361–372.

Zuckerman, M., Kuhlman, D. M., Thornquist, M., & Kiers, H. (1991). Five (or three) robust questionnaire scale factors of personality without culture. *Personality and Individual Differences, 12,* 929–941.

Zuckerman, M., Kuhlman, D. M., Teta, P., Joireman, J., & Carroccia, G. (1992, April). *The development of scales for a Five Basic Personality Factor Questionnaire.* Paper presented at the meeting of the Eastern Psychological Association, Boston.

Zuckerman, M., Kuhlman, D. M., Joireman, J., Teta, P., & Kraft, M. (1993). A comparison of three structural models for personality: The Big Three, the Big Five, and the Alternative Five. *Journal of Personality and Social Psychology, 65,* 757–768.

Żmudzki, A. (1986). *Poziom reaktywnoźci a powodzenie w trakcie startu u zawodników w podnoszeniu ciężarów* [Level of reactivity and success during competition in weight lifters]. Warsaw, Poland: Institute of Sports Publisher.

Index

Page numbers followed by *f* refer to figures; page numbers followed by *n* refer to footnotes; and page numbers followed by *t* refer to tables.